Flash 5 Studio

Nikhil Adnani
Kevin Airgid
Michael Bedar
Sham Bhangal
Andrew Bruntel
Brendan Dawes
Alric von Gerbig
Tracy Halvorsen
Peter Holm
Joni Leimala
Richard Mapes
Niko Nevatie
Andries Odendaal
Simon Robertson
Shawn Ryder
George Shaw
Jake Smith
Bill Spencer
Jessica Speigel
Chris Styles
Phill Taffs
Andreas Tagger
Andrew Zack

friendsof

DESIGNER TO DESIGNER™

Flash 5 Studio

First Printed March 2001

Trademark Acknowledgments

Published by friends of ED
30 Lincoln Road, Olton, Birmingham, B27 6PA, UK.

Printed in USA

ISBN: 1-903450-30-6

Flash 5 Studio

Credits

Authors	Nikhil Adnani, Kevin Airgid, Michael Bedar, Sham Bhangal, Andrew Bruntel, Brendan Dawes, Alric von Gerbig, Tracy Halvorsen, Peter Holm, Joni Leimala, Richard Mapes, Niko Nevatie, Andries Odendaal, Simon Robertson, Shawn Ryder, George Shaw, Jake Smith, Bill Spencer, Jessica Speigel, Chris Styles, Phill Taffs, Andreas Tagger, Andrew Zack
Content Architect	Andy Corsham
Editors	Andy Corsham, Jon Hill, Matthew Knight, Ben Renow-Clarke
Technical Reviewers	Jeremy Beacock, Kristian Besley, Garrett Carr, Kim (Bimmer) Christiansen, Richard Chu, Gahlord Dewald, John Flanaghan, Peter Fletcher, Simon Guerney, Vicki Loader, Glain Martin, James Penberthy, Patrick Rey, Rita Ruban, Oliver Shaw, Gabrielle Smith, Jake Smith, Jessica Speigel, Kevin Sunderland, Gobhi Theivendran, Phillip Valdez, Pete Walker, Michael Walston, Andrew Zack
Graphic Editors	Kristian Besley, William Fallon, Katy Freer, Deborah Murray
Author Agent	Gaynor Riopedre
Project Administator	Fionnuala Meacher
Index	Alessandro Ansa, Adrian Axinte
Cover Design	Katy Freer, Deborah Murray
CD	William Fallon
Proof Readers	Jez Booker, Laurent Lafon, Alan McGann, Ciara McNee, Fionnuala Meacher, Deborah Murray, Catherine O'Flynn, Mel Orgee, Andrew Tracey, Hesan Yousif

Flash 5 Studio

Nikhil Adnani   www.groovechamber.com

Nikhil Adnani is an independent artist and animator who lives in Canada. His work on GrooveChamber is inspired by his experiences and travels. Since moving to Canada he has been employed on a dairy farm, in a coffee shop, for a jewelry maker and most recently as a research engineer in the area of wireless systems. He is currently working towards a Ph.D. in Electrical Engineering. "I would like to thank my wife, Alison for her love and support."

Kevin Airgid   www.airgid.com

Kevin Airgid has worked exclusively in interactive design since the inception of Mosaic, the first graphical web browser. Kevin's work has been featured in the Macromedia Showcase and has won numerous awards. He has extensive experience designing web sites for various Fortune 500 companies. He has created multimedia projects for the Detroit Tigers, Bell Canada, and GM including Cadillac and Chevrolet. "I would like to thank God for giving me creative talent! I would like to thank my wife Crona for her positive energy, and Brian Reindel for being the sounding board for ideas good and bad!"

Michael Bedar

Michael C. Bedar is a freelance multimedia designer in Boston, MA. He is contributing author and assistant webmaster for www.flashaddict.com,and a founding member of the Boston Flash MMUG. His work can bee seen at FlashAddict, as well as at www.virtual-fx.net. Michael is a self-professed computer geek, and a devout Mac Evangelist. Michael enjoys reading books that have as little to do with reality as possible, and practicing martial arts. Michael's worst fear is that some day he will be forced to write about himself in the third person.

Sham Bhangal

Sham Bhangal originally started out as an engineer, specializing in industrial computer based display and control systems. His spare time was partly taken up by freelance web design, something that slowly took up more and more of his time until the engineering had to go. He is now also writing for friends of ED, something that is taking more and more time away from web design...funny how life repeats itself! Sham lives in Manchester, England, with his partner Karen.

Andrew Bruntel   www.vehicle-m.com

Andrew Bruntel is a student at the Maryland Institute, College of Art. He is currently in his senior year, studying Graphic Design and New Media. He has taught himself Flash over the last two years, and thinks of Flash 5 as a long term girlfriend that never yells at him but is a bit hard to dance with at parties.

Brendan Dawes   www.brendandawes.com

Brendan is Creative Director with interactive agency Magnetic North. His portfolio includes work for Fox Kids, Disney, Coca-Cola and Kellogg's as well as personal projects such as Saul Bass On The Web, a critically acclaimed homage to the late, great graphic designer. Bren is a regular speaker at industry seminars across the world including Flashforward, Macromedia Web World and the New Media Age Congress. When not working on commercial projects, he likes to put together non-sensical Flash experiments for his website at www.brendandawes.com.

Alric von Gerbig

I graduated (just barely) from Twin Valley High-School in Elverson, Pennsylvania, then spent three years at Kutztown University studying Geology. I quickly dropped out to play DOOM full time. The blood and gore took its toll and I went on walkabout in northern California for a year to clear my head. When I returned I set out to use technology for good, instead of evil. Currently I'm leaning heavily towards evil again.

Tracy Halvorsen   www.atomicelvis.com

Tracey Halvorsen is co-founder of Fast Spot Interactive Media (www.fastspot.com). She is also a painter, photographer and designer. She obtained a B.F.A in painting from the Cleveland Institute of Art, and her M.F.A. in painting at the Maryland Institute, College of Art. She has taught herself Flash through many late nights and heated conversations, mainly with the other authors of her chapter in this book.

Peter Holm   www.helpfish.com

Peter Holm, born in 1974 in Denmark. Living in Copenhagen, Denmark. Partner in and co-creative director at Titoonic ApS (www.titoonic.dk), doing Flashed 3D animation and graphic design. The work is a game and an expedition where you find your self on thin ice, learning, always learning, but never learning quite enough. Animation and composition are key terms in the understanding of communicative visual arts. Think in terms of "animating" posters and "composing" animation and motion graphics. Design contrasts and messages and un-design the rest. Creator of Flash Film Festival nominee site www.petergrafik.dk and www.chaseace.com.

Joni Leimala

I was nine years old the first time I came upon a computer. Since then it has been a part of my life. At times it's a tool for work, a way to relax, a teacher and, maybe most importantly, a source of my creativity and flair. My energy I get from sports. I think that's a good balance. I am really eager to learn new things, and I just want to improve my skills as much as I can. Maybe that is why I chose new media and especially Internet. There's no doubt it's the best way for me to express my feelings and myself.

Flash 5 Studio

Richard Mapes   **www.moonfruit.com**

Richard Mapes writes code. Whereas most other Flash developers started life doing design, Richard came from a software engineering background and somehow fell into Flash. This means he can do all sorts of whizzy stuff with ActionScript, but can't draw to save his life. He currently works as chief technical architect for www.moonfruit.com where he is surrounded by people to do the drawing for him.

Niko Nevatie

I must have been the child who breaks things apart, just to assemble them back again. The whole of computing and arts has been a hobby of mine since I was ten and I'm still not bored with it. Little by little I've learned how simple pieces come together and form larger, complex entities. If I had to choose a single word to describe myself, it would be 'curious'. Although desktop programming with traditional programming tools has probably been my strongest points, I have lately concentrated firmly in Java mobile communications technology and I'm currently employed by a Finnish company Wapit Ltd.

Andries Odendaal   **www.wireframe.co.za**

I completed a national fine arts diploma in printmaking and sculpture in the early 1990s, and went on to lecture in this area, specializing in sculpture and drawing. Then I went freelance, began dabbling in computer design, got interested in 3D animation and the multimedia industry, and eventually joined Wireframe Studio in 1998, where I could freely indulge my fascination with multimedia and get to grips with the applications I needed, like Flash. Today I work in studio production, specializing in Flash development.

Simon Robertson   **www.srobertson.com**

Ever since I was young I have always loved working with image and sound, creating music and animations on computers such as the Spectrum, Amiga and now PC. My primary passion is music and I have written soundtracks for many video games including Extreme-G, Forsaken, Re-volt and FurFighters. I also enjoy creating animations, images, games and web sites using programs such as 3DS Max, Photoshop, and Flash. I look forward to the day when the Internet is fast enough to allow people to view, and interact with, high quality full screen animation with stereo sound and music. It will be amazing!

Shawn Ryder   **www.webryder.com**

Shawn Ryder is the owner of Webryder Internet Design and Consulting located in Canada. Having worked with numerous local and International clients, he's learned the importance of excellent design skills. Having taken Computer Programming in college, Shawn decided that there was a necessity to become more creative. With it being the early 1990s, he found the Internet an exciting opportunity, and built visually appealing yet purposeful web sites, with Flash being a major part. This writing certainly is a highlight of an eventful year, with many thanks to Jocelyn, Devin, my parents, along with all of my very supportive friends and family.

About the Authors

George Shaw   www.onetendesign.com
I spent a lot of time when I was a kid in my grandpa's printshop watching him set lead type by hand. Maybe he taught me about design without even knowing it. In high school, they offered to let me go to an art school for half of every day to learn to draw – cool. I ran out of money in college, so I started freelancing, doing T-shirts and magazine ads for surf and skate companies. Then the Internet showed up. Perfect! Now I could make art AND play with computers all day. Once I grew up, my wife and I started up One Ten Design, working in a closet in Santa Monica, but now we have a great big space with lots of dogs and motorcycles and people who work with us.

Jake Smith   www.subnet.co.uk
Jake has worked at the "bitface" of digital media for 4 years now, currently as Interactive Director at northern media house Subnet, working for esteemed clients such as Disney, Golden Wonder and Kellogg's. Everyday influences range from Dr. Seuss to Shigeru Miyamoto and pretty much any digital content will keep him amused for hours at a time. Jake is also the resident video games console expert, owning over 30 different gaming systems, ranging from the early 8 bit consoles like the Atari 2600 right up to the PS2."Work hard, play harder" are the few words he lives by.

Bill Spencer   www.popedeflash.com
Bill Spencer is a visual information specialist for the Naval Surface Warfare Center, Carderock Division where he specializes in web technologies, distance learning, multimedia development and interface design for the USA Navy. Bill is best known as "Pope de Flash" serving as a senior moderator at flashkit.com and the i-us community boards. Bill has written articles about Flash third party tools for various Flash portals, and serves as a beta tester for Swift 3D and other third party ware. He has also served as a spokesperson for Flaskit.com at Flash Forward, and as a judge for both the Flash Film Festival and New Media Designs Awards.

Jessica Speigel   www.were-here.com
Born and raised in Seattle, WA, Jessica Speigel is co-founder of We're Here Forums, a very popular and comprehensive web site that coordinates developer questions and information about Flash. At her day job, Jessica works full time integrating Flash user-interfaces with Java and Oracle to create rich front-ends for web applications. Special thanks go out to Aaron Adams for all his help and support.

Chris Styles   www.bionicbox.com   www.atacokai.com
Chris Styles is the Director of Design Technology at BionicBox, Inc. With a Fine Arts and Design background, as well as formal education at the Maryland Institute, College of Art, he brings a sense of tactility, composition, and design expertise to the mix. He began with HTML six years ago, as well as Flash when wasn't Flash (remember FutureSplash Animator?) and moved up to other programming languages and technical disciplines with the intent of finding new forms of media for creative expression.

Flash 5 Studio

Phill Taffs   **www.subnet.co.uk**

Phill is the Subnet resident video and animation expert. Using high-end applications such as Adobe After Effects, together with Flash, Phill creates some of the most stunning visuals ever seen online or on video. He has worked for 3 years at Subnet where he has produced outstanding work for the likes of Disney, Coca Cola, Fox Kids and Kellogg's to name but a few. Following Phill's ground breaking article on the use of Flash in MacUser, Subnet were contacted by renowned design company "Amaze" to create some visuals for the Saatchi & Saatchi innovations site using the video flash technique that he has truly perfected.

Andreas Tagger   **www.projectangora.com**

Andreas graduated with degrees in multimedia design and digital painting. Currently, Andreas works professionally as a web designer for Ecko Unlimited clothing (www.ecko.com), and as a commissioned artist for the Geist Modeleur Foundation. In the past year, Andreas has sold a number of his flat screen digital paintings to a geographically diverse spectrum of institutions, collectors and graphic designers. From August 2001 Geist Modeleur Foundation will be exhibiting and auctioning Andreas' current works as fundraiser for the United Media State Association; please check www.projectangora.com for further details.

Andrew Zack   **www.fiestanet.com**

After being rejected by the worst law schools in the US twice, Andrew Zack took the next not so rational career step and moved into Multimedia, then the Internet arena. Currently Andrew is a Senior Partner at Zack and Schwartz Consulting Group, a Technology Consulting Firm. Mr. Zack specializes in Internet Marketing and Partnership Development, helping clients understand how to conduct business in the Internet world.

Palette and Table of Contents

Flash 5 Studio

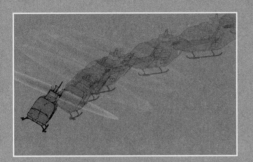 

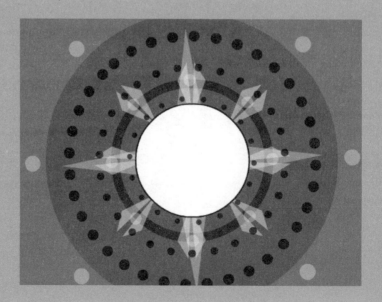

ACTIONSCRIPT

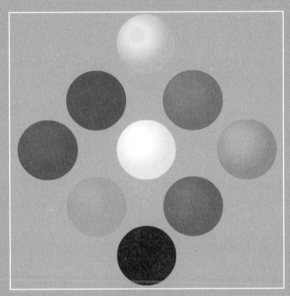

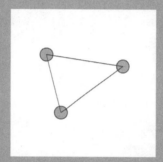 

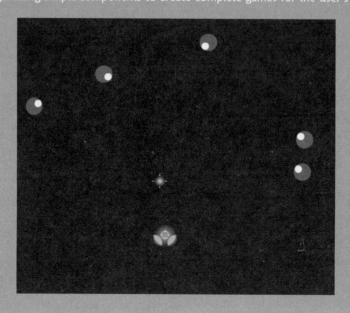

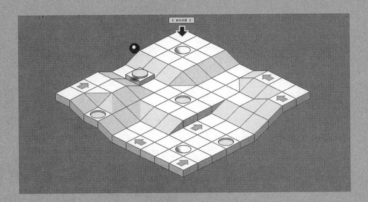

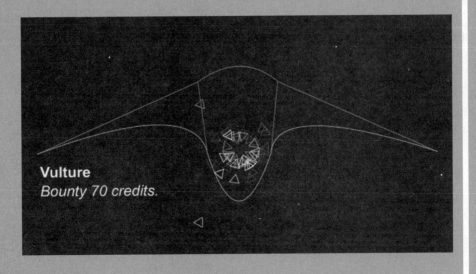

Vulture
Bounty 70 credits.

DYNAMIC CONTENT

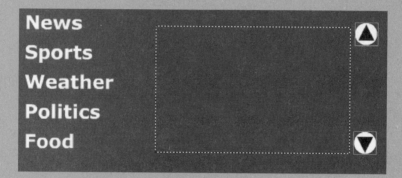

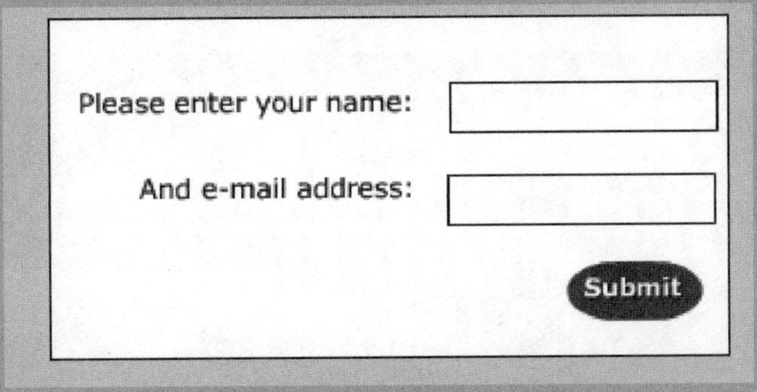

Please enter your name:

And e-mail address:

Submit

Next   Previous

Address Count

addressCount

Current Record

curRecord

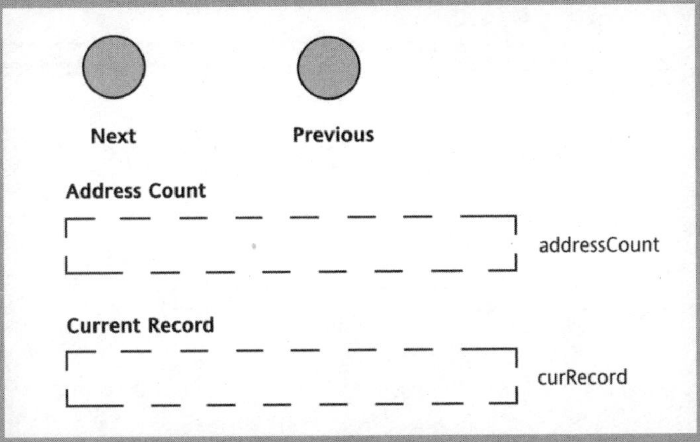

Flash 5 Studio

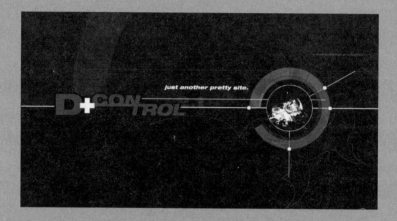

your content starts.

CHAPTER 23   OPTIMIZING FLASH FOR SEARCH ENGINES   711
ANDREW ZACK

Making sure that your hard work is rewarded with the maximum number of visitors!

Flash 5 Studio

Table of Contents

Table of Contents

Table of Contents

Table of Contents

Table of Contents

Flash's
Undiscovered
Country

Flash 5 comes in a pretty small box, but it packs a massive punch. Flash exploded onto the web scene a couple of years back, and it's now emerging as a serious tool for high class, visually rich site content. But it's more than that: the Flash 5 ActionScript implementation has turned Flash into the complete front-end tool, letting you build true interactivity, all the way from the user interface to the back-end data store. This book is all about helping uncover the full extent of what's possible with Flash, and the authors aim to help you choose where you want to go next with this powerful tool.

Every contributor to this book is a working web designer or coder, and they face the same kind of problems as you every day: "Just how should I do this? How *can* I do it? What options are open to me? How is this technology going to develop in the future? How can I make sure this site's seen by the maximum audience? What does my client want, and how can I give it to them?" This book's contributors have been out there in the trenches, battling with clients, technology and code, and they share their hard-won knowledge with you here.

We want to help you break into the world of *serious* Flash content.

(What's so funny 'bout) Depth, Breadth, and Understanding

If you've been to one of the big Flash conferences, you'll know that they're a melting pot of ideas, where Flashers of all abilities find their vector hunger satisfied by the wide range of speakers. Some of the sessions will be tough and some will be much simpler, but if you're lucky you'll find something to take away from each and every session – a new technique, maybe, or a new way of thinking about a problem. That's what we want to do in this book: give you a collection of new tools and new ideas that you can think about, absorb, adapt, and use in your own work.

We've assumed that you already know the basics of Flash, and that you don't need your fingers guided through every keystroke. We've concentrated on covering the material at a deeper technical level, and on explaining things so that you can fully understand them, internalize them, and add them to your toolkit.

If there's a mantra that sums up this book, it's "deeper, more serious, more fully explained".

Sliced and Diced

We've organized this book's material into distinct sections. You can read the book sequentially or dip into individual chapters as your preferences dictate. The sections are:

Prelude

This is a single chapter that encapsulates the site and graphic design principles that should influence how you put a great site together.

Content Creation

These chapters cover a range of techniques for embedding richer Flash content in your movies, including sound, video, animation and 3D.

ActionScript

This is a big section, and takes you deep into the theory and practice of ActionScript: how it's structured, how to use it effectively, and it shows a host of different applications built, dissected and fully explained. From loops to object-oriented Flash, you'll find serious but accessible ActionScript techniques in abundance.

Dynamic Content

Provides a taste of one of the areas that looms large in Flash's future – feeding content dynamically into the browser from separate data sources in response to user interaction.

Contexts

This section finishes off the book by discussing the global issues you need to think about when getting your site content out there in the world – embedding your Flash movies in HTML, streaming principles, and optimizing your site for search engines.

Layout Conventions

Firstly, we assume that you're using Expert mode in the Frame/Object Actions windows. We also use the authors' own symbol/variable naming conventions: we don't think that Flash code is yet subject to the more 'formal' constraints of established conventions. This also chimes with the book's principle of laying out the possibilities and letting you make your choices about what suits you best. We've also retained the authors' own platform choices of PC/Mac.

We've tried to keep this book as clear and easy to follow as possible, so we've only used a few layout styles to avoid confusion. Here they are...

- Practical exercises will appear under headings in this style...

Build this Movie now

...and they'll have numbered steps like this:

1. Do this first

2. Do this second

3. Do this third etc...

- When we're showing ActionScript code blocks that should be typed into the Actions window, we'll use this style:

```
Mover.startDrag(true);
Mouse.hide();
stop ();
```

- Where a line of ActionScript is too wide to fit on the page, we'll indicate that it runs over two lines by using an arrow-like 'continuation' symbol:

```
if (letters[i].x_pos==letters[i]._x &&
    ➡ letters[i].y_pos==letters[i]._y){
```

Lines like this should all be typed as a single continuous statement.

- And when we discuss ActionScript in the body of the text, we'll put statements such as `stop` in a code-like style too.

- When we add new code to an existing block, we'll highlight it like this:

```
Mover.startDrag(true);
variable1 = 35
Mouse.hide();
stop ();
```

- Pseudo code will appear in this style:

```
If (the sky is blue) the sun is out
    Else (it's cloudy)
```

- In the text, symbol and instance names will use this emphasized style – instance1, symbol1.

- Really important points that you ignore at your peril will be highlighted like this:

> **This is a key point, and you should read it really, really carefully.**

- `file names` will look like this.

- Web addresses will be in this form: www.friendsofed.com

- New or significant phrases will appear in this **important words** style.

- Finally, references to color images on CD will look like this:

THIS IS A COLOR IMAGE REFERENCE

What's on the CD?

The CD in the back of the book contains full support for the book's content. It includes:

- FLAs (and SWFs where necessary) for the worked examples, plus any supporting text/image files

- Color images from selected chapters

- Trial versions of key packages, including Flash 5, Dreamweaver 4, Freehand 9, Swift 3D, Swish and Poser

Support

If you have any questions about the book or about friends of ED, check out our web site: there are a range of contact e-mail addresses there, or you can just use the generic e-mail address – feedback@friendsofed.com.

There are also a host of other features up on the site: interviews with renowned designers, samples from our other books, and a message board where you can post your own questions, discussions and answers, or just take a back seat and look at what other designers are talking about. So, if you have any comments or problems, write us, it's what we're here for and we'd love to hear from you.

OK, that's the preliminaries over with. Let's explore the vast, sunlit landscape of Flash.

Section 1
Prelude

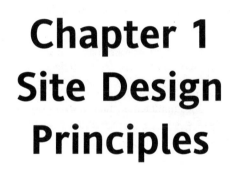

Chapter 1
Site Design
Principles

Technical Flash competence is one part of the Flash designer's toolkit – but you also need design skills if you're going to create professional sites. This chapter aims to provide you with a set of universally applicable web site design principles and creative techniques. Whether you're a relative newcomer to Flash or a more seasoned campaigner, we hope that you'll find plenty of insights into how to refine your creative processes and build better sites.

When a company or individual decides they want a web site, the reason is usually that they have a message or a piece of information they want to convey to a particular group of people, or perhaps to all the people of the world. The primary task of a web designer, therefore, is to ensure that the web site they create to meet this brief communicates their client's message effectively. This chapter will look at how a designer goes about achieving this, and aims to give constructive advice on producing focused, user-friendly – and therefore successful – designs for professional web sites.

Everybody wants their web site to be 'sticky'. They want it to be easy for the user to find their way around, they want the user to be able to get hold of the information they've come to see, they want the user to hang around and browse through the site, and they want the user to come back again and again.

Although as designers it may not be our primary motivation, the reason most web sites are created is to turn *users* into *customers* – happy customers. If a site is difficult to use, regardless of how good it looks, the user won't be able to get the information they've come for, they'll get annoyed – or bored – and they'll leave the site prematurely. And they won't come back. This chapter's going to look at the multifaceted task a web designer faces when communicating a message to a group of people, and discusses how a designer can ensure the site they create is usable and engaging.

In the first two-thirds of the chapter we'll look at the theory and practice of creative web design, and in the last third I'll walk you through these processes as I applied them to a real-world development project. I'll start here by discussing the critical issue of **usability**.

Usability

Usability is a complex subject that requires extensive study to master and apply. We're not going to go into too many specific and heavyweight usability issues here, but what we *will* do is look at the whole concept of usability and why it's important for designers to think long and hard about how a user will react to a site. By becoming aware of these issues you can improve your designs and make your web site much more usable – without sacrificing all those new Flash techniques and toys you've learned and want to incorporate into your work.

Usability is the science of making web sites efficient, understandable and, well, usable. It's based on intensive human-computer interaction studies and user testing and interviews. Usability studies are usually founded on the notion that the Web is a collection of sites that hold large quantities of text-based information and whose goal is to turn visitors into customers, and then make them repeat customers. Usability researches have unveiled a variety of issues that can improve or reduce a web site's level of usability.

Flash Usability

The world of web design has recently been involved in a heated debate on the form web pages should take: on one side we have the 'usability gurus' who've sworn loyalty to HTML and hold firm to their faith in a text-led, business-based notion of the Web; and on the other we have a swarm of post-modernist designers who've sworn loyalty to bleeding edge technology, with a much freer and expression-based notion of the Web. These are the two extremes, obviously, and in reality the task of the web designer – if he or she wants to remain at the forefront of their field *and* earn a living – is to find a workable position somewhere in between.

Some web designers don't want to hear about usability, believing that artistic freedom of expression should always be valued above usability. Some even talk about 'usability fascism', which they claim is a narrowing, creativity-stifling burden that the designers of today have to carry, while many designers claim that the issue of usability is irrelevant when using Flash – believing that for some reason the usual rules of design don't apply.

I don't think there has to be a conflict between usability and innovative design. The two shouldn't be polar opposites, but rather two sides of the same coin. A designer's job is to communicate information, and usability is all about making that information easily accessible.

As a designer, you speak a *visual* language. In order for people to understand you, you have to work inside some sort of common frame of reference so that the viewer will understand the visual language you're using. But before people can understand the visual language you choose to employ on your web designs, they must first be able to confidently *navigate* the site it's contained in.

If information is presented in a printed brochure, there's really only one way it can be accessed by the reader: page-by-page, referencing the sections they're interested in by the index and the table of contents. However, when viewing a web site the user has to deduce how the designer has constructed the site – and where the information they've come for is located within it. If the designer doesn't make this clear, the user will not bother viewing the site for long – no matter how 'bleeding edge' and fashionable the design itself may be.

The extent to which you explain to the user how to navigate your site and find information will, of course, depend on who your audience is going to be. If you're designing a concept-led 'user experience' aimed at the web-savvy, the site will not need to hold the hand of its viewers to guide them along to the same degree as, for example, an e-shopping site aimed at new or inexperienced computer users.

Balance is the key. A society does need an avant-garde group of artists that can bring evolution to mental, visual and philosophical issues. We need cutting-edge visuals from designers who are prepared to push back the boundaries of design, but we also need to ensure that these discoveries are put to a beneficial, practical use. The designers who incorporate usability into their web sites not at the *expense* of innovation, but in *addition* to it, are the ones who will prosper most from this developing technology.

Common Flash Site Usability Problems

Derived from everyone's favorite Flash critic, Jakob Nielsen, and loosely based on his **Top Ten Mistakes in Web Design** and the follow-up, **Top Ten New Mistakes in Web Design,** here's a summary of common usability criticisms that are leveled at web site design – and which are by no means exclusive to Flash sites:

- **Use of 'bleeding edge' technology**
  Although the Flash plug-in is now being included with current browsers, the fact that many users still have to download and install a plug-in means that the decision to use Flash technology poses a usability issue in itself. Being largely a plug-in based technology, Flash is thus a 'non-standard' solution. In general, non-standard solutions affect usability because they require the first-time user to learn a new way of interacting with an otherwise standard-based and relatively well-known medium.

- **Constantly running animations**
  Use animations with care – animations can monopolize attention and focus. For example, placing a looping animation next to important text-based content will make it virtually impossible for the user to concentrate on the information they are trying to take in.

- **Breaking the BACK button**
  The browser's BACK button is one of the most-used navigation features. By altering the way it functions, either by using redirects, pop-up windows, or full-screen windows, you take away a lot of the user's autonomy, which can cause them to become *extremely* frustrated.

- **Opening full-screen windows**
  Launching a site in a full-screen window is *pure selfishness*. By doing this, you take away the user's navigation bar, the favorites list, the address bar, the underlying windows and the desktop. You impose your web site on the user and force them to see the site as the center of the universe. While the novelty value of this effect can be pleasing at first, over time it leads to lots of irritation for the user – who becomes stranded whenever they visit the site.

- **Overly long download times**
  This is one of the main reasons behind Flash's poor reputation in usability circles – long preloads and long response times. It's vitally important that you design your Flash movies to optimize download and response times.

- **No navigation support**
  Users need to know where they are on your site. They need to know how to get back to where they were previously, and they need to know where they should be going. Though these points no doubt appear self evident in theory, in practice they are overlooked again and again.

- **Advertising-style content**
  Most users don't want advertising, they want content. By creating elements that look like advertising you make sure that users don't look at them.

The issues above all need to be addressed by you, the designer, at the initial stage of site-creation. By thinking of the user early on in the design process, you can make your Flash site more usable and more successful.

The links below will show you more about issues concerning usability, including some rather more colorful views on the use of Flash than the ones expressed here:

Usability Links

- **Jakob Nielsen's web site**: www.useit.com featuring:
  - Top Ten Mistakes In Web Design: www.useit.com/alertbox/9605.html
  - Top Ten New Mistakes In Web Design: www.useit.com/alertbox/990530.html

- **Usable Web** – Links about usability: www.usableweb.com

- **Dack.com** – Flash Is Evil: www.dack.com/web/flash_evil.html

The Web Designer's Role

A web designer is hired to set up a channel of communication between two parties: the client and the user. This communication is made through text, images, and graphics.

The web designer is almost acting as a dating agency for the client. They know all the client's best features and what they have to offer, and are trying to set them up with some customers for a long lasting and fruitful web site/user relationship.

The designer has to make it as easy as possible for these two parties to meet and communicate over the Internet, and the ease with which the user can do this can make or break the relationship. If the user finds their experience with your site is a bad one, perhaps due to one of the reasons we highlighted earlier, they'll hold it against the web site, leave, and probably never come back.

In order to succeed as a web designer, your sites have got to make the user feel good and, crucially, *in control*. When people feel good, they are open to new experiences and new information, which in turn makes your primary task as a designer – conveying information – that much easier.

The colors, sounds and 'mood' of a site can give the user a positive feeling, but these things alone are not enough. The way the site works and how easy it is to use significantly affect the way the user feels: if the user enters a beautifully designed site, but can't figure out how to use the navigation bar, the user will feel bad. They'll get annoyed either with the web site or the web designer, or even start to feel that their own computer skills are lacking and that it's their fault that they can't find what they want on the site. If a user feels like this, it's bad news for the web designer and their client. When they visit your web site, you want the user to feel good about their computer skills and good about the computer system they purchased that can download your high technology site in no time at all. If you help these things to happen, the user will also feel good about your work and the content of the site.

Defining the Message

In order to communicate the message of the web site, you'll have to know what the message is. To make the web site usable and understandable to the end user, you need to get a grasp of the goal your site hopes to achieve. If you're not clear about what your site is trying to say, the chances are nobody else will be either.

The following section will give you some pointers on how to determine the core message your client wants their web site to put across.

The 'message' your client will want you to communicate won't simply be a written message, like the company motto or an advertising campaign tag line. The 'message' in this context also means something a little more abstract: defining the message, from the designer's point of view, is mainly about pinpointing what sort of **mood** and **feel** your design needs to impress upon the viewer in order to reinforce the basic information you've been given. Your design must make an impression on the user that fits in with the image and market positioning that your client is aiming for. In a site for an established banking firm for example, you would want your design to give the user an impression of a responsible, trustworthy and successful company. The design must be appropriate for both the company it represents, and the audience it wants to get its message across to.

A typical goal of a web site could be to increase the turnover on the sale of a particular product. By opening a web site, the client will be hoping to open another sales channel, use the site as a marketing tool, or guide the company's image in some particular direction. Typical client messages you may be asked to convey could be: "This product is a quality product from a reputable company" or "This company knows how to relate to the younger generation".

These messages are not suitable to base a design on, but they *are* a start. You can't build a decent design just on a message that says: "Buy this!" You have to dig deeper than that and drill down into the emotional and conceptual heart of the client's messages.

The average client usually has some idea why they need a web site and probably wants to communicate a lot of important messages to their customers. The company's mission statement, the quality of their products, the brand name, the solidity of their organizational structure are all things they'll want to make known to potential customers. For the designer, successfully defining the message largely depends on your interpretation of the material made available by the client. The following advice should help you to get to grips with the brief:

- Take the time to talk with your client about what they feel is important to them. The more you get to know about the client and their project, the easier it will be to associate them with non-product related ideas and notions.

- 'Brainstorm' - This is a creative thinking method used by designers to formulate appropriate ideas; simply scribble down as many brief sentences as you can that describe the client and their mission, and write down words you associate with the client, their product, and the site project. Next, associate moods with the words on your list and try to imagine a suitable atmosphere. Do this several times to refine the collection of words and finish up with a rich collection of words relevant to the project.

- Try to simplify the message as much as possible. The more of the 'sales clutter' you can trim from the full manuscript, the more you can dig into the essence of what the client stands for and the nearer you are to a point where you can start communicating your client's message.

- If all this 'mood' and 'feel' business isn't your thing, you can go for another method. Instead of feeling your way through it, you simply make a choice. Choose your message. Cut away everything else and boldly define the message. Decide what you want to communicate and stick to it. Needless to say, make sure your decision communicates something that has a large degree of relevance to the problem in hand.

If at all possible you should end up with a single sentence or phrase that you feel describes the mood, feel, atmosphere, mission, product, and client. This is the **defined message**.

Editing the Manuscript

As a designer, it's often not your task to act as a *text* editor for the client: rather, it's your job to communicate the manuscript that they have provided you with. However, there'll be occasions when you have to intervene and modify the content that the client submits.

The written material for the web site that seems so important to the client may well be less than crucial to the web site *user*. A typical example of this is the internal organization of the client's company, which the client is involved with every day: the chain of command, the different units of the firm and the names of the assistants may all be very interesting to the client, but are usually unimportant to the user.

By retaining material that isn't 100% relevant to what the client wants the web site to achieve, and that will be of no interest at all to the user, you cause a slight shift of focus and concentration away from the core message of the web site. Adding extra topics increases the amount of information the user has to sift through, but if some of the choices the user makes take them to superfluous pieces of information, they may not stay at the site long enough to discover its real message. If they *do* stay, their route to the real message will have been made unnecessarily long, and its impact may have been diluted by the irrelevant content they've seen. You need to be aware of these issues when you're discussing and finalizing site content with the client.

Defining your Audience

The definition of the target audience is an important part of creating a web site, both in terms of usability and graphic design. As the purpose of a web site is to communicate information to a group of people, it's important to know exactly what group of people you're going to be addressing.

As in all other kinds of communication, a web site uses a distinctive language. Before doing anything else, find out *who* you're talking to. If you don't know who they are, there's a fair chance you'll end up speaking a language that this particular group doesn't understand or identify with.

Imagine that you're a salesman doing a product demonstration in a marketplace. Maybe you've got a crowd of ten people in front of you as you speak. You can't possibly be talking to, and keeping eye contact with, all of them at one time – you have to choose one or two people that you're primarily targeting. If you happen to be talking directly to the most receptive person in the audience you'll probably make a quick sale. You'll have chosen the person who is most willing to buy your product.

Narrowing down your audience improves the impact of your message. The better targeted the user, the more relevant the message is to that particular user. In other words, you should not attempt to *guess* who your target audience is. Instead, you should choose who your target audience is going to be. Having chosen the main target group, you can dig into the demographics of that group in order to get to know them better. If you're really lucky, the client might even have some existing research.

Ask yourself and the client questions about your potential audience, such as:

- Who do I want to sell the product to?

- How old are they?

- What are their interests?

- Where do they spend their money?

- What are they used to?

- What do they expect as a minimum?

- What are their quality standards?

- What would be new to them?

- What would impress them?

- What do they find appealing?

- How long have they been on the net?

- Have they tried downloading and installing plug-ins?

- What platform are they on?

- What browser do they use?

Remember, it's probable that neither you, nor your client, will be able to give the *exact* answer to all of these questions, and even if you're getting close, there'll always be a group of visitors that doesn't fit into your predictions. But asking these questions will help get you closer to your core audience.

Bandwidth Targeting

In order to make sure that you and your client are spending your energy and budget on the right type of site, it's also important to establish a **bandwidth target group**. This will ensure that you don't, for example, create a broadband site aimed at an audience with no more than dial-up modems.

Connection speed is one of the major limitations of web design. Your audience's connection may vary from a 14.4K dial-up to major broadband link. Again, there's no way you can faultlessly predict what connection your target audience will be using, but you *can* ask some general questions about your audience, and the answers to those questions will give you some valuable pointers:

- Are your audience young, rich and tech-savvy?

- Are they older and not so used to the net?

- Is your audience school kids who usually connect via the school network?

- What are the bandwidth averages for the given area/country?

Failure to target your audience's probable bandwidth may kill your web site instantly. Users on dial-up connections will have a low tolerance when it comes to broadband sites, and until broadband solutions become the cheaply available norm, the number of broadband users will be considerably lower than the number of dial-up users.

While the current bandwidth conditions hold, always go with the lowest common denominator of your target group when determining your ideal bandwidth. By aiming low you'll make sure that the users with dial-up connections don't get depressed about their connection speed and associate your web site with their bandwidth depression, and the broadband surfers will celebrate their lightning fast connection. Everyone's happy.

Until broadband solutions become the standard, creating a broadband-only web site will radically diminish the number of potential users. On the other hand, broadband users will be hungry for quality broadband content. One trick here is to use 'smart' Flash solutions that appear to utilize broadband fully: for example, using `loadMovie` actions to pull in requested content rather than loading everything at once. Another alternative is to have different versions of your site for users with different quality bandwidth.

Solving the Problem

Having defined the core message and the target audience, we've attained the knowledge we need to find the solution to the challenge we've been given. The solution to the task posed by the client should always be found by defining the intended message and the target audience. These two elements should guide all the creative and technical decisions you make throughout the rest of the design process.

Having decided on the technological level of your audience, make sure that you don't always automatically choose to create a full-scale Flash site. Sometimes HTML might be more appropriate, and sometimes a combination of Flash, HTML, and other technologies might be preferable.

Structural Design

When dealing with web sites, you usually have a substantial amount of information that needs to be made available to the user in the most efficient and engaging way. For this reason, **structural design** is important. A good structure makes it easy to find and access different topics in a web site. Having defined the real core of the site's message, you'll find it a lot easier to make a coherent structure to manage the information at hand.

Structural design is not just a way for you to manage the large amounts of information on a site – it's also a way of improving your web site's *usability*. If you can manage to create a logical and transparent structure, your users will benefit from it: it will be easier to navigate the site, users will be able to access the information they want more easily, and the user experience will be correspondingly improved.

To structure the information in a way that reflects your core message you need to think of it in terms of **importance**, **popularity**, **context**, and **focus**. Try to imagine a novice user as he or she navigates your web site. Under what topic headings would they be looking for a given piece of information? What would they think would be logical? Each time you make a structural change ask yourself: "Would a novice user understand this intuitively?" If not, then a proportion of your audience will be alienated from the site.

Asking the following questions will well help you to organize the content of your site structurally:

- **Which topics are most important to the *client*?**
  Arrange the content in order of importance to the client. Speak with the client, read through the material and try to come to a decision on the level of importance each topic should have. The most important topic obviously deserves prominence on the site. Related topics should be linked together so that the larger context and relationships become apparent to the user.

- **Which topic do you expect to be the most popular with the *user*?**
  It's a fact that most users want access to the most popular topics. Try to estimate which topics will become popular with the defined target audience. If your target audience were kids, they'd probably be more interested in playing games than in reading the company profile. Popular content will, by its nature, be accessed most often and therefore it's common sense to make it easily accessible.

  Note that there might be a significant difference between what the client wants to stress, what you think is popular, and what the users will find interesting. It's part of the designer's role to overcome this tension.

- **Focus on the most important message**
  Don't stress all topics equally. Bear in mind that if *everything* is emphasized, *nothing* is emphasized. By increasing the focus placed on a topic, you automatically reduce the attention given to others. Accept, and make your client accept, that only one element can be emphasized at any one time. The real art of emphasizing lies in choosing the *right* topic to stress. For example, the most eye-catching element on a front page does not necessarily have to be the most 'important' one. Instead it could be the most

popular one, highlighted in order to attract the user and encourage them to stay at the site long enough to become intrigued by the most important one.

A number of internal technical issues may have an impact on the way you structure the site, and these should be considered and discussed between you and the client – you may need to 'gloss' these for the client to ensure that they fully comprehend the meaning and implications of these issues. However, these technical aspects should *not* be allowed to influence the communicative structure you conceptualize: they aren't of any concern to the user and should remain invisible to them – all they're interested in is the site's message and the available content.

Some technical issues to consider could be:

- **How will the site be updated?**
  Future updating of the 'finished' site is an important issue to consider in the structuring process. Who is supposed to do the updating, and what are their qualifications? When you are sorting the information that'll be included on the site, you should distinguish between **permanent** information and **dynamic** information that will change from time to time.

- **Should users be able to add content?**
  Sites that contain elements such as message boards, chat rooms and file sharing, where users have a high degree of interaction, call for specialized structures.

- **Does the scale of the site call for database solutions?**
  Is this web site project so large that a database solution would be appropriate? Large, information heavy, regularly updated sites are nearly always resolved most efficiently with a database solution.

- **Should you be using Generator?**
  Flash sites with dynamic content may require a Macromedia Generator, Swift Generator or other 'middleware-based' solution to feed content dynamically into the Flash front-end.

File Sizes, Preloading, Streaming and loadMovie

The first ten seconds a visitor is at your web site can make or break your future relationship. If the web site doesn't perform, or fails to meet the user's expectations, you've lost your customer. It's crucial that something interesting happens within these ten seconds. Having defined your target audience, you should have a good idea of how much bandwidth they'll have, and what they're likely to be interested in.

The SWF format has an important built-in quality: it's **streamable**. Streaming simply means that the SWF file begins playback before it's fully downloaded, allowing the designer to exceed the file size we'd expect the user to download before they got bored waiting for our site to load. This process can actually render the preloading of a complete site obsolete. By authoring your Flash movies carefully, you can provide the user with a fluent and fast-loading site, even when relatively large file sizes and slow modem connections are involved. It follows that file size is not as important a consideration as efficient streaming strategies and accurate bandwidth targeting.

In order to optimize the streaming performance of your Flash file, you'll have to understand how the SWF format is loaded.

By going to File > Publish Settings you can select how you want your file to be downloaded by altering the Load Order of your Flash movie. The default setting is Bottom up and the alternative is, not surprisingly, Top down:

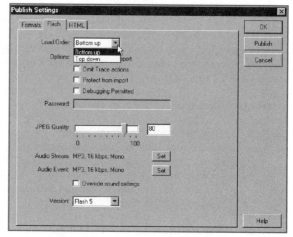

The Load Order determines whether the layers at the top or the bottom of the exported SWF will be loaded first.

Having been told whether to start at the top or the bottom layer, Flash now downloads the content of each frame as quickly as the user's bandwidth allows. Adding a preloader to the first couple of frames in each layer...

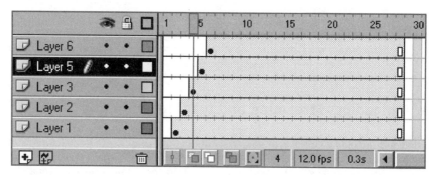

...makes the playback pause for a defined amount of time while the downloading continues as normal.

Knowing how your SWF will be downloaded allows you to arrange the content of your Flash movie in a way that will greatly improve its download performance, which in turn will lead to an improved user experience.

By introducing the elements of your page one frame at a time, keeping the different elements on separate layers, you can make any preloading unnecessary. As long as the size of the individual elements is kept down and the display order is set in a visually pleasing and content-relevant manner, the user will feel that something is happening, even though the site is still loading.

Flash's Bandwidth Profiler is extremely useful when optimizing your web site's loading performance. It allows you to simulate the streaming of your SWF file and check it will download smoothly:

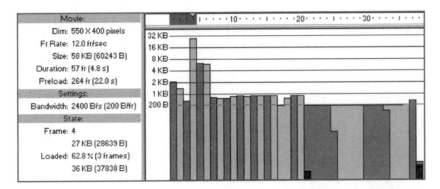

In order to ensure your Flash site downloads swiftly you will probably need to chop the whole thing up into several independent movies. Combining the `loadMovie` command with an efficient streaming arrangement for the separate movies will make your site perform very well.

> *For further in-depth technical discussion of streaming and preloading, take a look at the Preloading and Streaming chapter*

You won't be able to precisely predict which sections of your site a given user will find interesting and which ones they won't care less about. Using the `loadMovie` command affords the user a feeling of control by allowing them to decide when to use their precious bandwidth to download more information.

In contrast, forced preloading of an entire site leaves the user with only two options: they can either sit through the long preload and wait in the hope that the site's content will be relevant to them, or they'll leave the site prematurely to avoid wasting their time.

It's my guess that unless the user is a fellow Flash designer with a professional interest in your site design, or is on a very fast connection, they won't endure a long preload and will be surfing somewhere else before they've even laid eyes on your work.

Once you've decided upon your loading strategy, you can move on to the next step – creating a **prototype** of the working site.

The Functionality Prototype

A prototype is a structural skeleton of your web site. The prototype holds absolutely no content (except section or topic headings) and no graphical elements of any kind. It's a representation of structural and navigational functionality in its purest form. Here's the prototype that I used in the production of the Titoonia site that I dissect later in the chapter:

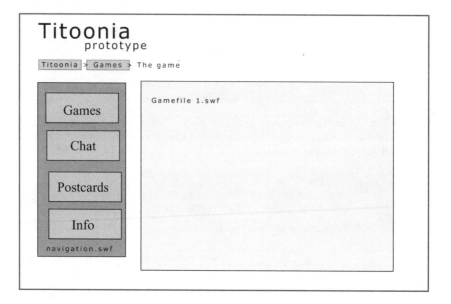

Making the prototype a common and familiar part of your web site creation process can pay great dividends. Using a decent prototype can save considerable amounts of time and help you to spot errors before the live site goes out. It allows you to test the internal and user-oriented usability of the structure you've designed, as well as the efficiency of your user interface.

While you're creating the prototype, think about what questions the user may have as they travel round the site. For example:

- How can I work out where I am inside this site?

- Where should I go next?

- How do I get back to where I was before?

Think of the prototype mostly as your own tool, a strange hybrid of lab assistant and lab rat. Use the prototype to build, test, and refine models that help you solve structural and navigational problems, or simply to get an overview of the information that you need to process and communicate.

Here's how I recommend you structure your site design process:

Start with pen and paper
Don't turn on the computer yet: it's much better to form your ideas on paper first. Make a quick list of the site's main topic and sub-topic headings.

Draw a simplified flowchart
Use pen and paper, or, if you insist, a flowchart program such as Microsoft Visio. Work through the different topics, pages and transitions. Imagine that you're using the finished site for the first time. This should be as much a process in your mind as a process on paper or the screen: you're thinking your way through the architecture and experience of the site.

Estimate your file size
Think about the content that should be visible as a default and which sections the user will want to be able to choose whether to view or not. If the file size gets too high, separate the section into several SWF files that you load as and when they are needed.

Consider file sharing
Think about what files can and should be shared between several pages, and make notes on what methods you imagine using to do this. The use of shared libraries in Flash 5, where several of your files are using the same elements, can help you to address this issue – *and* keep a check on your file size.

At this point, when you're satisfied with the topic categories and the flowchart, you can begin working on the computer.

Create the directory structure
Create a skeleton site that will be the local root directory of the final site. Create dummy HTML and FLA files named according to the pages and Flash movies shown on your flowchart. Then create sub-directories for sub-sections, images, video footage, downloads and so on, and create empty HTML and FLA files as necessary in all of these directories as well. Continue until you've created dummy versions of all the files your finished site will hold (except images, video files etc.). You'll now have a complete model of the finished site. It won't contain any real content at this stage, but you'll now have the means to simulate all the possible paths and jumps through your site.

Organize site navigation and links
Open the empty HTML and FLA files and create the internal navigational structure of the site using hyperlinks. Do one – and only one – simple button in Flash, and reuse it throughout your movies. Make all the main links you'll need in the finished site – you may find another flowchart helpful here to determine whether your navigation is set up correctly and allows users to move between appropriate sections.

Test thoroughly, and correct
Use your blank – and ugly – prototype to test the functionality of the site's navigation, the directory structure and the loading and unloading of movies. Make corrections, optimize and experiment. If possible, incorporate some testing of users from the target audience at this point as well. Listen to feedback and fix the site's flaws instead of explaining them.

If you use these techniques, you'll give yourself a great chance of ironing out a whole host of problems before you start creating the site's detailed content. Chances are you'll also end up with a solid navigation structure and strong insights into the working shape and functionality of the site.

Now let's drop down a level of detail and look at presenting visual information effectively within a single HTML page or Flash movie.

Usability and the User Experience

When presenting information in the form of text, people obviously have to be able to read it in some form – print, braille, monitor display – for it to be usable. In the same way, users have to be able to understand, or 'read', graphic images. The term given to the art of making graphic information accessible and usable is **Graphic Usability**. This is extremely important to consider in your design work if you're to help ensure that your defined message is reinforced by the graphic elements you use to put that message across.

The animators from the golden age of Disney Studios worked intensely with the term 'readability'. They had to draw characters whose actions could be easily interpreted, or read, by their audience, because if the viewers couldn't read what the character was doing in a specific scene, the point of the story could easily get lost and the audience would lose interest in the film. Ever since, animators around the world have worked with this term, knowing that readability can make or break a scene, or an entire film. This concept can be translated into our chosen field of graphic communication.

When animators plan a scene and sketch out how they want to position their characters throughout it, they spend a lot of time on finding the right **poses** for the characters. A certain pose has to express exactly what the animator wants to get across. The pose has to clearly and unambiguously communicate one single message – an emotion or a feeling such as anger, remorse, confusion, happiness, or doubt.

In addition to its pose, the **motion** of the character can add to the viewer's reading of its mood and further underline the core message of the scene. However, if the initial pose doesn't communicate at least part of the scene's message, then no matter how much fluent motion you add, you won't make the scene readable and your message will not by conveyed effectively to the viewer.

Animators check how readable a pose is by looking at it as a dark profile, as I've done below with the friendly robot from the Titoonic site. If the character's gesture works when only the outline or silhouette of the character is visible, this indicates that the signal will be even stronger when the actual details of the character are added.

Even though we can't see the character's facial expression, we understand that he's waving his hand at us. The waving gesture is universally recognized as a positive greeting. The body is relaxed in the way it's standing, and there are no obvious signs of aggression. Now we can add the details:

The facial expression and the further details of the character underline what we've already read from the blackened pose. The character is smiling and the eyes are friendly and relaxed.

A pose has to stress what the significant point of the scene is and point to the core of the message without obscuring it. If the audience has to pause to think about how to interpret it, the pose has failed, and the message is lost. A strong pose that works well signifies a focused message that the audience can read immediately. The pose should not have to work on a conscious level, but be *instinctively* understandable.

This concept can also be applied to graphic design and motion graphics. A graphic element in a web page has to be **readable**: it has to clearly indicate whether or not it holds information and, if it does, whether or not the information is important to the audience. In this context it's important to distinguish between **style-bearing** graphic elements and **information-bearing** elements in a web page.

The stylistic elements are freestyle graphic areas where you can express your artistic nature, and create the feel and ambience of the web site. These areas should not hold information, but rather express feelings, moods and sensations. Stylistic elements could be, for example, background images, ornaments, or decorative stripes, whereas examples of information-bearing graphic elements could be photographs of products, informational diagrams, graphical explanations, topic headings, buttons, or navigation bars. Such elements should contain a limited amount of clearly specified and targeted information. As a rule, the informative areas should be kept free of too much 'artistic' clutter.

If an information-bearing graphic looks like a stylistic element, the user is likely to misinterpret it, and therefore miss the information. If the information graphic is made to appear merely ornamental, it will be interpreted as an ornament and the user will discard the information it holds. On the other hand, when a stylistic element looks like it holds information or has some sort of practical function, the user will get confused. If an ornament looks like a button, for example, the user is likely to try and click it and will assume it's not working when it doesn't take them anywhere.

So, the graphical elements on your web site should clearly signal what they are and what their purpose is. All of this should be discernable by the viewer purely from the way each element appears on the screen. The characteristics you have given to each one – shape, position, color and so on – should instantly reveal the purpose of the object to the user.

Choosing and Formatting Text

The way you create and lay out your text also contributes to the usability of the site. Failure to make the text on your web site easy to read means failure to communicate with the user. One way to make communication more difficult is to use complex fonts:

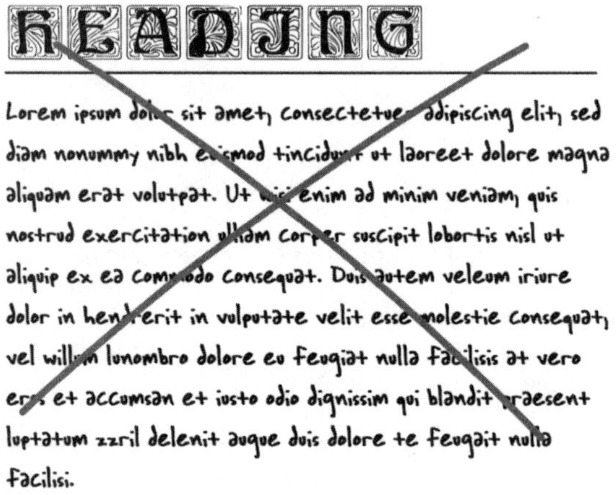

If you present information that you actually want people to read, you should always choose a font that is easily legible. Remember that the user has to read this text on a computer monitor, and as long as monitors have lower image resolution than paper, reading from a monitor will continue to be relatively painstaking.

As a general rule, no more than two fonts should be used in your design:

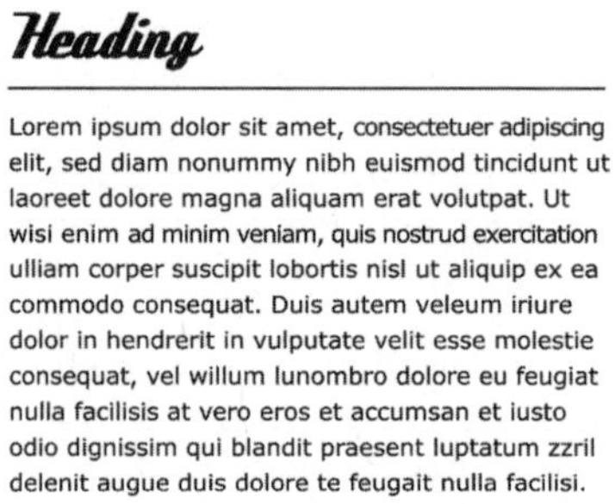

If several fonts are used, it tends to give the site an inconsistent feel and, unless the design is brilliantly executed, makes the layout seem amateurish. An exception to this rule would be the limited use of an extra font to represent a particular type of information, such as source code.

As long as it's still easily readable, you can afford to make the font you choose for your headings slightly more ornamental than that used for the main text. Generally, the font used for the main text needs to be as plain, simple and readable as possible. Avoid serifs, decorative typefaces and italicized characters as much as possible. Serifs and italics tend to be hard to read on a computer monitor.

When formatting your text there are some basic guidelines you should follow:

Choose the text justification carefully. With the possible exceptions of headings and tag lines, all main text should be either left aligned or justified. Never use centered text for long passages and avoid using right aligned text, as this makes it very hard for the user to change lines when reading.

Heading

Lorem ipsum dolor sit amet, consectetuer adipiscing elit, sed diam nonummy nibh euismod tincidunt ut laoreet dolore magna aliquam erat volutpat. Ut wisi enim ad minim veniam, quis nostrud exercitation ulliam corper suscipit lobortis nisl ut aliquip ex ea commodo consequat. Duis autem veleum iriure dolor in hendrerit in vulputate velit esse molestie consequat, vel willum lunombro dolore eu feugiat nulla facilisis at vero eros et accumsan et iusto odio dignissim qui blandit praesent luptatum zzril delenit augue duis dolore te feugait nulla facilisi.

Heading

Lorem ipsum dolor sit amet, consectetuer adipiscing elit, sed diam nonummy nibh euismod tincidunt ut laoreet dolore magna aliquam erat volutpat. Ut wisi enim ad minim veniam, quis nostrud exercitation ulliam corper suscipit lobortis nisl ut aliquip ex ea commodo consequat. Duis autem veleum iriure dolor in hendrerit in vulputate velit esse molestie consequat, vel willum lunombro dolore eu feugiat nulla facilisis at vero eros et accumsan et iusto odio dignissim qui blandit praesent luptatum zzril delenit augue duis dolore te feugait nulla facilisi.

Heading

Lorem ipsum dolor sit amet, consectetuer adipiscing elit, sed diam nonummy nibh euismod tincidunt ut laoreet dolore magna aliquam erat volutpat. Ut wisi enim ad minim veniam, quis nostrud exercitation ulliam corper suscipit lobortis nisl ut aliquip ex ea commodo consequat. Duis autem veleum iriure dolor in hendrerit in vulputate velit esse molestie consequat, vel willum lunombro dolore eu feugiat nulla facilisis at vero eros et accumsan et iusto odio dignissim qui blandit praesent luptatum zzril delenit augue duis dolore te feugait nulla facilisi.

Note that both left alignment and justification can cause problems. The left aligned example above produces a flaw where a line seems to have been cut off short. A similar glitch appears in the justified example, where the spacing between the words in one sentence is too big. These problems can be easily overcome by adjusting the tracking of the problematic line or by splitting the long first word you can see on the following line.

Be careful not to make text fields too *wide*:

Heading

Lorem ipsum dolor sit amet, consectetuer adipiscing elit, sed diam nonummy nibh euismod tincidunt ut laoreet dolore magna aliquam erat volutpat. Ut wisi enim ad minim veniam, quis nostrud exercitation ulliam corper suscipit lobortis nisl ut aliquip ex ea commodo consequat. Duis autem veleum iriure dolor in hendrerit in vulputate velit esse molestie consequat, vel willum lunombro dolore eu feugiat nulla facilisis at vero eros et accumsan et iusto odio dignissim qui blandit praesent luptatum zzril delenit augue duis dolore te feugait nulla facilisi.

This necessitates the user's eyes moving a long way to read the text. This long range of movement requires a greater effort of concentration and makes it harder for the user to move from line to line. It also tires the eyes, making the reader less receptive to the content of the text. If the text is to be placed over a wide area, the obvious solution is to split the area into columns.

Don't obscure the important text that you want the reader to absorb. By adding background colors that are either too close to that of the text or make an ugly contrast, you'll make the text very difficult to read:

TEXT/BACKGROUND CONTRAST

Remember that this kind of picture label is a reference to color images on the CD

25

Remember that it can be hard even to read clear text on a monitor. It's generally much easier to read dark text on a light background, rather than light text on a dark background.

Consistency: a Usability Tool

User interfaces like Windows or Macintosh are built around standards. Standards mean that, for example, one button in one part of the operating system (OS) is a 'clone' of the other buttons in the rest of the OS. The user will be able to understand and recognize buttons throughout the OS because they all look and function the same. **Consistency** is the unifying principle that GUI (graphical user interface) standards are built around.

The average web surfer is familiar with the interface standards they have used with the operating system of their computer, their programs and from their previous use of the Web. Programs authored for a specific OS generally implement the same GUI standards. All buttons and clickable icons are designed in a way that conforms to a standard format that is recognizable and therefore easily understood. By establishing GUI standards we can make sure that users don't have to learn new ways of interacting each time they use a new program or visiting a new web site. You'll understand how testing this can be if you're usually a PC user and are suddenly confronted with the Mac interface (or vice versa) – you can almost hear the gears meshing as your brain tries to make the necessary adjustments to move the mouse to the right places and press the right buttons.

When designing UI elements like scroll bars, buttons and windows – sometimes referred to as UI widgets – you establish a range of **metaphors**. A button in an interface is not *really* a button; it's simply a graphic representation of a real button. But in your head, subconsciously, you know that hitting that button is going to make something happen.

A good metaphor is all about **familiarity**. In order for UI metaphors to work, the user has to know what the metaphor refers to – it must relate to something the user is already familiar with. The common button metaphor works because we all understand objects from the physical world that contain similar buttons. Making the graphical button behave like a real button when it's clicked reinforces the effect that was set up by the initial mimicking of a button's appearance. For example, a metaphor for a volume control could be based on the actual volume control of a home stereo system. A Flash representation of the volume control would look and work in a similar way to the physical object, which most people would be familiar with, and is therefore a well-established UI metaphor even before the user enters the web site. However, the way to actually use the volume control metaphor will obviously be quite different from using the physical version – the user can't actually grab the on-screen control with their hand and twist it. You have to ensure that the implementation of the metaphor is intuitive and workable – this issue can be considered a potential source of problems.

Obviously, some aspects of our interaction with the computer cannot be based on real life objects. Drop-down menus, scroll bars, and indeed the actual concept of selecting information with a mouse pointer are all things we have become familiar with due to their consistent appearance across a wide range of applications. Because they have always been represented in near-identical ways, people have become as comfortable using these devices as they are using the average stereo volume controller.

Establishing a metaphor means introducing a UI widget to the user, and having the user feel comfortable and secure about using it. The user will have to use the new UI widget a couple of times to get used to how it works. When establishing UI metaphors, you have to relate to the knowledge a user has already acquired. Once a UI widget metaphor has been established, the user will feel that they are in control: they will have a presentiment about what will happen if they click a particular button, and they will know how to get back to where they started. Every time you introduce and try to establish a *new* UI widget metaphor, you delay the user's use of the web site: the user has to pause in order to figure out how this new widget works. You don't want to force users to spend time learning how to use your web site and, more importantly, users don't *want* to spend their time learning how to use your web site when there are billions of other web sites they could be visiting. If a user doesn't figure out how to use your web site within about ten seconds, chances are that they'll leave and never come back. Your site is not the center of the web-universe, and if the user gets impatient with it because they don't know how to use it, they'll quickly move to one they *do* know how to use.

When you're designing and prototyping your web site, try to think through the different types of user interaction you'll need on the site. Keep the number of metaphors used to an absolute minimum so that you won't have to teach the user how several new UI widgets work. Although it may look fantastic and be extremely clever, if you add a complex scrolling-pull-down-multi-button device to your site, it will only add to the amount of secondary information the user has to absorb before engaging with the *real* content.

Use widgets the way they were established. If you're using variations of major user interfaces that are based on commonly accepted standards – like Windows or Macintosh – make sure you use them correctly. When you, as a web designer, are using interpretations or redesigns of commonly known UI widgets it's crucial that you refer directly to the way they are used in their 'pure', original form. Significant deviations from this form either resemble the introduction of a new UI widget or a misuse of a standard widget, which can have a detrimental effect on the user's experience.

If you were designing a feedback form using multiple-choice questions, you'd probably use radio buttons or check boxes at some point. Both are commonly known in both the Macintosh and Windows interfaces, and have a similar (but not identical function) and meaning. Radio buttons only allow the user to choose one option from a list of several – when the user makes their choice, the button currently selected is depressed – whereas check boxes allow the user to select several options simultaneously from a list. It's a slight but important difference as using the check boxes as radio buttons, or vice versa, would ruin the established standard, confusing the user and spoiling the usability of the feedback form.

Viewable Web Design

Having looked at issues that are relevant to a web site's usability, and to the user, in this section I'll discuss some different aspects of the creative graphic design process. Though I won't mention usability as much as in the previous section, it's very important to constantly keep in mind that as a graphic designer you're *always* communicating your defined site message to whoever views it.

In this section I'm going to air some of my own thoughts on the graphic design process; I'll go through what I define as the cornerstones of the process. The methods I describe are based on my own experiences as a web designer and on various theoretical sources, and therefore in no way represent the only way to carry out the process. I can only tell you what methods work for me, and hope that the advice I pass on will prove useful and a spur to you creating processes that work effectively for you.

Creativity through Limitation

No matter what medium they're working in, a designer's task is to produce the most creative result possible within whatever restrictive boundaries the medium, or the brief, imposes on them. Being creative means making the most of the limited options at hand.

Think of young children playing – let's say a bunch of kids playing at 'soldiers' in the park. Maybe they've just met after school, and none of them have brought their toy guns – but that doesn't pose a problem. Some of them might be using a stick, others only their finger. When you think about it, that's quite creative. These kids are making the most of the situation, and have designed a refined interactive experience with, at best, a stick as their only external tool. In order to give the game structure they have to define a set of rules, such as: "When you're hit, you have to stay still and count to ten", "This side's the goodies, and that one's the baddies", "This tree is our base". They realize that if anyone cheats, the entire game will lose its realism and, the defined rules having been broken, won't be fun any more. Remember how deflated you felt as a kid when someone spoiled the game?

In the world where we're currently flexing our creative muscles, the Web, we have a scenario where almost everything is intellectually allowed but many things are *technically* prohibited. Things like bandwidth, processing power, screen sizes, user skills, and clients are all limitations the web designer has to work within and around as they try to present their message in a creative way. However, rather than perceive these things as obstacles that restrict our work we, as designers, should look upon them instead as boundaries that guide and challenge our creative minds. If a group of school kids can create an entire virtual reality based on a couple of sticks, we professional designers should be more than capable of overcoming the restrictions imposed on us by the Web.

I believe, in fact, that these restrictions actually *help* the progress and development of the creative process. A trained designer might find limitations annoying and counter-productive, but the novice will often find it very hard to come up with any creative idea at all if the client just says: "Do whatever you like". By its very nature, design is about problem solving – as we've already said, the designer's job is to communicate their client's message to the viewer. The boundaries imposed on you by your medium and your brief will help to guide and form your creative ideas, and ultimately help you to produce a purposeful, structured design. To get used to working inside this sort of framework, try the following exercise:

Design in Action

Pose yourself some small graphic communication exercises where you communicate a very simple message while obeying a very simple set of rules. For example, the design overleaf is intended to show the words 'construction' and 'deconstruction' as related opposites. In producing it I specified that only one font was allowed to be used, and only three colors: black, white and red:

CONSTRUCTION/DECONSTRUCTION

Work fast and spend no more than half an hour on each design. Bear in mind that these are exercises, and the results are not supposed to be fully resolved solutions for professional briefs. Here are the generic rules that I use in this kind of exercise:

1. **Define a message**
   Choose a very simple message, like a saying or maybe just one word – for example, 'Hope springs eternal', or 'Peace'. It doesn't matter what word or phrase you choose, but remember: the more subtle the message, the harder the task will be. You could start by choosing words like 'cold', 'warm', 'love', or 'anger', then write down the moods, colors, feelings, people and so on that you associate with the words.

2. ***Do not* consider the target audience**
   In this exercise, you don't need to think about who your message is aimed at because *you* are the target audience. Simply communicate the message in the way that means the most to you.

3. **You make the rules**
   Write down a simple set of rules like 'Use one font, two colors and only circles' or 'Use diagonal lines, squares, grayscales, and only two colors: red and purple'. Try writing several sets of rules for the same message.

4. **Create**
   Start creating your design using your usual techniques and creative habits. Stick to your rules and try to be as innovative as possible without straying beyond the boundaries you've set yourself. Every time you face a creative choice, look to your set of rules for an answer. Work fast, then work faster; it's important not to dwell on a problem for too long, as it's a luxury you won't be afforded in a professional environment.

5. **Evaluate**
   Quickly do a couple of designs before you lean back and evaluate what's working and what isn't. Don't fix any mistakes, but start over on a new design, keeping your mistakes in mind.

Sketching, Thumbnails and Doodles

Most every 'real' artist makes sketches and doodles before creating the final piece. It's not necessary to be a fine artist to benefit from basic sketching techniques. Don't say: "I can't draw!" Even if that's the case, you can still benefit from this process.

The sketching process should always be the first part of the graphical production line, and the process should be as free and open-minded as possible. Sketching is a wonderfully unlimited and informal process: everything is allowed and nothing is ruled out as 'technically impossible' at this stage. The key thing is to drive the creative ideas out of their hiding places. It's not important that what you're sketching looks like anything specific or concrete, it doesn't have to be a 'polished' work of art, and it doesn't have to make a lot of sense. What's important is to get your creative juices flowing. Don't limit yourself to following the laws of physics, conventions, or established graphic profiles. Start out in a vivid and wild way, and reduce and make practically realizable afterwards. Everything you've learned about the project at hand should serve only as a discreet source of inspiration, and not be a source of 'achievement anxiety'. Once you've concluded the initial sketching, you can start looking at the goals, deadlines, and expectations again.

In the initial stage of the sketching process you should *not* consider the fact that you're supposed to be designing a web site. The final goal should be obscured, or even better forgotten. The more you are able to let go of deadlines and limitations, the freer and better your sketching result will be.

The Sketching Process

The successful sketching process includes several steps that should be followed patiently and thoroughly. Give each step enough time and attention:

1. **Inspiration**
    Read through the material supplied by the client, go through your briefing notes, take a look at web sites for similar clients, and look at the client's existing web site (if any). I also find it very useful to spend a great deal of time looking at web sites that have nothing at all to do with the project at hand. Note down what's inspiring to you.

2. **Warm up**
    If your computer is turned on, turn it off. You probably know the feeling of being on the phone, and suddenly finding yourself with a pen and a piece of paper filled with nonsense doodles. Grab a pen, a pencil, or whatever drawing tool is at hand, a blank piece of paper, and start scribbling to try to get into this state of mind. Strive to draw non-figurative doodles on the entire piece of paper. Try not to think too hard. Leave your rational brain in the desk drawer and let yourself get tied up in both the details and the bigger picture.

3. **Sketch away**

   Make graphic 'notes' of whatever ideas pop up in your head. Details of navigational elements, backgrounds, transitions or shapes that might work or might not – all these should find their way onto the paper in no particular order. Don't worry too much about the overall layout of the site – spend more time on the various elements and their details than on how it's all tied together.

4. **Evaluate**

   Once you've got a pile of different sketches you'll have to go through every one of them to evaluate and extract the essence of the best ideas. Grab a red pen or a highlighter and circle the sketch elements you like and find usable or inspiring. Don't discard any of your sketches but save all of them in your project folder. Mark all sketches with your name, the date and project name.

5. **Refine**

   Having selected the key drawings and details, work them over again. Think the different ideas and concepts through, and maybe make some technical sketches or notes on how it should be implemented in Flash or HTML. Continue until a relatively clear image of where you are going begins to emerge.

6. **Repeat steps 3 – 5**

   Repeat the process as many times as you feel you can to extract new ideas from it. If you reach a dead end with an idea, don't continue with it just because you've invested a certain amount of time in it already – be prepared to ditch ideas that won't fit the brief or won't be usable.

When you feel you've squeezed as much as you can out of this process, decide which idea you're going to follow to its fully resolved conclusion.

Composition

The way an image is **composed** plays a large part in how successful it is in communicating its message. A successful composition can effectively lead the viewer's eye along a predefined path. Every image or design we see around us holds a built-in composition, which is its fundamental expression. Below all the layers of color, technique and expression, the image is carried by its composition.

You can think of composition as a way of making the image field interesting and appealing to look at, and as a way of pointing out what's important. A good composition emphasizes the message being communicated and brings the viewer's attention to the most relevant parts of the image. The composition you choose will go a long way towards determining the feel of your site, so it needs to be appropriate for your target audience. For example, a games site for kids would be composed in a far more dynamic and busy style than, say, a site for an up-market department store.

In Flash, the area where you compose your image is the stage. The format, or aspect, you choose predetermines a great deal of your composition. Let's take a look at the elements that you should bear in mind when composing the contents of your stage, your Flash movie, and the overall site.

The Elements of Composition

An image field's overall composition is made up of compositional elements. These elements, and the use of them, build the foundation of the image field. Some of the important elements are described below – these are all things that you should experiment with yourself in your trusty sketchbook.

The Image Field
The image field is the whole area that you have available to play with. In Flash terms, this is the stage, and for a pure HTML site, this would be the whole browser window.

Lines
Any image contains a large number of lines, visible (actually drawn and rendered) or invisible (for example, implied by areas of color and blank space). These lines cut through the image field, leading the eye and imposing either tension and conflict, or balance and harmony. The lines of a composition are both borders between different fields, and pointers or 'highways for the eye' which the eye can travel along.

Fields and Areas
Colored or shaded fields and areas cover an image. The arrangement and shape of these fields builds the overall background, or bottom layer, of the image. The blank area around these fields is called negative space and is as important as the fields themselves – so its appearance needs to be fully considered throughout the design process.

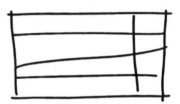

Shapes, Tension and Contrast

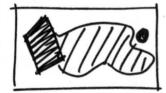

Within your image, there are likely to be a number of different types of contrasts, all influencing the overall feel of your composition. Differences between straight and curved lines, square and round shapes, light and dark areas, and different colored sections all create contrasts that can be used to bring an emotion into the image. In the central example above, the concept of contrast is used to describe size, tension, direction and conflict. The large ship appears threatening because of the contrast in size between it and the smaller boat. Tension is closely related to contrast, and adds to the lively, organic and dramatic feel of a composition. Tension arises in the field between two objects in contrast, along a curved line, or when strongly contrasting colors are arranged in a way that suggests conflict.

Dynamics

 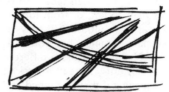

When you incorporate dynamics into your composition, you add a sense of movement, speed and direction. It's essentially done by adding lines – and the style of lines determines the form of dynamics produced. Smooth swirling lines give a soft, flowing feel, while straight – perhaps converging – lines will give off an impression of aggressive, direct movement.

Balance

Add balance to your composition to make it work. Balance grows from symmetry, but shouldn't be understood as symmetry alone. Balance is about distributing the visual weight evenly across the image. A large heavy field on one side of the image should perhaps be balanced by a small brightly colored element on the other side.

Harmony

As an alternative to creating tension and dynamics, you can give your composition a harmonious feel. Harmony is achieved using smooth flowing lines and uncluttered arrangements. Think of a wide expanse of blue sky with fields below, or a circular clearing in a forest on a summer day. No aggressive contrasts of color or size, and no fast movement:

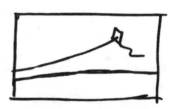

Colors

Colors can accentuate or minimize all of the compositional elements discussed above. Your choice of color can produce feelings of tension or harmony, balance or aggression. The use of either warm or cold colors, for example, can make parts of your image more or less prominent in the overall composition.

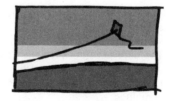

COLOR IN COMPOSITION

In the image above, color is used as a compositional tool in the terms of adding to the contrast between the large sky area and the small kite. The red color of the kite also adds balance to the image by acting as a counterweight to the blue area. The large green and blue areas at the top and bottom of the picture give the image a sense of calm. We'll look at colors in a little more detail later on.

Reading Direction

My view of composition is founded on the way I'm used to reading text and images. Because of the culture I've grown up in, I've been taught to read from left to right. Other cultures read in different ways, such as right to left, or from top to bottom, and therefore they have a different way of reading images as well. Although it may very rarely affect you, this is something that's worth noticing and keeping in mind when you're thinking about your design work, because you can exploit these cultural habits to achieve different effects. Things like a newspaper comic strip wouldn't make a lot of sense if you read it backwards, and even very simple compositions can change their feel and meaning if they're flipped and read backwards:

The way I would read this image, from left to right, is something like this:

Man swimming > Big shape> Big shark!

If I flip the image...

...and read it again, this time I would see it as:

Eye > Shark > Little guy swimming for dear life!

It's a small difference in this example, but the difference is there, and should be taken seriously.

The Composition Sketch

A useful technique for producing better composition in your design work is the composition sketch.

The difference between the composition sketch and the general sketching process I discussed above is that where the general sketch should focus on the individual elements of your project, the composition sketch should focus on the overall image and how the individual elements are combined.

Working on reasonably large-scale paper and using a permanent marker or a soft, thick pencil, sketch out possible layouts that incorporate all the aspects you need to include in your composition.

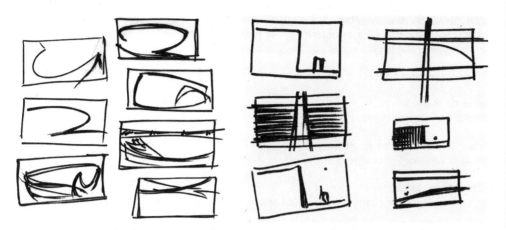

As in the sketching process described earlier, try to let go of any thoughts on specific elements of the site you're working on. Try instead to concentrate on the *mood* you want to communicate – visualize the emotional content of the message. For example, if you're doing an intro for a horror movie site, think about what horror means: maybe it's chaos, drama, tension and conflict. Try to visualize images in your mind that contain these elements – and then use them to create a composition.

At this point it's important that you choose the format of the site and stick to it. Then, as with the sketching we did earlier, work quickly: in a concentrated period of about 30 minutes do lots of small sketches, spending no more than ten seconds on each one. Try not to analyze too much: instead of thinking about where you're placing the separate image elements, like the navigation bar or particular buttons, try to consider the image as a whole. In this way, you'll resolve all the parts of your image as a whole rather than getting little sections finished but finding that they have to be altered later on to accommodate other elements as they are added.

Go through your sketches and choose the ones you think work. Then rework these sketches and gradually your layout ideas will be refined into a workable composition.

Color Schemes

When talking about and describing colors we have to use a lot of subjective terms, as, despite the existence of color theory, color usage is still an extremely subjective topic. Different people see color differently and, depending on how they are used in a design, color combinations can seem either gaudy or clean and crisp. Very often, the use of color is simply a question of personal taste.

However, the elements you've decided upon earlier on in the design process will have a strong bearing on the colors you decide to use in the final design. The defined message and the target audience determine the mood and feel you want for the site, but the colors you choose will also determine the mood and response you evoke. The color scheme also has to fit in with the composition you've chosen.

Again, think of your target audience, the defined message and the choice of composition. Dynamic or relaxed? Young or older? Boys or girls? Stick with, and get inspired by, the decisions you've made in the previous steps of the process.

Color's three most important qualities are:

Color or Hue
The color's name or defining property

Value, Luminosity or Brightness
The light value or light content of the color

Intensity or Saturation
The color's degree of clarity in proportion to the color's 'maximum'

There are a number of principles that you should consider when planning your site's color scheme. Let's take a look at these next, starting with the idea of **color contrast**.

Color Contrast
By contrasting colors intelligently, you can produce extremely effective results. When we simply place different colors next to each other, the contrast achieved is a result of the different hues of each color:

COLOR CONTRAST

Light/dark Contrast
If we use the same hue – a single color – throughout, but alter the brightness of certain sections, we can produce a **light/dark** contrast:

LIGHT AND DARK CONTRAST

Traditional graphic artists use this type of contrast in woodcuts and charcoal and pencil drawings.

Cold/warm Contrast
We're conditioned to link colors to different temperatures, and we can use the contrast of warm and cold colors to good effect:

TEMPERATURE CONTRAST

The temperature contrast is what tells your intuitive faculties "if you turn this handle you'll get cold water, and if you turn *this* one, you'll get hot". Red-orange is the warmest color and blue-green the coldest. The use of color in a room, for example, can psychologically inflict changes in your perception of the physical experience of temperature. Note that the colors in the sample shown here have the same lightness – only the hue is changed from color to color.

The Complementary Contrast

Complementary colors are direct opposites of each other, and so produce a definite contrast when used together:

COMPLEMENTARY COLORS CONTRAST

When mixed, complementary colors blend into a neutral gray-black. The use of complementary colors creates dramatic effects and can bring clarity and balance to an image. The complementary color pairs are:

- Yellow & Purple

- Yellow-Orange & Purple-Blue

- Orange & Blue

- Red-Orange & Blue-Green

- Red & Green

- Red-Purple & Yellow-Green

The Quality Contrast

Using sections with the same hue but different levels of saturation can create a subtle contrast. The saturation is really the intensity of the color, 100% being the full hue, and 0% being a lackluster gray:

QUALITY CONTRAST

The Quantity Contrast

Two factors determine the way a color works: the color's light intensity or luminosity, and the area the color covers. The quantity contrast is the harmonic relation between two colors' luminosity and the size of the area they cover. By comparing the colors to a neutral gray, we can get a notion of the color's luminosity.

Yellow is roughly like this: 9, Orange: 8, Red: 6, Purple: 3, Blue: 4 and Green: 6

QUANTITY CONTRAST

The harmonic area: size relation between yellow and purple in the example above, is $^1/_4$: $^3/_4$, whereas the relation between red and green is $^1/_2$: $^1/_2$

Deciding on your Color Scheme

Settling for a color scheme is about translating the defined message into a kind of 'color melody'. The message should be reflected in the colors of the site, and the mood of the message should be emphasized in the choice of colors – although you may well find yourself hindered by the corporate colors the client will want to use. You will probably have been aware of this restriction from the outset of the project, and it's just one more rule you've got to bend your creativity around.

Generally, you'll be better off trusting your intuition when it comes to choosing colors. As long as you have an understanding of basic color use and structure, which we've just gone through, you should be able to choose some effective color schemes. Of course, all we've been able to give you here is a sketch – there's plenty more theory and practice to explore in art classes and dedicated color theory books.

Your intuition knows a lot more about color than you might think. Your intuitive brain is constantly interpreting color at a subconscious level, and knows, for example, that the black and yellow warning stripes on a wasp represent possible danger – in the form of pain.

The way I work with colors is mostly an intuitive process, the result of my graphic design training and practice, practice, practice: I seldom think about what colors to use, or whether they work or not. I try to avoid thinking too hard, and instead I focus on *seeing*. I try to subjectively see and experience what's working and what's not. This skill is something that can complement the rational analysis and color planning that you do.

One of the most important things to avoid, and the most common mistake, is using too many colors. Getting a large number of colors to work together will always prove to be pretty difficult. Remember that each color sends a psychological message to the user's brain: these messages are unconsciously interpreted into a mood or a feeling, and if too many different messages are received at once the overall message will become muddled and the user will be confused – even if they don't know *why* they're feeling confused! Similar problems arise if you attempt to use several of the contrasts described earlier in one design – you'll send too many messages to the user and your site will lose its focus.

Flash is a great tool for the color-selection process itself. When I'm doing color styling for a site I usually use Flash and a digitizer tablet, like a Wacom PenPartner. By scribbling fairly mindlessly in Flash, using random colors, I try to narrow down the look I'm seeking. Again, I try not to think too hard about it, but instead try to analyze how I personally react to the colors, and how they make me feel. I compare these impressions with the defined message I'm communicating and the audience I'm trying to target. Once I've found the selection of colors I want to use, I do a 'quantity sketch' with them in Flash, sketching the amount of each color that should be used in order for the design to work:

COLOR SKETCH IN FLASH

From this sketch I can extract some color-application guidelines to use when I get to design the actual site elements.

When you've worked with color for some time, you'll probably realize that you've got a personal set of **color preferences**. Unconsciously, you'll acquire a favorite palette of colors that you use regularly. This palette has not come to you as the result of an intellectual process, but as the result of repeatedly working intuitively with color. It is an unconsciously acquired thing, and you are using it almost totally unconsciously. The personal palette contains your favorite colors and colors that you know work effectively. You feel safe about the palette, and, in some way, the palette expresses part of your personal style. The potential problem here is that you not only feel safe about this palette, you also have a hard time diverting your color attention *away* from it. In other words, *the personal palette can easily become a limitation in your creative development*.

Once in a while, therefore, it's a good idea to seek new color input to revitalize your color tool kit. Look at objects and environments around you for inspiration: stare at trees, sidewalk tiles, cornfields, cars, trashcans, skin, hotdogs and whatever you can lay your eyes on, and consciously work through the colors the item contains. For example, when you look at a tree in the summertime you're probably expecting the leaves to be green – only when you look properly will you see that they're not just shades of green; they're yellow, orange, bluish-purple, and many shades in between. Next time you find yourself sitting in traffic, take a good look at the automobile in front and see how the light reflects off its curves, angles, glass, and tires. These activities are a way of becoming more conscious about your color preferences. The more you know about the group of colors that make a tree's leaves green, the more you improve your basis for renewing and refining your personal palette. Although, as I've said, choosing colors should ideally be an intuitive process, the revitalization of your personal palette requires intellectual intervention. You have to *choose* to revitalize your palette and you have to *choose* to use a new color for the first time. Look around you – the world is full of inspiration!

Color Examples

Now I've shown you how I choose my colors, I'll show you some of the work my choices have gone into.

Chaseace.com

WWW.CHASEACE.COM

This is a promotional site for a PC action game in a retro-arcade kind of style. The game is a fast-paced, highly explosive experience, so the site obviously had to signal emotive responses – with words like 'action', 'aggression', and 'danger' cropping up in the early brainstorming process.

My primary source of inspiration were warning signs and wasps. Warning signs signal danger in a manner similar to the way the wasp signals aggression. I therefore went for the colors black and yellow, and red and blue – with a little green to balance the composition, and white fields to make the text readable. These colors were all used in a bright and undisguised way, with yellow as the most dominant color, and blue used least. The end result is a very 'loud' site, with a tendency to lack focus. In some circumstances, the use of signal colors in the background can shift the focus from the actual content, which can cause problems with the user not being able to tune into what's actually going on. In this case though, I felt that it didn't matter all that much after all. The target audience would be used to visiting obscure underground gaming sites with all-black backgrounds and blinking text, so coming to this site would make them look twice.

Helpfish.com

WWW.HELPFISH.COM

Helpfish.com is another promotional site, this time for an animated feature film called "Help! I'm a Fish". The creators of the film put a lot of effort into the preliminary designs and layouts that were to define the look of the film and enable the artistic quality and aesthetics to stand out. The message this site needed to communicate was an interpretation of the movie artwork's classy feel.

Due to the visual simplicity of the movie, and the underwater theme, I chose a blue and pale purple color scheme. The blue colors were used in a very pure form, but by altering the saturation – as I described earlier – I was able to produce different intensities that contrasted nicely. Three different purple tones were used, each with different luminosities, producing a light/dark contrast. Small dots of green, orange and a reddish hue were then added to prevent the design appearing flat, and to balance the blue and purple. I think that the end result succeeds in communicating aesthetic simplicity and that my color usage adds focus to the content. What's your view?

Petergrafik.dk

WWW.PETERGRAFIK.DK

Petergrafik.dk is my personal web site and, as you'll have noticed, it's all brown. In creating this site I didn't really follow my own advice! I didn't have a fixed idea of the content or message of the site – it was intended merely as a portfolio site and its main aim was to look different and interesting. There's a smooth contrast of colors from light brown through to black, with hints of different colors such as the yellow Chase Ace 2 logo and bits of green and orange, while the text is white to aid legibility.

I'm happy with the end result. It's certainly an individual site – I haven't seen one that uses brown to the same degree. The site has won several awards and has been very positively reviewed in several magazines. I have to admit, though, this site has a lot of usability defects, and so shouldn't be looked at as a model for the things we discussed earlier in the chapter. One day, when I get the time, I'm going to go back and fix that...

Consistency Revisited

I mentioned **consistency** previously as an agent for improving usability. However, as well as improving the usability of your sites, consistency can be used to help you design them as well. Consistency is one of the cornerstones of good design, and when carried out rigorously it can move decent design up a level to good design - and then make good design even better. Consistency is a unifying principle of design.

One of the reasons I introduced the graphic communication exercise in the beginning of this chapter was to show you a way of working with the consistency principle. In the exercise I described how to get some creative juices flowing by setting up a simple message and some simple rules, and then sticking to them through the creation of your design. To avoid creating inconsistent designs, you should create a set of design rules of your own, similar to the ones described in the exercise, but tailored to your own personal style and habits. Rules are what consistency is all about, and the foundations for these rules are built on the ideas we've been talking about throughout the chapter. Defining the message, defining the target audience, thinking about usability, and proper use of color contrasts are issues you'll need to deal with for every design you do. You have to ensure that all these things are fully resolved, and you need to have a meticulous eye for detail to spot and fix even the smallest deviations from your master plan. It's that extra bit of attention that makes the difference to your design, and having a set of rules and techniques that you always use will help you attain that higher level. When you start out you may well find it hard to check and correct every little detail, but once into your stride you won't be able to let a design go until you're certain every aspect of it has been checked. By training and nursing your eye for detail you'll find yourself always striving for perfection as your goal.

The concept of consistency is a form of 'object-oriented' thinking, and by thinking in terms of *objects* you may find it easier to apply consistency to your designs. This essentially means not focusing too hard on the *specific* element that you're working on, but instead thinking generically about that *type* of object: 'What do these kinds of objects have to do?', and 'What kind of characteristics should they have?' If, instead of thinking of 'this lump of text in the top corner of this particular page', you try to think of 'the text object', you might find it easier to remember and apply the rules we defined for the text object earlier in the chapter. Similarly, by thinking of 'the link object' instead of 'the second link from the top of the page' you'll know how to treat *any* link on *any* page of a site you're doing: all the link objects you've done before will give you the answer. The Flash architecture actually encourages this way of thinking and designing: by designing one button and then using multiple instances of that object, you ensure that the look of a button is consistent throughout your site.

The look, feel, and usability of a web site is greatly affected by the use of colors, fonts, UI widgets, the look of buttons and links, and the placement of your different elements. If, from page to page, the way you address these issues is inconsistent, your site will lose its focus and the user will become confused as to the message it's trying to communicate. Something as simple as placing the navigational links on the same spot on every page of the site, for example, means that the user always knows exactly where to look for them. If the navigational tools are placed inconsistently across the pages of the site, the user will have to search around for them every time he or she wants to move to a new page. Similarly, deviations in the placing of a header or a logo from page to page will make that particular element flicker and jump in transitions between pages or sections, while using one background color on one page, and another on the next may make the user think they've left the site, and entered another.

Consistency signals professionalism and responsibility. It gives a sense of unity between the different parts of a design and makes them connect to one another and appear to be related in the eyes of the user. Inconsistency gives exactly the opposite impression to the user. In its extremes, inconsistency can mean changing the message, the target audience, and the usability of the site each time a new section is selected.

The Graphical Profile

To ensure consistency in your designs, and to make your job as a graphic designer a whole lot easier, you can create a graphical profile – a design manual or 'rulebook' – for each of your projects. As you work your way through the preparation process, you'll learn a lot about the image, message and look of your project. All this knowledge should be organized so that you and your client can use it in the rest of the process, and for future reference. If you make it a habit to set up the graphical profile at the beginning of the process, you can add elements and notes along the way, as and when they're decided upon.

A graphical profile contains written and visual information on what graphical rules and elements are used in a particular project. The document should be created so that other people – and you – will be able to understand it. Important items to list in the document could be:

Colors
A complete list of the colors used. Include color samples, plus RGB and Hex values. Make notes on how the colors are used, for example: "background", "frames", "shadow", "ornaments", etc.

Fonts
A list of all fonts used. Include name, filename and platform, a font sample, and information on sizes, spacing, kerning, and line spacing, as well as notes on use, for example: "heading", "subheading", "normal" etc.

Logos
Any logos used should be included in the document in their final form. Write guidelines on how the logo should be used and make notes on color use in the logos. Include the filenames of the logos used – and keep the original file.

Styles
Make notes on any special approaches taken with the style and look of the project. Include the conclusions found when defining the target audience. Describe special image formats and composition or layout guidelines used on the project.

Dimensions
Include any important layout or composition dimensions. Make sure that movie sizes, image sizes or aspect, margin widths and other important measures appear in the description.

Placement
Placeholders in the layout should be part of the profile as well. An example could be specific margins when it comes to the placing of the logo. Use composition sketches to define the placeholders of the design.

Dos and Don'ts
Add examples that explain what to do, and what not to do. Make sure that the 'right' solutions are clearly separated from the 'wrong' solutions.

A good idea when creating a graphical profile is to create it in Flash or HTML format. This way, you'll have all the guidelines in the actual format you're going to use them in, and in addition you can put it online for your client or colleagues to see as well.

Improving your Designs

To take the step from decent designer to good designer, you'll have to strive to improve your designs. You need to seek creative development and new challenges. Inspiration and an urge to keep pushing the envelope are what make the difference.

A simple method to improve your designs is the **crash method**.

Crash Method

Computers tend to crash every once in a while, and when they do, the people using them sometimes lose a significant amount of their work and have to recreate it. If you're on a tight deadline, this can be extremely annoying, but in fact it can often be a benefit to your creative progress: weirdly, being forced to recreate a design, from scratch within a very short period of time is almost certain to improve the design compared to how it looked *before* the crash. By working quickly with something you're very familiar with, your unconscious self will take over much of the process. The work you're doing becomes a sort of 'inferior work', where you don't think too hard about what you're doing. The conscious self, or the logical part of your brain, will be occupied with dealing with the pressure of the deadline, the frustration of having lost a day's work, and reproaching the IT administrator about your loss. The creative part of your brain, helped by a surge of adrenalin, gets room to perform the task at hand without being disturbed. This is a great feeling to have – a natural high.

You should always be prepared to discard your best work and start over. This is hard to accept and can be very frustrating, but nevertheless it is something that every designer should learn how to cope with. By discarding work, I don't mean deleting or throwing away permanently, merely putting what you've created to one side and starting over from scratch.

When you do use this method, make sure you *save the work you've done*. Indeed, it's a good idea to keep *all* the design work you do. Each time you finish a project or make some sketches, mark every one of them with the date and project name, and then collect everything – doodles, sketches, layouts etc. – in a back catalog of your work. By collecting and saving your old stuff, you're creating a reference resource that you can return to when faced with briefs that are similar to those you've tackled in the past. More importantly, you'll be able to use it to track your creative development and prove to yourself that your work has evolved over time. Analyzing your old work allows you spot errors you missed at the time, and makes you more likely to spot them in the future. Conversely, looking at your old work can also restore your faith in yourself when energy, confidence, and time are running low.

Try to *train the way you look at things* so that you fully take them in and analyze them, rather than just glancing at them. By seeing and analyzing in this way you'll gain access to a new world of graphical knowledge. Train your eye for detail: details are what make the difference. Tiny alterations can significantly enhance or diminish the look and quality of your design. If you've created a good, consistent design it's important that you have the ability to spot the small deviations from the consistency conventions that you've set yourself.

Search for inspiration. Listen to people, look at people, look at their work and mimic all you can. Yes, that's right – mimic. Infants learn to communicate by mimicking. Why shouldn't you? By mimicking, you learn new techniques that you internalize and add to your repertoire.

Remember, however, that there's a very thin line between inspiration and *theft*. Generally, you shouldn't mimic people's work unless it stays behind your closed doors at home. Never pretend that you've invented a design that you haven't. If you do this, the monsters in your closet will come and get you in the night – alternatively, back in the real world, you might find yourself on the receiving end of a law suit.

Look at your surroundings for ideas. Sometimes it's hard to remember that there's a whole world outside the computer and off the Web. This world actually has a tendency to be inspiring. Next time you're looking for inspiration, try taking a walk while looking at people's shoes, even that can be inspiring. The day after you might take another walk where you try to focus on something else, thus getting a whole new batch of inspiration from the same walk. Don't *force* your ideas; let them come to you.

One of the most enriching and inspiring experiences is when you let yourself and what you do *stand out*. Being original isn't necessarily all that difficult. I think originality is often more a matter of courage rather than a matter of abilities. Just as copying is good for practice and inspiration, originality is good for life. If you can let yourself go enough to come up with an original piece, you'll feel a surge of satisfaction.

Producing original work is a road to immortality. If you produce a design that's like nothing that has ever gone before, it'll immediately be the most recognizable site on the Web, and will become one of the most famous as more and more designers start to mimic you.

The suggestions and guidelines I've given you in this chapter will help you to understand the process and execution of design, and your skills will grow and grow as your experience increases. When you combine this knowledge with the technical expertise the rest of this book will give you, and then add just a smidgen of creative inspiration, that original idea will be just around the corner – with immortality not far behind it!

To finish off this chapter and reinforce the things that I've discussed, let me walk you through these techniques as I applied them when creating the Titoonia.com site.

Designing Titoonia.com – a Case Study

To exemplify some of the theory and techniques that I've covered in the previous pages, I'll be using www.titoonia.com as a case study. All graphical resources from the creative process, including the graphical end result, are available for download at www.titoonia.com or at www.friendsofed.com.

Overview of the Site

Titoonia is a multi-purpose in-house entertainment and showcase site that we're creating at Titoonic (www.titoonic.dk). The primary purpose of the site is to serve as a proving ground for some of the ideas we generate at Titoonic. We want a site where we are in charge and where we can show some of the stuff that we like to do. The primary content will be games of different kinds that we've developed, as well as, in time, other fairly advanced experiments with game or entertainment relevance.

Secondly, the site should become a completely functioning, full-scale, standalone showcase of our skills. The site should be something we could show potential customers in an attempt to make a good impression on them, and to show them the potential of the medium.

Thirdly and not least, we're eager to explore the potential of creating Flash and entertainment-based sites with a strong community feel.

We want an easy to manage, flexible and well performing Flash 5 based site. As we're creating it on a low (no) budget we want it to be easily updatable and extensible once we're ready to add content. The site should have a low maintenance level and should not depend on frequently updated material. The site should work as a whole even when only a limited amount of content is available. At the same time, it should be easily expandable with the addition of pages in certain categories, or with the addition of whole new categories.

The site is a showcase, so the core functionality, the structure and the framework should perform effectively. As the site is an experimental area as well, we'll have to expect some performance glitches in some parts of the content. The site in general should perform well on virtually any connection and on virtually any hardware, whereas heavier and more demanding features will be expected from some parts of the content.

"What?" – the Message

As the site is an in-house showcase and thereby a direct reflection of our company and of what we're doing, we of course want the message to be a rewarding and positive one. People shouldn't come to this site and get the impression that we're unpleasant and incompetent. We want to impose an impression on our visitors that reflects the way we see our company, what we do, and our values. We're dealing with several sub-messages for this site: the site's content calls for the expression of fun and entertainment, and the site's various purposes call for some business-oriented terms.

In order to pin these disparate messages down, I created a list – in no particular order – of some words that I associate with the imagined mood, purpose and content of this site:

- Fun

- Quality

- Trustworthiness

- Originality

- Pleasure

- Leisure

- Entertainment

- Break

- Vacation

- Community

- Calm

- Tranquility

- Warmth

This list of words now needs to be further refined into something that's more directly usable. This kind of list can prove very useful in itself, and should be kept for future reference as a part of your project guide or 'rulebook'.

Next, I try to establish a single sentence (or a single word) that embraces or somehow relates to the most important – if not *all* the – words in the list. This process can typically take place when you're having a coffee break, when you're on your bicycle, in the shower etc. It shouldn't be a too intellectual process where you concentrate on the exact words or the syntax or typing: rather, it's a free process where *the* word or sentence emerges from your thoughts when you're hardly noticing it. What you're doing here is filling up your brain with the raw material and letting your subconscious do the work of filtering out the dross and delivering you a sudden nugget of essential truth and elegance.

The final message that I decided to communicate in this case is: 'This is a lovely place to be'. It somehow embraces the words on the list, the purposes, the content and my imaginary image of the project. The 'This is a lovely place to be' sentence will be ringing in my ears as I continue the creative process, and that sentence will be the first place I look to find answers to creative problems that may arise during the site development.

'This is a lovely place to be' – it doesn't have to be any more complicated than that...

"Who?" – the Target Audience

As the purpose of this site is multi-faceted: so, therefore is the target audience. Being both a showcase site, an experimental area, and an actual end-user based site, we're facing at least three types of target audience:

- Potential customers

- In-house game geeks and design weirdoes (my colleagues and myself)

- Actual gamers (whoever they might be)

In order to avoid too much confusion of the message, we decide to focus on only *one* audience group. If we attempt to communicate directly and equally to three different groups of people via the same channel, we're making sure in advance that the message will get muddy and that all of our audiences will feel like they're not the ones we're talking to specifically. We've got to maintain some sort of focus here...

The group of 'actual gamers (whoever they might be)' is by far the largest of the three target groups. The number of 'potential customers' is, let's face it, sadly limited, and the in-house geeks are not to be counted on at all in this matter – they should only be concerned with delivering content to the site. Even with this decision made, it's clear that 'actual gamers' is not the type of narrow targeted definition that we're after – it's not even close yet. We'll have to narrow it down some more, and this is where the real choice making is taking place. People that like to play games online, in this case small Flash-based games, can be anyone from school kids to younger grown-ups working in an office. The group could be composed of women and men, but probably with a majority of men.

Note that in other cases we would have to go deeper into the details and demographics of the target audience. If we had a certain product to push and we had to make the site an e-tail success with high profits and a big marketing budget, the target audience definition below wouldn't do at all. We'd need statistics, demographics and analysis on a much larger scale.

Eventually, we decide to define our target audience like this:

- A tech-savvy, rather youthful audience, with a great appetite for coffee break entertainment. We expect the audience to be web site 'nomads' – they surf around to a fairly limited number of places they know, and they occasionally bump into a site they've heard of, or have had recommended.

- A large portion of the audience has a penchant for emailing funny or interesting clips, images and games to their friends and colleagues. They probably depend extensively on email attachments when they're finding and deciding to visit new sites.

- The average visitor is between 20 and 35 years old. There's a slight over-representation of male visitors. Tech-wise we're looking at an audience that's familiar with the Web and spends a lot of time there, both at the office and as leisure entertainment. The majority are permanently connected either via LAN at the office, or via xDSL, or some similar technology at home. When it comes to hardware we shouldn't necessarily expect state of the art, but rather relatively up to date office machines.

- The typical visitor will have a fairly new browser, but probably won't update every time a new version comes out. A Flash plug-in will be present in a large majority of the cases, but a large portion of the audience maybe yet to upgrade to the most recent Flash player. Most of the visitors will have previous experience in installing the Flash player.

At this point, I take a look at how to solve the task at hand. It's about getting an overview of what you're about to get into, and it's about ideas and inspiration. In this case we know the technologies to use right from the beginning, so that's not a concern for us here. Instead, we need a conceptual or thematic approach, and a uniting idea for the project.

When we first had the notion of creating a showcase/entertainment site where we could feature some of our work, we wanted a name for it that was closely related to the Titoonic company name, but still different. Somehow the name Titoonia came up and we bought it. Now I get inspired about the name we'd found. To me, it sounds like some small, unspoiled utopian island kingdom somewhere in the Pacific: sunny beaches and palm trees, and girls in grass skirts with flowers in their hair. Browsing through some books, I also get inspired by the crisp 50's post World War 2 propaganda poster look, combined with some diffuse notion of Japanese pop-culture. Both styles features clean, tension-filled lines; flat, relatively bright colors: and a strong iconographic way of communicating. With this inspiration in mind I continue my work.

Structural Design

As mentioned before, we want an easy to manage, flexible and well performing site. Even though our target audience has relatively fast connections, we're still facing hardware limitations. It's crucial to us that the site performs well and fluently under almost any hardware and connection configuration. We'll accept the fact that some content on sub-pages will require more power or speed, but the core of the main site structure should be swift.

The next step is to come up with that structure. To do that, I utilize a few creative techniques to generate a list of the site's main sections and a description of their relationships...

Headings and Flowcharts

Titoonia.com will be a relatively simple and small site with only a few top sections and no more than five sub-sections per top section. I briefly make some notes on a piece of paper, writing down the section and sub-section names and their content. I do this maybe four or five times until I'm convinced that I've found the right way of organizing things logically:

DEFAULT. HTM
- GAMES
  - GAME 1
  - GAME 2
  - ETC.
- POSTCARDS
  - SEND
- CHAT
  - DEFAULT
- INFO
  - DEFAULT

Next I do a flowchart where I indicate the most important pages and sections. In this case I have to take into consideration that the games themselves will be added at some point in the future, so I simply add 'placeholders' instead of a detailed description of the pages the different games will require:

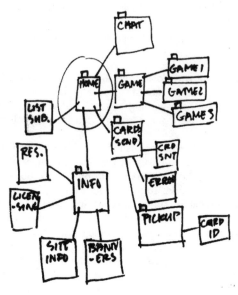

As I am a designer and not a programmer, I do not include scripts etc. in the chart. I only include the pages that need to be *designed*.

The reason I do the flowchart by hand is that I don't want to be distracted by the workings of a flowchart program which could have me focusing my efforts on neatness rather then the task at hand – I don't need a polished, ready to print flowchart, so I won't waste my time and energy on creating one.

File Strategy

By splitting what we see on the site's different pages into several different movie files I can easily reuse the most frequently used scene elements, such as the navigation and the background design. This also means that I won't burden limited bandwidth users with downloads they have no interest in. One of the most important tools to make a Flash-based site fast and high-performance is the loadMovie action, which allows us to incorporate streaming optimization in our site. For instance, loadMovie is also useful for bringing in more sophisticated sound or music to a Flash site – by putting the music in a discrete Flash movie that's loaded on demand, we can maintain better control of it and avoid holding back the loading time of the main Flash movie.

The shared files will be placed in the root directory so they're easily accessible from all parts of the site.

On the different sub pages I'll add `loadMovie` commands that load (for example) the commonly used navigation into place. This way the user will only have to download the navigation movie content *once* – the rest of the time it will be fetched from the cache.

Besides this type of movie sharing, where we reuse the same navigation movie across the site, the 'shared libraries' feature in Flash 5 allows us to reuse *individual symbols* across movies. In this site I use a very limited number of sharable symbols, so I decide not to use this option.

Directory Structure

In order to avoid some of the most common usability issues that are usually connected with the creation of a Flash site, and to optimize the site's overall performance, I settle for a structure where every piece of content is placed on its own HTML page. Each HTML page is then arranged in a directory according to its content. For example, if you need to access a pong game, the URL will be www.titoonia.com/games/pong/. The pong game itself will then be placed in an HTML document called default.htm inside the pong directory.

I create an initial directory structure according to this decision – it's a good idea to develop a file structure before you begin detailed content development, so that your files are easily accessible and locatable.

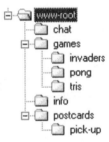

The creation of a directory structure is a very easy way to get a good overview of the site. In fact you could say that the creation of a directory structure is sort of a 'pre-prototype'.

The type of structure shown here, with a page and/or a directory for each piece of content, allows the user to use the browser BACK button just like 'regular' web sites. This also means that the user will be able to bookmark a certain page on the site for future visits. Furthermore, the URL will always give the user an indication of where they are located within the site. The downside of using this type of structure is that you won't be able to make 'soft transitions' between sections or pages.

To test the structure I've sketched and to get an idea of how to build the site in Flash I make a quick **prototype**.

Prototyping

The prototype has the sole purpose of mimicking the behavior of the finished site, without having to look good. It's a working model that lets us test the basic functionality of the site.

When constructing a prototype I make sure that when I press the navigation buttons the various movies are loaded into their proper place and that they have some indication of their type of content, plus maybe a line with their name. That's it – don't waste any more time on detail at this stage. Here's the site's front page in prototype, with a rough interface and a MENU button:

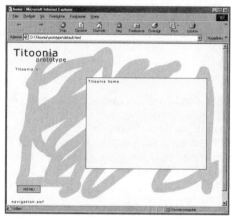

TITOONIA SITE PROTOTYPE

At the prototype stage, I also set up the FLAS and HTML files I need to test the loadMovie functionality and the directory set-up. I usually make a couple of prototypes during the design process to test different solutions:

chat
games
info
postcards
bg.fla
bg.swf
default.html
home.fla
home.swf
navigation.fla
navigation.swf

By creating the entire file structure you'll need before beginning the detailed graphic design process, you'll come across – and solve! – a lot of structural issues that will affect your design decisions, thereby avoiding a lot of corrections later on. Once you've created the prototype, you'll know for sure if your structural ideas will work or not.

Later on, when you've finished the main parts of the graphic design, you can copy and paste the graphic elements directly into the dummy prototype files where they're needed. You won't have to create a new file structure; you'll simply be replacing graphics and movies in the pre-defined and tested site structure.

Satisfied with the structure, I can now move on to the content design and creation.

Sketching

At this point in the design process, I've gathered a lot of loose, more or less usable ideas for the project. I do some sketches where I add whatever else comes into my mind. Sometimes I do a lot of sketches, sometimes only one. Sometimes they're very detailed and sometimes they're only a line or two to help me remember or imagine. For the Titoonia site I did the two rough sheets shown here:

Along the way more small sketches are done on envelopes, napkins or on the back of the phone book. Some of them, for example, test a layout, while others are used to figure out how to solve some particular technical issue. Again, it's important to think your way through the site and try to visualize problems as they might arise when the site is in use.

By sketching on the same piece of paper for a couple of days through the creation process, you'll accumulate a source of inspiration on this sheet. By the end of the process, go through the sketches and save all those you find even remotely usable or interesting.

Composition

I want a friendly, calm and slightly dynamic composition to support the message and feel of the site. I do a great number of composition sketches while keeping the message and the target audience in mind. The drawings shown here represent a selection of the sketches I did and actually used or treated as candidates:

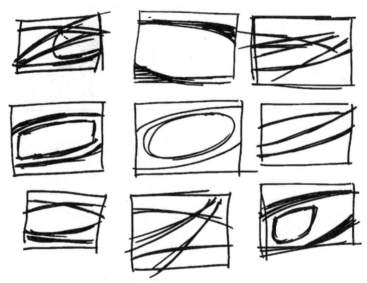

A lot of sketches were done as warm up and were not used, and some just seemed out of kilter and were subsequently discarded.

No matter how messy and strange they may seem, these sketches actually contain answers to most of the layout and design problems I bumped into on this site. By looking back to these sketches during the rest of the creation process, I find inspiration. As with the 'regular' sketches, I always save my composition sketches for future reference.

Color

As our message is 'This is a lovely place to be' and our target audience is a relatively young one, I figure it would be right to go for some crisp, warm and slightly twisted colors of nature. The colors should not be too childish or too 'old' in their expression, nor should they be gloomy or sad. The color scheme should reflect the words on the list we made when we defined the message, and they should appeal to the target audience.

I start in Flash by making a lot of dots with more or less randomly picked colors – other designers might use Photoshop, and this is really just a matter of personal preference. The colors are all evocative of the 'color mood' I've outlined above, but a lot of them will be discarded when I go through the next steps of refinement:

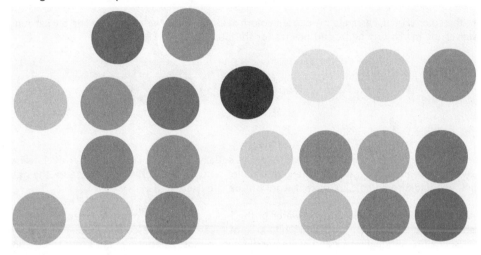

COLOR SCHEME TRIAL

Each color should be as closely related to the message, the audience, and other expressional parameters that I've found. Colors that stick out in too many ways are discarded. Furthermore it's important that I don't end up with *too many* colors. I'd rather end up with only a few well-balanced colors than with a lot of semi-balanced ones.

In Flash, I create a color doodle where I experiment with some of the colors I envisage using. The first attempts are usually way off, but by fiddling around and replacing and tweaking, you'll end up with a selection of colors that work for you:

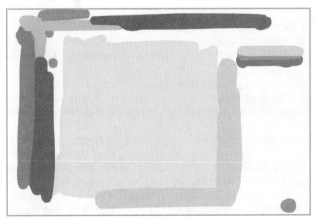

COLOR SKETCH

The color sketch is not only a proving ground where I find the colors to use; it's also a way of finding the right balance of color to use, and relationships between the colors. The quantity relations of this color sketch will be roughly those that will dominate the finished site.

By determining in which quantities the colors should be used, I learn a lot of how the color scheme works and how it doesn't work. If, instead of the pale sand color, I had used one of the green ones as the background, the expression of the site would have changed completely, into something far more wet and dark – more like Martian chewing gum than a South Pacific paradise isle.

From the color sketch, I arrange my chosen colors over the color I've chosen for the background. This gives me my color scheme and palette for the site:

SITE COLOR SCHEME

By arranging the colors according to their values in equally sized dots I'll get a better overview of the overall flow and temperature of the general color scheme. If it works here and sends the right signals, I should also be able to make it work on the site itself.

I finally settle for grass in the greens, water in the blues, sand in the orangey range, and a pink for contrast and 'spicing-up'. Black and white are not regarded as true 'colors', so they're not part of this selection. Although black and white are defaults in most palettes, I'm not going to be using them anyway.

OK, I've got my structure and my colors. Now I need to determine the fonts I'm going to use to convey my site's message.

Fonts

I want to choose two main fonts – one for headings and one for main text. I want the headings to reflect my main source of thematic inspiration, and to blend nicely with my mental impression of the site, with the color scheme, and with the sketches I've made so far.

The primary concern when it comes to choosing the font for the main text is that it shouldn't be too hard to read (that is,. it should be a sans serif font), and it shouldn't signal or emphasize something that's graphically 'off topic' – in other words, it should be a simple, almost *neutral* font.

After having spent some time testing, browsing and researching, I settle for a freeware font by Ray Larabie (www.larabiefonts.com) called **Deftone Stylus** for the headings. This font embodies several qualities that I'm after: it's decorative, but still relatively simple and clean, and not too hard to read. It combines some of the qualities of the '50s diner and poster style with a very modern yet classic look. The lines tend to be a bit 'space age', which links it to the vague definition of Japanese pop-culture that I'm also after. And, last but not least, it's freeware...

For the main text, I go for the easy, classic solution. I choose the standard font **Verdana**, which I think combines the virtues of the simple, readable, fit-for-screen font in the best manner. It has a wider and more open feel than, say, Arial or Helvetica, and while it's a bit plainer and less classy than both Arial and Helvetica, it has the friendly feel I'm after:

Deftone Stylus is nice for headings
Verdana is a simple readable standard font

Having made the generic design decisions, I can now drill down further into the content design.

Building the Titoonia Content

Having created a message definition, a target audience definition, a structure that works, sketches of different kinds, a supporting composition, a cool color scheme and made a font choice or two, we're ready to get into the site-creation in Flash. All that we have done so far has to be translated and refined into the design of the web site.

In this case, I create all the graphic elements directly in Flash. Using the line tool and a lot of pulling and stretching I draw the elements, starting out by creating the header and logo. These, I imagine, will be the most significant graphical elements:

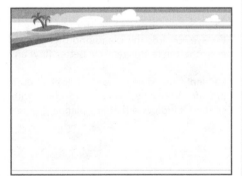

SHOWCASE 1

Next, I create and add the **logotype** – the titling at the top of the page:

SHOWCASE 2

However, I'm not entirely satisfied with how this works. The elements work fine individually, but when I compose the logotype on top of the background, it doesn't seem to 'read' very well. The way I see it, the background detracts from the logotype too much, and I also suddenly feel like the lines of the background go the wrong way according to the reading direction. I don't want to start 'reading' the image down where the bottom line of the background begins...

To improve the reading and weight distribution of the image, I flip the background and leave the logotype where it is:

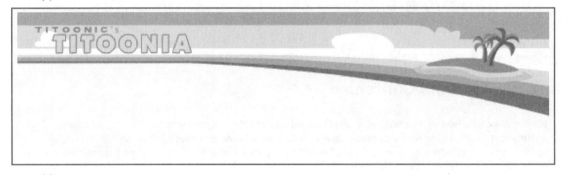

SHOWCASE 3

This way, the logo will be the first thing the visitor reads. The lines in the background will lead the eye towards the island and then down towards the content (in an ideal world, that is...). This gives the entire image a far better flow and slightly more dynamic feel, I think.

Suddenly, for some reason, I'm losing confidence in my initial choice of background color, so I try out an alternative background color with some other screen elements – movies that act as content windows – that I'm planning to use in the finished site:

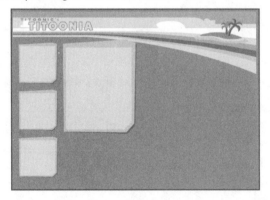

SHOWCASE 4

I often have to do this kind of double-checking and alternative-testing at some point in a project. Testing other options than the one you've settled for initially is always a good way of checking and re-checking your concept and design. More often than not, things work best if you go with your first idea, but don't be afraid to try out alternatives if you need to reassure yourself that you're still on the right trail.

If you look back at the sketches I did previously, you'll recognize the 'windows' or text field backgrounds that I've started experimenting with here. I realize though, that it somehow doesn't work and decide to discard the 'window' model. I try to come up with a new text/content field model:

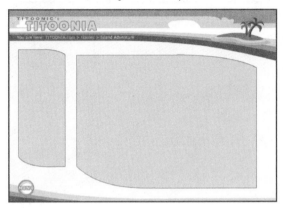

SHOWCASE 5

Here, I reuse the shape of the background lines in an attempt to make the layout work as a whole. Even more importantly, I add the bottom version of the header lines. These lines are added to 'close' the page and to add to the feeling of unity. Also the lines at the bottom conclude the slight revolving movement of lines and of the viewer's eye. Note that the lines at the bottom of the screen are bent upwards to echo the lines at the top, which bend down.

Unfortunately, this layout has to be discarded as well, because the two big text/content fields work against each other and the compositional whole. The lines from the big field on the right don't follow through in a convincing way to the small field on the left. Back to the drawing tablet...

Next, and with fresh inspiration drawn from the composition sketches I did before, I try to emphasize the composition and give a more light and soft impression by letting the lines from the two separate text/content fields blend into one, thereby allowing a more fluent flow of the eye:

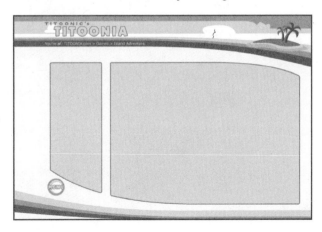

SHOWCASE 6

I realize that the pink outlines around the text/content fields seem to taking an awful lot of attention compared to what might actually be *inside* the fields. Another solution must be tried...

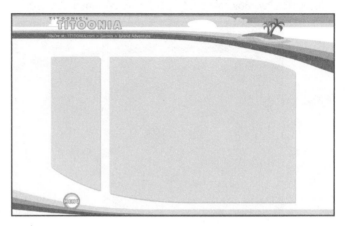

SHOWCASE 7

Note the change of aspect – the movie is taller now. I realized that, previously, the entire layout seemed squashed and somewhat out of proportion. By making the image field taller I add more space to hold the actual content, as well as aiming a bit more for the computer monitor aspect ratio. Additionally, the text/content fields have received a slight drop shadow effect to separate them from the background color in a subtle way. The shadow effect also gives an impression of light and warmth.

I do a 'full screen' version of the text/content fields to see if the text/content field concept will work on a larger scale:

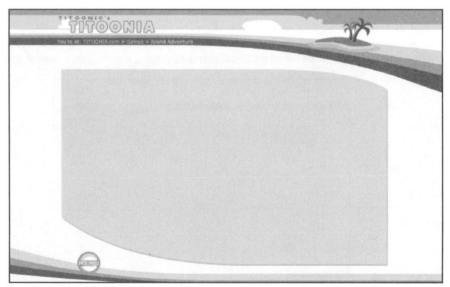

SHOWCASE 8

Being basically satisfied with the look of the background elements, I try adding text to see if my choice of fonts will work in this layout:

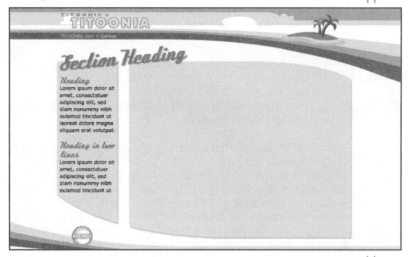

SHOWCASE 9

To counterweight the island graphics and the dominant lines of the layout, and to reduce the slanting effect of the italic-style font, I've decided to tilt the heading a bit. This, I think, also adds to the '50s poster feel I was initially inspired by.

Not quite satisfied with the effect of the subheadings left alone on the text field background, I add a small bullet to separate it further, and I also do a bit of user interface widget design – an input box and a button – to test how the different elements work together. With the background elements being fairly loud, I'm after a relatively discreet look for the widgets:

SHOWCASE 10

With the design of a simple input text field and a simple button, I have covered most of the creative questions that will arise with the rest of the UI widgets – I'll use these generic objects throughout the rest of the site to achieve a consistent look and feel.

Done!

Now I've got enough graphical elements and the design is complete enough to serve as a guide for the rest of the creation process. Now it's 'just' a question of adding content until the site is filled to the brim. Along the way, throughout the rest of the production, I can look back to the already created material and generic objects to find the answers to the page- and movie-specific design challenges that will turn up.

I seldom go deeper into the detail during the overall design process. I don't think through *every* aspect of the site to figure out how many different types of widgets and text fields I'm going to need. By creating a single, well thought-through page with the main design elements present, I'll have the key to the rest of the site's design. I have the basic themes in place now, and the rest of the site implementation will be variations on these basic, consistent themes. To ensure that I – and my co-workers – can easily extract the core design information from what I've created so far, one thing remains to be done – creating the graphical profile or the 'style guide'.

The Graphical Profile

As the different aspects of the design become clear and defined, I add descriptions and definitions to the graphical profile. The graphical profile will serve as a rule book or style guide as my colleagues and I continue the work on the subsections and pages of the Titoonia site.

Every time I get confronted with some creative/graphic challenge or question in the rest of the actual site production, I'll seek the answer in the graphical profile. To maintain consistency and ensure that I remain true to the message and feel of the site, everything I create on this project in the future will have to relate to the rules I have set up by creating the initial design and these design guidelines. For instance, if I can't figure out what colors I should be using for some of the content, I'll look at the graphical profile, and use some of the colors I have defined here, or some colors that are closely related to them. And if I need a new design for a button, I'll take into account the buttons that I have previously made for this project, just as I will when it comes to lines, composition, page and field divisions, fonts, and so on.

It's important to mention that the graphical profile isn't finished at this point. It probably never really will be finally complete as long as the project is alive and is being developed further: part of the concept with the graphical profile is that it changes and expands along the way. Every time you refine a design element or introduce a new one, the profile should expand as well.

If we eventually did any marketing of the site or started a product line of merchandise, the graphical profile would serve as a style guide in this work as well. When new material is created it will also be added to the guide.

The message and target audience definitions, the keyword list, the good bits of the sketches and the composition sketches should be part of the graphical profile. By collecting all this material I, or the other people that will be working with the site, only have to look in one place for inspiration and solutions.

Here are a couple of pages from the Titoonia.com graphical profile:

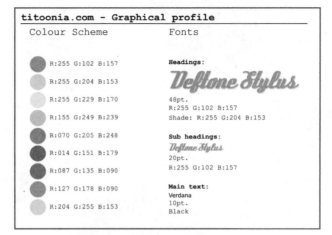

GRAPHICAL PROFILE 1

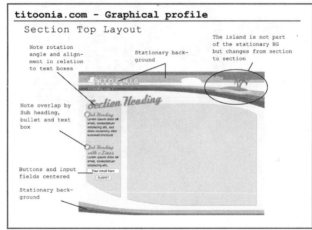

GRAPHICAL PROFILE 2

Closing Time...

As I said right at the start, this chapter has aimed to introduce you to a universal set of creative design principles and techniques that are widely applicable in the field of web site design, and particularly in Flash sites. With an awareness of the theory and practice of web site-related graphic design, you can explore each aspect in more depth, refine the techniques so that they're a better fit for your personal needs, and apply them in your own work.

By combining sound graphic design and usability principles with your technical Flash skills, you'll increase your chances of producing highly functional, attractive and professional-looking sites time after time.

Go design!

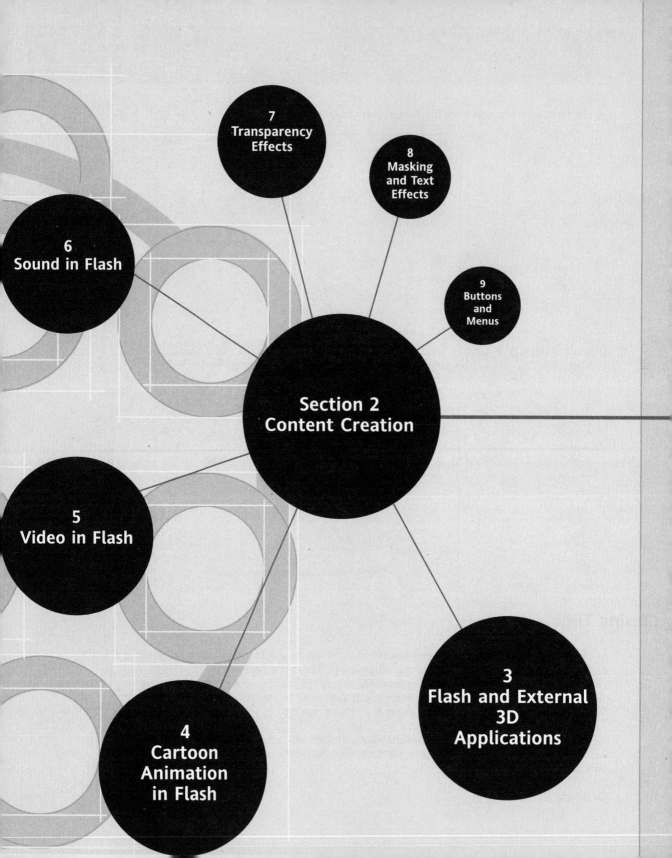

Chapter 2
Smart Clips

Smart clips are one of the best of the new features in Flash 5. They allow you to alter the ActionScript settings within a movie clip without ever touching any code. This means that a programmer can write complex ActionScript code to control a movie, and then pass that on to a designer who can make changes to how the movie will behave, without the need for further code manipulation.

For instance, let's say that you build a movie clip that fades out an image by using the alpha channel. This is done through a variable called *maxFade*, which contains a figure for the maximum alpha ranging from 0-100. Normally to change *maxFade* we'd have to go into the actual code, find the variable, and then alter it. If we make the movie clip into a smart clip however, and make the *maxFade* variable a parameter of that smart clip, then we can employ a user friendly dialog box to change the *maxFade* value simply, and without dirtying our hands in code. Used well, smart clips can save a great deal of valuable production time, and the range of uses to which they can be put is limited only by your imagination.

Creating a Simple Smart Clip

To give you a flavor of what smart clips can do, we'll create a button that'll direct the browser to a new URL when you press it, but with the twist that the URL will be specified as a parameter in a smart clip. To alter the URL, you just bring up the Clip Parameters panel and type it in, rather than having to open up the button, open the ActionScript for the button, and *then* alter the URL. Well-designed smart clips reduce the need to amend ActionScript code, so the chances of accidentally breaking that code while making changes to it are similarly diminished.

1. In a new movie, use the Rectangle tool to draw a vaguely button-shaped rectangle on the stage. Convert the rectangle into a button symbol, and give it a sensible name, such as button:

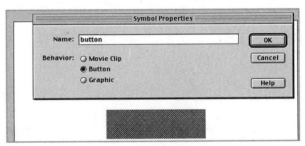

2. Next, convert the button that you just created into a movie clip symbol (mine is simply named button clip). It's this movie clip that'll become our smart clip. Open up the movie clip and select the button symbol within it. Bring up the Actions panel, and ensure that you're in Expert mode before typing the following:

```
on (release) {
  getURL (url, target);
}
```

The first thing that you'll have noticed about this code is that we haven't explicitly specified a web address or a target for our getURL action. Instead, we've given it the names of a couple of variables called url and target. These will be set to the correct values in the Smart Clip Parameters panel.

3. In the Library, right-click on button clip (or whatever you called your movie clip symbol) and choose Define Clip Parameters... from the pop-up menu that appears:

This brings up the Define Clip Parameters dialog box, which is where we specify the variables for our smart clip that'll be passed to the movie clip. Click on the + icon at the top-left of the dialog box to add our first parameter:

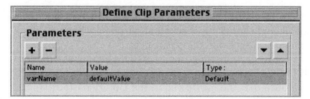

4. Now we just need to define it. Double-click on varName in the Name column and type in the name of the first parameter variable, which in this case is url:

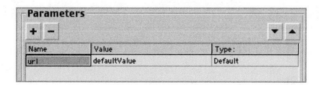

If you want to ascribe a value for this parameter that all instances of your smart clip will use by default, you can do so by double-clicking on defaultValue. If you don't put anything here, then each new instance created with the clip will just have a blank value field, waiting for input. I've entered the address of the friends of ED web site. Remember that all web-addresses used in Flash must give the absolute address, that is prefixed by http://

You can leave the Type column set to Default for now. The other options are:

- Array for dynamic lists

- List for static pre-defined lists

- Object for related elements with individual names and values

5. Click the + icon again to add our second parameter, the target variable. Double-click the varName box and enter target. If you want to you can add a default value such as _self, which will open the page in the current frame of the current browser window:

At the bottom of the dialog is a check box labeled Lock in (In Windows this is Lock in instance) that should be checked at all times. This prevents people from altering the parameter names inside the smart clip.

6. Click OK to finish setting the parameters for your smart clip; if you look carefully, you'll notice that the movie clip in the Library has acquired a new icon to indicate its new status. The new icon is a combination of half movie clip and half script, and is the Flash representation of a smart clip. Notice though, that Flash still refers to it as a movie clip:

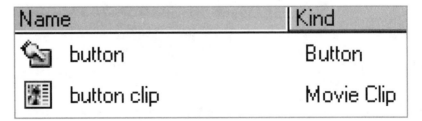

And that's it, the smart clip is now ready for use.

> *Before you can start to use your smart clip, you'll need to delete the original movie clip from the stage. This is because the new parameters that you define in a smart clip don't show up in instances that have already been placed on the stage.*

7. Delete the movie clip from the stage, and then drag a new instance of the smart clip onto the main stage. To set the parameters for the clip, right-click on it and choose Panels > Clip Parameters to bring up the Clip Parameters panel:

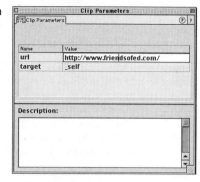

8. Double-click on the Value box for our url variable, and enter the address of a different web site. You can leave the target variable box as it is, or enter another value (such as _blank). When you're done, simply close the dialog box. You've now set the parameters for the button, which in this case are the URL, and the target for that URL.

All you need to do now is go to Control > Test Movie to see if it works as you expect. You should find that when you click the button, the requested URL loads up inside your browser window.

The Versatility of Smart Clips

The great thing about the smart clip that you've just created (and in fact, any smart clip) is that you can have multiple instances of it in your movie, all with different settings. Try dropping a few more of your smart clip buttons onto the stage, setting the parameters for each one with a unique URL, and then testing the movie. You've now got a movie clip that can be set up to do different things. How much time do you think that could save you?

Of course, creating a smart clip that enables you to alter a URL isn't exactly going to set the world on fire. After all, it's not *that* much hassle to alter the getURL command in the more conventional way. As our second example in this chapter, let's look at something that really does save time.

Creating a Universal Sound Smart Clip

When I'm using sound in Flash 5, I usually attach it dynamically from the Library. This allows me to have individual control over sounds, but each time I want to add a new one, I have to run through a sequence of five operations:

■ Create a blank movie clip for the sound to be attached to

■ Create a new sound object

■ Attach the sound to this new object

- Set the volume

- Set whether or not it should start immediately

Anyone who knows me will tell you that I'm all for an easy life, so having to do all that every time I need to add a sound is a real nuisance. What I need is a way to drag and drop a movie clip, set a few parameters, and no more. What I need is a smart clip for sound.

1.   Open a new movie, and create a new movie clip symbol called soundObject. Double-click on the first frame to open up the Frame Actions panel, ready for code to be added. Make sure you're in Expert mode, and enter the following line of code:

```
s = new Sound(_parent[this._name]);
```

s is the name of your new sound object. When we define s, we give it the name of a movie clip so that it can be controlled independently. Usually we'd just put the name of a clip, but on this occasion we don't know what the clip is going to be called. That's no problem, though, because we can get the name of the clip dynamically by using _parent[this._name].

2.   On the next line, we attach the sound to the sound object by typing:

```
s.attachSound(chosenSound);
```

The chosenSound variable will be set later on by our smart clip.

3.   Next, we set the volume with:

```
s.setVolume(initVolume);
```

4.   Finally, we want to allow the user to make the sound start straight away if they so wish. To do this, we use a small conditional statement:

```
If the autoStart parameter is set to true,
  Then the sound will start playing immediately;
If it's false,
  The sound does nothing.
```

In ActionScript terms, this becomes:

```
if (autoStart == "true") {
 s.start(0, loopAmount);
}
```

Notice that we've also used a variable called loopAmount. In the smart clip, you'll be able to set whether the sound should loop or not, and how many times it will loop.

5. After all the sound code, simply add a `stop` action so that the clip doesn't keep looping round and round. Your Frame Actions panel should now look like this:

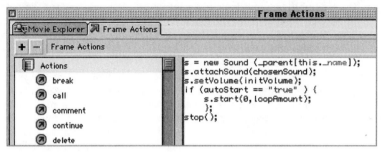

Now that our movie clip is written, ready to be turned into a smart clip, we need some sounds to work with.

6. Back on the main stage, choose File > Import... to bring up the Import dialog box, and locate some suitable sounds to use from your hard drive. I've gone for some Herbie Hancock and a bit of Run DMC, but feel free to use whatever you'd like:

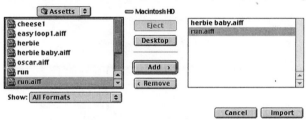

7. In the Library, locate the first sound, right-click on it, and then go to Linkage... in the menu that pops up:

8. To attach a sound dynamically from the Library, you need to export it, and give it an identifier. I've named my Herbie Hancock loop `herbie`:

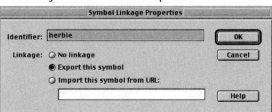

9. Repeat this procedure for every sound you've imported, giving each one a unique name.

10. Once all of the sounds have been set up correctly, we can set the parameters for the smart clip. Right-click on the soundObject movie clip in the Library, and go to Define Clip Parameters... to create two variables, chosenSound and loopAmount, with default types and values.

11. For the other two parameters we'll use a new type: a **List**. To see how this works, add a new parameter using the + icon, and call it autoStart. Then, in the Type column, double-click on the Default setting to invoke a menu that allows you to choose various types for this parameter. By selecting List, you'll be able to constrain the values to which the parameter may be set to a group of your choosing. Notice that when you do this, the Value column changes from saying defaultValue to saying (List[]).

12. We know that autoStart should only have two possible settings: true or false. Double-click on the box in the Value column to bring up the Values dialog box. From here, you can enter the values that the user will be able to choose from. As in the Clip Parameters dialog box, use the + icon to add two values, and name them true and false respectively. When you're done, click OK:

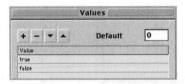

The default number refers to which menu item should appear by default when you open up the clip parameters. All menu items start at 0, so in this case, the 'default' setting in the menu would be 'true'.

13. Finally, add a fourth parameter called initVolume, making it another List type. Add some values for the volume settings by repeating the previous step. I chose 0, 25, 50, 75, and 100, meaning that the user can only select one of these numbers, and not enter an illegal value for the volume.

14. Now we can simply drag an instance of the soundObject smart clip symbol onto the stage. As in our earlier example, we can use the Clip Parameters dialog box to set the parameters to our desired values, so let's start by entering the name of the sound loop in the chosenSound field. Remember: this is the linkage name, not the name of the sound in the Library:

15. Set the other parameters as required. You'll notice that the parameters that you set to List earlier will now open up a list box that only allows you to select the values from that list. Now test your movie. As long as you set autoStart to true, and initVolume to a value other than zero, you should hear your sound loop kick in.

16. As a further trial, drag another soundObject smart clip onto the stage, set it up to play a different sound, and then test again. You should now hear two sounds playing. We've created a smart clip that allows us to attach sounds to our movies quickly and easily, without touching any code. Over time, it's possible to put together a common library of cool smart clips that can be used in any project you desire. Save this away on your hard drive as soundobj.fla.

Creating Custom User Interfaces for Smart Clips

In the previous example we saw how we could set the volume by using a drop-down menu. Though this was better than having to type the initial volume into the code, it still wasn't great interface design. What if the user wanted a volume different from the ones we had stipulated in the menu? What we need is a nice, friendly volume slider that can be set to any volume between 0 and 100. Clearly, we can't create a slider in the Define Clip Parameters dialog box, but we can create one in Flash and use that as the interface for setting our parameters.

1. Create a new Flash movie with a size of 250 x 150 pixels. Set the background color to a light gray. You can of course set the color to anything you want, but gray is just the standard interface color. You want the background to be just that:

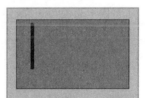

2. Name the initial layer of your movie slider back, and then use the Rectangle tool to draw out a slim, round-edged box. This will be the 'runner' for your slider. Make the box 100 pixels high.

3. Create a new layer named slider and then create a slider-shaped button on it. I used a simple rounded box, 30 x 13 pixels. Use the Align panel to place this slider right in the middle of the runner:

4. Convert this newly created shape into a button symbol called slider button, and then into a movie clip symbol named slider. Bring up the Object Actions panel for the button symbol within the movie clip and type in the following ActionScript:

```
on (press) {
 startDrag ("", false, left, top , right, bottom);
 dragging = true;
}
```

```
on (release, releaseOutside) {
 stopDrag ();
 dragging = false;
}
```

This piece of code allows us to drag the button up and down. Notice, though, that we haven't hard-coded the constraints of the rectangle when we start to drag — we simply use variables that are set when the movie runs. This allows us to put the slider anywhere on the stage, and it will always work correctly.

We've also set a variable called dragging to true if the button is being dragged, and false if it's not:

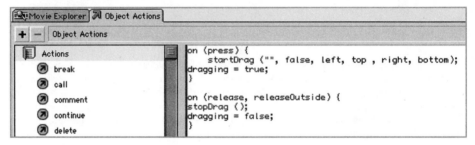

5. Now go back to the main timeline, make sure that the slider knob is selected, and bring up the Object Actions panel. We need to set some variables when the movie clip is first initialized (that is, when it loads). Type in this code:

```
onClipEvent (load) {
 top = _y-50;
 bottom = _y+50;
 left = _x;
 right = _x;
}
```

The variables top, bottom, left, and right are used for the dragging action. They constrain the slider knob so that it can only go up and down, and even then only fifty pixels either side of its starting position. This is why we put the slider knob in the middle of the slider runner, which is 100 pixels high.

If you now preview the movie, you should be able to drag the slider up and down.

6. Finally in our slider set up, add a text field under the slider on the main stage, making sure that it's set to Dynamic Text and named initVolume:

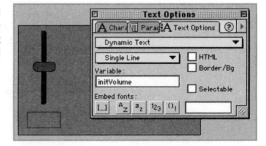

So we now have our slider, but for it to be of any use we have to be able to pass on the selected value of the slider to our smart clip.

7. Create a new layer called exchange and, making sure that nothing else is selected, create a new movie clip symbol called xch.

> *It's worth pointing out that the communicating movie clip that passes information between the custom UI smart clip and the host file must be called xch. This is something that's built into Flash, and nothing else will work.*

8. From the Library, drop this new movie clip onto the stage, anywhere you like. Then, most importantly, name this clip xch in the Instance panel. This instance name is important because it's going to act as a sort of middleman between your Flash movie and the smart clip:

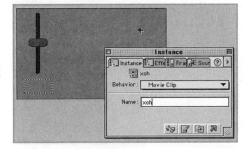

9. We need to set up the slider so that it passes the relevant information on to the smart clip. Select the slider knob and head once again for the Object Actions panel, where you should add the following code after our previous onClipEvent (load) actions:

```
onClipEvent (enterFrame) {
 if (dragging == true) {
 _root.initVolume = int(100+(top-_y));
 _root.xch.initVolume = _root.initVolume;
 }
}
```

The enterFrame event loops around as the movie clip loops around, so the actions specified above are being performed constantly. The if line is a conditional statement that asks whether the dragging variable is set to true. If it is, meaning the slider is being dragged, then Flash will do the following:

■   Set the initVolume text field to the value of the slider's position. A simple expression works out the position of the slider knob.

■   Set the smart clip's initVolume parameter, using the xch movie clip as a middleman. In this case, we set it to the value of the initVolume text field, which we've just set with the slider knob.

Smart Clip Panel   Sound Object

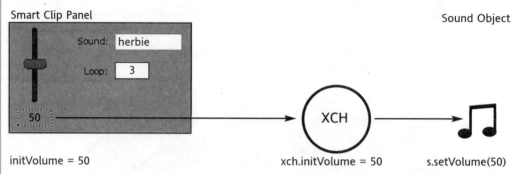

initVolume = 50   xch.initVolume = 50   s.setVolume(50)

We've now set up our Flash movie so that it passes a value from a user-friendly slider to the relevant parameter. Before we use this movie as our interface, let's add the other parameters too.

10. Create a new layer called input, and lay out two Input Text fields with the variable names chosenSound and loopAmount. You can also put names next to these text boxes so people will know what they're for when they come to use them:

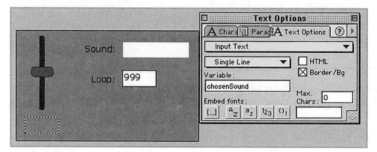

11. We also need to add a check box for the 'auto-start' function. Create another text label on the stage called Auto Start, and next to it draw a check box-sized square. Convert this square into a button symbol called checkbox. Then convert the button to a movie clip symbol with the name checkbox clip.

12. Double-click this new clip to edit the symbol, and rename the first layer button. Double-click on the first frame to bring up the Frame Actions panel, and enter the following ActionScript

```
stop ();
_root.xch.autoStart = "true";
```

The second line here tells the smart clip (via the xch movie clip) that autoStart is set to true.

13. Create a new layer and call it check. Add a simple graphic of an X over the check box that's visible in the first frame of this layer:

14. In the same layer, add a blank keyframe on frame 5. Then, back in the button layer, add a keyframe to frame 5. Double-click on this keyframe, and in the Frame Actions panel that appears, add:

```
stop ();
_root.xch.autoStart = "false";
```

We're going to be calling the keyframes in the button layer from another piece of code, so we need to add some labels to them. Using the Frame panel, add the label true to the first frame, and false to the fifth frame:

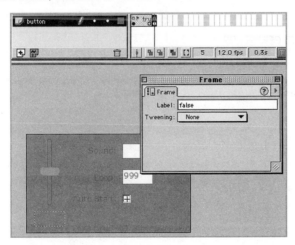

15. Move the playhead to frame 1, select the check box button, and bring up the Object Actions panel. Add the following piece of code to it:

```
on (release) {
 gotoAndStop ("false");
}
```

16. Do the same for the button in frame 5, but this time make it go to the "`true`" label, instead of "`false`".

We now have all of our interface elements in place, but we need to take one more step to finish this section of our custom GUI:

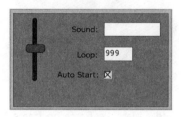

17. On the main stage select the slider knob and bring up the Object Actions panel once again. Insert the following two lines of code after the line that reads `onClipEvent (load) {`

```
_root.oldchosenSound = _root.chosenSound;
_root.oldloopAmount = _root.loopAmount;
```

18. Inside the `enterFrame onClipEvent`, enter the highlighted ActionScript:

```
onClipEvent (enterFrame) {
  if (_root.oldchosenSound != _root.chosenSound) {
  _root.xch.chosenSound = _root.chosenSound;
  _root.oldchosenSound = _root.chosenSound;
  }
  if (dragging == true) {
  _root.initVolume = int(100+(top-_y));
  _root.xch.initVolume = _root.initVolume;
  }
}
```

This code is a conditional statement that checks whether our `oldchosenSound` variable, which we set when the movie started, is not equal (`!=`) to the current value in the `chosenSound` box. In other words this means that the user has entered something new. If it *has* changed, then it sets the `chosenSound` parameter to the required value via the `xch` movie clip. Finally, we set the `oldchosenSound` variable to the new value.

Why don't we just constantly send the value to the `xch` movie clip, without checking whether the value has changed? Because if you keep communicating with the `xch` clip in a loop like this, it seriously degrades the performance of your custom interface. In this case that would mean that the slider would be very jerky indeed. To avoid that, we only communicate with the `xch` clip when we know that something has changed.

Finally, we need to add a similar condition for the `loopAmount` variable. Add the highlighted code after the last piece of ActionScript that you entered:

```
OnClipEvent (enterFrame) {
  if (_root.oldchosenSound != _root.chosenSound) {
  _root.xch.chosenSound = _root.chosenSound;
  _root.oldchosenSound = _root.chosenSound;
  }
  if (_root.oldloopAmount != _root.loopAmount) {
  _root.xch.loopAmount = _root.loopAmount;
  _root.oldloopAmount = _root.loopAmount;
  }
  if (dragging == true) {
  _root.initVolume = int(100+(top-_y));
  _root.xch.initVolume = _root.initVolume;
  }
}
```

19. All that remains now is to export our clip. Export it as soundui.swf into the same folder as your soundobj.fla that you created earlier when you tested the soundObject smart clip.

20. To use your new custom interface, you first need to open up soundobj.fla. Then, right-click on the soundObject smart clip in the Library and choose Define Clip Parameters... from the pop-up menu. Click on the folder icon next to Link to custom UI, locate the custom interface SWF that you've just created, and click Open. Once that's done, click OK to close the Define Clip Parameters box:

21. Now either drag an instance of the soundObject smart clip onto the stage, or use one of your existing ones. Right-click on it, and go to Panels > Clip Parameters from the pop-up menu. You should now see the Clip Parameters panel appear, but instead of the default dialog box, it's become your custom interface. Alter the parameters to suit, and then preview your movie. You should hear the sound you specified, at the volume you set with the slider:

22. After you've previewed your movie, return to the editor, deselect the smart clip, and then select it again. If you go back to the Clip Parameters panel, you'll find that the changes you made don't show up in the custom GUI. This is because each time you

select it, the custom GUI movie loads up in its initial state. Your parameters are actually still set, but they haven't been communicated back to the custom GUI. Fortunately, with a bit of tweaking, we can fix it.

23. Go back into your soundui.fla. First, you need to attach instance names to your slider and your check box on the stage. Call the slider initVolumeSlider, and the check box checkbox. Next, make a new layer named feedback, and add a second frame to all of the layers. This second frame is very important, as without it none of the code will work:

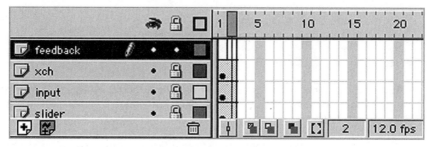

24. Create a keyframe in the second frame of the feedback layer. Double-click this keyframe to bring up the Frame Actions panel. All we need to do to get back the parameters that we set in the smart clip is use our xch clip; to set our initVolume text field, we write:

```
_root.initVolume = _root.xch.initVolume;
```

25. We then set another variable to the value of xch.initVolume with:

```
theinitVolume = _root.xch.initVolume;
```

26. We must also move the slider into the correct position by offsetting the slider knob movie clip in the y-axis, like this:

```
if (_root.initVolume >= 50) {
 initVolumeSlider._y = initVolumeSlider._y-(theinitVolume-50);
}
if (_root.initVolume < 50) {
initVolumeSlider._y = initVolumeSlider._y+(50 theinitVolume);
}
```

27. We've set the value for the slider, so now we need to set the values for the chosenSound name and the loopAmount:

```
_root.chosenSound = _root.xch.chosenSound;
_root.loopAmount = _root.xch.loopAmount;
```

28. Lastly, we need to put the check box in the correct state, depending on whether `autoStart` is set to `true` or `false`. We do this by simply controlling our checkbox movie clip by typing the following code after the previous section:

```
if (_root.xch.autoStart == "true") {
  _root.checkbox.gotoAndStop("true");
}

if (_root.xch.autoStart == "false") {
  _root.checkbox.gotoAndStop("false");
}
```

Also, add a `stop` action on the last line, so the movie doesn't keep looping round. Your ActionScript should look like this:

29. Now simply export your finished GUI, using the same name as before and replacing your previous version. Go back to your sound object source file and try it out. You should now see that the GUI always reflects the current parameter settings:

And that's a basic designer-friendly GUI done and dusted. Easy wasn't it? But there's so much more you can do. As it's really just a Flash movie for a front end embedded within a panel, you can do anything that you can in a normal movie. The only thing to bear in mind is that a smart clip's purpose is to make things simple and functional, so while you can make all your panels spin and fizz, it probably wouldn't endear you to the people who have to use them everyday. It's possible however, to add more interesting effects, and increase functionality.

Enhancing your Smart Clip

Because you can create your own custom GUIs, you can add non-standard controls, as we did with the slider, but why stop there? You could take the slider further: why not add a sound loop that starts up each time the slider is moved, reflecting the current volume, thus giving audio feedback to the user and making it easier to set the required volume.

1. Go back into your `soundui.fla`, and import a new sound loop. Ideally, this would just be a constant tone so that the user could hear the volume difference quickly and easily. For now though, anything will do.

2. Open up the Library and locate the newly imported sound, right-click on it, and choose Linkage from the menu that appears. From here, choose to Export this symbol, and give it the identifier loop:

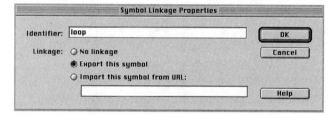

3. Add a new layer in the main timeline called actions. Then bring up the Frame Actions panel for the first frame of this layer.

4. We now need to add our sound. First off we'll initialize a new sound object and attach our sound to it in the same way that we did before in `soundobj.fla`:

```
s = new Sound();
s.attachSound("loop");
```

The name inside the brackets is the one that we set in the Linkage dialog box.

5. Finally we'll add a line to set the initial volume to 0:

```
s.setVolume(0);
```

6. Now we need to use the current position of the slider to set the volume of the sound. On the slider layer, select the slider knob and bring up the Object Actions panel. Locate the `if (dragging==true)` condition, and inside those curly brackets, add the highlighted line of code:

```
if (dragging == true) {
    _root.s.setVolume(int(100+(top-_y)));
    _root.initVolume = int(100+(top-_y));
    _root.xch.initVolume = _root.initVolume;
}
```

This is basically the same code that we use to set the initVolume variable, only this time we'e setting the volume of the s sound object, that is our loop sound.

7. At the moment if we tested the code, we'd hear nothing, as we haven't told the sound to start. We don't want the sound to play constantly, as that would get very annoying, what we want is to only hear the sound loop when we press on the slider knob. That way, when we adjust the slider, we'll hear the sound at the specified volume.

8. Double-click on the slider knob clip to edit the symbol. Select the actual slider button inside it, and bring up the Object Actions panel.

9. Inside the on (press) event handler add the highlighted line of ActionScript to start the sound playing:

```
on (press) {
    startDrag ("", false, left, top, right, bottom);
    dragging = true;
    _root.s.start(0, 999);
}
```

This tells our sound loop to start to play as soon as the slider is pressed. The number 999 tells Flash that we want to loop the sound 999 times, which is near enough forever, so you can guess what the next piece of code will be...

10. ...that's right, next we need to stop the sound when the slider is no longer being pressed. So in the on (release, releaseOutside) handler add the following highlighted line:

```
on (release, releaseOutside) {
    stopDrag ();
    dragging = false;
    _root.s.stop();
}
```

This stops our sound when the slider is released.

11. Finally test your movie. You should hear the sound getting louder as you move the slider up, and quieter as you move it down. You've now got an immediate audio preview of the volume setting. The last thing that you need to do is to export the custom GUI with the same name as your previous custom GUI and then try out the sound object.

As you can see, smart clips are incredibly useful for making mundane tasks quick and easy, streamlining workflow, and saving you time. In fact it's quite conceivable that you could build a smart clip that could create an entire Flash site. So what are you waiting for? It's time to get out there and make your movie clips smarter.

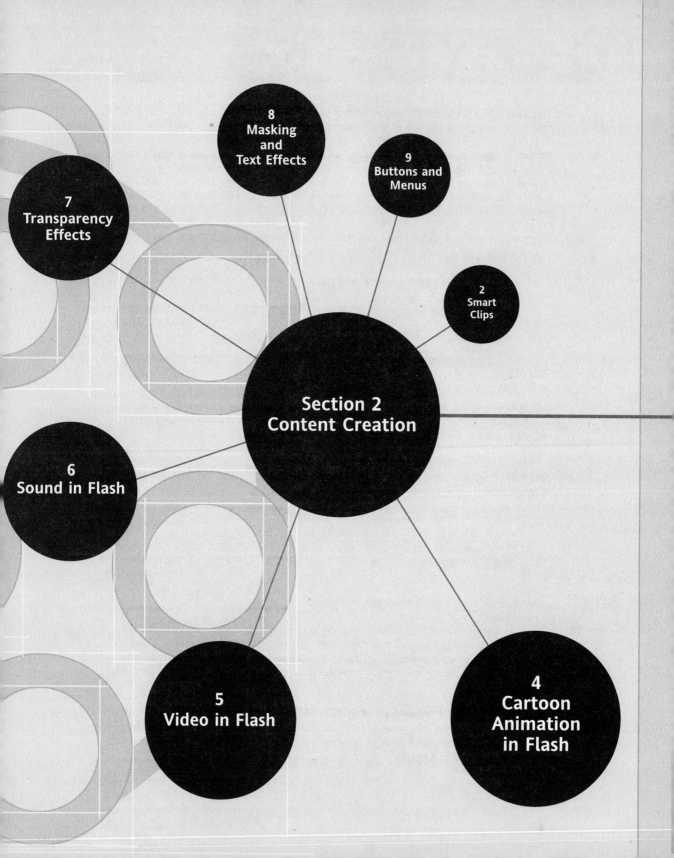

8
Masking
and
Text Effects

9
Buttons and
Menus

7
Transparency
Effects

2
Smart
Clips

Section 2
Content Creation

6
Sound in Flash

5
Video in Flash

4
Cartoon
Animation
in Flash

Chapter 3
Flash and
External 3D
Applications

Since its debut on sites like mano1 and WackedUSA, 3D has been gaining a lot of momentum and interest (see the Resources page in this chapter's folder on the CD for a bigger list of sites). People are seeing that the Flash canvas can truly be made to come alive by incorporating these elements. 3D only stands to gain more ground in the web-world over the next few years, and the chance is there for you to shape its look and feel.

3D software has traditionally been focused on producing raster images, with its research and development being mostly focused on high-end rendering for photo-realistic output. The assets created by these programs are usually still images and animations for the entertainment industry, illustrations for paper publications, or visualizations of things such as engineering projects. However, due to the limited export capabilities of the available content creation packages, the combination of the two worlds of low file size vector animation and 3D images – while very intriguing as a concept – was just not possible. Until now.

Just over a year ago, creating 3D objects in Flash was a long-winded and painstaking operation, with very few options available to you. You could create an image in a 3D program, import it into Flash and then, in a layer above it, hand trace over the outlines of the image. But if you wanted to produce an animation, you'd have to hand trace a series of images, then remove the bitmaps and hand fill the shapes you'd drawn. This would mean hours of tedious work, just to create a short animation. Another method was to turn your bitmap image into a vector using the Modify > Trace Bitmap menu option in Flash, or some other bitmap-to-vector solution. This process tends to create an extremely large number of vectors and often results in a file size larger than that of the original bitmap. When using this technique, there's also the danger of losing essential lines from the object, reducing the detail and definition of your image and damaging your animation.

As an alternative to these processes, you could use a program like Adobe Dimensions. You can create 3D models with this package and then export them as Adobe Illustrator AI files, ready to be imported into Flash. While all of these early solutions worked, they were overly time consuming and therefore not practical for large-scale animation. This chapter will show you how to use the present crop of 3D programs such as **Swift 3D**, **Illustrate!** and **Vecta 3D**, to create native vector images for Flash.

Let's begin by talking about 3D theory.

Basic 3D Theory

While we'll be calling the work we produce in Flash in this chapter '3D', in truth it isn't that at all. Strictly speaking, it's a 2-dimensional **projection** of a 3-dimensional object from a viewpoint within a 3D content creation program. Each keyframe can implement the necessary changes to create the illusion of 3D movement, but in reality, when we create 3D images we're using nothing more than **linear perspective**. As I've already said, the alternatives to using these programs are extremely time consuming and not particularly effective, but once you grasp the basics of using these new tools you'll be surprised how easy it all is, and you'll be more than ready to create your own 3D content with Flash.

Linear Perspective and Orthographic Projection

Before we start talking about the main systems of 3D, let's discuss the **planes** of the canvas. On all canvases we have the **X** and **Y** planes. These planes run from 'left to right' and 'top to bottom' respectively. There's also a third plane known as the **Z plane**. This plane runs from 'near space' to 'far space'. It's the addition of the Z plane that gives artwork a realistic 3D look:

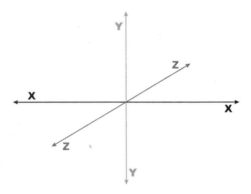

Using just the X and Y planes we can make the illusion that the Z plane is present. We do this through a number of methods such as **scale**, **overlapping**, and **color** to give an illusion of depth. Most of what we perceive as 3D, though, is defined through **converging parallels** and **inter-penetration**. These two systems make up much of what's called **linear perspective**.

While there are many other rules and systems for 3D to 2D projection content creation, the system of linear perspective is the motor that drives it. Linear perspective utilizes a horizon line and a vanishing point (or points) along that line to achieve the perception of 3D. There are three major systems in linear perspective: one-, two- and three-point perspective. When we create still images we can incorporate all three into a single image but it's not essential to do so. However, when we animate a series of images we employ all of them through the various movements of the objects. Let's take a look at the three major systems utilized in linear perspective.

- Using **one-point perspective**, where all of the drawn lines converge at the same spot, results in the front and back edges of the object you create being parallel with the plane of your canvas:

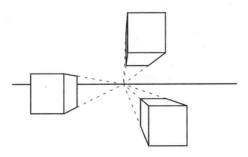

- Using **two-point perspective** allows you to create an object that appears to be **at an angle** to the plane of the canvas. One vertical edge is prominent in the foreground, and all of the top and bottom edges recede and converge to the left and right vanishing points on the horizon:

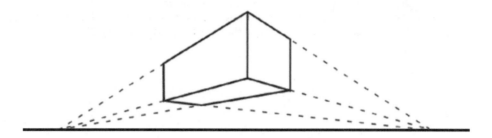

- **Three-point perspective** is used to suggest a viewing position far above or below the drawn object. Whereas in two-point perspective some of the drawn lines were parallel, in this method all of the lines extend from one of the vanishing points:

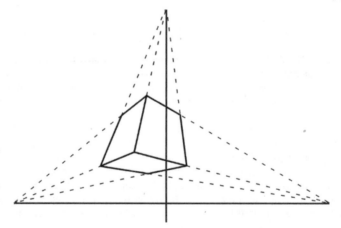

These methods allow us to see objects in 3D space. However, when creating our objects we also need to see their 2D planes, which we do using a system called **orthographic projection**. This means that we look at the object from different sides – as if it were encased in a cube – and build up our 3D representation from the 2D views. So, whereas linear perspective showed the object in 3D space, orthographic projection accentuates the outlines of the object in 2D form to give the object perspective and the impression of being 3D.

This image, taken from 3D Studio Max, shows the top, left, and front views of a plane, as well as the perspective view constructed from the other three:

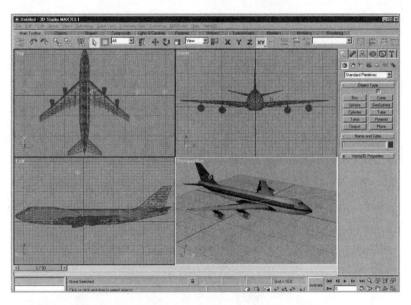

ORTHOGRAPHIC PROJECTION

This is the point where many people become confused by the many different views that they're confronted with. Hopefully, as you go through the tutorials in the chapter, you'll familiarize yourself with the interface and the orthographic planes, and begin to feel at home in a 3D world. The important thing to remember here is that we create our content using **both** orthographic and linear perspective, but render out to a 2D linear perspective output. The 3D content creation package does the hard work of calculating the convincing 2D projection based on the 3D description that we create using the X, Y and Z planes.

Now let's look at actually creating 3D content for Flash.

Creating 3D Content in Flash

In this section we'll start investigating the various techniques available for producing 3D elements for your Flash movies, and we'll also address file economy and structure. Firstly, we'll look at hand tracing and bitmap tracing, and finally at three automated products: Swift 3D, Vecta 3D and Illustrate!

Hand Tracing Within Flash

Hand tracing is the original method of creating Flash 3D content. Some sites like mano1 and WackedUSA keep their old hand traced sites up, so you can compare what was done using the 'trace by hand' technique with the more modern automated process that we'll talk about later in this chapter. These sites are still considered to be some of the best work on the Web today, partly because when you hand traced you had to take the time to plan your site out, and not just pump out a product. However, the technique is a bit slow for production work and is a painstaking process. We're going to use hand tracing techniques to create a simple cube and then a more complex shape with curved edges.

Hand Tracing within Flash

The items you need for the first exercise – the simple cube – can be found in the ht_1.fla file on the CD:

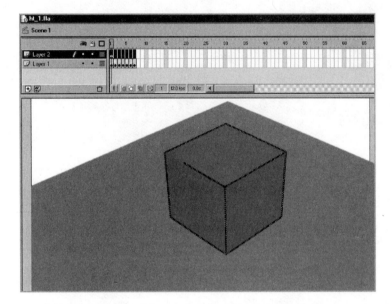

Notice there are only seven frames in the entire animation. As you can see, I've already placed a sequence of bitmap images in the layer containing the animation that we want to trace – Layer 1. This sequence represents the different stages of the cube being rotated. I've also placed a new layer – Layer 2 – above the images with a blank keyframe over each of the bitmaps. We'll use the frames on Layer 2 to trace the shapes from the bitmap images on Layer 1. If you look at the FLA, you'll see that I've started tracing the outlines of the cube in the first frame:

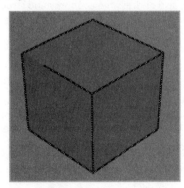

The key point that you must keep in mind is this: we only want to trace the elements that embody the movements needed to complete the animation cycle, nothing more – for example, we don't need to trace the colors and shading from the bitmaps. This will save time and make your final file size smaller.

Let's take this step by step.

1. Before you begin, ensure that the Snap to Objects option is turned on (View > Snap to Objects), as this will make it easier to connect the intersecting lines at the edges of the cube. Now select the Bezier-drawing Pen tool to start tracing the object and set the fill color to No Color. If you don't do this, when lines intersect the area formed will fill with color and make your task of tracing almost impossible. We could use the Line tool to create the trace – in fact, this is the way it was done in the past – but it seems quicker and easier to me to just use the Pen tool to trace the image.

> *There is a bit of a glitch that you need to be aware of when using the Pen tool in Flash. It will connect all of the intersecting lines to one another perfectly, except for the last line that needs to be created to complete the network of traced edges. If you try to connect the last two intersecting lines Flash will start to delete the nodes that you've already placed. You'll need to fake Flash out a bit by first selecting a point between the last two points to be connected – here's how:*

2. First of all, click frame 1 of Layer 2 to highlight the nodes that I've pre-drawn for you. Next, click on the node of the unfinished line to select it...

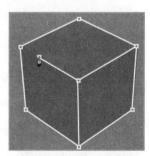

...then click on its destination corner node to draw a line between the two...

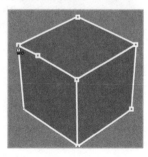

...and finally, click back on the mid-line node to delete it.

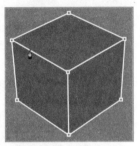

Now, if you hide Layer 1, you'll see that you're left with a perfectly traced 3D cube in frame 1 of Layer 2:

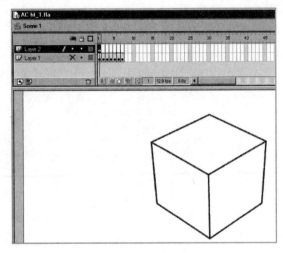

3. Now you can work your way through the rest of the frames and trace the remaining states of the spinning cube.

4. Once you've traced all of the frames, delete the background layer (Layer 1) containing the bitmap images so that only your tracings remain. Now test your movie. You should see your first Flash 3D item spinning away.

5. Finally, let's dress the cube up, so to speak. You can do this by filling the sides of the traced cube with different hues, or by using only one hue with different intensities to illustrate spatial movement and give an impression of the way the object is lit:

6. Open the `ht_shaded.swf` file from the CD to see a completed example.

You could also indicate lighting on the objects using gradient fills. This is a bit trickier, but if it's done correctly, it will make the movement and appearance of your object more life-like. One trick to getting your lighting to line up is to create the gradient that you want to use to fill an angle and, once you have it, choose the Eyedropper tool from the toolbar and select the gradient fill. This will lock the fill, making Paint Bucket tool the current cursor, and it will also keep the fill in the same **aspect**, meaning the fill for the various frames will be easier to line up. As long as the lock is selected the gradient center will remain the same on the canvas.

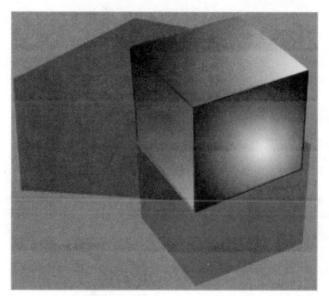

7. Open the `ht_lit.swf` file from the CD to see a completed example of this.

Now that we've completed a simple cube let's move on to more complex items that contain curved edges.

Open the `cone.fla` file on the CD and, using the same technique we demonstrated above, trace the cone. You may find that it helps to add the points running from the apex to the base:

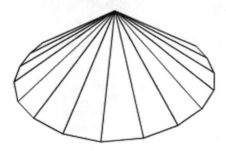

If you've worked your way through this exercise you've no doubt gained a greater appreciation of the way that 3D sites used to be created, and your respect for the skill and patience of the pioneers of high quality hand traced 3D has probably gone through the roof. While the tools in Flash have improved over the years, and it's possible to trace items in this way, it's still not easy. You may want to consider using FreeHand or another drawing program to do more complex tracing so that you'll have more robust drawing tools available to you, and then do the color fill in Flash.

To produce efficiently hand traced items you'll need a 3D program to produce the basic images to trace. If you don't already have one, there are several free programs you can download listed in the resources appendix.

If you *don't* want to learn a 3D program, then there are alternatives that you can use to create the images that you want to hand trace. You can use segments of home video and convert them into a series of images, or you can use still images from a digital camera as you would in stop-motion animation. To ensure that the camera angle doesn't change, use a tripod to steady the camera, and then place your object in the viewfinder and make the various turns needed to create the animation. When creating your animations you should import your images into a movie clip or graphic so that you'll be able to place the tracings anywhere on the stage and scale the animation with ease:

Take a look at the files in this chapter's Stop Motion folder on the CD to see how I used these images in Flash.

Another option for creating web-deliverable 3D content is auto tracing a bitmap image using Flash's **Trace Bitmap** option. While this seems like a logical choice, it can actually create larger files that need more cleaning up than the hand traced bitmaps that you produced previously! However, it can be a helpful option to use on graphics with more complex shapes than the simple cube we've been using here.

Tracing Objects Automatically

One trick to creating traced bitmaps is using images that have been created in black and white or just as flat, solid colors – the flat fills will speed up the tracing process and provide a smaller finished file. Tracing creates separate vectors for the various color areas, so if you use solid flat colors fewer areas will be created and you'll need to spend less time cleaning up the image after you've traced it. We'll take the cube again as our example, but this time get Flash to trace it for us automatically.

1. Open the `tb_1.fla` file from the CD. Select the bitmap in frame 1 and go to Modify > Trace Bitmap. A dialog box will appear:

    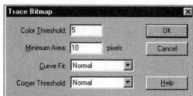

    You'll have to adjust the tolerances appropriately to achieve your goal. Since you've imported an image with few colors in it, the process will be a bit easier for your machine to perform.

2. Set the Color Threshold to 5 and Minimum Area to 10 pixels; leave Curve Fit and Corner Threshold set at Normal. Now click OK.

    Notice that the various color areas have been made into separate vectors – as you can see, the trace feature has picked up that the two front faces of the cube are the same color and converted them into a single vector shape.

    We can now remove the areas that we *don't* want to keep – the background color behind the cube. We do this in a slightly backwards fashion for something seemingly so simple, but when you start using more complicated images, you'll see why we do things this way – it's far easier than trying to select all the traced elements of a complicated background.

3. Select the two vectors that we *do* want, the top and front faces of the cube, and cut them from the stage:

4. Now select what's left on the stage and delete – *not* cut – it from the stage, including any little wisps and fragments that you can find.

5. Finally, paste the two cube components back onto the stage using the Edit > Paste in Place command. This will leave you with the cube on a blank stage.

If you zoom in on the object you'll notice the edges are jagged:

You can fix this by removing the superfluous nodes using the Subselect tool:

Keep in mind that cleaning the nodes up can be tedious in a large project, and in the process of removing nodes you may change the shape of an item and have to then make hand adjustments to ensure that the animation stays smooth. You have to be *really* dedicated to follow through with tracing work done inside Flash...

General Guidelines for Using Trace Bitmap

There are several attributes to consider when you trace a bitmap image:

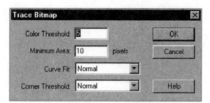

These can be a little confusing if you don't understand exactly what the tool does. Here, we'll quickly run through the various options and give you some examples of the commonly used settings.

Color Threshold Setting

The Color Threshold setting modifies the way that Flash traces a bitmap. Influenced by the Color Threshold setting, Flash takes two pixels and compares the difference in their RGB color values. If the difference is *less* than the color threshold setting, then the two pixels are considered to be the same color. As you increase the threshold value, you therefore decrease the number of colors in the finished – traced – vector image. I tend to start at a low setting like 5 since I'm usually bringing in an image that I really only want the edges of, and I plan to fill these items by hand after they're traced, to suggest lighting. If your item is more detailed, move the threshold up until you get Flash to reproduce in vector form the range of colors that you want.

Minimum Area

The Minimum Area attribute is used for assigning a color to an area of pixels. This can be set to a value from 1 to 1000, and the larger the minimum area, the smoother – but less detailed – the final image will be. Since most of the time you'll be bringing in a short series of frames from a 3D program and you'll be using only the colors needed to separate the areas, you can set the minimum area at 10. However, if you have a large image with many colors – such as a photograph that you're trying to trace a building from – you may want to bump the number up a little so that you only get the major areas/lines of the building or other object.

Curve Fit

Curve Fit determines how smoothly outlines are drawn. You can choose from Pixels, Very Tight, Tight, Normal, Smooth, or Very Smooth, and the names really speak for themselves. I tend to leave this at the Normal setting or go to Tight or Very Tight to retain the straight lines. If you have a lot curved shapes you may want to try the Smooth and Very Smooth, but for the most part I find that the Normal setting is adequate.

Corner Threshold

Corner Threshold determines whether sharp edges are retained or smoothed out. Here again, the names speak for themselves, and here again I tend to stick with the Normal setting.

There is no silver bullet to this technique: it's just a case of trial and error, learning which settings to use, and when, through experience and personal preference. Here are some tips on a couple of the common settings that I've found most useful in my work:

For accurate settings to create a vector graphic that looks most like the original bitmap, enter the following values:

- Color Threshold: 10
- Minimum Area: 1 pixel
- Curve Fit: Pixels
- Corner Threshold: Many Corners

But this can produce more nodes than you need most of the time, and it means more clean-up. These are the settings that I tend to use:

- Color Threshold: 5
- Minimum Area: 10 pixels
- Curve Fit: Normal
- Corner: Normal

You'll have to experiment with the settings to get exactly what you want, but this will at least give you a running start.

OK, that's all for our look at creating 3D content inside Flash. Now we'll turn to the external 3D packages that you can use in conjunction with Flash.

Creating 3D with Third Party Software

There are several different third party solutions that you may want to consider for creating your 3D content. While all of the products share some common points and have similar output, they take different approaches in their authoring environments. This section will look at each of these and, with the aid of some practical exercises, give you an idea of which ones you'll be most comfortable using.

Swift 3D

Swift 3D is probably the most developed authoring environment out of all of the standalone products, and it's the only third party 3D solution that comes in both PC and Mac versions. This product has the ability to create quite a complex level of modeling and is the only one of the applications we're looking at that'll create drag-and-drop animation. It's also the only standalone program that'll take a 3DS file (output from Discreet's 3D Studio Max) and render its animation paths, lights and materials.

> *It's important to note that Swift 3D wasn't created to be a 3D modeling solution, but to give you a way of creating animation in a drag-and-drop environment and as a tool for doing basic modeling for those who don't have any other environment in which to do it.*

We've provided a trial version of Swift 3D on the CD for both the Mac and PC. While this demo version is limited, it will give you a feel for what the program can and can't do. We'll run through an example showing you how to use Flash and Swift 3D together to create a simple 3D image. We've also provided some FLAs on the CD for you to study that show some uses of 3D elements and how to combine them with interaction.

Modeling in Swift 3D

Using a combination of Flash and Swift 3D, we'll create a model of a castle to get you familiar with the program's interface and rendering capabilities and to help you make your mind up about whether to purchase the full version or not.

1. Open the file `castle.fla` in Flash. For the sake of this tutorial, using the orthographic view system of drawing, I've laid out the castle components already, separating the different shapes – walls and tower bases – into different colors:

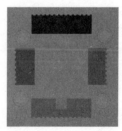

CASTLE COMPONENTS

However, when it's imported into Swift 3D everything is gray, so it's not strictly necessary to separate the shapes out in this way – as long as there are outlines to define the shapes, Swift 3D will be able to separate them out

You can see that all of the walls are laid out on their sides and the towers are set in place as if we were looking at them from the top down. In the second frame of the FLA I've also included a shot of the kind of effect we'll be able to achieve:

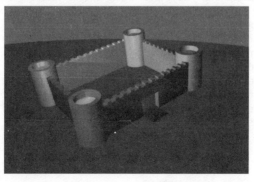

2.   Export frame 1 (the flat, orthographic layout) of the FLA as an EPS file from Flash by using the File > Export Image option, and then selecting EPS 3.0 from the drop-down menu that appears.

3.   Now open up Swift 3D, click on File > New, and choose to create a new empty Swift 3D document when prompted. Select File > Import, navigate to the EPS that you just exported from Flash, and import it. Imported images are automatically converted into 3D objects with a depth of 0.05. Giving the two dimensional images *depth* turns them into 3D objects:

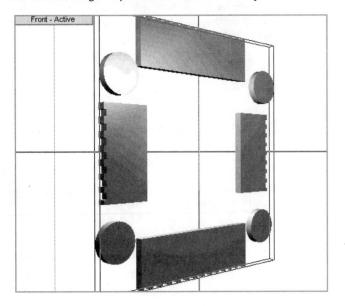

4.   To zoom out of the image, right-click (CTRL-click on a Mac) on an empty part of the stage and drag the mouse down away from the image. You should see the image get smaller the further you move the mouse. To zoom back in, just move the mouse the opposite way. It's important that you don't click on the actual object, as you'll start to move it, rather than the camera.

All models that you import into Swift 3D that are made up of multiple objects are automatically grouped together. If you want to change the characteristics of an individual part of the group, you must first ungroup it by using the Arrange > Ungroup command. Once you've done this, deselect the group by clicking on an empty part of the stage. You should now be able to select the individual parts separately:

5. We want to give our towers a bit more depth, which we can do by **extruding** them. Extrusion is just the term used for the process of stretching or squashing an object along one axis to alter its depth.

6. Select the outer ring of one of the towers and go to the Property Toolbox on the left of the screen. From here, select Sizing, and change the Depth from 0.05 to 0.4, then click on Apply. You should be able to immediately see the change reflected in the picture in the main view area:

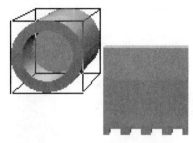

7. Now select the inner ring of the tower and, using the same steps as above, change its depth to 0.3:

8. That's the tower completely finished, so group both the inner and outer rings together as an object by selecting one, holding SHIFT, and clicking on the other. Once they're both selected, use the Arrange > Group menu to link them.

9. To complete the extrusions, repeat steps 6, 7 and 8 with the remaining three towers.

10. All good castles need walls that actually stand up. Since they've already been extruded slightly when they were imported, we don't need to alter their size, we just need to move them. It's handy to be able to see your object from more than one side when you're moving it, and this is made possible through the Secondary Camera function in Swift 3D. To turn this function on, just click on the Show Secondary Camera button (the one with two cameras on it) on the main toolbar:

Show Secondary Camera button

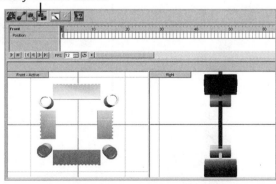

You should now be able to see the effects of your extrusion more clearly.

11. Notice that there are buttons in the top-left corner of each window that show which view you're currently looking at. Leave the first view as is, but change the second view to show your castle from the top:

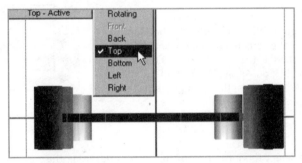

12. Now in the first view select the topmost wall. This will be the back wall in our finished piece. Notice that it's now displayed in the trackball in the bottom-left corner:

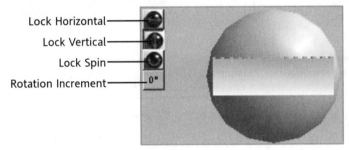

13. Click on the Lock Vertical button, the middle one of the three buttons with arrows. Selecting this option means that you'll only be able to move the wall vertically. Drag the trackball until the wall is edge-on, with the crenellations facing you:

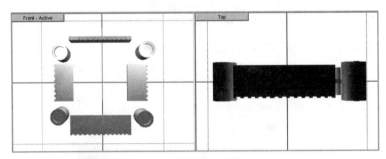

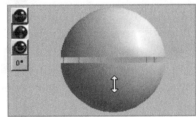

You'll see that the wall looks upside down in the view window, but remember that this is an orthographic view of the model. Because we're using the front as a top-down view, the real top view is the equivalent of standing on our head behind the castle.

14. Now do the same for the rest of the walls, changing the second view to the right, left and bottom, and turning the walls appropriately. We've included a drawbridge on the front wall of the castle. Feel free to do what you like with this, open it, close it, or just delete it all together. You should end up with something a bit like this:

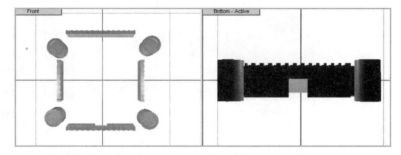

15. The walls may now be standing, but there are still some pretty huge gaps between them and the towers. We're not quite impregnable yet. Next, we need to drag all of the separate objects together to form the completed castle. Using the front view, select a tower and drag it to the corner at the front left of the castle:

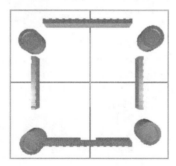

16. Next, line up all of the other walls and towers in relation to this:

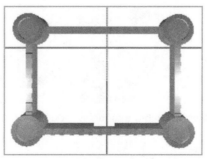

17. Now if you look at the second view, you'll see that the bottoms of the towers are not lined up with the bottoms of the walls. Put them in position by selecting the necessary views and dragging them into place:

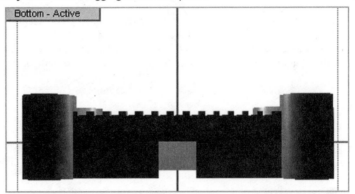

18. Now go to Edit > Select All, then go to the Arrange menu and group them all together.

19. We can now color the model by using the drag-and-drop coloring system at the bottom right of the screen:

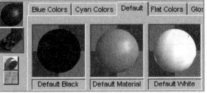

Each of the spheres represents a color and texture that can be applied to an object. There are about a dozen different material palettes to choose from, and to use them you just drag the color that you want onto the object that you want it on:

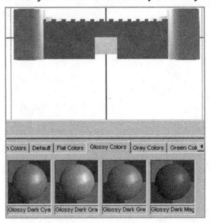

Notice that even though the model is grouped together, the individual pieces can still be colored separately.

Once you've finished with your model, it's time to render it out as a SWF file. **Rendering** is effectively taking a picture of it. It can be a very processor-intensive process though, because the computer has to take into account what can be seen in each picture, and then work out how each pixel will look depending on its position, color and texture, and the position, color and intensity of the light or lights that are shining on it.

Rendering in Swift 3D

Swift 3D offers several different rendering options. We'll take a look at them all and explain the pros and cons of each.

You bring up the rendering options via the File > Export menu on the PC...

...and on the Mac by using File > Export, filling in the file name details, and hitting Save:

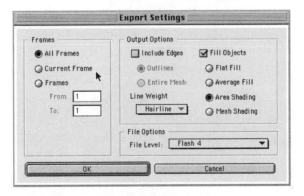

On the Mac, take care to save your file and read Electric Rain's documentation on memory settings before rendering out your construction.

The first option on the Export dialog box is to decide whether to Include Edges or not. This will determine if you want to be able to see the **mesh** that the object is made up of. Choosing Entire Mesh will show every single visible line in the model, while selecting just Outlines will give a more viewer-friendly image:

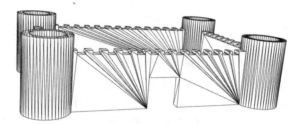

ENTIRE MESH

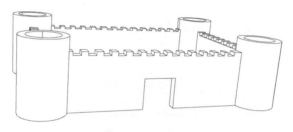

OUTLINE

You can also use the outlines in conjunction with fills. This is especially useful when you're exporting as a flat fill, as it helps to give definition to the model. I'll quickly run through the different export fill options, and give an example of each.

- **Flat Fill**: this will give you just the filled areas of the model minus any lighting or other effects. Most of the time, this will be the quickest and smallest of the render modes. I've given an example both with and without outlines here so that you can see the difference it makes in clarity:

The file size for the flat filled SWF on the left was 3k, while the flat outline filled SWF on the right was 7k.

- **Average Fill**: this is the same as the Flat Fill but it also partially takes lighting into account. It does this by calculating the average lighting on each surface, then flat filling that surface in the one average color. This brings more detail to the item but keeps it in flat colors:

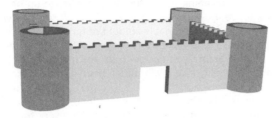

The file size for this SWF was 4k.

- **Area Fill**: this will fill the various color objects with a gradient using the light sources. This option is still not perfect though, as it only displays *one* reflected light source on each surface. This is fine for most simple renders, but if you want the best of the best, there's still one more step to take:

The SWF here is 9k.

- **Mesh Fill**: this option uses all the polygons to create the rendered surfaces. It also fully light-sources the image showing the accurately colored reflections of each light on each surface. This is the best quality render for lighted objects, but – as is always the case – it also gives the largest files:

This SWF is 26k.

The combination of mesh and fills that you opt for will be influenced by a number of factors:

- Where you're publishing to:

    - If you're planning on putting the final image up on the Web, it's best not to go above an Area Fill as the file sizes will soon grow too large for people to download in a reasonable amount of time. In fact, it's usually worth outputting your image at a low quality Average Fill first and seeing how it looks in your Flash file before you decide to go any higher. You'll be surprised at how often a lower quality image will suffice when it's incorporated into a full web site.

    - If you're planning on putting the image on a CD, or just running it from a hard drive, then by all means Mesh Fill every frame. The only thing holding you back here is the amount of patience that you have waiting for the scene to render. A fully light-sourced animation can take a *very* long time to process.

- How complicated the model is:

    - With a simple model, you can use a better quality output and still achieve a relatively small file. Also, with a simple model you'll sometimes find that you get a better quality image with an Area Fill rather than a Mesh Fill. The only way to verify this, unfortunately, is to render using both settings and see which you prefer.

- What effect you're trying to achieve:

    - Ultimately of course, it's down to you to decide which effect you prefer in the rendered image. You may only want the cartoon shading that's achieved by a Flat Fill with Outlines, in which case you'll be perfectly happy with the lower quality. On the other hand, you may only get the effect you require from the highest quality Mesh Fill, in which case you may try and compromise by lowering the quality/content of another part of your web site to try and maintain a comfortable download time.

There are examples of each output type in this chapter's folder on the CD, in the Swift 3D Castle Exports folder.

There's much more to Swift 3D that we haven't had space to touch on here, the most obvious of which is probably **animation**. Swift 3D uses a timeline and keyframe system very similar to Flash, which allows you to quickly and easily animate your 3D models. The instructions on how to do this, and much more, can be found amongst the Swift documentation, which is in the folder where you installed the Swift 3D demo.

Once you've exported your animation as a SWF file, you can easily integrate it into a Flash movie either with the use of the loadMovie command, or by importing the SWF into Flash as a series of keyframes. To keep them clean and easy to work with, I'd recommend pasting all of the frames into a movie clip so you can easily control and keep track of them.

As I write, the guys at Electric Rain are busy working away on some great new features for the next version of Swift 3D, and we've been lucky enough to be given a preview of the things they're aiming to include. Keep in mind that this is just a list of probables, and that nothing is yet set in stone. RAViX, Swift 3D's rendering engine, has undergone a significant overhaul. Not only will it be incredibly fast, it will provide new export options, improved file size optimization, and will easily handle models with very high polygon counts. V2 will import the most common 3D file formats including 3DS, DXF, and LWO. New features are being added to improve the ability to create 3D objects within the program and to allow for more precise control over those objects. There are a ton of other seriously exciting things being considered for V2. I can't wait for the full version!

3D Studio Max

You can also use 3D Studio Max's 3DS models in Swift 3D to create your animated (and static) 3D images. The trial version of Swift 3D on this book's CD includes a single model for you to experiment with – it'll be automatically imported when you choose the 3D Studio file option in the New File Wizard dialog box:

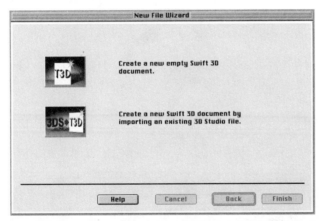

3DS models saved out of 3D Studio Max will retain their color, lighting and animation, which can be a big plus when you're doing serious animation. The model provided is a single piece and is not animated. Using the same techniques as above, you can easily animate and then export the file. As we'll discuss further in the chapter, there are hundreds of sites and sources to obtain free 3DS models from, which can save you time and money on your projects.

While Swift 3D will import 3DS models, it's not necessary to use them to create compelling models for your sites. Swift 3D has serious limitations on the types of models it can produce, but understanding the program's limitations and planning ahead will give you the ability to create dynamic interfaces and supporting props for models that you can get off the Web for free.

We'll now turn to look at some of the other 3D modeling solutions that can be used with Flash. Towards the end of the list we'll also take a peek into our crystal ball and examine some of the programs that were just appearing over the horizon as this book went to print.

Let's start with Vecta 3D.

Vecta 3D Standalone

The Vecta 3D product is comparable to Swift 3D in that it's standalone, but it takes a completely different approach to its interface and modeling tasks. It has a few unique features, such as a perspective button, and the ability to edit the center of the model, but it's limited in its ability to animate an object in that it can only rotate it around its center point. It also only has limited features for creating models from your AI files, as you can only import a single file and extrude it. You're not able to break the file apart into separate pieces or import other AI files to build a more complicated model. This limits your creativity for making your own models with Flash, but it serves its purpose elsewhere for things like logos. Let's take a quick look at the Vecta 3D interface:

Most of Vecta 3D's controls are located on the front panel and are grouped according to functionality. The animation tools differ greatly from other packages in that you set the rotation of the model or the camera using **degrees of angles**. Although Vecta 3D uses precise math to create the animation, it doesn't let you drag the object to the next point or rotation for animation. This math-based method takes a bit of guesswork and is not as user friendly as drag-and-drop animation, but it does allow you to perform some very precise animation. While there is also an automated method of animation, it's quite rigid and can be hard to use.

Vecta can light models, but it's limited to one light and that light can only be one color – white. To see an example of a lit model from Vecta 3D, look at the vectalit.swf file on the CD:

The easy way to create animation in Vecta 3D is to move the model by hand just a fraction of an inch and then do a render as an Illustrator file. Then move the model again, repeating this process until you have the necessary movements needed to create the animation. This can be both a good thing and a bad thing: while it will help you control the number of images it takes to make up the movement, the controls can make it difficult to handle the model smoothly. There's no demo copy of the Vecta 3D standalone product as I write, but if you come across a copy of it, it'd be well worth trying out the interface and the animated output to get a feel for the program and how it compares with others that you've used.

Vecta 3D is a simple solution: it can render out to the SWF and AI file formats and has a solid and fast render engine. However, it's limited by the program's internal animation facilities. It can bring in a series of 3DS models and render them out as animation, or it can make very simple extruded shapes from imported AI files. It's a product to watch, but at the moment it doesn't feel as fully developed or mature as Swift 3D.

Illustrate! 5.0 and Vecta 3D-Max Plug-ins

There are two plug-ins for 3D Studio Max that'll render out to SWF files: Vecta 3D-Max and Illustrate! 5.0. Also as we go to print erain have just released a 3Dmax plugin.

The Vecta 3D-Max Plug-in renders the same output as the Vecta 3D Standalone, but without the lighting. The problems with camera views don't exist in this version because the content is being rendered inside the 3D Studio Max environment. If you use a plug-in it's much easier to create a good 3D model and then export it in a Flash-friendly format.

Illustrate! 5.0 has just been released as I write, and looks to be very promising as it offers a huge collection of new and advanced features. You can produce flat fills, cartoon shading, cel shaded, and lit gradient models. It also allows you to cast shadows and reflections, a new development in Illustrate! 5.0 that gives you much greater realism in your final renders. You can download a free trial version of the software from the davidgould site, but don't forget that you need to have 3D Studio Max to use it. There is also an Alias|Wavefront Maya plug-in in the works that'll deliver the same as the 3D Studio Max version. Please visit www.davidgould.com to see some examples and more information on this product.

Amorphium Pro

This is a great-looking new product that was in its late beta stages as the book went to press, and looks like it has real promise. We've provided a trial of the software for you on the CD. It's a fully functioning package and will save out content with a watermark over the output.

Amorphium Pro provides a true modeling environment in which you can create complex shapes and models in no time. There are so many features in this program that I will only touch on the main points.

Amorphium was originally released a few years ago aimed at the non-3D artist. It has already been used to create effects for some major Hollywood productions. The creators decided that they would approach the problem of modeling the same way that artists do in real life – working in clay. You start with either a primitive shape (sphere, cube, cone, cylinder, torus, plane or text) made up of polygons, or 'digital wax'. You can then mould this shape using melting methods, picking and pulling at the object, or by using the Boolean tool to add or subtract matter from it. While the program is missing a few features that 3D artists are used to having, it does do a great job of modeling in a novel yet intuitive environment. Its SWF output is excellent for cartoon shaded work, and its ability to cast shadows is a great feature for 3D Flash lovers. Its only problem is that its gradient fills and outlines can be a bit 'soft' compared to the output of Swift 3D. Overall, though, it's a solid product that should cause the market to mature even more. I have provided a few example files for you to look at on the CD in the folder called `Amorphium Pro Examples`.

Let's take the quick tour around the main Amorphium Pro features. First stop is the main interface.

The program uses an unconventional interface that takes a bit of getting used to. You pull sub-menus out of the main menu bar on the left, which then sit out on screen as floating toolbars, like the two shown in the upper part of this screenshot:

The other parts of the screen will be a little more familiar, consisting of the main work area, in which you can have multiple views of the model, and the timeline. The timeline is where you assign your lighting and animation and, much like Swift 3D, it's a drag-and-drop editor. Every item is listed on the timeline, giving you the ability to add keyframes and animation for each object on its own line.

Next stop on the tour is the Tools area:

As you can see, the tools are a little unconventional. Rather than use the normal extrusion methods, you hammer away at the primitive shape or pull and pinch it to get the shape that you want. For a traditional 3D artist this concept takes a little getting used to, but it's a great new way to model. On the screenshot of this on the previous page you can see some of the brush settings that you can adjust for the various tools on the tool bar. For an example of this, take a look at ball1.swf, which shows an example of the stretch effect used on the ball to express volume and movement.

The next stop on our whistle-stop tour is the Wax Factory:

This is my favorite area of the program. Inside here, it's like playing with warm candle wax when you were a kid. As in the other interface, you just cut away at your wax primitive until you get the shape you want, but it allows some beautifully organic effects. Take a look at the ice.swf example of an ice cube melting to see a quick illustration of the power of this program. The way that you animate something like this is to go to the Composer, set a new keyframe in the timeline at the point that you want the action to finish, and then just melt away the area that you want to disappear. And that's it, the program does the rest. There are all sorts of other aspects to the program including a Paint Shop where you can carefully add color to individual parts of your model.

Amorphium Pro is a great step forward in creating SWF output for 3D. Its environment is packed with innovative tools and goodies to model with, and its output to shaded cartoon is small and clean, with good render times. The program can sometimes have problems with rendering gradient or outline models, but hopefully this will be corrected soon. The other problem is the price. At $375 (February 2001) it may be a bit steep for those who are just getting into 3D, but if you're looking to create great models and think that you may want to do more than just create SWFs, then you might do well to invest in this program.

Poser

Curious Labs has just entered the SWF fray with Poser. Poser is a character-modeling program that allows you to create a huge array of human and animal forms. It has been going for a number of years now, but has just been given the ability to export to SWF format. The final version wasn't complete at the time of going to press, but you can see some examples of SWF output on their web site. File size is always a concern, and large animations will still be a problem, but if you want excellent stills of people posed, then you need look no further.

Poser's interface gives an easy way to animate and pose human figures for natively created scenes, composite pieces or to export as models for other programs. At present, the SWF export facility comes as part of an add-on pack for the standard Poser 4 software. The pack is expected to retail at about $140, and will be an essential for anyone who uses or wants to use both Poser and Flash.

Which Product Should You Use?

There are some hard choices to be made about creating 3D elements for Flash, but perhaps the biggest of these is cost. While plug-ins for 3D Studio Max or Maya are good ideas and relatively cheap in themselves, their one caveat is that you must first own the original piece of software, and high-end 3D software doesn't come cheap.

For the designer who has no access to upscale 3D modeling software, Swift 3D is the clear choice. It gives you the capability to create compelling animation in an easy-to-learn environment. If you find that the thing holding you back in Swift 3D is the model creation, fear not. You can either wait for the new and improved version 2, or you can download a free 3D authoring package such as Strata 3D from www.3d.com, or Blender from www.blender.nl. These will increase your capabilities ten-fold, allowing you to create detailed 3D models and export them as 3DS files ready for import into Swift 3D. The other option is to go for a package like Amorphium Pro that'll allow you to both create a model in a professional environment *and* export it as a SWF file.

If you have 3D Studio Max you may want to consider either Swift 3D or Illustrate! 5.0. Both of these products have advantages and disadvantages. Illustrate will output right out of 3D Studio Max, giving you integrated use and a host of great features. Swift 3D will animate your 3DS files with lights and motion paths. I suggest you play with the demo of Swift on the CD and download the trial version of Illustrate! to compare them and help make your mind up.

Creating Interactivity

3D output doesn't only have to be for quick, illustration-only animations. You can create great interactive games and interfaces using some of the techniques mentioned above. I have provided the source files to my old site for you to look at. While this site is very light in the ActionScript department it will give you an idea of how to structure an interface to achieve the best file economy that you can. While it's a little larger than it could be, I wanted the nice shading, so I was prepared to pay the size price. I support open source file code – we can all learn from one another and improve our own projects. Enjoy the file, it's called `interface.fla`, and it's in the `Interactivity` folder in this chapter's area on the CD.

Real 3D

People are also creating 3D effects using either pure ActionScript, or ActionScript combined with objects in movie clips. While much of this work is still in its early, experimental stages, some of it shows great promise. A chapter by Andries Odendaal, a star in this field, follows this one. Andries' site, www.wireframe.co.za, and sites like www.digitalorganism.com show off the beauty of simple design and the use of 3D in code. Another great example is www.andyfoulds.co.uk. Andy has fine examples of 3D code menus that he's developed, especially his click and spin that he created with the help of Chris Glaubitz and his 3D engine. That engine can be downloaded from www.flashkit.com in the Movies section. Others, like Branden Hall of www.figleaf.com are working on 3D engines that support shading and lighting. There's a SWF example of what you can do on this book's CD called `coma2_cons.swf`. The guys at www.coma2.com developed this construction kit, which shows off just what you can do with ActionScript in Flash 5. If you want the specific code you'll need to contact the developers for it, but these are excellent examples of where things are going.

Optimizing 3D Content for Web Delivery

While creating 3D animation with automated methods is possible, it's not very efficient for web delivery, as files can be several hundred kilobytes – if not megabytes – in size. So how can we overcome the file size issue and create something complex and interesting, and yet still web deliverable? Let's take a closer look at how our 3D images are made up.

A model inside a 3D content-creation program is really nothing more than a lot of polygons connected together to create a tessellated object, thus forming the 3D shape. These small shapes are **surfaces**, an the more surfaces and object has, the larger its file size. Here's an example of a shape with thousands of surfaces which, as you can imagine, will create a huge file when exported:

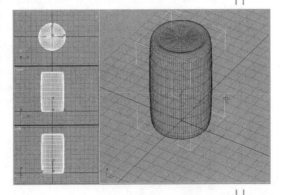

One standard technique for decreasing file size is to reduce some of the polygons on the models before they are rendered into vectors. This will reduce the number of surfaces, making the file smaller and also the render times much faster. On the down side, though, it can make your image appear to have more jagged and unnatural edges than you may want:

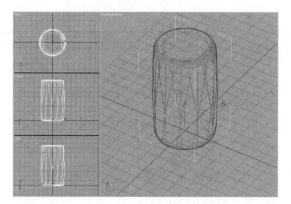

Most of the high end programs like Maya and 3D Studio Max give you the ability to do this, and even some lower end packages like Strata 3D and MetaCreations' Carrara will allow you to reduce the polygon count on a model.

The key problem here is how do you know when to stop removing polygons from the model? And the simple answer is that you *don't* know just by looking at the model in design mode – you'll have to do some test renders to see how the model looks and decide whether you can cut down the polygon count any more.

The next step to take is to optimize the render output method. We've already looked at this with the different export render settings of Swift 3D, so I won't go into it again here. There are also other ways that you can shave some valuable kilobytes from your SWFs. Here's how...

Limit Motion Renders

It's possible to render out only the movements that are necessary for creating your animation. You can then use Flash's own tweening and symbol economy features to bring down file size. To do this, you must identify which frames are required to export for things like turns, and which you can safely create with a motion tween in Flash. Open the example file Bell.swf on the CD and notice that the helicopter actually only turns a few times throughout the whole animation:

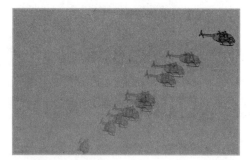

Many people make the mistake of rendering the entire motion path in the 3D package, but if a model is only being scaled or moved along the X or Y axis during animation, you can actually use Flash's built in tools. Look at Bell4.fla on the CD for an example.

Reduce Surface Areas

If you have to do a model render that'll require more than one light source, you can sometimes achieve this by hand. You can do this by going into Flash and selecting various areas of rendered surfaces then filling them with a purpose-built gradient. This may take some time, but it can vastly reduce the size of your file. Let's walk through this process and see just how much you can save in Kilobytes by using this technique.

Reapplying Gradient Renders in Flash

We'll begin with a mesh-optimized render of the can example we saw earlier:

While this file may look a bit rough at the moment, when we're done it will look almost as good as a full mesh render, but at a significantly smaller size. The full mesh render was 102 KB, but by the end of this process, we'll have got the file down to almost a tenth of that size.

1. Open the opt.fla file from the CD in Flash.

   As you can see, we've imported the optimized mesh render of the model into frame one. The first thing that we need to do is to create the gradient that'll fill the main body of the can.

2. Click on the Dropper tool, then select one of the gradients from the middle of the can's body. The Fill tab will now contain the gradient that you chose:

In this situation, since the gradient we need has five to six colors in it and the Dropper can only collect two at a time, we'll have to add the rest of the colors needed for the gradient ourselves. To do this, go to the Fill tab and add a few more colors to the gradient. You can ensure they are the correct colors by using the Dropper again to pick the color from the image:

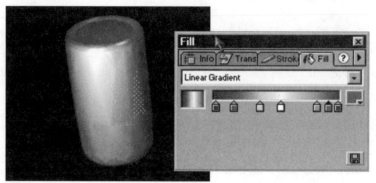

Once you've built the gradient, be sure to save it away for later use.

3.   Now that we have the color that we want, we can begin to remove the polygons from the middle of the can. After we've removed them, we'll fill the can surface with the gradient:

4.   Do this to the can in frames 1 and 2. Sometimes, you may run into a polygon whose fill runs into other polygons and may then leave gaps. We have a situation like that in this file.

Looking at frame 3 you'll see that I have drawn a line to separate the two sets of polygons: ———————

You can either remove these now or just fill the area with the gradient that you created and then finesse it later.

5. In frame 4 you'll notice that we've filled in the large area but there are some edges that don't match up to the gradient. We can simply lock the paint bucket on the Toolbar and then, by clicking on the rest of the outer polygons, fill them with the gradient to make the area one surface:

Now remove the line that you created to separate the polygons, and your file is optimized. The size of the optimized file is about 14 KB. As we said earlier, a huge reduction on the original 102 KB, and it looks a lot better too.

You can try this out with another file that we've provided on the CD called apg.fla

Now for our next optimization technique...

Render Parts of Frames

Don't render the entire file in every frame, only the parts that are needed. For example, if we have a model of a car and we want the wheels to turn as it drives across the stage, we can render just the wheels and drop them into a movie clip. We can then attach this movie clip to a static, single-frame render of the car's body. By doing this, we'll save vast amounts of information and cut down on render time and file size. To see an example of this open the CD's car.fla and car.swf files and look in the library to see the various separate parts that make up the files.

The key to successful web delivery is to be creative and experiment with your output. Remember to optimize your files, spend time storyboarding your projects, and plan your animation tasks, allowing ample download time to facilitate smooth downloads. Knowing who your target audience is and their bandwidth capabilities will help determine the amount of intensive keyframed animation that you create.

Finding Free Models on the Web

You may not have the time or the means to create your own 3D models. This doesn't mean that you can't create 3D content for your Flash projects. There are many CDs available with collections of 3D models, and there are literally hundreds if not thousands of sites on the Web that provide free models, plus tutorials on how to create your own. There are even online communities like www.3Dcafe.com and www.3d.com that are dedicated to 3D content creation. There are also Flash communities like www.flashkit.com and www.popedeflash.com that provide free models and forums to deal with Flash 3D related issues. See the Resources page on the CD for a list of great 3D sites. You may also e-mail me directly if you have any questions or would like to receive my monthly newsletter on flash 3D solutions, techniques and news at pope@flashkit.com.

Conclusion

I hope that this chapter has given you an insight into using 3D content in Flash using hand tracing methods or 3D content from third party packages. This is an exciting and growing area, and as more and more packages incorporate Flash compatible output the field can only get richer. This is a great time to be exploring the world of 3D web (and other platform) content, and I hope you'll get out there and explore some more.

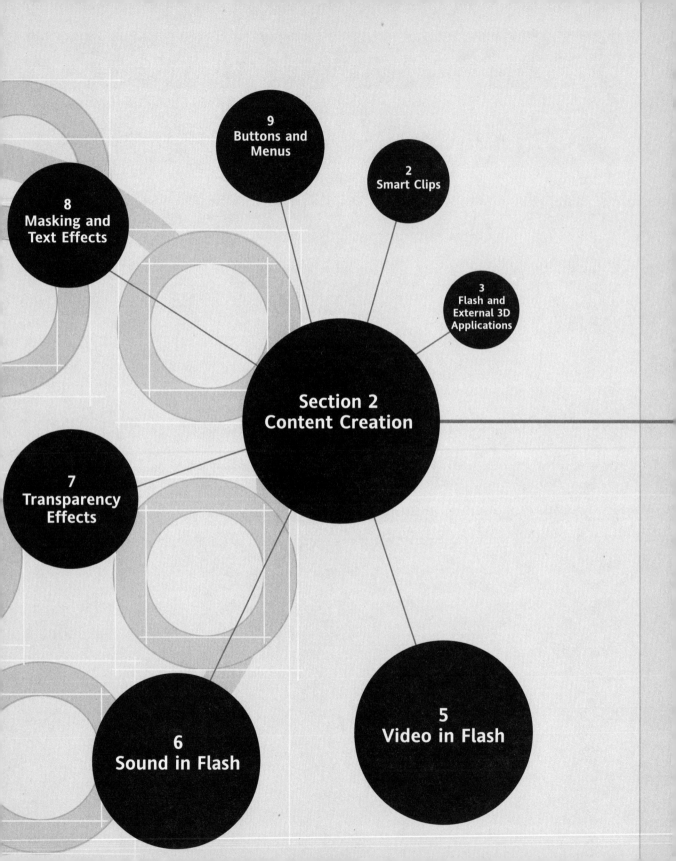

9
Buttons and
Menus

2
Smart Clips

8
Masking and
Text Effects

3
Flash and
External 3D
Applications

Section 2
Content Creation

7
Transparency
Effects

6
Sound in Flash

5
Video in Flash

Chapter 4
Cartoon Animation in Flash

The past decade has seen some very exciting technological developments that have had significant influences on art and design. Many illustrators and artists now use computers both as a tool to create their art, and as a medium for displaying it. Additionally, the connectivity offered by the Internet has opened up new possibilities for artists to showcase their creations.

Animation is another medium that has been influenced by technology. In the past, creating broadcast-quality animation involved expensive equipment to create, and it was the privilege of only the select few who had access to those machines. Over the last couple of years, however, this art form has gained in popularity and accessibility thanks to relatively inexpensive tools such as the home computer and software like Flash. This new technology offers the animator a means by which to create movies and then to distribute them relatively easily over the Internet:

Animating for the Web presents a unique set of challenges. Bearing in mind the time constraints that the viewer might be under, the form of animation best suited for the Web is that of the short movie. Additionally, in order that the broadest audience possible is able to view the animations, it's important to remember that people connect to the Internet at different speeds. It can be a major task making the animations modem-friendly by restricting their size using various optimization techniques. A further concern is managing the download efficiently. However, while these challenges are restricting, they can also inspire creative solutions. We'll cover all of this later in the chapter, but first, we should begin at the beginning with the thing that all good animations need, inspiration.

Getting Started

There are many methods for stimulating the creative process, doodling is one of them, and it's an excellent way to get your mental juices flowing. Take a blank piece of paper and fill it with continuous lines, circles, rectangles, uneven shapes, and anything you feel like without actually thinking about what you're doing. Although this is an exercise to loosen up, it can often trigger the imagination and produce unexpected ideas for stories:

Music and literature can also inspire you. Try opening a book at a page at random, picking a line from it, and then illustrating it or incorporating it into an illustrated plot. To demonstrate this technique, I have used the first line in Chapter 15 from *Dirk Gently's Holistic Detective Agency* by Douglas Adams:

"Some of the less pleasant aspects of being dead were beginning to creep up on Gordon Way."

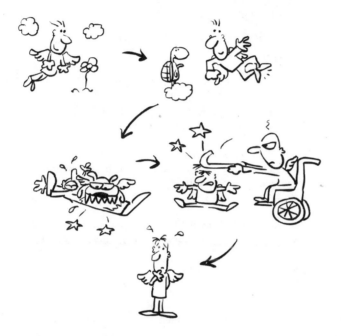

Another technique is to go at it 'freestyle', which involves beginning a movie with a basic concept and a few drawings, then going where your imagination takes you without planning any beginnings or endings. Often, the best animations come from the simplest ideas, and a sequence of frames drawn directly into Flash can lead to an interesting story. These drawings are spontaneous images, created without thought and not necessarily connected with one another. This is a very non-linear approach and one that I follow in my own work. Drawings executed directly in the Flash environment without pre-meditated rough sketches lend the animation a kind of spontaneity. Experiments and resulting accidents are then an integral part of the animation process, often leading to interesting effects and techniques not covered in any animation manual. Terry Gilliam summarized this neatly when he said that his approach to animation "has always been to keep an eye open for lucky accidents or mistakes."

The best stories often stem from your own real-life experiences, or from slightly exaggerated versions of them. Contrary to popular belief, it takes more than just drawing all day to be a good animator. What you draw and write about reflects who you are, which in turn is a result of your experiences. Because of this, it's always good practice to keep a notebook to record your ideas and experiences even if you don't use them right away – they might be of some use to you in the future.

Yet another technique is to design and illustrate a simple joke in panels:

This kind of short visual gag would be perfect for a small Flash animation. It exists only for the punch line, and it's obvious what the contents of the frames in-between would be.

In summary, there are ideas all around and inside of you, just waiting to be animated. All that's required is to be a good listener and a good observer. Although this might be hard work requiring conscious effort in the beginning, it's only a matter of time before you'll have more ideas than you'll have time to animate them.

Once you have your idea you need to commit it to paper, or to the computer screen. The traditional way of expressing your animation ideas is through the use of a storyboard.

Planning your Animation

Storyboards are used to plan the development of a movie and consist of the key components or scenes in the movie. I often work with the main visuals in my head to keep the drawings spontaneous, as mentioned earlier. As well, I rarely have a completed storyboard when starting on the animation. However, when working in a team it's a very important aid in communicating ideas with other animators.

Most traditional animators aren't very comfortable drawing in Flash, and prefer to stick with pen and paper. They then scan these drawings and import into the Flash environment. While sometimes necessary, this approach can be fairly time consuming. The approach I prefer to take is to draw directly into Flash using the tools within the Flash environment. A graphics tablet is highly recommended for this though, as using the mouse can sometimes prove to be difficult.

The following storyboard consists of the main keyframes for the short movie entitled *Zemi One Morning (A Love Story)*, which is included on the CD accompanying this book. Take a look at the movie to see how the preliminary sketches map directly onto the finished movie:

zemi one morning

Of course, we're no longer limited to linear animations like this, Flash has opened up a whole new dimension: interactivity.

Interactive Content

There are many different elements that comprise the presentation of a story or narrative in animated format. An interactive narrative might unfold in different ways depending on viewer input. A non-interactive narrative on the other hand, will follow a linear path. This example shows both types. The story can be followed through in a non-interactive fashion by just taking the vertical route through the story or, by introducing interactivity, the user can choose to branch off horizontally into a whole new story:

Although all narratives are interactive to some degree in that they involve the reader, and the reader can bring their own interpretations to the tale, Flash animation on your desktop has the ability to offer the most obvious kind of interactive user experience, where the user can directly affect the story by using the mouse or the keyboard. A story told in an interactive manner can evolve in different ways depending on viewer input at various stages of the movie.

Once you have your idea, and perhaps a few sketches scribbled down, it's time to translate it all into a language Flash can understand. As we'll see, Flash borrows a lot of techniques from traditional animation, but it applies its own computerized twist to them.

Basic Animation

The introduction of transparent Celluloid to the animation process enabled the reuse of certain static elements such as backgrounds over several scenes. Layers are similar in concept to these Celluloid sheets (cels), and can be used by the Flash animator to achieve the same level of economy. An added advantage is the reduction in file size that may be obtained by placing static and dynamic parts of an object on different layers, and only modifying the latter across two or more frames. In Flash, you can create as many layers as you like without affecting the final file size. Unlike conventional cels, however, Flash also allows you to place sounds and actions on layers:

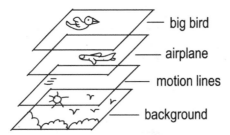

Animation can take place on any of the layers through a number of different methods. In a traditional animation sequence, content is changed in every frame, which is known as **frame-by-frame animation**. The file size corresponding to such a sequence in Flash can be quite large due to the significant number of keyframes filled with individual frames of animation.

The other main method that Flash uses for animation is tweening. This results in smaller file sizes than animating with keyframes, due to the fact that Flash only needs to store the values for the *differences* between frames, and not the entire frame. However, tweening several elements at once can be pretty processor intensive, resulting in an inconsistent animation speed (frame rate) across different computers with varying processing power.

Another aspect of animation that requires careful planning is the use of layers in dividing the elements visible in one frame. Usually, elements that are static over a number of frames, such as backgrounds, are placed on separate layers with only one extended keyframe over several frames. This will also apply in a dialog-driven sequence to a character of frames who only moves their mouth. The lips, which move from frame to frame, could be placed on one layer whilst the rest of the body is placed on another. Remember that there is no penalty in terms of file size for additional layers. It can also be helpful to break your story up into scenes. This prevents you from having to scroll through a large layer listing in the timeline. Sounds and actions can also be placed on separate layers for better organization.

Onion Skinning

Another trick that Flash borrows from conventional animation is onion skinning. It's often necessary to view two or more successive drawings in relation to one another simultaneously. For this purpose, a light box would normally be used to illuminate the surface under the paper on which the drawings are made. In Flash, a similar effect can be achieved across successive keyframes by using onion skinning. This enables you to simultaneously view the contents of all the frames between the two onion skin markers, which can prove extremely useful when creating frame-by-frame animations. The contents of the frame currently being 'played' are distinguished by being in full-color, whereas frames at other positions between the onion skin markers become increasingly transparent the further away they are from the 'live' frame.

So, with our inspiration and our basic theory behind us, it's now time to finally put it all into practice and examine some useful animation techniques.

Animating in the Flash Environment

The intent of this section is to provide you with ideas on how to analyze and apply the principles that you learned earlier to create short animated sequences, which can then be incorporated into a larger project. At the very outset I'd like to emphasize that all of these are only guidelines and not rules – the final goal is to create your own animated world, one in which your imagination defines how things work.

An essential component of animation involves creating the illusion of motion. Other equally important ingredients include the story, the artwork, and the manner in which these components interact with one another to create an engaging viewer experience. Although critics may pronounce some animation as not being truly representative of the art form, the truth is that there are many approaches to the art of animation, each equally beautiful in their own way. Animation is a skill best learned through practice, and Flash offers us a convenient way to do just that. In the following sections we'll cover various animation techniques which you may apply either after or while you construct your storyboard.

Character Design

It's through a character that a story is told, hence character design is very closely connected to the mood and theme of the story, and often also to the personality of the animator. In the case of Flash and distribution over the Internet, bandwidth limitations determine the complexity of character design, so simple lines and uncomplicated shapes are often used to represent a character in the Flash environment.

It's recommended that you also use and reuse symbols wherever possible. Prior to animating a movie, it might be good practice to start with what's known as a **model sheet**. Model sheets are used to describe a character in terms of its dimensions and dynamics from all angles. This ensures consistency of design when more than one animator is working on a project. You can also ascertain from these model sheets which elements of a character's structure could be reused as symbols:

In the above model sheet, for example, you could decide that the character's left arm could be converted into a symbol and rotated appropriately when he is in a different position throughout the movie.

While designing a character in Flash, it's necessary to bear in mind which parts are going to be animated. For instance, if a character does nothing but move her arms, it's good practice to reuse the body and legs, which are static components across many frames, while animating the arm on a separate layer. We'll see this in practice in the following example.

Dissecting your Animations

1. A girl and a dog are first drawn on the stage in layer 1. We've included this drawing on the CD (`girl_pats_dog.fla`) for your use, though it might be good practice to draw your own:

2. Insert another layer and create three additional keyframes in it. Then extend the first keyframe on Layer 1 to frame 4:

3. Using the Lasso tool, select the portion of the arm to the right of the solid line:

4. Cut and paste-in-place the arm into the second keyframe on Layer 2, and lock Layer 1 so that you don't accidentally modify the image.

5. Draw the other two positions of the arm, here labeled 1 and 3, into frames 1 and 3 respectively:

You may find it helpful to use the onion skinning feature for this purpose.

6. Select the arm in frame 2 and convert it to a symbol called mid-arm, then copy and paste an instance of this symbol into frame 4.

7. Now you can watch the animation cycle as it repeats across 4 frames.

This example demonstrates the use of symbols to create a simple animation from a static character drawing.

It's common practice among animation studios to build these libraries of characters and their motions, which are reused from one movie to the next. This is an excellent way to achieve both consistency and production economy. However, I prefer to redraw characters and animated sequences every time I start a new movie. I feel that reuse is often a hindrance both to the characters' natural evolution and to my personal growth as an artist. Every time I draw a walk cycle I learn something new about it.

We'll now turn to look at a different example of animation using a non-human character. We'll also start to look at applying the laws of physics to the motion of our characters.

The Bouncing Ball

The bouncing ball animation is often used to demonstrate the effects of weight and motion as governed by the laws of Physics. These principles can be applied to almost any animated character or object, as will be shown in the following section. The objective of this exercise is to demonstrate the exaggerated squash, stretch, acceleration and deceleration that the ball undergoes as a result of gravity. Additionally, in the Flash implementation of this exercise we'll demonstrate how to optimize the animation by reusing symbol instances of a ball. The effect we wish to achieve is this:

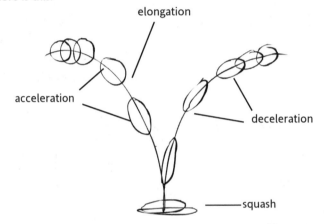

The important things to note are the acceleration, deceleration and transformation of the ball's shape as it falls, bounces and rises. The ball's constitution and the speed at which it's travelling determine the deformation.

Create a ball using the Circle tool and turn it into a graphic symbol. Try to use the same symbol over the whole animation, but in each keyframe, scale and rotate it as necessary to match our diagram.

I've demonstrated the bouncing ball here in 11 stages. This can be found on the CD in `bouncing ball.fla`:

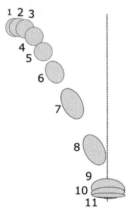

Drawings 1, 2, and 3 represent the 'slow-down' at the peak of the ball's cycle. Between stages 4 and 8, the acceleration due to gravity becomes very prominent, and the distance covered over each successive interval increases as a result. Furthermore, the object is stretched to accentuate the motion and the flexibility in the ball's structure.

Drawings 9, 10, and 11 represent the 'squash'. The more flexible the nature of the ball, the more pronounced is this compression. The images can now be mirrored to show the ball climbing again to its apex. It then recoils and undergoes deceleration as a result of gravity. Following its deceleration, the ball returns to its normal circular shape accompanied by a slow-down, and the cycle then repeats. In a more realistic scenario, the height to which the ball climbs should be slightly lower than the height from which it fell.

If you like, you can experiment with simulating varying degrees of 'solidness' of the object. A more solid or inflexible ball will have less of a stretch, so drawings 9, 10, and 11 and their mirrored bouncing back may be reduced to only a few drawings with little modification of the symbol. In the case of a lighter ball, the air might cause it to hover about at the top for longer (stages 1, 2, and 3).

It should be noted that this animation could be done using the motion tweening feature in Flash, and using the Easing property in the tweening operation. However, the level of control you're able to achieve using this approach is far less than if you did it manually as described above. It is of course possible to combine these techniques by using keyframes at important points, say every other frame, and letting Flash shape tween between them.

The Bouncing Man

In the following example, we've used one symbol and the same squash, recoil, acceleration and deceleration principles that we used with the ball, to create a very simple animation. It consists of a man bouncing up and down along a vertical line. The reused symbol has been modified in each frame using Flash's scaling feature. Modified shapes of symbol instances add very little overhead to the overall animation in terms of its file size. I've split the diagram up horizontally here, so you can see more easily the effect we're trying to achieve:

Here is an example of a more organic, hand-drawn approach to the human spring. It can be found on the CD as human spring.fla:

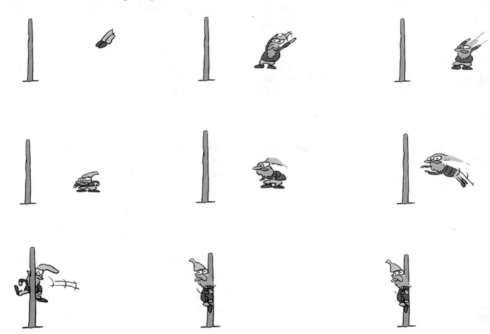

Motion lines have been used to enhance the effect of speed. Which method you choose depends on the constraints you're up against and the effect that you wish to achieve. However, it's very important that you maintain consistency across the entire movie. If you intend to draw your character movement frame by frame without reusing symbols (as I usually do), then motion tweening in only one isolated section of the movie might seem awkward and disturb the flow of the animation. I usually limit the use of tweens for moving text, background elements or object translations over short distances only. Motion tweening represents a more efficient use of resources but is not necessarily the most aesthetically elegant solution owing to its mechanics. Additionally it often takes a lot of tweaking to achieve a desired effect. The only way to discover which way works for you is to try both and see which you prefer.

After the bouncing of our human springs, it's time to move onto a more natural, but slightly more difficult, animation.

Movement Cycles

In this section we'll deal with a character motion more often encountered in reality, namely, walking. The walk cycle is one example of a cycle in which a set of drawings is repeated periodically to establish continuous motion. An analogy to this is a pendulum whose position follows a certain unique trajectory over a period of time and then repeatedly cycles through the same values. The basic unit of this cycle is the single step of one leg. Cycles are well suited for use in Flash because the basic unit may be contained in a symbol and reused in another symbol or symbols with little overhead.

We'll demonstrate a walk cycle by using and reusing symbols. Apart from learning how to draw a walk cycle, the goal of this exercise is to understand how to analyze and understand motion in terms of its simplest constituent parts.

Our first example cycle is divided into eight steps, and the animation consists of four layers:

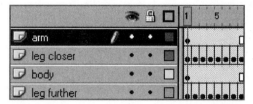

The walker's leg closest to the viewer is animated on the second layer, and the eight symbols that comprise this animation sequence are reused on the bottom layer, which holds the animation sequence for the leg further away from the viewer. The walker's body is placed on the third layer, and his arm on the first layer

Creating a Walk Cycle

Again, the graphics for this example are on the CD (walk cycle.fla), but it's always better to draw your own.

1. First, draw a one-legged character on layer one and split it into sections using the Lasso tool. The three parts are: his arm, his leg, and the rest of his body including his face:

2. Next, cut and paste these three elements on to separate layers named: arm, leg closer, and body. Convert each of these drawings into a symbol, and call them body1, arm1, and leg1. Alternatively, you could begin by drawing the different elements on different layers. I prefer to do it the first way, all on one layer, but again, try both and see which you prefer.

3. You can now complete the drawings of the leg in motion in eight moves. It's often helpful to deconstruct a moving figure into its simplest form for a better understanding. The steps are thus described using a stick-figure approach:

Notice that the heel follows a path that's roughly elliptical. Also notice that the spacing of the heel along the elliptical path is not at regular spaced intervals. You may experiment with different positions along the path and add in more drawings between the ones presented to see how it affects the motion. In particular, try to include additional positions between the last and first steps, and note the difference.

Here, as a guide, I've drawn out all of the steps that make up the animated walk cycle:

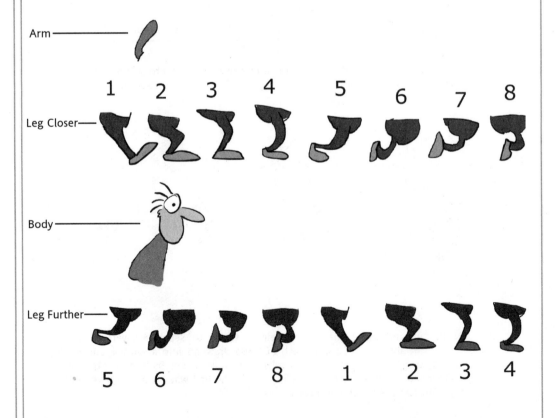

4. Drawings 1 to 8 on the leg closer layer are converted into symbols because we intend to reuse them for the other leg. The first four frames of the leg further layer are identical to frames 5 to 8 of leg closer, while the last four frames are identical to frames 1 to 4 of leg closer.

5. We now need to modify the properties of the symbol instances on leg further. An animation convention is to make things that are further away slightly darker than those that are up close. To emulate this, reduce the brightness of each instance to a suitable value (I picked -39%).

6. If you like, the instances on every layer can be moved until they are positioned appropriately. To give the body of the walking figure a more dynamic feel, you can scale the body by a small amount (I chose 98%), and shift it a little lower and to the left of the instance in frame one. This is done to simulate a minor compression as the body bobs up and down. You may use the onion skinning feature to accomplish this.

7. Finally, create a motion tween between frames 1 and 4, then reverse it between frames 5 and 8. The following figure shows the onion skinned outlines:

In this example, you can either use the arm as part of the body – in which case, leave the character's hand in his pocket – or you can draw a hand onto the arm and have it sway in time with the cycle.

You could also experiment with adding more complexity to the animation. For instance, the hair on the man's head could be converted into symbols and tweened to move up and down as he walks. Additionally, to make this animation more interesting, you could create a background pan using tweened animation with objects that move in the background. Don't go overboard though. Depending on your processor speed, you might notice that the more elements you tween simultaneously, the slower the animation gets. This is because tweening can be very processor intensive.

The personality of the character that you're drawing can have a huge impact on the shape of the walk cycle. For example, here we've demonstrated a strut:

Notice the motion of the body, which is more pronounced in this case. If you examine the drawings, however, you'll notice that the head retains its basic shape in most frames, with the exception of frame 2. This means that it could probably be converted into a symbol and reused across several frames.

Also, the speed at which the character's moving makes a difference to its motion. A run cycle is not just a speeded up walk cycle. The footwork is completely different from the two walk cycles that we've looked at before:

Often, if the size of the figure that's either walking or running is very small, it's not necessary to describe the steps in such complete detail. The following is yet another variation on the walk cycle: a sideways walk and sweep. The FLA is included on the CD accompanying the book:

Notice that the character only moves a very short distance, and that his left leg only really moves in frames 3 and 4.

If however, you hate drawing walk cycles, there are several ways in you can avoid it altogether. An example of this is to use a fence. Here, an individual walks across the stage but has her body hidden from view by a fence. The walker consists of two keyframes with the same symbol shifted vertically to create a head-bob. As well as saving you from having to describe the walk cycle, the resulting file size is smaller because it requires fewer key drawings.

Sometimes, a simple motion tween is inadequate to express quick movements across the stage. At times like this it might be worthwhile considering the use of motion or speed lines. You could draw such lines on another layer and make them follow the path of the object that's moving. The motion lines get progressively shorter and eventually they disappear. An example of this effect may be found in the FLA for *Zemi One Morning*.

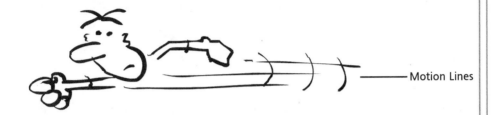

Motion Lines

Other Movement Cycles

Yet another example of a cycle can be found in Superduperman.fla. From the main menu, choose Control and make sure that Loop Playback is checked, then hit RETURN or ENTER to view the animation. This Flash file contains a four-frame animation of super-duper-man flying that contains just two symbols. The total size of the animation is only 2.2 KB:

I've used scaled instances of the cloud symbol on three separate layers to give the impression of motion. These instances were then positioned frame by frame across the stage:

Two of the cloud animations are in the background layer, while the third is in the foreground. The main character is moved slightly over four frames to create a dynamic jitter. The movement of clouds from left to right on the stage creates the effect of the main character flying from right to left. Hence, only two symbols, or rather instances thereof, are reused and cycled over the four frames to create the animation.

As another example of symbol reuse, here's an eight-frame dance cycle that uses only three unique drawings (a, b, and c).

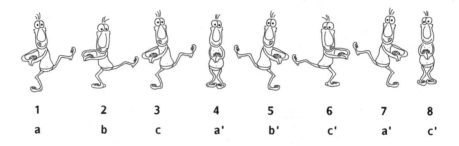

| 1 | 2 | 3 | 4 | 5 | 6 | 7 | 8 |
| a | b | c | a' | b' | c' | a' | c' |

The apostrophes here mark where a symbol has been mirrored to create its opposite image.

Hopefully, this has given you an idea of some of the variety of cycles that can be produced, and the methods of symbol economy that can cut down your file size, and the amount of work you need to do. While this is enough for traditional animation, Flash allows us to take things a step further and optimize the amount of strokes in our actual drawings.

Optimization

If a Flash animation is to be distributed via media such as CDs or floppy disks, optimization is not as critical a step as it is when the animation is intended for distribution over the Internet. In the latter situation, it's essential to keep file sizes to a minimum if the intent is to reach a large audience with varying modem speeds. A simple first-order optimization process would involve scanning through the movie and ensuring that symbols are used as often as possible. These symbols could comprise entire objects, or parts of objects. Unused symbols within a design file (FLA) don't increase the final size of the movie file (SWF). They do, however, increase the size of the FLA. If this is a concern, once the project is complete, choose Select Unused Items from the Library Options menu. This will highlight unused items so that you can delete them. Once this is done, save the FLA under a different name using File > Save As from the main menu. The new file should be smaller in size than the original file. This won't be very noticeable for small image files, but when you start to use sounds in your compositions, a forgotten dog bark can make quite a difference to the size of your FLA.

Another type of optimization involves smoothing the lines that comprise a symbol or drawing within the movie. You can do this in Flash by using the Modify > Optimize Curves command:

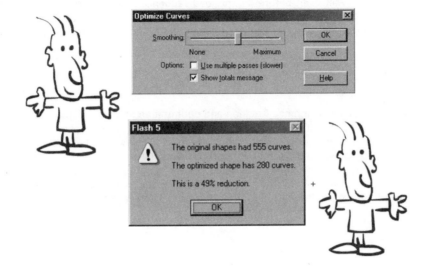

Moving the Smoothing slider affects the smoothness of the lines and curves in the optimized version. By checking the Use multiple passes box, maximum optimization will be achieved, but this can sometimes alter the drawing beyond recognition. When you optimize the drawing, Flash reports the savings due to this action. A 49% reduction is obtained in the above case when the drawing on the left is optimized to create the one on the right. If you're dissatisfied with the result, click OK and choose Edit > Undo from the main menu. Notice that for all intents and purposes, the drawings are identical, yet the second one contains almost half the number of curves as the first. By optimizing all of the drawing in your animations like this, you can shave valuable seconds off their download times.

It's also possible to optimize only a portion of the drawing. To do this, zoom in on a section and use the Lasso tool to make a selection, and then optimize it. It's a trial and error situation, finding out what works best for you.

Flash content is *designed* to stream over the Internet and it's necessary to manage this download efficiently to create an enjoyable user experience. Flash offers an effective means to simulate this performance and its dependence on the parameters of the movie – the Bandwidth Profiler. This can be used to view how the movie is divided in terms of its memory requirements per frame, and by using the different modem settings, you can simulate the download times for slower connections. This can then be used to ascertain which frames will most likely hinder a smooth download, and therefore need to be optimized a bit more. You'll find that it's often sound files that cause the bloated frames.

Playback prior to downloading an adequate number of frames might cause the animation to pause in order to catch up with the download. A popular technique to get around this involves the use of a preload sequence to keep the user engaged while the animation downloads in the background. There are a few things to keep in mind while constructing a preload sequence. It's advisable to use simple shapes to minimize unnecessary overhead to the main content. It's also preferable to use symbols from the main movie if they aren't too memory intensive, thereby resulting in a long wait even before the preload sequence loads. Another good practice is to include a progress bar, which informs the viewer where they are in the download process. Looping sounds are not recommended for lengthy preload times as more often than not they can lead to viewer insanity.

Conclusion

Web animation is still in its infancy. Creation and optimization of animated movies for distribution over the Internet in order that a wide audience may view them presents one of Flash animation's biggest challenges. As explained earlier, animations should always be optimized to account for the viewers' computer power and Internet connection speed. Often, this limits the bells and whistles that can be incorporated into an animated feature and requires a minimalist approach to movie making, but on the other hand these limitations force the artist to devise creative solutions. Additionally these constraints play an important role in influencing Web animation's aesthetics and defining its style.

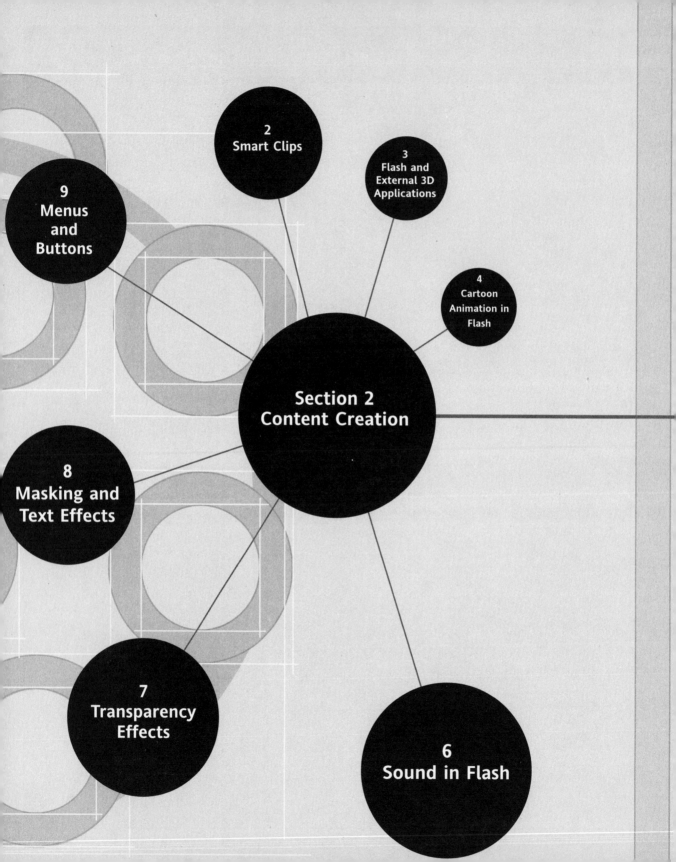

2
Smart Clips

3
Flash and
External 3D
Applications

9
Menus
and
Buttons

4
Cartoon
Animation in
Flash

Section 2
Content Creation

8
Masking and
Text Effects

7
Transparency
Effects

6
Sound in Flash

Chapter 5
Video in Flash

Over the past couple of years, Flash has become a serious and powerful tool for web content and animation. However, it's still not possible to embed a movie within the Flash file and export it as a SWF for the Web, or as a self-running projector file. It *is* possible to embed your Flash file in a QuickTime movie, but not the other way round. Happily, though, there is a workaround: video animation *can* be produced in Flash, and this chapter is going to explain how. The following pages will introduce a technique to convert digital video into a vector-based version of the same video, opening up a new area of animation to you as well as adding video skills to your Flash portfolio.

We've all seen Flash sites where the text comes spinning across the screen, fading in and out as it goes about its business. While this is all well and good, a site containing something a little bit different is always a pleasure to find. It was this that made me want to experiment with combining other applications with Flash in the hope of pushing my animation further. As well as being a fan of Flash, I also enjoy the power and image control of Adobe After Effects, so I decided to find a way to combine the two – in the hope of creating something not just incredibly cool, but useful too. I am by no means an experienced After Effects user but I feel that, when used with Flash, there's huge potential for producing interesting and innovative work that'll spice up the Web no end.

In basic terms, the following pages will show you how to convert a video clip into a series of black and white bitmap images in After Effects, and also in Photoshop. If you don't have After Effects, a trial version can be downloaded from the Adobe web site www.adobe.com, or there's a link to the download page on this book's CD. Although you won't be able to *save* the work that you do in the demo version of After Effects, we've included the PICT files that it would output on the CD, all ready to be imported into Flash. Once inside Flash, they'll be turned into a series of vector images to create a vector-based video animation. Why? Well, because it looks good, it's a very useful aesthetic tool, and – with a bit of imagination – it can be used to make a variety of different effects.

These next two images show the use of vector video animation in Flash. The first is from a screensaver for a band, and the second was part of a client pitch for a mineral water company:

  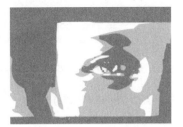

The first stage in the whole process is deciding what video input to use.

Choosing the Right Clip

There are (of course!) limitations to what you can do in Flash with vector animation, and the final results will depend very much on the original footage you choose. You need to be aware that you're going to be converting the footage into a series of simple black and white images; you *could* keep the footage in color but this would necessitate much more complex processing, and you'd need to fully understand the process in real depth before you started experimenting with it.

So, for instance, footage of a man dressed entirely in black, running on the spot against a white background is going to be a lot easier to convert than a blurred and distorted movie with lots of detail and light effects. Obviously there's a wide range in between these two points, and once you've used this effect in Flash you'll start to get a feel for which movies will work better than others. You may even find yourself wanting to use specific movie clips – possibly filmed especially for exporting into Flash. So, as a general rule, the less detailed and complex your original movie is, the easier this chapter's conversion process will be to apply.

The *length* of the movie and the *frame rate* you're going to use should also be considered. This is particularly important if you intend to use the finished video on the Web, where file size is always a factor. In addition to this you need to consider that content-rich video animation with lots of activity on-screen makes more intense demands on the machine showing it, and older, slower machines may start to struggle as a result. Also remember that, as in the traditional methods of 'true' animation, you'll be working on a frame-to-frame basis. Whereas many Flash animations use keyframes in combination with tweening, with this technique there is no tweening, and *every* frame will be a keyframe.

When you start converting your video images into vectors and optimizing them, you'll have to work on each frame individually. This means that you need to decide at the outset how long you want the movie to be, and how much time you're prepared to spend on it. For example, if your movie is 1 minute in duration and you want a very smooth animation, you might decide to keep the frame rate at the 25 fps it was filmed at. If this were the case, then you'd have 60 x 25 frames to attend to. That's 1500 keyframes. Not impossible, but hardly a great night in. The longer the movie clip that you choose, the more work you'll have to do and, in all likelihood, the bigger the file size you'll end up with.

With this in mind, we'll take a small section of a video from the CD and convert it into an animation in Flash. Open up `ready made cable video.swf` on the CD and run it. This is the effect that we'll be producing. Notice that the entire file weighs in at about 60 kilobytes.

Now let's work through the stages of building this kind of movie.

Treating the Clip in After Effects

For this example, you'll need a video clip that you want to bring into Flash. If you don't have a clip ready to use, or you'd just prefer to be able to follow the exercise exactly, then you can use the `cable-bluebirds are blue.mov` video clip, which can be found on the CD.

Once you've chosen the movie you're going to use, it's time to start work in After Effects. There are other tools that could perform this technique, but After Effects is my choice for video processing software in this context. We're going to import the movie, turn it into black and white images, and then export it, ready for use in Flash, as a series of separate image files. The format that you choose depends on the system that you're running on; I use PICT files on my Mac, but PC users can use JPG or TIF files if they prefer.

1. In After Effects, create a new composition by going to Composition > New Composition... (If the Composition menu remains inactive then go to File > New Project first.) You'll see the Composition Settings panel:

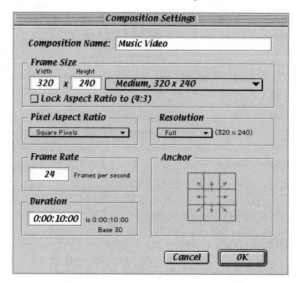

This panel allows you to set the frame size of your composition. Make this the same size as your movie so it will fit perfectly. My frame size is 320 x 240 so it needs a 320 x 240 composition. Set the frame rate to the same value as your original video clip, in my case 24 fps, and set the duration that you've decided upon. I'm going to make a ten second long composition. You can also give your composition a name; I've chosen to call mine Music Video. When you've finished all of this, press OK. If you configure these settings inaccurately initially you can always alter them by going to Composition > Composition Settings... later on.

Now you need to import your video clip.

2.   Go to File > Import > Footage File...

3.   Locate the clip that you're using – in our case, cable-blue birds are blue.mov on the CD – and click OK. If the Interpret Footage dialog box appears it means that After Effects is asking you how it should treat an alpha channel. Tell it to ignore any alpha channels by pressing the Ignore button and click OK. Your screen will now look like this:

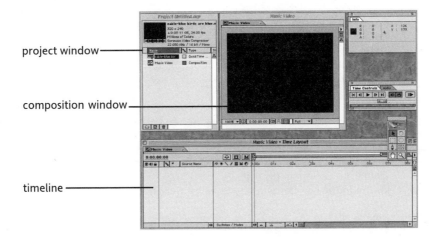

project window

composition window

timeline

Don't worry that everything on the display screen appears to be black; this is just because we've imported the video, but not actually put it anywhere visible yet. It's the equivalent of importing something into Flash; it appears in the Library, but you can't actually see it until you drag it onto the stage. In After Effects, rather than place an object on a stage, you just drag it onto the timeline.

4.   Select the imported movie in the Project window and drag it onto the timeline (the Time Layout window at the bottom of the screen).

It's important that the playhead in the Time Layout window is at the start of the composition, that is: 00:00:00, as you want to make sure you line up the start of your movie with the start of your composition. The frame that the playhead is on when you place something on the timeline denotes where that object will appear in relation to your whole composition. The composition window will still look blank, but this is just because the movie starts from a black screen.

You can tell that you've added the movie to your composition because you can see its name in the Time Layout window:

You can play the complete movie now if you like by hitting the SPACE bar, or by clicking the big fat 'play' button in the Time Controls panel:

If the Time Controls window isn't visible, go to Window > Show Time Controls. Bear in mind that when After Effects plays a clip it processes every frame individually, and therefore it doesn't play them at 'real life' full speed. You can see the speed that the movie is playing at in the Time Controls window. When you've finished watching the movie, hit the Rewind button to take you back to the beginning of the clip.

As the `cable...` movie is about three minutes long, it's really a bit too big to bring into Flash as it stands. At the moment, the movie contains 4584 frames. Even if we reduce it to 12 frames per second that's still 2292 frames, and I don't know about you but that's certainly more than I'd like to process one at a time in Flash. Because of this, I'm only going to use a small section of the movie to take into Flash – about ten seconds should do. Conveniently, After Effects allows you to select specific parts of your clip for use in the composition and to adjust their length to fit in properly.

5.   Double-click in the Composition window and a new window will open, showing the name of your movie file across the top:

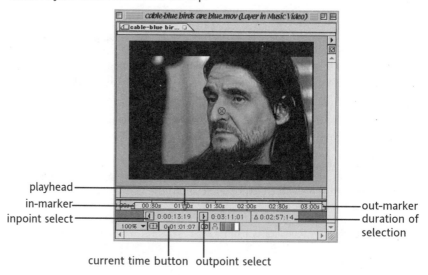

This window allows you to edit the footage that you're putting into your composition.

6. Click on the Current Time button, enter `0:01:01:07` into the box that appears, and hit OK. This will move the playhead to that specific point in time clip.

7. Now click on the Set IN Point button to mark that point as the time you want your selection to begin. Next, click on the Current Time button again and enter `0:01:11:07`, which is ten seconds later than we started with, and hit the Set OUT Point button to mark that as the point to *finish* the selection on.

You can check the length of the selection by looking in the Duration of selection box, it's the one with the little triangle icon on it, next to the Set IN and OUT Point boxes.

8. Finally, close the window to accept that selection.

9. It's now time to turn each frame into a simple black and white image. First of all, hit the Rewind button in the Time Controls panel to send the playhead back to the start of your clip. Making sure that you've selected the clip in the Time Layout window, go to Effect > Adjust > Threshold.

The movie clip in the Composition window will immediately lose its color information and be made up of only block sections of black or white, with no shades of gray in between:

You'll also notice that a new window has opened: The Effects Controls window, showing the current Threshold setting:

In After Effects, every layer that has an effect applied to it has its own Effect Controls window. This window lets you change all of the values for the currently selected effect – in this case the threshold level – to achieve the final look that you want. It's possible to have different threshold levels at different points in your composition by adding keyframes at various points. For now though, we're just going to apply the effect to the whole composition.

10. With the Composition window highlighted, play the movie through by pressing the space bar or the play button on the Time Controls. This gives you a rough idea of what the movie will look like in Flash. You can now use the Effects Controls window to alter the Threshold level by either moving the slider along, or clicking on the current value in the center of the window and typing in a new value.

> *If you're new to After Effects, something worth noting is that anything that has a dotted underline can be clicked on to bring up a dialog box, where you can adjust the relevant settings.*

It's often best to find what you consider to be a vital part of the movie when choosing your threshold setting. For example, if it were a movie of someone looking at their wrist to see the time, then the frames containing the actual face and hands of the watch would be the most important ones. You'd need to make sure that these frames were legible by moving the playhead so they were showing in the Composition window, and then chooing an appropriate threshold level. Then you should check the rest of the movie again and make sure it still looks OK as a whole.

The lower you set your Threshold level, the more white will be in the image, and vice versa, for example:

Threshold Value 64   Threshold Value 127   Threshold Value 165

It's worth rendering the composition as a QuickTime movie at this point to help you see what's changing. Render it out at low quality to reduce rendering time and help you determine if it's usable or not. This can be done through the Composition > Make Movie menu, but remember that you won't be able to render out with the demo version.

Remember also that the content will lose a small amount of detail once it's treated in Flash, so the better you make it look now, the more quality you'll be able to keep in the finished version. Even if you're happy with the results, it's worth playing around with effects levels as the smallest changes can have very different outcomes. I was happy with the standard threshold setting of 127, so that's what I used as output on the CD.

The final After Effects step is to get the movie ready to be taken into Flash. We're going to export it as a series of files which, when played back one after another, will create the illusion of being a motion picture. Of course, the final piece will have the stylized look given to it by the Trace Bitmap function in Flash.

11. Go to Composition > Make Movie. From here you can name your movie and choose where to save it. As you're about to produce a lot of files at once, it's best to create a new folder for them all to go in. Name the folder and the movie, and click on Save. This will bring up the Render Queue window:

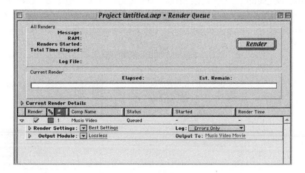

12. Select Custom… from the Render Settings drop down menu and set Quality to Best and Resolution to Full. Then press the Use this frame rate radio button in the Time Sampling area. This will allow you to set the frame rate for your exported movie:

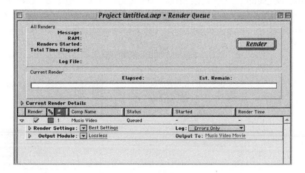

Whatever frame rate you prefer to work with in Flash is ideally what you'd work with here as well. However, the more frames you have, the more information there is in the movie, and the bigger your file size will be. Bearing this in mind, you have to find a happy medium between smooth animation and acceptable file size. It would be easy for me to say that you should work at 12 frames per second but it can depend just as much on the user's preference as on the detail in the movie itself. There's only one way to learn what's best and that's by getting used to the process as a whole and practicing.

As a suggestion though, anything between 8 and 12 frames per second should work very well, and it's very rare to go over 15 frames per second – if only because of the amount of work you'll be creating for yourself when you get to the Flash processing stage! I chose to render out at 8 frames per second, which meant a manageable total of 80 frames to process later on.

13. Once you've chosen your frame rate click OK. Now, back in the Render Queue window, select Custom… from the Output Module drop down window. Select the file format that you prefer from the Format drop down menu at the top, and click OK. I found PICT to be the best for the Mac, and JPG to be the best for the PC:

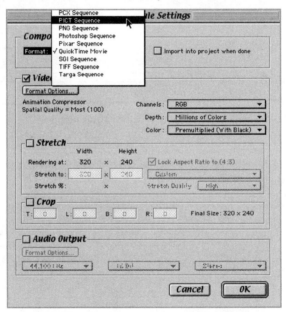

14. You'll now be back in the Render Queue window. Click on the Render button to export your files into your chosen folder.

Remember that if you're working on the demo version, you won't be able to render your movie, as the demo doesn't allow you to save or render your work. However, the files that you'd have created are included on the CD, ready for you to import into Flash. If you've no intention of ever getting After Effects then you'll probably now be thinking that this technique is of no use to you at all. Not so. You can obtain the files that you need for your Flash video by using QuickTime Pro and Photoshop. I'll quickly run through these methods now.

If you have an old version of Photoshop that doesn't have the Actions function then you'll have to apply the threshold effect to each frame, one at a time, as opposed to all in one go as I'll show below. If you don't have QuickTime Pro but do have QuickTime then you can always screengrab the individual frames of the movie and take those into Photoshop – by no means a perfect solution, but a workable one for people with a lot of patience.

Using QuickTime Pro and Photoshop

The first alternative method is to export the movie as a sequence of images from QuickTime Pro (I'll just call it QuickTime for short here) and then import the files directly into Flash. This is a very simple process.

1. First, create a new directory to hold all of the images that you'll be exporting, then open the movie in QuickTime by going to File > Open Movie.

2. Now you need to select the portion of the movie that you want to use. To do this, first move the Selection End marker to 01:11:

current location

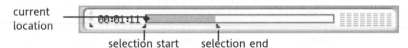

selection start   selection end

3. Then move the Selection Start marker to 01:01:

4. Now we have to trim everything except for the selection that we've chosen. The way to do this is by using the Trim command under the Edit menu. On a Mac, this is done by holding OPTION, and then opening the Edit menu, or on a PC by holding CONTROL-ALT, and then Edit.

5. Once this is done, you're ready to export the file. Go to File > Export to bring up the Export dialog box, and enter a name for your image sequence to be saved as. QuickTime will add a number to the end of this name to keep the files separate:

6. In the Export drop down menu select Movie to Image Sequence, then click on Options... and select the required format from the Format drop down menu. Again, I recommend PICT on the Mac, and JPG on the PC:

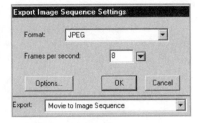

7. Now enter the frames per second value you wish to work with – I've chosen 8 again – hit OK, and then press Save to export your image sequence. This may take a while on slower computers, but it shouldn't be *too* long.

Of course, your images won't have been treated with the threshold effect that the ones in After Effects did, so although your Flash video will have lots of detail it'll have a huge file size too. The way around this is to open all of the exported files in the sequence into Photoshop and treat them with the threshold effect there. They'll then be ready to be imported into Flash.

Now, if you have lots of files then the thought of opening up every single one, applying the effect and then saving them all is not going to light your fire. Well, don't worry because you can do them all in one go. Photoshop has an 'actions' window that allows you to record a process and then apply it to any number of images. The first step is to show Photoshop what the process is.

> *The main instructions in this exercise are for Photoshop 5.5, but we've included the differences that need to be made for Photoshop 4.01 as well.*

8. In Photoshop, open some frames from your sequence and find one that's high in detail or is a key moment in the sequence. Go to Image > Adjust > Threshold:

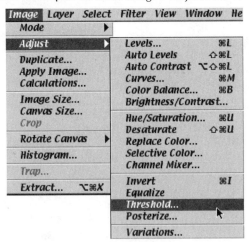

9. Change the threshold setting, again by either moving the slider or typing in a value, to produce the best block black and white image that you can. *Don't* press OK – at the moment, you're only finding the right setting. Make a note of the setting that you're happy with and then press Cancel.

10. With your image still open, go to Window > Show Actions. Then, in the Actions window click on the option arrow at the top right and select New Set... and name this set as Set 1. Now click on the arrow again and select New Action. In Photoshop 4, there isn't an option to create a new set, so just dive straight into creating a new action. Name this Flash Effect.

New Action		
Name: Flash Effect		Record
Set: Set 1	⬍	Cancel
Function Key: None ⬍	☐ *Shift* ☐ *Command*	
Color: ☐ None ⬍		

When you click Record Photoshop will record whatever actions you make next. While it's taping your every move, you'll see that the Record button at the bottom of the Actions window turns red to signify that recording is in progress.

11. Click Record and then, as before, go to Image > Adjust > Threshold, enter the value you noted down previously, and click OK. Now click on the Stop button on the left of the Record button to finish recording the new action. Your action will now be added to the Actions window ready to be applied to any image:

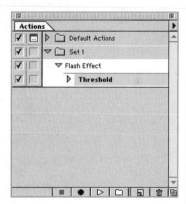

12. Close the image that you used to set the action, but *don't save over the original image*.

> *Before we apply the effect to all our PICT files, it's a good idea to make copies of them in a separate folder just in case you don't like your results.*

13. In Photoshop, with no files open, go to File > Automate > Batch:

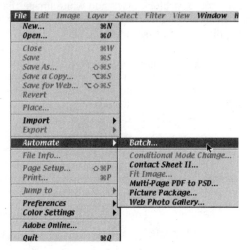

In Photoshop 4, the Batch command can be found from the Option arrow of the Actions window.

14. In the Play section of the Batch window select Set 1 from the Set drop down menu and the action Flash Effect from the Action drop down menu. In the Source section press Choose… and locate the original folder containing your image sequence. Select it and press OK, which will take you back to the Batch window. Now select Save and Close from the Destination drop down menu. Photoshop 4 users can follow almost exactly the same sequence of commands, just ignoring the Set menu:

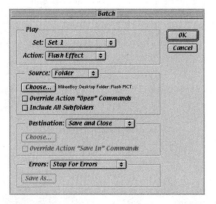

Photoshop will now open each image, apply the effect and save and close the image without you having to do anything. Put your feet up and enjoy a nice cup of coffee.

15. To start the automation sequence, just click OK.

You now have a series of files ready to take into Flash. As I've mentioned, the pre-prepared files ready for import are included on the CD. You may feel it's taken a while to get to this point, but I think you'll find it was all worth it as we get into the next section – actually creating our very own vector-based Flash video.

Creating the Vector Video in Flash

1. In a new Flash movie, go to File > Import and locate the folder containing your image sequence. Select the first file in the sequence and click Import. Flash should ask you if you want to import the rest of the images in the sequence:

    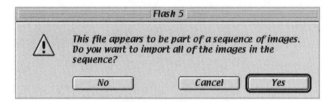

    Click Yes to this excellent timesaving feature before Flash changes its mind. When Flash has finished importing, you should see all of the files in order on the timeline, with each one given its own separate frame. If you saved your images in a non-native format, Flash may ask you if you want to import them via QuickTime. If it does, click Yes.

2. Test the movie to see how it looks. Is the frame rate that you've used in After Effects too slow, or do you think you could quite easily get away with fewer frames? If so, now is the time to go back into After Effects and change the frame rate when you re-export the treated video clip.

    If you're happy with it the way it looks at the moment, go though the timeline and try and spot any two images that are identical. Some of the initial images of the guard's face are probably good candidates for this; look at frames 12 – 14:

| Frame 12 | Frame 13 | Frame 14 |

This can sometimes happen when using files in this manner, but it just means that at that point the camera concentrated on one spot and as a result produced a lot of similar or identical images.

3. If you find some frames that are essentially the same, then delete the duplicate images from the timeline, *not* from the stage; highlight the frame that you want to delete in the timeline, then go to Insert > Clear Keyframe. The selected frame will be removed, although the image will still be in the Library. Cutting one or two images out of eighty may seem pointless, but in Flash every little helps and this could save file size and download time which, as we all know, are absolutely vital to the web user.

We're now ready to convert our sequence of bitmap files into vectors by using the Trace Bitmap command.

4. Play the movie through again and find, as we did before, a section that's important or has a high level of detail. Select the image you've chosen on the stage and go to Modify > Trace Bitmap:

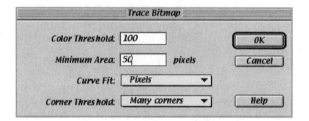

This is the moment that all of the earlier work was preparing us for. You should now see the Trace Bitmap dialog box. This contains settings for Color Threshold, Minimum Area, Curve Fit and Corner Threshold. These four settings can drastically alter the appearance of the soon-to-be-vector graphic so I'll take a moment here to briefly explain each one's function.

Color Threshold
Here, you enter a Color Threshold value between 1 and 500. When two pixels are compared, if the difference in the RGB color value is less than the Color Threshold value, the two pixels are considered to be the same color. Therefore by increasing the threshold value you'll reduce the number of colors. As we've already done this in After Effects, it doesn't really apply to this example so you can set it as high as you like. If you're working with unprepared, or multi-color, images though, you'll want to experiment with different settings to find an effect you like.

Minimum Area
Takes a value between 1 and 1000. This value will set the number of surrounding pixels to consider when Flash is assigning a color to a pixel. The lower the number, the smaller the area Flash will look at and the more detail your image will keep – but the higher the file size it will have. The value that you set depends on the style of the movie that you're looking for; there are a couple of examples at the top of the next page.

Minimum Area 5   Minimum Area 35

Curve Fit

The setting you choose from this menu will determine how smoothly Flash draws the outlines as it traces the image that is. how many points a curve will have:

Pixels   Very Smooth

Corner Threshold

This setting will tell Flash whether you want to keep sharp edges on the shapes that are created or if they can be smoothed out. This setting probably won't have a huge effect on this particular movie:

Many Corners   Few Corners

The combination of the settings that you choose will be instrumental in determining the look of your vector images. Play around and see what you like. Ideally, you're looking for each frame to be a simple block image that's still easily recognizable. It's hard to advise or suggest which settings to use without knowing the image that's being traced. However, experimentation based on the general guidelines on the previous page will give you the results you require, but also try using these settings to stylize your Flash movie. Some strange and interesting visual effects can be found here.

Once you think you've got the look you're after, you then have to apply it to each and every one of your imported bitmaps.

5. Go to the beginning of the sequence and, using your chosen settings, trace all the bitmaps in the movie. I warn you now this will be time-consuming – especially with slow machines – but once you get into a rhythm, it's not so bad. It's at times like this when keyboard shortcuts really come into their own – ALT+M, B on a PC, or you can use the Edit > Keyboard Shortcuts menu to define your own shortcut for both Mac and PC. When you become more experienced with the process you might want to start applying different Trace Bitmap settings to more detailed or important frames from those that you apply to simpler frames in order to reduce file size, or simply as an effect. There's no right or wrong answer here, as long as you're happy with the results. However, if the work is for a client then the look you achieve may well be decided for you!

6. Export the Flash movie and take a look at it. Let it play through a few times and see what you think.

Ask yourself if you're happy with the visual results. What's the file size like? Do you think it's too fast or too slow? Try changing the frame rate and then seeing what you think. Increasing the frame rate will make the animation appear smoother but will also make it play through more quickly, while decreasing the fps value makes it play through more slowly but may make it look jittery. This might add to the style and look you're after, but then again it might not. You may want to slow down certain parts of the movie and speed up others. This is easily done; to speed up an area of the animation, go to that point in the movie and remove every other frame over the area that you want to speed up. Always play through the results afterwards to check them, and then either delete more frames as necessary or be thankful for the many levels of *undo* that Flash can perform. To slow part of an animation down, highlight the frame in the timeline, then go to Insert > Frame. You'll see it simply adds an extra frame to that graphic. Go to the frame with the next graphic and do the same again, and repeat as necessary once more.

The next thing to do is to turn the entire sequence of single frames into one movie clip. This is done for a variety of reasons.

- it's easier to work with a movie clip later on down the road of most projects unless they're incredibly simple

- it's easier to apply effects like color change and alpha values when all of the frames are contained in one place

- it'd be very hard and awkward to apply any motion to the animation (by which I mean the video moving across the screen while it plays)

- it also means that it's very easy to resize the movie, which of course you can do now that it's a vector-based animation movie clip – something you couldn't

- it also means that it's very easy to resize the movie, which of course you can do now that it's a vector-based animation movie clip – something you couldn't do before when it was just bitmaps.

7. To do this, first highlight all of the frames on the timeline, and then use the Edit > Copy Frames menu to copy them.

8. Next, highlight the first frame in the sequence on the stage, group it, and convert it into a movie clip.

9. Now double-click on the new movie to open it for editing, select frame 1 in the timeline, and paste the copied keyframes into the movie clip by using the Edit > Paste Frames menu:

You can now delete all of the original frames from the timeline, and just drag a copy of your movie clip into the first frame.

Your movie's pretty much finished now, but if you're willing to sacrifice a bit more quality, there are some more optimization tricks that you can use to cut down on that all important file size.

Optimization

If you've ever optimized images before in Flash, you'll know that the results can sometimes be a little different to what you originally set out to achieve. Sometimes this'll be for the better, with abstract images appearing within what was your straight-laced video, but more often than not it'll just look like poor quality.

When you optimize a vector image in Flash you're essentially smoothing the curves of the graphic. The fewer curves a vector graphic has, the less information there is within the image, and the smaller the file size will be. If you overdo the optimization though, you'll end up with meaningless shapes that hold no visual information no matter how 'artistic' it might look. So how do you optimize a series of vector images? Well, I'm afraid the only answer is that you have to look at each frame on the timeline individually. It's not the most enthralling of jobs, but it can save considerable, and valuable, file size.

Optimizing the Movie Clip in Flash

1. Go into your movie clip in Flash, select the first frame in the sequence, and choose Optimize from the Modify menu to open up the Optimize Curves dialog box:

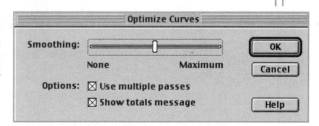

2. The best bet here is to leave the bar in the middle. It's worth trying maximum optimization first, because if it looks OK, you'll save the most file size but you may well find yourself just hitting the undo keys straight away when you see the result. The additional Options should usually be left on, too. Ultimately, remember that no matter what the file size saving, the image still has to be recognizable or the whole movie is pointless – at least in most applications.

3. Repeat this process for every frame. It's worth zooming right in on every frame and checking that there are no tiny spots or artifacts in the image, as they're not necessary to the essential image, and they all add to file size:

4. If you have unnecessary information such as a white background in all of the frames, then select the Eraser tool, turn on the Faucet, and click on the unwanted blocks of color.

Once you've fully optimized your animation, there's not much more you can do to lower file size short of deleting frames in order to shorten it. This only refers directly to the video-sourced animation that you're creating at the moment though, as other elements of a Flash movie (such as other graphics, fonts, and different types of animations) can always be left out, or changed, in order to reduce file size. Here's a list of some general hints and tips that you can use to reduce the size of your Flash files so that you can maximize your video input:

■ Avoid over-using special line types such as dashed, dotted, ragged, and so on. Solid lines are smaller.

■ All lines created with the Pencil tool require less memory than Brush tool strokes.

■ Use symbols, animated or otherwise, for every element that appears more than once.

■ Group elements as much as possible.

- Try to use layers to separate elements that change over the course of the animation, and give those that don't their own layer.

- Whenever possible, use tweened animations as they take up less file size than frame animations.

- If you have sound in your animation use MP3 compression, as it's the smallest format for sound.

- Use embedded fonts carefully as they increase file size, and limit the number of fonts you use.

- Try and avoid animating bitmap elements. It's best to use bitmap images only as background or static elements.

- Limit the area of change in each keyframe – make the action take place in as small an area as possible.

- Use the Mixer and Swatches tabs to match the color palette of the movie to a browser-specific palette. Filling an area with gradient color requires about 50 bytes more than filling it with solid color, so keep gradient use to a minimum.

As one more step, let's look at changing the colors in the video-based movie clip.

Changing the Video Colors

Throughout these last few pages we've emphasized the fact that the video's been black and white. This is not essential to the process though, it merely helps to approach it this way the first time to get you used to the concept, and to see it at its most basic. If you want to add color simply do so as you would to a normal image by using the Effect panel:

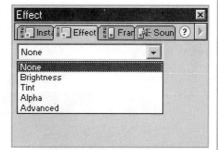

In here you can set color and transparency options for your animation. Remember that this will affect the whole animation and not just the first frame that's visible on the stage. When you edit the movie however Flash will show you it in its original form displaying all of the keyframes as you left them. The easiest way to add color effects to your video is by using the Advanced menu:

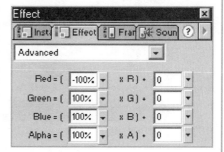

If we take a black and white video as a reference point, then the percentage values will control the color of the white parts of the image – though you won't be able to see the changes that you make on the stage, only when you play the movie – and the + values will affect the black parts, which you'll be able to see as you change them. If you've removed the white parts from your video, then you just need to set the movie background color to change *them*.

You can also achieve interesting effects by changing the color of the actual images themselves within the movie clip. If there's a key moment or specific element that runs over a few frames, then try altering the color by just using the Paint Bucket. You can even try a staggering effect, changing the color in alternate frames. Be careful not to go overboard though, or it might just look awful.

You may want to experiment with not using the Threshold effect in After Effects at all, but using the Posterize effect instead, or even *tint* the movie with the Threshold effect. All sorts of effects are possible within After Effects, and if you combine this with the different results that can be achieved with the Trace Bitmap function of Flash, you've got a whole range of different outcomes at your fingertips. You'll also find that the more you use After Effects, the easier it becomes, and the more you can understand what results can be achieved and the many ways that this can enhance your Flash work.

Once you've brought your video into Flash and converted it into vectors, there's a lot more that you can do to it than just changing the colors. Perhaps the most obvious of these is the ability to cleanly *resize* the video.

Scaling Your Movie

Ah, the power of Flash. This is one serious advantage of this process. You now have a video that's fully scalable with no loss of quality, due to the fact that it's completely made up of vector images. You can now scale the movie to fit the stage, or shrink it right down and stick it in a corner, which looks just as good:

Try tweening the size of the movie or fading it in, or turning the Alpha channel down and using it as a subtle but highly impressive background image. It can also, of course, be thrown around the stage the same way you would with any graphic, but this starts to test the machine a little if you're not running on tomorrow's hardware.

Conclusion

These are just some of the basics of video animation in Flash. Remember that experimentation is an important part of the process, and some great results can be gained from different settings both in Flash and After Effects. Try to think of new ways to use the animations that you're doing, and if you have your own video camera then think about what you'd like to see in Flash, and what hasn't been seen before. Hopefully you'll find that this kind of video animation can be used in many ways, from a simple loading graphic, to part of a navigational method, to the entire content of a screensaver.

Here are some more examples of Flash video animation, which can be found on the accompanying CD in the Examples of Other Work folder:

As Flash takes off in popularity, the video facilities are bound to be extended so that there's much more flexibility and integration with other packages. By all means have a vision, but don't be afraid to change it as the technology changes and the possibilities extend.

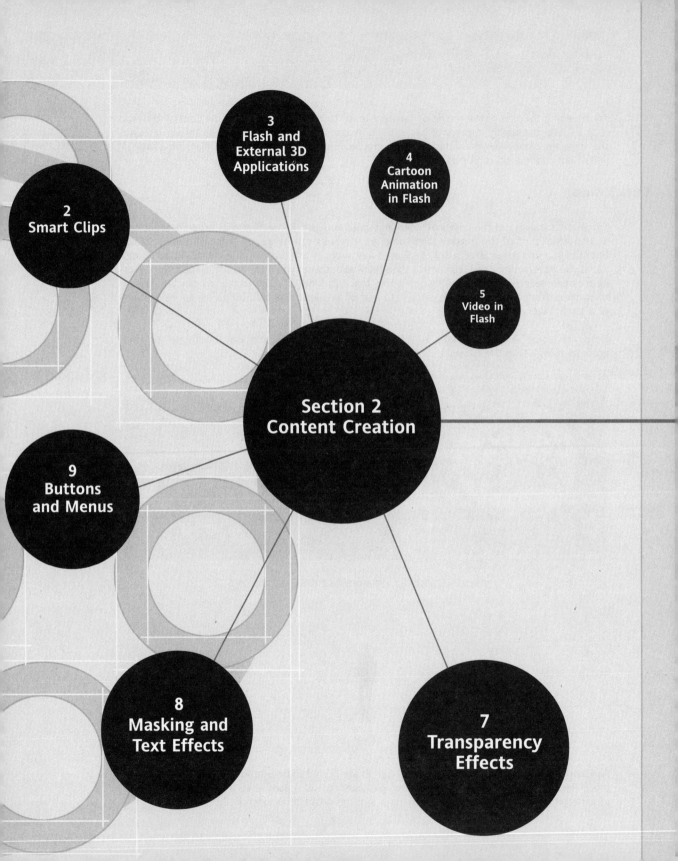

Chapter 6
Sound in Flash

A couple of years ago, when Flash really started getting a foothold on the Web, and sites that incorporated it really started to shine, one thing that made them stand out even further from the crowd was **sound**. Audio effects and music in web sites weren't unheard of, but they were never really used effectively, in terms of either the presentation or the delivery. But now, with Flash, you no longer need to embed a soundtrack in your page and download a WAV file before any other graphics have loaded. Also gone for good is the two-second delay while a rollover sound downloads and plays because the site creator doesn't have a good enough grasp of JavaScript. Flash features sound that can be played immediately a rollover or mouse-click occurs, because the sound is embedded directly into the Flash movie – it's integral.

Despite the advances that Flash brought to web sound, before Flash 5 was released there were still some fairly harsh limits on what you could do with sound in your movies. You could import the sound and stream it, or have it play in response to an event. You could also pan the sound from side to side, have it coming from one speaker only, or fade it in and out... just as long as you determined *in advance* how the effect would work – there was no possibility for interaction. This was fine, for a while, but it was restricting – through no fault of their own, Flash designers were constrained to using the same techniques from site to site.

But now, with Flash 5, there have been some major improvements in the way Flash deals with sound. For a start, it's now treated as an **object**, which has built-in properties that we can manipulate and track. The long and the short of this is that we've a lot more control over how, where, and when we use sound clips in our movies, because they can be controlled by ActionScript. This means that sounds can be loaded and controlled interactively, based on user input, and it also means that you don't have to hard-code every behavior into the movie when you roll it out; instead, the user can control what happens to the sounds based on the things that they do to the movie in their browser.

In this chapter, we'll be focusing on Flash 5's new **Sound object**, and looking at how it can be used in conjunction with graphics to bring a new lease of life to Flash movies. We'll then move on to more advanced and indirect uses of the Sound object to create effects with a more 'three-dimensional' feel to them, such as altering a sound the 'further away' it gets from the user.

The first example that we'll look at is a music mixer. We'll start off by just defining the basic sound controls, and then attach some graphics to them to create a more dynamic experience. Since the mixer only needs to use a few specific aspects of Flash 5's built-in Sound object to achieve its effect, the actual mechanics that we'll cover are fairly straightforward.

Creating a Music Mixer

Here, we'll be creating a simple music mixer that'll have six tracks, six pan dials (one for each track), a volume control for each track, and a *master* volume control:

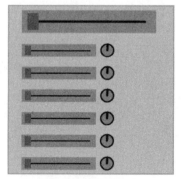

We also want to tie the sounds to some visual movie clips that we'll be creating. Just knowing this much, let's determine how to start setting up our file. Since we'll need the sounds first (in order to tell the controllers how to manipulate them), this is where we'll begin.

Creating and Importing Sounds

For this example, we created our sounds using keyboards, guitar, and drum machine, but if you're not musically inclined, there are plenty of sites out there where you can get copyright-free loops. Some great resources are:

- http://www.sonicspot.com – for links to freeware and shareware downloads

- http://www.flashkit.com – for loads of copyright-free music loops

- http://www.angrycoffee.com – some great info and tutorials on using sound on the Web

However you've done it, let's assume that you've got some music together – even simple sounds will work for the sake of this example project. You now need to get your tracks set up for the mixer, which means six different sets of sounds. We're using a drum track, a bass track, a keyboard track, a melody keyboard track, a guitar track, and a xylophone track, which we've edited down using an audio-editing program.

> *The sound files we've used here are included in the* `mixer_exercise.fla` *file on the CD. You can drag them out of that file's Library and into your own.*

If you're going to have multiple tracks that need to be in sync, it's a good idea to record all the tracks using a multi-tracking program. This way you can hear how the song sounds as a whole, as well as what each track sounds like individually. You can find freeware audio editors and multitrackers at http://www.sonicspot.com.

Here's an example of a sound displayed as a waveform in an editing program:

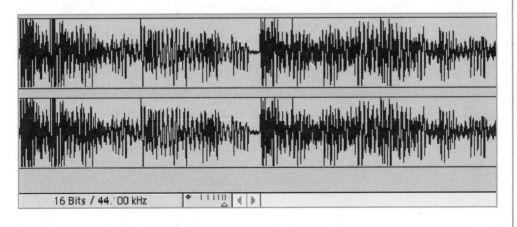

16 Bits / 44. 00 kHz

If you look at the bottom left of the window, you can see the legend 16 Bits / 44.100 kHz. This is the equivalent of CD quality sampling rate. Also, you can tell that the sound is in stereo because there are two waveforms. Wherever possible, it's important to start with the highest quality sound that you can find. It costs you in terms of memory and hard drive space, but the more information in the sound file to begin with, the better job Flash can do of compressing the sound for your movie when it's exported.

The bigger spikes you can see on the previous page are the loud parts of the sound, and the smaller spikes are quieter areas. From looking at this sound, you can tell a lot about it and its suitability for use in Flash. For example, you can tell that it may cause trouble if it's used in your Flash movie, because the loud parts are just a bit *too* loud. You can see this because the biggest spikes actually touch the upper and lower boundaries of the window that constrains the possible dynamic range. When these parts of the loop get compressed, there's a good chance that they'll just produce what sounds like 'clipping' noise, which is the sort of thing that you hear when the TV is turned up too loud and the sound starts to distort. Also, your target audience is likely to be using normal computer speakers, and these poor little machines aren't usually very good at handling sounds that are too loud. To avoid this we just need to reduce the volume of the sound clip a little, and this can be done easily in most sound-editing programs. Simple preparations like this can make a huge difference to the quality of the sound on your finished web site.

After recording the rough versions of each track, we used the audio editor to make them into loops, so that they'd play smoothly and continuously when we brought them into Flash. For our purposes here, we found the best technique to be looping the drumbeat first. If you've created the beat with a drum machine program, it's probably already a perfect loop – which is great, because you can just crop the other sound files to the same length as the drum beat, and they'll sync. However, if you recorded the beat in a different way, it's a bit trickier. You'll most likely have to play with the loop for a while, but after you have it playing smoothly, you can edit the other tracks down to the same length as the drum beat. You can test the loops by bringing them back into the multi-tracking program and seeing if they're still in sync.

> *It's very important to make the sounds the same length. Later, when we bring them into Flash, we'll be setting each sound to loop about a thousand times, so if they're even a fraction of a second out, they'll start sounding really screwy partway through the cycle!*

We're now ready to get into Flash and do the rest of our preparation there. This is where we actually start building the mixer.

Sound Importing and Tweaking

1.   Start a new movie, and import your sound loops into the Library. (Again, remember that you can just use the ones from `mixer_exercise.fla` if you wish.)

2. Once they're all imported, create a new folder in the Library called Sounds and put all of the sounds into it.

It's always good practice set up appropriately named folders in the Library to organize the different elements of your movies. Then, as you import things, we can stick them out of sight into folders and stay organized – at least superficially. It's like your mother always said: "When you get stressed, clean your room – it's good for the soul." Same thing in Flash.

3. Double-click on a sound file in the Library, and you'll open the Sound Properties dialog box where you're given several options – one of which is the method of compression to use when exporting your movie.

If you look at the drop-down menu at the bottom of this dialog, you'll see that it says Default:

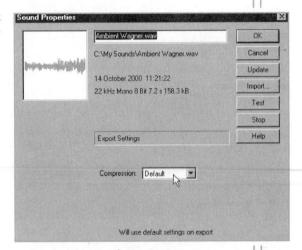

In this mode, which is Flash's default for all the sound files that you import, Flash compresses the audio at the rate specified in the Publish Settings menu:

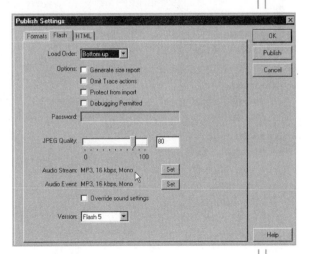

You can change the global compression options by clicking on the Set buttons, bringing up the dialog box...

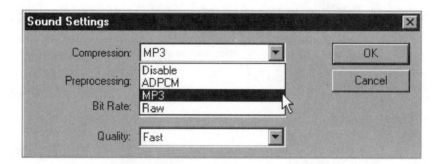

...and altering the setting in this menu to one of ADPCM, MP3, and Raw. For our example, we'll be using MP3 compression.

> *Note that there are two Set buttons – one for streaming sound, which will start to play as soon as Flash determines that it has enough 'frames' worth' of sound to begin, and one for event sound, which is dependent on the complete download of the sound before playback will commence. See the* **Preloading and Streaming** *chapter for more coverage of controlling sound during the streaming process.*

Back to the Sound Properties dialog box. You can set the sound properties for individual files here – and we're going to choose MP3 again here. On the off chance that you've been trapped under a rock and out of touch with civilization, MP3 compression allows you to shrink the size of your audio file significantly, depending on the settings that you choose. Because most people will be viewing your movie on their computers and listening through multimedia speakers, it isn't necessary to produce CD quality sound.

We've found that setting the Bit Rate to 32kbs or 48kbs, and the Quality to Medium yields the best sound quality results with the quickest download.

If you're using sound in a file that's intended for CD-ROM or other multimedia presentations, you can opt for 'higher quality' settings.

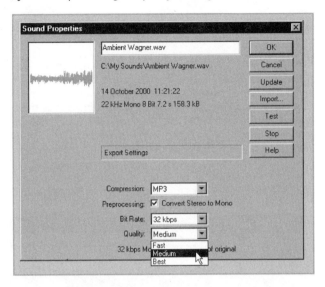

You can see how changing these settings affects the file size outcome by hitting the Test button on the right of the dialog box – Flash will tell you (at the bottom of the screen) exactly how much you've trimmed from the original file size:

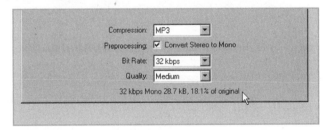

Having got our sound into Flash and optimized its compression rate and quality, we now need to let Flash start treating it as an object. To use Flash 5's new Sound object, we need to give each of the sound loops a **linkage name**.

Giving the Sounds their Linkage Names

This process uses the same principle as giving an instance name to a movie clip. It allows us to tell the sound to change volume, to pan, and to 'have a relationship' with other objects in the movie, in the sense that we can link certain events – say, a mouse-click – to these objects with ActionScript.

1. Right-click on a sound in the Library, and select Linkage... from the menu that appears. This will open up the Symbol Linkage Properties window.

2. From here, choose the Export this symbol radio button, which will allow us to give the sound an Identifier.

   It's this identifier that we can use in ActionScript, to reference the sound that's stored in the Library. Doing this allows us to use the sound in the movie, even though the sound itself won't actually appear anywhere on the timeline or stage. Notice that we *don't* have to use the same name for the identifier as the clip has in the Library, but you *do* have to remember that the name we use in ActionScript is the *identifier* and not the sound file's displayed name in the Library. (If you've copied our sound files from the CD, your sounds should already have these linkage names.)

3. Name the first sound loop1, and the second loop2, and carry on until you've named all of the sounds in your Library. We've got six sounds named loop1 to loop6:

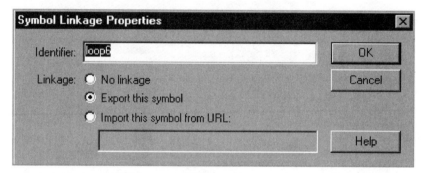

Once you've done this, expand the Library window and take a look under the Linkage column. You'll see that there's an entry reading Export for each loop that we've just exported:

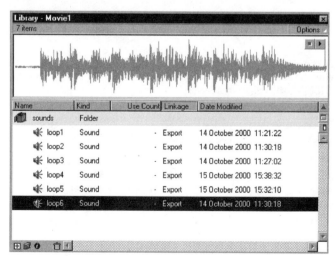

This has now made each sound available to our movie through ActionScript.

The next step is slightly more complicated. On the Flash movie front end, we have to create the volume sliders that'll control the volume of each of these sound loops.

Creating the Volume Control Sliders

In the finished movie we want a master volume control and six individual volume controls (one for each track):

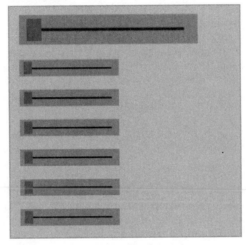

These will work just as a traditional (physical) mixer would: by setting the master volume of our mixer, we prevent any individual audio track from being set to a higher volume than that of the master.

To save time, we'll be using an 'object-oriented' method to create the volume slider clip. This means that we'll only need to create one clip and then we'll be able to drag as many sliders as we need onto the stage, and that they'll all work independently of each other without any need for alteration. The only thing that we'll need to do is ensure that we give each one an individual instance name.

1. Create a new movie clip symbol and name it slider. Within this symbol, create two new layers, and name the layers Code, Pan, and Slider from top to bottom:

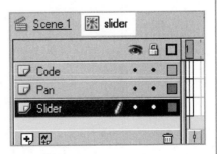

2. On the Slider layer, draw a 20 x 120 pixel rectangle and position it at 0,-10 using the top-left registration mark:

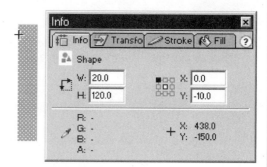

This is the background image for the slider.

3. Now convert the gray rectangle into a graphic symbol called slider_back. Go into the symbol and create a new layer, and, on this layer, draw a 100 pixel long line and center it over the slider graphic:

This is the 'slot' that the slider knob will move up and down in. Groovy.

4. Now go back into the slider clip and draw a 15 by 10 pixel rectangle, which will be the control knob on the slider. Convert this little rectangle into a movie clip called vlm_slider, then go inside the new vlm_slider movie clip and convert the rectangle into a graphic symbol called slider_graphic. You'll now have a graphic symbol inside the vlm_slider clip, which is in turn inside slider:

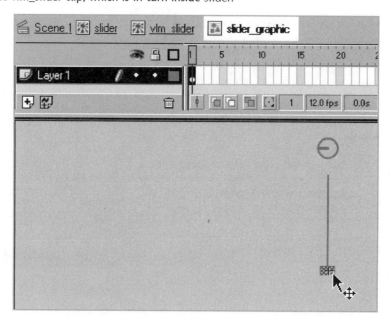

5. Open up the vlm_slider movie clip and set the top-left registration point of the graphic to 0, -5:

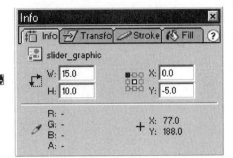

6. Inside the slider clip, position the new vlm_slider clip at the bottom of the groove:

7. Next, create a new button symbol called invis_button. Insert a keyframe in the Hit state of the button, draw a 15 x 10 rectangle in this frame and, finally, set the new rectangle graphic at a central 0, 0 registration point.

    The effect of this is to make the button transparent. Transparent buttons are extremely useful in situations where you wish to use graphical elements that have the functionality of a button. They can be placed over *any* element, transforming it into a button without having to create a unique one, and therefore reducing file size and saving time.

8. Go into your vlm_slider symbol and create a new layer called Button. Drag a copy of invis_button out of the Library and line it up over the top of the existing graphic:

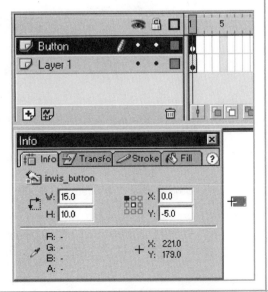

Now for some scripting. This code allows vlm_slider to be dragged up and down against the slider_back background rectangle.

9. Open up the Object Actions window for invis_button and key in the following ActionScript:

```
on (press) {
    startDrag ("", false, 2.5, 100, 2.5,
    ➥_root.slider_master1.vlm_master1._y);
}
on (release, releaseOutside, dragOut) {
    stopDrag ();
}
```

The 2.5 value for the Left and Right properties is the X position of the vlm_slider inside the slider movie clip. By setting both of these to the same value, we've prohibited any left and right movement of the slider and tied it to a single axis – the vertical. Notice also that, rather than setting an absolute value for the Bottom limit, we've set it instead to the _y property of the master volume slider – slider_master1. (This is a named instance of the slider clip that we'll place on the stage shortly.) The reason we do this is so that once we have a master slider on the stage we won't be able to drag the individual volume sliders higher than that of the master volume. Because we don't yet *have* a master slider, Flash will insert a default value of 0. Luckily, this is exactly what we want, as it allows us to test our slider.

10. Drag a copy of slider out of the Library onto the root stage and run the movie. You should be able to drag the volume slider up and down within the limits of the slider background. That's funky, no?

11. Go back into slider and give vlm_slider the instance name vlm_slider1:

Now that we've created a basic slider and prepared it to communicate with a master volume slider, we'd better go ahead and make one of those too.

12. Create a new movie clip called slider_master and drag a copy of slider_back onto its stage. Again, set its top-left registration point to 0, -10.

13. Now drag copies of slider_graphic and invis_button out of the Library and onto the stage. Select *both* slider_graphic and invis_button and convert them into a movie clip called vlm_master. This combination will act together to form our master volume controller.

14. Inside vlm_master, select both the button and the graphic again, and set their top-left registration point to 0, -5:

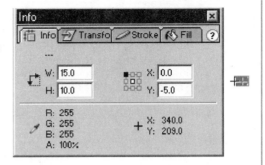

15. Back in slider_master, position the newly-minted vlm_master clip over the bottom of the groove and give it an instance name of vlm_master1.

Now we need to put some code onto the transparent button inside our master volume slider – this will allow us to drag it up and down.

16. Open up vlm_master and bring up the Object Actions window for the button inside it. Type in the following code:

```
on (press) {
    startDrag ("", false, 2.5, 100, 2.5, 0);
}
on (release, releaseOutside, dragOut) {
    stopDrag ();
}
```

Now we can test our sliders.

17. Drag a copy of slider_master onto the root stage, and give it the instance name slider_master1. You may also want to apply a transform or a tint to the master slider so that you can easily tell it apart from your normal slider. Once this is done, test your movie:

You should find that if you set your master slider to halfway, then the normal slider can't be dragged any further than halfway. There's a slight problem though: you can set the master volume to a lower position than the normal volume, and then when you click on the normal volume it suddenly jumps to the same level as the master. Let's see if we can fix this.

18.   Go back to the FLA and open up vlm_slider in the Library.

19.   Create a new layer and call it Code. Insert a keyframe in frame 2 of this layer, and then insert frames in the other two layers to line them up with the Code layer. Open up the Frame Actions window for frame 1 of the Code layer, and enter this ActionScript:

```
if (this._y<_root.slider_master1.vlm_master1._y) {
    this._y = _root.slider_master1.vlm_master1._y;
}
```

This code checks to see if vlm_slider (this) is higher than the master slider. If it *is*, then vlm_slider is set to the same level as the master slider. The code looks slightly odd because we actually say, "if this has a *lower* _y property than the master..." when we mean *higher*. This is because Flash treats the top of the stage as 0, so the higher up the stage you get, the lower the Y value. It's slightly confusing at first, but you soon get used to it...

The next thing to do is to create a loop so that the slider is constantly checking its position. This is easily done:

20.   Open the Actions window for frame 2 of the Code layer and enter:

```
gotoAndPlay (1);
```

When you test the movie this time, the normal volume slider should never be able to be higher than the master.

We're now ready to do what we came here for, and actually attach a sound to the volume slider.

21.   Give the slider movie clip that's already on the main stage an instance name of 1. This may seem like a bit of a strange name at first, but you'll see why it's called that in a minute.

22.   Open the original slider movie clip in the Library and type the following ActionScript into the first frame on its Code layer:

```
slidername = String(this._name);
mysound = ("loop"+slidername);
s = new Sound(this);
s.attachSound(mysound);
s.setVolume(0);
s.start(0, 1000);
```

Let's explain this code. First we set up a variable called `slidername` that contains the name of the current movie clip – we'll be using this variable later on when we add some color to the movie as well.

Then we create another variable called `mysound`, which combines the word 'loop' with the name of the instance that the code is sitting in – in this case, '1'. So for the specific instance of `slider` that's sitting on the stage at the moment, `mysound` is set to be `loop1`, which, you may remember, is the linkage name of the first sound in our Library. You can see now why we gave that copy of `slider` such an odd instance name.

The third line creates a new Sound object and assigns it to the current movie clip. `loop1` is then attached to the movie clip and set off playing the first of a thousand times. The first number in the `s.start` line tells Flash how far into the sound (in seconds) we want it to start playing. We've left this at 0 because we want the sounds to start right at the beginning, and we've also set the *volume* to 0 so that the sound doesn't 'click' briefly before we get to the next frame – where we'll be setting it to the position of the slider. The beauty of this is that each `slider` we drag onto the main stage will automatically assign itself to the sound that matches its instance name. Funky.

We want the volume to be updated regularly, but we only want the sound to be initialized once. We can easily achieve this by setting the volume in frame 2, and then constantly looping this frame.

23. Create two new keyframes in the Code layer and, in frame 2, type this code:

```
s.setVolume (100-this.vlm_slider1._y);
```

24. Then in frame 3, add this:

```
gotoAndPlay (2);
```

These two pieces of code simply set the volume relative to the position of the volume slider, and then constantly update it by looping back to frame 2.

25. Finally, add a keyframe at frame 3 in each of the other two layers so that their content will be visible throughout the movie.

We're now ready for the biggest test.

26. Play your movie. If everything has gone to plan you should be able to alter the volume of your first sound by dragging its volume slider up and down, and its level will be limited by the position of the master volume slider.

The next thing to do is to create a pan dial and attach it to the sound in a similar way so that we'll be able to control both the volume *and* the position of our sounds. First of all though, it's time for another spring clean. I'm doing it, mom...

27. Create a folder in your Library called Sliders and drag everything except for invis_button (and the Sounds folder) into it.

Our next step is to create a dial that'll let us *pan* our sound loops from speaker to speaker.

Creating the Pan Dials

The pan dial has three parts: the graphic of the dial, the indicator line for the direction of the pan, and the button that'll trigger the response when the dial is moved.

1. Create a new movie clip called dial_body and draw a 20 x 20 pixel circle in the center of the movie clip:

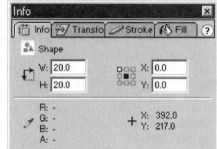

2. Make a new graphic symbol called dial_line and draw a 10–pixel long vertical line in the center of the stage.

3. Go into dial_body and drag a copy of dial_line onto the stage. Line it up on the center of the dial_body like this:

That's the main graphic of the dial done. Now we just need to make the button.

4. Create a new movie clip called dial_drag and pull a copy of our trusty invis_button onto the middle of the stage.

5. Use the Info panel to resize invis_button to 20 x 20 pixels, ensuring that it's still in the exact center of the stage:

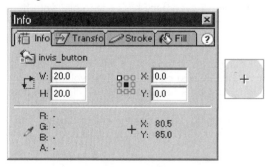

6. Next, open up the Object Actions window for the button and enter the usual dragging actions:

```
on (press) {
    startDrag ("", false, -10, 0, 10, 0);
}
on (release, releaseOutside, dragOut) {
    stopDrag ();
}
```

Here, we've set the button to be dragged 10 pixels left or right, but we're *not* allowing it to be dragged above or below its starting point.

7. Create a new layer in dial_drag called Code. This is where we'll perform a little bit of math trickery to rotate the dial depending on where we move the button. In the first frame of the Code layer, type the following:

```
_parent.dial_body1._rotation = _parent.dial_drag1._x*9;
```

This is an easy, cheat's way of controlling dials so that we don't have try and work out any difficult angles. The code here sets the rotation of the body of the dial to the position of the button. Our dial is really a direction indicator showing which speaker we're panning to, and by what amount. This means that we only want the dial to be able to turn 90°, as this will represent 100% pan in that direction:

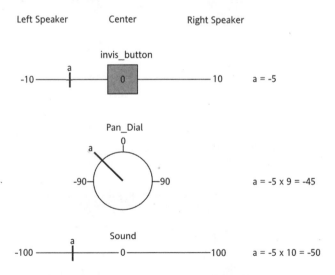

The maximum amount that we can move the button is 10 pixels either way, so we multiply that by 9 to get the rotation. This means that by dragging the button we can rotate the dial 90° to –90° from its original orientation. Of course, you can make the dial turn more or less than 90° by altering the multiplier.

8. Insert another keyframe in the Code layer at frame 2, and enter this ActionScript:

```
gotoAndPlay (1);
```

This just creates a loop to make sure we're constantly checking and updating the dial position. Insert a frame in the other layer as well to bring it into line with the Code layer.

9. Now we have to combine the two elements of the dial together so we can see if it works. Create a new movie clip called pan_dial, and give it two layers, called Button and Graphic.

10. Drag a copy of dial_drag onto the center of the stage on the Button layer, naming this instance dial_drag1. Pull a copy of dial_body out of the Library and onto the Graphic layer, and position it in the middle of the stage under the button. Give it an instance name of dial_body1:

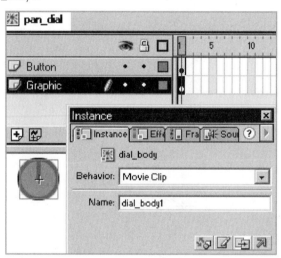

11. Now go back into the slider movie clip in the Library and drag a copy of pan_dial out of the Library and onto the Pan layer. Call this instance pan_dial1:

It only takes one more line of ActionScript to connect the pan dial to our sound. So rather than going ahead and testing the dial, let's add that line and then we'll be able to hear the whole thing in action.

12. Bring up the Frame Actions window for the second frame of the Code layer in slider, and enter this underneath the existing setVolume command:

```
s.setPan (this.pan_dial1.dial_drag1._x*10);
```

This line just sets the pan of the sound to 10 times the position of the button, giving it a range of values from -100 to 100. This matches the Flash setPan command perfectly, as it has a range from -100 (all in the left speaker) to 100 (all in the right speaker).

13. All that remains now is to test the movie. You should be able to hear the sound moving from the left to right speaker as you move the pan dial left or right.

You may be wondering what's happening to the other five sounds in the Library. This isn't much of a music mixer if you can only play with one track. Well, as promised, our object-oriented sound slider should be pretty foolproof, and we should be able to cater for the rest of the sounds too.

14. Drag another five copies of slider onto the main stage and apply the corresponding instance names 2 thru 6:

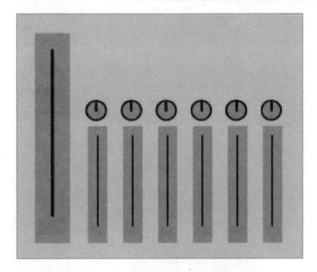

That's all you should need to do *functionally*, but you may want to make things a bit more *aesthetically* pleasing as well by lining them up. For instance...

15. Select all of the sliders on the stage and rotate them 90° clockwise, then use the Align panel to arrange them however you like. You'll notice that now you've rotated it, your pan dials are all facing the wrong way. Go into your slider movie clip, select the pan dial, and rotate it 90° counter-clockwise. Now when you go back to the main stage, everything should be right again:

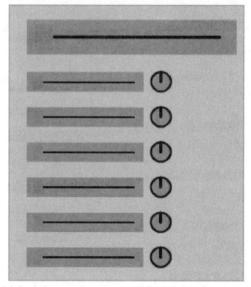

If you play your movie now, you should find that each volume slider, and its partner pan dial, control an individual sound. You should also be able to limit and lower the overall volume of all of the sounds by using the master volume slider.

Remember that we promised we'd tie some graphics to the sound controls? Let's achieve that by taking a glance at the Flash Color object.

The Flash 5 Color Object

Now it's time for some fun stuff: adding a relationship between the sliders, dials, and some visual color elements on the screen. There's an example on the CD, musicmixer.fla, which illustrates linking the pan dials to the alpha values of movie clips as well:

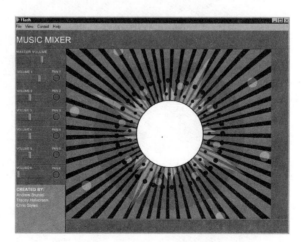

COLOR MIXER

Although there were some experiments with color sliders in Flash 4, the effects were faked using different levels of color and by setting the properties of the alphas for the different layers. You weren't really supposed to be able to do color changes in Flash 4, but as usual, someone worked out a way to get around it...

In Flash 5, changing colors is not so much magic as ingenuity. The Flash 5 Color object allows you to have full control over the RGB and alpha settings for a specified movie clip. Since this feature is now built in and doesn't have to be invented by you, we can only guess that everyone and their chinchilla is going be using it. Don't get us wrong – it's still a really cool feature – but now it may be better to use it in more subtle ways. In this example, we've tried to make the color change just *one* element of the imagery, and to keep it secondary to the actual sounds. Bearing this in mind, we decided to make the background color of our mixer dependent on where all the sound sliders were set.

Adding Color to the Mix(er)

1. Create a new layer on the root timeline, call it Background, and make sure it's at the bottom of the layer stack:

2. Draw a borderless white rectangle on the Background layer, and use the Align panel to set it to the height and width of the stage. Now convert the rectangle into a movie clip called background, and give it the instance name bg_color.

3. Go into the new movie clip and create another layer called Code, and then insert another two keyframes into this layer so that it has three in all. Open up the Frame Actions window for frame 1, and enter this ActionScript:

```
c = new Color(this);
mycolor = new Array();
```

Here we've defined two new objects. The first, c, is a Color object, which we've attached to the current (background) movie clip. The second, mycolor, is an Array object. This is going to be where we hold the values of our volume slider positions, which will in turn influence the visual display. We've initialized it as a blank array at the moment, but we'll fill it up in the next frame.

4. To apply a color transform to something, we first need to set up a generic object and populate it with our color component values. To do this, add this script to frame 2 in the same Code layer:

```
bg_color_new = {
 ra: mycolor[0],
 rb: mycolor[1],
```

continues overleaf

```
ga: mycolor[2],
gb: mycolor[3],
ba: mycolor[4],
bb: mycolor[5],
aa: _root.slider_master1.vlm_master1._y+100,
ab: _root.slider_master1.vlm_master1._y*.5
};
```

Here, bg_color_new is the generic object that'll act as a container for the values, and ra, rb etc. are the components of the Color object. The first letter (r, g, b, or a) stands for the red, green, blue, and alpha property of the movie clip. The second letter (a or b) represents either the percentage multiplier (a), or the offset value (b) to apply to the color. The six color values are set by the position of the volume sliders that we'll be passing into our array. The alpha values are set by the position of the master slider. We added 100 to the alpha percentage to keep the alpha from going below 0, and multiplied the offset by .5 to keep it from getting too high.

5.   Now we need to apply the transform to the background. Add this next piece of script under the code we just entered:

```
c.setTransform(bg_color_new);
```

This just fills the setTransform method with the values in our bg_color_new object.

6.   The last piece of code to go in background is this in frame 3:

```
gotoAndPlay (2);
```

This code constantly loops the setTransform to keep updating the color of the movie clip. Finally, make sure that Layer1 has the same number of frames as the Code layer.

7.   Now we need to go into our slider movie clip and enter the code to pass our vlm_slider position into our color array. This new line of code goes in frame 2 of the slider clip's Code layer, after the existing two lines:

```
s.setVolume(100-this.vlm_slider1._y);
s.setPan (this.pan_dial1.dial_drag1._x*10);
_root.bg_color.mycolor[(slidername-1)] = this.vlm_slider1._y;
```

At the moment, slidername contains a value from 1 to 6, but all arrays in Flash begin at 0. To allow us to easily reference each of the values in the array, we subtract 1 from slidername so that it runs from 0 to 5 and is in sync with our array.

8.   Now you can play the movie. You should find that when you move any of the volume sliders, the color of the background changes as well.

This is pretty crude at the moment, but what we're trying to do here is just establish the principles. Take a look at the `muscimixer.fla` file on the CD for some more subtle effects, which use both the volume and the pan controls to influence the screen display. As a next step in the simple mixer we've created here, you might want to think about making the sliders blend in a little better with the background.

You're now ready to step back and look at sound another way. Rather than building a movie purely to display sound, we're going to look at how to incorporate sound into other projects. Sound isn't just a nice extra feature to add to a Flash movie, it's an integral part of the new web world, and without it, your movies are just a little... mute.

Next, we're going to look at ways in which you can control sound in your movies without using something as obvious, or manual, as a volume slider.

Controlling Sound Indirectly

The first thing that we'll look into is tying the sound controls to the mouse cursor, so that when we move the mouse left or right it will pan, and when we move it up and down we'll fade the volume in and out.

Attaching Sounds to the Mouse Cursor

To make this example work, we need to get some sound clips ready. We could use one of the loops that we used earlier for the music mixer, but for variety I've chosen something else. I have a three-second loop that I created for a project some time ago that fits our purpose perfectly. You can find this sound inside the `mousesound.fla` file on the CD.

1. Start a new movie and import a sound into the Library.

2. Right-click on the sound in the Library, select Linkage, and give it the Identifier loop:

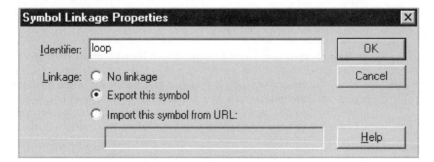

If you're wondering about the last option, Import this symbol from URL, it's for when you're using shared libraries and you need to load the library from a URL.

3. Insert two keyframes into the main timeline and open the Frame Actions window for frame 1.

4. The first thing to do is to insert the now-familiar ActionScript to create a new Sound object and attach our sound to it:

```
loud = new Sound();
loud.attachSound("loop");
loud.setVolume(50);
loud.start(0, 1000);
```

Here, we've attached our loop sound to a new Sound object called `loud`.

5. Underneath this code, enter the next two lines:

```
xStage = 550;
yStage = 400;
```

These two variables contain the height and width of the stage, and if we happen to change that later, we won't have to wade through code to alter the number 550 – it can simply be changed here, on the first frame.

The next frame is going to contain the majority of our code, but before we get to that code it's worth thinking again about exactly what we're trying to do. As we move the mouse up the screen, we want the volume to increase, reaching 100% at the top. Conversely, we want it to go down to 0% at the bottom of the screen. We can write this in mathematical terms as follows:

$$\text{Volume} = \left(\frac{\text{stageHeight - mouseHeight}}{\text{stageHeight}} \right) \times 100$$

Remember that Flash takes its 0, 0 reference point from the *top left* of the screen, not the bottom left as normal math does – which may explain why the equation is slightly more complex than you'd expect.

In terms of panning, we want the right pan to hit 100% at the right edge of the stage, and the left pan to hit 100% at the left edge. We also want the pan to be 0 when the mouse is in the center of the stage. Remember that pan is measured from -100 (left) to 100 (right), with an equal balance being 0. This can be written in English as 'mouse position divided by half the stage width, multiply that total by 100 to get a percentage, then subtract 100 to get a value in the range of –100 to 100'. Here's the equation for that:

$$\text{Pan} = \left(\left(\frac{2 \times \text{mouseWidth}}{\text{stageWidth}} \right) \times 100 \right) - 100$$

This, you'll be pleased to know, is as hard as the math we'll need is going to get. We're now ready to put this into ActionScript.

6. Bring up the Actions window for frame 2 and enter the following:

```
loud.setVolume(((yStage-_ymouse)/yStage)*100);
loud.setPan((((_xmouse*2)/xStage)*100)-100);
```

All that's left to do now is to carry on updating the sound as we move the mouse. This is done in the usual way, by creating a loop between frames 2 and 3.

7. Put this line in frame 3:

```
gotoAndPlay (2);
```

8. At this point, I know that you're anxious to give it a whirl and test your movie, but first it's probably wise to import a picture or draw a box on your stage that fills it exactly. This is so that you can tell when the mouse reaches the edges of the stage, and therefore check that the volume and pan are at the correct values.

9. Finally, let's publish the movie, preview it in a browser, and then *listen* to what happens when we move the mouse around the stage.

Extending this Example

We've proved that we can control sound properties with the mouse, but that's not where it ends. Taking exactly the same principles and applying them to other projects, we can do some cool things to enhance our web sites and games.

For example, imagine we're writing a Flash Space Invaders game. The rockets our ship fires from the bottom of the screen can get louder and pan when they move to the middle of the screen, and the lasers can make a noise that fades away the further up the screen they get. Similarly, the enemy can stomp left to right, and the sound can follow. Or a more pacifistic example might be interactive menus that pan in and out from the edge of the screen when they appear. Going further still, a 3D interface could involve having sound attached to a point on one side of a cube, so that when the cube rotates away from the user, the sound fades away to give aural feedback. These commands can be applied to any objects to create more feedback for the end user, and increase the enjoyment they'll get when using your Flash creations.

For a further example of how sound can be manipulated by ActionScript to provide audio cues, we're going to look at how it might work in a simple game scenario. We've used the classic game of Space Invaders as a starting block. This is for two reasons – one, taking the ship as our main sprite, we can use it as a good focal point for our exercise – and two, the mechanics of the game are pretty intuitive.

Game Sound Demo

Unfortunately, much as we'd love to, we're not going to recreate the whole game here – that's not what this chapter's about. After you've finished this book, though, you should be in a good position to take the project to the next level yourself – take a look at Sham Bhangal's chapter for some games programming ideas. The accompanying FLA for this demo is on the CD as GameSound.fla.

1. First of all, for that authentic old arcade machine feel, set the movie dimensions to 300 x 400 pixels. Next, put a keyframe in frame 3 on the timeline, then create a new layer called Code with three keyframes in it.

2. We'll need a spaceship, a laser beam, and a star field for the game. The first two of these will be created in Flash, but we used Photoshop to create the last. If you don't own Photoshop, you can either find the graphic that we used on the CD (starfield.gif), or just leave it black.

3. Rename Layer1 to Background, and create another two layers called Laser and Ship respectively.

4. If you're using our star field graphic, import it into the Library and then drag it onto the Background layer. Resize your graphic to fit the stage if you need to. It's a good idea to lock the Background layer now, as otherwise it's extremely easy to click on it by mistake.

5. On the Ship layer, draw an approximation of a space ship and convert it into a movie clip called ship.

6. And on the Laser layer draw a simple laser graphic (just a vertical red line will do) and convert it into a movie clip called laser. Here are our finished laser and ship:

7. Position ship at the bottom-center of the stage, and put laser just above it, but off the left-hand side of the stage. Give the two movie clips instance names of ship and laser respectively:

    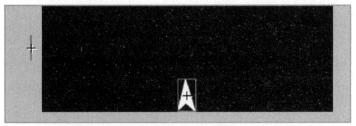

We've situated laser like this so we can use the duplicateMovie command to create more laser beams as required. When we call duplicateMovie, it'll make an exact copy of the laser movie clip and position it wherever we tell it to on the stage. We want the lasers to come straight out of the front of the space ship, so by putting the laser where we have, we can tell a new laser to appear at the horizontal position of ship, and at the vertical position of laser. This is an easy way of making sure that the lasers always appear in the right place.

We need to create one last layer for the hit area that'll trigger the lasers.

8. Insert a new layer above the Ship layer and call it Hit Box.

9. It's time for our old friend, the invisible button. Create a new button symbol called invis_button in the Hit Box layer. Insert a keyframe into the Hit state and draw a rectangle in the center of the stage. It doesn't matter how big it is, as we'll resize it in a minute.

10. Go back onto the main stage, and drag a copy of invis_button into the Hit Box layer. Scale and position the button so that it covers the width of the stage, and the height of the space ship:

I've chosen to do this so that the mouse has to at least be over the ship's movable area to fire. The reason why we didn't just make the button the size of the space ship is that we'll be adding some inertia to it later on, and it wouldn't be quite as practical. This will all become a lot clearer later on when you see it in action.

Lastly, we shouldn't forget the point of this exercise, the sounds. We've provided a laser and engine sound inside the FLA on the CD, but feel free to experiment – a ship that fired braying donkey lasers would be interesting to say the least.

11. To use the sounds, just open GameSound.fla and drag the sounds out of that Library and into your own. Once you've imported your sounds, give them linkage names of engine and laser.

Before we start entering code, let's reiterate our objectives:

●   We want to make the spaceship move about the stage when we move the mouse.

●   It can only move left and right, but when we click on an area close to the ship, it'll make the ship fire.

- This will produce a single laser beam that'll move up the screen at a constant rate.

- As we move the ship left and right, the engine noise of the ship should pan left and right.

- When we fire a laser, we want the sound to trail off, giving the impression that the laser is getting further from our space ship, thus getting quieter (I know sound doesn't travel in a vacuum, but this is a game, not real life...).

With these ground rules in place, we can look into implementing them in our movie.

12. We'll use the first frame of the Code layer to initialize our sounds and our variables. Open it up and enter the following ActionScript:

```
speed = 15;
n = 1;
xStage = 300;
yStage = 400;

engine_noise = new Sound(ship);
engine_noise.attachSound("engine");
engine_noise.setVolume(50);
engine_noise.start(0,1000);

laser_noise = new Sound(laser);
laser_noise.attachSound("laser");
laser_noise.setVolume(0);
laser_noise.start(0,1000);
```

Here, the speed variable represents the speed of the laser. Yes, by definition lasers should travel at light speed, but we don't have time to work out how much this would be at 12 frames per second. (OK, for the curious, we think speed would have to be about 71065954416, but don't take our word for it). n is simply a counter that'll be used when we start shooting lasers like crazy and need to have some control over them. Whenever the mouse is clicked on the hit area, 1 will be added to n, and the new n value will be used in the new laser's name. We've also defined the size of the stage.

The next two code snippets initialize the two sounds using the now-familiar Sound object notation and attach the sounds to their relevant movie clips. Note also that the last two lines in each sound's code chunk set the sounds' respective volumes and set the sound to loop 1000 times. We've set engine_noise to a volume of 50 because the whirring is a repetitive noise at best, and more of an ambient sound than a crisp, clear soundtrack. The laser_noise initial volume value has been set to 0 because we don't want it to play until we fire a laser.

13. Next, enter the main body of the ActionScript in frame 2 of the Code layer:

```
// ship inertia and limit checks
xPos = ship._x;
xMousepos = int(_xmouse);
xVal = xPos + xMousepos;
newxPos = (xVal/2);
if (newxPos < 0) {
    newxPos = 0;
}
if (newxPos > xStage) {
    newxPos = xStage;
}
ship._x = newxPos;
```

This first block of code makes sure that the ship doesn't go off the edges of our stage. It also handles the slight inertia of the ship, which will make it come to a gradual halt instead of stopping dead under the mouse. The actual line that does this is:

```
newxPos = (xVal/2);
```

This means that if the distance from the ship to the mouse is 16 pixels, it'll move 8, then 4, then 2, etc. We also have a couple of `if` structures to ensure that the ship always stays on the screen.

14. The next chunk of code handles moving the newly created laser sprite up the screen. Add this next chunk after the existing code in frame 2:

```
// for all lasers currently being fired
i = 1;
while (i <= n) {
    // get Y position of this laser - speed = new Y position
    newLaserY = getProperty("laser"+i, _y) - speed;
    // if laser hasn't reached top
    // move this laser, set its volume according to Y pos
    if (newLaserY > 0) {
        setProperty ("laser"+i, _y, newLaserY);
        laser_noise.setVolume(newLaserY/(yStage/100));
    } else {
        // if laser is off top of screen, delete
        removeMovieClip ("laser"+i);
    }
    i++;
}
```

Here, we check to make sure that the laser actually has a positive Y value, which means that it's still on the stage. It uses the `n` variable to keep track of how many lasers there are, and cycles through each active one performing `setProperty` commands to define the laser bolt's new position. The routines to actually *create* the laser beam will all be attached to the invisible button over the ship. If the laser has a *negative* Y value, meaning that it isn't on the screen, then it's deleted by the `else` statement.

15. Finally, the panning effect of the engine noise is dealt with swiftly in one line. Add it to the end of the frame 2 script:

```
engine_noise.setPan((((newxPos*2)/xStage)*100)-100);
```

This is a little easier: we simply take the position of the spaceship (newxPos), multiply by two, and then divide by the stage width. We then multiply by 100 and subtract 100 to obtain a value that ranges from -100 to 100, with 0 being dead center for the pan.

16. That's the majority of the code done. The third keyframe is a lot easier, as it just invokes the loop that provides constant updating of our stage. Add this goto action in frame 3:

```
gotoAndPlay (2);
```

If we test the movie at this point, we should get the star field with the spaceship at the bottom of the screen. The ship should move smoothly from left to right, but go no further than the edges of the screen. The noise of the ship should also pan smoothly with the ship itself, from left to right and back again. Lastly, the ship should have a slight slowdown instead of a dead stop when we stop moving the mouse.

Notice that no lasers are produced when we shoot, because we haven't yet set up the scripts for the transparent button. It seems obvious then, to move right along and remedy that now.

The final piece of our puzzle is actually spawning the lasers when we click the mouse button in the hit area.

17. Select the instance of invis_button on the stage and bring up the Object Actions window. Now enter the following ActionScript:

```
on (release) {
    n++;
    // create new laser clip
    duplicateMovieClip ("laser", "laser"+n, n);
    // tell it where to be
    setProperty ("laser" + n, _x, getProperty("ship", _x));
}
```

Broken down, this means that when the mouse is released, 1 is added to the value of n, the counter variable we defined earlier. The movie clip laser is then duplicated and given the name lasern (where n is our cumulative value) and placed on level n. When we setProperty with lasern, we're telling it to appear exactly above the ship movie clip, wherever that may be. This works by setting the _x value of the laser to the _x value of the ship. In English, we're firing a new bullet from the front of the ship whenever the mouse is clicked.

When you test your movie, notice how the volume for the laser fades away and the pan of the ship hums gently behind it all... it sounds just like those old Williams Defender machines! Smell the nostalgia...

Now you just need to put in some enemy ships, add a bit more code, a high score table, and of course some more sounds, and you'll have a Space Invaders game ready and raring to go. As we said earlier, take a look at Mr. Bhangal's chapter and see where you might like to go next.

Conclusion

In this chapter, we've tried to stay focused on the ActionScript that we used to create the sound effects, and to explain it in enough depth that you can take the concept and apply it to your own projects. We firmly believe that the Web is moving quickly towards media-rich content, and Flash 5 really gives us detailed control over our media elements. Of course, any mixer is only as good as the music it's mixing, and a game's only as good as the playability it's built on – no tool, no matter how versatile and powerful it is, can create these things for you. They come from talent, experience, hard work and practice.

It's interesting to imagine the learning curve for creative digital artists. When you're painting, it doesn't take long to get the hang of oils and the brush – then it comes down to the creative mind and the journey of discovery. With the computer, things are different: there are tutorials, upgrades, plug-ins, platforms, browsers, languages, versions... the list goes on. With all that to worry about, it's easy to lose track of the important part: the creation. You have to know the tools in order to break them – to get them to do things they were never intended to do. After all, that's how we got where we are today with the Web. Now everyone else is catching up, modems are faster, broadband is nearly here, and computers are fast enough to handle the information.

Now it's our responsibility to push the envelope again, to keep the medium evolving and to be responsible for what we create. We assume that most of the readers of this book are people just like us, working in web/multimedia design, having to answer to clients that pay the bills, and create designs and interfaces that function and deliver for the project at hand. It's important to remember, however, that as much as we're the ones learning these new tools and how to communicate with them, we're also the *teachers*. It's up to us to guide the client, the viewer, and to surprise and engage them. You have to remember: they don't know what they *want* to see; they only know what they *have* seen. What comes next is up to us.

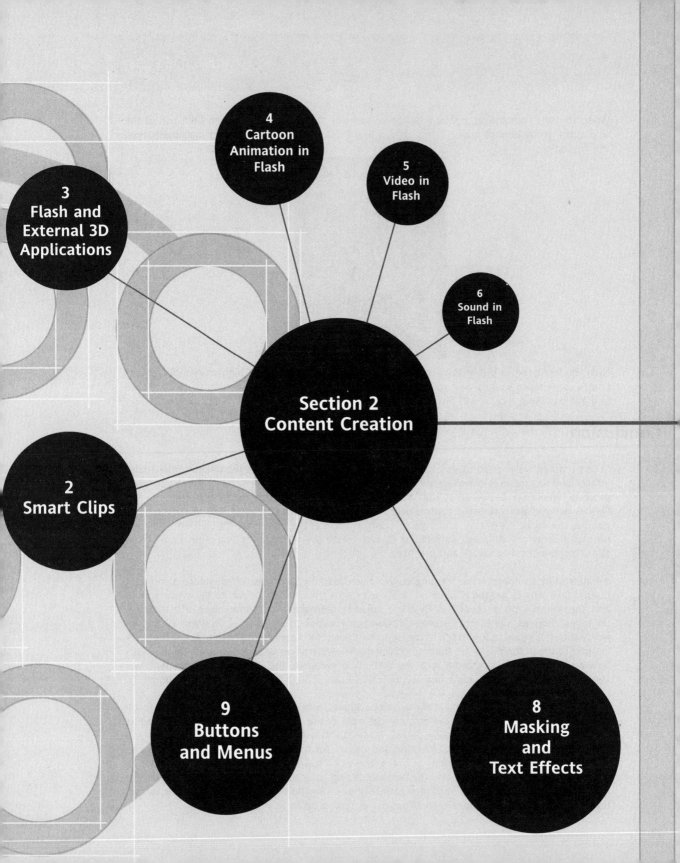

4
Cartoon
Animation in
Flash

5
Video in
Flash

3
Flash and
External 3D
Applications

6
Sound in
Flash

**Section 2
Content Creation**

2
Smart Clips

9
Buttons
and Menus

8
Masking
and
Text Effects

Chapter 7
Transparency
Effects

In this chapter we're going to look at a relatively undocumented trick that can help you to create highly layered designs and animation in Flash. The first part of this chapter involves using Photoshop, with which we're going to create a collage by using the Alpha transparency of PNG files. Then, with minimal effort, we'll duplicate the design in Flash and animate it.

Flash has been hailed as the champion of vector animation on the Web, but this chapter will demonstrate that it can also be used successfully with bitmap images. Bitmap images are made up of tiny differently colored squares called pixels, whereas vectors are constructed using flat lines and curves. Although vector-based animations have very small file sizes, they don't achieve the texture and depth that bitmap images (also called raster images) can offer.

In this chapter, you'll see how it's possible to use raster images in your animation, but still keep your file size down. Because Flash shares the layered image structure of Photoshop, designers can use it to get the same style of collaged images they've traditionally produced. There are still limitations when using raster images in Flash: scaling a movie without decreasing the quality of the raster image is difficult, and animating rasters can be taxing on the CPU. However, the advantages outweigh these limitations. Used well, raster images can add a distinctive texture and richness to your designs – here's how:

Designing your Photoshop Collage

In the first stage of this chapter we'll create a collage of images in Photoshop by making areas of each image transparent. Each image will be on a separate layer and, once our collage is complete, we'll save each layer as a separate file – ready to be imported into Flash.

The first stage – importing the individual files into Photoshop – has been done for you.

1.   Open the file collage01.psd and you'll see that all the components of our collage have been imported into this file: a picture of a clock, a landscape picture taken in Ireland, and a picture of a woman. Open the Layers panel by going to Window > Show Layers and you'll see that each image has been placed on an appropriately named layer:

> *It's advisable to name each layer to help you identify them at a later date. Also, if you work in a production environment with other designers, it helps to get into the habit of naming layers. This allows the designers to open your Photoshop file and still understand your layer structure.*

We'll start by removing the background from the woman layer. There are a few ways to remove the background from images, such as the Magic Wand tool or the Color Range menu found under the Select option. In this example, however, we're going to use the Eraser tool.

2. Select the Eraser tool and double-click on it to display its Options panel. Select the Paintbrush mode (the Airbrush mode can also be effective) and make sure all of the panel's other options are at their default settings. To do this, click on the arrow in the top right-hand corner of the panel, and then select Reset Tool:

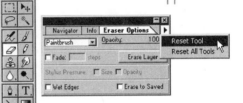

3. Open the Brushes panel by going to Window > Show Brushes and select the brush with 100 underneath it. This has a diameter of 100 pixels. Making sure the woman layer is selected, erase the white background around her. Use different sized brushes to create different degrees of feathering around the image; the more variations you create along the edge, the more interesting your collage will be. If you erase too much of the image, use the Edit > Undo command or go to Window > Show History which will show you all the recent changes you've made to your file and allow you to go back several steps:

4. Now hide all of the layers except for the ireland layer by clicking on the eye icon of the other two. Using the same technique as described above, erase both ends of the photograph using the Eraser Tool. This time, however, use a larger brush with a diameter of 300. Be sure to leave no corners on the photo, so that the picture fades out evenly. This is important; attention to detail gives your collages more depth. Now turn the woman layer back on by clicking on where the eye icon used to be. Your collage is starting to take form:

5. Now turn on the clock layer and move it to the top of the pile of layers by clicking and dragging it up to the top of the list in the Layers panel. Using the same technique, feather the edges of the clock gears until you can no longer see any of the brown wood in the photo. This will create a very abstract image, which will add interest to the collage. Now click on the Create new layer icon: it's the central icon at the bottom of the Layers panel that looks like a page with the corner folded over. Double-click on the new layer to bring up its Options window and change its name to horizontal lines:

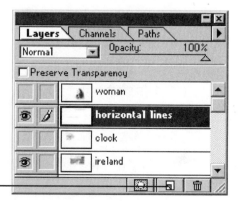

Create new layer

6.   On this layer, use the Line Tool to draw lines at the top and the bottom of the Irish landscape picture. To choose the thickness of the lines, double-click on the Line Tool to open its Options panel. Type 1 in the Line Width field. Now draw the lines, keeping SHIFT held down as you do to ensure they're perfectly horizontal. Feather the edges of the lines using the Eraser tool:

7.   Finally, reduce the size of the woman and the clock. Select one layer at a time and go to Layer > Transform > Scale. Holding the SHIFT key to keep the image's proportions, drag the square boxes that appear around the image – like they do in Flash's Scale tool – until you've made the image the appropriate size. Arrange your images in a well-balanced collage composition, making sure that the woman layer is above the others by dragging it to the top of the list in the Layers panel:

Now that we've created our collage, we need to get the individual images ready to import into Flash. In order to make them as easy to work with in Flash as possible, we're going to save them in a web-ready format that will optimize their file size.

> *At this point, it's a good idea to save your Photoshop file to a separate folder. You don't want to overwrite the file accidentally, destroying what can easily be hours of design work. Speaking from experience, I know just how devastating this can be.*

8. Save your file as `collage.psd`. Go to Image > Duplicate to create a copy of the `collage` file, and then delete all the layers apart from the woman layer by selecting the layer to be removed and clicking on the trash can icon at the bottom of the Layers panel.

9. Click and hold on the Marquee tool and select the Crop tool from the far right of the sub-panel that appears:

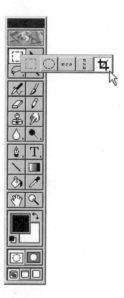

Click and drag a box around the image of the woman, close to the edges, and double-click inside it to crop the image. Save this image as a new file entitled `woman.psd`.

10. Go back to your original `collage` file and repeat the steps above for the other three layers. At the end of the process you should have four files named `clock.psd`, `horizontal_lines.psd`, `ireland.psd` and `woman.psd`. Save these files to a folder called `roughs`. This is where we're going to store all of the files that we'll generate in preparation for creating our Flash movie.

> *It's important to keep your files organized and named accordingly, as these types of projects generate a lot of files and they may be hard to discern if you revisit the project at a later date.*

11. Working on the woman.psd file, go to File > Save For Web. From the Settings drop-down menu select PNG-24, and then check the Transparency check box. You'll notice the white background disappears, revealing the default Photoshop checkered background:

This tells you that the background will be transparent when it exports as a PNG. Now click OK and save the file to the roughs folder as woman.png. Repeat these steps for the remaining Photoshop files.

At the end of the process, you should have four additional files in the roughs folder called clock.png, horizontal_lines.png, ireland.png and woman.png. That's the Photoshop work complete – we're now ready to import our files into Flash.

Importing your PNG Files

1. Create a new Flash movie and change the stage size to 700 x 400 pixels by going to Modify > Movie. Save this file as collage.fla.

We're going to put all our ActionScript code, which controls the movie, on the same layer and keep this as the top layer in the movie. By using the top layer as your ActionScript layer for every movie, you'll ensure easy access to your scripts for later editing.

2. Change the name of the default layer to actions.

The next thing we're going to do is set the publishing settings for this movie.

3. Go to File > Publish Settings. Select the Flash tab and set the JPEG Quality to 30. By giving thisa low setting, we ensure all files will be exported at a small size. If you're unhappy with the image quality, you can always increase the JPEG quality later and re-save the file.

4. Check the following Options check boxes: Generate size report and Protect from import:

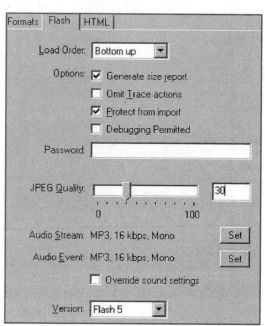

Generate size report will create a text file which we will use later to help reduce the file size of the movie. Protect from import helps prevent other Flash developers from stealing your work. (Note: this feature is not perfect, and any file can be hacked. In fact there are several free utilities to hack protected Flash files that enable a user to get at the source images. But this feature will stop the common user from stealing your source files.)

5. Go to File > Import and import the four PNG files you saved earlier in the roughs folder. When prompted by the Fireworks PNG Import Settings window, leave all of the options at their default settings and press OK. All the images will be placed straight onto the stage.

6. Select the woman image and go to Insert > Convert to Symbol. Make it into a graphic symbol called womansymbol. Repeat this for the other three images, calling them clocksymbol, irelandsymbol and linessymbol. When an image is converted to a symbol, Flash automatically centers the image inside the new symbol. This is helpful later on when we begin working with an instance on the stage, as Flash will treat the center of the image as the center of the symbol when doing things like scaling or rotating the instance.

7.   Select all the symbols and delete them from the stage.

If you look in your Library panel, you'll see that the original PNG images are still there alongside the new symbols. Note that whether the PNG file extension appears at the end of a bitmap's name will depend on the personal settings of your computer:

When you're working on a movie with a lot of symbols and imported images, it's a good idea to keep your Library organized by creating folders to keep groups of items in.

8.   Create a new folder in your Library by clicking on the orange folder icon in the bottom left-hand corner of the Library panel. Name this folder bitmaps – when you create the folder, the Name field will automatically be highlighted, so you can just type the new name straight in.

9.   Now select each bitmap. (the files with the green tree logo next to them) and drag them all into the new bitmap folder one at a time. The folder will open to expose its contents. Double-click on the folder to close it.

Updating your Original Images

Now, if you're halfway through a project and you want to add something to one of your bitmap images, ireland.png for example, it's very simple to update it. Back in Photoshop, open the ireland.psd file from the roughs folder. Make any adjustments you need to make, like changing the size or the color, for example, and go to File > Save for Web. Save the file as a transparent PNG file overwriting the old ireland.png. Switch back to Flash and open the bitmaps folder in the library. Double-click on the ireland bitmap and simply click Update to carry your changes through. You can update your bitmap files as you build your project, and it is even possible to change the look of your finished animation simply by updating your bitmap files.

Animating Bitmaps with Color

Now that our images are in Flash and ready to use, we can duplicate our Photoshop collage design and set about animating it. As well as adding a touch of movement, we're going to use the Advanced menu from the Effect panel to fade in the elements of our collage in interesting ways.

1. Create four new layers in the timeline, and then give your layers the following names: clock, lines, ireland and woman. Arrange the layers as shown, and then drag each of your symbols onto the appropriate layer:

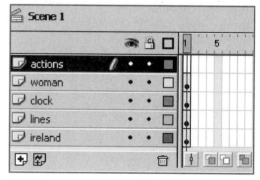

If you drag the bitmaps onto the stage instead of the symbols, then your animation won't work. Flash can't apply physical changes to or animate the original bitmaps, only the symbols they're embedded in.

2. Working on the lines layer, drag linessymbol up towards the top of the stage. Open the Align panel (Window > Panels > Align). With the To Stage option selected, center the symbol to the horizontal middle of the stage:

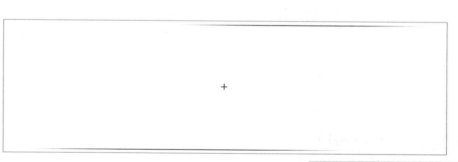

3. Now rearrange the other elements so that the stage looks like your Photoshop design. You might want to open the original file to use as a reference.

4. We're now going to create an introduction animation sequence. Insert keyframes at frame 70 in the timeline on all the layers, then pull the playhead back to frame 1. Now click and drag the first keyframe in the lines layer to frame 10, making linessymbol disappear from the first nine frames. Next, drag the first keyframe on the clock layer to frame 20, and the first one on the woman layer to frame 30. Your timeline should look like the one below:

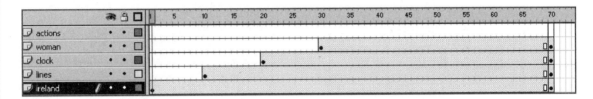

5. Insert keyframes at frames 10 and 20 of the ireland layer. Working on the image at frame 1, open the Effect panel (Window > Panels > Effect) and select Alpha from the drop-down menu. Set the image's Alpha value to zero, making the picture disappear from the stage. Now select the keyframe at frame 10 and choose Advanced from the Effect panel, where you'll be presented with several options. Set the Alpha value to 30% and the Red value to –28%. You should see the image take on a blue hue:

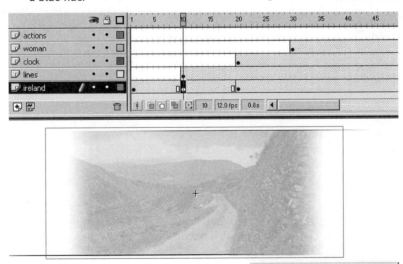

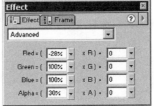

6. To animate the image, create motion tweens between frames 1 and 10, and 10 and 20. Hit ENTER to test the animation.

You should now see your animation starting to take form; irelandsymbol should fade from white to blue and then into its original color. Now let's form the rest of the collage.

7. Add a keyframe at frame 20 of the lines layer, and then select linessymbol at frame 10 and move it over to the left. Holding down SHIFT while moving an object constrains it to horizontal or vertical movement only, and will allow you to move the lines across in a straight line. This is important because we're going to animate the lines and they need to slide in horizontally. Using the Effect panel, set the initial Alpha value of linessymbol to 0%. Now create a motion tween between the two keyframes and, when tested, the lines will appear to fade in from the left.

8. Select the clock layer and insert keyframes at frames 30 and 40. Select the keyframe at frame 20 and set the Alpha value of clocksymbol to 0%. At keyframe 30, use the Advanced menu to set the symbol's values to the ones shown:

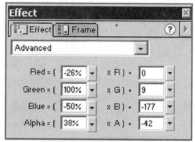

Feel free to experiment with other values, but be sure to select a low Alpha value so that the image still dissolves in slowly. By playing around with the advanced color variations, and combining them with different levels of transparency, you can produce some very interesting effects which can make pictures appear to fade in from the center outwards, or from the edges inwards. Create a motion tween between frames 20 and 30, and 30 and 40. When you test the scene now, notice the way the clock appears and fades in.

9. Select the woman layer and insert keyframes at frames 40 and 50. Set the Alpha value of womansymbol at frame 30 to 0%, and at frame 40 apply the following settings from the Advanced menu, leaving the other settings alone:

Green = 78%
Blue = -100%
Alpha = 74%

At frame 50 bring up the Advanced menu again and set the right-hand Alpha column to –255. Finally, create motion tweens between all the keyframes on the woman layer. Your timeline should now look like this:

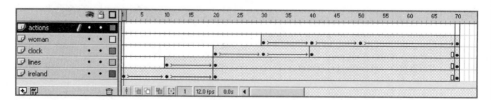

10. So that your animation will stop once the collage is complete, add a stop action in frame 70 of the actions layer. Now test your movie, and watch your completed animation.

Optimizing your Animation's File Size

When you're preparing your animation for publication you'll need to choose a file size for each component of your collage, striking a balance between image quality and the space it takes up. You can view the size of your components by testing the movie and opening the Output window (Window > Output) while you watch your animation:

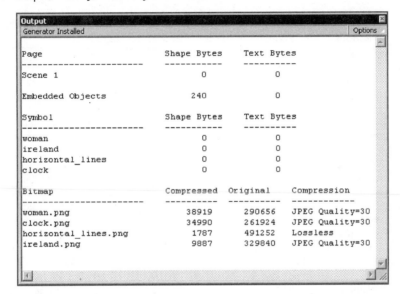

We earlier set all of our bitmap images to have a default quality of 30, but what if, for example, you were unhappy with the quality of the image of the woman in your collage. Well, you could increase the quality of it like this:

Optimizing Image Quality

1. Double-click on the woman.png bitmap in the Library panel. This will open the image's Bitmap Properties window. Uncheck the Use document default quality field and enter 40 in the Quality field that appears:

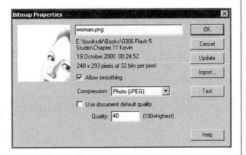

Although, from Flash's promptings, you may think you're reducing the quality from 50, you are in fact increasing it from the default setting of 30. This alteration won't affect the appearance of the file during editing, just the published version.

Having increased the file size of one element of your animation, you need to make up for it by reducing the quality of a less important part of the design. We can afford to reduce the quality of the clock image in this example, as it's in the background, and it may in fact look older and rustier as a result of this deterioration.

2. Double-click on clock.png in the Library and set the Quality to 15, redressing the earlier increase in file size. Now publish your movie and review it in the browser.

3. While your movie is playing go to File > Open and, from the same directory your Flash file is located in, open the text file collage Report.txt.

    If you scroll through this file you'll see a detailed account of the file size of all your Library members. You can use this file to help chip away at the overall file size of your movie by hunting down large Library members whose size needs reducing.

Before I draw this section to a close, here are some final thoughts on animating bitmaps in Flash using this technique.

As you're changing the color values of your bitmaps, remember that the larger the bitmap the greater CPU usage it will take to produce the effect. Not everyone has the latest multimedia computer so it's important that as you build your animation, you review it on other computers with less memory and slower chip sets than your own. It's a good idea for either you or your client to decide what the minimum computer requirements are for your Flash movie to ensure the success of your project.

If your movie is running slowly on your test computer, try taking the following corrective steps:

- Reduce the space between keyframes and lower your movie's frame rate

- Reduce the height and width of your original bitmap images – then update the versions that you import into Flash

- Avoid having too many objects tweening on the stage at once

- Embed the Flash movie in an HTML file placed by pixels, not percentage, so that the movie can't scale to a larger size

Advanced Bitmap Animation

It is possible to create very complex animation in Flash with relatively little work. For example, by duplicating a simple animation loop you can create complex-looking animations. In this final section we're going to look at this technique.

Making Bitmaps Into Movie Clips

1. Create a new Flash movie, name it animation.fla, and import the clock.png
    image into it from the roughs folder. Now convert the bitmap into a graphic
    symbol, as we did in the previous exercise, and call it clocksymbol.

2. Create a new movie clip symbol and call it clockmovie. Drag clocksymbol from the
    Library into the first frame of the movie clip and center it using the Info panel.
    Create a keyframe at frame 15 and, with this frame selected, bring up the Effect
    panel. Select the Advanced menu and in the right-hand Alpha column set a value of
    -255. Create a motion tween between the two keyframes:

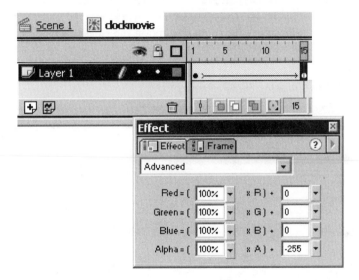

    When you play this animation, the clock mechanism should appear to fade out from
    the edges to the center, and then to white.

3. Create a second movie clip symbol and call it clockmovie2. Inside this movie clip,
    create two new layers and then make all three of the movie clip's layers 45 frames
    long. Place your first movie clip, clockmovie, in frame 1 of Layer 1 and center it.

4. On Layer 2, create a keyframe at frame 10 and place another copy of clockmovie in
    the center. Turn this instance onto its side by going to Modify > Transform > Scale
    and Rotate and entering 90 in the Rotate field.

5. On Layer 3 create a keyframe at frame 20 and drag another instance of clockmovie onto the center of the frame. Rotate this instance 60 degrees. The final timeline for this movie clip will look like the one shown:

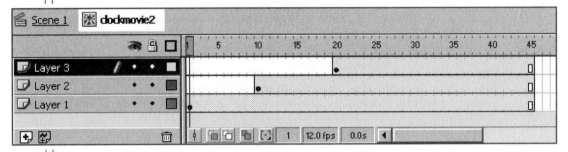

6. Drag an instance of your completed movie clip clockmovie2 onto the main stage and center it using the Info panel. Make the default layer 30 frames long, and then create a second layer. On Layer 2 create a keyframe at frame 15 and center another instance of clockmovie2 in this frame. Rotate this instance 90 degrees and set its Alpha value to 50% using the Effects panel:

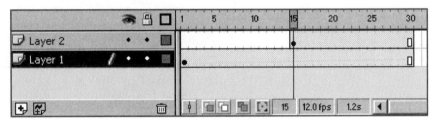

7. Now publish your movie and review it in your web browser.

In this exercise we've used bitmaps to create an interesting, and rarely seen, visual effect. Starting from a simple fade, layered over itself again and again, we've made quite a complex and apparently random effect. The clock mechanism appears to be exploding from the center of the screen, and then fading away. This technique can be applied particularly well to creating things such as explosions or raindrops. You can even create patterns that give the impression of being fractal.

I hope I've shown you in this chapter that animating bitmaps in Flash can bring new depth to your work. By combining vector animation with rich raster design work you can open new doors of creativity and experimentation. In Flash, the advanced color and alpha options can be used to provide a wide range of different animations, incorporating dissolves, blends, and color shifts. The main thing to remember while discovering these new techniques, of course, is to keep your eye on that all-important file size. Many people are put off these bitmap-based effects by the prospect of large file sizes and slow downloads, but if you can keep the amount of memory they use under control, you'll be able to create a usable and distinctive animation for your web site.

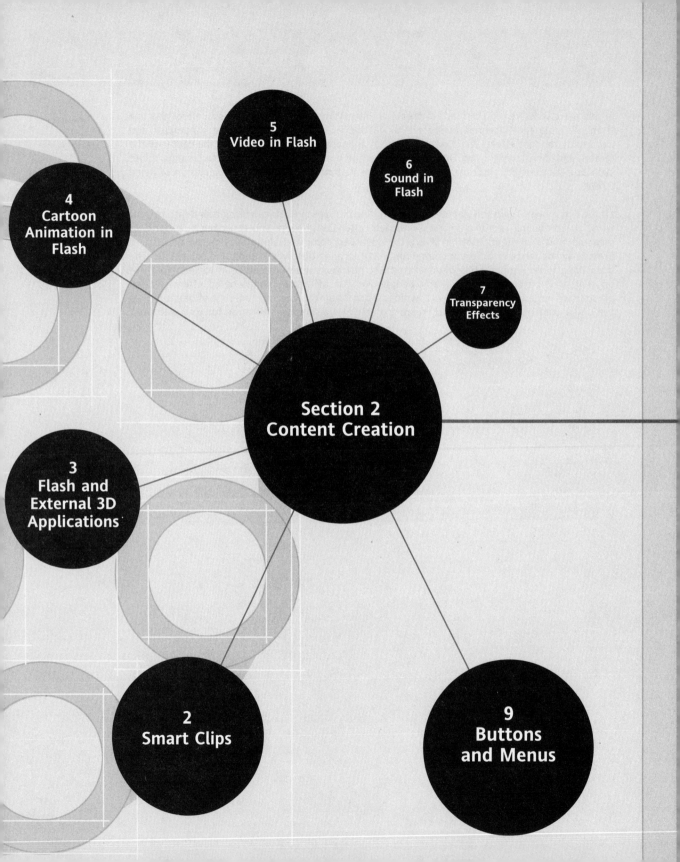

Section 2
Content Creation

5
Video in Flash

6
Sound in
Flash

4
Cartoon
Animation in
Flash

7
Transparency
Effects

3
Flash and
External 3D
Applications

2
Smart Clips

9
Buttons
and Menus

Chapter 8
Masking and Text Effects

Flash content provides you with refreshing movement, depth and rich visual effects. The ability to add bandwidth-friendly animation to a static web page is what draws people towards Flash as a tool, and the techniques that enable you to maximize the visual impact of movies are manifold. This chapter will be looking at using **masks** and **text** in Flash to achieve a variety of different animated effects. The purpose here is not so much to enable you to duplicate the specific content used in the examples, but rather to allow you to add the generic techniques to your toolkit so that you can add your own inspiration and your own effects.

Let's start by thinking for a moment about **layers** in Flash.

Layers

In Flash, you can have as many layers as you want, name them as you like, and arrange them in any way you choose. In fact, from a programmer's standpoint, layers in Flash are effectively invisible as movie components: by that, I mean that there's no way that you can use the *layer* name, or any layer variable or property, to reference a movie clip that's on a particular layer. Nor can you change the order of layers at runtime.

This can be confusing for newcomers to Flash, especially if they're coming from a Director background. In Director, you can only have one 'object' per layer, and you *can* reference these objects by using the layer name. In Flash, layers work similarly to how they do in graphics packages like Illustrator. You can put as much as you want on one layer, and you're not limited to just one 'object'.

Flash layers are not designed for programmatic manipulation, and are really only intended to help you organize your work. The creation of a large Flash movie or a very complicated effect can leave a great number of elements lying around. The use of named layers to organize your work can make life a lot easier for you as your movie progresses.

When I create a new movie, I have my own scheme for layer creation: first I make a Background layer to hold any background graphic. The top two layers in my larger movies are always a Labels layer for – you guessed it - labels, and an Actions layer to house any ActionScript. As many Flash designers will tell you, separating out your content in this way makes your movies much easier to develop and debug.

Careful use of layers is essential for creating sophisticated masking effects, and it's the combined use of layers and masks that the first section of this chapter will deal with.

Masking Essentials

A mask is a special layer in Flash that creates a 'hole' through which one or more layers grouped under it are visible. Mask layers and the layers grouped under them can be treated in the same way as any other layer, in the sense that you can put whatever content you like on them, and manipulate that content with tweens, or programmatically using ActionScript.

The way masking works is essentially straightforward: if there is any content on the mask layer, the content on the layers underneath will be revealed whenever it falls directly underneath the mask layer content:

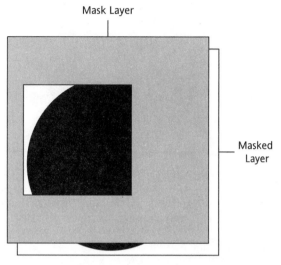

Mask Layer

Masked Layer

In this diagram, the Mask layer is empty, apart from the filled rectangle in the middle, and the Masked layer has a circle on it. Where the circle falls under the rectangle, the circle is revealed. The content you draw on the Mask layer opens a window on the layer(s) below.

It's a common mistake to think that the color or alpha settings of the objects on the mask layer will have an effect on the degree of masking of the content below – this is not true! Masking in Flash is all or nothing. Even a completely transparent fill placed on the mask layer will reveal the layers underneath it.

Just to ensure that everybody's basic knowledge of masks is on the same level, I'm going to quickly reiterate how to create a standard mask before going on to create some much more interesting mask effects.

A Basic Mask

1. Create a new Flash movie with two layers. Name the top layer mask and the bottom layer masked:

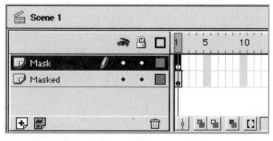

2. Draw a square on the Mask layer and a circle on the Masked layer. Center them something like this:

Nothing in the Mask layer will ever be seen in the finished movie, so don't be afraid to use bright colors to make the masking content a little easier to see. Indeed, I'd encourage you to use a distinctive, bright color on your mask layers, as this will help you distinguish between different types of content when you revisit your movies in the future.

3. Select the Mask layer and make it into a mask, either by selecting Modify > Layer to bring up the Layer Properties window and clicking the Mask radio button...

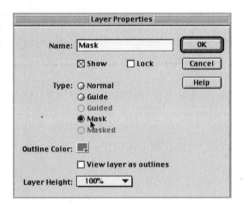

4. ...or by right-clicking on the layer name (control-click for Mac) and choosing Mask from the pop-up menu.

5. Now use the Layer Properties box to alter the masked layer, this time selecting the Masked option:

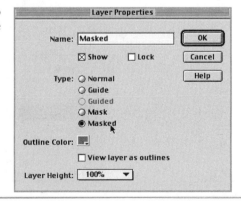

The icons in the layers list should have changed to indicate that the layers are now a mask and masked respectively...

...but otherwise you won't see a difference in your image yet. This is because the masking effect will only be previewed in the Flash design environment once all the layers involved are **locked**.

You can view your simple mask effect by locking both layers...

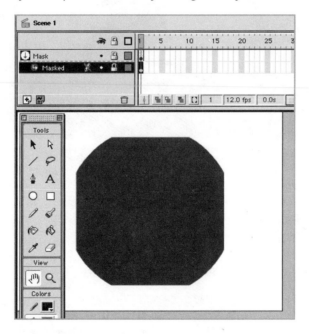

...or by testing your movie.

As you can see, the square on the mask window just acts as a window on the circle below: where the window 'glass' is, we see the content beneath, but the rest of the Masked layer remains hidden.

So much for the basic mask. Let's look at some of those more interesting *animated* masking effects.

Animating Masks

One of the easiest ways to get more out of masking is to use an **animated mask**. As I said earlier, a mask layer is really just like any other layer, which means that it has a timeline to which you can add keyframes, tweens, and even ActionScript. Motion tweens in particular can help to produce some interesting masking effects, as we're about to see...

Masked Text

Imagine that you wanted to create a big text title composed of letters whose interiors are filled with an image. It would be pretty simple to use a mask that contains the text over a masked layer that contained a graphic, say a few vector-based clouds:

With the clouds on a masked layer, however, you could also animate them to float behind the mask layer. This is a much more dramatic effect and one which would be nearly impossible to do without using masks.

Masked, Animated Clouds

1.   In a new movie, set up three layers called clouds, mask, and outline:

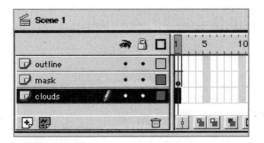

2. Type some *big* text on the mask layer using a large font. When you're happy with the look of your text, break it apart:

3. Select the text and copy it, and then paste it **in place** on the outline layer.

Since we're going to be animating clouds drifting (and visible) behind our text, we don't want the letters to be filled in. However, we also want the text to be readable at all times, so we need to be able see the text's outlines constantly. To satisfy both these aims, we're going to turn the pasted text into outlines that will sit on top of the mask to better define the text.

4. With the text on the outline layer selected, use Modify > Shape > Soften fill edges and specify a Distance of around 10 pixels, and using the Expand option:

This will create a distinct visible outline:

5. Now go to each letter individually and select its middle fill. Use the Mixer panel to bump down the Alpha to about 10% (you'll probably want to hide the mask layer so that you can see this clearly).

6. This should leave you with an overlay that has strong edges and a faint fill. Alternatively, you could just delete the fills if you wished.

   If you use the Soften fill edges approach and the 10% Alpha, you'll end up with this kind of effect:

   Now for those clouds...

7. On the clouds layer, use the drawing tools to draw a simple freehand cloud. When you have your cloud, group it. Make as many clouds as you want, putting each on its own layer, and ensuring that each cloud layer is *underneath* the mask layer:

8. Use your cloud layers and some motion tweens to set up an animation of clouds drifting behind the text area. Experiment a little to get it to look smooth and continuous. Don't forget to make sure that your text mask and outline layers are extended far enough in the timeline to cover the animation.

9. Convert your mask layer to a mask and all of your cloud layers to *masked* layers. Lock the Mask layer and all the masked cloud layers:

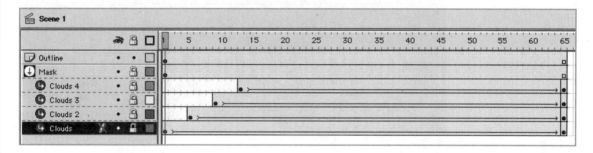

When you play your movie, you'll see your clouds drifting through your text:

Spotlight Effect

A common effect using a motion-tweened mask layer is the spotlight effect. In this effect, a background layer is masked by a layer that contains a small circular graphic. The circular graphic is then animated using a simple motion tween to move back and forth like a spotlight. Combined with a black background, this gives the illusion that the 'light' is illuminating the other content. Unfortunately, you can't combine a masking effect with a motion guide layer, so using a motion guide to direct the movement of the spotlight isn't possible – you have to use a tween.

Make the Spotlight

1.   In a new movie, make sure that you have a black background, and then create some content on the first layer. I'm using text, as you can see from the screenshots:

They've got me covered!

2.   Create a new layer above the content layer (mine's called spotlight) and draw a circle. Group the circle so that you can motion tween it:

3. Animate the circle traveling across the screen by adding a keyframe at frame 30 or so and using a motion tween. Add frames to the content layer so that it's the same length as the tween:

4. Turn the spotlight layer into a mask and the content layer into a masked layer. If you drag the playhead across the timeline or play the movie, you'll see the circle revealing the text beneath as it moves across the screen:

5. This spotlight doesn't look too realistic, I'll admit, but you get the idea. We'll make a better one next.

A More Convincing Spotlight

One problem with masks is that there are no varying degrees of transparency – they're either *on* or *off*. This is a shame as it would be nice, for instance, if we could put a slightly softer edge on the circle for our spotlight effect, as it's pretty harsh at the moment. Unless you want to sit and hope that Flash 6 has Photoshop-like masking capabilities, there's no perfect solution to this problem.

One simple approach would be to put a gray background underneath the content layer, and to make that a masked layer too:

When this is played back, you get a better effect, as the background appears to 'light up' as well as the text:

In Flash, you can often combine a few different effects to achieve what you're after. For instance, to add a softer edge to our spotlight, we can take the effect we have and add an extra layer to soften the edge of the circle. What we need on this layer is another circular graphic that we can animate on top of the mask layer – somewhat like the outline around the text in the cloud effect that we saw earlier. The second circle can be filled with a radial gradient that goes from the background color on the outside to transparent in the center, using the Alpha setting to tone down the effect:

Shadow the animation of the mask, and you'll achieve a soft-edged effect. You can experiment with colored gradients too in search of that elusive 'psychedelic 30s mobster movie' effect.

You can use this kind of Flash radial gradient in this context and it will look fine, but, if you're willing to increase your file size in exchange for a more 'natural' looking effect, then I recommend going into Photoshop and creating your 'soft circle' graphic as a bitmap graphic.

Once you're in Photoshop (or your preferred imaging program), draw a circle the same size as your circle mask and fill it with a gradient that has the movie background color on the outside, and which is completely transparent in the middle.

When you're creating the transparent part, the natural tendency is to take a black to white gradient and make the white part transparent. However, this will leave you with a white halo in the middle, so you need to pick the same color as the background color of your Flash movie as a transparent color – in other words a black to black gradient.

Export the graduated circle as a PNG24 file with transparency intact. Import your graphic into Flash, place it on a layer of its own and animate it in coordination with the original spotlight circle. You may want to bump up the scale one or two percent to fully cover the edges, but you should now have a fairly realistic looking spotlight.

Color Wheel Effect

As well as solid or graduated fills, you can also use a fairly complicated animation as a fill for a simple shape. An example application of this is a 'color changing' effect that you can use to fill text – we'll have a look at that here.

A Color Changing Text Fill

1. Create a text layer in a new movie and type in some text in a very large font:

Color Wheel

2. Add a new layer and draw a circle about twice the diameter of the text block:

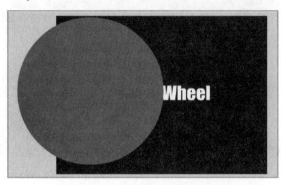

3. Fill the circle with a multi-color linear gradient...

MULTICOLOR GRADIENT

4. ...and give the colors varying degrees of transparency using the Mixer and Fill panels – click on the individual paint pots in the gradient and alter their transparency levels (you may want to save the gradient first to avoid overwriting Flash's default gradients):

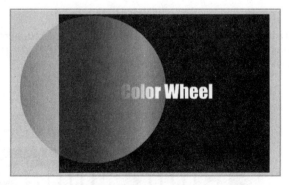

MULTICOLOR, VARIABLE TRANSPARENCY GRADIENT

5. Now place the circle so that the right half of the circle covers the text block completely:

6. Group the circle so that it's tweenable. On the circle layer add a key frame at frame 50 and create a motion tween, entering a clockwise rotation value of 1 in the Frame panel. (Don't forget to make the text layer the same length as the circle layer.)

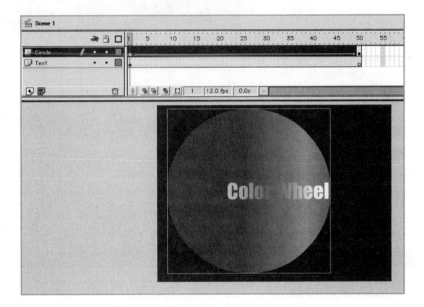

7. On frame 50, open up the Frame Actions window and add a gotoAndPlay(1) command.

8. Now create a similar animated circle in another layer, but this time place the circle's center point on the opposite side of the text, and set it to rotate *counter clockwise*:

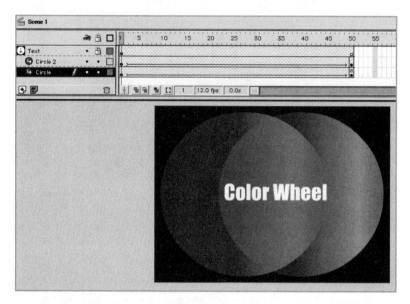

TWO MULTICOLOR, ROTATING GRADIENTS

Using this technique, the two colors in the wheels will add together to make the color of the text, which will be constantly changing.

9. Make the text layer a mask, and the other two layers *masked*:

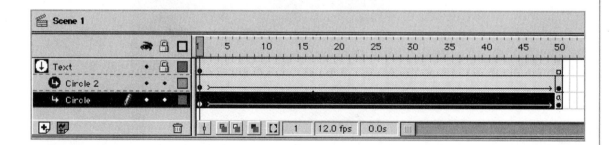

10. Play back the movie and take a look at the effect.

COLOR WHEEL IN MOTION

How subtle the effect is depends on the difference in the colors and transparency you chose, and the speed of the animation. Try this effect using different colors, or patterns – two striped patterns look very good together.

Masks and ActionScript

We've put a lot of things behind masks so far, and animating objects behind a mask can create some great effects. But it can also be a lot of work. For instance, our cloud effect looked pretty good, but if you wanted to make the cloud movement look really natural and non-repetitive, you would have to spend a long time tweaking the animation. Luckily for us, it's possible to control objects on masked layers with ActionScript – and this is what we're going to look at next.

Duplication Effects: Bubble Effect

For this effect, I want to create some text that has bubbles rising in the background, a little like looking into a fish tank. I'll set up the text the same way as in the cloud movie, with outline and mask layers. However, instead of using a motion-tweened cloud layer, I'm going to create a movie clip containing random rising bubbles.

1. Start by setting up the text mask and outline layers just like in the cloud movie, positioning your text roughly in the center of the stage. Using some blue colors here would look very aquatic:

We now need to make a movie clip that will generate all of the bubbles for us.

2. Create a new movie clip and call it bubble.

3. In your movie clip, draw a bubble. You could go back to Photoshop to make a photo-realistic bubble, or you could opt for the cartoon look again and draw a circle in Flash. Mine's blue with a white surround and a conventional bubble highlight:

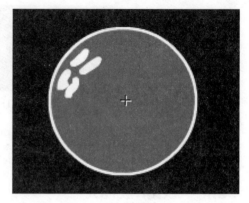

4. Create another new movie clip and call this one manyBubbles. Give it a new layer called actions and make three key frames on this layer.

The first key frame will hold the initialization script, the second the guts of our bubble producing script, and the third will loop back to the second frame to make sure that those bubbles just keep on coming.

On the first key frame, then, we need to set up some of the variables that will make our bubbles work. Here's the code:

```
ba=new Array();
howmany=0;
counter=20;
rate=4.0;
```

First, we need an array to hold a representation of all of our bubbles. For those of you still new to the idea of an array, you can think about it in simple terms as a list. This list has a number of items in it, and you access a particular item by referencing the list name followed by a specific item number in square brackets. Thus the tenth item on a list called testArray would be accessed by the statement testarray[10].

The command ba=new Array creates a new array called ba. Luckily for us, Flash 5 has a built-in Array object that we can base our own arrays on. The ba = new Array() statement says to Flash 'use your generic Array object as a template to create me an array called ba'. So ba will automatically inherit all the array-like characteristics that we need.

To accompany this array we need two counters: the first, called howmany, will track the number of bubbles, and we'll initialize this to zero; second, we have a variable called counter, which we'll use to space out the creation of our bubbles – this is initialized to an arbitrarily large number. In this case, 20 will do just fine, but you can alter this to suit your taste once you've got the FLA up and running. I've also set up a variable called `rate`, which we'll use to determine the rate at which the bubbles are manufactured.

5. Make sure that you've got the following script in the first keyframe of the manybubbles movie clip's actions layer:

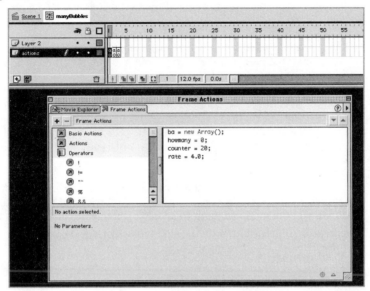

6. In the next keyframe on the actions layer (frame 2) add the script that actually makes the bubbles. I'll admit it, this script might look a little nasty to the uninitiated. Here it is in full (you can check it out in the Bubbles.fla file, too):

```
if (counter>=20) {
    howmany++;
    duplicateMovieClip (bubble, "bubble"+howmany, howmany);
    ba[howmany] = this["bubble"+howmany];
    ba[howmany]._x = random(600)-300;
    ba[howmany]._y = 100;
    ba[howmany].rate = random(3)+1;
    ba[howmany]._xscale = random(90)+10;
    ba[howmany]._yscale = ba[howmany]._xscale;
    counter = 0;
} else {
    counter++;
}
for (i=0; i<=howmany; i++) {

    if (ba[i]._y<-100) {
        removeMovieClip (ba[i]);
        ba.splice(i, 1);
        howmany--;
```

continues overleaf

```
        } else {ba[i]._y -= ba[i].rate;}
}
```

This is a little long, so we're going to take time to go through it to see exactly what's happening. As I said, the aim is not that you can perfectly repeat these exercises, but that they open your eyes to some of the possibilities and techniques that are there for you.

The script is divided up into two main sections. The first part (the if...else loop) creates new bubbles, and the second segment animates the *existing* bubbles.

The first decision we have to make in this code is 'how many bubbles do we want to make?' This is where the counter variable we set up in frame 1 comes in. We're going to increment the counter each time we run through the loop, and we're only going to make a new bubble when the counter gets up to twenty – otherwise we'd be generating a carwash full of bubbles. Obviously, you can change the counter variable value to make more or less bubbles.

So the first thing we do in the script is say if(counter>=20). If this condition is satisfied we move on through the body of the if loop. If the counter is still less than 20, we skip the loop and jump to an else statement that adds 1 to the counter:

```
} else {
    counter++;
}
```

Inside of the if loop itself, we create a new bubble – using the duplicateMovie clip command – and initialize it:

```
howmany++;
    duplicateMovie clip (bubble, "bubble"+howmany, howmany);
    ba[howmany] = this["bubble"+howmany];
```

As you can see, the first thing we do is increment the howmany variable. You'll recall that we initialized howmany to zero, so now that we find ourselves making our first bubble, it makes sense to increment it by 1. The next line is the duplicate bubble command. The general syntax is duplicateMovie clip (*movie clip, new name, level*). In this particular movie, we're duplicating the bubble movie clip and giving it a new name. The three parameters that we pass the duplicateMovie command are therefore:

- Movie clip = bubble

- New name = the literal variable "bubble", concatenated with the current value of howmany

- Level = the current value of howmany

The third line...

```
ba[howmany] = this["bubble"+howmany];
```

...simply takes that new movie clip and puts it into the array so that we can reference it later.

The next step is to initialize the newly created bubble on the screen. All that this involves is setting its scale, x and y position, and the speed at which it will move:

```
ba[howmany]._x = random(600)-300;
ba[howmany]._y = 100;
ba[howmany].rate = random(3)+1;
ba[howmany]._xscale = random(90)+10;
ba[howmany]._yscale = ba[howmany]._xscale;
```

Notice that we're accessing this bubble through its entry in the ba array. We've set the x position to a random number between -300 and 300, and the y position to 100. We set the rate to a random number between 1 and 4, and the scale to a number between 10 and 100. These bubbles will have a lot more variety in terms of position, size, and speed compared to the 'hard coded' tweened clouds that we animated in the earlier example. The last step in the if statement is to reset the counter to zero. And then there's the else statement that increments the counter if we *don't* make a new bubble on this loop through the if statement.

The second part of this script moves each bubble on the screen. To do this we use a for loop to iterate through the bubbles, and move them up a certain number of pixels based on their rate value. If we keep on making new bubbles without deleting old ones, we're going to slow down the animation and – eventually – run out of memory. To avoid this, we'll delete each bubble once it moves above the text. Look at the for loop below:

```
for (i=1; i<=howmany; i++) {
if (ba[i]._y<-100) {
    removeMovie clip (ba[i]);
    ba.splice(i, 1);
    howmany--;
}
else { ba[i]._y -= ba[i].rate;
}
```

As you can see, we simply loop through each bubble instance using the array again, and the value of howmany to generate a loop control variable, i. We check to see if the y position is less than −100, and if it *is*, we delete it. If it's not, we increment its position. You may well have text that is a little different to mine, so if the bubbles don't make it to the top of your text before bursting when you test this, you need to increase this value. An alternative approach would be to turn the text into a movie clip and code the movie clip's position and size to calculate the 'cut-off' point where the bubbles 'burst'.

239

7.   Still in the actions layer of the manyBubbles movie clip, add a `gotoAndPlay(2)` action to the third frame. This will loop back to the script in frame 2. We're almost done.

8.   Create a new layer inside manyBubbles. Drag an instance of the bubble movie clip that we prepared earlier out of the library and onto this layer, placing it at the edge of the screen:

9.   Give this instance of the bubble movie clip the instance name of bubble. This is important, as this is what the script above refers to – so if you miss this step then your bubble will just sit there and not do very much at all!

10.   Create a new layer called masked. Drag an instance of manyBubbles out onto this layer and position it to the left of main stage:

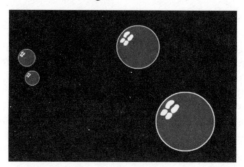

11. Test your movie now and you should see some lovely bubbles rising up the screen:

12. The final stage is to turn the text into a mask, play the movie, and watch those bubbles rise behind the text:

The nice part about this effect is that you can re-use a lot of the code any time that you want to duplicate an object or group of objects and move them across the screen, whether you want bubbles, clouds, birds or pretty much anything else really.

Text Effects

You may have noticed that most of the effects that I've presented so far are text-based. This is because, in a professional work situation, you're more likely to need a cool text transition than a lightning bolt effect. We're going to concentrate exclusively on text in this section.

Simple Text Effects

The first kind of text effect that we'll look at in this section is the type that treats a complete line of text as a single object. This is probably the least versatile category of text effects, because what you can do with a single block of text – all one object – is limited to effects that involve drawing on the screen and Flash's built in transformation and tweening tools. Later, we'll see that more extensive effects can be achieved with text that's broken up into individual letters.

Let's look at our first simple effect.

Flipping Text

This flipping effect simulates the effect of a spinning sign, like the kind that you used to see outside gas stations or stores. Those signs used to have a different message on each side, and when the wind blew the sign would rotate, clanking, and you'd be delighted to see two different messages every second or so. And then a tumbleweed would blow past and Ry Cooder would hit that slide guitar. In Flash, we can use some very simple skew transformations to give some text a kind of 'two and a half dimensional' quality:

Take a look at FlippingText.fla on the CD to see this in action.

Let's build it.

1. Start by creating two movie clips in a fresh new movie, each containing a single static text field. Type a word in each field in a fairly large font size.

2. In the main movie timeline, create a separate layer for each 'word' movie clip.

    This effect works by using a horizontal skew. The movie starts with the first word displayed, and then that word skews until it's invisible – imagine the rectangular text box morphing and flattening into a line. Once the first word has become invisible, the second word skews from a line into a rectangular box.

3. On the first layer, insert a keyframe at frame 10 and drag the movie clip for the word that you want to appear *second* out of Library and onto the stage. Insert further keyframes at frames 24 and 36.

4. Select the text at frame 10, and use the Transform panel to set the horizontal skew to –90. At the second keyframe, set the horizontal skew to 0, and at the third, set it to 90.

5. On the second layer drag the word movie clip that you want to appear *first* out of the library and onto the stage at frame 1, and then insert keyframes at frames 12, 34, and 48. Use the Info panel if necessary to make sure that the two words are pretty much lined up. I've put mine right at the center of the stage.

6. In the keyframes at 12, 34, and 48, set the horizontal skew to 90, −90, 0 respectively.

7. Now make the two main transitions on each layer into motion tweens – these should be between frames 10 and 24 and frames 24 and 36 on layer 1 and between frames 1 and 12 and frames 34 and 48 on layer 2.

    If you play your movie, you should see the two words flipping. You can try adding a few variations to this effect. It's particularly effective if you use the same *word* for each movie clip, but render them in different colors. Extending this idea, using a skew value of plus and minus 180 on the second word will make that word appear upside down, further enhancing the idea that you are see both sides of that old sign...

For our next example – blurry text!

Blurry Text

There are several ways you can make text objects appear to lose or gain focus, and this can create some beguiling effects. The simplest method by far is to create a copy of the text and use the Soften Fill Edges menu option to blur it. This copy is then faded in to give the impression of the text blurring, or faded out to make the text appear to sharpen. Let's try this out in an example.

1. Type some text on the first layer of a new movie – anything between a word and a short sentence will do. Then break it apart and duplicate the layer twice.

2. Add a blank frame on the bottom layer around frame 30, and then lock and hide the layer so that you can modify the top two layers more easily.

3. Start with the middle layer. You might want to hide the top layer so that you don't accidentally select anything on it. Select everything on the middle layer and modify it using the (by now familiar) soften edges command – the pixel distance is up to you. The further out you go (the higher the number in the Distance box) – the blurrier the text will look.

4. Once you're happy with the way the blurry text looks, convert it into a movie clip, and use the Effects tab to ensure that the Alpha transparency is 100. Add a keyframe at frame 15, and set the transparency to 0. Then add a motion tween between the two keyframes to make the blurry text fade (in conjunction with the other layers) into the regular text.

5. You can now hide this layer and reveal the *top* layer. On this layer, use the soften edges command on the text again, this time with a pixel distance of less than 5.

    This part is a little bit tricky, as we only want the *outline* of the letters. While softened edges *seems* to blur a shape, what it really does is duplicate the object several times, adding more transparency and scale to each successive layer.

6.   After you've applied the soften edges function, click on the background and then click in the center of one of the letters (you may need to zoom in if your letters are small). You should be able to select the center fill and delete it while leaving the edges intact. Delete the center of each letter in this way. Once you've finished your 'outline only' graphic, select it all and convert it to a movie clip – again, you may have to hide the other layers to see it properly.

7.   Add a keyframe on the same (top) layer at frame 30. Use the Transform palette to adjust the scale of the outline on the last frame – I set mine to 200 horizontal and 200 vertical. Add a motion tween between 1 and 30, and you're all set. (An alternative here is to scale the *first* frame instead of the last one.)

Test the movie and see the results of your hard work – this effect can look great, especially if you have several words right next to each other and stagger the animation so that successive words fade into clarity.

Now let's try another simple text effect – an outline effect.

Outline Effect

We're going to make use of the soften edges command again here.

1.   Start as always by creating a layer with some text on it. This is quite a busy effect; so one or two big words should do nicely. Break apart the text, copy it, and lock the text layer. Now make a new layer and paste the copied text 'in place'.

2.   With the text on the new layer selected, soften the edges. You need to specify at least 2 Steps and a 2 pixel Distance. You can experiment with different settings here – it all depends on how fuzzy an outline you want. Delete the center fills and, when you have your outline, convert it to a movie clip. Make three duplicates of this layer.

You should now have five layers in total, four of which have the outline text on them:

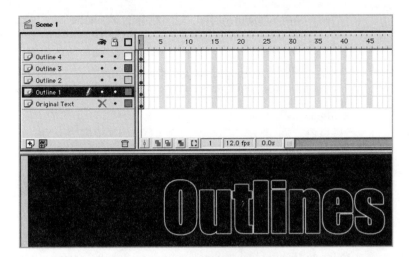

3. Now insert keyframes (and move around the default keyframe) on each of the outline text layers so that the *first* outline is visible between frames 1 and 10, the second between 5 and 15, the third between 10 and 20, and the fourth between 15 and 25:

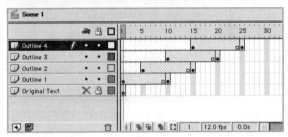

4. Once you've got this set up, change the size of each of the outlines layers' movie clips to 100% at the beginning of their ten-frame life, and 125% at the end of it. Then add a motion tween to each of the four transitions so that all of the outlines gradually scale up to 125%. Now set all of the 'end position' movie clip instances to have 0 alpha.

5. Add frames to the original text layer so that it's extended to frame 25 too.

    If you test the movie at this stage, it looks OK, but I really want it to play for a little longer. Instead of duplicating more layers, let's use a little scripting.

6. Create a new actions layer for the script and, in frame one, set up a variable called counter and initialize it at zero:

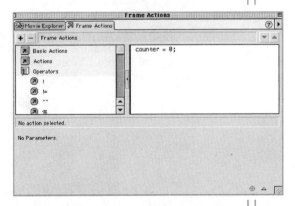

At the moment, frames 10 and 15 look pretty much the same. What I want to do is set up a loop that will repeat these frames a specified amount of times, and then go on to finish the animation.

7. In the actions layer, on frame 25 (which should be the last in your animation), add a stop action. Now add the following script to frame 15:

```
if(counter<=5){
counter++;
gotoAndPlay (10);
}
else{
gotoAndPlay (16);
}
```

As you can see, this script uses a simple if...else action to generate the desire value in the variable counter we set up earlier. When it's looped five times, this script goes to frame 16, after which there are no more looping commands, so it continues on to stop action in frame 25.

8. Test your movie and you should see your text pulsate and then stop – the perfect sort of effect to attract a user's attention and then stop before it becomes annoying or unnecessary. This is especially effective if you crank the frame rate up high. You could, for example, save this kind of element as a movie clip and put the movie clip into the Over state of a button. Clearly, you can change the number of loops specified in the first line to fine-tune the length of the effect.

More Sophisticated Text Effects

We've just been seeing what can be done with text when you apply effects to whole words and lines of text. The *real* fun begins when you start to break these text blocks into individual layers and give each letter its own layer. Before you start worrying about how much work this entails, try the next few exercises and see how much power this gives you in terms of the results you can achieve.

Layered Text

1. Open a new movie and type your text on the first layer. You may or may not want to leave this layer in the finished effect, but it's essential at this point to have a complete copy of the text to start from. Break the text apart:

2. Now comes the fun part. Duplicate this layer repeatedly, so that you end up with one layer for each letter. Once the copies are made, go into the original version and delete all the letters except the first. You'll probably need to hide all the other layers except the one you're working in, or things will get very confusing indeed!

3. On the original layer, select the remaining letter and group it. On the next layer up, delete all the letters save for the second and group it, and so on until you have your original layer with the first letter, and each subsequent letter on its own layer:

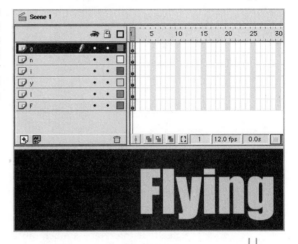

The finished effect will have the letters on the individual layers making a staggered entry, so that one letter comes in at a slightly different time.

4. To do this, add keyframes to each of the layers at frame 15 and change the scaling of each letter in each frame 1 – I've gone for 200%. For added effect, try converting the text to outlines in each frame 1, too. Now move each frame 1 letter off to the side somewhere:

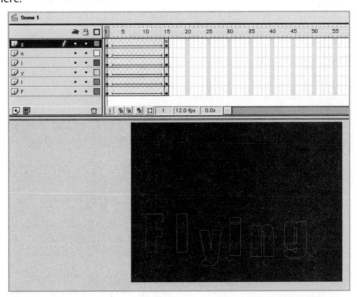

5. Add motion tweens to each layer.

6. Select each motion tweened set of frames and stagger them out along the timeline – with about a fifty percent overlap – so that the letters appear one by one, and add frames to the end of each layer so that they're all the same length:

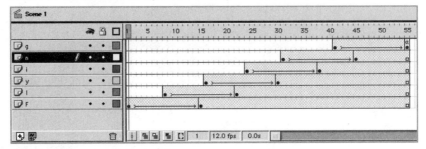

I've inserted a stop action at the end of the movie, too.

7. Test the movie and watch the letter outlines fly into place.

Again, if you crank up the frame rate (the FLA on the CD is at a crunchy 90fps) you'll see that the effect is much more convincing.

You might be tempted to think that there should be an easier way to do this sort of thing without resorting to the use of all these multiple layers and manual manipulation of individual letters. Well, the good news is that there is a better way. As with so many of the good things in Flash, it involves using ActionScript. Picking up the principles of manipulating text with scripts will bring some great effects within your reach.

Let's explore this idea with an effect that'll take a string of text, automatically split it up into separate letters, and mess them around on the screen.

Dynamic Text with ActionScript

We are going to use a script to create moving text on the screen, and we're going to hook that text up to the mouse so that the text will truck around the screen like a hyperactive caterpillar. This means a fair bit of scripting work up front, but you'll find that most of what we are doing is highly reusable, unlike the more mechanical layers and tweens approach.

1. In another new movie, create a movie clip – I've called mine seed – and place a dynamic text field in it. Set the Variable field to equal text:

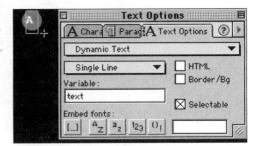

2. You can put a letter in it for now to see how it looks. Set the size, color and font the way you want – this will ultimately be applied to all the letters in the text string that we supply it with. I've chosen a font size of 14 to keep things nice and compact, and white text for clarity. I recommend that you use a nice simple font, such as Courier, to start out with, as it will make things easier to arrange later. We'll be using this movie clip as the basis for all the letters that get displayed on the screen, so the setup you create here will carry over.

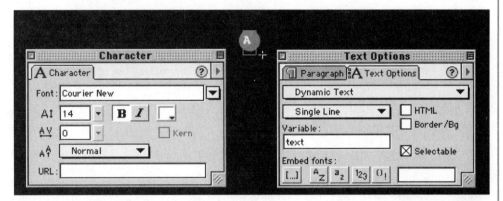

3. You can also add a background graphic to your letter. I'm using a simple circle graphic behind the text box to provide a little contrast and interest in the finished movie.

4. Place the seed movie clip on the main stage outside the visible stage area. In my example movie, I'm using letters that look like balls, so I named this instance of my seed movie clip ball0. You will see why I have the zero there in a moment.

Now that we've built the basic seed movie clip, we need to start writing the script that'll work with it. The script part of this effect is divided up into two parts: setting up the text, and then animating it.

5. Create a new layer in your main movie and call it actions.

6. Start out by defining an array. I love to use arrays to organize information. We need a list to store all of the individual letter movie clips we're going to be making in a second.

7. Add this statement in the Frame Actions window at frame 1 of the actions layer:

```
balls = new Array
```

Remember that this is just the way you ask Flash to construct a new array. Now that we have a place to store references to our movie clips, we need to define exactly what content we want those movie clips to contain. Remember how in the previous examples we wrote text out on one layer before we split it up? The next part of the script will be the equivalent of that, except that this time Flash will do all the breaking up for us in code. All I need to do is put my text string in a variable.

8. Add this next line of code to the script:

```
theText = "Dynamic Text"
```

Here, theText is just a plain old variable, and Dynamic Text is the actual text that I want to appear on screen and manipulate for my effect.

Remember that I already have one movie clip instance on the stage called ball0. We're going to use this clip to store our first letter, making use of the text field inside the movie clip. Then we'll duplicate this movie clip for each additional letter.

9. Set the first item in the balls array as the ball0 movie clip by adding this code as the next line in your script:

```
balls[0] = ball0
```

Remember that we put a text field in that original movie clip, with an associated variable called text? Our next problem now becomes how to get the first letter of our dynamic text string (which is Dynamic Text in this case) into that text field and display it. We're lucky again, because Flash provides us with a text function that will return us any character in a text string, based upon its **index value** – that is, its position in the string. Therefore, if we say balls[0].text = theText.charAt(0) then Flash will take the first letter of theText (the index values are zero-based) and place it in the input text field in our movie clip.

All we would need to do next is repeat those last two steps for each letter. We could, knowing the length of the input string is, code something like this...

```
balls[1] = ball1;
balls[1].text = theText.charAt(1);
balls[2] = ball2;
balls[2].text = theText.charAt(2);
balls[3] = ball3;
balls[3].text = theText.charAt(3);
    . . .
```

...repeating the two basic statements until we covered all of the letters in the string. However, that looks like a lot of repetitive work, and the whole purpose of this exercise is to avoid that.

10. To make this a whole lot easier, we're going to use a loop. Before we show you the loop, add this code to your script:

```
balls[0] = ball0;
balls[0].text = theText.charAt(0);
```

What we're doing here first is adding a reference to our single movie clip instance to the array as item 0 in that array. The second line uses the charAt function to set that same movie clip's text variable to the first letter of the text string – 'D', in this case. So we now have a movie clip that contains the first letter of the text, plus the graphic background that we built into the original clip.

If you pull that instance onto the visible area of the stage right now and run the movie, you'll see the letter D appear against the graphic background.

Now that we've established the groundwork, we can set up the loop that will process all of the other characters in the text string.

11. Add this loop code to your existing script:

```
for (i=1; i<theText.length; i++) {
    duplicateMovieClip (this.ball0, "ball"+i, i);
    balls[i] = eval("ball"+i);
    balls[i].text = theText.charAt(i);
    balls[i]._x = 20*i;
}
```

In the opening line we're defining the conditions that'll control how many times the loop runs. We set a loop counter, i, to an initial value of 1, and then tell Flash to run the loop as long i is less than the number of characters in the theText variable:

```
i<theText.length;
```

Note that this uses the in-built length property that every string variable has. The i++ increments i by 1 at the end of each iteration of the loop.

So much for initializing the loop – now for the body of the process. The next line of code...

```
duplicateMovie clip (this.ball0, "ball"+i, i)
```

...duplicates the original movie clip, creating a copy of ball0 and naming it by concatenating the literal string "ball" with the current value of the counter i, which means that successive iterations of the loop will generate movie clips called ball1, ball2, ball3 and so on.

Duplicating the clips is only part of the process. We also want to add them to the array so that we can manipulate them using their array index numbers. That's what happens in the next line:

```
balls[i] = eval("ball"+i);
```

This evaluates the movie clip represented by the combination of "ball" and i, and creates a reference in the array for that movie clip.

Now that we can access the movie clip through the array, we use the `charAT` function, plus the counter value ...

```
balls[i].text = theText.charAt(i);
```

...to set the latest duplicated movie clip's `text` field to the next letter in the `theText` variable. The last line in the loop sets the initial `x` position value for the new movie clip:

```
balls[i]._x = 20*i;
```

Here, we use the counter, `i`, multiplied by a constant number of pixels that I call the **offset**. Put simply, the offset is the number of pixels between the center of `ball0` and the center of `balln`. You'll see that I've specified the offset here as 20, which works with the fairly small circles I've been using, but you might need to alter this value to fit the size of background graphic and text you use. As you'll see if you try it, without the offset, the letters will separate when you move the mouse but land on top of one another when the mouse comes to rest. An alternative here would be to store this offset value in a variable instead of writing it directly in the script.

That's the end of the movie duplication script, which should now look like this:

```
balls = new Array

theText = "Dynamic Text"

balls[0] = ball0

balls[0] = ball0;
balls[0].text = theText.charAt(0);

for (i=1; i<theText.length; i++) {
    duplicateMovieClip (this.ball0, "ball"+i, i);
    balls[i] = eval("ball"+i);
    balls[i].text = theText.charAt(i);
    balls[i]._x = 20*i;
}
```

If you run your movie now, and depending on where you've positioned your original seed movie clip, you'll be able to see each of the individual letters (including the space) displayed in their own movie clip:

We now have an array of letters in movie clips, but there's still some work to be done. We need to define a script to tell the letters where to position themselves and what to *do* on the screen.

There are so many effects that you could use with the letters – any effects based on springs, gravity and other physics-related systems work really well in these cases if you have the math knowledge to write the code. I want to make a simpler effect, so I'm going to make the string of text follow my mouse around the screen. This is quite a common effect these days, but it's still instructive and fun to do.

To create this effect, you have to append one line of code to the end of the existing script.

12. Add this code to the end of the script in frame 1:

```
startDrag ("ball0", true)
```

This will let us drag the first letter, the D, in the `ball0` movie clip.

Run the movie and you'll see that the D movie clip will follow the mouse around.

What we need to do now is make each of the other letters follow the letter immediately preceding it. This effect is very loosely based on gravitational attraction, but don't worry, the math is all done for you. This script will be in frame 2 of the main movie timeline.

13. Add this script in the Frame Actions window at frame 2:

```
speed = 2;
friction = 0.45;
offset = 20

for (i=1; i< theText.length; i++) {
    Xdiff = (balls[i-1]._x-balls[i]._x);
    Ydiff = (balls[i-1]._y-balls[i]._y);
    Xdiff += offset;

    balls[i].x_rate += (Xdiff/speed);
    balls[i].y_rate += (Ydiff/speed);
    balls[i].x_rate *= friction;
    balls[i].y_rate *= friction;
    balls[i]._x += balls[i].x_rate;
    balls[i]._y += balls[i].y_rate;

    updateAfterEvent(mousemove);
}
```

As you can see the first thing we do is to set three variables. Speed defines how quickly one number chases another, and friction determines how much energy the balls lose as they approach the previous letter. Finally, offset is used to help govern the distant between the moving clips on the screen. Note that for speed, higher numbers mean slower-moving letters. The settings here work pretty well but as a general rule when you code stuff like this, experiment in small increments until you get it right.

The purpose of this script is to determine an x and y increment that will move the movie clips around on the stage in an appropriate way. To do this, the script finds out how far away the current letter is from the previous letter, and then takes a small step *toward* that letter.

First we set up the loop to carry out this set of actions for as many letters as there are in our old friend theText:

```
for (i=1; i< theText.length; i++) {
```

The first two lines in the loop itself determine the distance difference values for x and y:

```
Xdiff = (balls[i-1]._x-balls[i]._x);
Ydiff = (balls[i-1]._y-balls[i]._y);
```

These values are derived by taking the x position property of each movie clip in the array...

```
balls[i-1]._x
```

...and subtracting the x property of the next movie clip in the array:

```
-balls[i]._x
```

And similarly for the movie clips' y position properties.

So, in the first iteration of the loop the code will compare the positions of the clips referenced in the array at balls(0) and balls(1), and assign the difference in their x and y positions to the Xdiff and Ydiff variables.

After adding the offset value to the x difference...

```
Xdiff += offset;
```

...we then increment each of the movie clips' movement rates by a fraction of the x and y differences and the friction variable value:

```
balls[i].x_rate += (Xdiff/speed);
balls[i].y_rate += (Ydiff/speed);
balls[i].x_rate *= friction;
balls[i].y_rate *= friction;
```

If left to their own devices, the balls would take a lot of time to slow down, so we give them a little help by degrading their rates every loop using this calculation, and make them move a little more easily by adding the x_ and y_ rates to the x and y values of the current movie clip:

```
balls[i]._x += balls[i].x_rate;
balls[i]._y += balls[i].y_rate;
```

And that completes the first iteration of the loop, which then moves on to the next movie clip.

The final line in the script...

```
updateAfterEvent(mousemove);
}
```

...ensures that Flash applies these changes each time that the mouse moves. Phew.

14. In frame 3, just add a simple:

```
gotoAndPlay(2)
```

This will keep the movie repeating this process.

15. Finally – and **absolutely critically!** – add frames to the balls layer so that it's the same length as the actions layer:

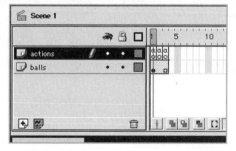

This effect won't work unless you do!

16. Try your movie and watch those balls and letters swarm:

Now experiment with different friction, offset, and speed values and see what effect these have on the behavior of the movie clips.

Without modifying the scripts too much, you could tell the ball0 movie clip where to go directly in the script instead of dragging it. Or you could assign each letter a final destination, and have them drift toward that point instead of the previous letter.

This example gives you an idea of the kind of things that it's possible to do by taking some text, breaking it apart programmatically, and using it inside dynamically created movie clips. Bear in mind that you can equally apply these principles to text that a user enters by taking data from an input text box, assigning it to a variable or variables, and manipulating those variables with this kind of code.

For the last example in this chapter, let's combine a masking effect with some script-manipulated text.

Masking Scripted Text

We're going to look at using a mask to put some small text inside some big text. Just to keep things interesting, we're going to make the fill text scroll from right to left, too.

1.   Start by setting up the text mask. As in a number of the previous examples, I've used the solid text on one layer as the mask layer, and created a separate outlines layer with softened edges to frame the mask:

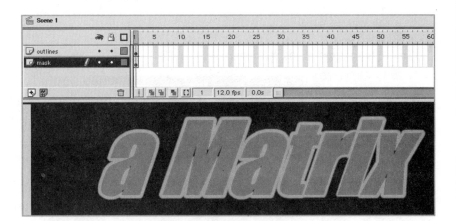

2. Now create a movie clip called maskedText. Inside this movie, add an empty dynamic text box that's the same width as the text on the mask layer. Make sure that you include the font outlines for this text box by clicking on Include entire font outline button in the Embed Fonts section of the panel:

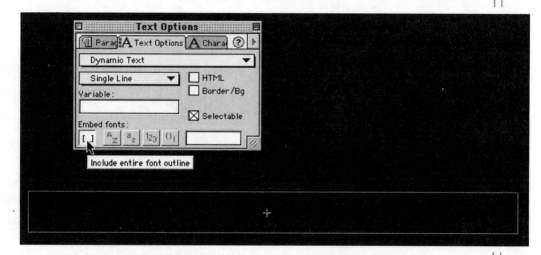

The masking effect won't work on the text unless the outlines are included.

Now we need to create another movie clip that'll contain the small text that will be generated in a script and scrolled across the screen behind the mask. This clip will be embedded inside the maskedText clip. In each iteration of a loop in a script, we'll create multiple copies of the small text clip, and add random text to one end of each line in this embedded clip while deleting a character on the other, causing the text to scroll.

3. Add a new movie clip called textLine. Create a dynamic text box inside it, roughly the same size as the one inside the masked text movie clip. Use a smallish font – I've gone for 14 point Courier. Give the text box the variable name text, and ensure that you embed the fonts again:

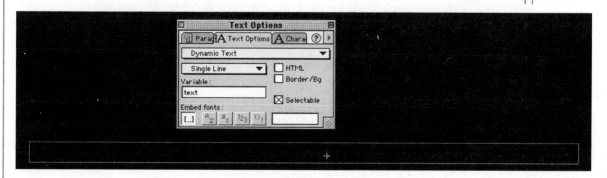

4.   Place an instance of textLine inside the maskedText clip and call the instance text0.

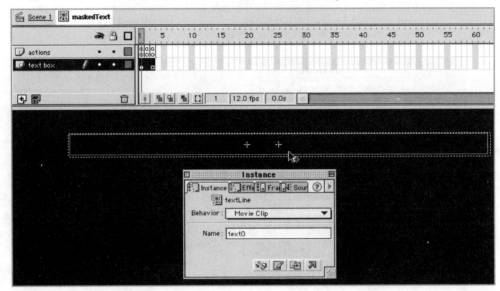

Now for the script that'll make the text live and breathe. This script goes inside the maskedText movie clip.

The structure of this effect is very similar to that of the bubble effect we looked at way back in the chapter. First we have to initialize our variables.

5.   Add an actions layer to the maskedText movie clip and insert this script in frame 1:

```
textArray = new Array();
textArray[0] = text0;
Counter =text0._y;
```

Here, we create a new array to house the text that we'll generate, and place the text0 movie (which is an instance of text line, remember) in position zero of that array. We then set up a counter variable to store the position of the first line of text.

The next step is to duplicate more of the lines from the original.

6.   Add the following code to the end of the existing script:

```
for (i=1; i<=20; i++) {
    Counter+=12;
    duplicateMovieclip (text0, "text"+i, i);
    textArray[i] = eval("text"+i);
    textArray[i]._y = Counter;
    textArray[i].text = i;
}
```

This will create multiple copies of the text-holding movie behind the mask. The only difference in this code from the duplication code in the bubble movie is the fifth line that moves the new movie clip down 12 pixels from the last one.

The last thing we need to do in this frame's script is fill all of the lines up with some random text before we start scrolling. (The code that we'll put in the next frame will add a letter to the right and remove one from the left, which will leave us with empty lines if we do not fill them up first.)

7. Add this final piece of script to frame 1:

```
for (j=0; j<=100; j++){
for (i=0; i<=20; i++) {
newChar=chr(random(150)+1);
textArray[i].text+=newChar;
}}
```

In order to generate random characters, what I'm doing here is translating a random number directly into ASCII text:

```
newChar=chr(random(150)+1);
```

This gives me a really high tech look, with all kinds of weird characters. Then I simply add the letter to the string:

```
textArray[i].text+=newChar;
```

In the second frame of the masked text movie clip, we want to run through the list of lines of text in the array, and then add a letter and delete a letter in each one.

8. Add this code to frame 2 to achieve that:

```
for (i=0; i<=20; i++) {
newChar=chr(random(100)+1);
textArray[i].text+=newChar;
textArray[i].text=textArray[i].text.substr( 1,textArray[i].text.length );
}
```

This is very similar to the code we used to fill the lines in the first place. Only the last line...

```
textArray[i].text=textArray[i].text.substr( 1, textArray[i].text.length );
```

...is really new. Here, we use the substr command to delete the first character in the string.

9.   In the third frame of the actions layer add this command:

```
gotoAndPlay(2)
```

This loops the animation back and produces the finished effect.

10.   Increase the length of the original layer in maskedText so that it's the same length as the actions layer.

11.   Now drag an instance of masked text out onto the stage in a new layer called masked. Like this:

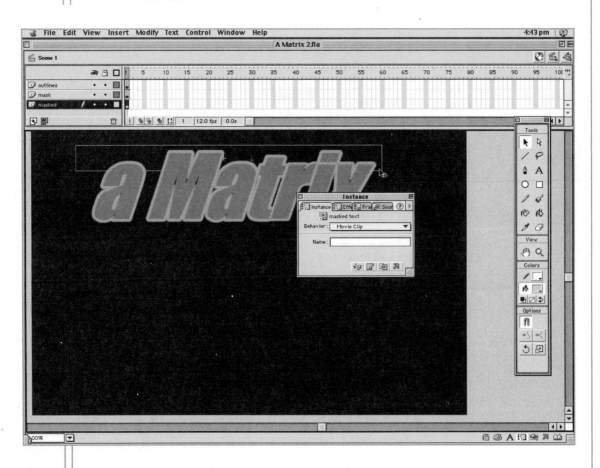

12. Set the mask and masked layers so that the text is behind your original mask...

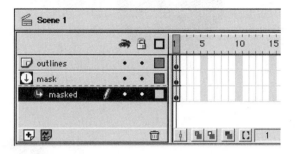

..and run the movie and see how it looks.

Now you can start messing with the precise movie clip positions, text sizes and so on to attain exactly the result that you're after.

Conclusion

With all the effects in this chapter, don't stop here, but use them as a stepping-stone to better ideas and effects. Mess around with the variable settings and movie clip placements to see the effects these have, and add extra bits of code to customize the movies.

If you see a great effect on the Web, have a look at it and see if you can figure out how it works, and then take it a step further. *Stealing* someone else's ideas isn't clever, but inspiration is freely available out there. Have fun.

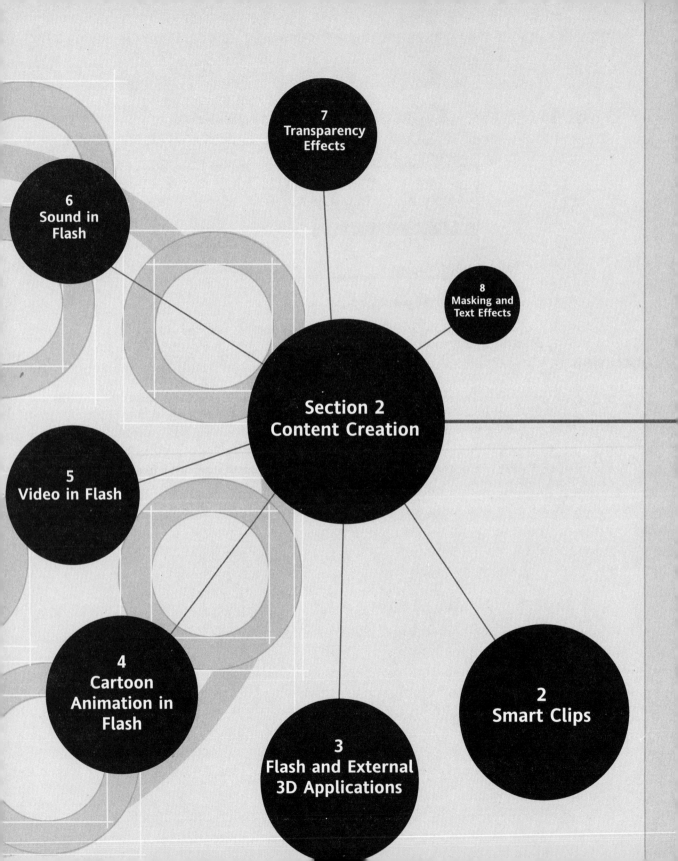

Chapter 9
Buttons
and Menus

Flash is an interactive medium. It provides you with a way to express your ideas, your artistic visions, and your product demonstrations in such an authentic and immediate way that you can almost forget you're looking at something web-based. However, the linear animation that you see in splash screens and banner advertisements will only get you so far. Learning how to create seamless, compelling interaction is the key to unleashing the full power of Flash.

This chapter will explore some of the many ways in which you can add interactivity to your Flash movies, but without going into heavy ActionScripting. Through clever use of Flash's basic functionality, you'll learn how to create dynamic buttons and other interface elements, how to build your movies so that they respond to the user's mouse, and how to streamline your sites' navigation with complete menu systems.

The two main interface components that we'll be looking at in this chapter are buttons and menus, and ways in which you can combine them to create more dynamic interfaces for your web sites. We'll start off by looking at buttons.

Buttons

Buttons are the basic unit of interactivity in Flash. In fact, until Flash 5 was released, buttons were the *only* way for the user to interact with a Flash movie – and even now, the button remains the most important way to give users some direct control over what happens in your movies.

The default button handling that Flash provides through the Up, Over, Down, and Hit frames is helpful for generating what you might call the minimum a user should expect from a button: some indication that it's active, and positive feedback that they've successfully clicked it. However, it's not difficult to augment the behavior of a button in ways that provide still better services to your users, and we'll look at some of these in this section. In particular, we'll be examining the effects that can be achieved by embedding movie clips in buttons, and by embedding buttons in movie clips.

Creating Buttons with Tooltips

When you're designing an interface for an application, space is at a premium. There's rarely enough room to position all of the elements in exactly the layout that you want them in. Often, for aesthetic and space-related reasons, designers use symbols rather than text to label their buttons. The job of a good interface designer is to make sure that the meaning of these icons is self-evident.

There is one trick that they use to make sure that the meanings of their icons are understood, and it can be seen in most commercial applications. In Flash, hold your mouse over one of the tools in the Tools window, and you'll see what I'm talking about: a small text box pops up near your mouse to give you more detail about that tool. These **tooltips** are priceless when you're designing an interface, and used effectively they can make a tremendous impact on your design.

As it turns out, it's very easy to add tooltips to your Flash buttons. The simplest technique of all would be to edit your buttons' Over states, and just add the text field. The problem with this is that the tooltip would appear as soon as the mouse was over the button, but what we *really* want is a slight delay between the instant when you roll over, and when the tooltip appears. One approach here would be to add a script to display the overlay, based on a timer function, but a very similar effect can be achieved by animating the button, through the use of an embedded movie clip.

Adding Tooltips to Buttons

To demonstrate this technique, we'll look at creating a Help button for a Flash movie that will display a tooltip if the mouse pointer hovers over it for a second. The basic button will consist of two graphic symbols containing the top of the button and its shadow respectively. We've already created the graphics for this example, and you can find them on the CD as `Tooltips.fla`. These symbols will be used as the basis for all of the button's states:

1. Drag the two graphic symbols out of the Library and onto the stage. Next, arrange them as shown, and convert them into a movie clip called Button_Movie.

2. Go into the new movie clip, and add a keyframe at frame 12:

The location of this keyframe on the timeline determines how long a delay will pass before our tooltip appears – twelve frames in a 12-frame-per-second movie will have the effect of pausing for 1 second, which is exactly what we're looking for.

3. Create a new layer called Tooltip, and insert a keyframe into frame 12. Now insert a Static text box slightly beneath and to the right of the square's center, containing the word Help:

> *You could type something more descriptive, but in general I recommend that you keep to the spirit of tooltips, and make the message short and to the point.*

You can also add a light-colored rectangle as a background for the tooltip.

4. Finally, open up the Frame Actions window for frame 12 of the Tooltip layer, and add a stop action so that the movie clip doesn't loop.

5. Now we're ready to make the button itself. Start by dragging another pair of the Top and Shadow symbols onto the main stage, and convert them into a new button symbol.

6. Open up the button, make sure that the graphics are laid out in the center of the stage, and add keyframes to all four of the states.

7. Next, delete the contents of the Over state, and replace it with an instance of your freshly produced movie clip. As long as the movie is aligned correctly with the symbols in the other frames (ours are set to 0,0), then any instances of this button will now have a descriptive tooltip that appears a second after the mouse has been moved over it, which is exactly the behavior that we required. It's this sort of detail that can bring an apllication to life

Buttons in Movie Clips

One aspect of Flash that confuses many new users of ActionScript is the difference between a movie clip and a button. Often, you want to create something that behaves like both, but by default, you can't detect whether the mouse has been clicked over a movie clip (not directly, anyway), and you can't name a button so that you can address it in your scripts.

To solve this problem, we can use the very simple technique of wrapping a button in a movie clip, and then using that movie clip in our movie just as we would have used the button – in a sense, this is the opposite of what we did in the last example. Through this technique, we're able to give the 'wrapped' button an instance name on the stage, apply color and alpha effects, and reference it in our ActionScript.

One particular example of where this functionality is useful is in the creation of draggable objects, where the goal is to make a small graphical object that, when clicked on, will stick to the mouse until the mouse button is released. The possibilities for this type of behavior are endless, and application can be found everywhere, from children's games to menu systems.

Creating a Draggable Button

Start this project by opening Draggable.fla from the CD. In the middle of the stage, you'll see an extremely straightforward Flash button, defined by the following four frames:

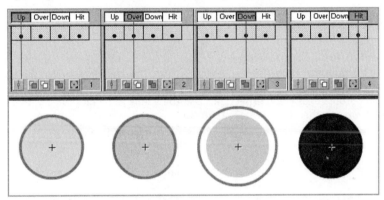

1. As explained above, to get the behavior that we want we need to embed an instance of the button in a new movie clip. This is as easy as selecting the button symbol on the stage and converting it into a movie clip called Drag_Button. If you test the movie at this point, you'll find that it operates in exactly the same way as an 'ordinary' button, but that's all about to change.

2. The 'drag-and-drop' effect is achieved by adding custom on (press) and on (release) handlers to the button – we want to pick the Flash button up when the mouse button is pressed, and then let go when the mouse button is released. The Flash functions that we need to do this are startDrag and stopDrag.

3. Bring up the button's Object Actions window, and add the following script:

```
on (press) {
    startDrag ("");
}
on (release) {
    stopDrag ();
}
```

In the `on (press)` handler, we're telling the `startDrag` function to specify the movie to be dragged – in this case, we've left it blank. Using an empty string tells Flash that you want to drag every object in the current timeline, and if we placed it on the main stage, the button would drag every other object visible on the stage at that moment. However, because we've placed the button in its own movie clip wrapper, it will drag everything *in that movie clip's timeline* – namely, the button itself, which is exactly what we want. If you test the movie now, you should find that when you click on the button, it attaches itself to the mouse and you can drag it around the screen until you release the mouse, where upon the button will stop where you left it.

In total, Flash provides support for handling *eight* actions that can happen to buttons: `press`, `release`, `release outside`, `key press`, `roll over`, `roll out`, `drag over`, and `drag out`. Also, the automatic handling that's inherent in the Over and Down states is great for people like me, who come from a background of working with Director. It's important to realize, though, that you're not limited by these built-in button behaviors, they're just blocks for you to build on. If you're comfortable doing a little scripting, you can solve almost any problem that presents itself.

Overriding Button Behavior

I recently worked on a Flash-based game for a children's web site. It had many draggable elements, like the ones that I described in the last section. The problem was that the client wanted the buttons to behave in a rather strange way: the game specification called for the buttons to be dragged and dropped, as you'd expect, but also to be able to be picked up with a single click, and deposited with another. If you think about the way we coded the last example, you will see the problem: sometimes a Release meant to start dragging, and sometimes it meant to stop dragging.

Now, "sometimes" is a horrible word for a programmer in any language, and my first response was, "You can't do that!" But on further contemplation, the answer came fairly easily. With a minimal amount of code, and one variable to add an extra 'state' to the buttons, the problem was solved. Let's work through the code and see how it was done.

Making a 'Sticky' Button

This example starts from where the previous one left off, so you can begin by opening up that one, or using the `Sticky_button.fla` from the CD. All we need to do now to add the new behavior is create a new state for the button to be in. I'll call this state `clicked`, meaning that the mouse was pressed and released while over the button.

1. In order to create the new state, we need a variable in which to store it. Open up the movie clip, bring up the Frame Actions window for frame 1, and enter this line:

   ```
   clicked = false;
   ```

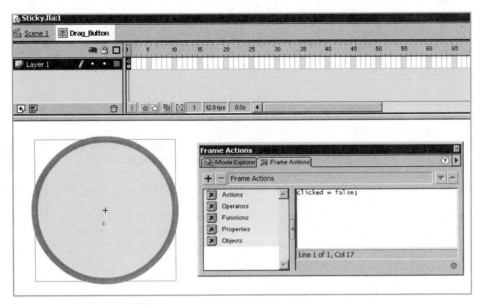

The line that's been added to the Frame Actions window here creates a new variable called `clicked` that we're initializing to a Boolean `false` value. We'll use this variable to determine whether the button has indeed been clicked.

2. Since we don't want the clip to loop and reset the variable without our say-so, you should also add a new keyframe to frame 2, and type a `stop` command into its Actions window.

3. The real meat of this example lies in an updated version of the code for handling actions that take place on the button. Make sure that you're in frame 2 of the movie clip, and bring up the Object Actions window for the button instance in that frame. Now make the following changes to the `on (press)` and `on (release)` handlers that we wrote for the previous example:

```
on (press) {
    if (clicked == false) {
        startDrag ("");
        clicked = true;
        loc_x = _x;
        loc_y = _y;
    } else {
        stopDrag ();
        clicked = false;
    }
}

on (release) {
    abs_x = Math.abs (loc_x - _x);
```

continues overleaf

```
abs_y = Math.abs (loc_y - _y);
if (abs_x > 20 || abs_y > 20) {
    stopDrag ();
    clicked = false;
}
}
```

The `on (press)` handler now features an `if` statement that branches based on the state of our `clicked` variable. We know that `clicked` starts its life being `false`, so the first time we press the button, `startDrag` is called immediately, `clicked` is set to `true`, and the `_x` and `_y` properties of the button are recorded as `loc_x` and `loc_y` for future use. Then, when we release the mouse button, the first thing that the `on (release)` handler does is to calculate the difference between the position where the button was clicked, and the position where it was released. The `Math.abs` function simply converts the number into an absolute number (that is, a positive one). This means that we can halve the amount of work that we need to do. We don't want to know which direction it's been dragged in, we just want to know how far it's been dragged. For this, we can just say:

If it's been dragged more than 20 pixels from its starting point then the user must have meant to drag it there, so we'll drop it

If the number is sufficiently large, meaning that the button was moved somewhere else on the screen while the mouse button was down, then the script calls `stopDrag` and drops the button, and the `clicked` variable is reset to `false`. *However*, if the two positions are within 20 pixels of each other, then the release handler does nothing, `clicked` stays `true`, and `stopDrag` is not called. This means that when the button is clicked *again*, `clicked` *is* `true` this time, so the `else` statement is executed, `stopDrag` is called, the button is dropped, and `clicked` is reset to `false`. That's it: you now have a button with a custom event handler. Test your movie, and try the two different ways of selecting the button.

One point that I've skipped over a little is the *need* for the test between the two positions. Why bother with the absolute values – why not just see if they are equal? That's actually the first thing I tried, but as I quickly discovered, it's difficult to not move the mouse a little between a click and release, and testing for equality led to some quirky behavior. Of course, the value you select to be the maximum allowed before you switch states is up to you; I chose 20 because I wanted to allow items to be grabbed with a 'swoop' of the mouse, but you can easily change it to 10 if you want it to be more precise.

Draggable Movie Clips and Drop Targets

To conclude this part of the chapter, we can add one last feature to our draggable, button-based movie clip. By using Flash's `_droptarget` property, it's possible to detect whether a clip that's currently being dragged is 'over' some other named movie clip, and then have a different action take place depending on this result.

If that sounds a little esoteric, it might help if I give you a couple of examples – the functionality can actually be surprisingly useful in a number of applications. Let's say, for instance, that you wanted to have the user drag an object from a group of objects, onto a specific area. This could come up if you were creating a children's game (say, dragging a geometric shape into a hole), or designing an online clothing store (dragging an article of clothing to the appropriate place on a mannequin, to preview an outfit before purchase). In both of these situations, you'd want the move to take place if the object has been dragged to (roughly) the correct location, but to be canceled otherwise. _droptarget can help you to do just that.

In order to use the _droptarget property, you need a draggable movie clip, and a named target movie clip. For the former, we can reuse the 'sticky' button from the last example, and for the target we'll use an instance of a simple, circular movie clip symbol. You'll find both of these in Droptarget.fla on the CD:

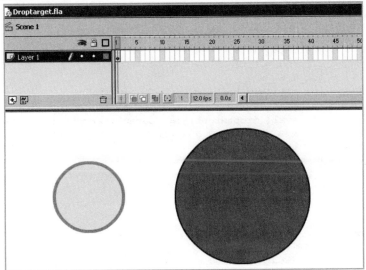

To illustrate its use, we're going to arrange that the button can only be dropped onto the target movie clip – if you try to drop it anywhere else, it will revert to its previous position.

1. Open up the FLA and give instance names to the two components: the button is called button, while the target has the name target. Obvious I know, but intuitive.

2. We've already got code in button that deals with the business of being picked up and put down with the mouse, so to get the behavior we want we just need to add some extra ActionScript to the code that's already there. Specifically, we want the movie clip to remember its starting location (in case it has to go back there), and to find out where it's been dropped.

    To address the first of these issues, we can simply reuse the loc_x and loc_y variables that we employed earlier to implement the button's 'sticky' behavior – so far, so good. Slightly more difficult however, is dealing with what happens when dragging ends. This is because we need to precede both calls to stopDrag with a conditional statement that tests whether the _droptarget property of button is the same as our target movie clip.

> *Annoyingly, the value that* _droptarget *returns is stored in pre-Flash 5 slash notation, so we have to use the* eval *function to get the information into a form that we can use. The* eval *function will just return a reference to the movie clip in dot notation.*

If we *are* over the target, we can just call stopDrag – but if we're not, we need to use the values that we stored earlier to reset the movie clip to its original position. Here are the changes that we need to make:

```
on (press) {
    if (clicked == false) {
        startDrag ("");
        clicked = true;
        loc_x = _x;
        loc_y = _y;
    } else {
        if (eval(_droptarget) != _parent.target) {
            _x = loc_x;
            _y = loc_y;
        }
        stopDrag ();
        clicked = false;
    }
}

on (release) {
    abs_x = Math.abs (loc_x - _x);
    abs_y = Math.abs (loc_y - _y);
    if (abs_x > 20 || abs_y > 20) {
        if (eval(_droptarget) != _parent.target) {
            _x = loc_x;
            _y = loc_y;
        }
        stopDrag ();
        clicked = false;
    }
}
```

The new code does exactly what we described above: if the drop target isn't the movie clip instance named target (!= means 'not equal to'), then we reset the position of the button clip before calling stopDrag. Notice that because both button and target are instances on the main movie's timeline, we have to specify the path to the target from the point of view of button, which involves using the _parent path.

You can now test the movie, and it should behave in the way that we wanted it to. If the button is released outside of the target area, then it'll snap back to its original position, but if the button is released while over the target, it will stop where it was dropped. The problem with this is that once it's on the target, it can't be taken off it again. There are different solutions to this problem depending on the project that it's placed in. In the child's shape game, you probably don't want the correct shape to be dragged out of its target anyway, so you can leave it as it is; but in the fashion mannequin example, you'd probably want another target – usually a container that it was dragged from in the first place – that you could drag it back to if you didn't want it. Using the knowledge that you have so far, you should be able to modify the example for any eventuality.

Menus

Up to this point, we've talked at some length about the two halves of interaction in Flash: the tools that the user employs to communicate with Flash, and the methods that Flash has of watching for those actions. I've tried to present information that will give you the building blocks to create larger, more complicated interactive pieces.

Now I'd like to shift the focus slightly to complete menu systems. Every good web site needs an intuitive way for its users to navigate through its content, and Flash is particularly effective at creating them – whether they're embedded within an HTML site, or part of a larger Flash movie. Menu systems appear in an amazing number of variations, but they're all based on the same framework: a group of buttons that together provide the required functionality. The buttons may be lined up in a vertical column, or they may be floating in a free-form 3D Flash sculpture, but at the end of the day, they all serve the same purpose.

The buttons in the menu can also have various responses when clicked on. Some menus are made up of simple buttons that take their users to a particular section of the movie or web site, while others have more than one level, where one button reveals a new set of options. As the designer, you have to look at the type and quantity of information that you have to present, and decide on the most efficient and aesthetically pleasing way to do it.

Simple Menus

Many people seem to think that a navigation system should be technologically impressive, but while there's no harm in that being the case, the most important thing to remember when designing a menu structure is *ease of use*. Don't make things so complicated that the user gets frustrated when they need to get somewhere quickly, and don't get caught up with creating such a dynamic experience that the user has to be a marksman to actually land the mouse on one of your fast-moving buttons.

We'll start our study of menu systems with the most basic variety. In the next exercise, we're going to create a very simple vertical menu bar that will link to different sections of our Flash movie. While this type of menu is easy to create, it is also one of the very best: if you have only a few categories in your project, it can make for a very elegant solution.

Building a Simple Menu

The first thing that we need for the menu is a bunch of buttons. Not just any old buttons though. What makes a menu a *menu* is a unifying design. The buttons in your menu should either all look the same, or have a very good reason for *not* looking the same. To this end, it's helpful to create the art for each state as a separate symbol, and then use this to create the rest of your buttons. Building your buttons this way also reduces movie size.

Remember: each state of any button can contain anything, from static graphics to other movie clips, sounds, and scripts. You can add text that the button needs when you're actually creating the individual buttons. If you *do* need text, create a new layer in the button – then, if you want the text to change between states, add keyframes to the text layer, and make the desired changes. Once you've created one button, you can copy it to create your other buttons. All you should need to do in the duplicate buttons is to edit the text layers.

The screenshot shows the Library and an image of the Simple_Menu movie clip that are contained in the `SimpleMenu.fla` sample project on the CD. As you can see from the symbol names, the construction of the buttons follows the recommendations that I outlined, and the buttons themselves are contained in the movie clip. Even if the buttons are just going to be on the stage, containing groups of elements like menu buttons in movie clips is a great way to organize your work, and makes editing your movies much easier later on.

To make this menu do something useful, we'll arrange for it to be displayed in the left-hand frame of an HTML page, and for the buttons to cause pages named `home.html`, `about.html`, etc. to be loaded into the right-hand frame of the same page.

1. Our first task, then, is to add `on (release)` handlers for each of the buttons in the movie clip. Open up the FLA, and then open the Simple_Menu movie clip inside it. Click on the Home button to select it, and bring up the Object Actions window.

Enter this code:

```
on (release) {
    getURL ("home.html", "target");
}
```

Here, the second argument being passed to `getURL` is a means of specifying the browser window into which the page should be loaded. When we come to write the page, we'll have to remember to give the name `target` to the right-hand frame I mentioned.

The other buttons contain the same script, but with the word "home" replaced for the appropriate word for that button. To save time, we've already filled in the ActionScript in the other buttons for you.

2.   Once all of the handlers are written, we only have one more thing to do in Flash, which is to resize our movie to match the contents on the stage. This is because when the movie is placed in a frame, that frame will scale the movie to fit into it. This means that if we published the movie, then the menu would come out as a small menu-like blob, it would still be functional, but not really usable.

3.   Finally, we can publish the movie. The publication process will generate a file called `SimpleMenu.html`, and as long as we make sure to include that in the left-hand frame, we should be all right. This is the HTML code for the controlling page, `TestMenu.html`, which can be found on the CD:

```
<HTML>
    <FRAMESET cols="175, *">
        <FRAME src="SimpleMenu.html">
        <FRAME src="home.html" name="target">
    </FRAMESET>
</HTML>
```

This code will produce a web site that looks like this:

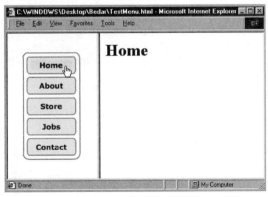

Clearly, it would be possible to be a bit more sophisticated than this, but it serves our purposes for the demonstration.

Floating Menus

Now that we've created our first menu, we can think about ways to improve upon it. If you're designing a Flash menu to be used in an HTML-based site (as we have), then you're fairly limited in how much space on the page you can take up. In these cases, a menu like the one we designed in the last section (or its horizontal equivalent) is fairly common. However, if you're designing a larger Flash movie, of which the menu is but a part, you have greater freedom as to the shape and behavior of your menu.

In the next example, we're going to turn our simple menu into a floating menu palette. This menu will be 'draggable' anywhere inside the Flash movie, and it will be collapsible, like one of the palettes in Flash itself. Floating menus work very well when the Flash movie has a lot of graphics with sizes comparable with the stage itself. The menu can be semi-transparent, and it could even include a drop shadow to enhance the 3D feel.

Letting Menus Float

For this exercise, we're going to need a copy of our simple menu, a new movie clip, and two buttons. One of the buttons will be a drag bar for the top of the palette, while the other will be a button to collapse the window. Together, their width should be a little less than that of the simple menu – something like what you see here is about right. You'll find these new button symbols by the names Button_Grab and Button_Open in FloatingMenu.fla:

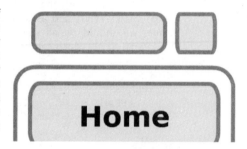

Now we're simply going to use some of the tricks that you learned earlier in the chapter to make the menu a little more dynamic.

1.   Select the menu and buttons on the stage, and convert them into a movie clip called Floating_Menu. Go into this movie clip, rename the first layer Menu, and add two new keyframes in frames 1 and 2:

2. Delete the content from the first keyframe, and create two new layers called Buttons and Background. Drag the Background layer to the bottom of the stack.

3. In the second frame of the Menu layer, cut the two small buttons from the stage, and paste them in place on the Buttons layer. Next, insert a keyframe into the second frame of the Buttons layer.

4. Now move to the Background layer, select frame 2 so you can still see the menu behind, and draw a tight rectangle around the menu and the buttons:

5. Next, add a second keyframe to frame 2 of the Background layer, click back on the first keyframe and scale the rectangle vertically so that it only covers the two buttons at the top:

6. Now that everything is arranged properly, we need to add the button scripts. Select Button_Grab in frame 1 and enter a basic drag script, like the one that we used in the draggable button example:

```
on (press) {
    startDrag ("", false);
}

on (release) {
    stopDrag ();
}
```

7. Repeat this in the second frame, and then, still in frame 2, select Button_Open and enter the following in the Object Actions window:

```
on (release) {
    gotoAndStop (1);
}
```

8.   Next, click back to frame 1, reselect Button_Open, and type this:

```
on (release) {
    gotoAndStop (2);
}
```

9.   Last of all, we need to add one final layer called Actions above the Buttons layer. If we don't act to stop it, this movie will happily loop forever, paying scant attention to any amount of clicking we might do. Put two keyframes in the new layer, and put a stop action in each.

And that's it, you can now try your movie out. The menu should be draggable if you click on the drag bar, and it should collapse when you click on the collapse button.

Now that you've got an understanding of how the basic elements of buttons and menus can be combined, we'll turn to a couple more implementations of menus – one horizontal, and one vertical. Rather than going back over how to make the menu and buttons each time, we'll just give you the essential new technologies that occur in each example so you can take them and apply them to your own projects.

Horizontal Hierarchical Menu

There are many different ways to build menus in Flash, but most can be identified as variations on the themes we've already seen. One very popular system makes use of hierarchical menus, which are really just simple menus with a twist: clicking on a menu button reveals several more choices. Menus like this are used when there are simply too many options to be represented all at once.

For instance, if you were creating a personal site to showcase all of your artwork, you might create a menu that has buttons such as Home, About, Portfolio, Resume, and Contact. In this case, you may want to break down the Portfolio section further, into sections for your drawings, Photoshop work, and Flash work. Using a hierarchical menu, you'd be able to design a menu system that loaded an HTML page when the user clicked one of the other buttons, but presented the subcategories when the user clicked on Portfolio.

An important consideration when designing more complex menu systems is how the menu will be incorporated into the main site. There are two basic ways to do this.

First, the menu could be a part of a large movie, and so the menu selections would point to different parts of that movie. From the standpoint of a Flash developer, this scenario is the easiest to implement as the menu would have far fewer space restrictions – it's not confined to a particular frame, or frame of reference. Special effects and transitions involving the menu extending farther out into the screen are possible. The downside is a loss of flexibility and ease of upkeep. If your entire site is created as one Flash movie, any update or upgrade to the site requires the master movie to be edited.

The other alternative for incorporating a menu in your site is to embed the menu in an HTML page. The benefit to this approach is that the menu is the item in your site least likely to change, so once you have it, you can update your pages by simply editing the HTML. The biggest problem with this approach is that it all but forces you to use frames, with the menu in one frame and the content in the other. If you *don't* use frames, you have no guarantee that the menu will remain available in the browser's cache between pages, creating the real possibility that your menu will have to be reloaded on each page, dramatically slowing down your site. Personally, I've no problem with sites that use frames for navigation, as long as the designer covers up any visible traces of the frames themselves, but many people seem to list frames as a definite 'don't' when it comes to web design. Only you can be the final judge and " – it's subjective."

To create this menu, we're going to use a movie clip with a keyframe for each section, and a button for each main category. As usual, start by creating a new movie clip, and decide how many main sections you're going to have – I chose to have four:

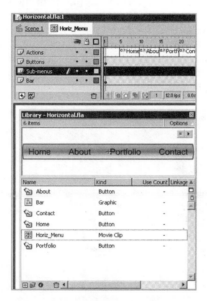

Looking at this screenshot, which shows the whole process a little further on, you can begin to see how this is going to work. The 'bar', and the four buttons that sit on top of it, are the constants in this movie clip – they'll always be around. The four script markers that you can see in the Actions layer betray the existence of stop actions; and the labels attached to each mean that in our button-handling code, we'll be able to send the movie to a place of our choosing. When we want a sub-menu to appear, we can place a new movie clip in the Sub-menus layer, in a position that coincides with the appropriate label.

> *Because we're going to be using frame labels to jump from one section to another, it doesn't really matter where you put these frames, or in what order. For organizational purposes, I like to space them out at intervals of five frames, giving enough room for the labels we're going to add to be legible. After the last keyframe, you might want to add a few blank frames, so that you can read the last label.*

With the movie clip in this position, the next step is to add on (release) handlers to each of the buttons. As so often, these are quite straightforward – the one for the Home button looks like this:

```
on (release) {
    gotoAndPlay ("Home");
}
```

And the others proceed in predictable fashion, gotoAndPlaying the About, Portfolio, and Contact frames respectively. At this point we have something that's functionally equivalent to our simple menu. It's built in a different way, but if we were to put all of the site's content into this movie clip, it would perform in the same fashion. However, we can and will do better.

We're going to give our Portfolio menu a sub-menu by placing another set of buttons in a second movie clip, and placing that in the appropriate location on our Sub-menus layer. In that layer, insert keyframes that correspond with those in the Actions layer, and move to frame 15. I created a smaller version of the main bar, with some new buttons on it:

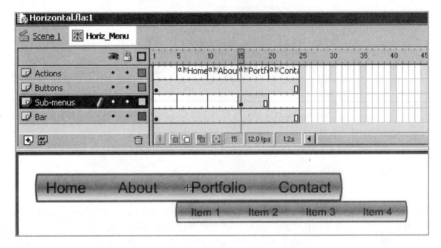

Now, when you click on the Portfolio button, the movie will jump to the frame that contains the additional buttons for that section. In order to get any further from this point, of course, you'd need to add 'go to frame' or 'URL' commands to the sub-menu button handlers – but that wasn't the object of this exercise. What we have is a space-efficient, horizontal, hierarchical menu – exactly what we wanted!

Vertical Hierarchical Menu

The horizontal menu is fairly straightforward, and perhaps its best feature is that you can easily add one or two more levels of information to your site structure without taking up much more space in your interface. Unfortunately, the horizontal menu's construction doesn't translate well into a vertical format. The problem is that if you have a main menu option expand downward to reveal sub-menus, any menu items beneath those sub-menus could be obscured.

Many sites use a vertical hierarchical menu that has sub-menus appearing to the side of the menu item clicked. The problem with this is that your menu takes up dramatically more room in your layout, and if you're using a Flash menu in an HTML page, this is probably unacceptable. One solution to this problem is to use a menu that expands *vertically*. To implement this type of menu, we could do something similar to the horizontal menu, creating a different layout for each menu selection. But, since this is the last example in this chapter, let's do something a little fancier. In the previous examples, I've tried to use as little scripting as possible. This one will use a lot more.

We're going to make a menu that has a dynamic hierarchical structure. Each item in the menu will be a movie clip that contains its own submenu items. We will use arrays to store information about the movie clips and where they're supposed to be on the stage at any given time.

The secret to this menu system is in the way you handle what happens when a menu button is pressed. For one button to 'expand', all of the buttons below it in the list have to move down – and precisely how far they have to move depends on how many submenus the original button has.

Let's express this situation a little more formally. If there were four buttons, and you clicked on (say) the first, then buttons two, three, and four would have to move. If you clicked on the second, then only the third and fourth buttons would be affected. A problem with characteristics like these is a strong candidate to be solved by a loop that iterates through the items in question, so I'm going to store the menu movie clips in an array called MenuArray. We're also going to store what I call **offset values** – that is, how much vertical space an expanded menu takes up – for each menu in a separate array. This is the only information we need to deal with when opening any menu.

Before we can think about moving them around, though, we first need to give some thought to *creating* the menu button movie clips, of which we have three (home, about, and contact). In fact, these are quite complicated little things in their own right, although you should also see some similarities with the menus we've developed elsewhere.

In terms of their timelines, the three movie clips look identical:

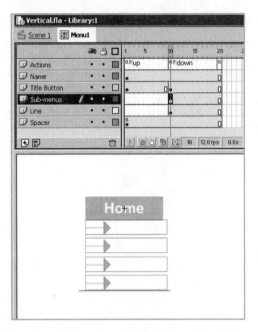

What on earth do we have here? *Seven* layers? Still, even with that apparent complexity, we can see what's going on quite clearly if we work our way down from the top. First, there's our almost-traditional Actions layer, which neatly divides this movie clip into 'up' and 'down' states. When the main button's 'up', or not expanded, the items visible on the stage are the button, its name, and the mysterious 'spacer'. With the button 'down', we also see the four sub-menu buttons, and the vertical line that joins them pictorially:

The arrows you see here actually form only part of the sub-menu buttons. They have text boxes to their right, containing the white text 'sub-menu'. This will become apparent when we eventually place our movie clips on a black background!

The Menu1 movie clip, then, consists of one 'main' menu button and four sub-menu buttons that are revealed when the former is clicked. If it's clicked for a second time, the sub-menus will be re-hidden. It's joined in this movie by Menu2, which is labeled Action and has two sub-menus, and Menu3 (Contact, three). When you've created all three clips (or better yet, loaded the Vertical.fla example from the CD), we can continue.

With the menu buttons done, we need at last to create the Menu movie clip on which they will be placed. On the surface, at least, this is quite simple: two layers (for background and buttons), and two frames (so that different ActionScript code can be placed in each):

The three movie clips have instance names of menu1, menu2, and menu3 respectively, and we can use those to prepare the functions that will be called when the buttons are pressed, to make room for vertical expansion. Frame 2 of the Buttons layer is easy – that just contains a stop action – but in frame 1 we have to do rather more work. I'll present the code first, and then explain it:

```
MenuArray = new array();
MenuArray[1] = menu1;
MenuArray[2] = menu2;
MenuArray[3] = menu3;
```

continues overleaf

```
offset = new array();
offset[1] = menu1._height;
offset[2] = menu2._height;
offset[3] = menu3._height;

function up(men_num) {
    var men_offset = offset[men_num] - 30;
    men_num++;
    for(i = men_num; i <= 3; i++) {
        MenuArray[i]._y = MenuArray[i]._y - men_offset;
    }
}

function down(men_num) {
    var men_offset = offset[men_num] - 30;
    men_num++;
    for(i = men_num; i <= 3; i++) {
        MenuArray[i]._y = MenuArray[i]._y + men_offset;
    }
}
```

This script does two things. First, it initializes the two arrays we talked about earlier, which is where that 'spacer' finally comes into play. Remember: we placed it right at the foot of the *expanded* menu movie clips, so the _height property will contain the amount by which the other menus will need to move when one of the menus expands.

The up and down functions will be called by the menu buttons' on (release) handlers, and you can see here that they're actually both quite short, and very similar to one another. The difference is that while up *subtracts* the offset from the current menu's _y value, down *adds* the offset. In calling these functions, a menu will pass its own number as the argument – so if menu2 calls it, men_num will equal 2.

The first thing the function does is set its internal variable men_offset by using the men_num variable to look up the value from the offset array. Now, the menu that we're clicking never moves – only the menus beneath it do that – so the next step is to increment men_num. Finally, we have a for loop that steps through all of the menus below the menu that was clicked, and moves them by our menu's offset value.

Very last of all, we need to add on (release) handlers to the menu button movie clips that call the up and down functions we just wrote, and switch the buttons themselves between their Up and Down states. You'll recall that each button had two keyframes in its timeline, so each one requires two handlers. By nature, these follow a symmetrical pattern; here are the two handlers (frame 1; frame 10) for menu1:

```
on (release) {
    _parent.down (1);
    gotoAndStop ("down");
}

on (release) {
```

```
        _parent.up (1);
        gotoAndStop ("up");
}
```

And, once you've added similar handlers to menu2 and menu3, that's it! You'll get a chance to explore much more scripting in later chapters, but for now you have written a pretty nice little movie script. This menu is incredibly useful, because you can store a lot of options in a small space. You could even add another level of sub-menus, if necessary. With a few small adjustments you could create a menu using our main menu movies as menu items.

Conclusion

When you add interactivity to your sites you know you're using Flash to its full potential. An interface should feel responsive as well as intuitive. It's really the small touches that leave the biggest impression. In this chapter, I have tried to show you some basic ways to add interactivity to your Flash movies, as well as a few tricks to make life easier. The possibilities, however, are limitless. As Flash expands in its capabilities and ActionScript becomes more and more robust as a scripting language, the more opportunity you have as a Flash developer to express your personal style in your work. You decide how you want elements in your movies to behave, and then go about figuring out how to achieve the desired effect. The best way to learn is by doing.

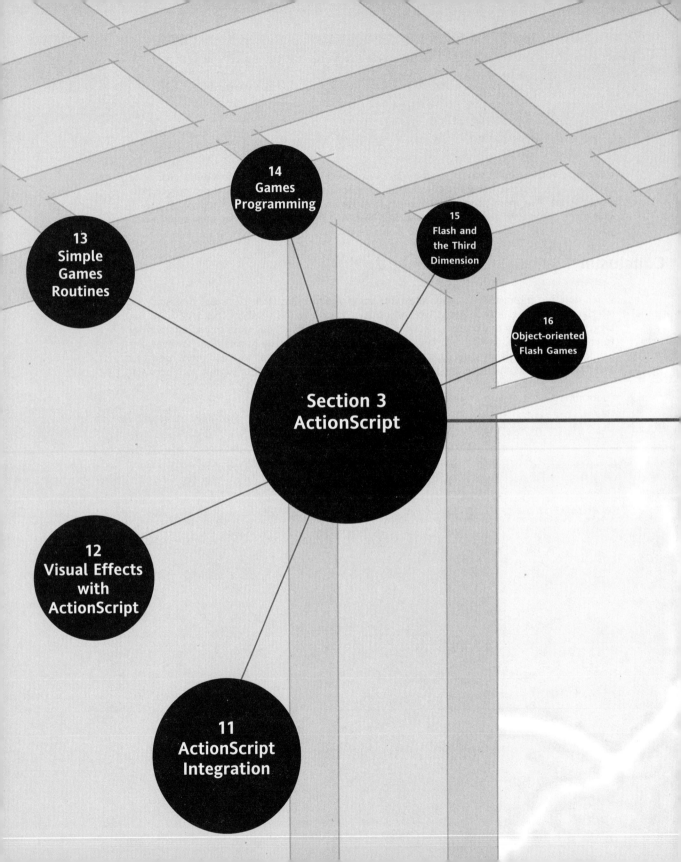

13
Simple
Games
Routines

14
Games
Programming

15
Flash and
the Third
Dimension

16
Object-oriented
Flash Games

Section 3
ActionScript

12
Visual Effects
with
ActionScript

11
ActionScript
Integration

Chapter 10
ActionScript
Programming
Principles

ActionScript is probably the most powerful tool that Flash developers have at their disposal to make their movies take wing. With Flash 5, ActionScript has started to become the norm rather than the exception, with almost every decent new Flash site or animation containing some sections of code. The variety, dynamism and richness that ActionScript facilitates is what sets Flash apart from all of its competitors, and it's almost certainly the engine of all the Flashed sites that make you go 'wow'.

In this chapter, we're going to profile the features that underpin ActionScript's power as a programming language in its own right. The aim is to help you to think about your movies and content as programmable systems, and give you some insights into how you can hook up Flash content programmatically to create great user interfaces and complete web applications with real functionality *and* small file sizes. Flash now has the power and flexibility of a mature programming language, and the ability to make use of back-end technologies (databases and other data sources) as well as the graphical interfaces that made Flash's reputation.

In Flash 5, ActionScript has been redeveloped as a fully featured scripting language using the ECMA-262 specification – itself a standardized hybrid of technologies, the most famous of which being JavaScript and JScript. A scripting language is essentially a tool to let you write strings of instructions that can be carried out when certain events occur.

In Flash, scripts written in ActionScript can be triggered in a frame when the playhead reaches it, or they can be set running by on-screen events invoked via active elements on the screen – such as movie clips, buttons, and the mouse.

We're going to start by looking at the key programming language features that ActionScript embodies.

Essential Programming Concepts

For simple scripts – for example, using `stop` commands to keep movie content on screen without the movie looping, or using `goto` to jump to a particular frame when a button is pressed – it's not really necessary to understand too much about programming theory and programming language components. However, as you become comfortable with ActionScript, you'll find yourself wanting to try and accomplish more and more complex tasks in your movies. It's *then* that it's essential to understand some of the concepts upon which the structure and components of Flash 5 ActionScript are based.

Let's start with the basic programming structure that stores data in programs – the **variable**.

Variables

Variables are simply containers for data. This data could be anything from a person's name through to a number that controls the speed with which a movie clip drifts across the screen. The key points are:

- You give the variable a *name* that you can use to reference it in ActionScript

- You give the variable a *value* that's stored in that named container

- You use the name to extract the value from the container whenever you need it

In more technical terms, a variable is a user-defined label attached to a certain location of the computer's memory – a physical location in the computer's circuitry, where a value is lodged. The variable name – the label – is there to make life easier for you: instead of having to remember the exact, *physical* memory address of a value, you can instead tell the computer to refer to that specific section of memory (you don't even have to know where it is) by using the label you give it. For instance, consider the following program:

```
myName = "Richard";
print (myName);
```

In this fragment of pseudo-code a variable called myName is created and given – *assigned* – the value "Richard". The stuff inside the quotes is the actual value stored.

> *The 'single equals sign' syntax assigns the value on the right of the equals sign to the variable name that appears to the left of the equals sign.*

With the myName variable's value safely stored in the computer's memory, the value is then printed out to the screen using a print function and the name of the variable. The effect of this is exactly the same as if we'd written the program like this:

```
print ("Richard");
```

So why use a variable? Well, because variables save us programming time and effort, and make our programs more flexible. Think about what would happen if I had a program that just printed out 'Richard' five hundred times in a row to make a nice pattern. Using the print ("Richard") method, where the name is hard-coded into the print statement, I'd just duplicate the statement five hundred times over. So far, so good. But what if I want to print "Mapes" instead of "Richard"? In the hard coded style, I'd have to manually change each and every one of those five hundred lines of code to read Mapes. However, when I use the myName variable to store the name, I need merely change the value of that one variable...

```
myName = "Mapes"
```

...and the new value will ripple through the whole program and be used wherever myName appears. Here, I'd still have five hundred statements, each one saying print (myName), but I'd only ever have to change the initial variable setting to achieve the result I wanted. The concept of using the same code, but with different values, is known as **reusability**. Flash also allows us to differentiate between different types of variable, lending us even greater control and flexibility in our code.

Variable Types

There are two categories of variable in Flash we need to discuss – **global** and **local** variables. Whether a variable is global or local defines its **scope**: that is, how widely its value can be disseminated throughout the whole program (or SWF movie, in the case of Flash).

Global variables are variables whose value can be accessed from *anywhere* in the movie. Global variables are a common store that any element in the movie can extract values from (and update, of course). The global variable type is the most commonly used because it's the default variable type in Flash. When you declare a variable in ActionScript by typing its definition in Expert mode or using the set variable action...

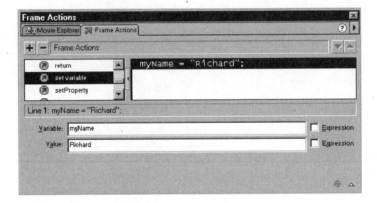

...you're implicitly setting the *global* variable myName to hold the text string 'Richard'. This value will be available to all movie clips and scripts in the movie.

This method is fine for most occasions, so why would you ever want to use a local variable instead? The choice-making difference comes when you're thinking about memory management. Memory is less and less a consideration with the advancing technologies of the age, but for the leanest, cleanest and most efficiently elegant code, it's still an issue you should ponder. When you set a global variable, you're effectively telling the computer to set aside a reserved memory location for exclusive occupation by that one variable. Even if the variable is only used once or twice in the whole Flash movie, that section of memory remains reserved for that single value. When you're running a memory-intensive movie with many variables, you can see that this could be a problem in terms of performance impact. The way to get around this is to use *local* variables.

With a local variable, the section of memory where the variable is stored is only reserved for a program-defined amount of time, and is then free to be reused. For example, if you had a piece of ActionScript code that used a 'loop counter' variable to track how many times an animation had looped, and if you declared the counter as a local variable, the variable will only be in memory while the looping is taking place. Once the desired number of loops has completed and the counter has done its job, the variable will be destroyed, freeing up memory. If it had been declared as a global variable, it would still be taking up memory even after the loop counting had finished. You can think of this as the program tidying up after itself, cleaning up any unnecessary garbage after it's been finished with, and putting it away. To define a local variable in Flash 5, you precede it by the keyword `var`:

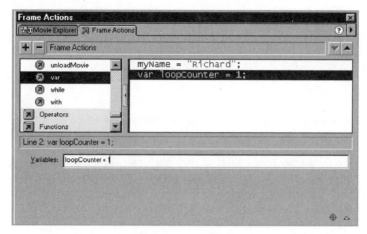

So what can you actually store in a variable? Well, pretty much *anything*. But to organize things and help us make sure we use the right kind of variables for the right kind of job, Flash, like other programming languages, defines a number of different **data types**, each of which has different characteristics and different ways of being manipulated.

Data Types

Different data types are used to store distinct categories of values. The following lines all contain valid variable assignments in ActionScript:

```
age = 17;

title = "Flash 5";

isAVariable = true;
```

Each of these assignments, however, represents a different data *type*. A data type, unsurprisingly, describes the *nature* of the data that the variable holds. There are several different data types available in Flash 5 ActionScript, and here's a quick description of each type, with an example:

Number
This is the simplest data type, which defines the variable simply as a **numerical value**.

Example:

```
x = 24;
y = 6;
```

Number type variables can have mathematical operations applied to them. For instance, using the above figures, you could add the x and y variables together like this – x + y – and the result would be 30.

String

This variable type holds a group of characters enclosed by quotation marks.

Example:

```
x = "Hello";
```

This kind of value is a *literal* value – that is, Flash will always reproduce the characters exactly as they appear inside the quote marks.

Strings are treated differently to numbers in that when two strings are added together they're *joined*, – or to use the technical term, **concatenated**. For example, if you stored two string variables like this...

```
x = "24";
y = "6";
```

...and then used the statement x + y to add them together, the result would be "246" as the two strings are simply spliced together. However, if you think about it, you couldn't sensibly *multiply* two strings together: when a value – even a number – is stored as a string, these are *literal* values, and you wouldn't, for example, want to multiply "Richard" by "Mapes", would you?

Booleans

A Boolean variable can only have one of two values: it can be either true or false. This kind of variable is used to evaluate things, which usually means the condition or status of other variables.

Example:

```
isMyNameRichard = true;
isMyNamePlantagenet = false;
```

Booleans are commonly used when you want to test if a specific condition exists before you execute another piece of code. For example, if you have a program where you want to check that the user's password is correct before you proceed, you would say:

```
if (isPasswordCorrect == true)
then proceed
```

Note that when you're checking to see if a variable is equal to a particular value or condition, you use the 'double equals sign' syntax. This double equals sign is called the **equality operator**, and it checks whether the value or expression on the right of the two equals signs is the same as the variable or expression on its left.

> *It's vital that you remember the difference between this equality operator and the single equals sign, known as the **assignment operator**, which is used to set a variable's value.*

Objects and Movie Clips

Objects are, in programming terms, groups of properties that have names and values. Flash has built-in objects, such as the Math object, which allow you to carry out collections of predefined mathematical operations.

Many of the things that you build in Flash – and, especially importantly, movie clips – are objects *implicitly*. This means that when you create a movie clip, it inherits the same kind of standard characteristics as all other movie clips. For example, you might build a movie clip symbol that displays a ball on screen. An instance of this movie clip placed on the stage and called BallClip would embody all the properties that Flash movie clips have by default – things like _width, _height, and _alpha. You can see these properties for an individual object on the stage by selecting it and then opening up the Properties book in the Object Actions window:

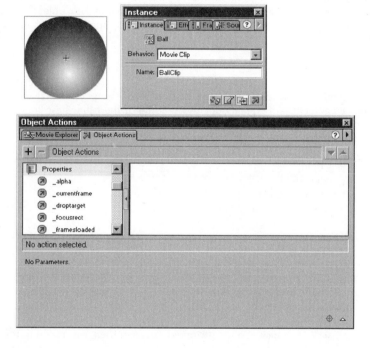

You can reference these properties in code and assign their values to variables. Likewise, you can set an object's properties to values stored in other variables. In ActionScript, you could set the _alpha property of this movie clip to a specific value by declaring a variable and then using Flash's dot notation to assign this value to one of the movie clip's properties:

```
alphaValue = 50;
BallClip._alpha = alphaValue;
```

Similarly, you can take the value of an object's property and assign that value to a variable:

```
widthValue = BallClip._width;
```

You'll already start to see that this provides us with valuable methods for passing data around inside a movie and changing things dynamically.

Constants and Literals

A constant, in most programming languages, is a predefined variable that can never be changed programmatically when the program runs, only *read*, like the read-only memory in your computer as compared to its RAM. Consider, for example, the constant *pi* (3.14 etc.). It would be counter-intuitive to try and change the value of pi – a bit like trying to change the color of the sky, which is just a *given*.

It isn't possible to *define* a variable as a constant in Flash; any variable that you declare will always be changeable in code when the program/movie runs. Flash does, however, come with a set of *predefined* constants: for example, the properties of the built-in Key object – Key.SPACE will always be set to the value of a press of the space bar, and it's impossible to change it to hold any other value.

Operators

Operators are symbols that perform some kind of processing on variables. We've already mentioned the assignment and equality operators. Some of the other best known operators are the arithmetic operators (*, +, -, /), and there are many other types, including the **comparison** operators, which you'll see used extensively in this book:

<	(less than)
>	(greater than)
<=	(less than or equal to)
>=	(greater than or equal to)

Comparison operators, like the equality operator, are extremely useful when checking conditions upon which further code is dependent.

Operators in Flash have an **order of precedence** just as they do in written math. The order of precedence for the basic arithmetic operators is *, /, +, -. This means that multiplication in an expression will always take place before addition. So:

1 + 2 * 3 = 7, because 2 * 3 is worked out first, then 1 is added to it.

To override this default order of precedence, you have to enclose part of the expression in parentheses. The expressions inside the parentheses are always evaluated before the rest of the sum. So:

(1 + 2) * 3 = 9, because 1 + 2 is evaluated first, then multiplied by 3.

Now that we've surveyed the basic elements, let's start looking at how they can be used to form program structures that fit together inside a movie and make it into something much more interesting and adaptable than a set of simple tweens that play one after the other.

ActionScript Programming Structures

The level of components that we've been discussing so far can be likened to the alphabet and punctuation used in a written language: variables would be the letters, and the operators would be the things that joined them together or separated them into individual words.

ActionScript also has a larger scale grammar and organization to overlay this lower level of detail. This grammar defines the order in which code should be written, and how chunks of code should be arranged and processed.

Expressions

If we can think of operators and variables to be the words of ActionScript, then expressions are the language's *phrases*. An expression is essentially any collection of code elements (a combination of variables and operators) that will generate a value. For example:

```
12 * 5

23 + 35

91 - 47
```

Statements

A statement generally equates to a single line of code, and can be thought of as the *sentences* of ActionScript. A statement is defined as a 'complete unit of execution', and is terminated by a semicolon. For example:

```
gotoAndPlay (2);

widthValue = BallClip._width;
```

Both of these statements are complete and self-contained. Running them will result in specific actions being taken and specific outcomes achieved.

When you're hand-writing ActionScript in Expert mode, it's vital that you remember those terminating semicolons at the end of each distinct statement.

Blocks

A block is a group of statements contained within braces – { }. A block of code is like a *paragraph* in a written language, and usually contains a set of related statements, all of which need to be run to achieve the desired result.

For example:

```
on (press) {

    alphaVal = 50;
    BallClip._alpha = alphaVal;
}
```

Forming code into blocks is important both in terms of organizing your ActionScript, and in terms of controlling the action.

To understand more clearly why we need blocks, we'll move on to look at **flow control**.

Programming Flow Control

Flow control is the manipulation of the order in which statements are executed, and it's concerned with how Flash controls a movie's behavior based on the instructions that we give it in the ActionScript programming structure. Implementing these structures is what allows us to escape from the straight linear playback of movies and movie clips, and what gives us access to more interesting and adaptable behaviors.

There are two groups of control structures that we need to sketch here: **branching** structures and **looping** structures. Each of these affects the order in which Flash carries out the ActionScript code as the movie plays.

Branching Constructs

These constructs are designed for making decisions, and are typified by the if...else structure. Generally, these are used when an action is conditional upon other data or circumstances.

For instance:

```
if (I am bored) {
        Go read a book;
        Make a drink;
        Write a string quartet;
}
else
{
        Carry on doing what I am doing;
        Grow and learn;
}
```

Here are the concepts of blocks and statements in action. Both the if and the else parts of this code have initial, *conditional* clauses, followed by separate code blocks, separated out using braces. Each block is made up of at least two statements, each of which is terminated with a semicolon.

What makes this a branching structure is that the code will take only *one* of the two routes provided – it will *never* carry out both blocks of actions in a single run of the program.

Looping Constructs

Unlike branching structures, which are designed to let the script choose between two alternate courses of action, looping constructs – loops – enable us to *repeat* complete blocks of code statements for as long as certain conditions exist. The key loop structures to look at here are:

```
for
while
do...while
```

The While Loop

For instance, this `while` loop...

```
while(I am hungry) {
        sit at the dining table;
        eat some food;
        take a drink;
}
```

...will re-evaluate the condition (`I am hungry`) and execute the code block inside the braces until the initial condition evaluates to `false`. This would happen when some other action triggered a change in that condition's status. Trigger events might include a user's button press, or a `poundsOfBeefConsumed` variable reaching a predefined threshold.

The For Loop

The `for` loop is like a `while` loop with self-control. Instead of being dependent on an external action or change to terminate the loop, the conditions for its completion are set up in the parameters that we use when we initialize the loop.

Consider this `for` loop:

```
for (i=0; i<5; i++) {
      print "hello";
}
```

The first line is the initialization statement. When you initialize a `for` loop, Flash will always require that you provide it with three arguments in the parentheses. In sequence, these are:

- The initial value of the variable that will control the loop. This variable (in this case, `i`) is the loop counter.
- The condition that will terminate the loop. In this instance, we're telling Flash to stop looping when the expression `i<5` is no longer true.

- What to do after running the statements in the code block each time through the loop. Here, we use the increment operator, ++, to add 1 to the value of i. Using this operator is a shorthand equivalent of writing "i=i+1".

After the initialization statement comes the code block that we want to execute in each iteration of the loop, the print statement.

Running the loop with this initialization statement will result in printing hello five times, once for each iteration of the loop, when the values of i are 0, 1, 2, 3 and 4. After this, i will be incremented to 5, the initialization condition will evaluate to false, and the code block won't be run again.

The while loop equivalent of this would be:

```
i=0;
while(i<5) {
    print "hello";
    i++;
}
```

Both of these pieces of code will print "hello" 5 times.

The Do...While Loop

The do...while loop is similar to a normal while loop, except that it always processes its code block at least *once* before checking the condition. For example:

```
x=15;
while(x<10) {
    print "hello";
}
```

...would not print anything, but...

```
x=15;
do {
    print "hello";
}
while(x<10);
```

...would print "hello" once before the loop condition was checked and the loop terminated.

Earlier on, we mentioned the concept of reusability – the idea that code can be used more than once. Next, we're going to look at one of the most important tools of reusability – **functions**.

Functions

A function performs a given task or set of operations whenever it's called by another piece of code. Whenever you identify a need for a chunk of code to be used in multiple locations in a movie, you should automatically think "This needs to be a function..." If the task that chunk of code performs is used frequently, it would be tedious and wasteful to have to rewrite the code in multiple locations. Equally, if you've got an error in that code, and have used it in several places, then when you find the mistake and try to fix it, you will have to fix it in a *dozen* places rather than just the one. This is the same principle as that 500-line program that we discussed earlier when we were talking about how useful variables are.

A function, then, is a lump of code that has a predefined purpose, and which can be called from elsewhere in the movie. The function will do its allotted job and then return a result to the movie clip or piece of code that invoked it. In order for this to work, the function has to be expecting, and be delivered, a specified quantity and type of input that it can then process.

Consider writing a function that multiplies two numbers together. The actual code in the body of the function could be as simple as this:

```
return the result of a*b to the code that's called this function;
```

For the function to do this job, we need to tell it to expect the calling code to pass it two variables – a and b – when it invokes the function.

When we create a function in Flash, we include the names of the variables that it will be passed in the definition statement:

```
function Multiply(a, b) {
```

Here, the word `function` tells Flash that this code will be called whenever someone invokes the function name `Multiply` in their code. The two variables specified in the parentheses are called as the function's *arguments*, and they act as placeholders into which specific values will be passed when the function is called.

So the function definition in full, complete with its actual code block, would look something like this:

```
function Multiply(a, b) {
    return a*b;
}
```

This function will take any two numbers passed to it, multiply them together and return the result. `return` is the command used to send back the result of the multiplication as a value.

To call this function from your program, you would use this line of ActionScript:

```
Multiply (3, 4);
```

This would then pass these two values in parentheses to the `Multiply` function where (taking the place of the placeholders in the function definition) they would be multiplied together. The `return` action would then pass the final value back to the main program.

If you wanted to display the result of the `Multiply` function, you could assign the result to a variable, like this...

```
result = Multiply (3, 4);
```

...and then display the variable in a dynamic text box on screen:

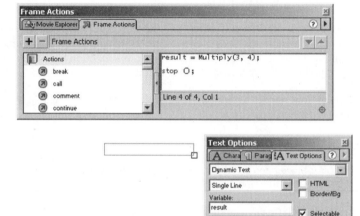

Admittedly this isn't a particularly exciting function, but if the set of instructions in the function's code block *is* long and complicated, then encapsulating them in a function will make maintaining the code a lot easier.

> *A useful rule of thumb is that a function should perform one task, and one task only. The best way to be sure of this is to use a simple naming convention – the name of the function should be a verb, and the name of any arguments should be nouns, for example:*
>
> *Throw (Ball);*
>
> *Eat (Eggs, Ham);*
>
> *If a function contains sub-tasks, then it should really be further broken down into sub-functions.*

Flash comes with a set of predefined functions such as `getVersion`, which returns the version number of the Flash player that the movie is playing in. Another useful function is `hitTest`, which returns a Boolean value when the bounding box of one movie clip is broken by another movie clip, allowing for simple collision detection.

Objects

Objects are essentially units of code functionality that are self-contained and know how to perform certain tasks. They are the most fundamental part of **object oriented programming** (OOP), one of the most significant developments in programming in the last two decades.

The process of designing programs has passed several milestones in its history. At first, programs were monolithic, starting at the first line, executing each instruction in strict sequence and then finishing when they reached the last line. The first big breakthrough came when it was found that tasks could be broken down into functions, simplifying the thought process and allowing common tasks to be isolated and called when necessary. However, both monolithic and function-based programming were still constrained by a rather rigid time dependence. Even when broken down into functions, each program would still start at the beginning and run to the end. Flow control concepts helped, but the introduction of graphical interfaces such as Windows meant that fewer and fewer programs were operating in a linear fashion. Now programs were expected to leap to attention at every click of the mouse, reacting to user input rather than following a set procedure.

To cope with this, the concept of objects was introduced. Instead of considering each program as a set of operations on data (functions), programs began to be considered as sets of data that interacted (objects). For instance, previously, the task of boiling a kettle had been broken down functionally as:

```
Fill (Kettle);
TurnOn (Kettle);
CheckBoiled(Kettle);
```

Now this task could be thought of as having a single kettle object with the following *methods* embodied in its code:

```
Fill
TurnOn
Boiled
```

The significance of this development becomes apparent when you try to work out *who* has responsibility for knowing when the kettle is full (or, indeed, when it has boiled). In the functional model, a variable that reflects the state of the kettle must be maintained in the core code. If the program is adapted to cope with two kettles, that change will ripple throughout the program, and you'll need a new set of 'fill', 'on', and 'boil' variables for each new kettle. If, however, you have a kettle object that contains its own set of states, each of which is represented *inside* the object, then you can add as many distinct kettles to the program as you like, without having to change the rest of the program.

ActionScript lends itself to an object-oriented approach through the use of movie clips. You can create small, functionally independent clips and then plug them into your main movie. Each may contain a certain number of properties and variables, and each may contain functions that are able to operate on those variables and properties. The great thing is that once these movie clips are spawned they can scuttle around, behaving independently of the tyrannical temporal flow of the main timeline.

Having introduced the key concepts involved in ActionScript programming, let's reinforce that by working through some practical applications of these concepts.

Illustrating the Concepts: Variables and Flow Control

One of the key uses of ActionScript is to animate objects where frame-by-frame animation is just not practical or desirable. For instance, to animate a bouncing ball frame by frame would take an immense amount of work – calculating the distance the ball should move in each frame, and painstakingly moving the ball to the right position – as well as requiring a large movie to allow for each frame of the animation. Let's take a look at how this can be much more easily accomplished by using ActionScript. You'll find the accompanying FLAs for these examples on the CD.

Animating a Basic Bouncing Ball

By programming the movement of the ball using ActionScript, we can get Flash to do the calculations for us, as well as reducing the movie to only three frames – one to set up the variables and two to perform the calculation loop.

1. We're going to need two objects in this particular animation, the ball and the ground. Make these as detailed as you like. If you're not feeling particularly artistic, a filled circle and a straight line will do. Make sure that the ball is high enough above the ground to allow for a good couple of bounces. Once you have drawn these, convert each of them into separate movie clips. It doesn't matter what you call them, but we have used ball and ground for clarity:

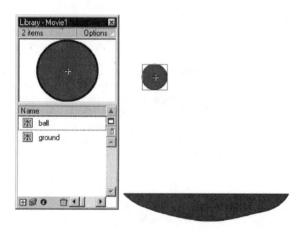

2. Click on the Edit Symbols button in the top-right hand corner, and select your ground symbol from the drop-down list to open it up for editing.

We want the top of the ground to be set to the Y position 0.

3. This can be achieved by selecting the whole shape and then using the Info panel, making sure the black square is in the top-left to ensure we're using the correct registration point, and then setting the Y value to 0:

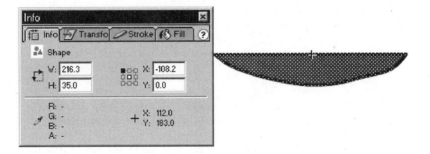

4. We're going to need two layers: one for the graphical objects on the stage and one for the code. This is a good practice to get into as it accomplishes several things:

- It separates out the code from the graphics, helping to keep things clear in our minds.

- It makes it easier to find and update the code when we need to.

- If we change the graphics, we know we're not going to accidentally delete the code!

These principles become increasingly important as you add more and more layers to complex movies.

5. Rename the current layer Graphics, then add a new layer and call it Code. Insert keyframes into frames 2 and 3 of the Code layer, and normal frames in the same place on the Graphics layer so that the layers are the same length.

6. You should now have a blank Code layer and a Graphics layer containing instances of your ball and ground movie clips. Use the Instance panel to set their instance names to ball and ground respectively:

7.   Now we've finished with the graphics, it's also a good idea to lock the Graphics layer from editing for safety.

Now we'll set up our variables.

8.   Add the following ActionScript to the first frame in the Code layer.

```
var groundLevel = ground._y;
var ballOffset = ball._height/2;
var gravity = 10;
var velocity = 0;
```

If you're using Normal mode, these are all var commands found in the Actions book, but when programming code, it's usually a lot easier to go into Expert mode and just type the code straight in.

This frame will only be run once. We're using it to set up the variables that are involved in the calculation of the movement of the ball. These variables are:

- groundLevel – this is the point at which we expect the ball to bounce. We extract this from the ground symbol instance's _y position property. If you're new to ActionScript, the dot notation here is referring to the y position (_y) of the clip with the instance name ground. Because we set the top of the ground movie clip to a 0 y value earlier, we know that the y position of any instance of it will relate to the 'surface' of the ground.

- ballOffset – as with the ground level, we will also be extracting the y position of the ball from the ball instance. However, in this case, we're looking for the *base* of the ball, which we know to be offset from the _y property by half the height of the ball. We therefore extract and store this value, which we'll later add to the ball's y position to give us the location of the bottom of the ball.

- gravity – this is a constant downward acceleration.

- velocity – the speed of the ball. This will be updated in frame 2.

Note that the first two of these values have been taken from the instances they're associated with, rather than being hard coded to a fixed value. This ensures that should we change the graphics in any way, either by moving them around the stage or changing their sizes, we won't need to alter the code. Another labor-saving bit of reusability.

Note also that we've given the variables descriptive names. This is good practice, as it means that when we come back to edit the program, we'll know what every variable refers to. A good set of variable names should be virtually self-explanatory.

9.   We'll now begin the animation proper at frame 2. We'll want to loop back to this point later, and we don't want to break the animation if we move it, so use the Frame panel to give it a label, FallingCalc:

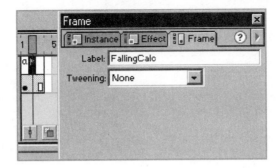

The animation will consist of two phases: updating the velocity, and updating the position of the ball.

10. Open up the Actions panel for frame 2 of the code layer and type in the following code:

```
// Update velocity

if ( (ball._y + ballOffset) < groundLevel)
{       //Gravity
        velocity += gravity;
}
else
{
        if (velocity > 0)       //Bounce
        {
                velocity = - velocity * 0.8;
        }
}
```

To see clearly what's going on here, we'll take the code line by line.

The first line is a comment, denoted by the // notation. It's a good idea to comment your code as fully and informatively as you can, so that you, or someone else, can come back to it at a later date and see exactly how it works and then update it easily. When the code is compiled into a file, all of the comments are ignored by Flash, so they won't affect the final size of your movie in any way.

The next line starts the program proper:

```
if ((ball._y + ballOffset) < groundLevel)
```

Here, we're checking if the current position of the base of the ball is above or below ground level. In Flash, the 0,0 point on the stage is in the top-left corner, so positive y values are in the downward direction. Therefore, we add the ballOffset to the ball's center coordinates to find the position of the base of the ball, and check if it's less than groundLevel to see if it's above ground.

Next, we have:

```
{        //Gravity
        velocity += gravity;
}
```

If we're above ground level, then we accelerate in the direction of gravity. The `+=` notation in this line is a shorthand way of writing: `velocity = velocity + gravity;`

This is followed by:

```
else
{
        if (velocity > 0)      //Bounce
        {
                velocity = - velocity * 0.8;
        }
}
```

If we're not *above* ground level, we must be at or below it. We therefore bounce by converting our downward velocity to an upward one. A constant factor of 0.8 is also applied to ensure that the bounces gradually fade away.

11. Now that we have our new velocity, we need to apply it to the ball. Enter the following code in frame 3:

```
// Update position
ball._y += velocity;

//And restart calculation
gotoAndPlay("FallingCalc");
```

The first of these lines updates the position of the ball by adding the velocity value to it. The second takes us back to the start of the loop in frame 2, recalculating the velocity and the new position of the ball.

12. Now play your movie. If your ball seems to bounce *behind* the ground, use the Modify > Arrange menu to send the ground symbol behind the ball.

It's not bad, but there are a couple of things you may want to play with to improve. You'll no doubt have noticed that the ball doesn't always bounce at the same place. This is because the check for a bounce in frame 2 isn't taking into account the velocity of the ball (that is, if the change in position indicated is greater than the distance to the ground, it will be *under* the ground before the next bounce). The way to solve this is to alter the position update in frame 3 so that if the ball's velocity will take it under ground level (remembering that in Flash, the higher the y number, the lower the level), the position is only changed to ground level. The implementation of this is left as an exercise for you to try yourself. Another thing you might want to try is playing with the variables in the first frame: try changing `velocity` by giving it a value between 0.1 and 1 and see what difference it makes. This is a good program to play around with, as any changes that you make to it can be easily seen when the movie is played.

Illustrating the Concepts: Functions

Now that you've toyed with some basic variables and loops, it's time to turn to functions. In this example we'll be creating a program to generate a fractal. Don't worry if when you're typing in the code you're not exactly sure of what you're writing – it'll all be explained at the end of each section.

Generating a Fractal

1. The first thing we need to do is set up the stage. As you did before with the bouncing ball example, create two layers, one for Graphics and one for Code. Once again, give the Code layer 3 keyframes, and the Graphics layer 3 normal frames.

2. On the Graphics layer, draw a straight horizontal line and convert it to a movie clip called Prim – short for **primitive**. Give it an instance name of Prim1:

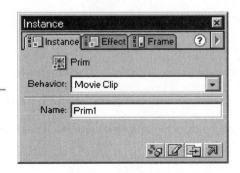

3.   Now we need to make sure that the registration point (the crosshair) for the Prim symbol is on the far left of the line. This can be done the same way as the ground was in the previous example: open the symbol up in its own edit window, then either move it by hand, or use the Info panel to set it at 0,0 to position it at the right of the crosshair:

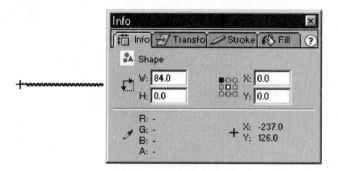

This primitive is going to be used as a line *generator* rather than as a line itself. Notice that there was no specific length given for the line – this is because when we run the program, the line itself will be invisible. We'll actually be using copies of the movie clip to display on the screen, and setting the length ourselves in the code.

4.   Time to start the hard work. Open up the Actions panel for the first frame of the Code layer and type in the following:

```
elementCount = 1;

//Generate a fractal at position x, y
x = 100;
y = 100;

//Init
l = 1;
w = 1;
h = 0;
rotation = 0;

Prim1._visible = false;
```

This is where we declare all of our initial variables:

- elementCount – keeps track of the number of elements

- x, y – the position to start drawing the fractal from

- l – the length of an element of the fractal

■ w, h – the width and height of each element at any given time (depends on rotation)

■ rotation – the rotation of each element

We also set our parent movie clip, Prim1, to be invisible at this point.

We'll be defining a couple of functions in this frame as well. The first of these functions is used to raise one value to the power of another. There is an existing Math.pow function in Flash 5, but this seems to have problems squaring a negative number. The function we'll be creating, Pow, takes two arguments: a number, x, and the power to which it is to be raised, n. Using a for loop, it multiplies x by another variable, result, n times.

5. Enter the following in frame 1:

```
function Pow(x,n)
{
    var result,i;
    result = 1;
    for(i=0;i<n;i++)
    {
        result *= x;
    }
    return result;
}
```

6. The second function, Turn(), is the workhorse of the fractal generator. The fractal is generated over a number of iterations, where at each iteration a new line is added at right angles to the previous one. Turn() calculates whether this angle should be clockwise or counter-clockwise, with 1 standing for clockwise and -1 for counter-clockwise. The value that we pass to Turn() is called i.

```
function Turn(i)
{
    //Find the turn direction of the i'th turn
    //1 = clockwise; -1 = counter-clockwise

    if (i<=0)
    {
        trace("Invalid Parameter in Turn : i should be > 0");
        return 1; //Avoid exception
    }

    //Reduce i to first odd number when dividing by 2
    var halfi, n;
    halfi = i/2;
    n = Math.ceil(halfi);
```

continues overleaf

```
        while (halfi == n)
        {
                halfi /= 2;
                n = Math.ceil(halfi);
        }

        //When number is odd, turn = (-1)**n where i = 2n - 1
        return Pow(-1,n);
}
```

Here, the first `if` statement is an error handling routine – we have to check to ensure that we've been passed valid parameters. If we're passed an `i` value of zero or less, the algorithm will continue forever. Therefore, even though we don't intend to pass this value, it's good practice to put in a check in case someone else uses our code, or we just forget. To make sure we keep everyone informed, we'll also use a `trace` statement to tell everybody that a problem is occurring if this happens. The `trace` statement will send our error message to the Output window if the error occurs while the program is running. By returning a value of 1, we're making sure that the program doesn't actually crash when the bug occurs, but instead warns the user and carries on running, using a dummy value for that iteration.

The `Math.ceil` function simply rounds up the number that we pass to it.

The second frame is where all of our movie copying and color changing will take place.

7.   First of all, enter the following:

```
        myMovieName = "Element" + String(elementCount);
        Prim1.duplicateMovieClip(myMovieName,elementCount);
        elementCount++;
        myElement = eval(myMovieName);
        myElement._x = x;
        myElement._y = y;
        myElement._width = l;
        myElement._rotation = rotation;
        myElement._visible = true;
```

The first line generates a unique name for our new element by appending the `elementCount` variable onto the end of the word `Element`. Eventually, we'll run into trouble when `elementCount` overflows and goes back to zero, but we can assume that by the time we reach that point we'll have probably run out of system resources anyway, due to the number of separate movie clips that will then be running.

The second line creates a duplicate of our Prim1 movie clip, gives it a new name, and puts it on a new level. The next thing we do is to add 1 to our `elementCount`.

The final lines are all to set the various properties of the newly duplicated movie clip. First of all, the variable `myElement` is used to hold a reference to the movie clip by assigning it the evaluation of the movie clip name:

```
myElement = eval(myMovieName);
```

This is a similar idea to creating a folder shortcut on the desktop on your computer – the shortcut is just a reference to the position of the original folder on your hard drive. Anything that you pass to the shortcut will be applied to the destination folder. In the same way, anything that we pass to myElement will be applied to the particular movie clip it's pointing to.

Underneath this code, we'll add a short routine to change the color of each new element. Luckily, one of the new features of Flash 5 ActionScript is a built in Color object that's perfectly suited to our task.

8.   Add this code after the previous chunk:

```
col = new Color(myElement);
colVal += 10;
if ((colVal & 0xff) > 0xf5) {colVal += 0x0900;}
if ((colVal & 0xff00) > 0xf500) {colVal += 0x090000;}
col.setRGB(colVal);
```

Before the Color object can be used, we have to use a **constructor** to create an instance of it. Using a constructor is similar to declaring a variable, in that we make the declaration that we want a new Color object, and Flash's built in constructors automatically build one for us based on the Color object's template. The code to do this is in the first line of this code:

```
col = new Color(myElement);
```

This works by setting col to be the name of the instance of the Color object, and then just gives the target that we want to change the color of, in this case using the same myElement shortcut to point to the current movie clip.

Once the new Color object instance is created, we can use its built in setRGB method to control the color of all the components of the movie clip. We use colVal to keep track of the current color, and increment it by 10 each time. The two complicated looking if statements simply allow us to increment the green value by 10 every time the blue value rolls over, and the red value by 10 every time the blue value rolls over. The number preceded by 0x is the hexadecimal (hex) value of the color; the 0x just marks it as being hex. (RGB colors are represented by two digits for each of the Red, Green, and Blue values in order, ranging from 00 to FF. The first pair of values represents Red, the second, Green, and the third Blue. So FF0000 is 100% Red, 00FF00 is 100% Green, and 0000FF is 100% Blue, and all of the other values represent the colors in between.)

Note that we don't initialize colVal with an assigned value. Any variable whose value is not specifically initialized will automatically have its value set to 0.

9.   The final set of actions in this frame tidy up the position and rotation of the cursor ready to put down the next movie clip. Add them now:

```
x+=w;
y-=h;
e = Turn(elementCount);
rotation += e*90;
tmp = h;
h = -e * w;
w = e *tmp;
```

This code moves us to the end of the current element, runs our Turn() function to tell us which way we should be facing, then turns and sets up the new dimensions of the next element.

The final piece of code needs to go in frame 3. It simply tells the movie to loop back to frame 2 and run through the whole process again.

10.   Here's the code to add next:

```
gotoAndPlay ("AnimStart");
```

11.   Now, finally, you can test your movie and watch the fractal grow. Again, try tinkering with some of the variables, and seeing what improvements you can make to the program.

Illustrating the Concepts: Objects

To build an object-based mouse trail, we're going to create an object that knows how to play follow my leader — each object in the trail will be trying to keep up with the one in front. If we then attach the leading object to the mouse, all of the objects will create a trail behind, whenever the mouse is moved.

Creating a Mouse Trail

The first thing to do is to create your object. We'll be using a sphere as our core element, but you can use whatever you'd like.

1.   Create your image and convert it to a movie clip symbol:

2. Now double-click on your movie clip to open it, and create three keyframes.

3. Next, open up the Actions panel for the first frame. Add the code to this frame that'll initialize the variables for our movie:

```
// Set up variables
this.Force = {x:0, y:0};
this.attractionCoefficient = 0.3;
```

The keyword `this` is a reference to the current movie clip. It means that we don't need to know the instance name of the object, we just refer to it as `this` and Flash understands that we mean the clip that this code resides in.

The first code statement creates a new object with the properties `x` and `y`, and it also initializes these properties to 0. The `Force` variable represents the attractive force between a mouse trail element and object that it's following. This value is proportional to the distance between them, so that the mouse trail element will slow down and stop when the distance is zero (that is, when it reaches the object it's following).

We then update the position...

```
this.attractionCoefficient = 0.3;
```

...by assuming that the mouse trail element is moving at a speed proportional to the force. The `attractionCoefficient` is the speed at which the clip moves towards its leader. We'll be adding more code to this frame – such as defining which movie clip is the leader – later on.

We now want to set up a two-frame loop to calculate the force attracting each sphere to its leader, and update the position it needs to move towards it.

4. Type the following into frame 2:

```
// Now play follow the leader
// Update positions as variables to allow flexibility
if (this._leader != undefined) {
    Force.x = 0;
    Force.y = 0;
    Attraction(this._leader._x, this._leader._y);
    UpdatePosition();
}
```

Firstly, we note that if there is no leader then we don't bother doing anything. The `!` means NOT, so we're basically saying 'if the leader is not undefined, then do this', or rather, 'if this clip has a leader then do this'. This allows us to set one object as the leader of the pack. Next we set the force to zero in both directions. This allows us to build up the force incrementally. In this example, we only have one function setting the force, but we might later want to add in a repulsive force to stop the balls getting too close to each other. Now we call two functions, one to calculate the force attracting the ball to its leader, and the next to update the position based on that force:

```
Attraction(this._leader._x, this._leader._y);
UpdatePosition();
```

The first of these functions calculates the force of each sphere's attraction.

5. To define the function, add this code in frame 2 beneath what you've just typed:

```
// Function to calculate attractive force
function Attraction (x, y) {
    // Attraction is proportional to the distance
    var xdiff = x - _x;
    var ydiff = y - _y;
    this.Force.x += this.attractionCoefficient*xdiff;
    this.Force.y += this.attractionCoefficient*ydiff;
}
```

This function simply sets the force to be proportional to the distance between the clip and a point defined by the coordinates x and y. By separating it out into a separate function, however, we can generate this force whatever we want.

The *strength* of the force is set by the attractionCoefficient.

6. The next function updates the position of the clip. Build the code for it now:

```
function UpdatePosition () {
    this._x += this.Force.x;
    this._y += this.Force.y;
}
```

This function just applies the positional information generated by the Attraction function to the calling movie clip instance.

If the attractionCoefficient is 1, then the balls will instantly move to the position of their leader. Setting a value of less than 1 gives a more satisfying feel to the motion by generating a lag to the movement.

Setting the attractionCoefficient to a value *greater* than 1 provides an interesting effect and is certainly worth a try. Providing the value is less than 2, the effect is that the balls will once more approach the leader, oscillating on either side of it, giving an appearance of planets in orbit.

If the value is greater than 2, then the motion will no longer decay, and the balls will all fly off the screen. Feel free to experiment with it and see what you can come up with.

7. Finally, complete the loop by putting this...

```
gotoAndPlay (2);
```

...into frame 3.

We now need to set up the stage properly by placing the necessary objects there, and then return to frame 1 to complete the program. At the moment we've only got one lead sphere, so I've added another seven to make eight spheres in total. There are two methods to creating the 'tail'.

I've gone here for the technique of dragging each object from the Library onto the stage explicitly, but it's equally possible to use a `duplicateMovieClip` action on our original clip to create another seven instances.

8. Create your extra instances by whichever method you prefer:

9. Either way, we must name our new instances. I've named the lead ball Head, and all of the subsequent balls Element1 through Element7.

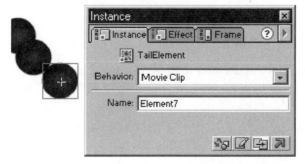

Finally, we need to add the last code to frame 1 of the main movie to connect all of our clips together. We'll also add a piece of code to make our clips incrementally smaller than the leader.

10. Add this code in frame 1:

```
var sizeChange = 4/5;
Element1._leader = Head;
Element1._width = Element1._leader._width * sizeChange;
Element1._height = Element1._leader._height * sizeChange;
```

```
for (i=2;i<=7;i++)
{
    myElement = eval( "Element" + String(i));
    myElement._leader = eval("Element" + String(i-1));
    myElement._width = myElement._leader._width * sizeChange;
    myElement._height = myElement._leader._height * sizeChange;
}
```

The first line sets up our sizeChange variable: this is just an arbitrary value to say that each sphere will be 4/5 the size of its leader.

The next line sets the leader property of the Element1 instance to be the original instance, Head. The next two lines change the size of Element1 based on the size of the leader, and the sizeChange variable we're applying to it.

The for loop runs through exactly the same actions for the remaining instances. It firstly sets a new myElement object to refer to the current instance:

```
myElement = eval( "Element" + String(i));
```

This code uses Flash's eval function to extract the relevant element name using the literal value inside the quotes, plus the value derived from the built in String function. Here, the String function just turns the current (numeric) value of the loop counter variable i into a string variable so that it can be concatenated with "Element".

Then we tell this element that its leader is the Element one number beneath it:

```
myElement._leader = eval("Element" + String(i-1));
```

Finally, it sets the size of the current instance based on that of its leader.

11. Absolutely the last thing to do is to actually attach the Head ball to the mouse. This can be surprisingly easily accomplished by adding the following code to the end of frame 1:

```
Mouse.hide();                //To hide the existing pointer
startDrag ("Head", true);
```

The leading ball will now follow the mouse wherever it goes, and with it comes its little band of followers.

Conclusion

If you haven't done so yet, go back over the examples here and play with them. Change some of the variables, even invent your own. Make your bouncing ball squash up as it hits the ground, then expand again as it rebounds. Exchange the color object in the fractal for a sound object with an appropriate noise, and with a bit of work you can turn it into a weird volume fractal. Add a bit more spark to your mouse trail, literally, by adding a series of smaller sparkles that spin off from each of the main balls, then fade away. Experiment: it's what Flash is there for, and it's what Flash is great at.

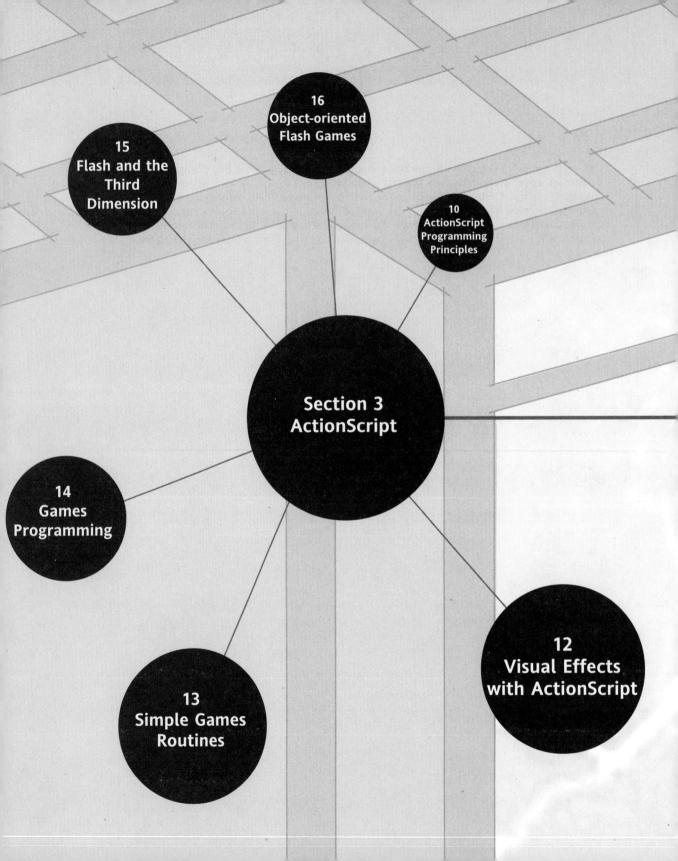

Section 3
ActionScript

16
Object-oriented
Flash Games

15
Flash and the
Third
Dimension

10
ActionScript
Programming
Principles

14
Games
Programming

13
Simple Games
Routines

12
Visual Effects
with ActionScript

Chapter 11
ActionScript
Integration

Timelines, Movie Clips and Objects

This chapter is designed to give you some insights into the timeline, movie clips and objects. You'll already have worked pretty extensively with the timeline and movie clips, but what I want to do here is step back and look at them in a larger context. I'll do this by looking at how different timelines in a movie interact, and at the order in which code is run when you have a movie with multiple movie clips and nested timelines. The rest of the chapter is concerned with sketching out how you might like to start thinking about movie clips as *objects* – essentially as lumps of code that can have a life of their own and built-in behaviors. Movie clips are massively powerful tools in Flash and can be put to terrific use when they have functions and other coded behaviors built into them.

This chapter is a mix of theory and practice, with the main concepts delineated at the start, followed by some worked practical examples that illustrate those concepts. As ever, you can find the relevant FLAs on the accompanying CD.

Let's begin by considering the Flash timeline.

The Main Timeline

The core of any Flash animation is the main timeline:

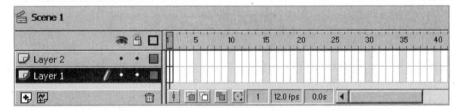

Whereas traditional programs follow a timeline determined by the flow control statements and at a speed determined by how long it takes to execute each statement, Flash has a built-in timeline that moves along at a precisely predefined **frame rate**, which is expressed in the form of the Flash movie's frames per second (fps) setting:

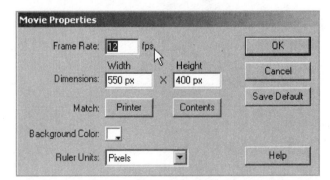

All the movie clips embedded in the main Flash movie also inherit this frame rate.

Any ActionScript code you create is either attached to a frame on the main timeline, attached to a frame inside a movie clip, or attached to any movie component (such as a button or a movie clip) that's on the main timeline or nested inside another movie clip.

The execution of the code in ActionScript can be thought of in the following terms:

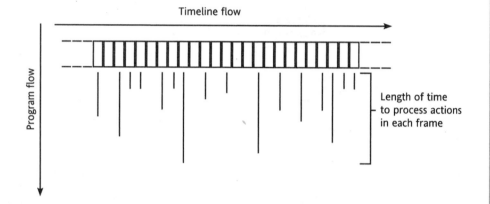

Each frame on the main timeline is played at the fixed fps rate, irrespective of how much content or code there is in that frame. Some frames have code, with the code in each frame differing in both length and the time it takes to execute. If the code takes *longer* to execute than the default time allocated to the frame by the frame rate, then the animation will 'block' the timeline: that is wait for the code to finish executing before proceeding to the next frame. If the animation is delayed by too great a time, Flash will issue a warning and offer to switch off the script. Hopefully though, this shouldn't ever happen if the code is divided intelligently between frames.

Avoiding Timeline Blocking

It's very important not to block the timeline. If an animation is delayed by slow code, then, at best, the animation will be jerky and poorly controlled and, at worst, a warning will be issued and the script disabled.

So how much time have we got to play with here? Well, first we need to work out the number of milliseconds it takes to play each frame. Assuming a frame rate of 12 frames per second (the default for Flash 5), and knowing that there are 1000 milliseconds in a second, each frame will take 1000/12 = 83.33 ms to play. So if our code takes longer than this to execute, we know that we'll likely to be disrupting the smooth flow of the timeline.

Furthermore, the time for a statement to execute will depend on the power of your computer; benchmarking on a 600 MHz Pentium shows that each ActionScript statement takes between 0.04 and 0.06 ms. On a PowerMac G4, the results were, similarly, in the range of 0.05 to 0.06 ms. This means that you'll begin to affect the timeline flow after about 2000 operations.

Ideally therefore, we should keep the amount of code per frame to a minimum. You're most likely thinking that there's no way you're ever going to have 2000 individual statements in your code for a single frame, and you're probably right. So why bother writing about it? Well, the complicating factor is that every time you run a loop, each of the statements in the loop will be run as well; run that loop ten times, and you've run each of those statements ten times too. Nest this loop inside another loop and you start getting a lot of statements. For example, here are a few lines of code that'll quite happily cause Flash problems:

```
for (a=1; a<100; a++) {
    for (b=1; b<100; b++) {
        for (c=1; c<100; c++) {
        }
    }
}
```

The issue here is that there are three nested loops; each iteration of the first loop will spawn a hundred iterations of the second one, and each iteration of *that* loop will spawn a hundred iterations of the *third* one. Which means 100 x 100 x 100 statements – considerably over that 2000 statement threshold.

The main problems of timeline blocking are caused by nested loops such as the one above, and by **recursive functions**. A recursive function is a function that *calls itself*. Say you have a range of numbers from 1 to 100, and you're trying to find a number within that range; you might have a function that cuts the range in half, and checks to see which half the number's in. It then calls itself again, cutting the new range in half... etc. etc. until it finds the number, and then ejects itself from the recursive loop.

To get around this problem, we should try and avoid using these constructs where possible. Recursive functions are easy to avoid, but steering clear of overactive loops can be more difficult.

There's nothing wrong with using loops in code, of course – they're a very useful construct in programming, but they're easy things to slip up on. We can get around this problem to some extent if we remember that we have *two* time dimensions to play with; instead of looping the whole code in one frame, we can loop it over a section of the timeline, as the following example illustrates...

Creating a Loading Screen Loop

To show the benefits of timeline loops over program loops, we'll look at a simple example: waiting for a movie to load. We'll create a movie that'll load another movie and then play it. We don't want to start playing the second movie until it's fully loaded into the first one, so we have a holding screen until the movie is ready.

1. First create three layers in a new movie: one for the code, one to hold the movie we're going to load, and one for the animation we'll play while we're loading the movie. Rename the layers Code, Final Movie, and Loading Screen respectively.

The `loadMovie` action can target the loaded movie clip into either a movie clip or a level in the parent movie. In this example, we'll be targeting a blank movie clip that will act as the 'container' – a kind of 'placeholder' – for the movie clip that we load in.

2. Create a new movie clip symbol called replace, and drag an instance of this symbol from the Library into the Final Movie layer. We'll need to give this instance the name movie1:

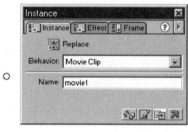

As you can see, a blank symbol in Flash 5 is represented by a small white circle on the stage.

Next we'll create our loading animation, which will display while the second movie is loading in.

3. Start this animation in the second frame of the Loading Screen layer. We've just got a simple looping shape tween, but you can make it as complicated as you'd like. Remember though that the loading screen is supposed to load instantly and play while we wait for the main movie to load, so don't make it too complicated:

There are three distinct steps to the process of loading the movie:

- Initiating the process

- Waiting for the movie to load

- Starting to play the loaded movie

4. To build these steps, create three keyframes on the Code layer and label them Initialize, Loading Loop, and Start Movie respectively. The Initialize frame goes in

frame 1, the Loading Loop frame goes in frame 2, and the Start Movie frame goes 2 frames after the end of your loading animation; in our case, this is frame 12:

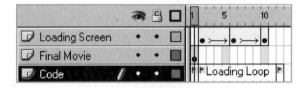

5. Add the following code to the frame labeled Initialize:

```
movie1.loadMovie("http://mysite.com/really_big.swf");
movie1.stop();
movie1._visible = false;
```

In this code, we first initiate the load process by calling the loadMovie command from within the empty movie container that we gave the instance name movie1. You'll need to replace the URL here with the location of the file you wish to load in. For test purposes, you can load an existing movie from your hard drive. To do this, the target movie needs to be in the same folder as the published movie that you're calling it from. So if your calling SWF is published in a folder called c:\flash examples, then the really_big.swf that you're going to be loading should be in the same folder. If this is the case, then your first line of code would instead be:

```
movie1.loadMovie("really_big.swf");
```

Notice that if you're targeting a local SWF rather than an URL, you *don't* include the path to the file, just the file name itself. To reiterate: to access a local SWF by using just its name with the loadMovie command, that SWF file must be in the same folder as the SWF that's calling it.

The next line ensures that the movie doesn't start playing until it has fully loaded. Then finally, we set its visible property to false so that we only see the loading screen and not the first frames of the partially loaded movie that we're pulling in.

To wait for the movie to load, we need to check the number of frames loaded against the total number of frames.

6. Add the following code to the Loading Loop frame:

```
movie1._visible = false;
if (movie1._framesloaded == movie1._totalframes) {
    gotoAndPlay("Start Movie");
}
```

The first line of this code again makes sure that the movie isn't visible. The if statement uses the built in framesloaded and totalframes properties to check if we've received all the frames of the movie that we're loading, and if we *have* it goes to the frame labeled Start Movie and starts playing. If the total number of frames has *not* yet been reached, then Flash will continue to play our loading animation.

7. To ensure that the loading animation is self-contained, add a keyframe to the Code layer, one frame after the end of the animation – frame 11 in our example – and add the following code to it:

```
gotoAndPlay("Loading Loop");
```

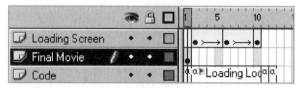

This just makes sure that we keep on looping our loading animation until we're ready to start playing the main movie.

Finally, we need to start the movie once it's loaded, then extend the timeline so that we can see it play.

8. To do this, add the following code to the Start Movie frame:

```
movie1._visible = true;
movie1.play();
stop();
```

With this piece of code, we first make the movie visible again, then start it playing. The stop command ensures that the timeline doesn't loop back to the beginning and attempt to load in the movie again.

9. Lastly, insert a frame in the Final Movie layer to match up with the last frame in your Code layer, in our case frame 12, so that you'll be able to see the movie when it starts playing.

Next, let's look at working with movie clips in some more detail.

Working with Movie Clips

Another concept in Flash that's often confusing to programmers is the separation into scenes, frames and movie clips. We dealt with frames in the last section – they're just individual slots in the timeline that hold content – and scenes are just a convenient way of dividing up the timeline into logical and manageable sections.

Movie clips, on the other hand, are more confusing. Not only can they appear and disappear at random points along the timeline, but they have their own timeline which operates in a way that's (semi-)independent of the main timeline.

Working with Multiple Timelines

One important point to remember when you're working with movie clips is that each movie clip contains its own timeline and can jump around that timeline without affecting the timeline of other movie clips. That's not to say that the timelines are strictly independent. Remember that the frame rate is constant across the entire movie, so movie clips are synchronized to this extent. For example, two movie clips containing four frames each will remain in tight synchronization with each other; two movie clips containing four and eight frames respectively will repeat every eight frames; and two movie clips containing three and five frames will repeat every fifteen frames.

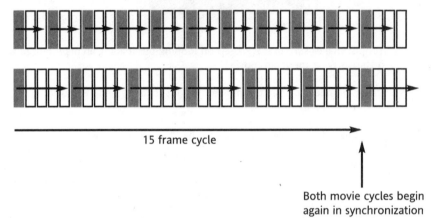

15 frame cycle

Both movie cycles begin
again in synchronization

The simple way of stating this is that the order of frames in movie clips is independent, but the frame rate is not. All movies take their frame rate from the top-level movie, whether they're defined as symbols in the Library of that movie or have been loaded in from an external source.

All extra movie clips in a given frame will potentially act as a drag on the frame rate, since all scripts have to be run before the playhead will move on to the next frame. This means that, in general, you should spread out lengthy operations over several successive movie clips. Spreading them out over several layers, or any other concurrent frames, won't really help much, and may even aggravate matters due to the overhead of moving between timelines. However, the reason for separating code into discrete timelines is usually more to do with attaching the code to its appropriate element (e.g. the code to perform collision detection for a movie clip should be within that movie clip). The best method is to optimize each timeline individually, not *across* timelines as this will usually lead to confusion of the code and cause more problems than it solves.

Working with Nested Movie Clips

Another issue to deal with is the nesting of movie clips. Not only can the main timeline contain numerous movie clips, each with their own timeline, but each of these movie clips may contain further movie clips and so on, ad infinitum. Perhaps the most difficult thing to grasp when working with nested movie clips is the **scoping** of variables and functions. When a variable is declared within a given timeline, then that timeline is its scope. You'll only be able to access the variable by just its name alone if you're accessing it from within the same timeline.

However, you may change your timeline path using the following syntax:

```
timeline_path.variable_name
```

If you're familiar with object-oriented languages such as Java, this should be looking very familiar. For example, if you create a movie which contains two movie clips, `bodger` and `badger`, and each contains a variable `count`, then you access them as `bodger.count` and `badger.count` respectively. The same applies to properties, as they're really just system-defined variables. So to access the `y` position property of `badger`, you'd use this syntax:

```
badger._y
```

To go up a level in a hierarchy of nested movie clip timelines is even simpler. Every timeline contains a pseudo object, `_parent`, which represents the timeline above it. We can also use multiple dots to access additional levels. Thus, to access a variable called `loop`, we could equally well use the syntax...

```
bodger._parent.loop
```

...which will take us down to the `bodger` timeline, back up to its parent timeline (that is, where we started) and then access the `loop` variable.

If we're getting very adventurous we can also use the `_root` and `_level0` pseudo objects. Like the `_parent` object, these take us to a different timeline, but this time, we jump all the way to the *top-level* timeline, the root of the whole movie.

In fact, there's a subtle difference between `_root` and `_level0`. The `_root` nottakes us to the highest level for the particular movie we're in, and `_level0` takes us to the timeline labeled `_level0` which *may* not be the same thing. For example, if the movie we're calling from has been loaded into another movie (using the `loadMovie` command), `_root` will take us to the level we've been loaded into, not the top level of the whole movie.

And before you ask, yes, there is a `_level1`, `_level2` etc. It just depends how many timeline levels exist in the currently playing movie.

Graphics, Movie Clips and Buttons

Have you ever wondered why there are three symbol types in Flash? Well, the difference isn't in the definition, but in the way that the symbols *behave*. Every symbol is, in effect, a movie clip: made up of a sequence of frames. However, the way these frames are interpreted depends on their repertoire of set behaviors.

A **graphic** symbol's behavior is the simplest; it just plays through the frames in the symbol. The symbol can't be manipulated from external code and any code in the graphic will have no effect on external symbols. In addition, the timeline of the graphic will be completely synchronized to the timeline it's contained in, so that a twelve-frame graphic in a two-frame timeline will play only two frames. The graphic may also have other play options selected, such as playing once, starting at a different frame, or displaying only a single frame.

Movie clip symbol behavior is what we've already been referring to implicitly in this chapter and the previous one, and it's the type of behavior that provides Flash movies with the most power and variety. As with the graphic symbol, a movie clip symbol contains a number of frames that will play in the usual way. However, the movie clip timeline is independent of the containing timeline, so that a twelve-frame *movie clip* on a two-frame main timeline *will* play all twelve frames in the movie clip. Each individual movie clip symbol instance on the stage can be given a name and manipulated within code. Furthermore, code within any movie clip instance can manipulate other objects and variables itself. Only a movie clip can have event code attached to it using the onClipEvent statement for things such as telling when a clip is loaded, or when the mouse is pressed. The effect of this is equivalent to adding a function that'll be called every time the defined event occurs (e.g. releasing the mouse button). This set of extended behaviors is what makes the movie clip symbol, along with ActionScript itself, a powerful engine in the most sophisticated and interactive Flash movies.

Finally, the **button** symbol has a completely separate set of behaviors. The button symbol only has four frames representing its four states – Up, Over, Down and Hit. Instead of playing its frames in order, as do the other symbol types, the button plays each frame in response to certain events. A button instance may have event code attached to it using the on command, so that ActionScript instructions are triggered – for instance – when the user moves their mouse over button or clicks on it. Buttons can have graphics and movie clips embedded in them.

When is Code Executed?

The order of execution of ActionScript is affected by many different factors. If a movie contains several movie clips, each containing several layers and several frames, then the order in which statements are executed will be affected.

The basic rules for ActionScript running order are as follows:

Within a single frame:

- Statements are executed in the order in which they're encountered. Code within a frame forms a single unit – no other code can be executed between the start and end of a frame's playing time.

Within a single layer:

- Frames are executed one after the other.

- Functions are executed when they're called; remember that they can only be called *after* they've been declared.

- Event handlers (the on or onClipEvent commands) are executed when the event occurs. Again, they can only execute after they've been declared.

Within a single movie clip:

- Code in frames playing at the same time is executed in layer order, from top to bottom (that is, from front to back).

- Frame ordering is sequential.

Within a movie:

- For concurrent frames, code in a movie clip is executed after any code in the parent.

It's also important to remember that the timeline of a movie clip will only start in the frame it's instantiated in.

The easiest way to check the order in which your actions are being processed is by liberal use of the `trace` action. For example, say you had variables called `Sheep`, `Gates`, `Count`, and `AmountOfSleep`. Imagine that they're all in different frames or movie clips, and that you want to know the order in which they're encountered. To do this you'd put a `trace` action after each variable was first used. For example:

```
Sheep = 24;
trace (Sheep);
```

Now when you test the movie, as soon as this line of code is run, the Output window will appear with the number 24 in it. To make this a little clearer, you can change the `trace` command to include the name of the variable; so using the previous example, the code would now be:

```
Sheep = 24;
trace ("Sheep = " + Sheep);
```

Which will give the result: Sheep = 24 in the Output window.

The following worked example illustrates the importance of code ordering.

Multicolored Pool Balls from a Single Symbol

Here, we're going to create an example for a proposed 9-ball pool game. The game won't actually be playable, but at least you'll be able to see the different color balls. For ease of example, we're treating the 9-ball as all white, rather than having to complicate things with a stripe at this stage. At the start of this example, we'll have a group of pool balls that are all the same uniform gray color, but by using a single function, we'll convert them all to different colors. The code shows you how to use a 'member' function to set up properties of a movie clip, such that a single symbol can be re-used effectively. It will also illustrate the importance of code ordering in ActionScript.

Rack of Balls

First we want to create a pool ball. We're going to use the `Color` object to set the color (using a color transform) so we want to start with a sphere which can be easily converted to any color.

1. To do this, create a circle filled with a gray and white radial fill, then convert it to a movie clip called Ball:

We'll be treating the pool ball as an independent object, so the first thing we need to do is give it some properties. The obvious properties of a pool ball are:

- Color

- Number

- Position

- Velocity

Of these, Position is already taken care of by the movie clip's built in x and y properties and, for pool balls, Color and Number are interdependent. Velocity would control the speed of the ball in the final game, but as we won't be taking this example that far, we won't include it in our code. Furthermore, none of these properties can be set until we have instances of the symbol: the Position properties will be set when we put an instance of the symbol onto the stage, so we only really need to worry about Color and Number here.

First of all, let's create an object that will contain all of the possible colors and numbers of the pool balls.

2. Double-click on the Ball movie clip to open it for editing, and bring up the Actions window for the first frame of the timeline. Type in the following ActionScript in Expert mode:

```
BallColors = {
Yellow: 1,
Blue: 2,
Red: 3,
Purple: 4,
Orange: 5,
Green: 6,
Brown: 7,
Black: 8,
White: 9
}
```

This syntax might be new to you. What we're doing here is using a very funky Flash 5 ActionScript component called the **object initializer**. This useful little beast allows us to create generic objects of our own, give them properties, and assign values to those properties. We're making use of it here to make a 'container' object that will store all of the values for the different balls and allow us to manipulate them easily in code: we'll be able to reference everything through the container object.

The first line is what tells Flash to create an object with the name BallColors:

```
BallColors = {
```

The opening brace after the equals sign tells Flash that what follows is the definition of the generic object's properties and their initial values. So the next line...

```
Yellow: 1,
```

...instructs Flash to create a Yellow property for the BallColors object, and the 1 after the colon indicates that we want to set that property's value to 1. Then we have a comma, followed by the rest of the property/value definitions for the BallColors object. Finally, we have a closing brace to tell Flash that our object definition is complete.

We can now read and write these properties' values using dot notation.

In the context of our pool balls, this does two things for us. Firstly, we can now refer to the colors by name when we set them. Secondly, it associates each color with a number.

Now we need to create a function that we can call in order to set the colors.

3. Type the following in the first frame after our previous statement:

```
function SetColor (ballColor) {
     col = new Color(this);
     trans = new Object();
```

The initial line is the initialization statement for our new SetColor function, which will be passed a single argument called ballColor. Inside the body of the function itself we create two objects: col, a Color object that we can use to alter the color of our pool balls, and trans, another generic object with no pre-defined properties. Later, after setting the appropriate values in trans, we'll use it to pass a collection of parameters to one of the Color object's predefined functions – setTransform, which we'll use to set the color transforms on the balls.

The Color object is a new addition to Flash 5 ActionScript, and it's an interesting object, in that it consists of a collection of functions which act on a target movie clip. For instance, the function SetColor doesn't act upon the Color object but upon its target *movie clip*. To be able to use the Color object, you first have to set up an instance of the object by using a 'constructor' statement – in this case new Color. This constructor takes a parameter that defines the target movie clip that it will act upon.

331

In this code, we want the target movie clip to be the one we're currently in, so we use the keyword this to tell Flash that we want the current instance (that is, the one that this code is running inside) to be the target of the new Color object.

After this, we need to enter the main body of the function, consisting of a series of if...else statements.

4.   Add this next block of code to the body of the function after the previous chunk. You may find that it's quicker to type in the first if, then copy and paste it eight more times before altering it:

```
if (ballColor == BallColors.Yellow) {
     trans.ba = 0;
} else if (ballColor == BallColors.Blue) {
     trans.ra = 0;
     trans.ga = 0;
} else if (ballColor == BallColors.Red) {
     trans.ga = 0;
     trans.ba = 0;
} else if (ballColor == BallColors.Purple) {
     trans.ra = 66;
     trans.ga = 0;
     trans.ba = 66;
} else if (ballColor == BallColors.Orange) {
     trans.ga = 66;
     trans.ba = 0;
} else if (ballColor == BallColors.Green) {
     trans.ra = 0;
     trans.ba = 0;
} else if (ballColor == BallColors.Brown) {
     trans.ra = 66;
     trans.ga = 33;
     trans.ba = 0;
} else if (ballColor == BallColors.Black) {
     trans.ra = 0;
     trans.ga = 0;
     trans.ba = 0;
} else if (ballColor == BallColors.White) {
     trans.rb = 40;
     trans.gb = 40;
     trans.bb = 40;
}
```

These statements set up the color transformation, dependent on the color that we wish to make the ball. At present, our ball is a white-gray gradient, and Flash will apply our color transformations on a per-pixel basis to each of the balls. This works by multiplying one of the RGB values of the ball by a set percentage. For instance, if we want to remove the blue from a ball, we multiply the Blue value by 0%. We'll look at how this works with a gradient.

We begin with a white to black gradient across the ball:

WHITE	LIGHT GRAY	DARK GRAY	BLACK
FFFFFF	999999	333333	000000

Next, we multiply the blue component (the last two digits of each six-digit hex color definition) by 0%, which gives:

FFFF00   999900   333300 .   000000

This has removed all of the blue pigment, leaving behind shades of yellow that run from lightest to darkest – black being the darkest shade there is. The ball still keeps its gradient, but we've changed its overall color.

You've probably noticed that the final color that we've set is white, and you're thinking, 'Hang on, if the ball's already white, why do we need to change it?' Good question: if you look closely at the code, you'll notice that whereas all of the other colors are suffixed by an 'a', e.g. `trans.ra`, the white values are suffixed by a 'b', e.g. `trans.rb`. The difference here is that while the 'a' values represent a percentage that the current color will be multiplied by, the 'b' values represent an amount to be added or subtracted to the current hex value of the color. For example, we want to lighten the gray shading of the ball to make it look more... well, *white*. We do this by adding 40 to the original RGB values, making the overall gradient lighter.

The last thing that we need to do is to apply our color transform. We do this by putting our `trans` values straight into our `color` object.

5.   Add the following ActionScript to the bottom of the code:

```
// Now set color
col.setTransform(trans);
}
```

And that's all the code done for the ball. Note that this function is for initialization only, as *reapplying* the color transformation may have some strange results: the color transform works by multiplying the red, green and blue components of the ball by specified fractions, and when this is applied to our gray-shaded ball, it gives the required color. However, if the ball has already *had* its color altered, then applying another color transform won't give the required color – usually resulting in the ball turning black.

For instance, we can set the ball to be red by multiplying the green and blue components of the ball by zero, leaving only the red component. This technique is used so that the shading of the ball is retained, and it will still resemble a sphere rather than a red circle. However, if we then try to change the color of the ball to green (by removing the red and blue components), we'll have problems, as we've already removed the green and the blue. This means that when we apply the new transform, it'll remove the blue and red components leaving nothing but a black disk.

Next we need to add the pool balls to the stage. There are a couple of ways we can do this. We can either add them manually, giving them instance names of `Ball1`, `Ball2`, `Ball3` etc., or we can use `duplicateMovieClip` to do the job for us.

6. In this case, just drag each instance onto the stage by hand so we can line them up correctly by eye. We want the balls in a diamond shape with `Ball9`, the white ball, in the center. It doesn't matter what order the other balls are in. The finished layout, with the appropriate instance names applied, should look something like this:

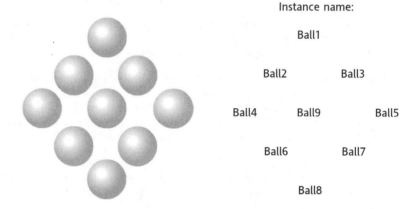

Instance name:

Ball1

Ball2   Ball3

Ball4   Ball9   Ball5

Ball6   Ball7

Ball8

The next thing that we have to do is tie the colors that we set up earlier to their respective instance names.

> *It's important to realise that we can't initialize the balls in the first frame that they appear in. This is because the function for initializing them doesn't exist until that frame has been executed. Remember that the order of code execution is parent first, then child. Thus the frame that defines the* `SetColor` *function won't be executed until after all of the code on the stage has run.*

7. To get around this problem, add a second keyframe to the main timeline and, finally, add the following ActionScript to frame 2 – this will call the function and apply the colors:

```
Ball1.SetColor(1);
Ball2.SetColor(2);
Ball3.SetColor(3);
Ball4.SetColor(4);
Ball5.SetColor(5);
Ball6.SetColor(6);
Ball7.SetColor(7);
Ball8.SetColor(8);
```

```
Ball9.SetColor(9);
```

```
stop();
```

This code sets each ball to its respective color by calling the SetColor function we created earlier for each instance of the ball on the stage and then stops. The first statement...

```
Ball1.SetColor(1);
```

...calls the function for Ball1, passing the function the argument 1, which is fed into the placeholder (ballColor) that we defined when we set up the function:

```
function SetColor (ballColor) {
```

Effectively, the function is now running like this...

```
SetColor (1) {
```

...with the number 1 representing ballColor. So what happens next? Well, look again at the first line of the if loop from the SetColor function:

```
if (ballColor == BallColors.Yellow) {
```

Remember, this loop will set the value for the color transformation of an individual ball. This line takes the current value of ballColor – 1 – and compares it to the value of the first property in the BallColors object that we created and stored the name/value pairs in earlier:

```
BallColors = {
Yellow: 1,
Blue: 2,
Red: 3,
Purple: 4,
Orange: 5,
Green: 6,
Brown: 7,
Black: 8,
White: 9
}
```

If the code finds that the current value of ballColor *is* the same as the Yellow property of this object, the if condition will be satisfied, and the next line of SetColor function will be executed:

```
trans.ba = 0;
```

This line will set the correct trans value to remove all the blue from the Ball1 instance, which will leave us with a yellow ball. As the if statement has been satisfied, the rest of the `else if` statements in the function will be ignored, and the function will jump to the lines that apply the `trans` value:

```
// Now set color
    col.setTransform(trans);
}
```

Remember that `col` is an instance of Flash's inbuilt `Color` object, and that it was set up to point at the current – `this` – movie clip when the function was initialized:

```
col = new Color(this);
```

So the `col.setTransform(trans);` line uses the Color object's `setTransform` method to apply the just-determined value of `trans` to the current movie clip – `Ball1`. At last, the ball is colored yellow.

The rest of the code in frame 2...

```
Ball2.SetColor(2);
Ball3.SetColor(3);
Ball4.SetColor(4);
Ball5.SetColor(5);
Ball6.SetColor(6);
Ball7.SetColor(7);
Ball8.SetColor(8);
Ball9.SetColor(9);

stop();
```

...performs this same processing for each of the remaining balls on the stage before stopping the movie so that we can delight at the sight of our rack of colored pool balls.

That might seem like a lot of work to change the color of a few spheres, but the real purpose of this exercise is to give you an insight into how you can combine Flash's built -in functions with your own functions, loops and code to create effects.

Another way to actually call the function and apply the colors would have been to use a loop in frame 2 to cycle through the ball instances, like this:

```
for (i=1; i<=9; i++) {
  eval("Ball" + String(i)).SetColor(i);
}
stop();
```

Here, we're using `i` as a loop counter and just adding its value to the end of `Ball` and `SetColor` in each loop iteration to pass the `SetColor` function the numbers it needs to make all of the color transformations.

8. The last thing to do is to change the background color to authentic blue baize, and then run your movie. You should see something like this:

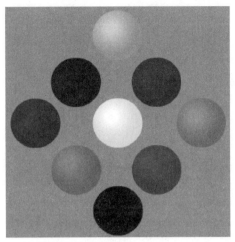

POOL BALLS IN COLOR

I'll leave the rest of the game to you. Check out the later chapters on games for some pointers.

This example demonstrates the point that movie clips are objects. They can use properties and functions, they're self-contained and they have a prototype – the original symbol in the Library – that can be used to generate instances. We'll look into the idea of movie clips as objects further in the next example.

Movie Clips as Objects – a Drop-Down Menu Box

To illustrate the use of movie clips as objects, we're going to embark on quite an ambitious project; we're going to create a configurable drop-down menu. In Flash 5 there are some menu item smart clips with similar functionality to the one that we'll build here, but this exercise will give you plenty of insights into coding techniques that you can apply elsewhere too.

> *There's plenty of code in this example, and we advise you to save your work often.*

Our drop-down menu will have the following characteristics:

- It can be filled with any number of items

- When dropped down, a maximum number of items will be shown

- If the list contains more items than this maximum, a scroll bar will be made visible, and the list will be scrollable

Taking all of that on board, the finished product will look something like this:

This is actually a little more difficult than it might at first look. For a start, the menu consists of several interacting parts, all with their own behaviors, and these must interact consistently to produce the total behavior of the drop-down menu.

We can break down the menu into two main parts: the text box – which displays the value chosen from the drop-down list box, and the list box itself.

The Text Box

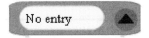

The text box must display the currently selected item. If the list contains no items, it may be empty; otherwise it will default to the *first* item in the list. To the right of the text box is a button that operates the list box. When it's clicked, the list box drops down and the arrow on the button faces upward. When it's clicked again, the list box is removed, and the arrow faces down again.

The List Box

The list box displays a set number of items (for this example we've made it four):

If there are fewer items than this to display in the list, then the drop-down will resize accordingly, and only the available items will be visible. If there are *more* items than this to display, then a scroll bar will appear beside the drop-down allowing the user to scroll through.

Before proceeding any further we need to think about how all of this will fit together from an object-oriented perspective. To properly utilize the object-like nature of movie clips, we need to think about the object-like nature of the menu that we're trying to build.

We can start at the top level by considering the properties we'll require from our menu and the states it can be in.

From the outset, we only require the menu to have two properties:

- A list of menu items

- An index value that points to the currently selected item

The menu can only be in one of two states:

- List box up

- List box down

The properties will convert directly into variables within a drop-down menu symbol, and the states will convert into sets of frames on a timeline. An initial guess at the drop-down menu symbol would therefore involve three frames: one to initialize the variables, and one to display each of the possible alternate states.

We've now defined our menu conceptually, and have all of the information that we need to go ahead and create it. The next things that we need to define are the text box and the list box.

To produce a text box in Flash terms we need a text display area – consisting of a background and a dynamic text box – and a button to drop down or put away the list box. The text box will only have one property: its currently displayed text.

The list box is slightly more complicated. It consists of a background, four text display areas (one for each item) and a scroll bar. It has one obvious property, which is the offset into the list at which it will start displaying list entries. This will be changed via the scroll bar, and will be initialized to 0.

Note that we've already identified at least four new objects, one of which is shared by both components. These are:

- Text display area

- Drop-down button

- List box background

- Scroll bar

> *You can easily see that when we begin thinking about components as collections of objects, we quickly generate long lists of things that need to be created. At first glance this may seem a little daunting. However, the important thing to remember at this point is that we haven't actually created any more work. When you think about it, every object we're identifying has to be present in the final component anyway. Without thinking about components as objects, we'd have to design the whole movie clip in one go. By separating the design for each object into a manageable chunk of functionality, we actually progressively simplify the work we'll have to do. In addition, we begin to find common objects, such as the text display area, which previously we'd have had to design twice. By creating such an element as a separate, self-contained movie clip, we can simplify our work, both in terms of constructing new components and in maintaining the system later.*

Fortunately, we're beginning to get to the bottom of our design. We've located our first three basic components – the text display area, the list box background and the drop-down button. Looking at the scroll bar, we can see that this too is made up of components: the background, the up and down arrow buttons and the scroll slider.

We've now identified the following components:

- The drop-down menu

- The text box

- The list box

- The text display area

- The arrow buttons

- The scroll bar

- The scroll slider

- The list box background

As we want to try and modularize the code as much as possible and let the components talk to each other, we're going to give them appropriate **interfaces** that will let them communicate with their compadres. These interfaces will be of two kinds: **incoming**, which will handle messages or instructions sent to the component, and **outgoing**, which will do the work of telling other components what to do. We'll discuss these interfaces as we come across them for each component. The idea of interfaces becomes increasingly important as you develop a more object-oriented approach to ActionScript programming.

The next thing that we have to do is build these components. We'll start with the smallest parts and work up from there. The text box and list box are made up of combinations of the other components, so we'll begin with a part that's common to both: the text display area.

Creating the Text Display Area

This component is used in two places: the text box and the list box, and in both of these it's used to display text and to allow it to be selected.

1. Draw an 80 x 20 pixel rectangle on the stage with a 30° corner radius, and convert it to a movie clip called text display area:

2. Double-click on the new movie clip to open it, and then convert the rectangle into a movie clip called text background. This gives us two advantages:

   ■ We can manipulate the background programmatically if we need to (for instance to resize the display area)

   ■ We can potentially load in any background that we want, by using `loadMovie` or `attachMovieClip` actions

3. Rename the layer in the text display area movie clip as Background, then create two new layers called Button and Text:

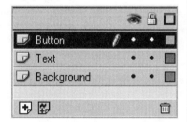

4. On the Text layer, create a dynamic text box over the top of the background:

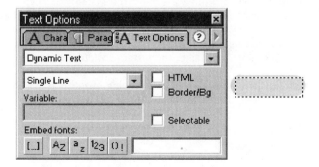

5. Select the text box a variable name of `value`, and make it non-selectable.

We now have an 'incoming' interface for the text display area: to set the text, we simply have to assign our desired setting to the `value` variable.

6. To allow the text box to respond to mouse clicks, we must add a button. Create a new button symbol called invis button, and drag a copy of text background from the Library into the middle of the screen. Set the top-left registration point of the button to 0,0 and use the Effect panel to change its Alpha value to 0.

7. Go back into the text display area movie clip, and drag a copy of invis button out of the Library and onto the Button layer. It will appear as a semi-transparent blue button. Use the Align panel to position the button over the top of the existing background.

8. Now type this code into the Object Actions window for the button:

```
on(release) {
    _parent.onTextBoxSelect(_name);
}
```

This forms the 'outgoing' interface of the text display area. In order to make the movie clip reusable, we want to delay specifying what happens when we select it until we attach it to something. We therefore generate an event (`TextBoxSelect`), which is fired every time this text box is selected. In order to respond to this event, any movie clip containing a set of text display areas should also contain a function called `onTextBoxSelect`, which takes the name of an object as a parameter.

We could conceivably have used `onClipEvent` to perform the task of responding to the text box selection. However, firing an event has the following advantages:

- `onClipEvent` would require the same (or very similar) code to be attached to every instance of the text display areas. The method we're using here keeps all of the code in one place.

- The parent knows nothing about the mechanism of selecting text boxes with this method. Therefore if we extend the system to accept keyboard selection as well as mouse selection, the parent doesn't need any changes made to it.

- Every time we add a new text box, it will automatically take care of notifying the parent of its events. This makes the system *scalable*.

We'll be coming across this idea of an outgoing event interface in several of the objects in this system. The next components to define on our list are the arrow buttons.

Creating the Arrow Buttons

These buttons are used three times: once as a drop-down button for the text box, and twice within the scroll bar. In each case the only difference is the orientation of the arrow and the effect of pressing the button. Each button will have interfaces – basically functions – that we'll build to handle their interactions with the rest of the world. We're therefore going to define their functionality like this:

Incoming Interface

> *SetOrientation(orientation)*

This defines the direction the arrow will face.

Outgoing Interface

> *{Button name}_onButtonUp()*
> *{Button name}_onButtonDown()*
> *{Button name}_onButtonOver()*

Here, we're take a slightly different approach from the text display area. There, we required a common event handling function to deal with all of the text boxes, but in this case we want to attach different functions to each button. Therefore, each function will be named after the button to which it's attached.

In order to allow the arrow and the background to be oriented separately, we'll create separate symbols for each, and add them as instances named Arrow and Background respectively. This also has the advantage that we could, if we so desired, set their colors independently, allowing the button to be completely configurable. We'll see in a moment how this is put to good use to indicate the state of the button.

Let's get on with building the thing...

1.   Go back to the main stage and draw a 20 x 20 pixel circle. Convert this into a movie clip, and call it arrow back.

2.   Next we need to create the arrow itself. I find that the easiest way to do this is to draw a 15 x 15 borderless square, and then use the Arrow tool to pull the top and bottom right-hand corners together to form a triangle:

3.   Once you have your arrow shape, convert it into a movie clip and give it the name arrow front.

4.   In the first frame of each of these movie clips, add this ActionScript:

```
function SetColor(newcol)
{
     _root.functions.SetColor(this, newcol);
}
```

This allows us to set their colors by using a simple function call.

5. The next thing to do is to combine the two symbols into a button and give it some code that allows its orientation to be changed programmatically. First of all, give each of them an instance name: call them Background and Arrow respectively.

6. Next, line up the two symbols, arrow over circle, and combine them into a movie clip called arrow full:

7. Open up arrow full, and rename the first layer graphic. Then create two new layers. Call the first layer code, and the second button.

8. Type the following ActionScript into the first frame of the code layer:

```
function SetOrientation (orientation) {
    if (orientation == "down") {
        Arrow._rotation = 90;
    } else if (orientation == "up") {
        Arrow._rotation = -90;
    } else if (orientation == "left") {
        Arrow._rotation = 180;
    } else if (orientation == "right") {
        Arrow._rotation = 0;
    }
}
```

We can now change the direction of the arrow programmatically.

9. Create a new button symbol called arrow button. Insert a keyframe into the Hit state of the button and drag a copy of arrow back from the Library and into the center of the stage. Note that by using the same shape for background and button we ensure that we have the right hit area.

10. Now go back into the full arrow movie clip and drag a copy of arrow button onto the stage in the button layer. Line the button up over the top of the existing graphic.

11. Next, open the Object Actions window and add the following code to the button instance:

```
on (press) {
    onButtonDown();
}
on (release) {
    onButtonOver();
}
on (rollOver) {
    onButtonOver();
}
on (rollOut) {
    onButtonUp();
}
```

This allows us to define functions to set the three states of the button.

12. The next thing that we need to do is add the final load of ActionScript to give functionality to our button. All of this code goes on the code layer below the existing ActionScript:

```
background.bdColor = 0x50ffff;
background.buColor = 0x4471ff;
background.roColor = 0xff71ff;
```

Here, we first set up default colors for the three states of the button. These states are: button down (cyan), button up (blue) and rollover (pink). These three states are identical to the states for a Flash-defined button. We define these colors as variables so that we'll be able to set them to different values if we like.

13. Underneath this, add the next piece of code:

```
function onButtonDown () {
    background.SetColor(background.bdColor);
    eval("_parent."+_name+"_onButtonDown")();
}
function onButtonUp () {
    background.SetColor(background.buColor);
    eval("_parent."+_name+"_onButtonUp")();
}
function onButtonOver () {
    background.SetColor(background.roColor);
    eval("_parent."+_name+"_onButtonOver")();
}
```

These three functions set the color of the background and fire the appropriate event whenever we enter the named state. The function call for firing the event is made by using the eval command to create a function name from the name of the button and the required event. Be careful to get all the parentheses in the right position – one slip, and the movie won't work!

14. Now add this final section of ActionScript:

```
function Refresh () {
    background.SetColor(background.buColor);
}
```

This provides a function to update the button if we change its colors.

We now have a button consisting of a single frame that can be given an instance name that allows it to be manipulated programmatically. The next component to make in our list is the scroll bar.

Creating the Scroll Bar

The scroll bar is yet another component that'll have an outgoing interface. This time we're intending that any object that we attach it to should consist of a list of items which will be stepped through when we move the scroll slider or click on the buttons. The finished scroll bar will look like this:

Furthermore, we're intending that the scroll bar should automatically scale the slider movements based on the number of list items to be stepped through.

This gives us an outgoing interface requirement of the following:

- refreshDisplay – recalculates the displayed list of items

- listItems – an array of items to display

- itemsToDisplay – the maximum number of these items that are visible at any one time

- offset – how far into the list to display the first item

The first thing to do is to create the background for the slider.

1. Draw a 22 x 150 pixel rectangle on the main stage with no fill, a line width of 2, and a corner radius of 30. Convert this into a movie clip called slider full and then, inside *that*, convert it again into a graphic symbol called slider back:

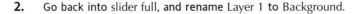

2. Go back into slider full, **and rename** Layer 1 to Background.

We need to add three buttons to our scroll bar: two arrows to step up and down, and the other a slider bar which can be dragged using the mouse:

The up and down buttons are easy to add, as we've already defined our arrow.

3.   Create a new layer called Arrows, and put a copy of arrow full at either end of the scrollbar on this layer. Give them the appropriate instance names – scrollUp and scrollDown. Although we have functions for orientating the arrows, it makes more sense to simply rotate the symbols here, since their orientation won't change during the course of the movie.

4.   We'll need to create a symbol for the slider bar, too. Create a new layer called Scroll Bar and draw a 20 x 30 pixel rectangle on the stage. Feel free to make it look more professional if you like by giving it some bevel effects:

5.   Convert it into a movie clip called scroll block, and give this scroll block the instance name scrollBar.

6.   Inside scroll block, select the rectangle again, and this time convert it to a graphic symbol called slider. Make sure that you're in scroll block and use the Info panel to set the top of slider to Y position 0. This makes it easier for us to position it correctly later.

7.   Rename the first layer of scroll block to Graphic, and add another two frames to it. Next, create another two layers and call them Code and Button.

8.   Drag the invis button that we created earlier for our text display panel out of the Library and onto the Button layer. This time however, instead of just covering the graphic with the button, make it twice the height of the graphic. This is because we want it to respond to mouse activity above and below the slider in order to drag it:

9.   To achieve this precisely, use the Info panel to resize the button to 20 x 60 pixels, and place it over the slider graphic with an equal overlap at the top and bottom.

To allow the slider to interact correctly with the scroll bar we need another outgoing interface with the following requirements:

```
onScrollUp
```

```
onScrollDown
```

Now we need some way of firing the events for this interface. We want the slider to react when the mouse is over the scroll bar and moving down but not at any other time. We therefore need to create frames for two states: drag, and nodrag.

10. Convert all of the frames on the Code layer into keyframes, then label the first frame nodrag and the second frame drag:

11. Open up the Object Actions window for invis button and add the following code, which will enable the button to switch between the two states:

```
on (release, releaseOutside) {
    gotoAndPlay ("nodrag");
}
on (press) {
    gotoAndPlay ("drag");
}
```

This will switch the slider to the drag state when the mouse button is down, and to the non-dragging state whenever the mouse button is released. And, in keeping with object-oriented ideas, the code is attached to the button itself – it knows how to behave.

12. The first state, nodrag, consists of one frame. Nothing should be happening in this state, so add this single simple line of code to this frame:

```
stop();
```

13. The second state, drag, must continually follow the position of the mouse. To do this, add the following two-frame loop. First, start the loop in frame 2 with this:

```
if (_ymouse<0) {
    _parent.onScrollUp();
} else if (_ymouse>30) {
    _parent.onScrollDown();
}
```

14. Now close the loop by adding this code in frame 3:

```
gotoAndPlay("drag");
```

This checks continually to see if the mouse is above or below the slider graphic, and fires the appropriate event. The number 0 is the top of the slider, and 30 is the bottom.

When we scroll, we want to know the limits that the scrolling slider should be able to move between. In order to automatically calculate these limits, even when the scroll bar symbol has been resized, we can use another graphic placed between the arrows and then just read the top and bottom position of that graphic.

15. Create a new layer in slider full and call it Scroll Range. Drag a copy of invis button from the Library and resize it to 20 x 110. It should now be the right size to fit between the arrow buttons.

16. Use the Instance panel to change the behaviour of invis button to a movie clip. This allows us to give it the instance name scrollRange – do that now.

17. Once this is done, position scrollRange snugly between the two arrows. We can now use its `y` and `height` properties to calculate the available scrolling range.

Now that we've added our scrolling buttons, it's time to wire up our scroll bar so it can react to events.

18. Create a new layer called Code in slider full and prepare your fingers for a typing assignment. Start by adding the following functions in frame 1 of the Code layer. These will react when either a scroll arrow is pressed or the slider is dragged up or down:

```
function scrollUp_onButtonDown () {
    SetOffset(_parent.offset-1);
}
function scrollDown_onButtonDown () {
    SetOffset(_parent.offset+1);
}
function onScrollUp () {
    SetOffset(_parent.offset-1);
}
function onScrollDown () {
    SetOffset(_parent.offset+1);
}
```

These call the `SetOffset` function (which we'll create next) and pass it the required argument so that it can update the offset whenever scrolling occurs.

19. The next thing to do is add the ActionScript to define this function. This goes straight after the functions you've just added:

```
function SetOffset (val) {
  if (val>=0 and val<=_parent.listItems.length-
    ➥_parent.itemsToDisplay)
  {
      _parent.offset = val;
      UpdateBarPos();
      _parent.refreshDisplay();
  }
}
```

This function first checks if the scrolling is attempting to go outside the valid offset range. If not, then the offset is updated, the list display refreshed, and the scroll bar position is updated.

20. The update is achieved using the next function – `UpdateBarPos`. Add this to the code next:

```
function UpdateBarPos () {
    if (_parent.listItems.length>0) {
        scrollBar._y =
        ➥scrollRange._y+(_parent.offset*(scrollRange._height-
```

continues overleaf

```
➥ scrollBar._height/2)/(_parent.listItems.length-
➥ _parent.itemsToDisplay));
    }
}
```

This function calculates the proportion of the scroll area, which represents the distance down the list we are, and moves the scroll bar appropriately. At the *beginning* of the list the scroll bar will be at the top of its range, and at the *end* of the list it will be at the bottom of the range.

Now that we've got all of our event code out of the way, we need to add some more code to set up the components.

21. Add this next chunk of ActionScript in the first frame, below the event code:

```
function SetupScrollButton (scrollBut) {
  scrollBut.background.roColor = scrollBut.background.buColor;
  scrollBut.background.bdColor = scrollBut.background.buColor +
  ➥ 0x101020;
  scrollBut.Refresh();
}
function UpdateScrollBlockHeight () {
  scrollBar._height =
    ➥2*scrollRange._height/_parent.listItems.length;
  if (scrollBar._height<50) {
    scrollBar._height = 50;
  }
}
```

The first function sets the colors for the buttons using the background color. The second function changes the height of the scroll bar to be appropriate for its range and sets the bar's position for its first update.

The button colors can't actually be set in this frame though. This is because the code that defines their default colors won't run until the code in its parent frame (frame 1 of the scroll bar) has finished. Thus, if we attempt to set up new colors in frame 1, they'll be overwritten. We get around this by not calling the function that sets these colors until frame 2.

22. To do this, add another keyframe to the Code layer, and enter the following ActionScript:

```
SetupScrollButton(scrollUp);
SetupScrollButton(scrollDown);
UpdateBarPos();
UpdateScrollBlockHeight();
stop ();
```

That's the last of our scroll bar code done, and almost the last in our list of basic components.

23. Finally, add a second frame to all of the other layers to bring them into line with the Code layer.

We're now in a position to create the first of our main two components, the list box.

Creating the List Box

This will consist solely of symbols that we've already defined, with the exception of our last basic component: the list box background. Thankfully, this is a pretty easy thing to make.

1. Draw a 130 x 110 pixel rectangle on the stage, with a corner radius of 30. Convert this to a movie clip called list box back, then give it the instance name boundingBox:

2. Still on the main stage, place four text display area clips on this box and give them the instance names textBox1, textBox2, textBox3, and textBox4. Also, drag an instance of slider full onto the stage and resize it to 20 x 80 pixels.

3. Now arrange all of the pieces on the stage until they resemble a list box:

4. Finally, select *all* of these pieces and convert them into a single movie clip called List Box.

We're now able to add in the functionality of our list box. Due to the fact that we've done most of the work already by coding basic functionality into the component parts, this is relatively simple.

5. Inside the List Box movie clip, rename the default layer Components, then create a new layer called Code. Add the following ActionScript to frame 1 of this layer:

```
listItems = new Array();
itemsToDisplay = 4;
offset = 0;
```

This defines `listItems` as an array ready to have items added, sets the number of items which can be displayed at any one time to 4 (since we have four text boxes) and initializes the `offset` to 0.

The next thing to do is enable the list box to react to events.

6. First, start adding the code for this function in frame 1. This function, when complete, will allow the list to scroll:

```
function  refreshDisplay() {
     getListItems();
```

This first function is the `refreshDisplay` event handler, which will be called every time the user scrolls the scroll bar. It first ensures that it has an up to date copy of the list items stored in its parent, using the function `getListItems` (which we'll code shortly).

7. Next, add this line:

```
    totalheight =0;
```

This initializes a variable, ready to calculate the height of the list box.

8. Then type:

```
        //Set visibility of scrollBar
        if (listItems.length <= itemsToDisplay) {
              scrollBar._visible = false;
        } else {
              scrollBar._visible = true;
        }
```

This means that the scroll bar is turned off if the number of items in the list is less than the number of items to display.

9. We now need to actually set some items in our list boxes. Add the following code:

```
        //Add list items to boxes
        for(i=0;i<itemsToDisplay && ((i + offset)
➡<listItems.length);i++)
        {
              eval("textBox" + String(i+1)).value =
➡listItems[offset+i];
              eval("textBox" + String(i+1))._visible = true;
              totalheight+=20;
        }
```

Starting at the `offset` position, this code iterates through the list, filling in the display boxes. We also increment the `totalheight` by the height of each displayed box. This will give us a final total of 4 x 20 = 80 unless the number of items in the list is three or less. If this is the case, we need to some more code: Add this now:

```
//Make rest invisible
for(;i<itemsToDisplay;i++)
{
        eval("textBox" + String(i+1))._visible = false;
}
```

10. If we *do* have fewer items than display boxes then we'll need to make the remaining boxes invisible, so the last thing to do here is change the box's dimensions to match its contents by adding this code:

```
boundingBox._height = totalheight + 20;
scrollBar._height = totalheight;
}
```

We don't *really* need to resize the scroll bar, since it will either be 80 or invisible. However, if we change the code later (for instance to have a flexible number of text boxes) then this will ensure that everything remains consistent and bug free.

Now we need to define the getListItems function to allow the list to be populated with information.

11. Carry on adding this code to frame 1:

```
function getListItems()
{
    for (i=0;i<_parent.listItems.length;i++)
    {
            listItems[i] = _parent.listItems[i];
    }
}
```

12. We also need to react to a list item being selected. Add the following code, which creates a new outgoing interface that passes on the effects to the parent:

```
function onTextBoxSelect(textBox)
{
    _parent.setValue(eval(textBox).value);
    _parent.gotoAndPlay("list_up");
}
```

First of all, this sets the selected value to that which was clicked on by the user, and then it closes the list box.

Now we have to ensure that our list box is reactive to changes in the list of items it's supposed to display – it needs to be kept up to date. To do this, we need to create another two-frame checking loop.

13. Add two new keyframes to the Code layer, and label frame 2 as refreshLoop. Add this line to frame 2...

```
refreshDisplay();
```

14. ...and this to frame 3:

```
gotoAndPlay("refreshLoop");
```

15. Finally, add a frame in frame 3 of the Components layer to bring it into line with the Code layer.

And that's almost it. After a great deal of effort, we're finally able to put everything together into a completed drop-down menu.

Tying it all Together

To reiterate: the menu will consist of the list box plus a text box made up of a toggle button and a text display area. We'll also add a background behind the text box and toggle button to make it look pretty.

1. On the main stage of the root timeline, select the entire list box, convert it into a movie clip called DropDownMenu, and give it the instance name myMenu. Inside this new movie clip, rename the default layer to List Box. Then create another layer and call it Text Box.

2. Drag a copy of arrow full, list box back, and text display area onto the stage on the Text Box layer.

3. Resize the list box back to 130 x 30 pixels, then arrange the other two elements over the top of it:

4. Give arrow full the instance name toggle_button, and text display area the name selection.

5. We now need to define some event handlers for these objects. Create a new layer called Code, and add the following ActionScript to frame 1:

```
//Init funcs and variables
listItems = new Array();

function toggle_button_onButtonDown()
{
    gotoAndPlay(nextState)
}

function setValue(val)
```

```
{
    selection.value = val;
    this.value = val;
}
```

First of all, we initialize `listItems` as an array. We also set up a handler for the drop-down button (`toggle_button_onButtonDown`). This handler simply toggles between states, using a variable `nextState`, which we'll define later. Finally, `setValue` is the function called when a value is selected in the list box. It does two things – sets the value to display in the text display area, and sets a property of the drop-down menu, `value`.

6. On the List Box layer, give the list box movie clip the instance name drop_down_list.

7. To complete the list box we need to create our two states: `list_up` and `list_down`. This can be done by adding two keyframes to the code layer, and labeling the first list_up, and the second list_down. Add this ActionScript to frame 2...

```
nextState = "list_down";
toggle_button.SetOrientation("down");
drop_down_list._visible = false;
stop ();
```

8. ...and a similar section of code to frame 3:

```
nextState = "list_up";
toggle_button.SetOrientation("up");
drop_down_list._visible = true;
stop ();
```

This is relatively simple. First, we define the `nextState` variable, which we first saw in `toggle_button_onButtonDown`. This sets the toggle action of the drop-down button. Next we set the orientation of the arrow – pointing down when the list is hidden, and up when the list is displayed. Then we set the list box to be visible before pausing the action.

9. Now add frames to the other two layers to make them level with the Code layer.

And that's pretty much it. By separating all of the code into defined areas within the components, we've progressively simplified each higher level of integration.

Now we can use the menu by simply making sure that we have an instance of it on the stage, and then filling the `listItems` property with items. Remember that we can't use the `listItems` array before it's been initialized.

10. To fix this, add the following code to the first frame of the root timeline:

```
//Init drop down menu
for (i = 0;i<10;i++)
{
    listItems[i] = "My Entry " + String(i);
}
```

11. Then add another frame to the first layer:

You should now be able to run your movie, and see it populated with a list of My Entry values running from 0 to 9:

You now have a drop-down list box that you can use in any application and populate by a simple loop like the one that we just used. The next step would be to integrate this list box into an application, perhaps by adding code to a button that the user could press when they'd made their selection. This code could trigger a purchase, for example, or be used to set some variables and properties elsewhere in the application.

Conclusion

This chapter has covered a lot of ground and there's been a lot of code. I hope that the theory and practice that I've covered here, plus the chance that you've had to pull apart the FLAs, will have given you some insights into using functions and other code in tandem, and will have set you thinking about encapsulating code into small components that can then be integrated into a larger whole.

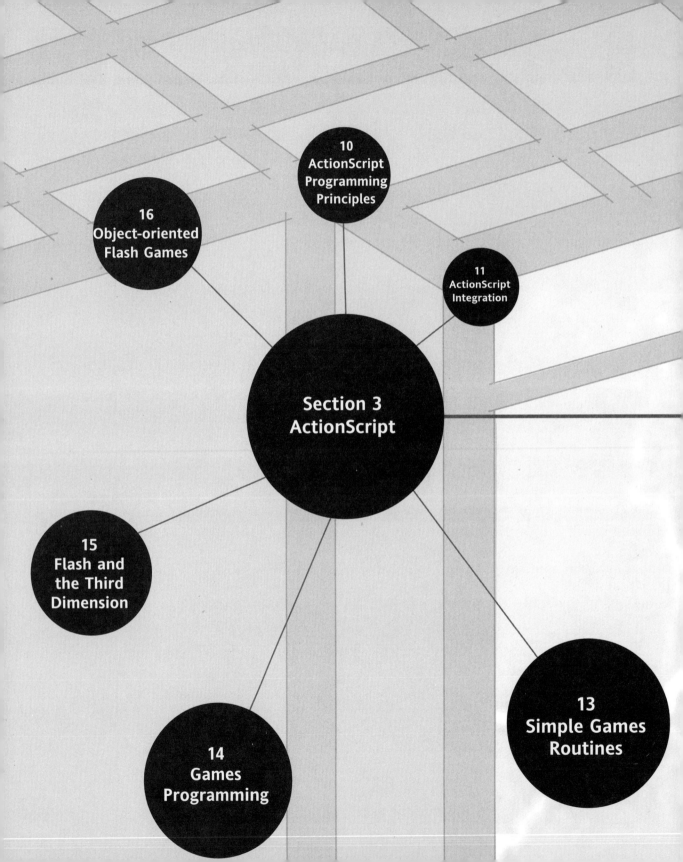

10
ActionScript
Programming
Principles

16
Object-oriented
Flash Games

11
ActionScript
Integration

Section 3
ActionScript

15
Flash and
the Third
Dimension

14
Games
Programming

13
Simple Games
Routines

Chapter 12
Visual Effects
with ActionScript

This chapter aims to carry on from other chapters in this book to show you why anyone – even the relative beginner in ActionScript – can use ActionScript to produce some really excellent effects on screen. What I'll be doing here is sharing some of my ideas and favorite little tricks, in the hope that you'll like what you see, understand the code, and be able to take that code and adapt it for your own ideas, building up your own repertoire of preferred techniques and creative methods. As ever, the FLAs for this chapter's worked examples are there on the CD for you to zoom in on and take to pieces for yourself.

Before we dive head first into coding the effects, I'll just reiterate the basics about one of my most trusted 'tools of the trade': **arrays**.

Arrays

In Flash you can often find yourself working with a great number of variables and objects at any given time. Whether it's a group of buttons, a set of movie clips, or just a series of variables, there are many situations where we need to store several similar objects for use in our scripts.

Flash provides a way to organize a series of objects or variables into a list that can be easily referenced: **arrays**. An array behaves much like a numbered list, in that it has numbered slots, each of which is available to store data. To declare an array in ActionScript, you simply use a statement like this:

```
myArray = new Array (10)
```

This will create a new array that can house ten values.

You can now start assigning values (or objects) to the array by using the array name followed by the storage slot number you wish to access in square brackets. Array items are numbered starting with 0. This next statement would create an array and populate the first three slots with values:

```
myArray=new Array ();
myArray[0]=100;
myArray[1]=256;
myArray[2]=34;
```

Note that you don't *have* to specify the size of the array to be able to populate it with values.

I could have achieved the same effect with this code:

```
myArray=new Array ();
myArray=[100,256,34];
```

The numbers included in the square brackets would automatically be assigned to the array's index numbers in the same order as the first piece of code.

How do we go through an array to edit or read each storage slot? The best way is to use a loop. If I wanted to do something to items in an array, I could use a loop counter variable as an index in the array to iterate through each item. This type of processing makes perfect use of `for` loop.

We'll be using a lot of `for` loops in the practical examples in the rest of the chapter, so you'll get plenty of practice with them.

Visual Effects

Let's start on our first example of using ActionScript to achieve effects on screen. This example uses that ever-popular favorite, the mouse chaser.

Mouse Chaser

We're going to begin with a simple mouse chaser that uses duplicated movie clips to create the 'tail'. This is a variation on a theme, and provides an alternative approach to that taken in a previous chapter. It is designed to show you that there are multiple programming approaches to the same basic problem.

Building a Mouse Chaser

Here's an image of the finished effect, which is a little comet-like:

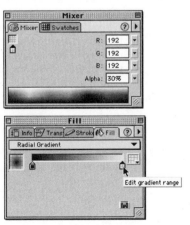

1. In a new movie, create a new movie clip and call it ball. In it, draw a strokeless circle and fill it with a radial gradient that goes from blue in the middle to transparent on the outside. Make sure that the circle is the exact size that you want to follow the mouse, because if you resize it after placing it on the main stage you'll get some odd results when the code manipulates the original (full sized) movie clip. Mine's 85.5 by 85.5 pixels.

2. To get the right gradient effect, highlight the solid blue fill and then select Radial Gradient from the Fill menu. You can then select the paint pot at the right hand side of the gradient range bar and set its alpha to (say) 30% using the option on the Mixer panel:

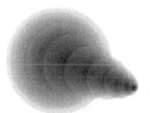

3. Place an instance of ball in the first frame of the first layer of the main timeline. Give it an instance name of ball0. Make this layer three frames long:

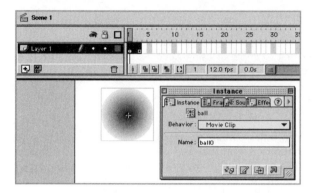

4. Create another layer, call it actions and give it three consecutive keyframes.

You'll probably be getting familiar with this three keyframe model as a standard setup for many movie clips: the first frame contains any initialization code, the second frame an iterative step, and the last frame a gotoAndPlay(2) statement to loop the iterative step in the second keyframe.

In this particular case, we'll set up an array to store our duplicated mouse chaser graphics in the first frame, and then run through the array to move each movie clip in the second keyframe. The third frame will loop this process so that the chaser keeps chasing...

Our first goal is to create an array to hold references to our ball0 movie clip and its duplicates. We'll then be able to refer to the movie clips using the index number of slot in the array.

5. Add this code to the Actions layer in frame 1 of the main timeline to create the array:

```
balls = new array();
```

We must decide how many duplicates to make of this clip in the script. I decided that this effect needed ten balls in total, which means that I have to duplicate my ball0 movie clip nine times. I'll use a variable to store this value so that if I want to change the number of chasing balls later I only have to change this variable value in the code.

6. Add this statement after the existing code in frame 1:

```
num_balls = 10;
```

7. Since we already have one ball on the stage, assign the ball0 instance to the first position in the array by adding this next statement:

```
balls[0] = ball0;
```

The next step is to create a `for` loop to build the duplicates of ball0 that populate the rest of the array.

8. Add this code to the existing script:

```
for (i=1; i<num_balls; i++) {
    duplicateMovieClip (this.ball0, "ball"+i, i);
    balls[i] = eval("ball"+i);
    balls[i].x_rate=0;
    balls[i].y_rate=0;
    balls[i]._xscale-=(i*10);
    balls[i]._yscale-=(i*10);
}
```

In the `for` loop initialization statement, we start with the counter variable `i` equal to 1 because we already have a ball0 in the array. The conditional part of the `for` loop is i<num_balls, which uses the value in the num_balls variable as the upper bound of the loop iterations. The first line in the body of the loop duplicates the clips, using ball0 as the template, assigning the new movie clip a new name and level. Both of these last two operations use the loop counter value to determine the correct values.

The next statement places the new clip in the array at the index position, again using the very handy loop counter variable:

```
balls[i] = eval("ball"+i);
```

Now that we have a new ball placed safely in the array, we can access it through the array to initialize it:

```
balls[i].x_rate=0;
balls[i].y_rate=0;
balls[i]._xscale-=(i*10);
balls[i]._yscale-=(i*10);
}
```

In this case that involves setting up two *rate* variables that we'll use to calculate the motion in the next frame, as well as setting up the size of the new clip. Just for variety, I decided to make the balls get increasingly smaller using a multiple of the current counter value. This block of code is a great illustration of how useful the counter can be inside a `for` loop way beyond its primary function

9. Now add this last action to this frame:

```
startDrag ("ball0", true);
```

This just uses the `startDrag` command to attach ball0 to the mouse.

Your complete code in frame 1 should now look like this:

```
balls = new array();
num_balls = 10;
balls[0] = ball0;

for (i=1; i<num_balls; i++) {
    duplicateMovieClip (this.ball0, "ball"+i, i);
    balls[i] = eval("ball"+i);
    balls[i].x_rate=0;
    balls[i].y_rate=0;
    balls[i]._xscale-=(i*10);
    balls[i]._yscale-=(i*10);
}

startDrag ("ball0", true);
```

The next keyframe, in frame 2, holds the motion script, which is a simple version of an attraction behavior that we'll be using again later in the chapter. This time, we want to see each ball being attracted to the ball immediately preceding it in the array.

To get the attraction motion to work, we'll set up two variables – speed and friction – which will be used to calculate the attraction.

10. Add this code to frame 2 of the Actions layer:

```
speed=2;
friction=0.45;
```

The speed value is actually the number of frames it will take a new ball to catch the last ball made. If speed is set to 1, the balls will never trail behind the mouse because they will catch up with each other too quickly. In turn, friction describes a simulated air friction, causing the balls to lose energy as the move through the air. The higher this number is, the more time it takes the balls to come to rest.

We'll give motion to the balls by adding the rates that we stored in frame 1 to the x and y positions of the duplicated movie clips. Again, we'll do this in a loop to make maximum use of the array.

11. Append this code to the existing code in frame 2:

```
for (i=1; i<num_balls; i++) {

Xdiff=(balls[i-1]._x-balls[i]._x);
Ydiff=(balls[i-1]._y-balls[i]._y);

balls[i].x_rate+=(Xdiff/speed);
balls[i].y_rate+=(Ydiff/speed);
```

This code uses the derived `Xdiff` and `Ydiff` variables to calculate the `x_rate` and `y_rate` values that will control the motion. These rates starts out at zero, but here we work out the distance between the balls, divided by our speed variable, and add that to the initial rate.

12. Now type this next block of code into frame 2 – this will actually apply the movement to the balls:

```
balls[i].x_rate*=friction;
balls[i].y_rate*=friction;

balls[i]._x+=balls[i].x_rate;
balls[i]._y+=balls[i].y_rate;

updateAfterEvent(mouseMove);

}
```

Here, we multiply the rate by the friction variable to simulate the loss of energy, change the `_x` and `_y` properties of the movie clip using the rate values from the last block, and then, finally, update the movie's position after the mouse moves.

This is the complete final script in frame 2:

```
speed=2;
friction=0.45;

for (i=1; i<num_balls; i++) {

Xdiff=(balls[i-1]._x-balls[i]._x);
Ydiff=(balls[i-1]._y-balls[i]._y);

balls[i].x_rate+=(Xdiff/speed);
balls[i].y_rate+=(Ydiff/speed);

balls[i].x_rate*=friction;
balls[i].y_rate*=friction;

balls[i]._x+=balls[i].x_rate;
balls[i]._y+=balls[i].y_rate;

updateAfterEvent(mouseMove);

}
```

All we need to add now is finish the movie off.

13. Add this to frame 3 of the Actions layer:

```
gotoAndPlay (2)
```

You can now test the movie and see the – pretty groovy – effect.

Now's the time to start experimenting: try the animation with different numbers of balls, and different variable values for friction and speed. Another exercise to try would be to make the trail turn on and off using a keystroke to trigger the on/off status. Trying different *graphics* can also have a great effect on the appearance of the chaser. You may also want to create a movie clip to hold the entire effect in order to let you import it into other Flash movies.

This example is a pretty direct use of the duplicateMovie action. It's nice and neat because we're doing all of the duplication in the first frame in a fairly controlled manner. In the next example, we'll be using duplication for a purely *visual* effect.

Particle Effects: Fire

Some visual effects are very hard to animate using traditional means. Imagine that you want to create an animation of a candle burning. If you try to draw this animation frame by frame in Flash, you'll probably end up with something resembling a cartoon unless you are an incredible vector artist.

You can achieve a fire effect with a much higher degree of realism by using duplication to simulate a dancing flame. This effect can be categorized as a 'particle' effect, as we'll be using many *small* objects to simulate a larger object. Particle effects can be used to simulate many things, from rain to flocks of birds.

Fire

An important aspect of most particle effects is that the component objects actively control their own behavior. To create the fire effect, we'll make a particle movie clip with a fairly simple, internally-defined behavior that tells it to travel upward. This will contain our spark, tweened to grow larger to simulate a flame. We'll duplicate flames so that they keep rising until they eventually die off.

All the main movie does is create the particle movies and set them free to move. After we finish, you'll be able to drag this movie clip into any movie that you want to set fire to.

1. Make a new movie clip to hold the entire effect and call it fire effect. Create an actions layer inside that movie clip and give it the standard three keyframes.

    Our movie duplication code will be called every cycle throughout the animation, so we can't use a loop counter to keep track of the number of fire movie clips we make.

2. To keep track of the total number of particles we've made, create a variable called count and initialize it to zero in the first frame of actions:

    ```
    count=0
    ```

    We need to create a movie clip called particle that'll contain our flame graphic (we'll do that shortly). Now that we've set the count variable in the frame 1 script, we need to set the visibility of that particle movie clip to false – we don't want to see the original movie clip, only the ones we duplicate.

3. To achieve this, add the following code to frame 1:

    ```
    particle._visible=false
    ```

4. The last initialization step is to create an array to store our particles called fireArray. Put this into frame 1 too:

    ```
    fireArray=new Array()
    ```

    Before we leave the first frame, we need to define a function that will delete a given movie clip from the array once its animation has completed. I've created a function called deleteMe(me) for this purpose. This function will be called by the movie clips themselves, passing the function their index number in the array. All the function must do is call Flash's standard removeMovieclip function.

5. Add this function to the frame 1 script now:

    ```
    function deleteMe(me){
    removeMovieClip (fireArray[me]);
    fireArray[me]=0;
    }
    ```

    This uses me – that is, the calling movie clip – as a parameter. As you can see, I set that position in the array to zero just to be neat and indicate that this movie clip is no longer in existence. Eventually, my array is going to be very large and consist mostly of zeros as a result of the removed movie clips. I *could* write the duplication function so that it looked at the array and placed a new movie clip in the first vacant slot instead of simply adding it to the end, but the animation would take a big speed hit from the while loop that I'd need to cycle through a big array every time.

    Instead, we're going to restart the animation every once in a while so that the array stays manageable. This means that every few minutes the flame goes out for a moment, but it speeds up the animation. You'll find that you often have to make trade-offs like this in your scripting, especially when you're working with graphic elements.

For this example, it's a good trade, but if I were building an array of important data that I couldn't easily replace, rather than flames that all look pretty similar, then the more rigorous scripting option would be better. If you had to do this, you could use the array's built in `splice` method to remove the data at that point and shift everything above it down one space.

Moving on to the script for the second keyframe, we have to set up a loop that will create a few new flames every time the main movie loops.

6. Create a variable called `flame_num` which will dictate how many new flames are made each cycle:

```
flame_num=1;
```

The higher the number, the more realistic the fire effect will look, but the slower it will run. It looks pretty good set to `1`, which eliminates the need for the loop, but I wanted to build in the ability to change this if necessary.

7. Create a standard `for` loop that uses `flame_num` as the end condition, and add the first line of code in the body of the loop:

```
for(i=0; i<flame_num; i++){
    count++;
```

The first thing we must do inside the loop is to increment `count`. If we're in the loop, we're creating a new flame, so `count` goes up by one.

8. The next step is to duplicate our particle movie clip. Instead of using the loop counter to set the name and level, use this code to add the `count` variable:

```
duplicateMovieClip (particle, "fire"+count, count);
```

9. After duplicating, we need to put the new movie clip in `fireArray[count]`. Add this code to do that:

```
fireArray[count]=eval("fire"+count);
```

Now that the new movie clip is in the array we need to initialize it, which in this case means first making it visible. If you remember, we made the original `particle` invisible to hide it from view.

10. Add this next line to frame 2:

```
fireArray[count]._visible=true;
```

11. Next, set the clip's x and y positions with this code:

```
fireArray[count]._x=0;
fireArray[count]._y=0;
```

In this case, they're both zero because the fire is intended to be a concentrated candle flame. If the fire was to be more diffused, you could use random numbers to spread out the initial placement.

12. The last step in the loop is to set a variable called myNum inside the new movie clip equal to count, so we know what number it is in the array. Do that now with this script:

```
fireArray[count].myNum=count;
}
```

13. To finish off our frame 2 script, we need to add that clean up function I mentioned:

```
if(count>1000){
    for(i=0; i<fireArray.length; i++){
        if(fireArray[i]!=0){
            removeMovieClip (fireArray[i]);
        }
    }
gotoAndPlay(1);
}
```

It only gets executed every 1000/flame_num times. When it does run, it deletes all of the duplicated movie clips and returns to frame one to reinitialize our variables. Notice that we use the != (not equal to) notation to zoom in on clips that haven't already been deleted.

Here's the finished frame 2 script in its entirety:

```
flame_num=1;

for(i=0; i<flame_num; i++){
    count++;

    duplicateMovieClip (particle, "fire"+count, count);

    fireArray[count]=eval("fire"+count);
    fireArray[count]._visible=true;
    fireArray[count]._x=0;
    fireArray[count]._y=0;
    fireArray[count].myNum=count;
    }

if(count>1000){
    for(i=0; i<fireArray.length; i++){
        if(fireArray[i]!=0){
            removeMovieClip (fireArray[i]);
        }
    }
```

continues overleaf

```
gotoAndPlay(1);

}
```

14. On the third frame, enter our trusty...

```
gotoAndPlay(2)
```

...command, and we're finished *scripting* the main movie.

Now we need the *content* for all that lovely script to work on.

15. Create a movie clip to hold the flame graphic and call it fire. Inside fire, on frame 1, draw a (roughly) 50 pixel wide circle with no stroke and fill it with a radial gradient. For fiery colors I chose a bright yellow for the center at 50% alpha, and a dark red on the outside at 25%. If you want, you can change the alpha of the individual colors in the gradient by selecting the little paint pots on the bar in the Radial Gradient option in the Fill panel and manipulating them with the Mixer settings:

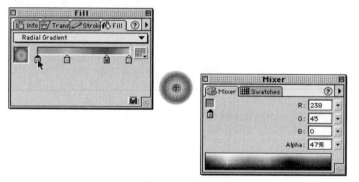

16. When you're happy with the result, add a key frame at frame 25.

17. Select your circle in frame 25 and use the Info panel to make it 100 pixels high, so that it's an oval shape. Now drag the little paint pots in the Radial Gradient part of the Fill palette to opposite ends to reverse the gradient in the circle's fill:

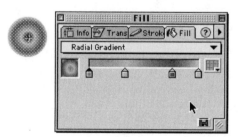

The flame should now be red in the center and yellow on the outside.

18. Add a shape tween between the two keyframes. Make sure the animation works properly by dragging the playhead through the tween before you proceed.

   The reason that we're changing the color of the circle is because fire tends to change color, from the heart of the flame to the top. Since we're going to set these movie clips to move up of their own accord, the color change will be streaked in that direction. Everything is semi-transparent, so things should blend nicely.

   Unfortunately, orange circles don't look *exactly* like flames. To get around this, I created a black and white picture of fire in PhotoShop and imported this into my movie clip, where I traced it and used it as a mask over the circle layer. You have the choice of creating your own mask, borrowing mine (the original is the flame.png file, and the traced version is the Mask symbol – they're both in the FLA's Library) or doing without.

19. If you *do* decide to use a mask, create a new layer and put your mask in there before turning it into a mask layer. Then double its dimensions in a keyframe at frame 25 as we did for the gradient filled circle and create a shape tween for the mask. Lock both layers and drag the playhead through the tween again to check that everything has worked well:

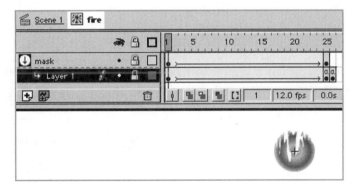

Our flame movie clip is almost done. All we need to do is arrange for each flame to go tell the main movie when it has finished playing. We're going to be duplicating a lot of movie clips in this effect, and our animation will slow to a crawl unless we get each flame to douse itself on its last frame.

We'll use the flame movie clip's last frame to call the main movie's deleteMe() function that we set up earlier. In this function call we're going to use _parent to travel up through the movie hierarchy to call the function in the main movie clip. The myNum variable, if you remember, contains each movie clip's position in the array, so we'll pass this to the main function so that it knows what to delete. Thus when the flame is finished it goes away, giving us a nice fire effect.

20. Still in the fire movie clip, select the last keyframe of the layer that has the fire effect on it, *not* the mask layer. Add this script:

```
_parent._parent.deleteMe(_parent.myNum)
```

21. Create a new keyframe immediately after this one and add a `stop` action.

22. For the next step, create another movie clip called particle. Now drag a copy of the fire movie clip into it and give it the instance name of fire.

23. Still inside particle, add an actions layer that's three keyframes in length – I've stuck to our three keyframe animation pattern even though the first frame is actually devoid of a script. Make sure you extend the original layer so that it's the same length as the actions layer.

24. On the second frame, enter two lines of code to increment the clip's x and y position:

```
this._x+=(Math.random()*2)-0.5;//spread
this._y-=(Math.random()*2)+1;//height
```

This will make the movie clip jitter a little bit from side to side while it moves upward.

25. On the third frame of the particle movie clip, add this command:

```
gotoAndPlay(2)
```

26. Now go back and open up the main fire effect movie clip. Create a new layer, make sure that it's three frames long, call it particle and drag your particle movie clip into that layer. Give it an instance name of particle:

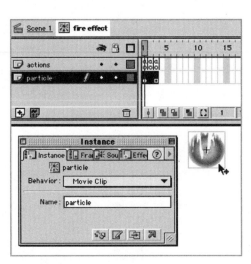

27. Finally, and very importantly, drag a copy of fire effect out onto the main stage and run the movie:

I drew a small candle to support my flame, but you can do whatever you want with it.

If you try the effect out, you should have a nice little flame burning. You can play with the settings to make the flame taller and wider. Changing the *color* is a little more difficult, but you can make blue flames or green flames without too much trouble. Best of all, because we've made this all in a movie clip, you can drag fire effect into any movie you want without any problems.

For our next example, we're going to look at integrating keyboard input with ActionScript.

Key Capture

Flash 5 contains several predefined objects that give us access to advanced features, such as the `Array` object that we've been using previously. We're going to use another one of the objects for this next effect – the `Key` object. In Flash 4, you could set up a button to execute a segment of a script if a certain key on the keyboard was pressed, but if you wanted different functions for several keys, you had to write a handler for each of them in your script. While you can still do this in Flash 5, Macromedia has given us a much better way to detect and distinguish user keystrokes with the new `Key` object.

To use the `Key` object effectively, we need to figure out how to detect when a key has been pressed. We're no longer using buttons, so we have to come up with another way of detection. We also have to figure out which key was pressed; and we need to know what we want to do about it.

In Flash 5, movie clips can be given event handlers just like buttons. While button handlers 'watch' for events like `press` and `release` that make sense for buttons, movie clips can also now wait, poised for events that affect movie clips, such as `load`, `unload` and `enterframe`. Movie clip events also include `keyUp` and `keyDown` 'handlers', which handle the processing that follows a given event. Using these keywords as parameters to the movie clip's `onClipEvent` handler will activate the code when the key is pressed. For example, when any key is pressed the `onClipEvent(keyDown)` handler will activate whatever code we specify after it.

Chances are that inside our `onClipEvent` handler we're going to want to distinguish exactly *which* key was pressed. How many keys we need to deal with depends entirely on what we're trying to accomplish in our movie, and how much interactivity we require.

We're going to look at two examples in this section, the first of which uses a very simple script to move an object around on the screen using the arrow key. The second example will be a little more complicated in that it requires us to distinguish *which* key was pressed.

Arrow Key Motion

1. Make a movie clip with a graphic – say, a circle – in it.

2. Place this movie clip on your stage and give it the instance name of ball. With the movie clip still selected on the stage, open up the Object Actions window.

We want our ball graphic to move when we press one of the four arrow keys. We can use onClipEvent (keyDown) to tell us that a key has been pressed, after which we need to know *which* key has been pressed so that we can invoke the proper motion.

The Key object also has a list of constants for some of the more common keys. The constants I am interested in are Key.RIGHT, Key.LEFT, Key.UP, and Key.DOWN. I can plug each of these into the test function, Key.isDown, to see which key is pressed at the moment. We have to use a series of if/else statements to see which of the four keys is down.

3.   Attach the following script to ball:

```
onClipEvent (keyDown) {

if(Key.isDown(Key.RIGHT)){
    _parent.ball._x+=5;
} else if(Key.isDown(Key.LEFT)){
    _parent.ball._x-=5;
} else if(Key.isDown(Key.UP)){
    _parent.ball._y-=5;
} else if(Key.isDown(Key.DOWN)){
    _parent.ball._y+=5;
}
}
```

4.   Test the movie and then click with the mouse in the browser – you should be able to move the circle around with the arrow keys. (You have to click first to bypass a built in Flash security feature.)

This simple procedure will allow you to start coding simple games...think PacMan!

As I mentioned before, it's possible for Flash to find out *which* key was pressed last. This provides another way to write this function. The Key object has a function, Key.getCode, which will return the code for the last key pressed. The advantage here is that you can detect keys that have no constant representation (which the arrow keys *do* have. You can detect the last key after it was pressed for an infinite amount of time afterwards.

5.   Rewrite the function to use this new code (the changed lines are highlighted):

```
onClipEvent (keyDown) {

theKey = Key.getCode();
if(theKey==Key.RIGHT){
    _parent.ball._x+=5;
} else if(theKey==Key.LEFT){
    _parent.ball._x-=5;
} else if(theKey==Key.UP){
    trace("UP");
```

```
        _parent.ball._y-=5;
} else if(theKey==Key.DOWN){
        _parent.ball._y+=5;
}
}
```

Now that we have a variable (theKey) set to the virtual key code of the last key pressed, we can use it in our conditional statement to compare against the symbolic constants instead of using the Key.isDown function, and kick off whatever code we desire based on the user's specific key press.

More on Key Codes

I've been using the term 'key code', but the Key object actually has *two* ways of recognizing each key press: the *virtual* code that we've been using, which is obtained by using the Key.getCode function, and the ASCII code, which you can get through the Key.getAscii function. The two methods are very similar in effect but actually work in different ways.

The key codes are directly related to the keys on your keyboard – each one of those keys has a code assigned to it. When you press a key, an internal variable in the Key object gets set to that particular code, which then sits there, waiting for a Key.getCode function to retrieve it. ASCII codes, on the other hand, represent *characters*. When you press a key, the computer figures out which character you want based on the key you pressed and any modifiers that may be in effect. This ASCII code then gets stored in another variable in Flash.

This means that the key code will tell you if the 'A' key was pressed, but not if it was an A, a, á, or Á, while ASCII will tell you *exactly* which 'A' variant was pressed. The general rule in dealing with key capture is to first get the key code, eliminate all non-text characters that have no ASCII equivalents, and then get the ASCII code for the remaining characters. You can find a list of all of the virtual codes in the back of the Flash ActionScript Reference Guide that came with Flash.

Next, we're going to do something much more interesting than move a circle around the screen. We'll create a small application that allows the user to type in letters that then appear on the screen. Each letter will live in its own movie clip, making it highly amenable to ActionScript manipulation.

Typing Text in Real Time

This effect has five parts. The first is the main movie script. This script will set up an array to hold our letter movie clips, and use information stored in various places to move the letters into position. The second part is the letter movie clip itself, which will contain a text field that displays a letter. We'll duplicate a copy for each letter we type. The third part is a text field on the stage that'll keep track of what's been typed. Fourth is a rectangular backdrop that's used to define the typing area. Fifth, and last, is the most complicated piece, a movie clip called listener that will house the key press handler code.

Here's a preview of the finished effect:

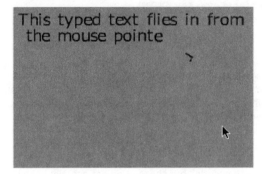

This typed text flies in from the mouse pointer

Most of the work in this effect is in keeping track of where each letter should go.

1. In a new movie, create a movie clip to hold the entire effect and call it typer. This way, you'll be able to drag the typer into any other movie.

2. In the main typer movie clip, create a new layer called display and draw a dynamic text field with the Multiline and Word Wrap options specified. Make the text field quite large – in the region of 450 by 100 pixels – and give the text box the variable name text. This will be the storage field that'll keep track of all the letters that have been typed in.

3. Create another movie clip, call it Drawing Board and draw a gray rectangle 300 pixels wide and 200 pixels high in it. This board is where the typed letters will be displayed.

4. Go back to the main typer movie clip, create a new layer, and drag an instance of Drawing Board onto the stage. Position it above the dynamic text field we've just made and give it the instance name board. Make absolutely sure that your board is positioned at 0,0, otherwise the text won't appear exactly lined up with it when we finish. We'll be designing our script to make the text appear on this board.

5. Next, create a movie clip for our letters and call it text_movie. Create a dynamic text box about 30 x 30 pixels, deselect the Multiline and Word Wrap options, and give it the variable name letter_text:

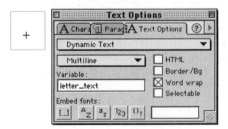

6. Put a capital 'A' in 20pt Courier inside the text box and resize the box until it's roughly the size of the A, and center the box at 0,0 in the clip:

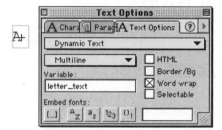

7. Now ensure that you check the Include entire font outline button in the Embed fonts part of the Text Options panel:

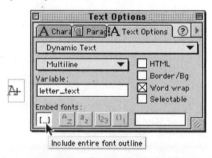

> *Double check that you've done this – it's imperative that you do, or the effect won't work, and you'll go crazy trying to work out why!*

8. Create another movie clip and call it letter_object. Drag a copy of text_movie into the center of letter_object and give it the instance name text_movie:

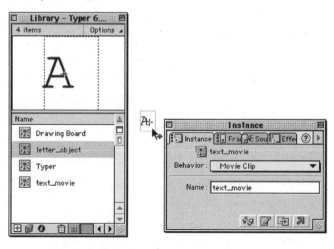

9. Make the layer with text_movie in it ten frames long by inserting a keyframe at the tenth frame, and then use the Frame panel to create a motion tween that rotates clockwise once. Also, check the Scale, Synchronize and Snap boxes:

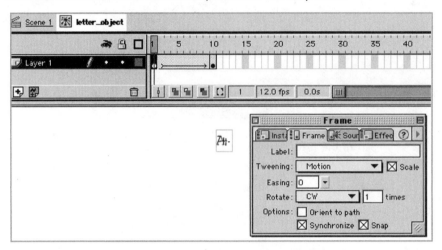

10. Add another ten empty frames after this keyframe by inserting a frame at frame 20 – this way, the letter will stay still visible for a second after it has rotated. Label frame 1 as text_movie so that we can refer to it later.

11. Still in letter_object, select the first keyframe and enter these actions:

```
a_code=0;
x_rate=0;
y_rate=0;
```

Eventually, this will set the contents of the tween to nothing, waiting for information about the typed letters to come from the listener clip.

12. Select the keyframe at the end of the motion tween (frame 10) and add a stop action to it so that the letters only rotate once before coming to rest.

13. In the main typer movie clip create a new layer and call it letters. Drag a copy of letter_object into letters, give it the instance name letter, and position it off to left of the stage:

14. Create an actions layer in the main typer movie clip and insert the customary three keyframes. In the first frame of the typer clip, we initialize all of our main variables. Add this script to do just that to frame 1:

```
h_offset = 0;
num_chars = 0;
line_counter=0;
letters=new Array();
kern=new Array();

BoardBounds=board.getBounds(this);
```

The num_chars variable stores the total number of characters that the user has typed, h_offset describes the amount of space to the left of the starting position a letter will be placed, while the line_counter describes the number of lines down we are at a given moment. The letters array stores references to the set of individual letter movie clips.

The BoardBounds=board.getBounds(this); statement uses the board graphic that we added to our typer clip to define the writing area. The built in getBounds method returns four variables, xMin, yMin, xMax, and yMax, which tell us the extent of the movie clip.

The kern array stores width values for each letter. Kerning is actually the biggest obstacle in this effect. If you look at a block of text, you'll see that, for most fonts, not all of the letters have the same width. Now that we're going to attempt to put the letters in a text paragraph, it's important that the spacing looks natural. Unfortunately, there's no direct way to record the width of a character at a given size of a given font. Damn.

There are four possible solutions to this problem. You could use one of the mono-spaced fonts, like Courier, where all of the letters are actually the same width. If the effect you're trying to achieve permits it, you could leave extra space between all of the letters so that the differences aren't noticeable, or you could create a background graphic for each letter, like a square or a ball, and use these to space out the letters. Lastly, and most tediously, you can estimate the width of each letter and use these widths to space the letters out. Masochistically, this is what I did, and if you look in the FLA you'll see that I've hard-coded the kern array in the first frame, starting like this...

```
kern[65]=15//A
kern[66]=15//B
kern[67]=15//C
kern[68]=15//D
```

...and continuing until I get to Z, plus some punctuation characters.

To save you the trouble of typing all this in, we've provided this code in a text file on the CD – KernCode.txt.

15. Open up the `KernCode.txt` file, copy all of the statements, and then paste them into the frame 1 code after the `BoardBounds=board.getBounds(this);` statement:

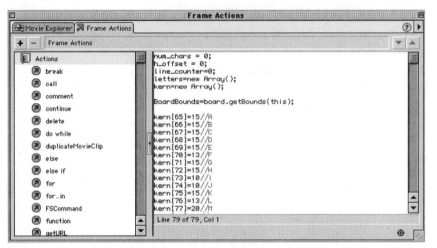

The script for the second frame will look a little familiar as it's almost the same as the motion behavior script we've used previously for the mouse chaser and candle. This time, we'll be looping through the `letters` array and moving the letters toward their final position.

16. Enter this code into the second keyframe:

```
speed = 2;
friction = .45;

for (i=1; i<=num_chars; i++) {

if(letters[i].moving==true){
    Xdiff = (letters[i].x_pos-letters[i]._x);
    Ydiff = (letters[i].y_pos-letters[i]._y);

    letters[i].x_rate += (Xdiff/speed);
    letters[i].y_rate += (Ydiff/speed);

    letters[i].x_rate *= friction;
    letters[i].y_rate *= friction;

    letters[i]._x += letters[i].x_rate;
    letters[i]._y += letters[i].y_rate;

    if (letters[i].x_pos==letters[i]._x &&
    ➡ letters[i].y_pos==letters[i]._y){
        letters[i].moving=false;
    }
}}
```

The key thing to notice here is the `if(letters[i].moving==true){` line. We'll be using the `moving` variable to control whether or not we want the clip to move. At the end of this code we set `moving` to `false`.

17. Add the usual `gotoAndPlay (2)` action to the third keyframe.

Now that we've set the effect up, we can move on to the heart of the effect, the listener movie clip itself. Remember, this is the clip that will actually respond to the user's key presses and trigger the code to handle them.

18. Create a new movie clip called listener, drag it into a new layer in the typer movie clip, and position it over the center of board. As it's an empty movie clip, it'll just show up as a little white circle when not selected:

19. Select it, give it the instance name of listener, and open up its Object Actions window.

20. Now add this code to the listener object:

```
onClipEvent (keyDown) {

    theKey = Key.getCode();
```

Here, we're using the built in `onClipEvent` handler to detect when something happens, so our first line is `onClipEvent(keyDown)`, which will be fired when the user hits a key on the keyboard. We then capture the key that was hit by using `Key.getCode` and storing the result in a variable called `theKey`.

Next, we're going to use a series of `if...else` statements to determine what we want to do now that we know which key was pressed.

21. Add this first `if` statement to the existing `onClipEvent` code:

```
if ((theKey>=48 && theKey<=111) || theKey == 32) {
    _parent.num_chars++;
    theKey = Key.getAscii();
    newLetter = String.fromCharCode(theKey);
```

Note the two 'pipe' symbols in the first line. On the keyboard, the pipe character is found on the backslash (\) key in 'shift' mode. In this code context, two pipes together represent ActionScript's logical 'OR' operator.

This first `if` tests to see if the key the user has pressed falls is one of the characters we want to turn into letter movie clips. The ASCII codes in the first line relate to all the values we defined for the `kern` array, plus the space bar (32). If the key code *is* alphanumeric, which in this case means any letter, number, punctuation character or the space bar, we increment `num_chars` to indicate that we're going to be making a new letter movie clip. Then we use the `Key.getAscii` function to reset `theKey` to equal the appropriate ASCII code. Next comes a line where we use one of Flash's built in string manipulation functions, `String.fromCharCode`, to convert the ASCII code into a one-character string, which we store in a variable called `newLetter`. At this point we've succeeded in *capturing* the letter entered by the user. The next step is to place that letter in a copy of the letter_object movie clip, and to add that to the array.

Do you remember that large text field we made in the typer movie clip? As I said, I just want to use that field to display a record of what the user has keyed in. One reason to store what's been typed in is to send the text somewhere when we're done, such as to an external CGI script that'll store the results in a file or database – but I'll leave you to play with that one after reading the dynamic content chapters later in the book. What we're going to do here is simply echo what the user types in.

To achieve this, all we have to do is add the `newLetter` to the text field.

22.   Add this next chunk to the existing script in the listener instance's `onClipEvent` code:

```
_parent.text = _parent.text + newLetter;
```

This syntax uses the + operator to append the value of the `newLetter` variable to the existing text value in the typer clip. Remember that we're working in the listener movie clip now, so the _parent prefix is necessary to get us back to the typer movie clip.

23.   Now we can go ahead and duplicate the letter movie clip. Add this next batch of code to do that:

```
duplicateMovieClip (_parent.letter, "letter"+_parent.num_chars,
➡  _parent.num_chars);
     _parent.letters[_parent.num_chars] =
➡  _parent["letter"+_parent.num_chars];
```

This may look more complicated than previous examples, but it's the same idea – duplicate the clip and add its reference to the array. We can use num_chars as the suffix on the name as shown, as well as for the level. We can also use that new name to add the new letter to the letters array at position num_chars. The letter is now safely in the array.

Now to initialize the letters movie clip instance and animate it using the motion script back in the typer movie clip.

24.   Append this next piece of code to the existing script:

```
_parent.letters[_parent.num_chars].a_code = theKey;
_parent.letters[_parent.num_chars].text_movie.letter_text =
➡  newLetter.charAt(0);
_parent.letters[_parent.num_chars].moving=true;
```

Initializing the clip is maybe a little more complicated than you might think. The first step is to store the theKey variable in the letter movie clip in a variable named a_code so that we can get at it easily in the future. Next we set that input text field to equal the first, and only, character of newLetter. If you remember, that text field was buried pretty deeply, which is why the path in the second line here is so long. We use the charAt string function to take the first character out of the newLetter string. Finally, we set the clip's moving variable to true, which indicates that the clip will be able to move in the motion code we built earlier.

The next part of the script handles assigning initial and final x and y positions to each letter clip on the screen.

25. To start achieving that aim, add this next code block:

```
if (_parent.h_offset>_parent.board._width-20) {
    _parent.line_counter++;
    _parent.h_offset = 0;
}
```

The first thing you see in the code is an if statement, which uses our board graphic to see if the next character will run outside our writing area. If it does, the text is sent to the next line. To do this, we use code that increments the line counter and resets the horizontal offset; the net effect being that the insertion point for new text goes down a line and back over to the left.

26. Now that we know we're ready to position a letter, add this next lot of code, which will precisely position each letter's host clip on the board:

```
_parent.letters[_parent.num_chars].x_pos =
➡ 20 + _parent.BoardBounds.xMin + _parent.h_offset;
_parent.letters[_parent.num_chars].y_pos =
➡ 20 + _parent.BoardBounds.yMin + (20*_parent.line_counter);
_parent.letters[_parent.num_chars].hoffset = _parent.h_offset;
_parent.h_offset += _parent.kern[theKey];
```

Setting the final positions, which will be stored each letter in the variables x_pos and y_pos is accomplished by using the line number and the horizontal offset. Naturally, both values must be kept updated as you add letters. Here, we get the x position by using a constant spacer (20), plus the right bound of the drawing board, plus the h_offset variable; the y position is calculated using the spacer value, the top bound of the box, added to the h_offset multiplied by the spacer. We then store the current offset in the letter's movie clip so that each letter knows what the offset was before it was added. Finally, we add the kerning value of the current letter to the overall offset.

Now to set the starting positions for each duplicated clip.

27. Add this code:

```
_parent.letters[_parent.num_chars]._x = _xmouse;

_parent.letters[_parent.num_chars]._y = _ymouse;
```

For the initial positions that the letters fly from, I've used the mouse's position, giving the illusion that the letters shoot out of the mouse pointer. You can of course use any point you wish.

That completes the character clip creation code. We have just two more types of key presses to deal with the ENTER key and the DELETE key. Don't worry; they're a lot easier than the last batch of code.

28. Add this next lot of code to cater for the ENTER key:

```
}

else if (theKey == Key.ENTER) {
    _parent.line_counter ++;
    _parent.h_offset = 0;
```

This just moves us onto a new line using the line_counter variable and the h_offset.

Lastly, we need to deal with the DELETE key (we'll also include the BACKSPACE key in this definition). The DELETE key doesn't capture properly on my Mac G3 and to get the key to generate the DELETE code, I need to hold down the OPTION key as I press it. The key works perfectly on PCs, so I think that it may just be a bug in the Mac version of Flash. The deletion process is a little longer than a new line, but you have actually been setting up this capability throughout the creation process without knowing it.

29. Add this final batch of code:

```
}

else if (theKey == Key.BACKSPACE || theKey == Key.DELETEKEY) {
            if(_parent.num_chars>0){

_parent.h_offset=_parent.letters[_parent.num_chars].hoffset;

removeMovieClip(_parent.letters[_parent.num_chars]);
    _parent.num_chars--;

    if(_parent.h_offset<=0 && _parent.line_counter>0){
                        _parent.line_counter--;
            }
        }
    }

}
```

To get started, we have an else if to cater for the two keys, then an if statement that checks whether there are actually some characters to delete. We then use the offset stored inside the letter we want to delete to revert the h_offset variable. Next, we remove the movie clip and decrement num_chars. Lastly, we check to see if this character was the *last* one on the line, in which case we decrement line_counter too. Overall, the deletion process mirrors the creation process quite closely.

30. Drag a copy of the whole Typer movie clip onto the stage. Test it and see how it works.

The DELETE and ENTER keys won't work unless you test it in a browser, as they're assigned to other tasks if you simply Test Movie from within Flash. You'll need to click once with the mouse before entering any text in your browser as a result of a security feature within Flash which stops you entering any text until you click. (This makes sure that it's not possible to load up a Flash file in a browser and then start to capture keyboard presses, which could include passwords and the like.) If anything doesn't work, check your instance names very carefully. The FLA for this effect – Text Typer.fla – is on the CD along with all the other code for this chapter.

There's plenty of room to make this effect bigger by adding support for more key combinations if you feel like twiddling.

For our next effect, which is a lot simpler to code, we're going to draw some lines.

Line Manipulation

There's a limitation inherent in a reliance on movie clips, which is that the smallest elements we use must always be predefined. In all of the effects that we've created in this chapter so far, you've seen how we create one object by hand, and then use ActionScript to duplicate it and manipulate it to create the finished effect. The problem is that we can never draw anything on a *pixel* level with ActionScript, and thus can never create our own objects to use at runtime.

If I asked you to program an application that took a set of data and displayed it as a bar graph, you can probably figure out that you'd need to duplicate some sort of *bar* graphic and scale it in one direction based on the data. It might take some time to make it work, but it's definitely feasible. However, what if I asked you to make a similar program that produced a *line* graph? I suspect that you might have a little more trouble with that: Flash just can't draw a line dynamically. Don't worry, though, there's a great trick you can use to draw a line in Flash from one point to any other point. We're going to build a function that does just that, and use that function in a few real applications.

In the first example, we're going to make a simple movie that has four draggable nodes. Each of these nodes will be connected to two other buttons with a line, so that the four nodes are the vertices of a quadrilateral:

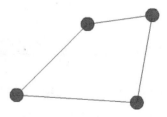

When the nodes are moved, the lines connecting it to its adjacent nodes will be updated dynamically, and the shape will change

Nodes and Lines

1. Start out by creating a new movie clip to hold the effect. Call it line drawing.

    Each of the nodes is actually a button embedded in a movie clip. The precise graphical component is actually unimportant, but I just made a small circle.

2. Create a small button, with, say, a 20 pixel diameter circle, and make sure that it has a Hit state as well as the usual Up, Over, and Down. Mine's called node button.

3. Place a copy of the button inside of a new movie clip called point and make sure that the button is placed dead center of the movie clip – use the Info panel to line it up at 0,0. The effect won't work unless you do this, so double check.

4. Select the *instance of the button* inside the movie clip and use the Object Actions window to give it the following event handlers, which will allow the button to drag its container point movie clip around:

    ```
    on (press) {
    startDrag ("",1);
    }
    on (release) {
    stopDrag ();
    }
    ```

5. Once you have the button set up inside its movie clip, drag four instances of the point movie clip inside the main line drawing movie clip. Give them the instance names point0, point1, point2, and point3:

To get this effect to work, we only have one object left to make – the graphic that we use to draw the lines.

6. Create a new movie clip called square, and draw a square inside it with no fill and a dark stroke, exactly 100 pixels high and 100 pixels wide – use the Info panel if necessary.

7. Align the square so that its upper left corner is in the exact center of the movie clip. Use the Align To Stage option in the Align palette, and the Align top edge and Align left edge buttons for precision:

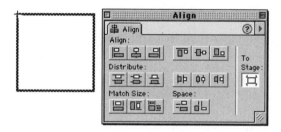

8. Inside square, carefully draw a *red* line from the upper left corner of the square to the lower right corner. It's very important that this line meets exactly with both the corners – any gaps will effect how well the lines drawn on-screen fit together later. Use the Snap to objects option and zoom in to make sure that this is absolutely perfect.

9. Select the line and save it as a separate movie clip called line. Go into edit on line and position its top-left corner at 0,0.

10. Now go back into square, select all of the lines in the square, and make sure that their thickness is set to hairline:

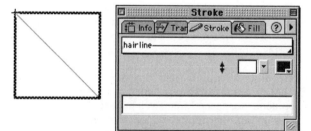

11. When you've done that, make a new layer called components in the main line drawing movie clip and drag your square movie clip onto that layer. Give it the instance name square.

12. Now drag a copy of the line clip onto the same layer, give it an instance name of line, and place it exactly over the top of the square instance, so that the two red lines are superimposed over each other.

At this point you should see four circular button movies and a square with a line in it in the main movie clip:

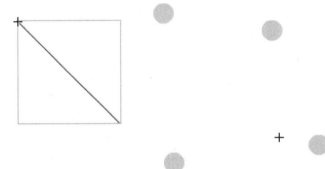

13. Add a new layer, call it actions and create the standard three keyframe layout.

14. In the first actions frame, begin as usual by defining some variables:

```
lines = new Array();
points = new Array();
points[0] = point0;
points[1] = point1;
points[2] = point2;
points[3] = point3;
```

All we're going to need are two arrays, one for the points and one for the lines. Since we already have our points, we have to place them in the array manually. Therefore, we set points[0] equal to point0 and so on. We'll come back to the lines array shortly.

The rest of the script is split up into two functions: an initialization function (CreateLines) and a drawing function (DrawLines). Once we have the drawing function done, our second frame will have to do nothing more than call it every cycle. The initialization function could be written inline instead, but for purposes of portability I've made it a function. I *love* functions.

The initialization function takes as input an array of objects that it will use as points. In this case the objects happen to be movable buttons, but any movie clip that has the required x and y position that the drawing function needs will do.

15. Create the initialization function now as a continuation of the code in frame 1 of the Actions layer:

```
function CreateLines (pointArray) {
    for (i=0; i<pointArray.length; i++) {
        duplicateMovieClip ("line", "line" +i, i);
```

```
        lines[i] = eval("line" +i);
        lines[i].p1 = pointArray[i];

        if (i == (pointArray.length -1)) {
                lines[i].p2 = pointArray[0];
        } else {
                lines[i].p2 = pointArray[i+1];
        }
    }
}
```

All this function does is make a copy of the lines movie clip for each set of two consecutive points in the input array. This function makes a closed polygon, so it makes a line between the last point and the first. This function doesn't actually do any drawing. What it *does* do is tell each new line object what its start and end points are by storing references to them (p1 and p2) in each line movie clip. The duplication code should be familiar by now, as it's the same code structure that we've been using all through the chapter. The if statement tests if the point in consideration is the last, in which case the function will link it to the *first* point, completing the shape.

16. Lastly, add the code for the drawing function:

```
function DrawLines (lineArray) {
    for (i=0; i<lineArray.length; i++) {
            lineArray[i]._x = lineArray[i].p1._x;
            lineArray[i]._y = lineArray[i].p1._y;
            lineArray[i]._xscale = lineArray[i].p2._x-
               ➥lineArray[i].p1._x;
            lineArray[i]._yscale = lineArray[i].p2._y-
               ➥lineArray[i].p1._y;
    }
}
CreateLines(points);
line._visible=false;
square._visible=false;
```

The function itself is fairly simple. It'll run through the line array and position each graphic in the right place. Understanding *why* the function actually works is a little more difficult. I'll explain the math, but I think you'll understand the effect better when you've seen it in action.

OK, here's the math: imagine a blank movie clip, and imagine that you place a dot at (0,0), which is at the center of the movie clip where the little cross mark is. Then place a mark at (100, 100). Do you remember the square graphic we made? Because it was a 100 x 100 square, if you place it in this movie clip with its upper left corner on the first mark, the lower right corner will naturally fall on the second mark. Now imagine that you move the second mark out until it is at (200, 200). How could you scale that square graphic so the its lower right corner again rests on that second mark? It's easy to see that the x any y scales need to be set to 200 to get the desired effect. What if I move the second mark somewhere where the numbers are *not* so obvious? You'll find that once you place the upper left corner of our 100x100 square on the first mark, you can set the x scale of the square to equal the x position of the second mark minus the x position of the first. Likewise, you can set the y scale to the y position of the second mark minus the y position of the first. In the case where we moved the mark to (200,200), this would equal 200-0, which of course is 200, the scale factor we need.

The last part of this code calls the initialization function, which takes lineArray as a parameter. I also make the original line graphic invisible for good measure.

Here's the frame 1 script in its entirety:

```
lines = new Array();
points = new Array();
points[0] = point0;
points[1] = point1;
points[2] = point2;
points[3] = point3;

function CreateLines (pointArray) {
    for (i=0; i<pointArray.length; i++) {
        duplicateMovieClip ("line", "line" +i, i);

        lines[i] = eval("line" +i);
        lines[i].p1 = pointArray[i];

        if (i == (pointArray.length -1)) {
            lines[i].p2 = pointArray[0];
        } else {
            lines[i].p2 = pointArray[i+1];
        }
    }
}

function DrawLines (lineArray) {
    for (i=0; i<lineArray.length; i++) {
        lineArray[i]._x = lineArray[i].p1._x;
        lineArray[i]._y = lineArray[i].p1._y;
        lineArray[i]._xscale = lineArray[i].p2._x
            ➥ lineArray[i].p1._x;
        lineArray[i]._yscale = lineArray[i].p2._y
            ➥ lineArray[i].p1._y;
    }
}

CreateLines(points);
line._visible=false;
square._visible=false;
```

17. On frame 2, simply call the DrawLines function with this line:

```
DrawLines (lines)
```

This will do all the work for us using the lines array as input.

18. On frame 3, your fingers should already be typing...

```
gotoAndPlay(2)
```

...from habit.

19. Drag a copy of line drawing onto the main stage and test the movie:

You can experiment by editing the graphic further, as long as you use a hairline that begins at 0,0 and ends at 100,100 you can do anything you want in the middle. Try some subtle curves, maybe.

Now that we know how to draw lines anywhere we want, let's use this functionality. At the beginning of this section, I kind of challenged you to think of a way to create a line graph in Flash. Let's do just that.

Line Graph

If you want to have dynamically generated graphs on your web site, you'd normally have to pay for expensive server side tools that generate the graph and then display the graph as an image. Using native Flash we can save a lot of money and make nice-looking graphs at the same time. In this example we'll create a graph based on figures from some input fields.

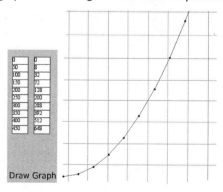

In real life you would probably want to read the data in as text from a text file, but that's beyond the scope of this chapter – again, check out the dynamic content chapters at the end of the book for some ideas in this regard. For now, we'll create a function that we'll draw our line graph given a data set that's entered by hand.

1. Create a movie clip to hold everything, and call it graph. Note that because we want to plot the graph in the traditional way, with the bottom left coordinate as the origin, you should position all this movie clip's content above and to the right of the clip's center point.

2. Use the File > Open as Library menu option to open up the previous exercise's FLA, and drag the line movie clip from its Library into *this* movie's Library.

3. Create a new layer in the graph movie clip called line and drag a copy of line into the top left hand corner of graph. Give it the instance name line:

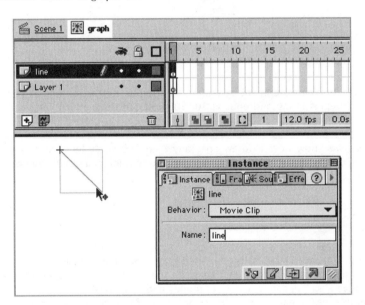

4. Create a new movie clip, call it point and insert a very small circular graphic into, about 5 pixels wide. Center it at exactly 0,0 using the Info panel.

5. Create a new layer called point in the main graph movie clip, and drag a copy of point into the top left hand corner, next to line. Give it the instance name point:

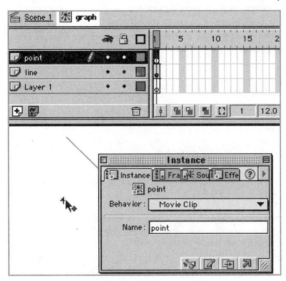

6. Now add another movie clip and call it field. In this, create an *input* text field about 40 pixels wide by 20 high and center it at 0,0. Give the text field the variable name text, select the Single Line option and check the Border/Bg box:

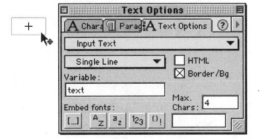

7. Make absolutely sure that you set the Max Characters box to something sensible – 4 should do it.

8. Create a button and call it drawGraph. Enter the text Draw Graph at a size of about 20pt in the first frame of the button and then add separate keyframes for all four states of the button:

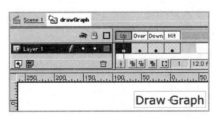

9. Make the text gray in the Up and Over states, and red in the Downstate. In the Hit state add a large rectangle – it doesn't matter what color, as you won't ever see it – that comfortably covers the whole text block. Create a new layer in the main graph movieclip, and then drag a copy of the button onto that layer at the bottom left hand corner:

Draw Graph

This effect can take a little more time to set up, because we need to set up a grid area where we can draw our graph. First we need to decide which quadrant of the x, y plane we wish to use for our graph. We'll use the upper-right quadrant for our example.

10. If you want to, create a grid out of pale lines for a background on its own layer. As you can see, I made a grid line every 50 pixels in the example movie:

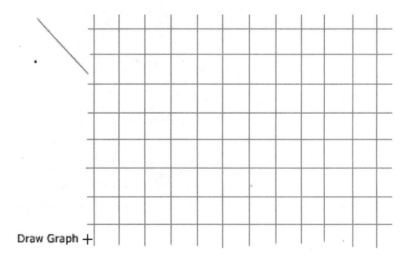

Draw Graph +

11. Drag two instances of the field movie clip onto the main stage. Name the two instances x0 and y0 and arrange them side-by-side on the left hand side, underneath where you put line and point earlier:

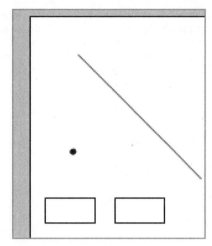

These movie clips will be duplicated in pairs nine times, to give us a place to enter a total of ten sets of x and y points, so make sure you've left room for this to happen underneath them. We could lay them out by hand, but I find it easier to make them and name them in the script.

This completely optional, but if you want to do what I've done and give the text fields a background, create a new layer in the main movie clip and do this:

Draw Graph

Speaking of the script, it's time to get started on it. This effect only has one script frame. We'll set up everything we need to draw the graph and then write a function to do the actual drawing. Then we'll attach that function call to the button, so that every time we update the text field, we need only press the Draw Graph button to redraw the graph.

12. Create an actions layer in the main graph movie clip and add this script to the first frame:

```
input_num = 10;
lines = new Array();
input = new Array();
points = new Array();
```

The script starts out by defining a variable to store how many x, y points we will have, and then initializes three arrays: one to hold lines, points and data sets respectively. The first two are standard arrays, but the `input` array will actually be a *two-dimensional array*, with each indexed location containing another array. Each slot in the second array will contain two values, with an x data item in the first position and a y data item in the second.

Now that we've declared the initialization variables, we must populate the `input` array.

13. Add this script to do that:

```
input[0] = new Array();
input[0][0] = x0;
input[0][1] = y0;
input[0][0].text = 0;
input[0][1].text = 0;
```

The first line here creates a new array *inside* the first slot in the existing `input` array. We can then use the 'double bracket' notation to populate both of the sublocations inside the first slot:

```
input[0][0] = x0;
input[0][1] = y0;
```

Thus the x0 movie clip is put in `input[0][0]`, and y0 is stored in `input[0][1]`. The `text` variable of each is the set to zero:

```
input[0][0].text = 0;
input[0][1].text = 0;
```

The next three blocks of code contain separate duplication loops, all very similar to those that we've seen before.

14. Add this code for the first loop now:

```
for (i=1; i<input_num; i++){
    duplicateMovieClip (this.x0, "x"+i, i);
    duplicateMovieClip (this.y0, "y"+i, (i+input_num));
    input[i] = newArray();
    input[i][0] = eval("x"+i);
    input[i][1] = eval("y"+i);
    input[i][0]._y += i*25;
    input[i][1]._y += i*25;
    input[i][0].text = i*50;
    input[i][1].text = Math.pow (i*2, 2)*2;
}
```

This loop will create the new data items. It's actually duplicating two movie clips, the x0 and y0 clips. Each is duplicated and then moved down using an offset technique that might look familiar from the keyboard capture example from earlier. The `text` properties of each clip are set to some initial values, using a multiple of the loop counter for the first location, and some output from the `Math` object's `pow` method for the second:

```
input[i][0].text = i*50;
input[i][1].text = Math.pow (i*2, 2)*2;
```

15. Insert the code for the next duplication cycle:

```
for (i=0; i<(input_num-1); i++) {
    duplicateMovieClip (this.line, "line" + i, (i +
        ➥ (input_num*2)));
    lines[i] = eval("line"+i);
}
```

This creates all the new lines that we need to draw the graph. We need one less line than the total number of data points, because the number of line segments in a graph equals one less than the number of points.

16. Create the script for the third and last duplication cycle:

```
for (i=0; i<input_num; i++) {
    duplicateMovieClip (this.point, "point" + i,
        ➥ (i+(input_num*3)));
    points[i] = eval("point"+i);
}
```

This makes some copies of the point graphic that'll mark the points on the graph. In the last example, the points determined where the lines would go, but in this movie, the points are added on afterwards as visual markers.

17. Finally, add the function that's the heart of this effect, the `DrawLines` function.

```
function DrawLines (inputArray, lineArray, pointArray) {
    for (i=0; i<(input_num-1); i++) {
        lineArray[i]._x = inputArray[i][0].text;
        lineArray[i]._y = inputArray[i][1].text;
        lineArray[i]._y*=-1;
        lineArray[i]._xscale = inputArray[i+1][0].text -
            ➥ inputArray[i][0].text;
        lineArray[i]._yscale = inputArray[i][1].text -
            ➥ inputArray[i+1][1].text;
    }

    for (i=0; i<input_num; i++) {
        pointArray[i]._x = inputArray[i][0].text;
        pointArray[i]._y = inputArray[i][1].text;
        pointArray[i]._y*=-1;
    }
```

continues overleaf

```
    }
line._visible=false;
point._visible=false;
DrawLines (input, lines, points);

stop();
```

While the math for drawing a line remains the same, the data structures have changed significantly from the last example. In this function, we have two `for` loops, due to the count difference between points and lines. We draw the points first, using the data from the `input` array. Note that we multiply the y position of each point by a negative one:

```
lineArray[i]._y*=-1;
```

This is because of the way the coordinate system works in Flash: we have to flip the results vertically to place the graph in the correct quadrant. The next `for` loop positions all of the lines in the `lines` array.

After the function definition is finished, we simply call it at the end of the script, using the three arrays as arguments:

```
DrawLines (input, lines, points);
```

This presents the user with the initial graph display when the movie starts.

I've also set the original line and point movie clips to be invisible. The last thing on the frame is a `stop` action – we don't want the movie to loop back and reinitialize everything.

18. Nearly there. Finally, go to the drawGraph button instance on the stage and add these actions in its Object Actions window:

```
on ( release ) {
DrawLines (input, lines, points);
}
```

19. Drag a copy of graph onto the main stage, position it appropriately, and test the movie out.

The graph should appear instantly, with the initial coordinate values generated by the ActionScript code:

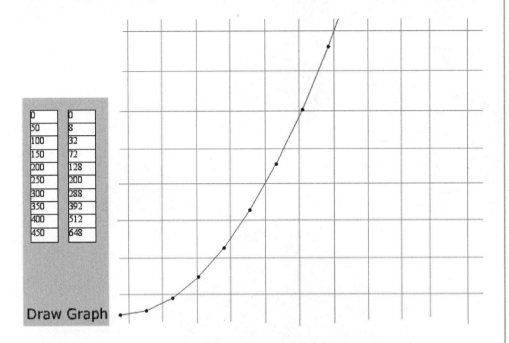

0	0
50	8
100	32
150	72
200	128
250	200
300	288
350	392
400	512
450	648

Draw Graph

Try editing a point in the graph by changing the numbers in the text boxes. When you press your Draw Graph button the graph should change to reflect the new numbers. It's still possible to make the graph draw outside of the graph area, so if you want a little scripting practice, you can make the Draw function refuse to draw a point that goes outside the graph area.

You could also start playing around with the calculations, and thinking about how to feed figures into the movie as a series of variables and using them as the point coordinates to plot.

Conclusion

I hope that this chapter has given you some useful insights into what's possible with Flash's immensely powerful scripting language.

The best advice I can give anyone who wants to learn ActionScript is to be patient. As with all code, expect to spend some time debugging and trouble shooting, scratching your head and toggling back and forth between different object's code Actions windows. This will be a great learning experience and proving ground for you, and it'll really fix ActionScript's tools and techniques in your mind. There's no shortcut – it's all about practice, experimentation and innovation. Good luck, and happy Flashing!

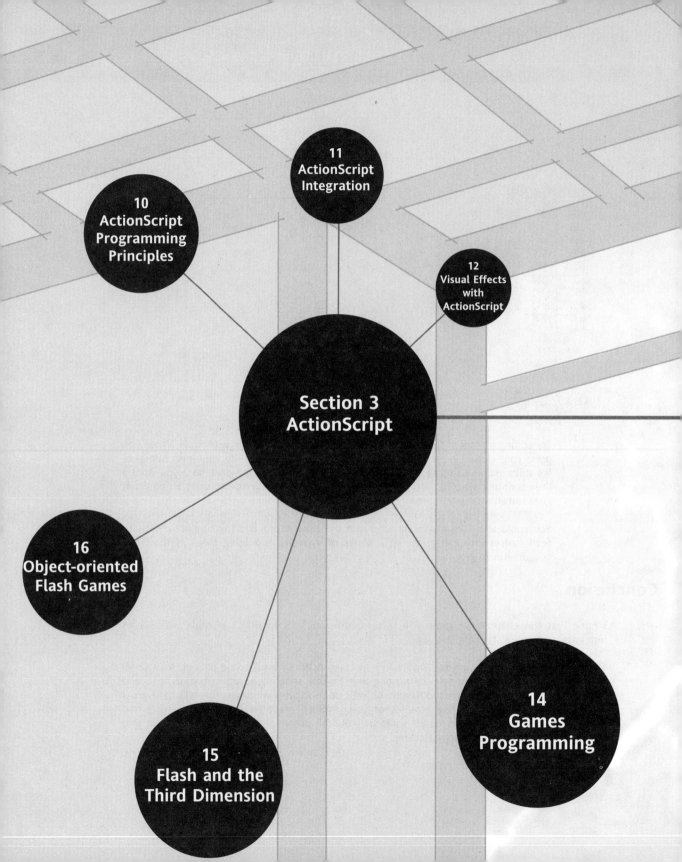

11
ActionScript
Integration

10
ActionScript
Programming
Principles

12
Visual Effects
with
ActionScript

**Section 3
ActionScript**

16
Object-oriented
Flash Games

14
Games
Programming

15
Flash and the
Third Dimension

Chapter 13
Simple Games
Routines

Like it or love it, web sites created with Flash are everywhere you look nowadays, but even though Flash is one of the most powerful web creation programs available, a lot of these sites aren't using it to its full potential. One aspect of Flash that people didn't often use previously was ActionScript programming, but with the advent of Flash 5, this is no longer something that can be ignored. With ActionScript you can create highly interactive interfaces and even Flash-based games, and this is what we'll be exploring in this chapter.

We'll be going through a series of programming tutorials that'll take you step-by-step through the process of creating games and interactive content for your sites. Even if you don't have much experience with ActionScript, the tutorials are designed to ease you into it, getting more and more advanced as we lead up to the final tutorial.

One thing that's essential to keep in mind throughout is the difference between a symbol name and an instance name. The *symbol* name is the name of a graphic, button, or movie clip that appears in the Library, and naming your symbols descriptively will make them a lot easier to identify, and it'll speed up your workflow too. An *instance* name however, can only be given to a movie clip on the stage, and it enables you to control the clip using ActionScript commands. The advantage of an instance name is that you can drag multiple copies of the same symbol onto the stage, and yet control them all separately by giving them individual names. The instance name and symbol name can be the same – Flash will never confuse them, as they're different *types* of object, so it's up to you to decide if you want the same name so you can remember it easily, or whether you prefer to have different names so you don't confuse yourself. As I said, it makes no difference to Flash, but it's something that you should think about as you develop your own particular working methods and habits.

OK, let's begin.

One of the most important things that you'll need to know when programming games for Flash is how to create a movie clip that knows where it is on the screen, and is capable of moving itself around. In this first tutorial you'll learn how to create a simple ball that moves around the screen bouncing off the sides.

The Rebounding Ball

The first thing you'll need to do is to set up the Flash movie for your ball to bounce around *in*.

1. Create a new movie and change its Width and Height to 400 pixels. For now, change the Frame Rate of the movie to 20 fps: you can play around with this to find your preferred speed, but I've found that 20 fps gives the movie enough speed to create convincing animations. Finally, set the Grid Spacing to 10 px and make sure that Show and Snap to Grid are turned on.

2. Draw some black lines around the edges of the stage. This will be your wall so you can clearly see where the ball bounces when it reaches the sides:

3. Now you've got your background sorted out, you just need to add the ball. Draw a filled circle anywhere on the stage, and use the Info panel to give it a Width and Height of 20 px. Once you've done this select the circle and convert it into a movie clip symbol called Ball. Next, use the Instance panel to give the instance on the stage an imaginative name... Ball.

4. That's the basics done. You're now ready to add your first piece of ActionScript and get the ball rolling. Open up the Ball movie clip ready for editing. Create a new layer, insert keyframes into frames 1, 2, and 3, and name this layer Code. Insert another 2 frames into Layer 1, and rename it Graphics:

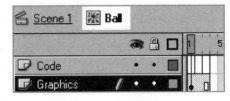

5. Open up the Frame Actions panel for frame 1 on the Code layer and add the following actions:

```
Xspeed = 10;
Yspeed = 10;
```

These variables set the speed of the ball by defining how far the movie clip will move in each frame.

6. In frame 2 on the Code layer add the following actions:

```
BallX = _x;
BallY = _y;
BallX = BallX+Xspeed;
BallY = BallY+Yspeed;
if (BallX>390) {
    BallX = 390;
    Xspeed = Xspeed*-1;
}
if (BallX<10) {
    BallX = 10;
    Xspeed = Xspeed*-1;
}
if (BallY>390) {
    BallY = 390;
    Yspeed = Yspeed*-1;
}
if (BallY<10) {
    BallY = 10;
    Yspeed = Yspeed*-1;
}
_x = BallX;
_y = BallY;
```

This is the core code of the ball's movement. _x and _y are the built-in properties that represent the position of the ball on the stage. The variables BallX and BallY are set to the current _x and _y of the ball, then a series of calculations are carried out on them, and at the end _x and _y are set back to BallX and BallY, updating the ball's position on the screen.

The if statements check to see if the ball has reached the edge of the screen. We know that the stage is 400 x 400 px, and the radius of the ball is 10 (half of 20). At the moment, Flash is set to measure the ball from the center, so if we take the radius of the ball away from the size of the stage we'll know when the side of the ball has reached the edge of the screen:

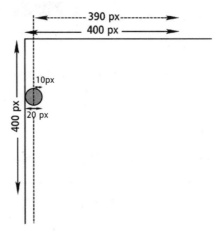

When we reach the edge of the screen we reverse the direction of the ball by 'flipping' the appropriate speed. This is simply done by multiplying it by –1: for example, 10*-1 = -10 and -10*-1=10.

7. In frame 3 on the Code layer add the following actions:

```
gotoAndPlay (2);
```

This simply sends the movie clip back to frame 2 to create a loop, updating the position of the ball ten times a second.

If you've entered the code correctly you'll see the ball bouncing about when you play the movie. If you find that nothing happens, or that the ball doesn't move around properly, double check the ActionScript, as one small mistake can make all the difference. If everything is working fine, then save the file to disk and name it Balltut1.fla because we'll be adding more ActionScript to this in the next tutorial.

Adding Randomness

At the moment, your ball will be bouncing around an invariable path, just looping round and round. The first thing we can do to change this is to alter the speed of the ball. By changing the Xspeed and Yspeed variables in the first frame we can make it cheat gravity. Try values of 8 and 15 respectively. These mean that the ball will move faster, and therefore further, along the Y (vertical) plane than it does along the X (horizontal) plane.

Adding random elements to your actions will make the ball act and move in different ways every time the movie is run. This is a good thing, as it adds an element of life to your movies and will make them more interesting for people to watch and eventually interact with. In this example we'll add actions to the ball that make it start in a random position on the screen and change to a random speed when it hits the sides.

1. Starting with your previous bouncing ball file, select the Ball movie clip and then either edit or edit-in-place to get to the Ball timeline. In frame 1 on the Code layer, alter your ActionScript to match the following listing (changed code is highlighted):

    ```
    Xspeed = 8;
    Yspeed = 15;
    _x = (Math.random()*300)+20;
    _y = (Math.random()*300)+20;
    ```

    These two new actions will make the ball start at a random position whenever the movie is run. We're using the Math.random() method here rather than the random() function, because it's the preferred command in Flash 5, and it's also a better approximation of a random number. The only problem with this method is that it returns a number from 0.0 to 1.0. This means that we have to multiply the result that we get by another number to get a wide enough range. For example, in Flash 4, you could write random(10) to receive a random number from 0 to 9, but now it's better to use Math.random(), and then multiply the result by 10. So, for a random number from 0 to 9, the code would be Math.random()*10. This, however, will give you a very precise number e.g. 8.945272636435, so to round it down to the nearest *integer* you could use Math.floor(Math.random()*10). This may look complicated and long winded, but don't forget that you can always put this into a function of your own. A simple example of this would be:

    ```
    function NewRand(a){
    return Math.floor(Math.random()*a);
    }
    ```

    You can now get a random number from 0 to 9 by calling NewRand(10);.

2. Next, go into the main Ball code and give it a random speed. To do this, add the following actions in frame 2 on the Code layer:

```
BallX = _x;
BallY = _y;
BallX = BallX+Xspeed;
BallY = BallY+Yspeed;
if (BallX>390) {
    BallX = 390;
    Xspeed = Xspeed+((Math.random()*10)-5);
    Xspeed = Xspeed*-1;
}
if (BallX<10) {
    BallX = 10;
    Xspeed = Xspeed*-1;
    Xspeed = Xspeed+((Math.random()*10)-5);
}
if (BallY>390) {
    BallY = 390;
    Yspeed = Yspeed+((Math.random()*10)-5);
    Yspeed = Yspeed*-1;
}
if (BallY<10) {
    BallY = 10;
    Yspeed = Yspeed*-1;
    Yspeed = Yspeed+((Math.random()*10)-5);
}
_x = BallX;
_y = BallY;
```

These new actions will tell the ball to change its speed and direction when it reaches the edge of the window.

3. When you run the movie you'll now notice that the ball never takes the same route as it did before, and here you can clearly see the effect that a few random numbers can have on a movie's movement. When you're happy with the movie save it to disk and name it `Balltut2.fla`. We'll be using this movie in the next tutorial.

Now it's time to add a bit of interactivity and basic mouse control to your movie.

Getting Interactive

Adding interactive elements into your movies gives you the opportunity to create some amazing animated menus and buttons. We've already looked at programming a movie clip so that it moves around the screen by itself, and now we'll add some actions that'll enable the user to stop and start the movie clip by moving their mouse over it:

1. The first thing that you need to do is to create a button that triggers some ActionScript when the mouse is moved over, and then moved away from the ball. Open up the Ball movie clip and select the ball graphic on your Graphics layer. Convert it to a button symbol and call it Button. You now have a button nested inside your movie clip that's ready to add actions to.

2. Click on Button to select it, then open up the Object Actions window and type the following code:

```
on (rollOver, dragOver) {
    Xspeedsave = Xspeed;
    Yspeedsave = Yspeed;
    Xspeed = 0;
    Yspeed = 0;
}

on (rollOut, dragOut) {
    Xspeed = Xspeedsave;
    Yspeed = Yspeedsave;
}
```

The Xspeedsave and Yspeedsave variables store the movement speed of the ball before the speed is reduced to 0. When the mouse is moved away from the ball the Xspeed and Yspeed variables are returned to their original values using the Xspeedsave and Yspeedsave variables.

That's all the ActionScript that you'll need to stop and start the ball with the mouse. Run the movie and see if everything is working correctly, then save the file as Balltut3.fla. Once again, we'll be building on this movie in the next tutorial.

Duplicating the Ball

We're now going to add a button to the movie, which will create a new ball every time it's pressed.

1. On the root timeline, open up the Library window and drag a copy of the button that we created earlier onto the bottom right-hand corner of the screen:

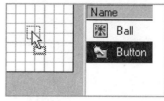

If you like, you can use the Effect panel to tint the button to make it stand out from the others.

2. Now open up the Object Actions window for the button and add the following actions:

```
on (press) {
    Count = Count+1;
    duplicateMovieClip ("Ball", "Ball" + Count, Count);
}
```

The Count variable stores the number of balls on screen and increases itself by 1 every time the button is pressed. The duplicateMovieClip action creates a new version of the ball and appends the value of the Count variable to the end of its name, so the first instance of the Ball clip will be called Ball1, the second will be called Ball2, and so on.

3. Once you've entered the actions run the movie and press the button as many times as you like. Each time you press it, a new ball will appear, and you should still be able to stop each ball by putting the mouse over them:

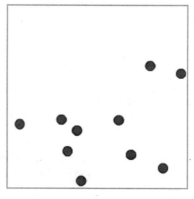

4. Once you've finished playing, save this movie to disk and name it Balltut4.fla.

OK, that's the end of the ball examples. So far we've covered the four basic ActionScript routines that are needed to create both games and some very lively Flash content on your sites. These four routines are:

■ Movie clip movement

■ Basic collision detection

- Random elements

- Movie clip duplication

You're now at a stage where you can create your first Flash based game.

A Basic Bat and Ball Game

It's time to create a Flash-based 'bat and ball' game using the routines we've just covered, plus some additional actions that'll take you deeper into the world of ActionScript.

The game will contain a ball which bounces around the screen, two bats controlled by the player, two score zones or goals for the ball to enter, and some text displaying the score.

Creating the Game

First you need to set up the playing area for the movie.

1. Create a new movie and set the Width to 600 px and the Height to 400 px. While you have the dialog box open, set the Frame Rate to 20 fps as well. Set the grid spacing to 10 px and make sure that Show Grid and Snap to Grid are turned on, then draw lines around the edge of the movie as you did before, so that you'll be able to clearly see the size of the window when you run the movie.

2. Now to create the ball that'll be used in the game. Draw a filled circle 20 px wide and 20 px high, and then convert it into a movie clip, giving it the symbol name Ball. Now click on the instance of the movie clip on the stage, open up the Instance panel, and give it the instance name Puck, for a change.

3. Next, you need to create a bat. Draw a filled rectangle 10 px wide and 40 px high. Select the rectangle and convert it into a movie clip called Bat.

    In this game, the bats will move in relation to the position of the mouse. To do this we'll create an invisible movie clip that moves with the mouse: this clip will tell the bats where they need to move to. This will become clearer when you see it in action.

4. Create a filled circle 10 px wide and 10 px high, and then convert it into a movie clip called InvisClip. Once you've done this give it the instance name MousePosition.

5. Click on the first frame of the main timeline and bring up the Frame Actions window. In order for the MousePosition movie clip to move with the mouse you'll need to enter the following simple actions:

    ```
    startDrag ("MousePosition", true, 0, 20, 600, 380);
    ```

    The startDrag action causes the MousePosition instance to lock itself to the mouse. The numbers define the border that the clip can be dragged into; you'll notice that this is a little smaller than the size of the stage. This is so that when the bats are moving they won't be able to go over the top or bottom boundaries of the stage:

You can see here that when the MousePosition clip hits its boundary, the bat just reaches the top of the stage as we predicted. The true property tells Flash that we really do want to tie the mouse cursor to the center of the clip.

6.   If you play the movie now, you'll see that the MousePosition instance happily moves around the stage, locked to the mouse cursor.

At the moment there's only one bat on the screen, but we'll need two for the game, so open up the Library window and drag another copy of the Bat movie clip onto the stage. Select one of the bats and position it so that its top-left corner is at the top-left of the stage, then give it the instance name LeftBat. Select the remaining Bat and position its top-right corner at the top-right of the stage and give it the instance name RightBat:

It's now time to program the movie so that both of the bats move up and down the screen with the mouse, but *not* left or right.

7.   On the main stage, select the MousePosition movie clip and open it for editing. Add a new layer called Code and create keyframes in frames 1, 2 and 3. On Layer 1 insert a frame into frame 3.

8.   Add the following actions to frame 3 on the Code layer:

```
gotoAndPlay (2);
```

This will create a loop between frame 2 and frame 3.

9.   Now add these actions to frame 2 on the Code layer:

```
MousePositionY = _root.MousePosition._y;
_root.LeftBat._y = MousePositionY;
_root.RightBat._y = MousePositionY;
```

These actions check for the position of the MousePosition movie clip and then relocate LeftBat and RightBat to match that position. If you run the movie now, you should be able to move the mouse around, and the bats will follow it when it moves up or down, but they won't move left or right.

That's all the programming you'll need to do for the bats, so let's move on to the ball.

The Puck movie clip will hold all of the ActionScript handling collisions with the edges of the window, collisions with the bats, and the game score, so now might be a good time to make yourself a cup of coffee because you've got quite a bit of programming ahead of you...

10. Select the Puck and open it for editing. Create a new layer and call it Code. Add a keyframe in frames 2, and 3 on the Code layer, and then add a frame in frame 3 in Layer 1.

11. Add this action to frame 3 on the Code layer:

```
gotoAndPlay (2);
```

Again, this will create the familiar loop between frames 2 and 3.

12. Add the following actions to frame 1 on the Code layer:

```
Xspeed = (Math.random()*15)+5;
Yspeed = (Math.random()*15)+5;
_root.Score = 0;
_x = (Math.random()*300)+150;
_y = (Math.random()*150)+75;
```

These set the initial random speed for the ball, the initial score value, and a random starting position for the ball.

Frame 2 will contain the main skeleton of the program: the ball's movement, the collision detection, and the game score.

13. Add the code to update the position of the bats and the ball:

```
LeftBatY = _root.LeftBat._y;
RightBatY = _root.RightBat._y;
BallX = _x;
BallY = _y;
BallX = BallX+Xspeed;
BallY = BallY+Yspeed;
```

The first two lines record the position of the bats, the second two record the position of the ball, and the last two set up the ball's new position.

14. Next, beneath that, we'll use a series of `if` statements to determine when the ball hits something, and define what to do when it does. The reactions that we want are as follows:

- Ball hits top or bottom – bounce off with a new random speed

- Ball hits bat – bounce off with a new random speed, and add 10 to the score

- Ball hits right or left wall – game over, restart game and reset score to 0

Let's take a look at the code step by step.

15. Enter all of this ActionScript in frame 2 beneath the last piece:

```
if (BallX>580) {
    if (BallY>(RightBatY-20)) {
        if (BallY<(RightBatY+20)) {
            BallX = 580;
            Xspeed = (Math.random()*15)+5;
            Xspeed = Xspeed*-1;
            _root.Score = _root.Score+10;
        }
    }
}
```

This first set of `if` statements discover if the ball has hit the right-hand bat. First of all they check to see if the ball has reached a certain point on the screen, which you can imagine as a vertical line drawn just in front of the bat. Then the code checks to see if the ball is at the same level of the screen (measured from top to bottom). If the ball is next to the bat then it bounces off and the score is increased by 10.

If, however, we miss the ball with the right-hand bat...

```
if (BallX>590) {
    _root.Score = 0;
    gotoAndPlay (1);
}
```

...then the score is reset, and the game starts again.

16. Next, we need a similar set of actions for the bat on the left-hand side. Add these now:

```
if (BallX<20) {
    if (BallY>(LeftBatY-20)) {
        if (BallY<(LeftBatY+20)) {
            BallX = 20;
            Xspeed = (Math.random()*15)+5;
            _root.Score = _root.Score+10;
        }
```

```
        }
    }
    if (BallX<10) {
        _root.Score = 0;
        gotoAndPlay (1);
    }
```

17. Now tell the ball what to do when it hits the top or bottom of the screen:

```
    if (BallY>390) {
        BallY = 390;
        Yspeed = (Math.random()*15)+5;
        Yspeed = Yspeed*-1;
    }
    if (BallY<10) {
        BallY = 10;
        Yspeed = (Math.random()*15)+5;
    }
```

18. Lastly, add this code to update the position of the ball:

```
    _x = BallX;
    _y = BallY;
```

That's all of the main programming done. There's still a bit of tidying up to do and the score to sort out, but we'll come to that in a minute. For now you can sit back, relax, and play ball:

OK, now for the final touches. First of all, we need to hide the movie clip that's underneath the mouse cursor. The easiest way to do this is just to delete it.

19. Go back to the main window, select the MousePosition movie clip, and open it for editing. From here select the filled circle and delete it. Don't worry – this won't delete the movie clip.

We can even take this one step further and hide the mouse cursor itself as well.

20.   Go back to the main timeline and open up the Frame Actions panel for the first (and only) frame in Layer 1. There's already a `startDrag` action in this frame. Underneath this, add:

```
Mouse.hide();
```

The cursor should now be hidden, and that's all there is to it. To display the game score you need to add another layer called Score to the main movie timeline.

21.   Create a dynamic text field on this layer and set the Variable field to `Score`. Move the text field to a position on the screen where you'd like the game score to appear; I've put mine at the top-middle, and you might also want to check the Border/Bg box so the score is easier to see:

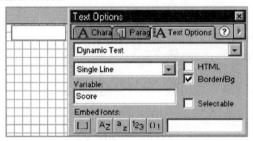

And now it's time for the big test. Run the movie and you should see the ball moving around the screen. If the ball reaches the far left or far right of the screen then your score goes back to zero. If you move the bats in front of the ball then it will bounce off them and you'll score some points. Of course there's still room for improvement – high score tables, better graphics, sounds, a start button to begin the game, etc. – but I'll leave that for you to play with. When you're done, save the game as `BatandBall.fla`

Creating a Virtual Pet

Virtual pets, eh? You see them everywhere these days: on computers, on games consoles, even on key rings. Although these virtual pets appear to use really complex programming to make them behave like real animals, it's possible to create a simple one using ActionScript and a little bit of imagination.

In this example I'll take you through the process of creating your own Flash-based virtual pet using nothing more than a few movie clips and some ActionScript. We'll start off with the movement and then move onto behaviors and finally interactivity.

1.   As always, the first thing to do is set up the stage for the new movie. Set the Width and Height to 500 px, and the Frame Rate to 20 fps. Also, set the Grid Spacing to 10 px and make sure that Show Grid is switched on. You may also want to draw lines around the edge of the movie so that you can clearly see the perimeter when you run the movie.

Now we can get on with making the creature.

2. Draw a filled circle 40 px wide and 40 px high, then select the circle and convert it into a movie clip with the symbol name Creature. Once you've done this, select it and open it for editing.

3. Now draw an arrow, pointing upwards, over the filled circle:

4. Select the filled circle and arrow and then convert this assembly into a graphic symbol called CreatureGraphic. Once this is done return to the main stage, select the Creature movie clip and give it the instance name Creature.

As you can see, the movie clip doesn't look much like a creature, but you can always make it look better by editing the CreatureGraphic symbol. To keep things simple for now it's best to leave it as is. You'll just have to imagine that it's small and black with lots of little moving legs.

It's now time to create the actions that'll make the creature move around the screen and rotate to face the way it's moving.

5. Select the Creature movie clip and open it for editing. Create a new layer and rename it Code. Add keyframes in frames 2 and 3 on the Code layer, and add a normal frame to frame 3 in layer 1.

6. Enter the following action in frame 3 on the Code layer:

```
gotoAndPlay (2);
```

This will create a loop between frames 2 and 3.

7. In frame 1 on the Code layer enter the following actions:

```
Direction = (Math.floor(Math.random()*8))+1;
Speed = (Math.floor(Math.random()*10))+5;
```

These actions tell Flash what direction to start the creature moving in, and what speed to move at. The creature will have eight directions of movement:

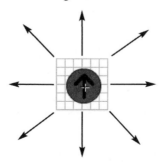

8. Next, add the following actions to frame 2 on the Code layer:

```
CreatureX = _x;
CreatureY = _y;
```

These two actions store the creature's current X position and Y position.

9. Beneath that, add this code:

```
if (Direction == 1) {
    CreatureY = CreatureY-Speed;
    _rotation = 0;
}
if (Direction == 2) {
    CreatureY = CreatureY-Speed;
    CreatureX = CreatureX+Speed;
    _rotation = 45;
}
if (Direction == 3) {
    CreatureX = CreatureX+Speed;
    _rotation = 90;
}
if (Direction == 4) {
    CreatureY = CreatureY+Speed;
    CreatureX = CreatureX+Speed;
    _rotation = 135;
}
if (Direction == 5) {
    CreatureY = CreatureY+Speed;
    _rotation = 180;
}
if (Direction == 6) {
    CreatureY = CreatureY+Speed;
    CreatureX = CreatureX-Speed;
    _rotation = 225;
}
if (Direction == 7) {
    CreatureX = CreatureX-Speed;
    _rotation = 270;
}
if (Direction == 8) {
    CreatureY = CreatureY-Speed;
    CreatureX = CreatureX-Speed;
    _rotation = 315;
}
```

These if (Direction == ?) actions check to see which direction the creature is pointing in, and then rotate and move it in that direction.

10. Next, add another series of `if` statements:

```
if (CreatureX>480) {
    CreatureX = 480;
    Direction = (Math.random()*8)+1;
    Speed = (Math.random()*10)+5;
}
if (CreatureX<20) {
    CreatureX = 20;
    Direction = (Math.random()*8)+1;
    Speed = (Math.random()*10)+5;
}
if (CreatureY>480) {
    CreatureY = 480;
    Direction = (Math.random()*8)+1;
    Speed = (Math.random()*10)+5;
}
if (CreatureY<20) {
    CreatureY = 20;
    Direction = (Math.random()*8)+1;
    Speed = (Math.random()*10)+5;
}
```

These actions check to see if the creature has reached the edge of the screen. If it has, then it'll be given another random direction to move in and a random speed.

We'll also add another random element to the creature's movement. This is so that every now and then (with a 1 in 30 probability) the creature will just take off in another direction.

11. Add this short piece of code to the bottom of the last section:

```
DirectionChange = (Math.floor(Math.random()*30));
if (DirectionChange == 1) {
    Direction = (Math.floor(Math.random()*8))+1;
    Speed = (Math.floor(Math.random()*10))+5;
}
```

If you'd like to make this direction change happen more often, just change 30 for a smaller number; for example, setting it to a value of 10 will give the creature a more erratic and frenzied movement.

12. Finally, we need to update the creature's position with our new values:

```
_x = CreatureX;
_y = CreatureY;
```

These actions control all of the creature's movement. If you run the movie you'll see the type of movement you've just programmed the creature to do – try to imagine it's a little bug with lots of legs!

It's now time to add some additional actions to the above ActionScript to enable the creature to pause for a random amount of time before it moves off again. This will give the impression that our virtual pet is stopping and checking out its surroundings, and thinking about where it's going to go next before it moves.

13. Make sure the Creature movie clip is open and add a normal frame to frame 20 of Layer 1. Also, add keyframes in frame 5, and frame 20 of the Code layer:

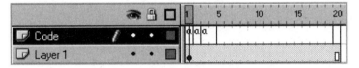

The gap between frames 5 and 20 will be our pause.

14. To make it work, add this next section of code after the end of the script in frame 2 of the Code layer:

```
Pause = (Math.floor(Math.random()*40))+1;
if (Pause == 1) {
    gotoAndPlay (5);
}
```

The Pause variable receives a random number between 1 and 40, and if this number is equal to 1 the movie clip jumps to frame 5 and the creature appears to pause for a second. This essentially gives the creature a 1 in 40 chance of pausing; if you want to increase this, just change the if condition to something like...

```
if (Pause <= 2) {
```

This would then give the creature a *2* in 40 chance of pausing.

15. Finally, add this action to frame 20 on the Code layer:

```
gotoAndPlay (1);
```

This is so that, at the end of its 'thinking' phase, the creature will be given a new direction.

We'll be adding some more behaviors to the creature at the end of this worked example, but before that let's start getting interactive.

You'll be programming two types of creature interactivity in this section: one will enable you to pick up the creature and move it around, and the other will enable you to move a block around the screen. If the creature hits the block it will be treated like a solid object and the creature won't be able to move through it.

16. Make sure that you have the Creature movie clip open and then create a new layer above the Code layer. Name this new layer Button.

17. Now create another filled circle that's the same size as the creature (40 px wide, 40 px high) on the Button layer, and then move it so that it covers the creature (don't worry, it won't squash the little fella). Select the new filled circle and convert it into a button called CreatureButton.

18. Select the CreatureButton and open it for editing. Add a keyframe in the Hit state, making sure that the filled circle is still visible, and then delete the graphics from the other three states, leaving you with an invisible button on the creature's 'back'.

19. Return to the Creature movie clip, open up the Object Actions panel for the CreatureButton on the Button layer, and add this code there:

```
on (press) {
    gotoAndStop (10);
    startDrag ("", false, 30, 30, 470, 470);
}
on (release, releaseOutside) {
    play ();
    stopDrag ();
}
```

What this does is stop the Creature movie clip from running when the button is held down. It then activates the startDrag action, allowing you to drag the movie clip around. When you release the button the Creature clip is told to play again and the startDrag action is stopped. The reason why we send it to frame 10 is so there'll be a short pause before the creature starts to move again after it's dropped.

Now we're going to create the block that can be moved around the screen with the mouse.

20. Back in the main movie window, create a new layer and call it Block. Create a filled square 80 px wide and 80 px high on the Block layer, convert it into a movie clip, and name it Block. Select the Block movie clip and open it for editing.

21. Once you've done this, select the filled square on Layer 1 and convert it into a button called BlockButton. Add a frame to frame 3 on Layer 1 of the Block clip.

22. Create a new layer and call it Code. Add keyframes to our usual frames 2 and 3 on this new layer.

We're now ready to start adding some actions. We'll start with the traditional method of a loop between frames 2 and 3.

23. Add the following action to frame 3 on the Code layer:

```
gotoAndPlay (2);
```

24. Now we'll get into the more serious scripting. Add the following actions to frame 2:

```
BlockX = _x;
BlockY = _y;
CreatureX = _root.Creature._x;
CreatureY = _root.Creature._y;
if (CreatureX>BlockX-70) {
    if (CreatureX<BlockX-40) {
        if (CreatureY>BlockY-60) {
            if (CreatureY<BlockY+60) {
                _root.Creature._x = BlockX-70;
                _root.Creature.gotoAndPlay(10);
            }
        }
    }
}
if (CreatureX<BlockX+70) {
    if (CreatureX>BlockX+40) {
        if (CreatureY>BlockY-60) {
            if (CreatureY<BlockY+60) {
                _root.Creature._x = BlockX+70;
                _root.Creature.gotoAndPlay(10);
            }
        }
    }
}
if (CreatureY>BlockY-70) {
    if (CreatureY<BlockY-40) {
        if (CreatureX>BlockX-60) {
            if (CreatureX<BlockX+60) {
                _root.Creature._y = BlockY-70;
                _root.Creature.gotoAndPlay(10);
            }
        }
    }
}
if (CreatureY<BlockY+70) {
    if (CreatureY>BlockY+40) {
        if (CreatureX>BlockX-60) {
            if (CreatureX<BlockX+60) {
                _root.Creature._y = BlockY+70;
                _root.Creature.gotoAndPlay(10);
            }
        }
    }
}
```

This chunk of code checks to see where the Creature movie clip is, and each of the sets of nested if statements controls one side of the block. If the creature's close to a side of the block, then the Creature movie clip is stopped and told to go to frame 10 and play – again, this will make the creature pause for a while, giving the appearance of thought.

25. To enable the block to be dragged around with the mouse make sure you have the Block movie clip open and then add the following Object Actions to BlockButton:

```
on (press) {
    startDrag ("", false, 80, 80, 420, 420);
}
on (release, releaseOutside) {
    stopDrag ();
}
```

This does the same sort of thing as the button that's used to drag the creature around, and allows you to shift the block anywhere on the screen.

The way that the block has been programmed allows you to have more than one of them on screen simultaneously.

26. Open up the Library and drag a couple of copies of the block on to the screen. If you now run the movie you'll see what I mean: each block can be moved separately, and the creature treats all of them as solid objects:

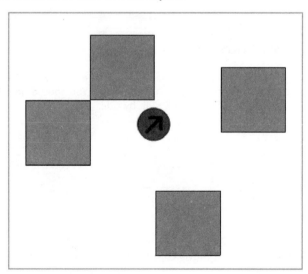

You've now created a basic virtual pet engine for Flash. With a bit of imagination and experimentation you'll be able to modify this to create your own virtual Flash-based pet, creating more graphically-rich and varied environments for the little fella to explore and nest in. The best way to do this is to sit down with a pad and pen and write down exactly what you want the pet to do before starting to program it. Good luck, and have fun. Before you start to change the program too much, remember to save it as Vpet.fla.

Distance and Connections

In this final example I'll show you a variation on the popular technique of calculating the distance between two movie clips and then have a line drawn between them both.

1. Once again you'll need to create a new movie that's 400 px wide and 400 px high. Set the Frame Rate to 20 fps and the Grid Spacing to 10 px, and make sure that Show Grid is turned on.

2. Draw a filled circle 20 px wide and 20 px high. Select the filled circle and convert it into a movie clip called Point.

3. Now select the Point movie clip and open it for editing. Once inside, select the filled circle and convert it into a button symbol named PointButton.

4. Select the PointButton button and give it the following Object Actions:

    ```
    on (press) {
        startDrag ("", false, 20, 20, 380, 380);
    }
    on (release, releaseOutside) {
        stopDrag ();
    }
    ```

    This code will enable you to drag the movie clip around the screen.

5. Return to the main movie window, open up the Library window, and then drag another copy of the Point movie clip onto the stage. You should now have two copies of the Point movie clip sitting tensely side by side:

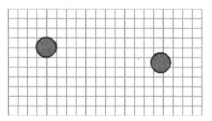

6. Give these two Point movie clips the instance names, A and B respectively.

    The line that'll connect the two movie clips will actually be a movie clip itself. You'll need to get the dimensions of this line perfect otherwise it won't connect the two Point movie clips correctly. If you've read Michael Bedar's chapter on ActionScript visual effects, you'll already have seen a similar technique.

7. Draw a square on the main timeline 100 px wide and 100 px high, with no fill. Now draw a line from the top left of the square over to the bottom right of the square:

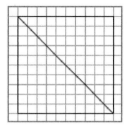

8. Now delete the square outline being careful not to delete the line you've just drawn. This should leave you with just a diagonal line:

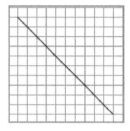

9. Select the line, convert it into a movie clip, and name it Line. Select the Line clip and then select Edit, **not** Edit In Place, to open up the movie clip.

10. Now select the line and then move it so that its top-left point is at the center of the movie clip. The easiest way to do this is by opening the Info Panel and setting the X and Y values to 0 using the top-left origin point:

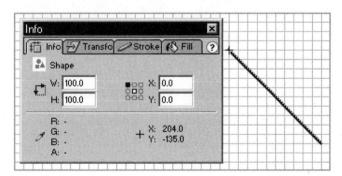

11. Now return to the main movie window, select the Line movie clip and give it the instance name Line.

This line is important for many reasons:

- It's 100 pixels wide by 100 pixels high when it's at normal (that is 100%) size. This means that when we scale the line by a percentage we know exactly how big it will be. For example, if we scale it 50% on the x-axis, and 30% on the y-axis, then the line will be 50 pixels wide by 30 pixels high.

■   We can also make the line flip along its axes by applying a negative scale value to it. So, for example, if we apply an x-scale of -100% to the line, it will just flip it along the y-axis:

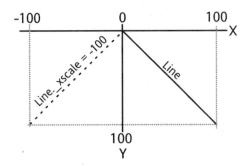

■   Its top-left is set to 0,0 on the stage. This means that we can place the line somewhere on the stage, and just by scaling the line like we did above, we'll know exactly where the other end of the line will be. This is an extremely useful, and fairly simple, way of drawing a line between any two points.

Now that everything's set up, we can get down to the business of adding the ActionScript.

12.   Make sure you're on the main movie window and then create a new layer called Code. Add keyframes to frames 2 and 3 on the Code layer, and add a normal frame to frame 3 on Layer 1.

13.   Add the following action to frame 1 on the Code layer:

```
_root.Line._visible = false;
```

This will prevent the movie from displaying the original Line movie clip when it's run.

14.   Next, add the following actions to frame 2 on the Code layer:

```
AX = _root.A._x;
AY = _root.A._y;
BX = _root.B._x;
BY = _root.B._y;
duplicateMovieClip ("Line", "NewLine", 1);
_root.newline._x = AX;
_root.newline._y = AY;
_root.newline._xscale = BX-AX;
_root.newline._yscale = BY-AY;
```

These actions store the coordinates of the A and B movie clips. They then duplicate, position, and scale the Line movie clip using the stored coordinates, as we explained before.

15. All you need to do now is to add a loop action to frame 3 on the Code layer:

```
gotoAndPlay (2);
```

You've now finished the first part of this movie. If you run the movie now, you'll see what effect the actions have:

Don't forget to save the movie with the name `Connect1.fla` because it will be used again in the next tutorial.

More Connections

I'll now show you how you can easily add more Point movie clips to `Connect1.fla` using only a few extra lines of ActionScript.

1. Once you have `Connect1.fla` open, bring up the Library window and drag another copy of the Point movie clip onto Layer 1. Give this new movie clip the instance name C.

2. Add the following highlighted actions to the existing actions on frame 2 of the Code layer:

```
AX = _root.A._x;
AY = _root.A._y;
BX = _root.B._x;
BY = _root.B._y;
CX = _root.C._x;
CY = _root.C._y;
duplicateMovieClip ("Line", "NewLine", 1);
duplicateMovieClip ("Line", "NewLine2", 2);
_root.newline._x = AX;
_root.newline._y = AY;
_root.newline._xscale = BX-AX;
_root.newline._yscale = BY-AY;
_root.newline2._x = BX;
_root.newline2._y = BY;
_root.newline2._xscale = CX-BX;
_root.newline2._yscale = CY-BY;
```

This code just records the coordinates of point C, duplicates another Line, and joins the line between points B and C. If you now run the movie you'll see that the new Point and Line have been added:

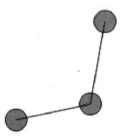

The final touch to this movie is to make a connection between the last two unconnected Point movie clips.

3. To do this, add the following actions to frame 2 on the Code layer:

```
AX = _root.A._x;
AY = _root.A._y;
BX = _root.B._x;
BY = _root.B._y;
CX = _root.C._x;
CY = _root.C._y;
duplicateMovieClip ("Line", "NewLine", 1);
duplicateMovieClip ("Line", "NewLine2", 2);
duplicateMovieClip ("Line", "NewLine3",3);
_root.newline._x = AX;
_root.newline._y = AY;
_root.newline._xscale = BX-AX;
_root.newline._yscale = BY-AY;
_root.newline2._x = BX;
_root.newline2._y = BY;
_root.newline2._xscale = CX-BX;
_root.newline2._yscale = CY-BY;
_root.newline3._x = AX;
_root.newline3._y = AY;
_root.newline3._xscale = CX-AX;
_root.newline3._yscale = CY-AY;
```

These new actions will now create the final connection. Run the movie to see the effect:

You've now completed the final exercise in this chapter. All you need to do now is save the movie as `Connect2.fla` and you're done.

What Can I Do Next?

During this chapter you've created the building blocks for more advanced Flash-based games and interactive web site content.

The first thing you'll need to do before creating any type of interactive content within Flash is to sit down with a pad and pen and write out what it is that you want to do. Do you want a menu-bar to be animated, to follow the mouse around the screen, bounce around the screen or do something completely different?

If you intend to create a game in Flash then you'll have a whole lot more thinking to do. In the following section I'll give you a brief description of some of the elements with which a typical game is built. Hopefully this will give you a better idea about how to go about programming each part of it, and then in the next chapter I'll run through the creation of a full Flash game from initial idea through to implementation.

Elements of a Typical Game

Here's a selection of traditional rules for most games, covering such things as the player and the enemies. Remember though, this list isn't the be all and end all. As long as you know the rules, then you're free to break them.

The Player

The player's character is one thing that needs to be in the game, but there are several different ways of implementing this. You can view the character from the side, from the top, from the back, or you can view the game out of the character's eyes in a 'first person perspective'.

The player's character normally always has some sort of health level that reduces when an enemy hits them or they wander over a harmful trap. Health is normally replenished when the player picks up a health-pack or some sort of power-up.

Depending on what sort of game you're designing, you need to decide if your player's character will use any weapons. If so, you now need to decide what type of weapons, how much damage they will do, how much ammo each weapon will use, and how the ammo will be replenished. If your game *does* include weapons then it's normally a good idea to introduce the weapons as the game progresses rather than giving the player *all* of the weapons at the start of a game.

You may also want to allow your player to increase their stats (maximum energy, strength, movement speed etc) as they progress through the game.

The Enemies

A typical game will include enemies that'll try and destroy the player. They'll have their own weapons, their own health levels, and their own movements.

You'll need to decide how each enemy will be destroyed, and if it's a big enemy whether or not it will have multiple parts that need to be destroyed.

Enemies normally get bigger and meaner as the game progresses and you'll find that most games have a 'boss' (a large, difficult-to-beat enemy) at the end of each level, and a *very big boss* at the end of the game.

Levels

Levels in a game set the atmosphere, whether the game's set in space, in a jungle, in an underground military base, or in a variety of places.

A good game will always have different stages (or levels) that a player has to progress through before completing the game. As the player progresses the levels should get more difficult and the enemies on these levels should also increase in strength.

All levels in a game should have some final goal that the player needs to reach in order to complete it. For example, you may wish the player to destroy all of the enemies on screen; you may want the player to complete a certain task or selection of tasks; or you may want the player to reach a certain score.

You'll need to decide how many levels you want your game to have and if the player can return to any of these levels. Most games just allow the player to progress through the levels in a linear way. *Good* games will allow the player to travel back to previous levels to unlock secrets that couldn't be accessed before. It's potentially more difficult to program a non-linear game, but the results will be well worth it for the player, giving them an added sense of freedom and achievement.

Objects and Hazards

Objects in a game can be anything from bushes through to an entire planet; it's all down to the sort of game you're creating. Objects can be used for many different things in a game. For example, the player can gain extra points, hidden pick-ups can be revealed if an object is destroyed, or you can have an entrance to a secret level hidden behind a large rock that blows up if the player shoots it enough!

Hazards in a game will decrease the player's energy if they come into contact with each other. Some hazards may destroy the player completely, and again it's up to you to decide what any hazards you use will do.

The Story

Any decent game will have a good story to it. The most playable and addictive games will have a story and plot that'll draw the player deep into the game world. Even if you're creating a basic shoot-'em-up game you'll want some sort of story to it, which can be anything from a convoluted multi-threaded plot with numerous possibilities and endings, down to the good old 'save the world from the alien invaders' setup. If there's one thing that most games players are good at, it's suspending their disbelief. Remember that it doesn't matter how fantastical the story gets as long as it's consistent within itself and it *feels* right. This is something that you'll pick up with experience, and it leads to some bizarre situations – people will quite happily accept that a monkey can fly, but only if it 'feels' right when it's flying.

You may also want to include other characters in the game that the player will meet while travelling. This can help to keep the story going and to encourage the player to continue and meet new characters. You may also wish to enable the player to control these new characters for a short period of time, or for the rest of the game.

Well, that's it, we've come to the end of this chapter. I hope that the examples have been helpful to you in establishing the basic ideas and components that can feed into simple games, and that they will help you create even more stunning content for your sites. Remember that above everything else, using your imagination is the key.

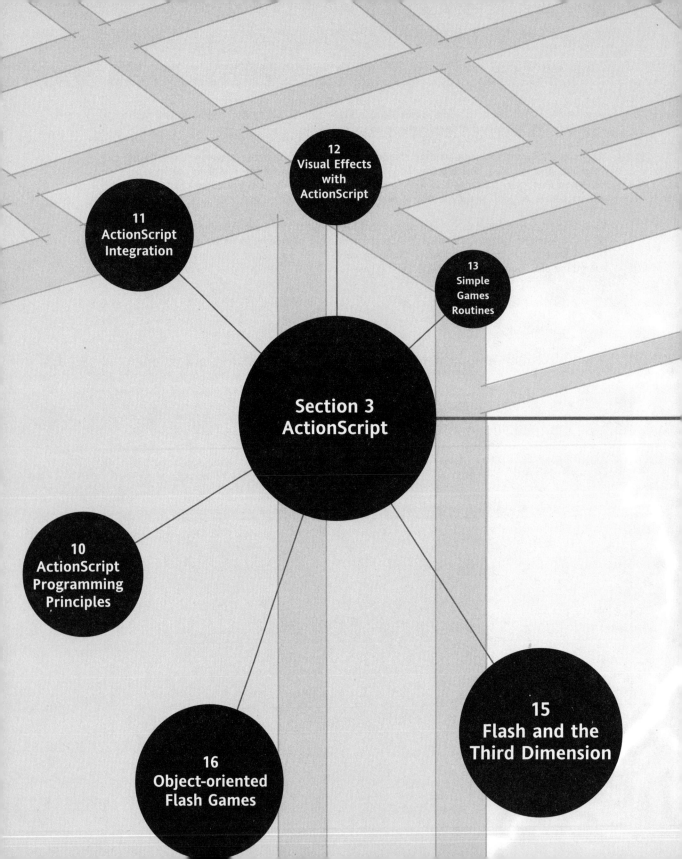

Section 3
ActionScript

11
ActionScript
Integration

12
Visual Effects
with
ActionScript

13
Simple
Games
Routines

10
ActionScript
Programming
Principles

16
Object-oriented
Flash Games

15
Flash and the
Third Dimension

Chapter 14
Games
Programming

You've just stumbled across what looks like a good Flash-based game on the Web. You wait for the game to load...you wait a bit longer...finally the game has loaded and you hit the 'start' button. What you're more than likely to see appear in front of you is something that doesn't even *resemble* a game. You can only fire one shot at a time, you only get a couple of enemies at a time, and to top if off the controls are terrible! Wouldn't it be great to have a Flash-based game that looked and played like a proper game? Well, you're about to make one!

The game we'll create is a good old shoot-'em-up, but with a slight twist. As well as the reams of enemies that'll swarm down the screen towards you, there's also an invincible mine that'll constantly swoop around your ship attempting to ram into and destroy you. Luckily you'll not only have your trusty blaster, but also a collection of power-ups dropping from the sky that you can collect to temporarily boost your ship. Be warned though, there's also a *bad* power-up that will slow you down and allow the advancing hordes to cut short your dreams of a high score. Be brave.

The Cosmic Game

Fire up `Cosmic_final.swf` from the CD and play through it a few times. Get to know the basic premise of the game, and the expected handling of the different elements. This is what you'll be making:

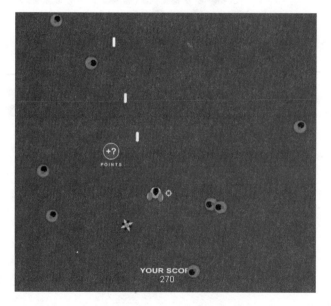

To make things a little easier, we've already created the graphics that you'll need for the game. We've done this so that you don't have to spend hours reading how to draw them precisely, and then build the movie. Instead, you can just get straight in there and start coding. The graphics that've been used are very simple, and you can easily create your own, or modify the existing ones to suit your own personal taste. We'll go into this at the end of the chapter because there are a couple of guidelines for the graphics (their size etc.) that you'll need to bear in mind when you're customizing the movie.

Before we begin, you'll need to load up the `Cosmic final (no_code).fla` file from the CD. This is the skeleton of the game, complete with the pre-drawn image symbols.

The first thing to notice when you load up the FLA is that the movie is made up of two scenes, one called START, and the other called GAME. The START scene contains the instructions and introduction to the game:

This scene just waits for the user to click on the button and then moves on to the next scene, which in turn starts the game.

There are three layers in this scene:

■ TEXT/GFX – Contains all of the text that's on the stage

■ MOUSE – Contains the Mover movie clip that replaces the mouse cursor

■ CODE – Will (soon!) contain all of the code for this scene

When you're creating your own games, it's a good idea to have an introductory scene like this so that the game only starts when the player is ready. It also gives you a chance to manage the loading times of large games by keeping the user engaged while the meat of the game is streaming through to them.

The second scene is the GAME scene:

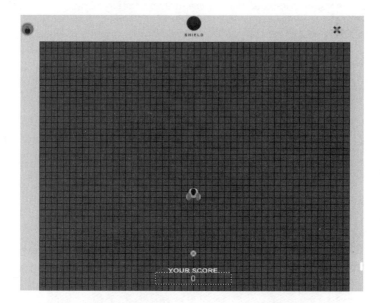

This is where all of the fun takes place. There are six layers in this scene:

- CODE – This is where the code for the game proper will go. It also contains the button that the user clicks on to start the game again when their ship is destroyed.

- GFX1 – Contains the main graphics for the game – the player's spacecraft in the center, two enemies off-stage at the top, and a white laser beam off-stage on the right. It also contains the 'Game Over' text and final score at the end of the game.

- GFX2 – Contains the custom mouse cursor that we'll be using.

- GFX3 – Contains the text box displaying the player's current score. It also contains a brief white-transparent fade, so the screen will flash when the player's ship is destroyed.

- GFX4 – contains the player ship-explosion animation off-stage at the top-left.

- GFX5 – contains the graphics for the power-ups off-stage at the top.

If you open the Library you'll see a list of nineteen items, the majority of which are movie clips. We'll also be adding a bit of code to some of these. We'll explain when and where as we go along. We've already given all of the items on the stage instance names, so here's a quick list of what they are, and an explanation, where needed, of what they do:

- PlayerShip

- Enemy – the 'normal' enemy

- Mine – the indestructible enemy

- PlayerShot – the player's laser beam

- Mover – the mouse cursor

- ScoreMovie – holds the player's current score

- PlayerShipExplosion

- Powerups

OK, that's the introductions out of the way. It's time to get stuck into the code.

Coding the Start Scene

The first thing we'll do is add the ActionScript into the timelines of the START and GAME scenes. We'll discuss what all of the ActionScript does as we progress. From this you should get some insights into how to modify the game code in preparation for creating your own Flash games.

1. Move to the START scene and add the following ActionScript to frame 1 of the CODE layer:

    ```
    fscommand ("allowscale", "true");
    fscommand ("showmenu", "false");
    ```

    The fscommand action allows the movie to call JavaScript methods in the web browser or Flash player that it's running in. The two commands that we're using here are specific to the Flash player, and they'll have no effect on a browser itself. The first command will allow the movie to be scaled, and the second stops users from bringing up a context-sensitive menu when they right-click on the movie.

2. After this, type the next two lines:

    ```
    Mover.startDrag(true);
    Mouse.hide();
    ```

    This attaches our Mover movie clip to the center of the mouse cursor, and then hides the cursor, leaving just the movie clip visible.

3. Now on frame 5 of the CODE layer add:

    ```
    stop ();
    ```

    This shouldn't need much explaining!

You can now test the first stage of your movie. When it plays, it should just display the opening screen, and you should be able to move our modified mouse cursor around. It's not very exiting, but it's essential preparation. The next thing is to add some code to allow us to get to the next scene.

4.   Back in the movie itself you'll see a transparent button covering the click here to start text. Select it, and then bring up its Object Actions window. Add the following script to it:

```
on (press) {
    gotoAndPlay ("GAME", 1);
}
```

This simply tells the movie to go to the GAME scene and start playing from the first frame when the player clicks on the button.

Believe it or not, that is all the programming that you need for the START scene. After all, it's just a holding area until the user's ready to start playing. It's now time for the next, admittedly more difficult, scene.

Coding the Game Scene

As promised, we'll add the ActionScript to the timeline first, and then later on we'll program the movie clips. The CODE layer is right at the bottom of the layer stack in the GAME scene.

1.   On frame 1 of the CODE layer add the following ActionScript:

```
Mover.startDrag(true);
```

This is the same as the code that we used in the START scene. It's important to note that certain commands, such as `Mouse.hide`, will affect every scene in a movie, whereas more specific commands such as our `startDrag` need to be restated in the different contexts that we want them to work in.

2.   After this, it's time to start the code proper. Enter this ActionScript below the `startDrag`:

```
PlayerShot._visible = 0;
EnemyNum = -1;
EnemySpeed = 2;
GameScore = 0;
Enemy.gotoAndStop(31);
PlayerShip.CraftSpeed = 10;
Mover.Laser = 0;
Shield = 0;
```

Here, we're setting up everything ready for the start of the game. First, we make PlayerShot invisible. This is done so that you don't see it shoot off up the screen to begin with. We then initialize a few variables for the game. EnemyNum is used for the duplication of the enemies, which you'll see later on. EnemySpeed sets the initial speed of the enemies and GameScore sets the player's score back to 0. The next command tells the Enemy movie to go to and stop at its last frame. We've done this to prevent the player seeing it at the start of the game. This Enemy movie clip is also the parent movie clip that'll be used to duplicate all of the other enemies. The three variables at the bottom, CraftSpeed, Laser, and Shield, are for use with the power-ups that we'll cover later on in the chapter.

3. Once we've set everything up, we can start to produce enemies for the player to shoot. To do this, add the following to frame 2:

```
EnemyNum = EnemyNum+1;
duplicateMovieClip ("_root.Enemy", "Enemy"+EnemyNum,
   ➡EnemyNum+100);
setProperty ("Enemy"+EnemyNum, _x, random(400)+50);
if (EnemyNum>6) {
    PlayerDeath = false;
    gotoAndPlay (19);
}
```

This is the main enemy duplication code. The first line increments the EnemyNum variable that we initialized in frame 1. This variable will be used to individualize the enemies. The duplicateMovieClip action causes the Enemy movie clip to be duplicated and then renamed. The new name of the movie will be "Enemy" plus the EnemyNum number. For example, if the EnemyNum variable is 5, then the name of the duplicated enemy will be Enemy5. The setProperty command randomly places this new enemy somewhere along the top of the screen. The movie has been set to be 500 pixels wide, and we've given the new movie clip an X position between 50 and 449. This is to stop the new enemies from appearing too close to the edges of the screen. The if command tells the timeline to go to frame 19 once six enemies have been placed on screen. This is to give the player a 'grace' period at the start of the game where they can't be killed. When this period is over, we set the PlayerDeath variable to false, making them mortal. We now want to loop around this frame to keep creating enemies.

4. On frame 18 of the CODE layer add:

```
gotoAndPlay (2);
```

5. We've set the loop to go to frame 19 after it's run six times, so we'd better put some code there. Type this in at frame 19:

```
if (PlayerDeath==true) {
    GameScore = _root.ScoreMovie.GameScore;
    PlayerShipX = _root.PlayerShip._x;
    PlayerShipY = _root.PlayerShip._y;
    gotoAndPlay (21);
}
```

This directs the timeline to frame 21 if the `PlayerDeath` variable is `true`, meaning that an enemy has destroyed the player. When this happens, the final score is recorded in the `GameScore` variable. This is set by reading it from the `ScoreMovie` movie clip, which displays the current score at the bottom of the screen. The `PlayerShipX` and `PlayerShipY` variables are set so that the `PlayerShipExplosion` movie clip can be moved to the correct position when it's game over.

6.   On frame 20 of the CODE layer add:

```
gotoAndPlay (19);
```

This simply causes a loop between frames 19 and 20 while the game is being played. As soon as an enemy hits your ship, it's game over, and the timeline will jump to frame 21, which we'll code right now.

7.   On frame 21 of the add the following ActionScript:

```
PlayerShipExplosion._x = PlayerShipX;
PlayerShipExplosion._y = PlayerShipY;
PlayerShipExplosion.gotoAndPlay(1);
Num = -1;
do {
    Num = Num+1;
    setProperty ("_root.Enemy"+Num, _visible, 0);
} while (Num<15);
Powerups._visible = 0;
```

The top two lines set the x and y position of `PlayerShipExplosion` to the final position of `PlayerShip` that we set earlier on in frame 19. We then tell the `PlayerShipExplosion` movie to play from this position. Next, we initialize a new variable called `Num`. We'll be using this variable as a counter for the `do...while` loop. The `do` command will keep looping while the variable `Num` is less than 15. The `setProperty` action within this loop causes the enemy movies to become invisible once the player ship has been destroyed. The last line hides the master `Powerups` movie, ready for the beginning of the next game.

8.   To finish off the main timeline code, add the following ActionScript to frame 30 on the CODE layer:

```
PlayerDeath = false;
Mouse.show();
stop ();
```

This sets the `PlayerDeath` variable to `false` and causes the mouse cursor to reappear. The `stop` command keeps the movie at the end screen until the 'click here to retry' button is pressed.

9.   For the final touch, add the following ActionScript to the button that covers the click here to retry text:

```
on (press) {
    gotoAndPlay ("START", 1);
}
```

This is used to send the game back to the initial title screen when the button is pressed.

That's all of the code for the timeline done, but if you try and test the movie now you'll see that it doesn't do too much. The player's ship will sit there and flash, and the enemies will do the same. It has a certain charm, but it seems to be missing a bit of playability. This will all come in the form of the ActionScript attached to the movie clips throughout the movie.

Coding the Movie Clips

It's now time to program the most important parts of the game: the movie clips. The easiest way to do this is by finding the appropriate clip in the Library and then double-clicking on it to open it. Remember that we've already given instance names to all of the movie clips on the stage, so now we've just got to put the code inside them.

Let's start with one of the enemies:

Enemy_One_B:

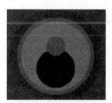

These are the main antagonists in the game. They begin by dropping down the screen with lemming-like fatalism, just turning to face their destroyer. But as each enemy is eliminated, another – increasingly intelligent – alien replaces it.

1. Double-click on the Enemy_One_B movie clip to open it up. Once again you'll see a CODE layer on the main timeline, which will be used for the ActionScript. Enter the following code in frame 1:

    ```
    EnemySpeedY = 2;
    EnemySpeedX = 0;
    ```

    This initializes the variables that we'll use for the enemy space ships. EnemySpeedY represents the speed that the enemy moves down the screen, and we'll be incrementing this value later on to make the enemies move faster and faster. EnemySpeedX does the same sort of thing, but controls the speed that the enemies move across the screen towards the player. Notice that this begins at 0, so to start with the enemies will just fall vertically down the screen, lulling the innocent user into a false sense of security.

2.   On frame 2 of the CODE layer add:

```
Death = false;
EnemyY = EnemyY+EnemySpeedY;
EnemyX = _x;
if (EnemyY>400) {
    EnemyY = 0;
}
```

Death is the variable that holds the status of the enemy movie clip, and when the enemy is destroyed it's set to true. The EnemyY variable is increased by the EnemySpeedY variable and is used to give the enemy its vertical movement. If the EnemyY variable reaches 400 or above, meaning that it's reached the bottom of the screen, then it resets itself to 0 and jumps back to the top of the screen, where it starts to fall again.

3.   Enter the next piece of code below:

```
PlayerShipX = _root.PlayerShip._x;
if (EnemyX>PlayerShipX) {
    EnemyX = EnemyX-EnemySpeedX;
}
if (EnemyX<PlayerShipX) {
    EnemyX = EnemyX+EnemySpeedX;
}
```

This section of code controls the movement of the enemy towards the player. The PlayerShipX variable is first set to the PlayerShip movie clip's X position on the main timeline. The if commands are then used to change the enemy's position using the EnemySpeedX variable: if the enemy is to the right of the player, then it will move left, and vice-versa. Furthermore, the higher the EnemySpeedX variable, the faster the enemy will move along the x-axis towards the player.

4.   Finally, we need to tell Flash to move the enemy to its new position. This ActionScript goes at the end of the code on frame 2:

```
this._x = EnemyX;
this._y = EnemyY;
this._rotation = (EnemyX-PlayerShipX);
```

We've also told the enemy to rotate to face the player. We do this by a simple calculation that will slightly exaggerate the rotation, but will give a weightier *feel*.

5.   Next, insert this script on frame 3 of the CODE layer:

```
PlayerShipX = _root.PlayerShip._x;
PlayerShipY = _root.PlayerShip._y;
EnemyX = _x;
EnemyY = _y;
```

```
if (EnemyX<PlayerShipX+20) {
    if (EnemyX>PlayerShipX-20) {
        if (EnemyY>PlayerShipY-20) {
            if (EnemyY<PlayerShipY+20) {
                if (_root.Shield == 0) {
                    _root.PlayerDeath = true;
                }
            }
        }
    }
}
gotoAndPlay (2);
```

This is the main enemy and player collision code. The PlayerShipX and PlayerShipY variables are first set to the x and y positions of the PlayerShip movie clip. The EnemyX and EnemyY variables are set to the current position of the Enemy movie clip that they're running inside. The if commands are then used to check whether or not the enemy occupies the same area as the player. The final if command here checks to see if the player currently has the Shield power-up active. If the player has hit an enemy, and the ship doesn't have a shield, then the PlayerDeath variable on the GAME scene timeline is set to true. Frame 19 on the main GAME is constantly checking to see if PlayerDeath is true, and when that condition *is* satisfied, it moves the playhead on to the 'explosion' and 'game over' screens. The gotoAndPlay command tells the enemy movie clip's timeline to go to frame 2 and keep looping around updating the position of the enemy, and then checking to see if it has hit the player.

It's worth noting that Flash 5 does come with an ActionScript command specifically for collision detection – the hitTest *command. Although this would seem to be the obvious thing to use in our game , as it gives much cleaner and shorter code...*

```
if (this.hitTest(_root.PlayerShip) && _root.Shield==0){
_root.PlayerDeath=1;
}
```

...when we tried it, it didn't give results as good as those of the nested if *constructs that we've used in the finished game. When we used a bounding-box, it seemed to slow down the game, as well as giving it Spectrum-style collision detection. When we used direct coordinates rather than a box, the detection was too late, allowing the player to be quite far over an enemy before the* hitTest *finally triggered. Feel free to try the different methods in your own games, though. A way round this might be to make a smaller movie clip that sits behind the enemy, and to use this for the collision detection , rather than the enemy itself.*

6. If you look at the GFX layer, you'll see a tween happening from frames 4 to 11. This tween is the animation that plays when the enemy is destroyed. On frame 4 of the CODE layer add:

```
Death = true;
_root.ScoreMovie.GameScore += 10;
```

The Enemy movie clip will only move onto this frame when the PlayerShot movie clip instructs it to. When it's in this frame, it means that it's been shot by the player, and destroyed. This bit of code sets the Death variable to 1 and adds 10 to the GameScore variable in the ScoreMovie movie clip, which updates the score. This is just a shortened way of saying _root.ScoreMovie.GameScore = _root.ScoreMovie.GameScore + 10.

7. When an enemy is destroyed, we want another one to appear at the top of the screen. Rather than removing the old movie clip, and duplicating a new one, we'll just recycle this one by putting it back at the top of the screen. Add this to frame 12 of the CODE layer:

```
_root.PlayerDeath = false;
EnemySpeedY += 0.5;
EnemySpeedX = EnemySpeedY/3;
this._y = -20;
this._x = random(400)+50;
EnemyY = -20;
gotoAndPlay (2);
```

When the player shoots the enemy this code increases EnemySpeedY and EnemySpeedX and then restarts the enemy at the top of the screen. This makes the enemy faster every time the player shoots it. It then starts up the movement and collision detection loop from frame 2 again.

OK, that's the first enemy done. If you test the movie now, you'll see the enemy fall down the screen. If you're lucky enough to have one hit the PlayerShip movie clip, the movie should move on to the 'game over' screen. It's now time to program the second enemy, so double-click on the Enemy_Two_B movie clip in the Library to open it up.

Enemy_Two_B:

This is the indestructible enemy mine that swoops around the player's ship attempting to collide with and destroy it. There will only be one of this enemy, meaning that we won't need code to duplicate it, but due to its added complexity we *will* need extra code for its movement.

1. On frame 1 of the CODE layer add the following ActionScript:

    ```
    MineSpeedX = 0;
    MineSpeedY = 0;
    MineX = _x;
    MineY = _y;
    MineMax = 1;
    ```

    As usual, we spend frame 1 initializing the main variables that the mine will use. MineSpeedX and MineSpeedY set the initial movement speed of the enemy, and MineX and MineY hold its starting x and y position. The MineMax variable sets the enemy's initial maximum movement speed.

2. Now we'll code the mine's movement in frame 2. We've split this code up into chunks to make it easier to explain. Start by adding this:

    ```
    PlayerShipX = _root.PlayerShip._x;
    PlayerShipY = _root.PlayerShip._y;
    ```

    These two lines record and store the position of the PlayerShip movie clip on the screen. We'll use this to work out where it is in relation to the enemy.

3. Insert this next section of ActionScript, which controls the movement of the mine:

    ```
    if (MineX<PlayerShipX) {
        MineSpeedX = MineSpeedX+.3;
    }
    if (MineX>PlayerShipX) {
        MineSpeedX = MineSpeedX-.3;
    }
    if (MineY<PlayerShipY) {
        MineSpeedY = MineSpeedY+.3;
    }
    if (MineY>PlayerShipY) {
        MineSpeedY = MineSpeedY-.3;
    }

    if (MineSpeedX>MineMax) {
        MineSpeedX = MineMax;
    }
    if (MineSpeedX<-MineMax) {
        MineSpeedX = -MineMax;
    }
    if (MineSpeedY>MineMax) {
        MineSpeedY = MineMax;
    }
    if (MineSpeedY<-MineMax) {
        MineSpeedY = -MineMax;
    }
    ```

This code checks the enemy's position and the player's position and then adjusts the enemy's movement accordingly. The enemy will always try and move towards the player's ship.

4. We then need to apply the calculations that we've made to the actual position of the enemy on screen. Add this to the bottom of the current code:

```
MineX = MineX+MineSpeedX;
MineY = MineY+MineSpeedY;
this._x = MineX;
this._y = MineY;
```

The MineX and MineY variables are adjusted using the MineSpeedX and MineSpeedY variables that we set in the last piece of code. These are then used to update the position of the enemy in the final two lines.

5. Now we've come to the last bit of enemy programming. This frame contains similar collision detection code to that we used for the first enemy. This ActionScript goes in frame 3 of the CODE layer:

```
MineMax = MineMax+0.025;
if (MineMax>15) {
    MineMax = 2;
}
PlayerShipX = _root.PlayerShip._x;
PlayerShipY = _root.PlayerShip._y;
EnemyX = _x;
EnemyY = _y;
if (EnemyX<PlayerShipX+15) {
    if (EnemyX>PlayerShipX-15) {
        if (EnemyY>PlayerShipY-15) {
            if (EnemyY<PlayerShipY+15) {
                if (_root.Shield == 0) {
                    _root.PlayerDeath = true;
                    gotoAndStop (4);
                }
            }
        }
    }
}
gotoAndPlay (2);
```

The first line increases the MineMax variable by 0.025 each time this frame is activated. Remember, the higher the value of MineMax, the faster the enemy will move. If the enemy's speed is too great, it is reset to 2. This not only stops the mine from becoming too fast to cope with, it also prevents it shooting off into space. The rest of the code is exactly the same as that for the other enemies and is used to check for a collision with the player. If a collision *does* occur then the variable PlayerDeath on the GAME scene timeline is set to 1 and the enemy's timeline is sent to frame 4. There's also an *if* statement that checks to see if the player's shield is active or not, just like we had before.

If you test the movie, you'll see that there are now *two* types of enemy attacking the helpless player: one that falls down the screen towards it, and one that circles around it once, taunting it, before crashing into it and ending the game. It's time to let the player fight back.

Mover

Mover is the crosshair that replaces the mouse cursor. The player moves the mouse to indicate the direction that they want the ship to move in, and the ship trails along slightly behind. This delay is present to add more challenge and a more realistic feel to the game. You'll see how much difference it makes when you're playing and you pick up your first speed power-up. The second, but no less important, function of the Mover movie clip is to hold the button that allows the player to fire.

1. Double-click on the Mover movie clip in the Library to open it up. On the Button layer you'll see a small circular button covering the crosshair. Select it, then bring up the Object Actions window and add the following ActionScript to it:

```
on (press) {
    gotoAndPlay (2);
}
```

This simply sends the timeline to frame 2 every time the button is pressed. This means that the player has clicked the mouse, and wants the ship to shoot.

2. Now go into the timeline of the Mover clip and find the CODE layer. Add this line to the first frame:

```
stop ();
```

This command is simple, but important. If it wasn't here then you'd get an unstoppable auto-fire effect in the game. As soon as the player clicked on the mouse, the ship would start firing from then until the end of the game. This action simply stops the timeline on frame 1. If you want to add some sort of auto-fire function to the game later on, then this is the place to come back to.

3. Next, add some functionality to frame 2 to allow the ship to fire:

```
ShotNum = ShotNum+1;
if (ShotNum>10) {
    ShotNum = 0;
```

continues overleaf

```
    }
    duplicateMovieClip ("_root.PlayerShot", "PlayerShot"+ShotNum,
    ➥ShotNum+500);
    if (Laser == 1) {
        _root["PlayerShot"+ShotNum]._yscale = 200;
        _root["PlayerShot"+ShotNum].Laser = 1;
    }
    if (Laser == 0) {
        _root["PlayerShot"+ShotNum].Laser = 0;
    }
```

Here, first of all, the ShotNum variable is increased by 1. The if command then checks to see if the ShotNum variable has a value higher than 10, and if it does, then ShotNum is reduced to 0. This prevents the player from having more than 11 (don't forget it starts at 0) laser blasts on the screen at once. The duplicateMovieClip command creates another PlayerShot movie clip, and renames it in the same way that the enemy duplication was done. The if (Laser) commands are used to check if the player has the laser power-up active. If they have then the shot is increased in size, and a variable is set in the PlayerShot movie clip that tells the laser 'bullet' not to stop if it comes into contact with an enemy.

Before we can test this new code and see the changes, we'll have to program some functionality into the shots themselves.

Player_Shot_A

These shots need to travel vertically up the screen from their start point at the nose of the space ship. If they come into contact with an enemy, then they need to destroy that enemy as well as destroying themselves. The only exceptions to this are: if the player has the laser power-up, in which case the shot won't be destroyed on contact with an enemy; and, secondly, that the enemy mine can't be destroyed by *any* type of shot.

1. Double-click on the Player_Shot_A movie clip in the Library and then add the following code to frame 1 on the CODE layer:

```
this._x = _root.PlayerShip._x;
ShotY = _root.PlayerShip._y-10;
ShotDeath = false;
```

The first line is used to keep the bullet on the same vertical line as the player's craft. The ShotY variable is then used to place the shot just above the craft. This is done so that when the player fires, the shot appears to come from the same position as the front of the ship. At the bottom of the code the ShotDeath variable is set to false. This will be set to true when the bullet comes into contact with an enemy.

2. On frame 2 of the CODE layer add the following ActionScript:

```
ShotX = this._x;
ShotY = ShotY-15;
EnemyNum = -1;
if (ShotY<-20) {
    gotoAndStop (4);
}
this._y = ShotY;
```

This sets up a few variables and checks to see if the shot's next movement will take it further than 20 pixels above the top of the screen. If it will, then it moves the timeline to frame 4, where the shot will be recycled.

Now it's time for probably the most complicated piece of code in the game. This covers the collision detection routine for the shots.

3. Add this script on frame 2, under the last piece of code:

```
do {
    EnemyNum = EnemyNum+1;
    EnemyX = _root["Enemy"+EnemyNum]._x;
    EnemyY = _root["Enemy"+EnemyNum]._y;
    if (ShotX>EnemyX-15) {
        if (ShotX<EnemyX+15) {
            if (ShotY>EnemyY-15) {
                if (ShotY<EnemyY+15) {
                    if (Laser == 0) {
                        ShotDeath = true;
                    }
                    if (Laser == 1) {
                        ShotDeath = false;
                    }
                    if (_root["Enemy"+EnemyNum].Death==false) {
                        _root["Enemy"+EnemyNum].gotoAndPlay(4);
                    }
                }
            }
        }
    }
} while (EnemyNum<12);
if (ShotDeath == true) {
    this._x = 600;
}
```

This chunk of code uses the `do...while` action to create a code loop. The code loop contains the commands to check if a collision has occurred with any of the on-screen enemies. The loop will continue while the EnemyNum variable value is below 12. If a collision has occurred then the ShotDeath variable is set to true, and the Enemy movie clip that was hit is told to go to frame 4 of its timeline. If you don't remember as far back as programming that frame (we don't), the code there told the enemy that it was dead, played its little animation, and added 10 to the score. After a collision has taken place the shot is then moved off screen using the final `if` command. The `if (Laser)` commands are used to check if the player has the laser power-up active. If they do then the bullet will continue on its journey up the screen taking out every enemy in its path – yeaaaaaah. After all of that coding, we'll take a bit of a breather in the next frame.

4. On frame 3 of the CODE layer add this next piece of script:

```
gotoAndPlay (2);
```

This loops the timeline round to frame 2.

5. Now add the following code to frame 4:

```
this._x = 600;
this._visible = 0;
ShotDeath = false;
stop ();
```

This code is used once the shot has collided with an enemy. The first command moves the shot off screen and the second one renders it invisible. The `ShotDeath` variable is set to `false` and, finally, the `stop` action stops the timeline on frame 4, where it will remain until another shot is fired.

That's all the code we need for this movie clip. If you test the movie, you should now be able to make the ship fire by clicking the mouse. If you're lucky, you'll be able to destroy any stray enemies that cross your path before the homing mine collides with your ship. This is all well and good, but there's still something missing. It's time to program the movement for the player's spacecraft itself.

Player_Ship_B

There isn't much coding to do for the player's ship. All that it really needs to do is follow the Mover movie clip around.

1. Double-click on the Player_Ship_B movie clip from the Library to open it up, and then enter the following ActionScript into frame 1 of the CODE layer:

```
MoverX = _root.Mover._x;
MoverY = _root.Mover._y;
PlayerShipX = _root.PlayerShip._x;
if (MoverX>PlayerShipX) {
    PlayerShipX = PlayerShipX+((MoverX-PlayerShipX)/CraftSpeed);
}
if (MoverX<PlayerShipX) {
    PlayerShipX = PlayerShipX-((PlayerShipX-MoverX)/CraftSpeed);
}
if (MoverY>PlayerShipY) {
    PlayerShipY = PlayerShipY+((MoverY-PlayerShipY)/CraftSpeed);
}
if (MoverY<PlayerShipY) {
    PlayerShipY = PlayerShipY-((PlayerShipY-MoverY)/CraftSpeed);
}
this._x = PlayerShipX;
this._y = PlayerShipY;
this._rotation = (MoverX-PlayerShipX)/3;
```

This code is used to move the craft towards the Mover movie clip (the crosshair). The MoverX and MoverY variables are first set to the position of the Mover movie clip, and PlayerShipX is set to the position of the player's ship. The if commands check to see where the Mover movie clip is in relation to the ship, and then increase or decrease the ship's x and y position accordingly. The commands at the bottom of the code update the craft's position and rotation on screen. The CraftSpeed variable is set to 10 at the start of the game, and will be changed after the player activates certain power-ups. Changing this variable to a value smaller than 10 will speed up the craft, while setting it higher than 10 will slow it down.

2. Now copy and paste that code into frame 2, and then change the last line as highlighted here:

```
MoverX = _root.Mover._x;
MoverY = _root.Mover._y;
PlayerShipX = _root.PlayerShip._x;
if (MoverX>PlayerShipX) {
    PlayerShipX = PlayerShipX+((MoverX-PlayerShipX)/CraftSpeed);
}
if (MoverX<PlayerShipX) {
    PlayerShipX = PlayerShipX-((PlayerShipX-MoverX)/CraftSpeed);
}
if (MoverY>PlayerShipY) {
    PlayerShipY = PlayerShipY+((MoverY-PlayerShipY)/CraftSpeed);
}
if (MoverY<PlayerShipY) {
    PlayerShipY = PlayerShipY-((PlayerShipY-MoverY)/CraftSpeed);
}
this._x = PlayerShipX;
this._y = PlayerShipY;
this._rotation = (MoverX-PlayerShipX)/3;
```

continues overleaf

```
gotoAndPlay (1);
```

As you can see, there's one slight change in the code. We've added a `gotoAndPlay` command to the end so it will loop back to frame 1. We did this so that the ship will react more smoothly: if we'd only had the `goto` line in this frame, then the ship's position would've only been updated every other frame. By including the code twice, we can ensure that the ship moves in every single frame.

OK, that's the code for the player's craft done. We now need to add a tiny bit of code to the Player_Ship_Explosion movie clip.

3. Double-click on the Player_Ship_Explosion movie clip in the Library and, on frame 47 of the CODE layer; insert this action:

```
stop ();
```

That's all you have to do. This simply stops the timeline when it reaches frame 47.

You'll now be able to test the basic game. The ship should follow the Mover movie clip around, and you should be able to shoot the enemies by clicking with the mouse. When you hit an enemy though, you'll notice that the score goes a bit weird: instead of giving a correct score, it displays a bundle of what looks like binary code. This is because we've told Flash to add 10 to GameScore when an enemy is killed, but we haven't yet defined GameScore itself. Because we've already put 0 in the dynamic text box that displays the GameScore variable, Flash thinks that we're trying to make a string of characters. It'll then just add 10 to the end of the string every time an enemy is killed. So you'll get 010 the first time you kill an enemy, 01010 the second time, and so on. Luckily, this is very easy to fix, as we just need to tell Flash that it's a number, and not a string. We do this in the Score_A movie clip...

Score_A

We've almost finished the game now. After we've sorted out the scoring, there are just the power-ups left to tackle.

1. Double-click on the Score_A movie clip in the Library, and add the following ActionScript to frame 1 on the CODE layer:

```
GameScore = 0;
NextScore = 200;
```

This sets the GameScore variable to 0, telling Flash that it represents a *numerical* value and not a string. We also define a new value called NextScore, which represents the next score that the player needs to get before they get a power up.

2. On frame 2 of the CODE layer add:

```
if (GameScore >= NextScore) {
GameScore = GameScore +10;
```

```
NextScore = NextScore +200;
_root.Powerups.gotoAndPlay (2);
}
```

This code triggers the power-ups when the player reaches a certain score. Every 200 points the movie will call the Powerups movie and a random power-up will drop down the screen.

3. Finally, add this to frame 3:

```
gotoAndPlay (2);
```

This sends the timeline back to frame 2, and keeps checking the score to see if the player has earned a power-up.

Your basic game is now fully playable. You can go out and face the alien hordes, send lasers sizzling into their midst, and rack up the highest score possible before the inevitable happens, and your valiant ship is reduced to a shimmering cloud of neutrinos. You get the idea. Now that the basics are all there and working, we can experiment with some enhancements to the gameplay. We'll do this by the addition of some power-ups.

Player Power-Ups

These power-ups will drop slowly down from the top of the screen, one for every 200 points the player scores during the game. The different power-ups will have various short-lived effects on the player's craft:

- **Speed-Up** – this will increase the player's speed

- **Slow-Down** – this is the bad power-up that slows the player's craft down

- **Bonus Points** – this will give the player an extra, random amount of points

- **Laser** – the laser will cut straight through multiple enemies

- **Shield** – the player's craft will be invincible for a brief period of time

The graphics for all of these are held in one movie clip (Player_Powerups_A) and the animation that plays when they're collected is contained in another (Player_Powerups_B). We'll have to alter both of these power-up movie clips, but we only need one line of code in the first, so we should be able to get that out of the way fairly quickly.

1. From the Library, double-click on the Player_Powerups_A movie clip to open it up, and add the following ActionScript to frame 1 of the CODE layer:

    ```
    stop ();
    ```

    This just stops the clip from cycling through all of the graphics when it first appears. We'll be calling specific graphics using gotoAndStop commands housed in the next movie clip we build.

2. We'll now move on to the Player_Powerups_B movie clip. Double-click on it from the Library window and add this code to frame1 of the CODE layer:

    ```
    stop ();
    ```

    You may have justifiable deja vu at this stage, but we really did mean to write that. This time it's used to stop any power-ups from being triggered when the game is first started, as we only want this to happen when the player reaches certain scores. Unfortunately, this movie clip's not quite as simple as the last one, and there's a lot more code to come yet.

3. On frame 2 of the CODE layer add:

    ```
    _root.PlayerShip.CraftSpeed = 10;
    _root.Mover.Laser = 0;
    _root.Shield = 0;
    _root.PlayerShip.Effects._visible = 0;
    _root.PlayerShip.Effects.gotoAndPlay(50);
    _root.Powerups._y = -60;
    ```

    These first six lines stop any currently active power-up and stop the graphical effect on the craft if it's active (which happens when a power-up is being used). The player shouldn't normally get two power-ups simultaneously, but with lucky use of the laser, they'd be just about able to. This code makes sure that if they do work hard to get a second power-up, we immediately take the first one away. It's cruel, but fair.

4. Now we need to add the code that determines which power-up the player will receive on each occasion that they earn them. Insert this code immediately after the previous snippet:

    ```
    Powerup = random(5);
    _root.Powerups.Image.gotoAndStop(Powerup+1);
    _root.Powerups._x = (random(400)+50);
    _root.Powerups._y = -60;
    ```

The first line generates a random number from 0 to 4 for the variable Powerup. We then tell Flash to play the specific power-up graphic for that number. Flash just goes to the frame in the Player_Powerups_A movie clip (which has the instance name Image on the stage) and stops. The bottom two lines of code set the start position of the new power-up so that it'll fall from a random location at the top of the screen whenever it's triggered. Now that we've got the right graphic on the stage, we need to give it some ActionScript, first to let the player collect it, and then to make it *do* something.

5. On frame 3 of the CODE layer add:

```
PowerupY = _y;
PowerupY = PowerupY+2.5;
if (PowerupY>440) {
    _root.Powerups._y = -60;
    gotoAndStop (1);
}
_root.Powerups._y = PowerupY;
PlayerShipX = _root.PlayerShip._x;
PlayerShipY = _root.PlayerShip._y;
PowerupX = _x;
PowerupY = _y;
if (PowerupX<PlayerShipX+20) {
    if (PowerupX>PlayerShipX-20) {
        if (PowerupY>PlayerShipY-20) {
            if (PowerupY<PlayerShipY+20) {
                gotoAndPlay (5);
            }
        }
    }
}
```

This is the movement and collision code for the power-up. It's very similar to the enemy's movement and collision code that we used earlier, the only difference being that the player isn't killed on contact with the power-up, and once the power-up has reached the bottom of the screen it doesn't reappear again. If the player misses the power-up they don't get a second chance, they'll just have to reach the next target score in order to trigger another one.

6. On frame 4 of the CODE layer add:

```
gotoAndPlay (3);
```

This causes a loop between frame 3 and 4, checking that the player hasn't collected the power-up, and that it hasn't gone off the bottom of the screen.

Now, after the player has collected a power-up, we need to make it work. The resulting actions depend on what number has been generated, and will trigger different power-up types depending on that number.

7.   Type this ActionScript into frame 5:

```
if (Powerup == 0) {
    _root.Shield = 1;
    _root.PlayerShip.Effects.gotoAndPlay(2);
    }
if (Powerup == 1) {
    _root.PlayerShip.CraftSpeed = 3;
    _root.PlayerShip.Effects.gotoAndPlay(2);
    }
if (Powerup == 2) {
    _root.PlayerShip.CraftSpeed = 40;
    _root.PlayerShip.Effects.gotoAndPlay(2);
    }
if (Powerup == 3) {
    _root.Mover.Laser = 1;
    _root.PlayerShip.Effects.gotoAndPlay(2);
    }
if (Powerup == 4) {
    _root.ScoreMovie.GameScore += (random(10)*10);
    }
_root.PlayerShip.Effects._visible = 1;
```

This code is used if the player manages to collect a power-up. Depending on the value of the Powerup variable, different variables in other movies will be set. If the Powerup value is 2 then the CraftSpeed variable in the PlayerShip movie will be set to 40, causing the craft to slow down. The final line of the code is used to trigger the graphical flashing effect around the ship when a power-up is active. At the moment, this effect is playing all the time, but we'll change that in a minute.

8.   To finish off the power-up code, add the following script to frame 200:

```
_root.PlayerShip.CraftSpeed = 10;
_root.Mover.Laser = 0;
_root.Shield = 0;
_root.PlayerShip.Effects._visible = 0;
_root.PlayerShip.Effects.gotoAndPlay(50);
_root.Powerups._y = -60;
```

We use this code as a timer for the power-up. Rather than specifying a loop or getting the actual time, we just wait until we reach frame 200 and then stop the power-up. All of the various power-up variables are reset and the Powerups movie clip is moved back to the top of the screen. The graphical effect around the player's craft is also turned off.

All that we have to do now is to add a small bit of code to the Player_Ship_Extra movie clip, and then we're done.

9. Open up the Player_Ship_Extra movie clip in the Library and add the following ActionScript to frame 1 on the CODE layer:

```
stop ();
```

This will (finally) stop our ship from flashing all of the way through the movie.

10. And now on frame 10 of the CODE layer add this:

```
gotoAndPlay (2);
```

This simply causes the graphical effect to loop while a power-up is active.

That's it. That's as far as we're going to take you with this game. Whether you choose to expand it or not is up to you, and we'll give you a few ideas on how do that in just a minute. First though, it's time to run the game and admire your handiwork. Have fun playing it, and remember: you're only as good as your last high score.

Changing the Game

Now that you've added all of the ActionScript to the game, you may want to go about modifying it and tweaking the game as you see fit. The first, and most obvious, thing that you can change is the look of it. You can easily customize the appearance of the game by changing the movie clip graphics. If you do this then it's a good idea to keep the graphics roughly the same size as they are now. The reason is that the code is programmed to work with a set size. If you *do* want to change the size of the graphics then feel free to do so, but you'll also need to edit the code for the collisions to match the new graphics sizes.

The next thing that you can change is the code. This can be slightly more daunting and difficult, but with careful planning and a bit of luck and trial and error, you should be able to make what you want. Here are a few suggestions of things you could change:

- Add *levels* to the game. To move onto the next level, the player will need to earn, say, 1200 points.

- Add different enemies for different levels, perhaps getting faster, but also worth more points. They could even begin to fire back at the player.

- Add 'end of level' guardians. These are unique, extremely tough enemies that are only found guarding the end of the levels.

- Add an auto-fire facility or power-up.

- Every 1000 points, reset the speed of the normal enemies, but materialize an additional *indestructible* enemy.

- Give the player more than one life, or perhaps an energy bar that decreases when the player is hit.

- Add a scrolling background or some nice vector gas effects.

- Add more power-ups, such as:

  - New weapons – homing missiles, bombs with a blast radius, double-shot, multi-directional shot, bouncing lasers...

  - Auto-fire

  - Smart bomb – destroys all enemies on screen in one blast

  - Score multipliers – doubles the amount of points that you get for each enemy

  - 'Aid droids' – little robots that the circle the player's ship, giving extra fire-power or shielding the ship from enemies

  - Reset – puts the enemies back to their starting speed

  - Extra health/life

As you can see, the things that you can do with this game are pretty boundless: all you need are the ideas and the desire to hone your ActionScript programming skills. Hopefully, this chapter's given you some ideas in both these respects.

Good luck, and don't be seduced by the dark side...

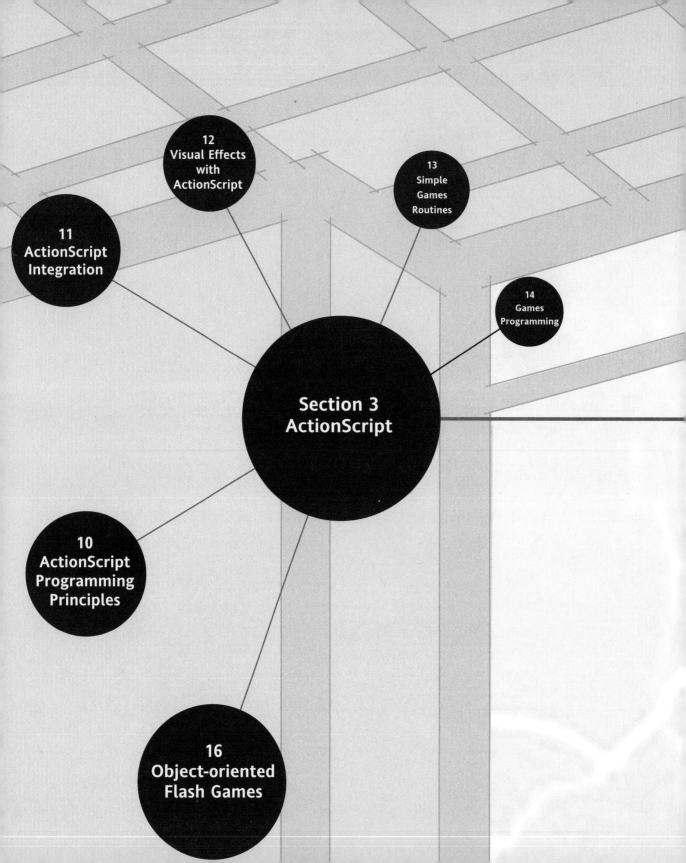

Chapter 15
Flash and the
Third Dimension

For as long as I can remember, Flash designers have gone to great lengths to include 3D content in their projects, and with the release of applications such as Vecta3D and Swift 3D, adding this content to a web site has become a relatively simple matter. Since then, it's been used in numerous web sites and online games with differing degrees of success. Three-dimensional effects are a consistently reliable crowd pleaser, but it's easy to fall into the trap of using them in unsuitable places. Even though this chapter deals with the subject of 3D Flash, I'm still wary about advocating the use of 3D effects on web sites with abandon. I believe that a 3D toolset *can* enable you to create some truly memorable user experiences, but I know also that it has pitfalls. It can be very processor intensive, and there's the ever-present danger of leaning towards the cheesy end of the design spectrum if you're not careful.

With the introduction and development of ActionScript in Flash 4 and 5 came the ability to perform real-time 3D calculations, rather than relying on pre-rendered ones. In spite of the improvements made to the new Flash 5 player though, the processor requirements for complex calculations in Flash at a decent speed are still pretty high. With a bit of lateral thinking, however, it's possible to find ways around these limitations.

The Possible and the Practical

With the above restrictions in mind, I came to the conclusion that for now, the value of real-time 3D in Flash is not going to be the recreation of complete, complex geometries – that's simply beyond the bounds of what's reasonable at the moment. What's more appealing is the ability to plot the positions of 'objects' in space by giving them spatial coordinates. An example of this approach is a 3D rugby game called Conversion Kings that my company created for Sportal, and which you can view on its web site at www.sportal.co.za/conversionkings:

To calculate the x, y, and z coordinates of the ball in space, we used a basic 3D engine that's similar in design to the one that this chapter is going to deal with. The stadium, the posts, and the ground are also given spatial coordinates, which enables us to do things such as detecting when the ball strikes any of these objects. We then superimpose this invisible 'matrix' of 3D coordinates on a pre-rendered 3D background to give the ball's movement a context.

Because the coordinates are calculated in a virtual 3D environment, we can also change the angle and perspective of the view, enabling us to create a series of different views from different angles – even a 'replay' option from behind the posts. The only positions that need to be calculated on a frame-by-frame basis are the ball and its shadow, and this makes it a viable use of 3D in Flash.

Similar in concept is the user interface of www.com-ebusiness.de, where again the only 3D calculation that has to be done is to plot the position of the ball in an isometric 3D space, as its x, y, and z coordinates are affected by physics calculations and the environment:

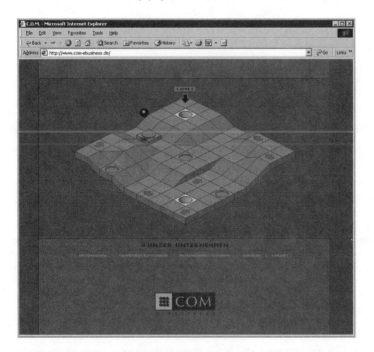

I believe that this combination of pre-rendered 3D objects and real-time 3D spatial calculations is one with great potential, especially as far as Flash game development is concerned – and so far, the opportunities that it offers are relatively unexplored. Of course, it can also be used quite creatively in designing multimedia interfaces.

All About Circles

Before we can even consider such applications, however, we have to understand what's involved in performing these 'basic' 3D calculations. That's going to be the focus of this chapter, which will walk you through the process of generating a basic 3D 'engine' in Flash. At the heart of this engine are some circle and angle-based calculations. To this end, I have created a series of FLAs that explain the various concepts and steps along the way.

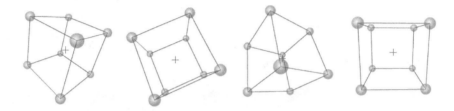

These FLAs can be found on the accompanying CD-ROM, and I would suggest keeping them close at hand while working through this tutorial. I believe that the best way to learn is to experiment, so do take the time to investigate the various stages of the tutorial, as represented by the sample files.

Before we begin, let's think about exactly what it is that we're hoping to achieve. Our aim is to create 3D effects in Flash 5 using ActionScript, and our final destination is represented by sample_13.fla, which uses ActionScript to calculate a cube's coordinates in space and create the illusion of 3D. Note that I use the word 'illusion' here not because this tutorial deals with pseudo-3D effects, but because a 3D object on *any* 2-dimensional surface is only an illusion. It's achieved by the combined efforts of setting the x and y properties of individual points in the 3D object, and by adjusting their scale properties as these points move in space. Our cube looks 3D because of the rules that we followed when drawing it, which allow our brain to rapidly associate and visualize the cube as an object in 3D space. Because we live in a 3D world, we intuitively recognize the effects of perspective, things like objects getting smaller as they get further away, and lines converging on vanishing points.

In sample_13.fla, a key characteristic is the illusion that the various points in the object seem to rotate around a central point. If you've been around for long enough to have used Flash 3, you'll probably recall having tried (or seen someone try) animating an object along a squashed circular (oval) path to simulate 3D rotation around a central point. This is important, because it gives us our first clue to how we can simulate 3D effects using ActionScript. It means that if we can *calculate* a circular path, instead of just *animating* it, we'll be well on our way to creating real-time 3D effects in Flash.

Sine and Cosine

I seem to recall my high school math teacher saying something about the relationship that the trigonometry functions **sine (sin)** and **cosine (cos)** have with circles. We won't be explaining how these functions actually work, that's the job of your math teacher, but luckily you don't *need* to know this to get through this chapter. If you're interested in finding out more about trigonometry functions, there are plenty of books, web resources, and colleges just waiting to be discovered. Without further ado then, let's have a look at them, and see what help they can offer us.

Given a particular angle, we can use sine and cosine to calculate the coordinates at which a line drawn at that angle intersects a circle. So in simulating 3D, sine and cosine can be used to calculate a circular path around a central point. Cosine represents the horizontal (X) value and sine the vertical (Y) value of the coordinate. Here you can see an illustration of how this works:

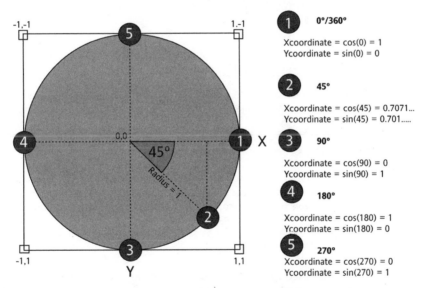

1 0°/360°

Xcoordinate = cos(0) = 1
Ycoordinate = sin(0) = 0

2 45°

Xcoordinate = cos(45) = 0.7071...
Ycoordinate = sin(45) = 0.701.....

3 90°

Xcoordinate = cos(90) = 0
Ycoordinate = sin(90) = 1

4 180°

Xcoordinate = cos(180) = 1
Ycoordinate = sin(180) = 0

5 270°

Xcoordinate = cos(270) = 0
Ycoordinate = sin(270) = 1

The sine and cosine values for an angle are based on a circle with a radius of one unit, also called a **unit circle** (as in the figure). The radius represents the distance between the central point (0, 0) and the edge of the circle. Using this, the equation for working out the x-coordinate on a circle is:

`Xcoordinate = radius * cos (angle)`

And the equation for working out the y-coordinate is:

`Ycoordinate = radius * sin (angle)`

The larger the value of `radius`, the larger the circle will be.

For an example, let's take an angle of 33 degrees, with a radius of 2:

X = 2 * cos (33) = 2 * 0.8387 = 1.6773

Y = 2 * sin (33) = 2 * 0.5446 = 1.0892

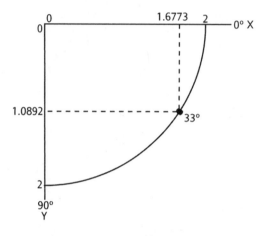

Unlike all of the previous versions, these trigonometry functions are built into Flash 5, and we can access them through the new Math object. So in ActionScript, we can write the equations like this:

```
Xcoordinate = Radius * Math.cos (Angle);
Ycoordinate = Radius * Math.sin (Angle);
```

It seems simple, but there's a small catch: the angles that are used by Math.cos and Math.sin are measured in **radians**, not degrees. Radians are basically just a more eloquent way of measuring angles, but if you feel more comfortable with degrees, you can convert by using the following:

*radians = degrees * (π / 180)*

The value of π (pi) that's used by the above equation can *also* be accessed through Flash 5's new Math object, so in ActionScript it'll look like this:

```
radians = Angle * (Math.PI / 180);
Xcoordinate = Radius * Math.cos (radians);
Ycoordinate = Radius * Math.sin (radians);
```

This should allow you to work out the x- and y-coordinates of any point that intersects a circle of a known radius.

Movement in a Circle

Let's put this to the test. If you take a look at sample_01.fla, you'll notice that in the _root timeline is a single movie clip instance in the center of the stage. It's inside this movie clip that all the action is going to take place, so double-click on it to edit its contents.

The movie clip contains two further movie clip instances: a circular shape with the instance name Point, and a crosshair movie clip with the instance name centerPoint. The _x and _y properties of centerPoint serve as a reference to the coordinate around which Point will travel; in this case, it happens to correspond to the center of the movie clip, (0, 0):

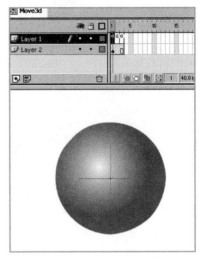

If you look at the timeline setup, you'll see that the movie clip contains just three frames. These contain the ActionScript that we're going to use. Frame 1 acts as the setup frame, and it's here where we store the various functions that we'll need. Double-click on frame 1 to reveal its actions:

```
Radius = 100;
degrees = 0;

// function setAngle
function setAngle () {
    Angle = degrees * (Math.PI / 180);
    degrees = degrees + 2;
}

// function drawPoints
function drawPoints () {
    Xpos = Radius * Math.cos (Angle);
    Ypos = Radius * Math.sin (Angle);

    // Draw
    Point._x = Xpos + centerPoint._x;
    Point._y = Ypos + centerPoint._y;
}
```

Throughout this tutorial, setAngle will be used to set the Angle values for any rotation that we might want to calculate. In this, our first sample, it's used to set Angle to the value of the conversion from degrees to radians, and then to increment degrees by 2 every time it's called.

drawPoints contains the code that calculates the point on the circle based on the equations that we covered earlier, and then finally plots Point's new position on screen by setting its _x and _y properties.

Frame 2 contains the code that calls setAngle and drawPoints:

```
setAngle();
drawPoints();
```

And the script in frame 3 is simply responsible for continually looping the script in frame 2:

```
gotoAndPlay(2);
```

As the value of Angle is incremented by continual calls to setAngle, and sine and cosine are used in drawPoints to calculate the new position of Point on a circle with a radius of 100. This results in Point moving in a circular path around centerPoint:

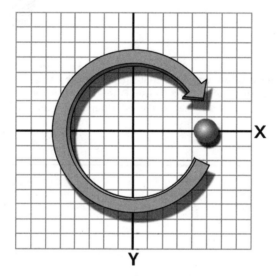

By changing the value of Radius, we can control the size of the circle. If, instead of giving it a set value of 100, we change our drawPoints function to increment the value of Radius every time it's called, the circular path will gradually become bigger (sample_02.fla):

```
Radius = 0;
degrees = 0;

// function setAngle
function setAngle () {
    Angle = degrees * (Math.PI / 180);
    degrees = degrees + 2;
}

// function drawPoints
function drawPoints () {
    Radius = Radius + 0.5;
```

```
Xpos = Radius * Math.cos (Angle);
Ypos = Radius * Math.sin (Angle);

// Draw
Point._x = Xpos + centerPoint._x;
Point._y = Ypos + centerPoint._y;
}
```

The result will have Point traveling in a spiral path around centerPoint:

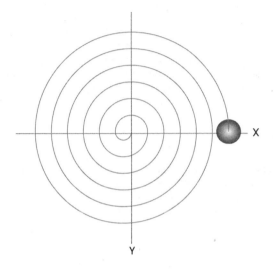

The Z-Axis

So, how is this spiral related to a 3D tutorial? The next figure shows a breakdown of the three axes in a 3D environment (x, y, and z). If you look at the first picture, you can see that in the two samples so far, we've been calculating rotation around the **z-axis** by using the point's coordinate on the x- and y-axis to plot a circular path. On a computer display, the z-axis could be imagined as the axis that comes towards us, out of the screen.

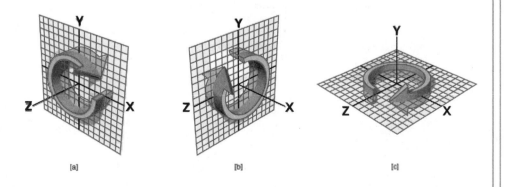

[a]   [b]   [c]

Based on this figure, we can say that in a 3D environment:

- Setting the x- and y-coordinate of a point using sine and cosine can calculate the rotation of the point around the z-axis.

- Setting the y- and z-coordinate of a point using sine and cosine can calculate the rotation of the point around the x-axis

- Setting the z- and x-coordinate of a point using sine and cosine can calculate the rotation of the point around the y-axis

In Flash, we can set the x- and y-coordinate of an instance using its _x and _y properties, but the z-coordinate proves to be a little more problematic. In a 3D environment, the position of an object on the z-axis usually represents its distance away from the viewer. If you think about it (due to perspective) the closer an object is to the viewer, the larger it appears — and vice versa. That means that we can use an instance's _xscale and _yscale properties to represent its coordinate on the z-axis.

Rotation Around the Y-Axis

Let's put this to the test. Based on our first experiment, sample_01.fla, I've modified the code in drawPoints to simulate rotation around the y-axis. According to the rules listed above, we do this by setting the x- and z-coordinates. The new code is in sample_03.fla, and it reads like this:

```
Radius = 100;
degrees = 0;

// function setAngle
function setAngle () {
    Angle = degrees * (Math.PI / 180);
    degrees = degrees + 2;
}

// function drawPoints
function drawPoints () {
    Xpos = Radius * Math.cos (Angle);
    Zpos = Radius * Math.sin (Angle);

    // Draw
    Point._x = Xpos + centerPoint._x;
    Point._yscale = Point._xscale = Zpos + 200;
}
```

There are only two changes here. First, the following line:

```
Ypos = Radius * Math.sin (Angle);
```

Was replaced with:

```
Zpos = Radius * Math.sin (Angle);
```

And instead of setting the _y property of Point, I now set its _xscale and _yscale properties
to Zpos + 200:

```
Point._yscale = Point._xscale = Zpos + 200;
```

Here, we're just setting both Point.yscale and Point.xscale to equal Zpos + 200. The value
of 200 that gets added to Zpos here is just to compensate for the fact that, with Radius having
a value of 100, the minimum value of Zpos will be -100 – and we don't want Point to have a
negative scale value. The movement of Point along the x-axis remains the same (as defined by
the cosine of Angle), but instead of moving up and down on the y-axis, Point now moves
'forwards' and 'backwards' on the z-axis – or more accurately, it *scales*, as defined by the sine of
Angle. The result is the illusion of Point moving in a circular path in space:

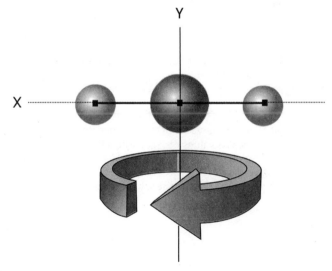

True Perspective

Although this motion is quite convincing, it's not yet entirely accurate. We've been adjusting the
scale of Point, but the *path* that our 'object' follows should also be adjusted for the scaling of the
point. In other words, because the path itself stretches towards and away from us, it too should
be seen in perspective. To deal with this, we can introduce a perspective variable, and set the
_x, _xscale, and _yscale properties of Point relative to it.

So, at the top of the script in frame 1 of sample_04.fla, the new perspective variable is set
to a value of 150:

```
Radius = 100;
perspective = 150;
degrees = 0;
```

continues overleaf

```
// function setAngle
function setAngle () {
    Angle = degrees * (Math.PI / 180);
    degrees = degrees + 2;
}
```

This variable is used by drawPoints to calculate the amount of perspective distortion that occurs. The smaller the value of perspective, the more dramatic will be the distortion, and vice versa. In drawPoints itself, a new variable called Depth is set, based on the values of perspective and Zpos:

```
// Function drawPoints
function drawPoints () {
    Xpos = Radius * Math.cos (Angle);
    Zpos = Radius * Math.sin (Angle);

    // Perspective
    Depth = 1 / (1 - (Zpos / perspective));

    // Draw
    Point._x = (Xpos * Depth) + centerPoint._x;
    Point._y = centerPoint._y;
    Point._yscale = Point._xscale = Depth * 100;
}
```

The value of Depth is multiplied by the value of Xpos to set the _x property, and multiplied by 100 to set the _xscale and _yscale values of Point. The 'closer' Point is to the viewer (in other words, the bigger Zpos is), the greater the value of Depth will be. If you take a look at the next figure, which is essentially a view along the y-axis (or, from the 'top'), you can see how the path around the center is distorted, and how different values of perspective would affect this:

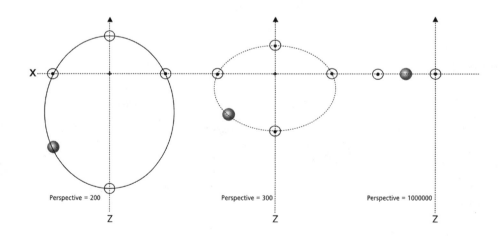

Perspective = 200   Perspective = 300   Perspective = 1000000

Viewed along the z-axis, this will have the effect of more dramatic movement and scaling as the object comes 'closer to' the viewer, and more subtle movement the 'further away' the object is. This can be likened to driving through a landscape where the immediate surroundings appear to move much more quickly than, for example, the mountains in the background. When the value of perspective reaches the region of 1,000,000, there will be hardly any distortion, producing an **orthographic view** (a view where no perspective distortion occurs). If we looked at our surroundings with an orthographic perspective, all objects would appear to be the same distance away.

At the moment, the perspective variable in frame 1 of Move3d is set to 1000000 so you won't notice much variation when you play the movie:

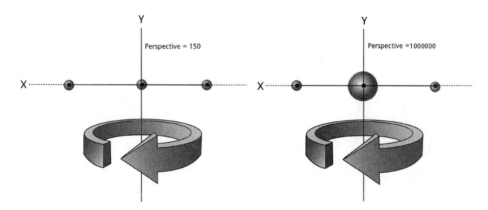

Try changing the value to 150, and then running it to get a really deep perspective effect. It's even possible to create an effect of moving outside of the screen; set perspective to 15, and try not to duck as it loops around your head. As you change the value of perspective, the variation in the motion and scaling of Point can be seen quite clearly.

Rotation Around the X-Axis

The same technique can be used to simulate rotation around the x-axis, by calculating the z- and y-coordinates. The view along the x-axis presents us with a plane where y will represent the vertical coordinate (sine), and z will represent the horizontal coordinate (cosine).

So, in the script to simulate rotation around the x-axis (sample_05.fla), drawPoints will look like this:

```
function drawPoints () {
    Ypos = Radius * Math.cos (Angle);
    Zpos = Radius * Math.sin (Angle);

    // Perspective
    Depth = 1 / (1 - (Zpos / perspective));
```

continues overleaf

```
        // Draw
        Point._x = centerPoint._x;
        Point._y = (Ypos * Depth) + centerPoint._y;
        Point._yscale = Point._xscale = Depth * 100;
    }
```

A representation of the results of these changes would look like this:

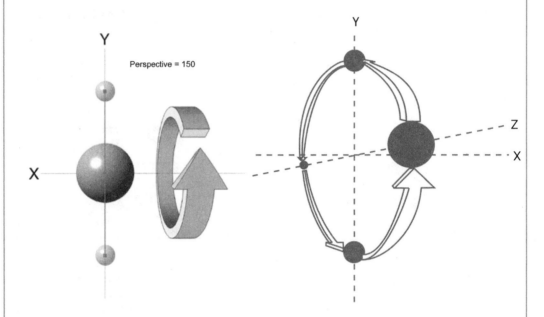

Perspective = 150

Our sphere now appears to rotate around the x-axis, getting closer, then further away as it swoops around.

Moving Multiple Points

Now that we have an idea of how sine and cosine can help us to simulate the rotation of a single point around an axis in space, let's look at how we might go about creating a system that will rotate more than one point around the center.

The first thing that we need to do is establish where we want the various points in the system to be, and how we're going to store that information. To make the explanation as simple as possible, I'm going to deal with this as a 2-dimensional concept first, and then apply a 3D solution later in the chapter.

The 2D system is going to allow us to set an x- and y-coordinate for each point that we want to include. These coordinates are set relative to the central point (0, 0), and will continue to operate on the same principle as the single-point systems that you've seen so far. That is, we'll follow the Flash convention of saying that any point situated *above* the x-axis will have a *negative* ycoordinate value, and any point *below* will have a *positive* y-coordinate value. The same also applies for the x-coordinates, where a point to the left of the y-axis will have a negative x-coordinate value, and vice versa:

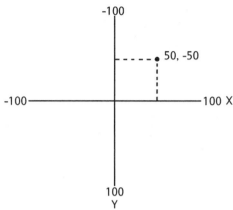

Rotation Around the Z-Axis

We're going to start with four points in our system. This figure illustrates the coordinates necessary to draw a square that's 100 units high and wide, and has its center aligned with the center of the grid:

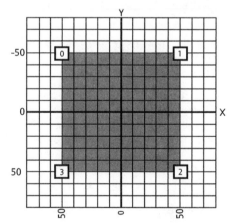

The coordinates for the corners of this square are as follows:

Point 0:	x = -50, y = -50
Point 1:	x = 50, y = -50
Point 2:	x = -50, y = 50
Point 3:	x = 50, y = 50

In Flash, we're going to use two arrays called x and y to store these values. So, based on the first frame of sample01.fla (the very first experiment we did), we're going to replace the line that sets the value of `Radius` with some code that sets the two new arrays. The new script (in `sample06.fla`) will look something like this:

```
// Set point xyz coordinates
x = new Array(-50, 50, -50, 50);
y = new Array(-50, -50, 50, 50);
verticeNum = x.length;
```

In this code, `verticeNum` is set to the `length` of the `x` array – that is, the number of points that we have in the system. Because we want four points in the system, I've included a routine that creates duplicates of `Point`, naming them `Point0`, `Point1`, `Point2`, and `Point3`, and renders the original movie clip invisible:

```
// Duplicate points
for (c = 0; c < verticeNum; c++) {
    duplicateMovieClip ("Point", "Point" + c, c);
}

Point._visible = 0;
```

The major change to `drawPoints` involves the equations that we've used until now to calculate `Xpos` and `Ypos`:

$$Xpos = Radius * cos\ (angle)$$
$$Ypos = Radius * sin\ (angle)$$

Instead of `Radius`, we're going to use the x- and y-coordinates that we just set to do more or less the same thing. So the new equations will look like this:

$$Xpos = x * sin\ (angle) + y * cos\ (angle)$$
$$Ypos = y * sin\ (angle) - x * cos\ (angle)$$

However, we now need to set `Xpos` and `Ypos` (and the `_x` and `_y` properties) for *every* point in our system. This is achieved by using a loop that will execute the actions responsible for setting these values four times. The loop uses a variable called `c` to keep track of how many times it has looped, and to access the values of the `x` and `y` arrays:

```
function drawPoints () {
    for (c = 0; c < verticeNum; c++) {

        // Z - Rotation
        Xpos = x[c] * Math.sin(Angle) + y[c] * Math.cos(Angle);
        Ypos = y[c] * Math.sin(Angle) - x[c] * Math.cos(Angle);

        // Draw
        this["Point" + c]._x = Xpos + centerPoint._x;
        this["Point" + c]._y = Ypos + centerPoint._y;
    }
}
```

In the Draw section of the above code, this["Point" + c] will change when the movie is running to the names of movie clip instances Point0, Point1, Point2, and Point3 in turn.

On running this new script (sample_06.fla), you'll notice that as the angle is increased (by setAngle), all four points are now moving in a circular path around centerPoint, keeping a constant relationship with one another:

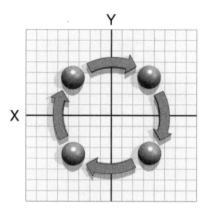 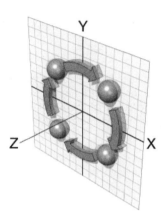

The real advantage of using this method is the ability to change the x- and y-coordinate of each point in the system. Let's do a little experiment that will illustrate this better: we'll change the values in our x and y arrays, using the shape in the next figure as a reference. This shape presents a whole new set of values that read as follows:

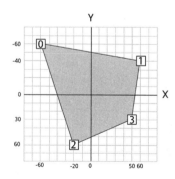

Point0:   x = -60, y = -60
Point1:   x = 60,   y = -40
Point2:   x = -20, y = 60
Point3:   x = 50,   y = 30

When we replace the value sets for arrays x and y with these new values (sample_07.fla), it results in a new configuration of the points in the system, resembling the shape in the previous figure. However, they still rotate around the centerPoint, keeping their relative positions as they do so. Experiment a little with changing these values yourself to see the results.

Rotation Around the Y-Axis

Similar to the very first sample that we looked at, we've just done the calculations that would represent rotation around the z-axis. So from here, we can do the calculations for the y- and x-axes, based on what you learned in sample_04.fla and sample_05.fla. Let's have a look at rotation around the y-axis first.

You know that in order to simulate rotation around the y-axis, we need to set the values of Xpos and Zpos, and for this we'll need a set of point coordinates on the x- and z-axes. For this purpose, we can imagine 'rotating' the x-y plane 90 degrees around the x-axis, with the result that the old y-coordinates now become z-coordinates, while the x-coordinates remain the same:

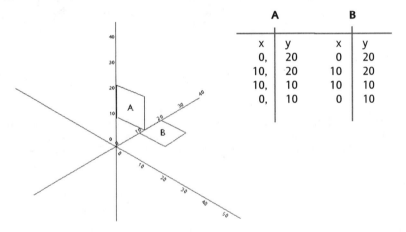

A		B	
x	y	x	y
0,	20	0	20
10,	20	10	20
10,	10	10	10
0,	10	0	10

The new equations for calculating the rotation around the y-axis will look like this:

```
Xpos = x * sin(Angle) + z * cos(Angle)
Zpos = z * sin(Angle) - x * cos(Angle)
```

You've also learned that we need some code that sets the value of Depth, and that this is used to set the _xscale and _yscale properties of Point. Depth is also multiplied by Xpos to give us the _x property of Point.

Because Depth relies on perspective for its value, we also have to remember to give perspective a value – and as before, we include this at the beginning of the script in frame 1. So, the code in drawPoints, simulating rotation around the y-axis, will look like this (you'll find it in sample_08.fla on the CD):

```
// function drawPoints
function drawPoints () {
    for (c = 0; c < verticeNum; c++) {
        // Y - Rotation
        Xpos = x[c] * Math.sin (Angle) + z[c] * Math.cos (Angle);
        Zpos = z[c] * Math.sin (Angle) - x[c] * Math.cos (Angle);

        // Perspective
        Depth = 1 / (1 - (Zpos / perspective));

        // Draw
        this["Point" + c]._x = (Xpos * Depth) + centerPoint._x;
        this["Point" + c]._y = centerPoint._y;
        this["Point" + c]._xscale =
                    ➥this["Point" + c]._yscale = Depth * 100;

        // Z-Sorting
        this["Point" + c].swapDepths(Depth * 500);
    }
}
```

The last line of code in this function is responsible for **z-sorting** (working out which points to draw in front of which others, as the points rotate). In Flash 4, we had to go through quite a process to do this, but in Flash 5 we can use the built-in swapDepths function. Basically, this moves the current instance to the new level specified by the expression Depth * 500 – so the greater the value of Depth, the higher up in the stack the current Point instance will be moved. This function doesn't *replace* the contents of the level it moves to, but *swaps* the contents of the two levels, which is particularly helpful when two points have the same Depth value.

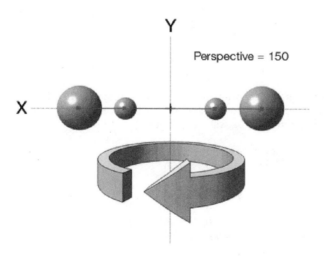

Rotation Around the X-Axis

Similarly, the equations for rotation around the x-axis, calculating the y- and z-coordinates, will look something like this (see `sample_09.fla`):

```
Ypos = y * sin (angle) + z * cos (angle)
Zpos = z * sin (angle) - y * cos (angle)
```

And the result will be similar to that of `sample_05.fla`, except that there are now four points rotating around the x-axis.

A 3D Object

Up to this point, we've been calculating the rotation around the individual axes separately, each time assigning two coordinates per point to do the calculation. However, to create the illusion of a rotating 3D object, each point has to be assigned an x-, y-, *and* z-coordinate, and the calculations for all three axes have to be done for each point. The next figure illustrates that when we extrude a 2-dimensional square to generate a cube, we need to generate four more points, and each point also has to be assigned a z-coordinate:

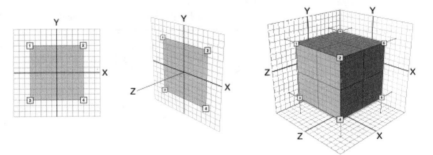

The final cube is floating in a 3D coordinate space with its origin at 0, 0, 0. Based on this figure, we can say that the 3D coordinates for a cube, such as this one, that's 100 units high, wide, and deep, with its center point at (0, 0, 0), will look like this:

Point0:	x = -50, y = -50, z = 50
Point1:	x = 50, y = -50, z = 50
Point2:	x = -50, y = 50, z = 50
Point3:	x = 50, y = 50, z = 50
Point4:	x = -50, y = -50, z = -50
Point5:	x = 50, y = -50, z = -50
Point6:	x = -50, y = 50, z = -50
Point7:	x = 50, y = 50, z = -50

Instead of doing the calculations for rotation around a single axis, as we've done up to now in our `drawPoints` function, we're going to do the calculations for all three axes at the same time.

Because of this, we need to introduce three new variables that will keep track of the rotation angle around each axis. We'll name these variables Xangle, Yangle, and Zangle, and they'll replace the generic Angle variable we've been using.

Xangle will represent the angle of rotation around the x-axis; Yangle the rotation around the y-axis; and Zangle the rotation around the z-axis. The new set of equations can therefore be clearly divided into three parts, and will look something like this:

x-rotation:

$$Ypos\_Temp = y * sin(Xangle) + z * cos(Xangle)$$
$$Zpos\_Temp = z * sin(Xangle) - y * cos(Xangle)$$

y-rotation:

$$Xpos\_Temp = x * sin(Yangle) + Zpos\_Temp * cos(Yangle)$$
$$Zpos = Zpos\_Temp * sin(Yangle) - x * cos(Yangle)$$

z-rotation:

$$Xpos = Xpos\_Temp * sin(Zangle) + YPos\_Temp * cos(Zangle)$$
$$Ypos = Ypos\_Temp * sin(Zangle) - Xpos\_Temp * cos(Zangle)$$

In these equations, Xpos_Temp, Ypos_Temp, and Zpos_Temp serve as temporary variables that are used in place of x, y and z to arrive at values for Xpos, Ypos, and Zpos.

So, having assigned values for Xpos, Ypos and Zpos, these equations are followed by the line that sets the Depth variable, and finally the new point positions are drawn to the screen by multiplying Depth with Xpos and Ypos, and setting each point's _x and _y property in the same way that we've done it in previous examples. Depth is also used, as before, to set the _xscale and _yscale properties of each Point.

Finally, the script that makes up our drawPoints function is (sample_10.fla):

```
// function drawPoints
function drawPoints () {
    for (c = 0; c < verticeNum; c++) {
        // X - Rotation
        Ypos_Temp = y[c] * Math.sin (Xangle) +
                ➡z[c] * Math.cos (Xangle);
        Zpos_Temp = z[c] * Math.sin (Xangle) -
                ➡y[c] * Math.cos (Xangle);

        // Y - Rotation
        Xpos_Temp = x[c] * Math.sin (Yangle) +
                ➡Zpos_Temp * Math.cos (Yangle);
        Zpos = Zpos_Temp * Math.sin (Yangle) -
                x[c] * Math.cos (Yangle);
```

continues overleaf

```
                    // Z - Rotation
                    Xpos = Xpos_Temp * Math.sin (Zangle) +
                       ➥YPos_Temp * Math.cos (Zangle);
                    Ypos = Ypos_Temp * Math.sin (Zangle) -
                       ➥Xpos_Temp * Math.cos (Zangle);

                    // Perspective
                    Depth = 1 / (1 - (Zpos / perspective));

                    // Draw
                    this["Point" + c]._x = (Xpos * Depth) + centerPoint._x;
                    this["Point" + c]._y = (Ypos * Depth) + centerPoint._y;
                    this["Point" + c]._xscale =
                                  this["Point" + c]._yscale = Depth * 100;

                    // Z-Sorting
                    this["Point" + c].swapDepths(Depth * 500);
            }
        }
```

At this point, it'd be helpful to pass on a useful tip: it's not always necessary to calculate rotation around all three axes to create 3D effects. It's *sometimes* necessary to rotate the object around the z-axis, but by no means is this always the case. Generally, cutting down on the code in Flash is a good idea, so we could just calculate the x- and y-rotations:

x-rotation:

```
Ypos = y * sin(Xangle) + z * cos(Xangle)
Zpos = z * sin(Xangle) - y * cos(Xangle)
```

y-rotation:

```
Xpos = x * sin(Yangle) + Zpos * cos(Yangle)
Zpos = Zpos * sin(Yangle) - x * cos(Yangle)
```

Doing things this way also removes the need for the extra temporary variables. (You can find this as sample_11.fla on the CD.) However, for the purposes of this tutorial, I'm going to continue with the original sample that calculates rotation around all three axes.

To get from sample_09.fla to sample_10.fla, we also need to change the setAngle function to set values for all three angle variables (Xangle, Yangle, and Zangle). We can do this simply by duplicating the existing script three times, and changing the variable names:

```
        function setAngle () {
            Xangle = Xdegrees * (Math.PI / 180);
            Yangle = Ydegrees * (Math.PI / 180);
            Zangle = Zdegrees * (Math.PI / 180);
            Xdegrees = Xdegrees + 2;
            Ydegrees = Ydegrees + 2;
```

```
    Zdegrees = Zdegrees + 2;
    }
```

The values that we add to the degrees at the end of the code are the amount that we want each axis to rotate. For example, setting this to 0 stop the cube rotating on that axis, and setting it to a negative value will make it rotate in the opposite direction. Of course, these values could also be set using any other expressions. For instance, to rotate the object based on mouse movement, we can change the script to look like this (sample_12.fla):

```
    function setAngle () {
        Xangle = Xdegrees * (Math.PI / 180);
        Yangle = Ydegrees * (Math.PI / 180);
        Zangle = Zdegrees * (Math.PI / 180);
        Xdegrees = this._xmouse;
        Ydegrees = this._ymouse;
        Zdegrees = 0;
    }
```

Setting Xdegrees and Ydegrees to the current location of the mouse pointer location is the most basic way of achieving this effect, but we could use more complex scripts to achieve other movement and interaction.

This brings us to the final step. At the moment, we have eight points in a system around the central point, but we might want to give the object some structure by connecting the individual points with lines. To this end, I'm going to create another function called drawLines that will loop for the number of lines we want to plot. To connect the points in a cube, we're going to need twelve lines, but unfortunately Flash won't let us set the individual point coordinates for a line using ActionScript. We're going to have to find another way around this.

The solution is to use a movie clip that contains a single diagonal hairline, and to scale this movie clip horizontally and vertically between the points that need to be connected. It's important that the movie clip should have equal _width, _height, and _scale properties when its endpoints correspond with points that need to be connected – in other words, we need a movie clip that's 100 units high and wide when it's scaled at 100%. This means that if we know the distance between two points, then we just need to set the _scale properties of the movie clip to that distance to make it the correct length.

To create this movie clip, simply draw a diagonal line running down from left to right at 45 degrees, and in the Info panel set its X and Y values to 0 such that the top left hand corner becomes the 'center' of the movie clip. Set its width and height to 100.

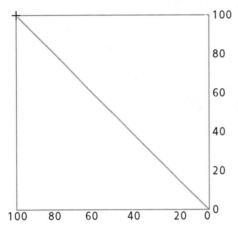

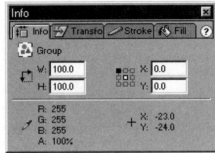

We'll name this movie clip instance Line.

In frame 1 of the Move3D movie clip in sample_13.fla, we then set a variable called lineNum to equal 12. This represents the number of lines that we'll need to connect all of the points in the cube:

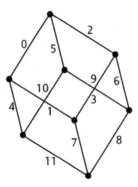

The next step is then simply to duplicate Line twelve times, naming the duplicates Line0, Line1, Line2, etc., and then setting the visibility of the original instance to 0:

```
lineNum = 12;

// Duplicate lines
for (c = 0; c < lineNum; c++) {
    duplicateMovieClip ("Line", "Line" + c, c + verticeNum);
}
Line._visible = 0;
```

To tell the script that's responsible for connecting the lines which points to connect, we'll set up a list of the points that need to be connected for each line. This is done by assigning variables called Line*X*Start and Line*X*End to each of the lines, where X is the number that we appended to the name of each movie clip in the last piece of code. The list will look this:

```
// Set line connection info
Line0Start  =  0, Line0End  =  1;
Line1Start  =  0, Line1End  =  2;
Line2Start  =  1, Line2End  =  3;
Line3Start  =  2, Line3End  =  3;
Line4Start  =  0, Line4End  =  4;
Line5Start  =  1, Line5End  =  5;
Line6Start  =  2, Line6End  =  6;
Line7Start  =  3, Line7End  =  7;
Line8Start  =  7, Line8End  =  6;
Line9Start  =  7, Line9End  =  5;
Line10Start = 5, Line10End = 4;
Line11Start = 6, Line11End = 4;
```

So, Line0 will have Point0 as its anchor (Line0Start), and it will be stretched to Point1 (Line0End). Line1 will connect from Point0 to Point2, and so on. The first four lines will look like this:

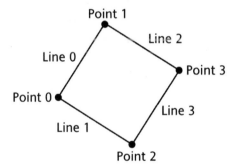

Next, we have to add a function to join the dots. This is the job of the new drawLines function in frame 1, which is responsible for looping the script that plots the lines:

```
// function drawLines;
function drawLines () {
    for (c = 0; c < lineNum; c++) {
        this ["Line" + c]._x =
            ➥this ["Point" + (this ["Line" + c + "Start"])]._x;
        this ["Line" + c]._y =
            ➥this ["Point" + (this ["Line" + c + "Start"])]._y;
        this ["Line" + c]._xscale =
            ➥this ["Point" + (this ["Line" + c + "End"])]._x -
            ➥this ["Point" + (this ["Line" + c + "Start"])]._x;
        this ["Line" + c]._yscale =
```

continues overleaf

```
➥this["Point" + (this["Line" + c + "End"])]._y -
➥this["Point" + (this["Line" + c + "Start"])]._y;
    }
  }
```

This script sets the _x and _y properties of each line to equal the _x and _y properties of the point that represents its starting point (LineXStart), and then scales the line using the difference between the _x and _y properties of the two points that it connects. This works because if we negatively scale something, then we effectively flip it across its axis. So, if we want Line to look like this:

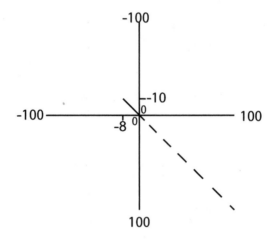

Then the math will be:

```
StartX = 0,  EndX = -8
StartY = 0,  EndY = -10
_xscale = -8 - 0 = -8
_yscale = -10 - 0 = -10
```

This means that we scale Line by -8% on the x-axis, making the width of the movie clip -8, and scale the y-axis by -10%, making the height of the movie clip -10.

Once we've applied this to all of the lines, we'll have what we set out to make: a cube in 3D space:

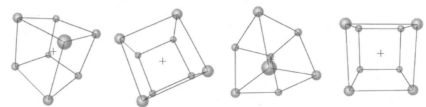

This completes the basic 3D engine, but it could quite easily be adapted for your own needs, depending on the application. The finished model can be found on the CD as `sample_13.fla`.

Conclusion

The next step from here is to experiment by changing the individual point coordinates to see how this affects the model. Also, try setting additional points in the system by changing the value of `verticeNum`, and setting initial point coordinates for these. It would be a relatively easy task to convert this to a dynamic system where the user could control the depth or the number of points through an input text field, or simple plus and minus buttons, and see their changes happen in real time.

Last of all, remember that these coordinates don't have to be static. The beauty of this system is that we can reset the positions of the points every time the script is looped, in much the same way that we set the variables that are responsible for setting the rotation angles. This gives us the ability to move points around within the system, and is the basis that the examples mentioned at the beginning of this chapter were built upon.

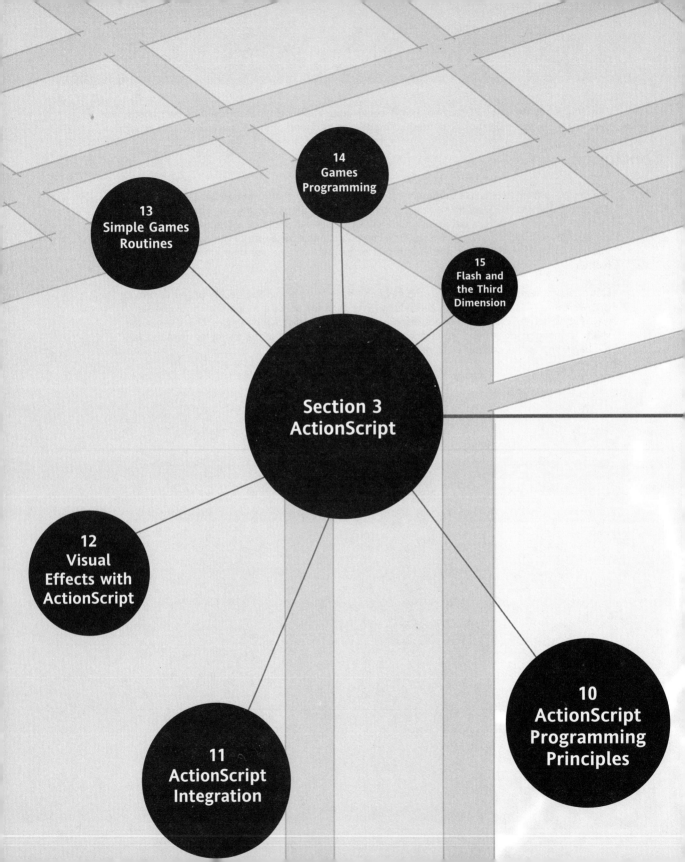

Chapter 16
Object-oriented
Flash Games

The top creators of Flash sites are just beginning to master the ins and outs of web site design and dynamic content, but it seems that's just not enough for some people. Increasingly, clients are seeking out designers with the ability to also write Flash games, puzzles, and other multimedia 'extras', in the belief that such things will keep users at their sites for longer. There's also a more subtle reason why your clients love these games and screensavers – they have the ability to be made into standalone downloads that the user can take away to play or watch offline. Their monitors are like thousands of free virtual billboards, all there for the taking!

> *Additionally, the word is that advertisers are getting exited about rich media in their web adverts and banners, and I can't think of anything richer than an interactive game to entice that all-important click-through to occur.*

Looking ahead, the Web is obviously moving away from its print-based origins (which involved pages with text and static content), towards something that more fully deserves the description "electronic media". With its interactive elements and animation, Flash started a lot of this, but we're seeing more and more advanced interfaces being developed. Some of these are so far removed from HTML, and even from basic Flash sites, that they're starting to steal concepts from the world of computer gaming, such as simulation of real-world movement, and dynamic, intelligent animation elements.

Our first conclusion, then, is that knowing how to design and code Flash games is not just something for the Flash ActionScript guru who wants to show off. Rather, it is an emerging mainstream skill that may get you (and your clients) ahead of the crowd.

Roadmap

There are, however, a number of reasons why designing games is fundamentally different from designing traditional Flash web sites, and you need to be aware of them before you start. Web design can be performed via a number of different programming routes, from 'no ActionScript' upwards. Games are different, in that a structured, ActionScript-based implementation is more or less a must, along with dynamic, property-based animation (timeline-based animation simply won't work). Before we get too excited, however, there are some limitations of Flash that we need to consider as well.

We will end this chapter by designing and coding a Flash game that circumvents all the disadvantages of Flash, and makes the most of all the advantages. I will attempt to introduce a common structured method that you can take away to use in your own game creations. I will also specify what I consider the two golden rules in designing and creating a game that people will want to play.

Despite the structured method, there are no shortcuts. Writing Flash games is one of the more difficult uses to which ActionScript can be put, and because the game I have created is pretty math-intensive, *Savior* is not for the fainthearted. It's something for you to look at using all of your newfound skills. Play with it, dissect it, and if you want to, improve it.

If you like, you can have an early peek at our game by looking at `savior.fla`, but before we get any further in describing it, let's get the bad news over with first.

Limitations of Flash as a Gaming Environment

There are a number of limitations inherent in trying to write a game for Flash, and I have described two of the biggest ones below. But before you get too pessimistic, I should say that they aren't so much "Why it can't be done", as "Here's where we have to focus our ingenuity". You'll see what I mean...

The browser is not a games console

Games consoles have the significant advantage of being displayed on television sets, which make a decent fist of showing resolutions much lower than the average computer's monitor. Early video games ran on screens with typically no more than 320 x 256 pixels, and 8 colors. Even as late as the PlayStation and Nintendo64 consoles, a resolution of around 400 x 300 pixels was pretty normal. Furthermore, video game consoles' processors are dedicated to the game being played, and the game code can assume total control of the hardware.

Within a browser, Flash has none of these benefits. It has no control of the screen resolution, which will be high (typically 1024 x 768 x 24-bit color, which is beyond dedicated games machines even now). Also, even though your target machine may have a 1GHz super processor with a gigabyte of memory, the poor Flash plug-in is pretty low down in the pecking order of system resources. It can't count on having free use of all that power, and it can't talk to that lovely 3D graphics card you bought the other day, either.

Flash has an inappropriate rendering engine for many traditional games

At the heart of most gaming hardware, you have one of two things: a bitmap-based, sprite/scroll/scale engine (as seen on the early Sega and Nintendo machines), or a real-time 3D/texture-mapping engine (as seen on most modern consoles). Occasionally you get both, as is the case with the Microsoft DirectX API that has set the PC games market alight.

Flash has neither of these: it has a 2D, filled vector-based rendering engine *that is optimized for low file size at the expense of speed*. The engine requires the Flash plug-in to build each frame of graphics *during runtime*, based on a compressed format that contains just the point and the fill data for each graphic element. This engine is slow when used with bitmaps (because it's not suited to them), and it can't handle real-time polygon 3D very well (because the plug-in just doesn't have the processor priority to tackle something so computationally intensive).

Creating Games Regardless

That's a pretty damning set of limitations – what, if anything, do we have to say in Flash's defense? Well, there are a few general ways out of these traps, and we have a rather good programming language on our side. Let's look at ways to overcome the processing bottleneck first. You can:

- Make the game's play area small. This is a favorite technique used by most Flash games. By making the game area small and not scalable, the graphics that Flash has to draw on screen are kept manageable. A little ingenuity goes a long way here, and it's entirely possible to make the *visible* screen size large, but to make the *active* game area much smaller, without making the game look too claustrophobic.

- Make the individual game sprites small. This is just a variation on the above, but it does allow you to have a larger game area. Remember, we're talking about Flash's *vector-based* rendering here, which takes 'small' to mean something very different from what a bitmap-based engine would. Flash sees a diagonal line from the top left of the screen to the bottom right as a 'small' graphic because it is easy and quick to draw, given knowledge of just two points. A bitmap-based game engine would see this as a full-screen bitmap, and rather more difficult. By creating graphics that use this fundamental difference to your advantage, you will be releasing Flash from many of the bottlenecks associated with trying to emulate a bitmap-based game.

- Use few moving sprites at any one time. To stop the game area looking too sparse, have lots of things moving, but *not at the same time*. The old video game classics suffered from underpowered hardware, but their developers got around that by using simplistic graphics and stylized game environments. There's a lot that can be learned by looking back at how they achieved this feat, and went on to create some of the most addictive games ever.

There's a good example of many of these workarounds being used within Flash 5 itself. Select Help > About Flash, and *immediately* double-click on the Macromedia 'M' logo on the About Flash window that appears. If you do this before the three buttons (team, thanks, and legal) appear at the bottom left, and then click on the thanks button, you get an addictive yet extremely simple game called *Gold Rush* (complete with a 'back to work' button for when the boss comes over) that actually works well on Flash's 'minimum specification' machine. As an aside, you can also try double-clicking on the Macromedia logo more than once to get the 'M' bouncing about, complete with comedy 'boing' sound!

This illustrates perfectly my main point about Flash games: you have limited resources, and you may have to use a small screen area, but that can be an advantage. It forces you to be *creative*, rather than relying on top-heavy, pre-rendered cut scenes, and the support of lightning-fast hardware.

The advantages that Flash offers us *can* get us out of most of these problems, if we work carefully and within our limitations. As Flash 5 users, we have the luxury of a structured, object-oriented language, a graphic object that supports animation directly (the movie clip), and the ability to introduce complex hierarchies not only within our code, but also within our *graphics*, via nested timelines. As we shall see later, this point is pretty fundamental, because it lets us do some otherwise complex things easily.

Although we don't have the ability to run our games at the hardware's optimum speed, we have the use of ActionScript, which has support for important elements like event-driven structures, collision detection, and screen layers already built in. We can extend our code structures to the graphics themselves, because Flash 5 treats *everything* as an object, irrespective of whether it is code or a graphic. This is great, because (as we shall see) it lets us organize our graphic structures into objects that emulate complex game elements.

A Flash Game Template

Before we go on to discuss the specific code for the game we'll be developing in this chapter, we're going to define a general template for game design that's suitable for Flash's authoring environment. Because games can be more complex than web sites, we need to be careful and design a structure early on, so that our game engine (that is, the code that runs the game) doesn't end up looking like a plate of spaghetti, structure-wise. The system described below is a way of adding this structure, and it's something I've refined over a number of Flash games. Although it isn't the *only* method you could use, it does employ the advances in ActionScript that Flash 5 has given us to create an object-based structure.

As mentioned earlier, the fundamentally new thing about Flash 5 is the way it treats *everything* as an object, including graphics (via the magic that is the new `MovieClip` object). Although Flash doesn't directly support the advanced animation elements needed for game design, they can be built from scratch within the Flash environment. My system uses movie clips as the essential basic object, and makes each game element animate itself via ActionScript code embedded within the movie clip. This defines a *local* structure for each animated game element, but it doesn't define a *global* structure to put all the individual pieces in. The system gets over this by defining a hierarchy that uses the fact that Flash lets us embed movie clips within movie clips – or, more fundamentally, lets us have a hierarchy of independent timelines.

Like so many things, the game system doesn't really come alive until you've seen a proper example, and walked through a stepwise demonstration of how the game template was 'filled in' to create a game. My advice, then, is to read through this section on the game template once, picking up as much as you can, but then to look at the coded example to see the application of the theory, because that's what leads to real understanding. Hold tight!

GameSprites

First of all, I'd better explain my terminology. The word 'sprite' is used by Macromedia Director to describe something that isn't the same as the meaning I intend to convey when I use the same word. What I'm referring to is actually closer to what a game developer would call a 'sprite', but to avoid any confusion, I will call my version a **gameSprite**.

A gameSprite is a dynamic graphic that controls its own movement and appearance. It doesn't need the timeline it's sitting on to tell it what to do, because it can do all that itself. Once released onto the stage, the gameSprite will do whatever it needs to do, without any external helping hand. Finally, a gameSprite can modify its behavior, based upon rules that the game environment has set up. If we took our gameSprite and placed it into a slightly different environment with (say) lower gravity, or greater friction, then the gameSprite would know this and start following the new rules.

GameSprites animate themselves by using a new Flash 5 pathname called `this`. When we're using property-based animation, we animate by referring to an instance name and its property, like this:

```
myMovie._x = myMovie._x + 10;
```

The above code would move the instance `myMovie` ten pixels to the right by increasing the movie clip's `_x` property – but it requires us to know the instance name. The `this` path, on the other hand, refers to the timeline the command is issued from:

```
this._x = this._x + 10;
```

If we wrote this in a frame on `myMovie`'s timeline, then the movie clip itself will move: the movie clip is actually causing itself to animate! This is the basis of our gameSprite construction. By writing ActionScript within movie clips, using the `this` path as a target, we are causing movie clips to be in control of their own destiny!

The Game World

For gameSprites to work their magic, we have to set up a game 'world' that a gameSprite will understand. To do that, we need to set up a structured relationship between our world and the gameSprite, something like this:

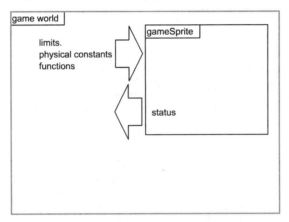

In this figure, the large box represents the game world, inside which is our gameSprite. The game world has to provide some information to the gameSprite as to how it's set up; this includes *limits*, *physical constants*, and *functions*. Similarly, the gameSprite will have to provide some information to the game world (or more likely, to other gameSprites in the world, rather than to the world itself) regarding what it's doing; this information is called its **status**. We'll discuss these ideas in detail in a moment, but first we have the more important task of tying all this back to Flash.

Paths

The game world is a Flash timeline, while a gameSprite is a timeline *inside* the game world – it will be a movie clip on the game world's timeline. The diagram represents this by placing gameSprite within the game world's box. For a gameSprite to get information from the game world, it would use this path:

```
_parent.information
```

If, on the other hand, the game world wanted to know anything from the gameSprite, it would use this path (where spriteName is the sprite's instance name):

```
spriteName.information
```

The use of the first of these is preferred, because no instance names are needed. Data is requested by a gameSprite from the _parent level (that is, the game world level), and if necessary it can be placed back there via the same path. If you think about it, that's how *our* world works: we interact with the world, rather than it interacting with us, because we are the things with intelligence. In our game world, the gameSprite has the intelligence, and it does all the data manipulation. The game world is just terrain to move around in, described by data.

Levels

What we have here, then, is a way of using Flash's ability to use nested timelines to represent two levels. The path of the game world will be either _root or _root.world, and any gameSprites within it are represented by a level beyond that: _root.spriteName or _root.world.spriteName respectively. Flash's timeline levels are being used to represent increasing detail.

We don't necessarily have to stop at _root.world.spriteName, because we could add all sorts of controlling movie clips within our gameSprites to modify their behavior (something I'll call **behavior movie clips** later on). Also, if we use the preferred path of _parent, we don't (in most cases) need to know the instance name of something in order to control it, and that frees us from a lot of bother.

When I'm designing my Flash games, I draw a lot of diagrams like the one above – they're the key to representing the complex structure of a Flash game in a simple way. In the object-oriented approach we're taking here, the diagram is showing two objects (the game world and the gameSprite), their relative positions in the game world hierarchy, and their interfaces (that is, the nature and content of the communication that must take place between them). In the ensuing discussion, the diagrams will underpin everything else, so here I'll go through each piece of information they contain in detail.

Limits

Limits are things that the gameSprite is not allowed to do. All game worlds must have at least one set of limits: the edges of the world, beyond which the gameSprite is not allowed to move. I will call these the **boundary limits**:

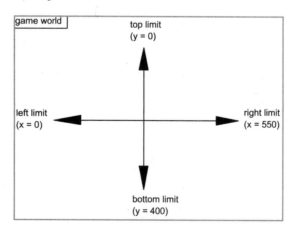

In the simplest type of game world, which consists of the Flash stage, these boundary limits refer to the size of the stage itself. The default stage size is 550 x 400, so the limits you would set are as shown above. The gameSprite would read these values from the world, and know that it mustn't cross those boundaries. For more complex games, there are other values that the sprite may need to know, such as its starting (or 'spawning') position – that is, the place where it's 'born' into the game world.

Physical Constants

The gameSprite will contain algorithms that set it in motion and cause it to stop. In the real world, we obey physical laws, such as gravity, force and acceleration relationships, and friction. We *could* build the values that tailor these laws into the gameSprite's algorithms themselves, so that it knows them as soon as it's spawned, but that's not a good idea for two reasons:

- The values may be different for different games. We want to make our gameSprite as modular as possible, so that we can drag and drop it into new games with different physics. By doing this, we also open up the possibility of defining a general gameSprite engine that we can just tweak and use afresh in new games.

- These physical 'constants' may change over time. Usually, we want our game to get harder and harder as it goes on. One of the easiest ways to do this is to make the game world easier for 'enemy' gameSprites to move within – we can reduce things like friction, or raise their maximum speed. The game world then becomes more inhospitable for the player, because the enemies appear to become more skilled.

The best way to tell the gameSprite what the physical constants in its world are is to make the gameSprite read them from the world each time it spawns.

Functions

As well as physical constants, we may sometimes want to set up whole new physical laws, or large tables of values. The way to do this is via a function. If, for example, we were modeling acceleration, the gameSprite would say to the game world, "My current velocity is *this* and the accelerative force acting on me is *that*. Given those two values, tell me what my new speed is."

GameSprite Status

We'll have more than one gameSprite within our world, and at some stage they are sure to need to communicate with one another. There are two ways to do this, depending on how many other gameSprites are likely to want the same information.

If there is a single gameSprite that has within itself a piece of information that many other gameSprites may want to know, we broadcast that information to the world by placing it in the world as soon as the originating gameSprite knows it. In effect, what we do is to make that information a special kind of game limit. In the game of Space Invaders, for example, all of the aliens want to know two things from the player's ship: "Where are you?" (so we can dive or fire at that position) and "Are you dead yet?" (so we know when we've won).

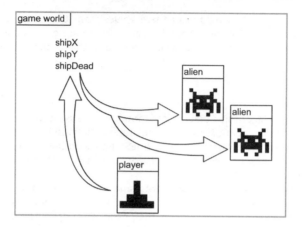

In the world above, the `player` gameSprite knows its own position thanks to its local variables `shipX` (x position) and `shipY` (y position). When the player dies, the `player` gameSprite will also set a Boolean value `shipDead = true`. If the `player` gameSprite makes these three pieces of data available to the game world on a constant basis (thus making it global data), then each `alien` can look at it with:

```
_parent.shipX
_parent.shipY
_parent.shipDead
```

> *Notice that transferring this information didn't require any instance names to be known by any of the gameSprites, which means that we can write generic routines that refer to a general game world.*

But we have a second communication option: if gameSprite A wants to know something from gameSprite B, *it has to ask B for that information*. This models what happens in the real world too: if I want to know where my brother is, I call him up and ask him – but to do that, I need to know his cellular phone number. In Flash, the equivalent of my brother's phone number is the path to clip B from clip A, and this can become problematic because an instance name is now required. Getting over this problem requires careful structuring of our game world to ensure that such data transfers happen in one direction only. (This is usually *from* a gameSprite controlled by the player, which is almost always the only gameSprite that the others are interested in, and therefore the only instance name that has to appear in the code.)

Another Level?

Sometimes, you want a level that's even more fundamental than the world level; I call this the **system level**. This looks after things that don't really belong in the game world, but which are required to set up Flash to be able to support the game. In a modern computer game, things such as initializing hardware, joystick support, and the 3D card would typically go here. My *Savior* game uses a system level because:

- The game world, including all the gameSprites, and everything else contained within it, scales itself (that is, it appears to zoom in and out). A more fundamental level was needed for things that I didn't *want* to scale with the world, such as the player's score.

- I used the system level to define the sound objects for the game, something we will touch on later.

Behavior Movie Clips

There is one final level of detail in our system: the things that go on inside the gameSprite itself. For that, we need to introduce the final block in this game-building system.

All intelligence is invested in our gameSprites. Inevitably, these can get quite complex, because they may be required to do several things at once. In general, a gameSprite may have to:

- Animate itself, making sure it's within the game world limits, at the same time as...

- Detecting collisions with any other gameSprites, at the same time as...

- Calculating where it wants to move in the next frame, based on its ultimate destination and game world physical constants, at the same time as...

- Taking input from the user

> *A gameSprite under the control of the user is sometimes called an* avatar, *from the Hindu word meaning 'a deity in human or animal form visiting the earth', but used by adventure gamers to mean 'human player in digital form visiting a virtual world'. Same concept, different levels.*

To be effective, the gameSprite has to do all these things *in every frame*. The code to do this could become quite tricky, to say the least, but there is another way: we can split up the gameSprite:

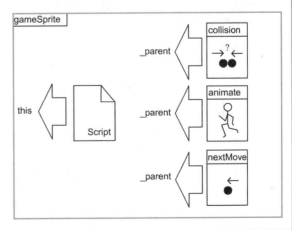

As well as ActionScript, we can embed further movie clips within the gameSprite that are dedicated to providing particular functionality, such as the things listed above. I call these **behavior movie clips**, because they control parts of the gameSprite's overall behavior within the game world.

A behavior is a nested movie clip, in the same way that the gameSprite itself is nested in the game world. To control the gameSprite's properties, or to set variables within it, the behavior movie clip uses the _parent path. To refer to the 'world' level, the behavior movie clip uses _parent._parent (that is, it goes up two levels). This is distinct from the ActionScript within the gameSprite, which (as stated above) would use the this path to impart control to itself.

There are three advantages to using behavior movie clips rather than handling everything using ActionScript code inside the gameSprite:

- **Modularity.** By splitting up the gameSprite into separate items, we simplify it. This also has advantages in reusability – we could, for example, use a 'collision' behavior in every gameSprite that needed it.

- **Parallel processing.** We can use the concept of nested timelines to perform several things at the same time. Each behavior is running at the same time as the gameSprite timeline, but separately from it, and each one is controlling particular parts of the gameSprite's behavior *at the same time as all the other behaviors are doing their thing*. Think of them as the crew of the good ship *gameSprite*: we have a sailor steering with the rudder (movement behavior), a sailor in the crow's nest looking out for land or other ships (collision detection behavior), and so on.

- **Creating complex gameSprite behavior via the interaction of simple components.** Each behavior tells the gameSprite to perform a particular function. If these functions overlap, the behaviors will be added together. For example, if we had a behavior movie clip that shrank the size of our gameSprite, and another that made it vibrate, the gameSprite would shrink and vibrate at the same time. By creating more useful interactions, we will begin to do what nature does: create complex (and even chaotic) behavior via the interaction of a few simple, separate rules.

And that's the full game system! Although there's a lot to grasp, bear in mind that there are really only three components: the game world, the gameSprite, and the behavior movie clip. Once you've used them all a few times, they will start to feel like second nature. You'll see the theory in this chapter start to creep into your web designs, and when that happens, the competition will be in trouble!

Creative and Design Input

After all that theory, I think we need to let our brains get back to their normal temperature. As they cool down, we can move away from the technical and consider instead the aesthetic: what will our game look like, and what should it do? Fundamentally, what makes a good game? I've seen lots of Flash games that look like they use cool ActionScript techniques, but the game designs themselves are playing second fiddle. The world is already full of top-heavy Shockwave games that have designs like:

> *"We'll have an octopus (rendered in a Disney style) throwing cans of your brand of soft drink, which the player's diver has to catch in an oversized clam shell. This is a great idea because your drink is called 'Aqua', and... well... divers and octopi swim in water!"*

I'll eat my words if this concept turns out to be a huge hit on the next generation of game consoles, but somehow I doubt that will happen. This is the game of 'catch', with lots of added cheese. If you *do* try this at home, please treat it as a practice attempt! By all means, have rich graphics if the client insists, but don't implement them until the gameplay is sorted out, using stick figures and outlines if you have to.

For the game I built for this chapter, I drew inspiration from what I believe to be the three all-time classic shoot 'em ups: Defender, Galaga, and Asteroids. I haven't just copied chunks of them to create some kind of Frankenstein game, though – I wanted to extend the genre by adding features that Flash excels at, but which just weren't possible at the time those games were coded. By definition, retro gaming is not new, but part of it is surprisingly current: the limitations and facilities that the early developers had are nearly identical to those we see when we use Flash to create games for the Internet.

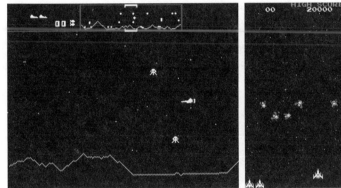  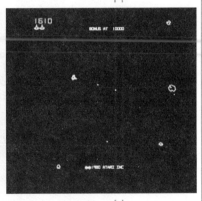

In writing this chapter, I looked at the basic principles that these classics followed, and tried to form a list of why I thought they worked so well. Here's the 'good game design' checklist that I came up with:

- The game must get harder with time, or the player should see a progression with time. In early games, this was simply a matter of going up game levels, but more recently it's included character development, being allowed into different areas of a game, and getting more advanced rules to follow.

- The player should have well-defined goals.

- The game should show a believable (or at least, self-consistent) world. In particular, the player should intuitively be able to see the rules the world is using (unless discovering them is the aim of the game). Note that neither 'believable' nor 'self-consistent' means 'accurate'. One of the main concerns in game design is how little of the real world we can get away with putting into our world, and still fool the player that they are 'there'.

- The game must be responsive, and this must have priority over graphical appearance (games that prioritize appearance are the epitome of what I call the 'top heavy' approach).

- Players must believe that when they lose, they lost fairly, and they should always be able to see the failure coming. If there's an alien diving at me, I should be certain that when it kills my ship, the reason I died is that I didn't move away fast enough, and I was given the chance to look ahead and avoid this.

- The player should believe that the opponent is *intelligent* and not just increasingly erratic. For example, if in the octopus game I described, I died because I was at the far left and *by chance* the octopus threw a can to the right of the screen, where I had no chance of getting to it, this would be bad design. If, on the other hand, I *knew* that there was a particular position I should try to keep to (the middle), and I got the impression that the octopus was *intelligently* trying to make me move away from there, I would feel like I was playing against a real opponent. (This is actually a very subtle thing to achieve, because in most games, the opponent gains in intelligence based on one or more random values that, on average, increase with time to make the alien faster, or the tennis player a better hitter, or whatever.)

- It must be possible to get better at the game with time. (This is another good reason to avoid any erratic behavior on the part of the opponent, which is difficult for the player to overcome even with practice.) This is the main cause of a player wanting to have another go, and the mark of a well thought out game.

> *This is the first of my golden rules of game design: know what makes a good game in the genre you are targeting. Do this before you start to code it – if you don't, you'll only look at what's easy to create, and miss the important question: "Will people play it?"*

I looked at how my three chosen games worked, at the rules they seemed to be following, and at what made them tick. A few points soon became apparent:

- Asteroids uses simple line graphics. If I could do the same, I'd be taking advantage of something that Flash is actually *very* good at: drawing vectors.

- Defender and Galaga use small sprites throughout, so the fact that I'm limited to doing the same in Flash is no problem.

- Defender and Galaga use game worlds that require scrolling, but the hardware they ran on at the time didn't support it. The games got over this by using a line representing a moving landscape and a star field respectively. In each case, they fooled the player that they were in a moving world just by moving little dots (stars) or the outlines of hills (drawn using lines). Flash is good at drawing *both* these things, because they're vector-based.

- Asteroids' spaceship rotates and thrusts around the screen in a manner that's a bit more realistic than the simple left-right or up-down motion afforded by the other two games. However, it doesn't scroll when you move off the edge of the screen – you simply reappear on other side, in a wraparound effect. I thought that Flash could do better than either scrolling or wrapping, but I wasn't sure exactly what.

The next stage was to start sketching ideas for my game. Quite apart from the fact that vectors are easier than bitmaps for Flash to handle, I was warming to them for design reasons too. Not many other Flash games have gone down this route; they tend to choose small symbols that consist of both vectors *and* fills. I tried drawing some alien spacecraft using lines alone, and came up with these:

> *This is the second of my golden rules of game design: don't be put off by limitations (usually, speed constraints caused by graphics). Look at what you* can *do, and build that into your design by simplifying and abstracting your world and the characters in it.*

The fact that I was using simple vectors meant that Flash would be able to do a bit more than just move these graphics about: it could also *scale* and *rotate* them pretty fast too. I figured that instead of scrolling the screen as things moved, I could *zoom out* (in the same way that a camera would when it wants to capture two people running in opposite directions). Also, instead of boring bitmaps, which move like cardboard cutouts, I thought that all the pieces in my game could spin at any angle. Taken together, this spinning and zooming would make for an outwardly simple and old-fashioned looking game, but once you played it and saw it moving, you'd see some pretty cool interactive animation at work.

That sounds like a plan, then, but notice that at this stage I haven't laid down a detailed specification (as I certainly would do with a web site design). Although the client may impose what will appear in a game, and give me a theme to work to, I prefer to leave the actual coding open because playability *can't* be designed in. You have to experiment as you go along, making the changes you see fit as development progresses.

In the Beginning...

To recap, I want to build a game with a retro feel, but under the hood I want there to be effects going on that outstrip what could be actually achieved by older games. I've decided that it will be a shoot 'em up, but I want the game to have enemies that move in a more intelligent way than the 'move down the screen' attacks typified by things like Space Invaders.

Let's start at the very beginning. We need to create a world, and fill it with physical properties that describe the digital terrain our gameSprites will move within. The Greeks tell us that God is pure thought pondering itself, but in my game world, *I'm* God, and I say that He's a little bit more hands-on than that. We need to look at the practicalities of our world, and ask lots of *what* questions:

- What do I want to happen, and can I break these things down?

- What will be inside my world, and what will it want to know from me?

- What can I get away with *not* including in the world?

There is a legend regarding the video game Defender. Its creator, Eugene Jarvis, spent months trying to create a new game for the manufacturer, Williams, and all he had to show at the end of this period was the scrolling landscape. Finally, when there were only a couple of days to go before the deadline, it all came to him, and he coded the aliens and the player's ship in a few hours. The lesson we can learn is that the game world is *the most important thing*. It's the bedrock on which the game is built. Once that's working, the rest will follow; if it's wrong, you won't get far.

In this chapter we have the benefit of hindsight, so I can show you in advance what the image in my head actually looked like. If you haven't been tempted already, have a play with the game in `savior.fla` before you continue. Here's a list of things that we need in order to create the world for this game:

- We need to build general rotation functions that allow a gameSprite to spin around on its axis.

- We need rules that a gameSprite can follow so that it can rotate itself to face another gameSprite.

- We need to know how to scale the game world in or out, so that all the gameSprites are always on the screen.

If we tried to build all this at once within a single FLA, it would be a pretty complex task. Instead, it's better to identify the main difficulties you will face as god of your game world, and tackle each one separately, via a test FLA. I identified the first and second bullet points above as being the most difficult problems to solve, and decided that I had to deal with them first. If I couldn't... well, the game relies heavily on these two things, and if I couldn't do them, I would have to go away and rethink my plans.

Rotational Dynamics

I chose to build rotational dynamics into my world, because it's computationally intensive to work out motion in an arc, as opposed to motion in a straight line. This demonstrates an important aspect of creating game worlds: the need to reduce complex calculations by calculating difficult things before the game starts. Flight simulators and their kin use pre-calculated tables to work out complex things like "What is the drag coefficient for this mode of flight?" or "At this speed and with this bomb loading, what is the minimum angle for the aircraft to stall?" These so-called **lookup tables** are used in many games to avoid complex, real-time calculations without having to resort to simplification (which would reduce the level of reality in the game).

The game of Asteroids involves no real rotational dynamics. The asteroids don't actually rotate at all, and the player's ship is nothing more than a movie clip of pre-drawn frames that, when seen in order, imply a rotating spacecraft.

For our game, I was looking for something a little more advanced, because I wanted to show you a way to apply complex math in real time, without slowing down your world model. Take a look at `savior_test01.fla`, in which you can rotate the ship with the left/right arrow keys, and thrust with the up arrow key. This was the test I used to define the player's ship, its interfaces with the user, a basic game world, and the rotational dynamics that the world will impose. This FLA demonstrates nicely how my world is set up, and it's summarized in this diagram:

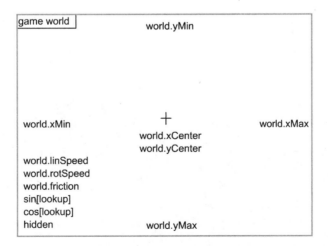

The first thing you should know is that this diagram was sketched before I wrote the ActionScript (which appears on frame 1 of the `_root` timeline), and you can see how useful it was simply by noticing how the script describes the diagram almost verbatim.

I created an object called `world` to hold all of the game world parameters. Although I could have defined them as separate variables, the use of an object makes for structure: I can *see* they are all world-level variables thanks to their names, which are always `world.something`.

Limits

`.xMin` and `.xMax` define my world's width limits.
`.yMin` and `.yMax` define my world's height limits.
`.xCenter` and `.yCenter` define my world's center (which will be used as the *spawning point* of the player's gameSprite).

Physical Constants

`.linSpeed` defines my maximum linear speed.
`.rotSpeed` defines my maximum rotational speed (that is, how fast my gameSprites can turn).
`.friction` defines a frictional constant that will slow down motion, and models the sum of all the retarding forces on the gameSprite.

The rest of the values aren't part of the `world` object because they're not world limits or constants. Rather, they're things that help me to build up physical rules.

Functions

To work out how the player's ship should move, I'll need to perform some trigonometry, and that's where my lookup tables enter the scene. In the first frame of the game movie, Flash will run through these functions to calculate the lookup tables, by storing the sines and cosines of a range of angles in a couple of arrays:

`sin[]` defines a lookup table of pre-calculated sine values, from 0 to 360 degrees, in increments of 1 degree.

`cos[]` defines a lookup table of pre-calculated cosine values, from 0 to 360 degrees, in increments of 1 degree.

> *The* Math *object's trigonometric functions use radians rather than degrees, where π (that is, pi, or 3.141...) radians are equal to 180 degrees. Mathematicians use radians in advanced geometry because π appears a lot in their calculations, and scientists and engineers use them for the same reason, but the rest of us find degrees easier because we can't visualize angles like 0.7854 radians very well (it's 45 degrees, or half a right angle). For this reason, and because array indexes have to be in whole numbers, I have expressed my sine/cosine tables in degrees.*

Other

`hidden` is a value that I added during development, and it represents the (x, y) position of an off-screen point where I can place something that I want to be hidden. It's better to define this as a variable rather than just using (-100, -100), for example, because it's one of those funny things you'll come back to six months later and think, "Why on earth am I putting that gameSprite there?"

The Movie

Here's the code listing for frame 1 of the `_root` movie clip in full:

```
// Create and initialize global objects
// World setup
world = new Object();
world = {xMax:550, xMin:0, yMax:400, yMin:0,
        ➡linSpeed:7, rotSpeed:5, friction:0.98};

with (world) {
    world.xCenter = (xMax-xMin)/2;
    world.yCenter = (yMax-yMin)/2;
}

// Misc constants
hidden = -100;

// Create and populate trig lookup array object
sin = new Array(360);
cos = new Array(360);
for (i = 0; i <= 360; i++) {
    radian = (i/360) * 2 * Math.PI;
    sin[i] = Math.sin(radian);
    cos[i] = Math.cos(radian);
}
```

Notice that even now, complexity is starting to creep in. The number of values we have is already as high as we'd normally expect to define in a complete Flash web site, and we've barely scratched the surface yet! That's why we need a game creation system to get anywhere fast.

The second thing to notice is that, as well as using movie clips as gameSprite objects, I'm using Flash 5's data objects (arrays, and the `Object` object) to create structured data variable management. If you ever wanted to see Flash 5 ActionScript's advances in object-oriented programming being used, you've come to the right place, because the final game makes great use of them.

In the Library for `savior_test01.fla`, you'll find three movie clips:

Because I'll be using movie clips for different types of task, I've organized my library names around a prefix system that differentiates them. 'ma' means 'movie clip ActionScript', and refers to a movie clip that contains only ActionScript only – typically, a behavior movie clip. 'sp' means 'sprite movie clip', and refers to a movie clip that will act as a gameSprite.

The Spaceship

The most important thing here is the `sp.player` movie clip, which defines the player's spaceship. Let's look at its object diagram:

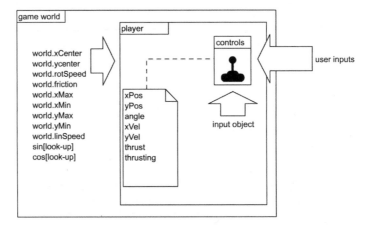

The gameSprite for the player's ship initializes its starting position by looking at `world.xCenter` and `world.yCenter` from the game world. It also takes in `world.rotSpeed` to define how fast it can rotate, and `world.linSpeed` to define how fast it can move. `world.friction` is used to define the retarding forces on the ship, and it reads the world limits, `world.xMax`, `.xMin`, `.yMax`, `.yMin`, so that it knows the extents of the game world. Finally, it makes use of the `sin` and `cos` lookup tables in its internal calculations.

The player's ship also creates its own internal variables: `xPos` and `yPos` (its current position in the game world), `angle` (its current angle or orientation), `xVel` and `yVel` (its current velocities in the x and y directions), `thrust` (the current thrust on the ship, moving it forward), and `thrusting` (a Boolean that tells us whether the player is actually firing the engines right now). It further employs an embedded behavior movie clip called ma.playerControls to interface with the user at the keyboard, and this association uses another user-defined object that goes by the name input.

The main ActionScript code that drives the player's gameSprite is in frame 2 of the movie clip called sp.player. It uses properties of the input object (.leftPress, .rightPress, .thrustPress, and .firePress) that will be set to true if the key on the keyboard corresponding to the action in question is currently pressed.

Maneuvering

The first code block in frame 2 handles the rotation of the ship. If we want to rotate left (that is, counterclockwise), we have to *decrease* the angle (by subtracting our rotation speed from it). If we want to rotate right (clockwise), we *increase* our angle by adding world.rotSpeed to it:

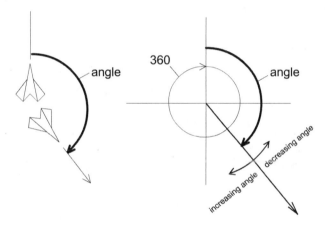

There's a problem, though. Because a full circular rotation is 360 degrees, we need to limit our angle to the range 0 to 360, and that's what the second part of this code does:

```
// Calculate new ship rotation
if (input.leftPress) {
    angle = angle - rotSpeed;
}

if (input.rightPress) {
    angle = angle + rotSpeed;
}

// Limit angle between 0 and 360 degrees
if (angle < 0) {
    angle = angle + 360;
} else if (angle > 360) {
    angle = angle - 360;
}
```

That's the easy bit done; now for the harder part. In Flash, we can only move our ship in two directions: left and right (the x plane, via changes in the _x property), or up and down (the y plane, via changes in _y). What if the ship's thrusting at an angle to these two planes?

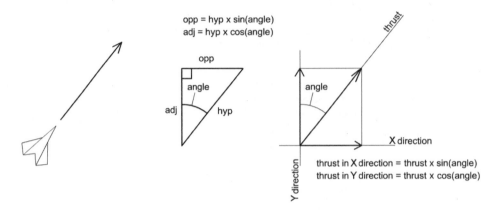

opp = hyp x sin(angle)
adj = hyp x cos(angle)

opp
angle
adj   hyp

angle
X direction
Y direction
thrust in X direction = thrust x sin(angle)
thrust in Y direction = thrust x cos(angle)

thrust

Some fairly simple trigonometry comes to our aid here, because we can calculate the two components of our ship's velocity by looking at its angle. By forming a right-angled triangle, where the ship's direction (or thrust vector) forms the hypotenuse, we can calculate the x component and the y component by using sine and cosine respectively. We want to limit our ship to linSpeed, so that comes into the equation as well, but all we're doing here is splitting out the x and y velocity components (xVel and yVel) by looking at the ship's angle.

Before we look at the code, one last thing to watch out for is that back in math class you used *Cartesian* x and y coordinates, in which the value of y increases as you go *up* the page. Flash uses web-based x and y directions, where y increases *downwards*, so a minus sign crops up in the yVel term when you might not have been expecting it. Because we're using a lookup table, using trigonometry doesn't slow us down. (Calculating sine and cosine values in real time requires Flash to use a long and processor intensive function, which we definitely don't want to happen.)

```
// Calculate new velocity vectors
thrusting = false;
linSpeed = _parent.world.linSpeed;

if (input.thrustpress) {
    thrusting = true;
    if (Math.abs(xVel) < linSpeed) {
        xVel = xVel + (thrust * _parent.sin[angle]);
    }
    if (Math.abs(yVel) < linSpeed) {
        yVel = yVel - (thrust * _parent.cos[angle]);
    }
}
```

We now have to change our ship's position (xPos, yPos), by adding our velocity terms (xVel, yVel) calculated above. To model friction, I multiply the velocities by the friction physical constant. Since this is less than one, it will tend to slow us down over time:

```
// Model friction (reduces velocity over time)
xVel = xVel * _parent.world.friction;
yVel = yVel * _parent.world.friction;

// Calculate new ship positions
xPos = xPos + xVel;
yPos = yPos + yVel;
```

The only thing that remains before we actually move our ship is to check that the new position we'll go to won't take us out of the game world. If it does, this code will 'wrap' us around to the other side of the stage, so that if we scoot off the left-hand side of the screen, the if statements will reset our position to the right-hand side:

```
if (xPos > _parent.world.xMax) {
    xPos = _parent.world.xMin;
}
if (xPos < _parent.world.xMin) {
    xPos = _parent.world.xMax;
}
if (yPos > _parent.world.yMax) {
    yPos = _parent.world.yMin;
}
if (yPos < _parent.world.yMin) {
    yPos = _parent.world.yMax;
}
```

In terms of calculation, we're all done. We can now move our gameSprite by drawing it at the new position and angle:

```
// Animate ship based on latest values
this._rotation = angle;
this._x = xPos;
this._y = yPos;
```

While playing about with savior_test01.fla, you'll see that the ship has a smoke plume behind it, which is created with the sp.exhaust movie clip. I used this as a visual cue to make sure that the ship was correctly converting the thrust vector into the x and y components, but it does look rather pretty. It doesn't make it into the final game, so I won't discuss it, but feel free to dissect and use it in your own projects if you like.

The best way to analyze how the FLA is working is to go into debug mode and see how the variables change as the ship moves about. Because there are two rather large arrays (sin and cos), you'll see the debugger window appear to lock up for a short time if you try to look at the variables in _root, but wait a few seconds and everything will be fine again.

In the final game (savior.fla), the player's gameSprite is almost identical to the one we've looked at here, except that it has interfaces with the bullet sprite as well. If you look at the final game, you'll see how I incorporated the results of this test FLA into it.

Facing Down the Enemy

The second thing that we want is for one gameSprite to be able to rotate so that it faces another. The alien ships in the final game use this when they're moving towards the player's ship. I think I feel some more trigonometry coming on.

Have a look at `savior_02test.fla`. *This* FLA uses a behavior movie clip called ma.point that makes any movie clip it's embedded in rotate until it's pointing at the current mouse position. ma.point isn't actually the brains behind this functionality, though, because it's calling a function named `arctan` that's defined in the ma.FastTrigLibrary movie clip. I'll go through the `arctan` function, because it's used in the main game, and it's the most complex part of `savior_02test.fla`. Open ma.FastTrigLibrary, and look at the script attached to frame 1.

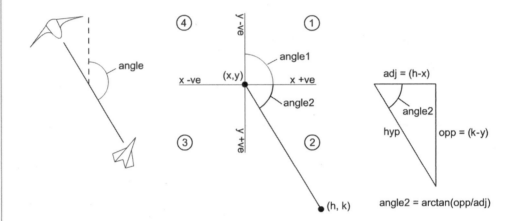

Suppose that we have our alien at a point (x, y), and our ship at (h, k). Our alien needs to know `angle`, because if it orientates itself to this direction, it will be facing our ship. Now, this angle can be between 0 and 360 degrees, but if we try to draw a right-angled triangle, we get stuck. The calculation will only get us `angle2` in the above figure, which is between 0 and 90 degrees, and equal to arctan((h-x)/(k-y)).

We can work out `angle1` by looking at which *quadrant* point (h, k) is in, with respect to point (x, y). We can determine this by looking at whether x is bigger or smaller than h, and whether y is bigger or smaller than k. This will tell us whether angle1 is 0 (quadrant 1), 90 (2), 180 (3), or 270 (4). This test is carried out in the first part of the `arctan` function:

```
function arcTan (x, y, h, k) {
    // Returns the angle of the vector[(x,y),(h,k)]
    // First work out angle to nearest 90 degrees by looking
    //   at quadrants...
```

```
if (h > x) {
    if (k < y) {
        // Quadrant 1
        angle1 = 0;
    } else {
        // Quadrant 2
        angle1 = 90;
    }
} else {
    if (k < y) {
        // Quadrant 4
        angle1 = 270;
    } else {
        // Quadrant 3
        angle1 = 180;
    }
}
```

That done, we need to find out what angle2 is – and as usual, there's a problem. If k and y are equal, (k-y) will be zero, and attempting to divide by zero will result in an error. However, this only happens when angle1 is 90 or 270 degrees and angle2 is 0 degrees, so in this case we can just set angle2 to zero without performing the calculation.

If h and x are equal, there *shouldn't* be a problem, because zero divided by anything is still zero. However, my career has been blighted by assuming this rule to be implemented properly (I had enormous problems with an industrial, computer-based control system that evaluated it as infinity), so I'm always rather wary of it. I therefore set angle2 directly to zero in this case as well.

Finally, if either the adjacent side or the opposite side (but not both) of the triangle has a length given by a negative number, the tangent calculation will work out the 'wrong' angle, so I've done a little extra trigonometry at the end of this function. This handles the situation by switching the sides around in the calculation, and making sure that tan always stays positive with the built-in Math.abs function. (This has the additional effect of resulting in a lookup table that's half the size it might otherwise be.)

```
// Work out tangent of the angle of the triangle of which
//   our vector is the hypotenuse...
adjacent = h - x;
opposite = k - y;
if ((adjacent == 0) || (opposite == 0)) {
    tan = 0;
} else {
    tan = opposite / adjacent;
    if (tan < 0) {
        tan = 1 / tan;
    }
    tan = Math.abs(tan);
}
```

To calculate `angle2`, I need to evaluate `Math.arctan(tan)`, but as usual I don't *want* to do this, because it's processor intensive. Instead, I've used a ladder of `if...else if...else` statements that will give me a result via comparison with pre-calculated values. This provides me `angle2` to the nearest five degrees, which is accurate enough for the effect I'm trying to create.

```
// Now work out remaining angle (via a lookup table)
//   to the nearest 5 degrees (which is a good enough
//   approximation for most games)...
if (tan > 5.67) {
   angle2 = 80;
} else if (tan > 2.75) {
   angle2 = 70;
} else if (tan > 1.73) {
   angle2 = 60;
} else if (tan > 1.19) {
   angle2 = 50;
} else if (tan > 0.84) {
   angle2 = 40;
} else if (tan > 0.58) {
   angle2 = 30;
} else if (tan > 0.36) {
   angle2 = 20;
} else if (tan > 0.18) {
   angle2 = 10;
} else {
   angle2 = 0;
}
   return angle1 + angle2;
}
```

Putting it Together

Once I'd built these two routines and got them working at a fast enough rate to be used in a game, I could say with certainty that I had the basic code to power the game world for the game I had in mind. All of which brings us to the game itself.

`savior.fla` contains the final game, but I'll go through the landmark intermediate steps that took me to it. Where an FLA in the sequence added nothing of importance, I haven't included it as one of the files for you to look at. This is the reason why the file `savior01.fla` isn't included, but `savior02.fla` is.

Savior02.fla

This was my first working attempt at a game world that scaled itself to fit everything on screen. Have a look at the Library in this FLA:

The sp.alien gameSprite doesn't *do* anything yet – it's just there to give a better visual indication of what's going on when the scaling takes place, and whether it updates quickly enough with a few graphic symbols in it.

The player folder contains things you've already seen in savior_test01.fla.

The world folder contains the basis of the game world, and it's the major addition to this FLA over the two previous test files. The game world defined by the movie clips in this folder is able to *self-scale*. Although this may seem more impressive than all the trigonometric mumbo-jumbo from the last section, it's actually far easier in principle, because scaling is something that Flash can do naturally. It works like this...

The game world consists of a movie clip called mc.world that represents the extents of the world. It also contains a second movie clip called mc.frame, which is a simple square outline, although it's not seen in the final FLA because its _visible property is set to false. What the frame does is to set a minimum size ('original size' in the diagram below) that the world starts at. The ma.worldScale behavior movie clip will always try to keep the world at this size by looking at the world's _height and _width properties.

If our ship goes outside the frame, it will change the world's _height or _width property (because it's embedded in the world, and therefore a part of it). This happens by virtue of some new code in frame 2 of the sp.player movie clip:

```
max_XPos = Math.abs(xPos)+_parent.world.maxS;
max_yPos = Math.abs(yPos)+_parent.world.maxS;
if (max_xPos>max_yPos) {
    _root.gameSize = max_xPos;
} else {
    _root.gameSize = max_yPos;
}
```

The ma.worldScale behavior will see this, and *shrink* the entire world by multiplying the _xscale and _yscale properties by (original size)/(new size), to scale it back down to its original size. The scaling routine is always working, so it's constantly scaling the world to make sure it stays the same physical size, resulting in a zoom in/zoom out effect.

> *Is that an idea to take away for a totally new web site zoom out/in navigation scheme? I think it might be!*

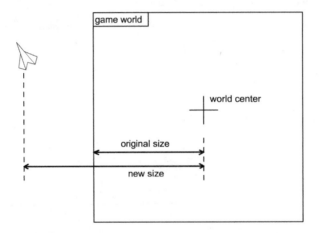

Once you know how the scaling functionality is going to work, the ActionScript to do it is surprisingly easy. Have a look at the ma.worldScale behavior movie clip, which will scale any movie clip it is placed into by controlling the properties of its _parent (in this case, mc.world). The whole zooming function is actually done in three short frames of ActionScript code.

Frame 1 simply initializes a variable called worldSize with our original world size. This will be the size of our world's enclosing frame, mc.frame. Our world will always be a perfect square, so only _height is used, because _width is identical:

```
worldSize = _parent._height;
```

Frame 2 creates two variables, xSize and ySize, which are the world's _width and _height respectively. It then takes the bigger of the two and sets it to a new variable called size ('new size' in the diagram above):

```
xSize = _parent._width;
ysize = _parent._height;
if (xSize > ySize) {
   size = xSize;
} else {
   size = ySize;
}
```

Then it's simply a matter of creating a scaling factor and applying it to the `_parent` via the `_xscale` and `_yscale` properties:

```
scale = worldSize / size;
_parent._xscale = _parent._xscale * scale;
_parent._yscale = _parent._yscale * scale;
```

There's one last issue: as our player pilots his ship back towards the center of the world, causing the world to zoom *in*, there's a chance that the outermost thing in the `world` object will be a blinking star, causing our zoom function to follow not the ship gameSprite, but the star. To avoid this, the stars are *outside* the world object, but they still need to know the scaling factor so that they can zoom in/out to keep up with the world. That's what the last line does:

```
// Pipe out scale factor to _root
_root.scale = scale;
```

Frame 3 simply jumps back to frame 2, causing these routines to run constantly.

The starfield folder contains two simple movie clips that control the blinking star field. If you've understood everything so far, you'll have no difficulty working these out – they use very similar techniques. I'll leave you to examine them in your own time, but as a quick hint, remember that the star field is *outside* the `world` object, and needs to scale itself constantly with:

```
this._xscale = this._xscale * _root.scale
this._yscale = this._yscale * _root.scale
```

These lines appear in frame 1 of sp.starfield, and frame 2 simply loops back to this frame.

The score and level text is simply a pair of dummy text fields that I placed in the FLA to prove that they wouldn't scale with the rest of the world.

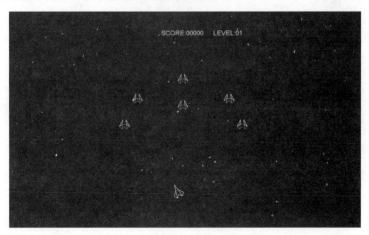

As you experiment with this FLA, you might notice that the ship seems to move more sluggishly than it does in the final game. The world parameters in `savior02.fla` haven't yet been fine tuned (an important final exercise), so issues like gameSprite speed haven't been addressed.

Savior03.fla

savior03.fla adds the aliens and animates the scoring system. It also includes the ability to fire at the aliens, but they can't kill you yet, which seems a little unfair to say the least. The important new features in this FLA are:

- Integration of all the math as a movie clip, ma.fastTrigFunctions, which you can see in the screenshot below at the top left corner of the stage.

- Animation of the aliens, and a collision detection behavior movie clip called ma.hitTest. Almost every video game will have one of these, so it's definitely something to look at later.

- A system based on smart clips that involves a single alien capable of taking several different guises and skill levels, to give the impression of multiple alien types. (This is another cool trick to dissect if you want to build your own games, because it lets you code a *general* gameSprite type, then tweak its behavior per instance with smart clips to create apparently separate game characters.)

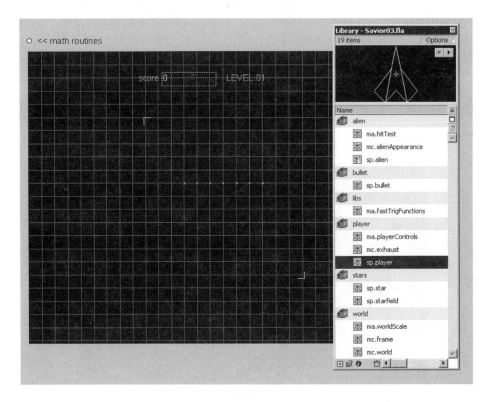

The Aliens

OK, aliens first. As well as using a number of values and functions from the `world` object, an alien will look at the player's `xPos` and `yPos` values to find out where the player is. You'll notice that the first few variables in the alien gameSprite object are identical to the player gameSprite object – it's always a good idea to standardize objects as far as possible, because this lets you reuse your behavior movie clips, and also lets you reuse code generally.

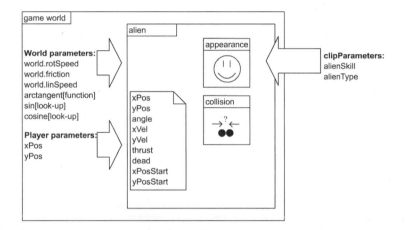

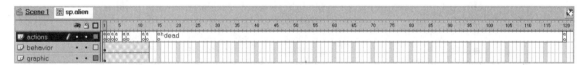

The sp.alien movie clip has a fun-packed timeline, with lots of good stuff in it! As you can tell from its icon in the Library, it's a smart clip, and if you select any of the aliens on the stage (they're on frame 2 of the mc.world clip) and bring up the Clip Parameters panel (Window > Panels > Clip Parameters), you will see the following:

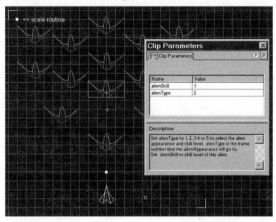

To change the value of either of these parameters, simply click on the Value field and enter a new number. The parameter can then be used in any scripts within the movie clip as a variable that will be initialized at the value you have just set. So, although our aliens all have the same ActionScript, each instance has the alienSkill and alienType variables set to particular values.

> For more information about creating and using smart clips, see Brendan Dawes' chapter.

Let's look at how the scripts in sp.alien work. Frame 1 initializes the alien's xPosStart and yPosStart variables to the _x and _y property values of the position in which it finds itself on the stage. Why? Because (as in most games) the alien never really dies – it simply 'pretends' to die by disappearing for a short time, and then re-spawning at its original starting point. Ultimately, therefore, shooting the aliens is a pointless exercise! I also set the scale values to zero, which means that the aliens initially have zero size, and are therefore too small to be seen:

```
// Initialize initial position in formation
xPosStart = this._x;
yPosStart = this._y;
this._xscale = 0;
this._yscale = 0;
```

Frame 2 is the initialization frame that the alien will jump back to just before it re-spawns, and it's labeled "init". This is where our smart clip parameters alienSkill and alienType are used to personalize each alien instance. You'll see that the speed at which the alien can rotate (rotSpeed) and its thrusting force (and therefore its acceleration) are modified by alienSkill. The alien's appearance is defined by an embedded movie clip called mc.alienAppearance that has a number of frames – each containing a particular alien graphic – and an instance name of alien. alienType refers to a particular graphic on a frame within mc.alienAppearance that's equal to the value of alienType, so to set the appearance, all we have to do is say alien.gotoAndStop(alienType). Simple!

```
// Initialize alien data
rotSpeed = _parent.world.rotSpeed * alienSkill;
angle = 0;
xVel = 0;
yVel = 0;
xPos = xPosStart;
yPos = yPosStart;
thrust = alienSkill;
dead = false;

// Set initial appearance
alien.gotoAndStop(alienType);
this._xscale = 0;
this._yscale = 0;
this._x = xPos;
this._y = yPos;
this._rotation = angle;
```

Frames 3 and 4 contain the *spawning* routine, which produces a little animation in which the aliens spin as they grow bigger. Frame 3 simply adds 5 to the scaling factors, making the alien slightly bigger. It also adds 18 to the rotation value, to give the spin. This keeps happening thanks to a gotoAndPlay command in frame 4, until the scaling factor has reached full size (100), at which stage we're able to jump to the "readyLoop" frame (frame 6):

```
// Spawn routine
// Scale it up over time...
this._xscale = this._xscale + 5;
this._yscale = this._yscale + 5;
this._rotation = this._rotation + 18;

if (this._xscale == 100) {
    gotoAndPlay ("readyLoop");
}
```

Frame 6 simply thinks of a random number between 0 and 1, and if it's greater than 0.999, the alien will start to dive and seek out the player's ship. The chances of this happening are once every thousand frames per alien, which is a bit high, but the figures used here are for proving purposes only. Frame 7 is a loopback to frame 6, so the two frames will constantly look at the random result until they can jump to "huntLoop" (frame 11):

```
// Stay put unless ready to dive
if (Math.random() > 0.999) {
    gotoAndPlay ("huntLoop");
}
```

Frame 11 contains the real brains behind the alien's behavior. In fact, you've already seen a lot of this code in the two test FLAs, so although this script might look intimidating at first, there's not much new here. Frame 12 loops back to frame 11, so the latter is executed constantly until the alien is shot.

Frame 11's first action is to get the player's position. The player's ship has an instance name player, so the path to it is _parent.player:

```
// Acquire player's position
targetX = _parent.player.xPos;
targetY = _parent.player.yPos;
```

The alien constantly attempts to face the player's ship, and does so via a call to the arcTan function we created in the second test FLA (savior_test02.fla) earlier:

```
// Point to player
targetAngle = _root.fn.arcTan(xPos, yPos, targetX, targetY);
errorAngle = targetAngle - angle;
```

```
      if (Math.abs(errorAngle) > 5) {
          if ((errorAngle>0) && (errorAngle<180) || (errorAngle<-180)) {
             angle = angle + rotSpeed;
          } else {
             angle = angle - rotSpeed;
          }
      }

      if (angle > 360) {
         angle = angle - 360;
      }

      if (angle < 0) {
         angle = angle + 360;
      }
```

The rest of the script is very similar to the code we used to control the player's ship in savior_test01.fla – in fact, there's really only one difference. The aliens base their velocity on how far they are away from the player: the further away they are, the harder they'll thrust, up to the maximum speed in linSpeed:

```
      // Calculate new velocity vectors
      // See how far away we are from our target (roughly)
      //  and base our linear speed on that...
      xDist = Math.abs(targetX - xPos);
      yDist = Math.abs(targetY - yPos);
      if (xDist > yDist) {
         linSpeed = xDist / 30;
      } else {
         linSpeed = yDist / 30;
      }

      // If we're not going faster than the max speed already,
      //  fire our engines...
      if (Math.abs(xVel) < linSpeed) {
         xVel = xVel + (thrust * _root.fn.sine(angle));
      }
      if (Math.abs(yVel) < linSpeed) {
         yVel = yVel - (thrust * _root.fn.cosine(angle));
      }

      // Model friction (reduces velocity over time)
      xVel = xVel * _parent.world.friction;
      yVel = yVel * _parent.world.friction;

      // Calculate new ship position
      xPos = xPos + xVel;
      yPos = yPos + yVel;

      // Animate alien based on calculated values
```

```
this._rotation = angle;
this._x = xPos;
this._y = yPos;
```

Getting Hit

How does the alien die? Well, a check is constantly being made to see if it has hit the player's bullet via the behavior movie clip ma.hitTest. This will cause the alien timeline to jump to frame 15 (labeled "dead"), where the alien will play dead (that is, it will disappear by becoming a movie clip with nothing in it) until frame 120, where it will jump back to frame 2 to re-spawn:

```
gotoAndPlay ("init");
```

Have a look at the sp.bullet movie clip as well, to see how that works, and how it interacts with the alien's collision detection behavior in ma.hitTest, which is an extremely simple behavior that uses a single conditional ActionScript command:

```
if (_parent.hitTest(_parent._parent.bullet)) {
    _parent.gotoAndPlay("dead");
    _parent._parent.bullet.range = _parent._parent.bullet.maxRange;
}
```

This uses ActionScript's built-in MovieClip.hitTest function to determine whether the alien and bullet movie clips intersect. As well as 'killing' the alien, we also get rid of the bullet by making it believe that it has suddenly reached its maximum range.

Assuming that you have a feel for how the player and alien gameSprites work, there's nothing new in the bullet movie clip – it just takes the angle of the player's ship at the point of firing, and travels in that direction for a given range. Feel free to have a look, it won't bite.

The Mathematical Movie Clip

The other thing to notice is how the trigonometry functions are set up. I've seen many people have trouble getting functions like these working, so the main things to remember are:

- The movie clip containing the functions must be on a timeline every time you make a function call.

- The frame containing the function definitions must have been passed before you make the function call for the first time.

The second bullet point above is why the world timeline looks like it does. The function library ma.fastTrigFunctions is read on frame 1 of the _root timeline, while the game proper starts at frame 2, giving the functions time to be defined beforehand:

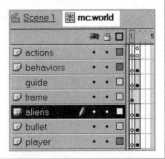

Savior.fla

All of this takes us to the finished game:

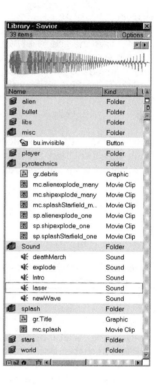

Looking at the Library, you'll see a few new symbols. There's now an introductory splash screen, which is just a simple, tween-based animation. There are also some sound effects, which I've set up using the new Flash 5 Sound object, and we'll examine those in a moment. First, though, we'll look at how the pyrotechnics work.

Explosions

The explosions are all basically the same (the 'wormhole' on the splash screen animation also works on the same principle, but uses an alpha-based fade effect as well). What we have is an explosion shard (the '..._one' movie clips) that starts at position (0, 0) (the 'start point' in the leftmost diagram below). This is moved by a piece of ActionScript that continuously increases its _y property (noting that positive y is downwards) until it is a distance 'range' away.

The movie clip also does something sneaky, which is to rotate itself by a random angle between 0 and 360 degrees. This means that the shard won't go straight down, but at a random angle this._rotation, which is the angle *the whole movie clip* is rotated at. The single-shard movie clip is repeated several times in the '..._many' movie clips to create a circular explosion of shards. This is a prime example of a single, simple animation being repeated to create a much more complex-looking effect.

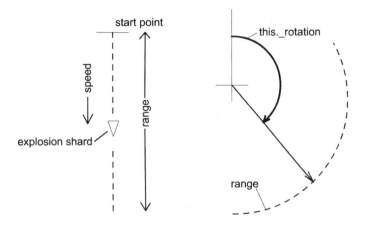

Making a Noise

The only other really new thing in the final game is the sound effects, which are defined in frame 1 of the _root timeline. The sounds themselves are not on the stage, but linked directly from the Library. Flash can't do this without something corresponding to an instance name, and we do this by selecting the sound file *in the Library* and selecting Linkage from the Options drop-down menu. In the Symbol Linkage Properties window that appears, click the Export this symbol radio button and give the sound an Identifier name.

It's this name that you must reference (in quotation marks) when attaching the sound to a Sound object, as shown in the listing below:

```
// Define player variables...
scale = 1;
score = 0;
level = 1;

// Define sound objects...
introSound = new Sound();
introSound.attachSound("intro");
laserSound = new Sound();
laserSound.attachSound("laser");
laserSound.setVolume(40);
explodeSound = new Sound();
explodeSound.attachSound("explode");
waveSound = new Sound();
waveSound.attachSound("newWave");
deathSound = new Sound();
deathSound.attachSound("deathSound");
stop ();
```

Because the sounds are defined in _root, you get them to play by using commands like:

```
_root.explodeSound.start(0, 1);
```

This plays the explodeSound object for one loop, with zero lead-in time (the zero is how many seconds into the sound you want to play; if the sound was 1 second long and you specified 0.5, the command would play the sound starting from 0.5s into the sound).

There. Finished!

Conclusion

I've explained all the key points of this game, but have a look at how it all works for yourself. You should find that the object diagrams are helpful in doing this, particularly because they're the only things I used in defining this game (no flowcharts required!), which is as it should be for the busy ActionScript programmer. More importantly, you've seen a general game-building system defined and used to create a moderately complex game world.

In following the game *Savior*, you have seen how the initial game design was based on a flexible gameSprite system, which forced me to think of the interfaces between each game element in a structured and modular way (or, if you want the technical term, in an *object-oriented* way).

The game design proceeded by:

- Looking at defining a game world

- Populating it with simple gameSprites

■ Adding additional features to the gameSprites by using behavior movie clips

Time and time again I hear on the newsgroups and at seminars that Flash-based, real-time games are not possible, or have to be postage-stamp sized to get them to work at a decent speed. But this is just not true if you plan your games like the professional programmers do, take care to minimize the work you make the game platform do during runtime (by pre-creating the data beforehand), and keep your sights on the true factors of good games: responsiveness and playability, not bloated and sluggish graphics.

Now... practice by writing your own game. The features you'll need to define and build it are the features that will appear in the next generation of Flash web sites. So if anyone asks, you're not playing games. You're practicing for the future.

20
Flash
and XML

Section 4
Dynamic Content

19
Flash and PHP

18
Dynamic Web
Applications

Chapter 17
Dynamic Content
from Text Files

One of the most powerful features of Flash is its potential to act as a front end for **web applications** – sites that provide interactive services and content that keep users coming back time and time again. The Flash player provides a universal means for delivering this kind of content, and, combined with the rich graphical environment that Flash makes possible, this makes a superb vehicle for providing users with interactive dynamic content that looks great visually. Dynamic content makes your site more interesting and exciting for the user, and it's an excellent way to give users a reason to return to your web site.

In this chapter we'll explore one of the simplest methods of integrating dynamic content into your Flash movies – data stored in text files that can be accessed remotely at the click of a button in a Flash movie. To implement this kind of content on the web, you're going to need a web server , we use Microsoft's Internet Information Server – IIS, part of Windows 2000 Professional – here, but you'll be able to work these examples through on your own machine even if you don't have IIS.

We'll be going through two separate projects here, the first a web site page with regularly updated topic sections, and the second a dynamically updated banner ad.

While there are a lot of tools out there that make the creation and updating of dynamic Flash sites easier, the text file option is easy to build and maintain. It may be that you're developing a simple site for a client who has very little knowledge of Flash and potential data sources, and who will need an easy way to update the site long after you've finished your development work. In this context, leaving that client just a series of simple text files to update periodically is a good solution. The arguments for combining such a simple data source with Flash in this scenario shouldn't need spelling out – to miss out Flash is to miss out on the possibility of a download-friendly motion web experience that places you streets ahead of your static competitors.

Dynamic Content from Text Files

As an example of a web site that could use quick, easy and frequent text updates (and maintenance by the web site owner), we're going to create a page with the latest in news, sports, weather, politics and food. By the time we've finished, anyone who can use Notepad (or any other simple text editor) will be able to change the content on the site and see their updates reflected the next time they visit the site online. This screenshot shows the overall example that we're going to create in our first exercise:

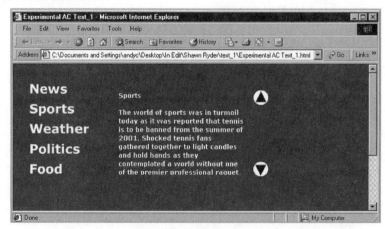

What we have here is a set of buttons on the left which trigger the display of text information on the right-hand side of the screen. There are also a couple of arrow buttons so that the user can scroll up and down the displayed text field. In this screenshot, the user has selected the Sports option.

Point your browser in the direction of...

http://www.webryder.com/flash_book/text_1.html

...to see the version of this on my own site.

Before we get into the detail of creating the Flash file that achieves this aim, let's establish how this all works conceptually.

Loading Text Data into Flash

To view and update dynamic text content in Flash, we need three things:

- A web browser
- A SWF sitting inside a web page
- A data source containing the updateable text

The user browses to our Flash movie, requests some content, and the Flash movie pulls in the desired text from the web site and displays it in the browser.

The way that this process works in action is illustrated in the diagram:

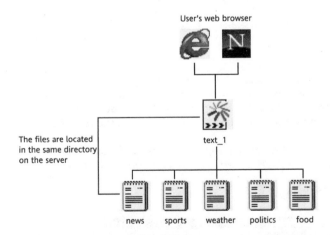

When someone calls up the host HTML page in their browser, the SWF that's embedded inside the page is displayed. Inside the SWF will be some predefined dynamic text boxes – like those that we'll create in a moment in our first exercise. Prompted by some simple ActionScript, these dynamic text boxes will import data from the text files and update the content displayed inside the Flash movie.

Creating a Movie Clip to House Dynamic Text

The first thing we need to do is use Notepad or a similar text editor to create the source files for the movie which will contain the different text elements that we want to display. For this exercise, we've chosen to mimic a news portal.

1. Let's start by creating our five text files to hold the information that will be displayed in the Flash movie on our web site. Keeping matters simple, we're going to call the files `news.txt`, `sports.txt`, `weather.txt`, `politics.txt`, and `food.txt`.

   As shown in the diagram earlier, we're going to store all five text files and the Flash file in the same directory on the server (or on your hard drive if you're storing the files locally), to keep things simple. Make sure that you save these five files in the same folder that will hold your Flash movie and its host HTML page.

2. You can put whatever text (or dummy text) you feel is suitable in each of the files, but you must include a special line at the start of each file. This is the line that will tell Flash the identity of the text that follows, and let Flash use that text in the movie.

   For the weather page, I created a text file that reads like this:

   ```
   textField=Weather

   DEC 6 Scattered Showers - lo 24°F

   THU DEC 7 Snow Showers hi 30°F - lo 15°F

   FRI DEC 8 Snow Showers hi 32°F - lo 13°F
   ```

   and so on...

3. Note the `textField=Weather` line at the beginning of the file. The `textField=` statement says to Flash 'look, here's some text that I want you to associate with the `textField` variable that I'm going to set up in my Flash movie', and the `Weather` part gives Flash a heading for the chunk of text that follows in the rest of the file.

4. Add `textfield=` elements as the top line of each of your text files, specifying: news, Sports, Weather, Politics and Food in turn as the headings.

   This is how my files look:

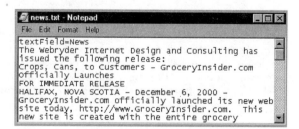

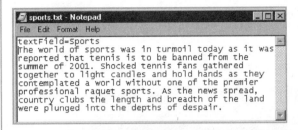

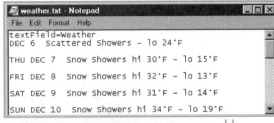

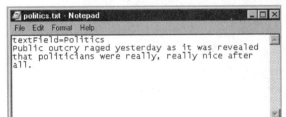

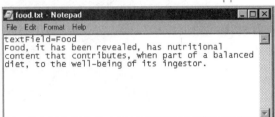

We now need to create a location in a Flash file that will allow us to display this text file information.

5. Open a new Flash movie, create a movie clip symbol and call it text_location.

6. Use the Text tool to create a simple text box in frame 1 of the movie clip:

Now we have to configure the text box so that it's a suitable vessel to contain the dynamic text content that we want to feed into it.

7. Choose Dynamic Text in the Text Options tab so that the field can be updated, but won't, like Input Text, allow users to input text into the box. We also need to ensure that we have the Multiline option selected, check the Word Wrap box so that the text will flow onto the next line when necessary, and check Selectable so that users can copy and paste the text if they want to:

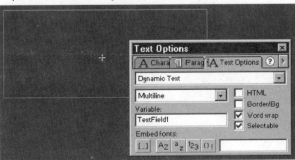

Our final step in configuring the text box is to associate a variable with it. We'll use this variable name to point to the text file content that we want displayed in the text box.

8. Enter our variable name, `textField`, into the Variable field on the Text Options tab This is the same name that we specified at the top of all of our source text files:

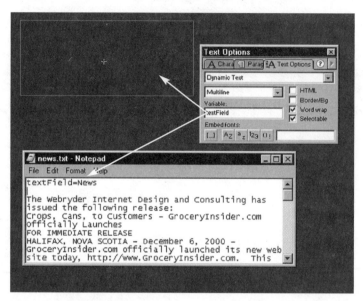

9. Using the Character option on the same panel, we can choose the font and color for the text that will appear in the text box. There's no text in this text box by default, but we need to make sure that the color is different to the background color of the movie. We can also set some rough values – in this case we know that there's likely to be quite a bit of text, so we can choose something like 12pt with a font that's nice and easy to read. We've gone for 12pt white Verdana:

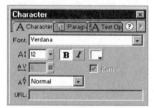

Now that we've got the text box defined inside the movie clip, let's test it by giving it some text to display.

10. Open up the Frame Properties window for the movie clip's frame 1 and add a `set variable` action that sets the `textField` variable to something like "This text box set aside for dynamic update from text files…":

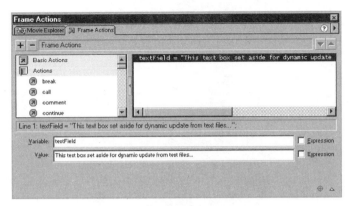

This will display some text in the text field until the user chooses a specific topic.

11. Drag a copy of your text_location movie clip out onto the stage, give it an instance name of textMovie, and run your movie. You should see something like this:

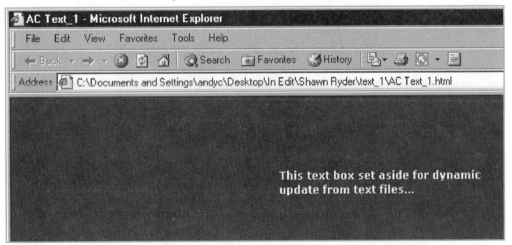

OK, that was simple enough – all we've done in this test is assign a 'hard-coded' value to the textField variable and used it to update the dynamic text box inside the movie clip. That's kind of dynamic, but not *that* dynamic. To take this a stage further, let's add the ActionScript that'll pull in the content of one of the text files that we created previously.

Pulling in the Dynamic Text

What we need to do here is point Flash at one of our text files and get it to read in the text data. To do that, we'll use a loadVariables action. We'll attach this to a button and pull in the text when the button is pressed.

Here's a schematic of the whole system:

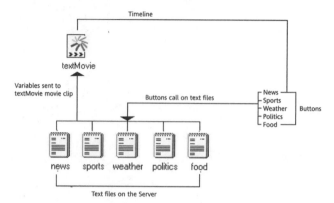

1. Start out by creating a simple button symbol labeled News. Do this in any way you like, but bear in mind that you'll probably want to create a button for each separate topic: News, Sports, Weather, Politics and Food. For that reason, I've created five separate buttons, each with a Hit state that covers the text:

I've placed the buttons on a separate layer in the main movie.

Now to hook the News button up to the news.txt text file.

2. Select the News button on the stage and bring up the Object Actions window. Then add a loadVariables action that uses the news.txt file as the source URL, and the textMovie movie clip instance as the target for the loaded variables:

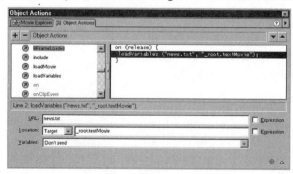

3. Now do the same for your other buttons, specifying the appropriate text file name as their respective URL source. When you run your movie this time and click on the buttons, you'll see that Flash pulls in the dynamic text content from the text files:

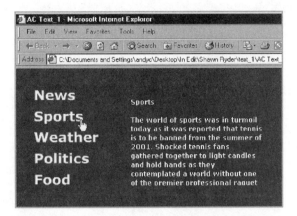

Depending on the size that you drew your text box, you may have some formatting problems, with text running over the edge of the text box. We'll come back to fixing that shortly.

> *This was quite a simple thing to do, but it encapsulates a really important principle – you can specify variable names, populate those variables with data called from a remote location, and display that data in the SWF. That's a powerful concept, and it's at the core of feeding dynamic content into the Flash front end.*

In this example, we're able to use a simple syntax in the URL field when we specified where we wanted to pull in our text from:

As the news.txt file was in the same folder as the Flash movie and its host HTML page, we could just use the file name, and Flash could easily locate the source file. Suppose, however, that our source file was somewhere else on our machine...

If, for example, my news.txt file was stored in the Testing/Flash folder of my C: drive, I could specify that location like this:

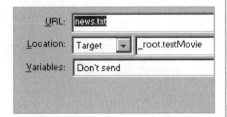

This would give me the following syntax in the `loadVariables` code:

```
on (release) {
    loadVariables("c:/Testing/Flash/news.txt","_root.textMovie");
}
```

Note also that we can use the ActionScript's dot notation to specify a Target Location anywhere else in the movie, too – provided that we've configured that target movie clip to accept the dynamic content that we want to send to it.

If our source text file was located on a remote server, we'd still be able to pull the data in, provided that we specified the syntax correctly. Suppose that the `news.txt` file was stored on a site called www.freshfroot.com, in a directory called `StudioText`. In this case, I'd need to specify the full web address, which I could do like this:

This is the syntax for fully specifying the source URL name.

Now let's get back to how our text displays in the browser. The way you format the text using this simple text file method will affect how the text appears in the finished movie.

For example, if you type in `textField=News` in the source Notepad file, hit the ENTER key to go onto the next line, and then continue entering your text...

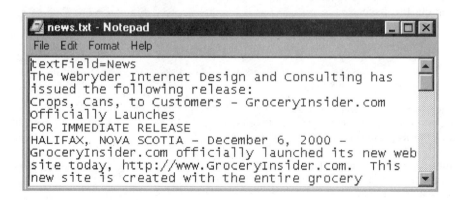

...the text will display like this in the finished movie...

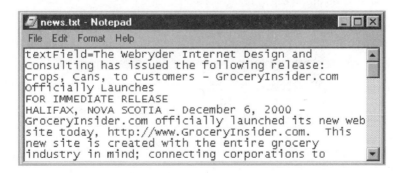

...with a nice clean line break between the News heading and the body of the text.

If, however, you were to add an extra, blank line after the heading, the text would display like this...

...with a BIG gap between the heading and the text.

If you left out the News heading part altogether, like this...

...your text would display like this...

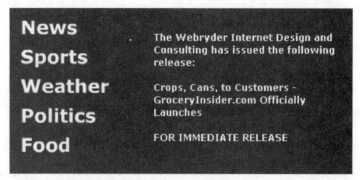

You can see from this that there are a number of simple things you can do with the basic formatting. You might also want to explore using multiple text source files and multiple text boxes, each with their own dedicated variables, to display different parts of the text in different point sizes and styles.

Given the fixed size of the text box that we created inside our text_location movie clip, it might be useful to provide the user with a means of scrolling through the text. It's possible to do this by clicking on the displayed text and using your keyboard arrow keys, but a more intuitive and elegant solution is available. Let's look at that next.

Making the Text Scrollable

The setup we'll use here will be to add a couple of buttons to our movie, one for scrolling up, and one for scrolling down. When the user presses the buttons, we'll set a variable whose value effectively controls the position of the 'cursor' inside the displayed text box.

First, we need to define the two variables that we're going to use to get our text scrolling.

1.   In the same movie we've been working on in the previous examples, open up the text_location movie clip symbol for editing.

2.   In a new layer, use two var commands (from the Actions book) to create two variables in frame 1, upScroll and downScroll, and set both their initial values to 0:

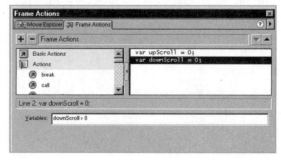

The `var` command defines a **local** variable. This is in contrast to **global** variables, which are declared using the `setVariable` command. We'll only be using these variables inside the movie clip, so we declare them as local variables here.

Now for the buttons that'll use these variables.

3. Create a new layer for the scroll buttons inside the movie clip, and add two new buttons to the right of the existing text box:

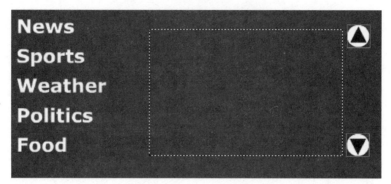

I've given my button two layers, with a white background circle on one layer and a black arrowhead over the circle in the other. On the Over state of the button, I've changed the tint color of the arrow from black to blue, so that it changes color when the user moves their mouse over the button. Once you've finished the first button, you can duplicate it in the Lbrary and rotate the arrowhead 180 degrees in the keyframes to create the second scroll button.

In my example, the buttons are called Up Scroll and Down Scroll.

4. Select the instance of the Up Scroll button on the stage, and add an `on` action.

5. Now use the check boxes to set the button up as follows:

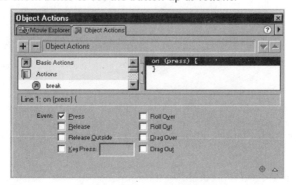

This script will now respond when the user clicks on the 'up' button in the SWF.

Now we need some ActionScript to scroll the text.

6. Use a set variable action (or just type directly in Expert mode) to set the upScroll variable we created earlier to 1. Your script should now look like this:

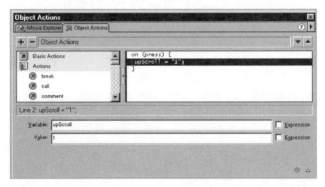

This means that when the user clicks on the Up Scroll button with their mouse, Flash assigns a value of 1 to upScroll, the local variable we created earlier. We'll make the text scroll for as long as the value of upScroll remains 1 – in other words, for as long as the button is pressed.

7. We want the value of the variable to return to 0 once the user moves away from the button. The next bit of code to add is:

```
on (release, releaseOutside, rollOut) {
    upScroll = "0";
}
```

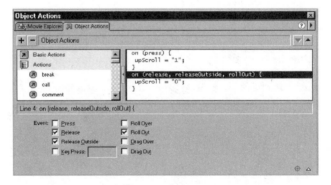

Make sure that you check Release Outside as well as Release and Roll Out, as shown in the screenshot. We want to stop scrolling (indicated by a value of 0) when the user releases the mouse button, whether the cursor is inside *or* outside of the scroll button.

We need to add some similar actions to the down button in order for the text to scroll downward. On this button we'll use the downScroll variable to achieve this effect.

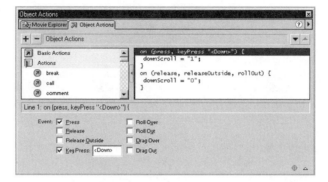
8. To make the Down Scroll button work, create the code shown here:

```
on (press, keyPress "<Down>") {
    downScroll = "1";
}
on (release, releaseOutside, rollOut) {
    downScroll = "0";
}
```

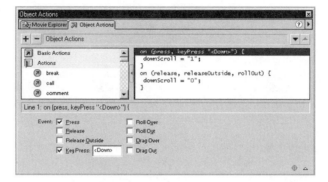

We now need to assign some actions to our textmovie instance on the stage – these will make the text scrolling actually happen in the text box.

Making the Text Scroll

Again, we'll be using the upScroll and downScroll variables that we created inside the textmovie movie clip.

1. Select the textmovie instance on the stage and open up the Object Actions window. Add the following code (we'll go through it in detail in a moment):

```
onClipEvent (enterFrame) {
    if (downScroll=="1") {
        this.textfield.scroll += 1;
    }
}
onClipEvent (enterFrame) {
    if (upScroll=="1") {
        this.textfield.scroll -= 1;
    }
}
```

> *Make sure that you use the 'double equals sign' syntax in the if statements – two equals signs together side by side.*

The very first part of the action is `onClipEvent`, which is given the trigger event `enterFrame`. This tells Flash to play the action as each frame is played. Our movie only contains one frame, so it plays continuously.

Then we use `if` statements to check the current values of both the `upScroll` and `downScroll` that we defined in the movie clip. If the value of these variables is `1`, this tells the clip to either scroll up or down.

The `scroll` property is predefined in Flash and is used specifically to scroll through text. So our `this.textField.scroll += 1` statement effectively says "Use the text associated with `this` movie clip's `textField` variable and scroll down". The `this.textField.scroll -= 1` statement uses the same principle except that it scrolls *up* instead.

And that's it.

2.   Test the movie with some largish text files, and you should see the text scroll up and down in response to the buttons:

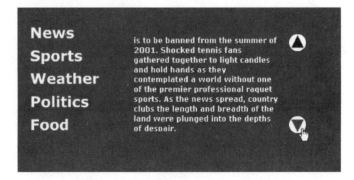

If there is a new news story or weather update, we can just make the changes to the text files and upload them to the server, replacing the old text files. As soon as the upload is complete, the file will be dynamically updated. In other words, our Flash file can now be easily updated without needing to upload a bunch of files that could take a while and interrupt the way users see the page. We don't need to touch the original SWF – we just change the text data file, a task that even the most basically computer-literate client would be able to do for themselves.

Now let's have a look at our example of a banner ad.

An Updateable Banner Ad

This time we're going to make a very simple banner ad that will call on easily updateable text files. We're going to use a new feature in Flash 5 that allows for some basic HTML formatting options inside of the text box itself. You can see how this should work in the diagram:

User's
Web
Browser

banner_ad   banner_ad

The text file is located on a remote server

If you want to see the finished product, then it's at...

http://www.webryder.com/flash_book/banner_ad.html:

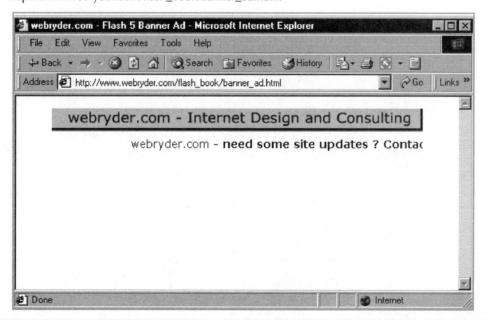

There are a number of reasons that you might want to change the text inside a banner ad periodically. For example, if you had a special offer on your web site, you could change fonts and font colors to draw attention to the offer. You could also update the text file to include a URL to take the users directly to the page with the special offer.

Let's make a banner of our own.

Building an Updateable Banner Ad

Before we start building, let me sketch the structure of the banner we'll be creating here. Essentially what we have is a main movie that hosts a movie clip containing the scrolling banner text. This 'scrolling text' movie clip in turn contains two movie clips, each of which retrieves its text from a single Notepad-based text file. The Notepad file can be manually updated whenever you or your client needs to update the banner text.

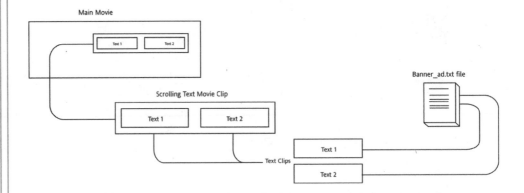

1. Open up a new movie and set the stage dimensions to 468 pixels wide by 60 pixels high – the size of a standard banner ad. This will be the main SWF that you can embed in an HTML page, and the stage will act as the background for the scrolling text.

   Now for the 'container' movie clip that will house the two text movies.

2. Create a new movie clip called textscroll. Give the movie clip three layers, one for some ActionScript, and one each for the two text movie clips that we're going to use to actually scroll the text:

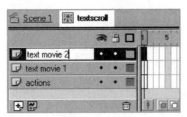

We're going to have two messages scrolling across the screen consecutively. We'll create the template for the two movie clips that'll do that next...

3. Create a new movie clip called textbox and add a dynamic text field in the first frame. Make the dynamic text field about half the height of your main movie and wider – mine's 30 pixels high by 800 wide to cater for a long piece of text. Specify the text field as Single Line and gave it a variable name of text. Make sure that the Selectable option is unchecked – we really don't want users to be able to copy and paste the text as it scrolls along the window. Check the HTML box, as this will allow us to use some tags inside the text file to change the appearance of the text in the finished movie. Don't forget to pick a text color that contrasts with your movie background, and use a font size around 16 point:

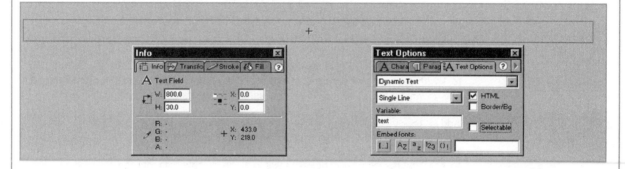

We'll use two instances of this movie clip symbol inside the textscroll 'container' movie.

4. Next, create a text file called banner_ad.txt. This file will eventually store three pieces of content that our movie will use:

    ■   Text content for the first textbox movie clip instance

    ■   Text content for the second textbox movie clip instance

    ■   A variable setting that will tell Flash when the content of banner_ad.txt has finished loading into the movie

We'll add the content to this text file shortly.

OK, we now have all of the structural components we need – all we have to do now is lash them together with some ActionScript and provide them with some actual content.

Remember that the textscroll movie is a container for the actual scrolling text movie clips. We'll also use it to control the action and coordinate things by issuing a loadVariables command and directing the text data from Banner_ad.txt to the movie clips that will scroll that text.

5.   In the textscroll movie clip, create a variable called go in the first frame of the actions layer and assign it a value of 0:

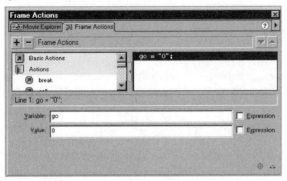

This is a control variable: while its value is 0, our movie won't start scrolling the text across the screen. This is because we want to be sure that all the data has loaded in from the text file before we set the banner scrolling in motion. We'll set the go variable to 1 with a line at the very end of the text file – once Flash has read in all of the text file, go will be set to 1, and this is the signal that we can start to scroll that text.

6.   Add a loadVariables command to a new keyframe in the *second* frame of the actions layer. Specify the banner_ad.txt text file as the URL, then select Target from the drop-down menu and enter this as the location for the variables to be sent to, checking the Expression box. This will pull the variable data into the calling movie clip:

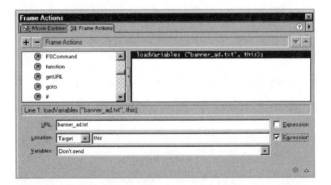

If the text file wasn't in the same folder as the SWF, you'd need to enter the full web address of the text file's location in the URL *box – for example,* http://www.webryder.com/banner_ad.txt. *Due to security issues, the Flash file for the banner ad has to be located on the same domain or sub domain (namehere.yourserver.com), as the main web site files or it won't work. It does work if you're just using a local hard drive, but it's easier just to enter* banner_ad.txt *in the* URL *box and make sure that all your files are in the same folder.*

To ensure that the text file is fully loaded before proceeding with the scrolling activity, we have to check on the value of the go variable that we initialized in the first frame. We *could* just carry on without checking that the text file is loaded, but this means that the text could suddenly appear while the scroll is halfway across the screen, which isn't very professional. If the value is 0, meaning that the text hasn't yet fully loaded in, we want Flash to carry on looping until the text *has* loaded in and the value of go is 1.

7. To implement this checking/delay loop, create new keyframes in frames 3 and 4 of the actions layer. Now add the following script to frame 4 of the actions layer. This will send Flash back to the blank frame 3 until the value of go is 1:

```
if (go == "0") {
    gotoAndPlay (3);
}
```

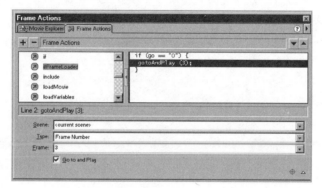

On the next two layers of the textscroll movie clip – text movie 1 and text movie 2 – we want to add the text field movie clips that will scroll across the screen.

8. In frame 1 of their respective layers inside textscroll, place two instances of the textmovie movie clip on the right side of the stage, which is where they will begin the scrolling from.

9. Position both movie clips identically in their respective layers, roughly as shown here, level with the center point of textscroll, and with the vast majority of the clip off to the right of the stage. Remember that you won't be able to see the outline of the movie clip once its extremities move beyond the stage area:

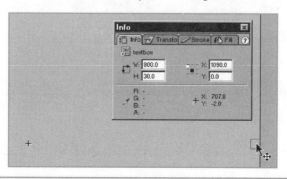

The two movie clips are right on top of each other, but on their individual layers so that you can access them easily by hiding one layer or the other.

> *It's not really an issue here, but if you ever do anything else like this, it's extremely important that the text fields are rendered in the movie before the text variables are loaded. If the text fields aren't there when the variables load, then the variables won't have anywhere to go and the text won't show up! This is why the frame order is so important.*

Give the two movie clip instances the instance names of text_1 and text_2 respectively:

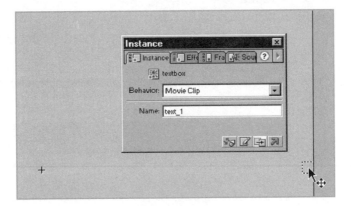

We want to scroll the two movie clip instances across the screen one after another.

10. On the layer containing the first movie clip, insert a keyframe in frame 5 (the frame *after* the `if go=="0"` statement in the actions layer) and then a keyframe further on – somewhere around frame 60 should do it. Shift the movie clip off to the extreme left of the stage in the keyframe at frame 60, and create a motion tween between the two keyframes:

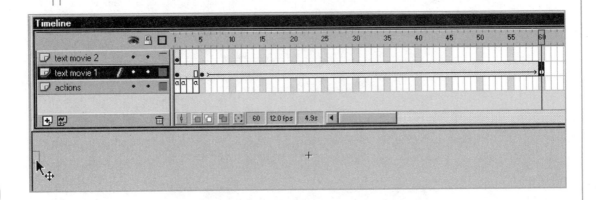

11. Do the same to the other instance, but this time start the tween where the first one ended – frame 61, in my example here:

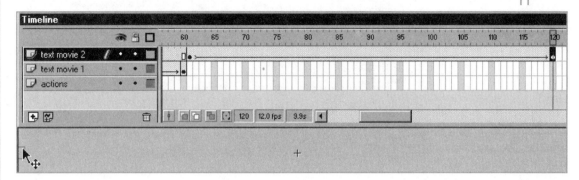

There may be a bit of testing involved in moving the boxes from left to right to get the placement right, because you want them to start off on the right side of the screen and end on the left side without seeing their beginning too early or the end for too long. If you *do* start or end too early it won't look right, so come back and experiment with this a little when you've got everything else fixed (after we test the movie – soon!).

Make the layers the same length by dragging the final frame on the text movie 1 layer to frame 120.

12. On the last keyframe of the text movie 2 layer, we need to tell Flash to begin over again in order for the text to scroll across the screen repeatedly. We can do this with a gotoAndPlay action that sends it back to frame 5 of the movie:

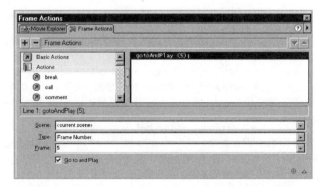

If you want more than two scrolls across the screen then just add more layers with an instance of the textbox movie clip given a different instance name in each layer. Then use tweens – as we've just done – to scroll them across one after the other.

13. Now that the container movie clip and all of its components are complete, we can place a copy of textscroll on the main timeline. Go back to the main timeline, place an instance of the movie clip on the first frame and give it the instance name textscroller. Position the movie clip off to the right of the stage, like this:

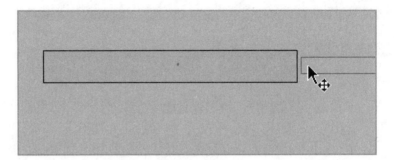

Finally, we need to create the text file that contains the information that's going to be sent to the text boxes. This is where the HTML that we told Flash to allow in our text box earlier comes in.

14. Open up your `banner_ad.txt` text file in Notepad and enter the following code:

```
text_1.text=<A HREF="http://www.webryder.com"><FONT
COLOR="#0000ff">webryder.com</FONT></A> - <B>need some site
updates ? Contact Us today!</B>
```

OK, this might look a little strange to you – let's deconstruct it. What we're doing here is supplying the text for the first dynamic text box and applying some HTML formatting to that text. Here's the low-down...

`text_1.text=` tells Flash the value of the `text` variable inside the `text_1` movie clip instance. Notice the HTML hyperlink `<A HREF=http://www.webryder.com>`, which allows users who click on the text to go to the specific URL web site location.

`<FONT COLOR="#0000FF">` opens a font color command using the hexadecimal value – blue in this example. We add the text that will link through to the URL we have just defined and then we use `</FONT>` and `</A>` to close the font tag and the hyperlink.

The `<A>` tag is actually used to define any link between different resources, whether it's a hyperlink like the one used here, or a bookmark that will send the user to that part of the page with a tag like this: `<A NAME="Link Name Here"></A>`.

We want the next text to be in bold, so we use the standard `<B> </B>` tags around the text. The standard HTML paragraph (`<P><P ALIGN="right">`), italic (`<I></I>`) and underline (`<U></U>`) tags all work in this context, too.

You can also use `<FONT FACE=" "></FONT>` to set the font, and `<FONT SIZE="+2"></FONT>` or `<FONT SIZE="6"></FONT>` to set relative/absolute font sizes. Note that Flash will take font size as a *point* size rather than the HTML value.

We have now mentioned all the HTML tags that Flash can read, as specified by Macromedia.

15. Now add this code to the text file after the previous section:

```
&text_2.text=<A HREF="http://www.webryder.com"><FONT
COLOR="#0000FF">groceryinsider.com</FONT></A> - <B><I>Our latest
site—Grocery Products, Careers and More !</I></B>
&go=1
```

The & symbol is used to let Flash know that this is another variable that we want to treat separately from the `text1_text` data that we defined in the previous piece of code. The code then defines the value of the second movie clip with `text_2.text=`. Just as with the other variable `text_1.text`, we define the hyperlink and the text that's going to be shown. We also make the text bold and italic.

The last variable to be defined, right at the bottom of the file, is the `go` variable, used to let Flash know that all of the information has been loaded and it is now safe to proceed with the scrolling across the screen. If you have more movie clips that are to scroll across the screen, then the text needs to be defined here as well, prior to the `&go=1` line.

Your final file should look similar, like this:

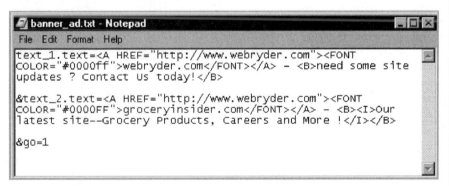

You may need to be careful with the amount of text you use in relation to the size of the dynamic text boxes we created. If there is more text than the size of the box Flash will cut off the end of the text, so make sure that the text box is big enough for the text. As with the positioning of the text boxes in the movie clip, you'll need to experiment with this to get the placement right.

Run the movie and watch that text scroll. Now you can start to refine it.

Conclusion

Using dynamic content from text files within Flash allows sites to combine the visual edge of Flash with updated content that gives users a reason to continue to come back to the site. Once the updateable content is there in Flash, updating and uploading a text file is easy.

There are a wide variety of reasons for using dynamic content from text files within Flash. You could, for example, post a question on a site and allow users to post their comments. You could create an executable file containing dynamic text from a remote URL that is updated daily and allow users to download it. (The security feature for the URL does not affect Flash movies that are playing in stand-alone projectors, only when they are playing in a web browser.)

Stir in some dynamic content and your Flash recipes are going to become even spicier than they were before.

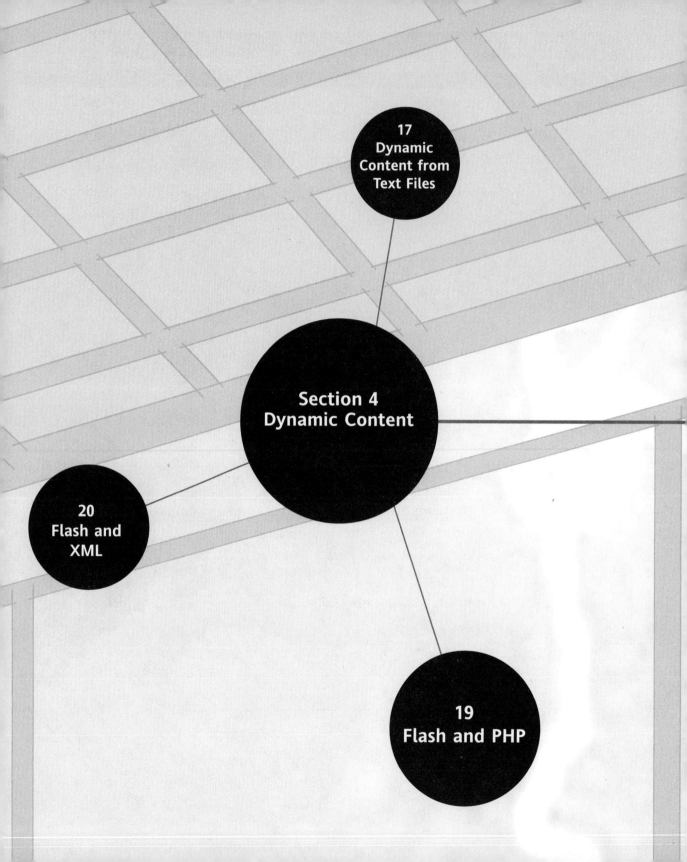

Chapter 18
Dynamic Web
Applications

The new Web is a place where static HTML and text-only sites are not the default option, and where you go to a site to truly interact, rather than merely be a passive visitor. The new web is a place where you get a sensory experience *and* some use value. It's a place where web sites are transforming into **web applications**.

What *is* a web application? The simplest definition is that it's an application that runs on a web server that users interact with, and which provides those users with some valuable experience or service. A search engine is a good example of a web application: the user brings up the search engine site, types in their query, and the application searches through the database before returning all the relevant listings to the viewer. The search engine on its own is a sad little machine in a darkened room, but when it gets together with the user it comes to life – and the user gets the service that they want.

An even better example of a web application is a shopping cart system, where viewers can look through items, add items they want to buy to their cart, go to the checkout, and buy the items that they selected. A system like this integrates different functions to create a unified user experience. Later in this chapter, we'll be looking at how to design a simple shopping cart using Flash.

There are two main components in any web application: the **back end** and the **front end**. The *back end* is the code that does the work, plus the database that holds the information that the user will see, interact with, or supply. The *front end* is the part that the user actually loads into their browser and interacts with.

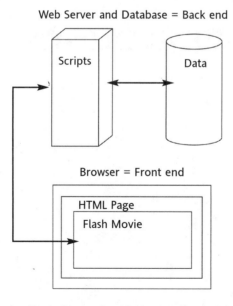

Flash, when used effectively, is the ideal tool for building the front end – and Flash's ActionScripting capabilities mean that it can hook up to the whole range of other tools and technologies that provide the back end functionality and feed dynamic content into the user's browser as they make choices on-screen. Flash could easily become the *de facto* standard for front ends on the new Web.

One of the reasons that so many of us love to use Flash is that it produces small, scalable vector graphics. This means you can use Flash to create incredibly intuitive user interfaces that make it much easier for viewers to use your application. For example, a built-in contextual help system is quite easy to do in Flash, but would never be possible in a web application using HTML for its front end. You can even use Flash to take the help system one step further and introduce a character or agent to guide viewers through each screen.

The visually arresting appearance you can create with Flash, coupled with the dynamic content that you feed in from the back end, provide incredibly rich and versatile ways to create an attractive interface that downloads quickly and is easy to use. In its current incarnation, Flash has all the tools necessary to become the standard front end to *any* web application.

Let's take a more detailed tour.

The Front End

We'll begin with a quick look at some ground rules for designing front ends in Flash.

Design Architecture

When using Flash to design the front end for a web application, architecture and usability are more important than ever before. When you build the front end for an application, you're essentially building a template for each screen the viewer sees and/or interacts with, leaving placeholders for the data that the back end will supply when the movie runs.

> *For global graphic design considerations in your Flash sites, take a look at Peter Holm's chapter.*

It's important to organize your movie(s) into a format that will be easy to come back to after the project is complete – for example, if new features need to be added, or problems arise with the existing movies. Generally, it's a good idea to organize your movie into separate SWFs that will be loaded into different levels. Level 0 is good to use as an interface level, and it should contain the art for the interface, the main navigation elements, standard instances that are referenced throughout other levels, as well as functions.

How the other levels are constructed really depends on the specifics of the project that you're involved in, but I like to break everything into logical sections by content. A good rule of thumb is that if you have a button that routes you to a section, then that section should have its own SWF. This makes it much easier to edit the different sections of your project discretely, and it's also easier on the client computer in terms of RAM and CPU usage.

You can also use **standard instances**, which are common movie clips used and referenced throughout the entire movie. The standard instance I find most useful in the web application context is storing all incoming data in a standard 'container' instance named vars, which makes the data easily accessible throughout. This isn't necessarily the best move for *all* projects, but it's well worth considering as part of your architecture design strategy.

I find that it's best to store all the functions used in the movie in the first frame of the main timeline on level 0, in their own layer, above the actions layer. If you call a function before it's been declared, the function won't work, so using this method ensures that all functions are declared before there's any chance of them being used in the movie.

> *By storing your functions in the main timeline of level 0, you can reference every function used in the movie with the same target path, `_level0.functionName`, which is much less hassle than having to reference main functions spread out over multiple timelines and levels.*

When you're working on a large project with many sections and multiple SWFs, you could go one step further and use a functions layer *in each individual SWF* to house the main functions for that section, and the main functions *for the whole project* in level 0. Within the SWFs, it's worth storing sound, actions and labels on layers of their own and making sure all movie clip instances are named – it's much easier to read and understand debugging output this way.

Modular components are the key to building a successful front end. In this context, **smart clips** are great timesavers. For example, if you have a lot of places where the viewer can select items from drop-down menus, it would be time consuming and difficult to make a different drop-down menu movie clip for each menu. This is where smart clips come in: instead of making the drop-down menu movie clip a hundred times, you can create the menu once and use **clip parameters** to enter the specific items that will populate that particular menu when you use it on the stage.

Smart clips were designed to make it easy for programmers to put together complex pieces of code that could easily be implemented by designers, but they also allow you to create common controls that you can use throughout a Flash movie. This makes it easier to be consistent, and will make your front end easier for viewers to use and understand. This method of developing controls also allows for rapid development, and easily updateable movies. Once you implement one smart clip, it's very easy to begin using them for everything. Over time, you can build up a library of modular controls that can be used in any number of projects by modifying the graphics.

> *Check out Brendan Dawes' chapter for more on building and using smart clips*

When a front end is organized well, and uses modular components, bugs will be easier to locate and fix, and might even be avoided altogether!

Planning Ahead

The most important step before you start building a web application front end is to plan, plan, and then plan some more. It's extremely difficult to just jump in and start building anything until you have some clear concepts and ideas on paper.

First, create a list of features that the front end should have – write a description of the *purpose* of the software, what it will do *for the user*, and how it will accomplish this goal. Then create a list of all the movies you'll need to satisfy the requirements that you've identified, give them names, and identify the levels at which they'll be loaded in. You've now created what's known as an **architecture document**.

When you're planning the front end, you might find that **storyboards** – on paper or on screen – are extremely useful for referring to in the development process. Simply create a quick graphic for each screen the viewer will see in the application, not forgetting error screens, help screens and the like. This may be time consuming, but it's an invaluable step in the planning process, and it shouldn't be skipped. Storyboards don't need to be pretty or have any design sense at all, as long as they convey what will be present on the screen. Creating storyboards will help catch most of the issues that would otherwise pop up later on during development.

In addition to storyboards, **flow charts** are also extremely valuable in the development process. Flowcharts show how the viewer will travel through the application, and what screens they'll see and interact with along the way, allowing you to define the 'flow' of the program and understand the different paths a viewer can take. This helps avoid the gaps in architecture that can later slow development to a crawl or even derail it.

When constructing your flow charts, remember to try and anticipate all possible errors that could occur, and mark those down. Here's a simple, sample flow chart:

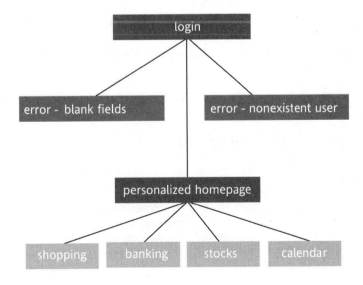

COLOR FLOW CHART

As you can see from the color version on the CD, I've used a different color for the top-level pages and the secondary pages, which makes it easy to identify key screens in the application. The two error screens are colored red. Using flow charts and storyboards in tandem is a great way to plan out your project. Label each item in the flow chart with the corresponding storyboard, and reference each from the other.

Using storyboards and flow charts can strengthen the architecture of your front end three times over. Your storyboards and flow charts will help to avoid holes in your architecture that would otherwise necessitate major reworking further on into the project. I'll be following my own advice by using these techniques as we go through our shopping cart example later in the chapter.

So, to make creating your web application as painless as possible:

- Create storyboards detailing each screen in the front end

- Create flow charts to complement your storyboards

- Use standard instances of movie clips like vars to organize code and data

- Separate content into logical pieces, and use the loadMovie action to load them at runtime

- Take advantage of smart clips to build modular components

- Plan your project thoroughly and completely

- Use functions to modularize your project

- Organize your timeline and movie in a manner that's logical and easy to understand

- Take advantage of tools such as Flash's Debugger when your scripts don't work!

- Don't replicate your code over separate timelines and levels – try to use commonly-accessed functions wherever possible

We've already said that a web application will typically use a front end and a back end. Next, we'll discuss how the two elements can talk to each other effectively.

Back End/Front End Communication

With actions such as loadVariables and the new XML and XML Socket objects, Flash has no problem communicating with outside scripting languages, which can, in turn, retrieve information from a database to display in the Flash movie. The only real requirement is that the applications *return the data to Flash in a format it can understand*. In most cases – XML being the key exception here – Flash can only accept name/value pairs separated by ampersands, and special characters in the values must be **URL encoded** – that is, translated into a form that can be safely sent to the browser without confusing it.

In our shopping cart example, the stream of name/value pairs that get sent to the browser are separated by ampersands – such as *variable1=value1&variable2=value2* and so on.

Flash does have some limitations: popular image formats such as GIF and JPG can't be imported at runtime without resorting to a middleware package – although there is a way around this. Since the SWF format is open source, it's possible to use a scripting language to encapsulate the graphic within an SWF file dynamically and use the loadMovie action to import it. Macromedia Generator or Swift Generator are also options in cases where loading images dynamically is a 'must have'.

Another Flash shortcoming is in the area of **browser incompatibilities**. Internet Explorer 4.5 on the Macintosh platform doesn't support the POST method of sending variables from a Flash movie to an external script. While this *is* fixed in IE 5, it's still an issue for developers to watch out for. A good workaround to resolve the POST problem is to use the GET method. Unfortunately, there's an issue with the GET method as well: it's supposed to be able to send up to the 256kb of data but IE will only send about 50kb of data – if too much data is sent, the loadVariables call will be ignored and the player may cause the browser to crash.

Many Flash designers are intimidated by the idea of using middleware to insert dynamic content into Flash movies. However, all you are really doing is loading a glorified text file. *All* server calls go through essentially the same process:

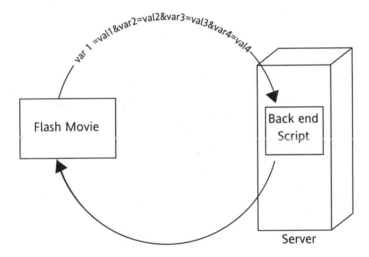

First, the Flash movie makes the call to a back end script and the server that hosts the script processes that script's contents. Next, the server returns the output to the Flash movie, which is a stream of URL encoded name/value pairs that you can see in the diagram. The output isn't *automatically* in the correct format for Flash as the scripts must be written to output the data in the URL encoded, name/value stream of variables.

In simplified terms, all that's happening is the server receives the script call, it's then processed, and returns the variable stream output into the Flash movie. The trick is writing (or getting a programmer to write) the back end scripts to return a stream of variables as the script's output.

Flash front ends rely on data for content, and data – just like graphics and movies – takes time to load. The script sending the data needs time to execute, and the data needs to be downloaded by the computer where the Flash movie is running. If your code tries to manipulate values that haven't been fully loaded from the server yet, you'll get some unpredictable results. What we really need to be safe is a mechanism that preloads the data and tells the movie to continue once the data has been completely received from the server.

Luckily, the Data option of the onClipEvent action makes it easy to know when all the variables have been loaded into a movie clip:

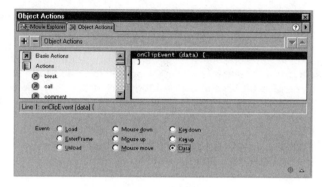

This event is fired when the last variable in the stream has been completely loaded into the movie clip.

Another easy way to check on preloaded data is to make a two keyframe movie clip, like this:

1. Create a movie clip called preloader with two keyframes. Leave the first keyframe blank, and in the second add some text that reads preloading data, please wait. Now put an instance of the movie clip on the root timeline with an instance name of preload. Add a stop action in frame 1 of the main timeline too – this will pause the movie while your preloader does its stuff.

2. Earlier, we talked about setting up a standard instance called vars to hold all incoming data – here's an example of how we'd use that: create an empty movie clip called variables and drag an instance of it onto the stage in frame 1. Name the instance vars. You now need to give the vars instance a loadVariables action to start loading in our data, and an onClipEvent handler so we can detect when the data is all loaded. Here's how...

3. Select the vars instance, and add the following actions to it:

```
onClipEvent (load) {
    //send the preload clip to the preload frame
    _root.preload.gotoAndStop (2);
    //load the variables.
    loadVariables ("textdata.txt", this);
}
onClipEvent (data) {
    //send the preload clip to the blank frame
    _root.preload.gotoAndStop (1);
    //tell the main timeline to go to the next frame
    _root.nextFrame;
}
```

Now, when the data event is fired by Flash detecting that it has read in all the variable data, the vars movie clip will send the preload clip to the blank frame and tell the main timeline to go to the next frame (where actions manipulating the loaded data may begin safely). You could alternatively tell Flash to go to a particular label in the last line of code, using a goto action.

Here, the preloading and loading of data is taken care of with two blocks of actions. We'll be using this technique in anger in our shopping cart example, which is up next.

Notice that the code above is liberally commented. Well-commented code is much easier to come back to after time than uncommented code. It also allows more than one Flash developer to work on a project, and know what the other one has done, and why. Comments won't add to the final file size of SWF as they're not exported with the code, so comment away.

OK, now let's take a look at that shopping cart.

A Flash Shopping Cart

As discussed earlier, we're going to use a shopping cart front end, to illustrate how a simple web application front end goes together. For simplicity's sake, we're going to use a text file to define the variable data that the cart uses, and use that to simulate the output from a back end script. We've provided the FLA and all the components for this walk-through on the CD.

First, in the real world of development, we should define the *goal* of the project. We can do that quite simply here: the shopping cart front end should provide site visitors with a mechanism for picking out products and adding them to their cart. While the user is shopping, a running total price of the items added to the cart should be displayed somewhere on the screen. We'll build that functionality in this example – in the real world we'd have to build or adapt the transaction/payment system too, but we don't have space to do *all* of that here, unfortunately. Maybe in another book...

Once we've defined the goal, the next step – determining the features the front end must have to satisfy the goal – is pretty straightforward. Here's my version:

- The cart needs to show the viewer the items they've already added to the cart

- The list of items will be scrollable: only 6 items will be viewable at any time

- The cart should show a running total of the items in the cart

- The products should be dynamically loaded SWF files (these will be defined in the text file that's substituting for our back end script)

- The front end should be modular enough to take as many products as necessary, and have scroll bars that take the viewer from page to page of products

Before we take a look at the FLAs, let's take a look at the storyboards I created for each screen. In the design and development process these are only meant to give a rough idea of what the final interface will look like, but they really do give us a great way of determining the positioning of the key elements.

This first storyboard is a sketch of the main screen:

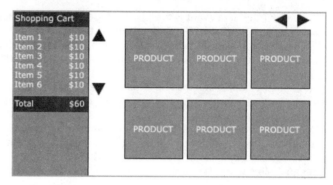

The main screen elements are:

1. The scrollable list of products on the right

2. The scrollable list of selected products and their prices, plus the total price, on the left side of the screen

And here's the second storyboard:

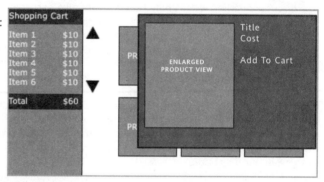

The key element here is the 'enlarged product view' on the right of the screen. This will be a separate movie clip that has a detailed picture of the product selected from the main screen (including its name and cost), and there's also a button that will add that product to the shopping cart.

The storyboards give us a good idea of the features we need to include, and how we can lay them out. They also help us visualize what Flash items need to be constructed in the FLA, and what the user will see when they are interacting with the interface.

Let's take this one step further and take a look at a flow chart that models how the user will progress through the front end:

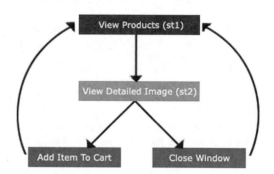

The first thing the viewer will see when they visit the site is the list of products (as shown in st1 - storyboard 1). Then, after a product is clicked, the viewer is taken to the detailed image screen (st2). Notice how the storyboards corresponding with the different nodes in the flow chart are cross-referenced with their identifiers – st1 and st2. This makes it easy to tie all the design charts and graphics together and organize your final application.

In the detailed view screen, the viewer is presented with two options – they can either add the item they are viewing to their cart, or they can close the window. Both options will take the viewer back to the list of products. This flow chart shows both round-trip paths the user can take through the front end.

See how the flow chart and storyboards make the application clear? Even with a small application like this, the flow chart and storyboards make planning the architecture of the front end much easier – this is one of the great strengths of visualization. The finished product will be much more stable after going through the rigorous planning stages before jumping into the code.

The FLA Architecture

Now that we've finished the planning stage, we're ready to take a look at the FLAs that make up the front end.

First, open up the main FLA for the shopping cart from the CD – it's called shoppingcart.fla. The other FLAs contain product images, and have just one frame each.

Let's take a look at the layer structure of the main timeline:

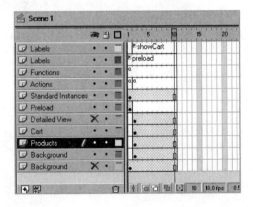

The movie is effectively broken up into two parts, as indicated by the two Labels layers at the top of the screenshot showCart and preload. There are two Labels layers because this allows the label names to be seen in their entirety.

I've followed my own advice and created a Functions layer and an Actions layer to hold functions and actions. The Standard Instances layer holds all the standard instances used in the movie, which in this case is only vars – the variable container.

The first frame of the movie (indicated by the start of the preload label) holds a Preloading data...please wait message, and there's a stop action in frame 1 of the Actions layer – this pauses the movie until all the variables have been loaded. The code to do this is inside the var instance, and it's based on the simple preloader example I described earlier.

When the variable data is all loaded, the movie moves on to the second frame. Frame 2, which corresponds to the start of the showCart label, is the main interface, showing the cart interface, products and scroll bars:

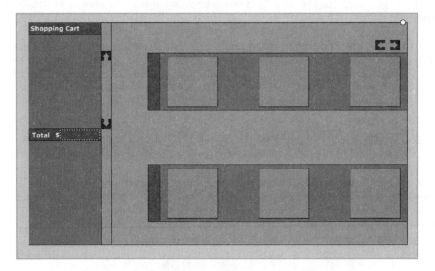

The Preload layer holds the message that tells the viewer that the variables are preloading. The Detailed View layer holds the detailed view screen with its individual product details. The layer visibility for Detailed View is set to false in this design view to make the interface elements underneath this layer easier to see and work with, but here's what the detailed view looks like in the FLA:

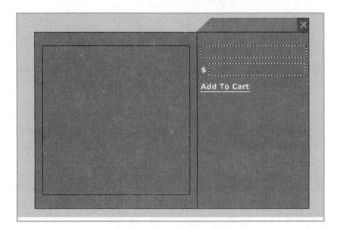

The Cart layer holds the shopping cart movie clip, while the Products layer holds the product placeholder movie clips – these get populated with actual images when the movie runs. There are two Background layers: the first holds the interface art while the second holds a square outline that encompasses the stage.

Before we dig down into the movie's code, let's examine that main screen in a little more detail – we've labeled some of the main points of interest:

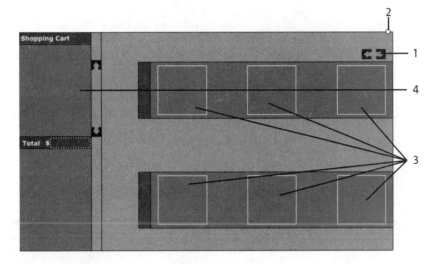

The key to the movie components labeled here is:

1. Scrollbars to scroll from page to page – instance names prev and next

2. Standard instance – instance name vars: this runs the preloader code and jumps us into the main screen when the variables are loaded

3. Product Placeholders – instance names product1 through product6

4. Cart – instance name cart

As we mentioned earlier, there's one other item on the main stage that's not visible in this screenshot – the detailed view screen, which we've kept invisible for reasons of clarity.

Since the detailed view screen is made up of quite a few important elements, let's take a look at it by itself:

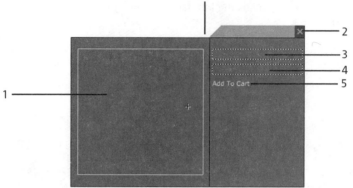

1. Product placeholder – instance name product

2. Close screen button

3. Text box to hold the item's name – variable name title

4. Text box to hold Item's cost– variable name cost

5. Add to cart button

6. Invisible button allowing screen to be dragged

Now let's take a look at the *cart* in detail. Remember, this is the area where the user's selected items will be listed:

It's easier to see how this is created if you open up the mc cart movie clip in the shoppingcart.fla file's library:

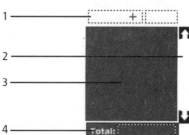

The cart item contains two textfields – labeled as 1 and 4 in this illustration. The area at the top (labeled 1) is composed of a separate movie clip called mc cart_items. This movie clip gets duplicated once for each item added to the cart. The scrollbars (2) work by moving the movie clip containing the cart items behind the mask (3).

The product placeholder movie clip – there are six of these arrayed across the main screen – is a key component as well, so let's examine it some more. In the Library, open up mc product_view – this is the symbol that all six placeholders are based on:

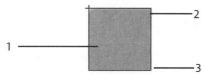

The components here are:

1. Invisible button. This allows viewers to click the product for a detailed view

2. Black outline. This is only for appearances

3. The movie clip the product image will be loaded into – instance name product1 – product6

The timeline of the mc product_view movie clip deserves a close-up look too:

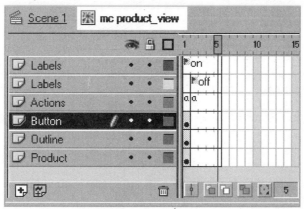

What's going on here? Well, the first frame of the movie clip contains the on state of the movie clip and the second frame the off state:

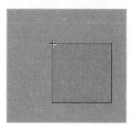

We need these two states in the movie clip because at times there won't be a product to display, and we don't want to leave the outline and the button when there is no product.

Looking at the items on the main stage, we can start to see how all the features we outlined in the very beginning will be implemented.

Standard Instances

This project utilizes one standard instance, vars. Located on the Standard Instances layer, you can find it at the top-right hand corner of the stage:

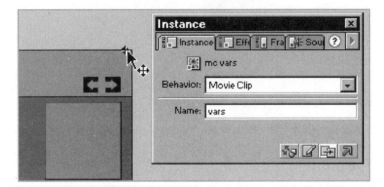

The vars instance serves as a container for the variables that the shopping cart pulls in from the text file (or server script, in the real world). This lets us access these variables from any other movie clip in the movie simply by using the same path reference syntax – _root.vars. This eliminates a lot of confusion and makes scripts easier to implement and understand. It also lessens the margin for error due to faultily-specified variable paths. Faulty variable paths are one of the most common causes of problems in more complex Flash movies, and we can save ourselves a lot of development time by limiting the chances of this happening.

The Text File Data

Open up cartParams.txt file from the CD in a text editor and you should see the following variables:

```
item1=Apple&cost1=10&url1=apple.swf&item2=Grapes&cost2=15&url2=grapes.swf&
item3=Pineapple&cost3=20&url3=pineapple.swf&item4=Coconut&cost4=25&url4=
coconut.swf&item5=Banana&cost5=30&url5=banana.swf&item6=Pears&cost6=35&url6
=pears.swf&item7=Fruit&cost7=50&url7=fruitbunch.swf&count=7
```

If we format that to make it 'human' - rather than 'Flash-readable', you can see things a little more clearly:

```
cartParams.txt - Notepad                        _ □ ×
File  Edit  Format  Help
item1=Apple&cost1=10&url1=apple.swf
&item2=Grapes&cost2=15&url2=grapes.swf
&item3=Pineapple&cost3=20&url3=pineapple.swf
&item4=Coconut&cost4=25&url4=coconut.swf
&item5=Banana&cost5=30&url5=banana.swf
&item6=Pears&cost6=35&url6=pears.swf
&item7=Fruit&cost7=50&url7=fruitbunch.swf
&count=7
```

Notice that there are seven main items – one for each type of fruit that we'll sell on our site. Each fruit has a series of three name/value pairs:

1. `item`/fruit name

2. `cost`/price of item

3. `url`/swf file name containing that item's image

Each parameter is also followed with the individual index number of the item – `item1`, `item2` etc. This allows us to reference each item and its parameters by the index number. It also allows us to loop easily through each item in the data file to create the display for the user. The `count` variable at the end tells us how many products are present in the file. As we discussed earlier, all name/value pairs are separated by ampersands.

Why the Movie's Built this Way

What we've done is create templates for each of the screens the viewer will see and interact with. In the main screen, the product placeholders serve as locations to display external SWF files containing product images. The 'detailed view' screen similarly has a placeholder for the enlarged image – and notice how the shopping cart uses the same image for the detailed view *and* the product view. The image added to the external SWF files is inserted at the size appropriate for the detailed view screen, but is scaled down in the main screen's product view when imported at runtime. This means we only need to use one picture for each product, but resize it depending on context.

The cart itself is fairly straightforward: every time the user chooses an item, a function called `addToCart` duplicates an mc cart_item movie clip, appending text fields for the chosen item's name and cost, and then positions it further down on the stage's cart area:

Shopping Cart	
Apple	$10
Grapes	$15
Pineapple	$20
Pineapple	$20
Banana	$30
Banana	$30
Total $ 125	

This happens behind a mask, so only six items will be viewable at once; this allows the scroll bars to be coded easily. The total price is also updated when an item is added to the cart.

The Code

It's the code that ties all of the different visual components together and transforms a nice-looking front end into a functional component of a web application. We'll walk through the code in detail so that you can see how the code acts as both 'glue' *and* 'communication system' in the application. If you have the FLA's Actions window open while you're reading this section, you'll be able to click backwards and forwards between components and start making the connections for yourself.

The bulk of the shopping cart's code is organized into five main functions – essentially, just reusable chunks of code – each of which takes care of a major feature in the cart.

Main Functions

These main functions can be found in the Functions layer on the main timeline: this allows us to reference each function with a path of `_root.functionName`. These functions contain the core functionality that make the shopping cart application work.

Let's take a look at the first function, which is called `initialize`. This function is run in frame 2 of the main movie's Actions layer:

```
//function to initialize the application
function initialize() {
    _root.cart.total = 0;
    _root.cart.noItems = 0;
    _root.pageNo = 1;
    _root.cart.minY = _root.cart.cartItems._y;
    _root.totalPages = Math.ceil (_root.vars.count / 6);
}
```

This function is pretty self-explanatory: it initializes the main variables used in the application. First it sets the `total` variable to `0` so that the running total in the cart shows $0 at the outset. The second line...

```
    _root.cart.noItems = 0;
```

...sets the `noItems` variable in the cart movie clip to `0`. This variable is used to keep a running total of the number of items added to the cart. This variable is also used in later functions, in the duplicate movie clip instance names process, and also to set the *depth* of each duplicated clip.

The `pageNo` variable...

```
    _root.pageNo = 1;
```

...keeps track of what *page* the viewer is on. Remember that there are only six placeholders on the main screen, but seven items of fruit in total. When the user presses the left/right scroll buttons on the main screen...

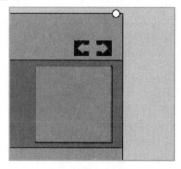

...the `pageNo` variable effectively toggles between values of 1 and 2.

The `minY` variable...

```
_root.cart.minY = _root.cart.cartItems._y;
```

...is used as a reference to scroll the cart items up and down. It's set – from the cart movie clip – to the Y position of the cartItems movie clip.

The final variable, `totalPages`...

```
_root.totalPages = Math.ceil (_root.vars.count / 6);
```

...is calculated by taking the `count` variable from the cartParams text file, dividing the value by six (which is the number of products viewable on a page) and rounding up the final value. This will allow us to expand the number of items we store in the text file without changing our movie code – this calculation will always give us the right number of pages to display the quantity of items we have in the text file.

The second function – `buildDetailedView` – is what gives the user the ability to look at a detailed view of the product. This function is called when the user presses the (invisible) button sitting behind any product image in the main screen:

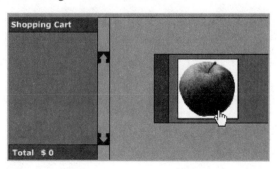

Let's walk through this function:

```
//function to build the detailed view when a user clicks on a
    //product.
function buildDetailedView (itemName, itemURL, itemCost) {
    loadMovie (itemURL, _root.detailedView.product);
    _root.detailedView.title = itemName;
    _root.detailedView.cost = itemCost;
    _root.detailedView._visible = 1;
}
```

When the user clicks on one of the products, the function is also passed a number of parameters:

```
function buildDetailedView (itemName, itemURL, itemCost) {
```

The values of these three parameters are determined from the specific product that's clicked on, and are generated by code inside the button: itemName is the name of the item the viewer has clicked on, and this will be displayed in the title text box on the detailed view screen; itemURL is the URL of the SWF file that needs to be loaded into the product placeholder; and itemCost is the cost of the product the viewer has chosen to see – this will be displayed in the cost text box in the detailed view screen.

The first line of code in the function...

```
loadMovie (itemURL, _root.detailedView.product);
```

...loads the external SWF containing the product image into the product placeholder movie clip, using the itemURL parameter. Next, the code sets the detailedView movie clip instance's title variable to the value of itemName parameter:

```
_root.detailedView.title = itemName;
```

After that, the code sets the cost text field to the value of the itemCost parameter and, lastly, the code sets the visible property of the detailedView movie clip to 1 (meaning visible):

```
_root.detailedView.cost = itemCost;
_root.detailedView._visible = 1;
```

The third function – buildProductView – is quite important, and a little more complex than the previous two functions. It takes care of building the list of products when the viewer either loads the front end or scrolls through different pages of products:

```
//function to build the view of the thumbnails of all the products.
function buildProductView () {
     var n = 1;
     for (i = _root.pageNo * 6 - 5; i <= _root.pageNo * 6; i++) {
          if (i <= _root.vars.count) {
               _root["product" + n].gotoAndStop ("on");
               _root["product" + n].itemNo = i;
                    loadMovie (eval("_root.vars.url" + i),
                    ➡ "_root.product" + n + ".product");
          } else {
               _root["product" + n].gotoAndStop ("off");
          }
          n++
     }
}
```

This function has several uses in the application. It builds the view the first time the viewer loads the movie, but it's also called each time the viewer clicks the forward or previous button to see different pages of products.

First, the code sets a local variable n to 1:

```
var n = 1;
```

This variable is used to reference each of the six product placeholder movie clips in a for loop. The for loop itself...

```
for (i = _root.pageNo * 6 - 5; i <= _root.pageNo * 6; i++) {
     if (i <= _root.vars.count) {
          _root["product" + n].gotoAndStop ("on");
          _root["product" + n].itemNo = i;
               loadMovie (eval("_root.vars.url" + i),
               ➡ "_root.product" + n + ".product");
     } else {
          _root["product" + n].gotoAndStop ("off");
     }
     n++
}
```

...perhaps looks a little confusing at first glance. Allow me to explain.

Since we need to refer to the different products based on the i variable, this variable needs to be initialized *based on the page number*. For example, if the viewer is on the first page, i will equal 1 through 6 as a result of the loop, but if the viewer is on the *second* page, i will equal 7 through 12. So this part of the code...

```
for (i = _root.pageNo * 6 - 5; i <= _root.pageNo * 6; i++)
```

...determines the number of times that the loop needs to run – once for each product.

After the `for` loop is initialized, the code checks to see if `i` is greater than the `count` variable in the `vars` instance:

```
if (i <= _root.vars.count) {
```

If it *isn't*, then we run the code throught the loop, and the code sends the product placeholder clip to the frame labeled on (in case it was on the off frame):

```
_root ["product" + n].gotoAndStop ("on");
```

Note that the value of `n` is concatenated with the "product" variable – this tells the code exactly which movie clip to operate on.

Next, we set the `itemNo` variable to equal the value of `i` in the product placeholder clip:

```
_root ["product" + n].itemNo = i;
```

This variable is referred to when the viewer clicks on the product to see the detailed view. The code then loads the SWF containing the product image into the product placeholder clip:

```
loadMovie (eval("_root.vars.url" + i), "_root.product" + n +
    ".product");
```

If `i` is more than the `count` variable, we know that there *isn't* a product image to display in that slot, so the code sends the product placeholder to the frame labeled off:

```
} else {
    _root ["product" + n].gotoAndStop ("off");
```

This removes from view the outline and the button the user can normally click on to see the detail view.

Finally, the loop code increments the n variable using the `++` operator, and the loop runs as many times as is appropriate. The `i` variable doesn't need to be incremented manually since we took care of that in the initialization of the `for` loop.

Phew.

The fourth function – `addToCart` – is pretty complex as well. It takes care of adding new items into the cart, and is triggered by the button on the detailed view screen:

Here's the code.

```
// function to update the cart when a user adds an item.
function addToCart (itemName, itemCost) {
    _root.cart.noItems++;
    duplicateMovieClip (cart.cartItems.item0,
    ➡ "item"+_root.cart.noItems, _root.cart.noItems);
    _root.cart.cartItems["item"+_root.cart.noItems]._y =
    ➡ _root.cart.cartItems["item"+(_root.cart.noItems-1)]._y+20;
    _root.cart.cartItems["item"+_root.cart.noItems].cost =
    ➡ "$"+itemCost;
    _root.cart.cartItems["item"+_root.cart.noItems].item = itemName;
    _root.cart.maxY = _root.cart.minY-(_root.cart.noItems*20)+120;
    if (_root.cart.noItems>6) {
        _root.cart.cartItems._y = _root.cart.maxY;
    }
    updateTotal(itemCost);
}
```

First, let's take a look at the parameters this function takes. itemName is the name of the item being added to the cart, and itemCost is its cost. Both of these are displayed in the text fields in the cart when the relevant movie clip is duplicated there:

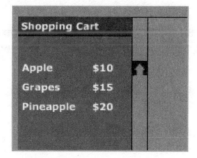

This parameter is also used in the call to the updateTotal function.

Now onto the body of the function itself. First, the noItems variable is incremented by 1 using the ++ operator:

```
_root.cart.noItems++;
```

This is so that the current number of items in the cart is accurately reflected.

Then a new movie clip is duplicated for the new item that was clicked on. The clip is duplicated from the master clip instance item0 – essentially two text fields – which you can find inside the mc cart_items clip:

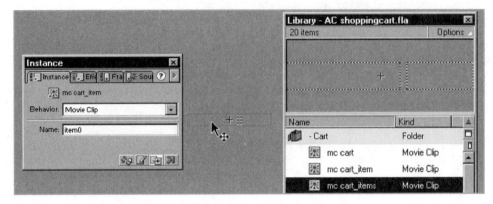

This serves as a starting point for positioning the duplicated clips. The new name is made up from the word *item* and the value of the noItems variable:

```
duplicateMovieClip (cart.cartItems.item0,
        ➥"item"+_root.cart.noItems, _root.cart.noItems);
```

The *depth* of the new movie clip is also set to the value of the noItems variable. The Y position of the newly duplicated movie clip is set to the value of the previously duplicated movie clip, plus 20:

```
_root.cart.cartItems["item"+_root.cart.noItems]._y =
    ➥_root.cart.cartItems["item"+(_root.cart.noItems-1)]._y+20;
```

The cost variable in the clip is set to the value of the parameter itemCost, appended to a dollar sign, and the item variable in the clip is set to the value of the itemName parameter:

```
_root.cart.cartItems["item"+_root.cart.noItems].cost ="$"+itemCost;
_root.cart.cartItems["item"+_root.cart.noItems].item = itemName;
```

The code next sets the variable maxY in the cart movie clip to equal the current number of items in the cart (noItems) multiplied by 20 (the space between duplicated clips) plus 120:

```
_root.cart.maxY = _root.cart.minY(_root.cart.noItems*20)+120;
```

The resulting variable is the *maximum* Y position the cartItems clip can reach before it can't scroll any further: maxY is referenced by the scrollbars when the user scrolls up and down.

After that, the code makes a check to see if the current number of items in the cart is higher than 6 (the maximum number of items that can be displayed at any one time). If it *is*, the code changes the Y position of the cartItems clip that contains all the duplicated clips to the value of maxY:

```
if (_root.cart.noItems>6) {
        _root.cart.cartItems._y = _root.cart.maxY;
```

This is used so that when the viewer already has more than six items and adds another item to the cart, the system automatically scrolls to the bottom the list of items, making it obvious to the user that the item was added successfully.

The last action this function performs is calling the separate updateTotal function:

```
updateTotal(itemCost);
}
```

This is how the total is updated with every call to the addToCart function.

The updateTotal function itself is quite simple:

```
//function to update the total in the cart.
function updateTotal (itemCost) {
    _root.cart.total += Number(itemCost);
}
```

This function takes one parameter – itemCost. This value of itemCost is added onto the current total, and the function is complete.

These are the main functions of the front end, but we still need to look at when and where they are called – there are small sprinklings of code in other places as well.

Scrollbar Code

First, let's take a look at the scrollbars for the items in the cart:

The scroll up button has the following code attached to it.

```
on (release) {
    if (cartItems._y < minY) {
            cartItems._y += 20;
    }
}
```

This code checks to see if the current Y position of the cartItems movie clip (the clip containing all the duplicated clips) is less than the minY variable that was set in the initialize function. If it *is*, then the Y position of cartItems is increased by twenty pixels.

The code for the scroll down button is quite similar:

```
on (release) {
    if (cartItems._y > maxY) {
        cartItems._y -= 20;
    }
}
```

This code checks to see if the Y position of the cartItems movie clip is greater than the maxY variable set in the addToCart function. If it is, then the Y position of cartItems is decreased by twenty pixels.

The horizontal scrollbars used to navigate from page to page of products use the same scrollbar button symbol, but the button is nested within a movie clip, which can be found in the library as mc page_scroll.

The actions in the button are as follows:

```
on (release) {
    _root.pageNo += dir;
    _root.buildProductView();
}
```

The actions for this button are designed this way so that we can use the same movie clip for both the previous and next buttons. The value of the variable dir is added onto the current value of pageNo, which holds the number of the page the viewer is currently looking at. The buildProductView function is then called to build the new page of products.

The actions for the previous button are:

```
onClipEvent (enterFrame) {
    if (_root.pageNo == 1) {
        this._visible = 0;
    } else {
        this._visible = 1;
    }
    dir = -1;
}
```

This movie clip uses the enterFrame handler to fire its actions. First, the movie clip checks to see if the current page number is 1 and, if it is, it changes its visible property to 0. If not, it changes the visible property to 1 in order to display the button. This makes the previous button disappear if the front end is displaying the first page of products, because a previous button wouldn't be necessary in that situation. The dir variable that's used in the button actions is then set to -1. To understand why this is, let's backtrack to the code used in the button within the movie clip, specifically the line _root.pageNo += dir. Since the value of dir is *added* to the value of pageNo whereas the previous button needs to *subtract*, we set the dir variable to -1 to subtract 1 instead of adding it, meaning that we can use the same movie clip symbol for both scroll buttons.

The actions for the next button are similar:

```
onClipEvent (enterFrame) {
    if (_root.pageNo == _root.totalPages) {
        this._visible = 0;
    } else {
        this._visible = 1;
    }
    dir = 1;
}
```

There's one major difference, however: instead of comparing the pageNo variable to 1, this compares it to the variable totalPages, which is set within the initialize function. By doing this, the button is hidden when the page being displayed is the *last* page that exists. Then the dir variable is set to a value of 1 to increment the value of pageNo by one when the button is clicked.

Preloader Code

This is the code that preloads the variables into the vars movie clip. Firstly, remember that the architecture of the movie is set up with two crucial frames in the main timeline, the first labeled preload and the second showCart. In the Actions frame for the preload frame, there's a stop action, which pause the movie until all the variables have loaded.

The following actions are attached to the vars movie clip.

```
onClipEvent (load) {
    loadVariables ("cartParams.txt", this);
}

onClipEvent (data) {
    _root.gotoAndStop ("showCart");
}
```

The load clip event loads the content of the cartParams.txt text file into the vars (this) movie clip. Then the data clip event detects when the last variable has been loaded into the movie clip and sends the main timeline to the showCart frame when it's detected – very similar to the example we discussed earlier in the chapter.

The actions in the Actions layer of the showCart frame call a couple of functions.

```
initialize();
buildProductView();
stop();
```

The initialize function is called to set the main variables used by the rest of the functions, and then the buildProductView function is called to build the first page of products.

The last piece of code I want to mention is attached to the detailedView movie clip instance:

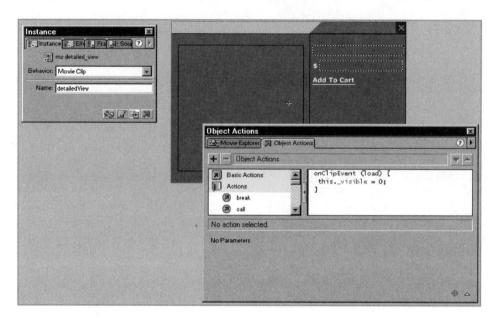

```
onClipEvent (load) {
    this._visible = 0;
}
```

This sets the visible property of the detailed view screen to false (0) when the interface first loads, ensuring that the user gets a nice clean view of the main screen.

OK, that's all the code I think we need to discuss here. I appreciate that there was a lot to take in, but you can now use the FLA as an experimental area where you can explore the way I built this code, and try out a few things of your own.

"I Love It when a Plan Comes Together"

Structurally, this Flash shopping cart comes together pretty easily, since most of the code is organized into main functions. Projects built in this fashion are much easier to edit, and upgrade, since all the main code is organized in one frame on the Functions layer.

Using storyboards and flow charts, it's clear how all the features will be implemented. Planning the project out thoroughly helps your chances of executing the features in a clear, concise manner, and the code is more modular. I can't emphasize enough the importance of meticulous planning when executing a front end.

Troubleshooting Techniques

When building dynamic front ends, things rarely work the first time around – and I speak from painful experience! Remember to enable debugging when you export your movie. You can always turn this option *off* before exporting a final version of the movie and it can really help. To turn on debugging open your FLA file and go to File > Export Movie. Select the folder you want to save the movie to, then select the Debugging Permitted option and enter your debugging password. The export dialog should look like this when you're finished:

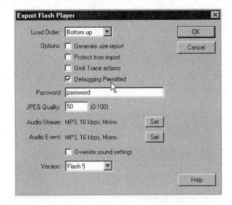

You'll also need to enable remote debugging from the debugger itself. To do this, go to Window > Debugger, and select Enable Remote Debugging as shown here:

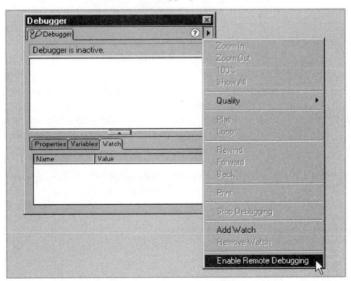

Note that you may need to experiment with the debugger a little: this feature can be a little... temperamental.

When you play your movie in the browser, as you will generally have to when testing dynamic content, you should be able to right-click (or CONTROL-click on the Mac) on the movie, and select Debugger. This will show you the timelines present in the movie, and the variables and properties belonging to the timelines. This is one reason why it's important to name *all* the movie clip instances on the stage even when they're not targeted – it makes them easier to locate in the debugger.

> *You can change all the variables and properties that can be set this way, and the changes are updated in the browser. This makes it easy to see what will happen when variables have different values, or properties are changed.*

The Watch tab is another handy tool. This allows you to...well, 'watch' variables that you want to keep an eye on as the movie runs. To add a new watch, right-click/control-click in the content portion of the Watch tab, and select Add:

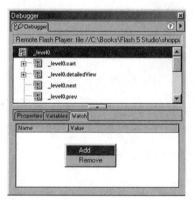

Type the name of your variable in the Name section and the variable's current setting will be shown in the Value section. You don't need to input a path to the variable – just select the timeline that your variable is on and type the name. If you want to *remove* a watched variable, just right-click or CONTROL-click on the variable you want to remove and select Remove from the context menu.

It's very important to test your back end scripts thoroughly before testing them within Flash. Development time can escalate very quickly when working with a buggy back end. Before you test a server call inside Flash, test it 'raw' through a browser to ensure that the script itself isn't causing an error. When you do this, it eliminates the possibility of searching for an error inside the Flash movie, when the problem *really* lies in the back end.

Conclusion

When approaching a project that includes dynamic content, it's important to keep things in perspective. All you're really doing is loading variables from a text field into your movies. These variables just happen to be dynamic.

Building Flash front ends can be very satisfying since the technology is so new. Amazing applications can be created by taking advantage of the power of dynamic content coupled with Flash's excellent vector graphics, animation capabilities, and – of course – the unifying power and flexibility of ActionScript. As long as you remember to include a rigorous planning stage to cut down on the problems that can arise when there are so many facets to a project, you can start to create some fantastic web applications. The world is waiting – what are *you* waiting for?

The next two chapters in this book introduce you to using a couple of important dynamic content tools with Flash – PHP and XML.

18
Dynamic Web Applications

Section 4
Dynamic Content

17
Dynamic Content from Text Files

20
Flash and XML

Chapter 19
Flash and PHP

PHP (which, for reasons that are unlikely to be immediately apparent, is an abbreviation of **Hypertext Preprocessor**) is a tool and a language for writing dynamically generated web pages. In this respect, it's not that dissimilar to Microsoft's ASP, which we've encountered elsewhere in this book. There are two important differences, though. First, PHP works on *all* the major hardware platforms: Windows, Macintosh, and UNIX, whereas ASP is Windows only. Second, PHP is open source software, which means that you can download and use it free of charge – an attractive proposition at the best of times! PHP has a massive installed user base and has proved a highly popular tool for people building sites with dynamic content, and PHP can be quite easily integrated with Flash to provide your Flash movies with that all-important dynamic, interactive content element.

In this chapter, we're going to look at how PHP can be used in the design and creation of dynamic Flash movies – that is, movies that can 'customize' themselves according to the prevailing conditions. We'll see how to use Flash and PHP together, explore some techniques for developing web sites using this combination, and go over some ideas for what's possible using these technologies in tandem. By the end, you should have a good idea of the role PHP could play in your movies, and be ready to learn more about this exciting technology.

Principles of using PHP with Flash

The PHP scripting language has come a long way since its birth in 1994. Although it's now recognized as a powerful web scripting language, it was originally intended only for the needs of its original author, Rasmus Lerdorf. At that time, PHP was used for simple HTML content creation, with a few macros that helped the user to create utilities like page counters and web guest books. As the years have passed, the community of open source code developers has contributed an enormous number of new features to the PHP scripting language engine, and the success has been amazing: rough estimates suggest that more than 1,000,000 sites around the world are using PHP. (Oh, and by the way, the name PHP is a hangover from the early days when the language was called *Personal Home Pages*.)

In order to create Flash sites and applications that are able to communicate with their surroundings, an understanding of some core theory is necessary. The next part of this chapter will describe how Flash communicates with the other building blocks in the world of the web application: PHP, web server, databases and the end user. We'll also examine the whole concept of creating dynamic Flash with PHP.

The first thing to grasp is how the browser running in your (client) desktop interacts with the remote server that's hosting a web site and providing it with content and services.

Client-to-Web Server Connections

The simplified diagram on the following page shows how web servers handle client connections and send responses that involve 'traditional' web content (that is, HTML), or other text resources, over an HTTP session:

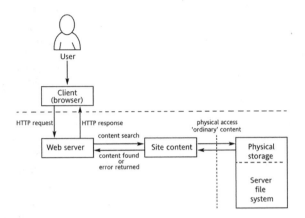

The connection between the browser and the web server is first triggered by the user requesting a piece of information on a web site. The browser generates a HTTP request that's sent to the destination web server along with any other required information about the requested resource. When the web server receives the request, it checks whether the request is valid. If everything is fine at this stage, the server returns the requested resource to the client, with a short HTTP status code. Should something fail during the processing of a resource request, a HTTP error status code is generated and sent back to the client browser.

Now let's look at how PHP is added to the mix.

The PHP CGI Executable

When it comes to requests for PHP scripts on the web server, the relatively simple diagram above becomes a little more complicated. Such requests are directed to the **PHP CGI** (Common Gateway Interface) executable. This is the part of the system that handles the processing of the *scripts* written using the PHP language. It's in these scripts that the intelligence to filter and manipulate data and variables resides. The PHP CGI component takes the necessary action in running the script and handling any data and file requests that the script invokes:

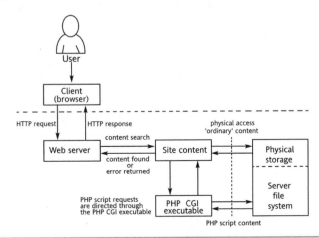

The web server directs the *output* of the PHP CGI executable – the data that was requested by the client, and which has been generated and processed by the PHP script – back to the client that originally requested the actual PHP script file. In this way, the client side sees only the *result* of the executed script, and not the script file itself. The advantages of this kind of *server-side* environment are manifold, compared to *client-side* task execution. The server-side processing is not limited to the environment and software of the end client, making it possible to carry out complex database operations, for instance. Additionally, the whole implementation of the process can be hidden and secured.

The PHP CGI executable works as a script language **parser**. The parser reads through the script, line by line, and carries out different functions as necessary. There's a huge collection of useful function groups in PHP, each concentrating on different areas of functionality. In this chapter, we'll just be zooming in on basic programming for PHP.

So where does Flash fit in this model?

Communication Between Flash and PHP

While PHP can be used as a tool for creating dynamic web sites on its own, here we're obviously more interested in the possibilities it can bring us when it's combined with Flash.

Essentially, what we're doing when we integrate a Flash movie with a server-side scripting tool like PHP is this: when we create our movie in the FLA, we define some variable names in ActionScript, which we associate with – say – a series of dynamic text boxes:

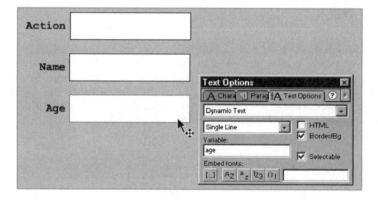

Then we code some ActionScript that calls a PHP script on the server, which dynamically returns a series of variable values. Flash then uses those variables to populate the text boxes, on the fly, inside the movie that's displayed in the user's browser. So, for example, we could use ActionScript to call a PHP script on the server that performed a search on a database, and then populated a whole series of text boxes inside the movie based on the results that the script returned to Flash.

With this step, our diagram representing the interaction between client and server becomes more complex still:

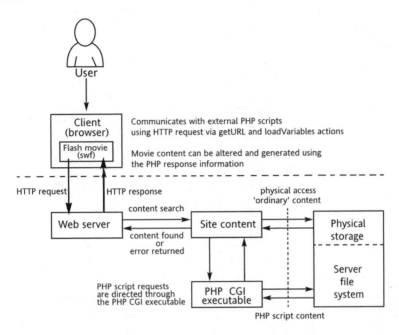

As you can see, it's now the Flash movie, rather than the browser, that triggers all the necessary HTTP requests to the web server. This means that the Flash movie can be quite easily influenced and modified using information gathered from the output of PHP scripts.

Since the browser and the Flash movie only receive the *results* of the PHP scripts that are executed on the server, it's essential that the PHP scripts produce their output in a form that's acceptable for the Flash movie to read. Essentially, this means that the output is a stream of name/value pairs, with each new variable name (after the first one) identified with an ampersand:

```
action=register&name=John+Smith&age=25
```

So in this data stream, we have three variable names and values:

Variable Name	Value
action	register
name	John+Smith
age	25

Does that data stream look familiar? It might well do if you've done some web development: the format of the variable strings to be used by Flash is the same as the URL-encoded HTTP request parameter strings, with a couple of exceptions. Flash variable parameters should be URL form encoded too, but it seems that spaces can be used as normal characters. All the variable parameters have to be separated with &, but the first parameter is not supposed to be preceded by anything. Let's say that you have a ready-made Flash movie with only three dynamic text fields named Action, Name and Age. Now, if the above variable string were taken into the Flash movie as input, it would change the contents of those three text fields to contain the variable values register, John Smith and 25:

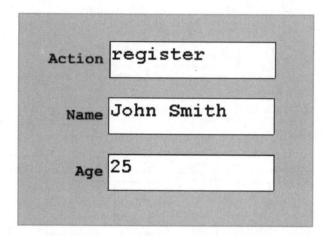

So how do we trigger a PHP script to run and return us some variable values? The key engines for us here are the loadVariables and getURL actions. If you haven't used the loadVariables or getURL functions of Flash 5 ActionScript before, it's time to learn!

When they're called as part of your ActionScript code, both of these actions generate an HTTP request and pass the identities of the variables defined in the current movie to the URL that's named in the ActionScript. In our examples, of course, that URL destination will host the PHP script that will perform our processing. The identities of the variables in the movie are used to match against variable names defined in the receiving PHP script. The getURL function will not wait for any response variables, but jumps directly to the URL specified. The loadVariables function, on the other hand, will wait, and feed the variables from the HTTP response stream (generated by the PHP script) into the movie that invoked the script call.

For example, the following piece of ActionScript uses the getURL action to load the content in the variable myURL to a blank browser window:

```
on(release) {
    getURL(myURL, "_blank");
}
```

Meanwhile, this next script inputs the variables produced by a PHP script called content.php, housed on the web server, into the current movie:

```
on(release) {
    loadVariables("www.mysite.com/content.php", 0);
}
```

This next schematic summarizes the process of sending and receiving variables via this route:

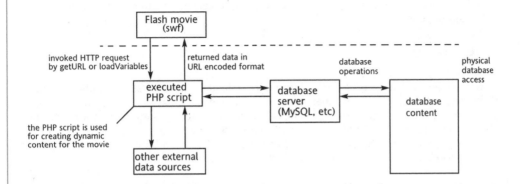

The database and the other data sources in this figure are completely optional. Sometimes, it's better to keep the script side as light as possible (by using text files as your data source input, for example) to ensure maximum efficiency for the running Flash movie – you don't want the movie to 'freeze' in your users' browsers while it's waiting for some data to be generated by a PHP script.

There's an important issue with the loadVariables function that can sometimes make life a little difficult. When the action is called, the Flash movie will not automatically wait for the group of variables to get loaded into the movie from the external source before continuing – instead, the default behavior is for the movie to keep on playing frame by frame, and it can be very hard to predict when the variable values have been safely loaded in their entirety. If this behavior is not handled correctly, problems are likely to arise. If you're using Flash 5, this problem is quite easy to get around: Flash 5 ActionScript contains the OnClipEvent(data) event, which is triggered when the last variable of the external variable stream has been loaded into the Flash movie. Flash 4 *doesn't* have this helpful event, so some other way of getting around the problem must be found. Luckily, it's quite easy to implement a solution to this by waiting for an extra 'check' variable to be read from the variable stream:

```
action=register&name=John+Smith&age=25&foo=ok
```

If Flash 4 is the target version for your movies, the extra foo variable should always be the last one to be output in your PHP scripts. You'll also need to add a checking loop that'll keep looping until the foo variable has been received, indicating that all the script-generated data is now present. If, for instance, the first frame of the movie uses the loadVariables action to start loading the group of variables from a PHP script, the *third* frame of the movie should have the following ActionScript check:

```
if (foo eq "") {
    gotoAndPlay (2);
}
```

It's that easy! After the looping between the second and third frame is over, you can be sure that all of the passed variables have been loaded into the Flash movie successfully, even if there were a lot of variables to load.

OK, that completes our initial tour of how Flash and PHP integrate in theory. Later in the chapter we'll work through some detailed examples to really drive home the practical side of working with Flash and PHP, but let's pause now and look at the supporting platforms that you need to run and test this kind of code.

Tools of the Trade

You may have heard that open source tools are unreliable, difficult to install, and difficult to use. That was arguably true once, but times have changed, and the creators of these utilities have responded to the needs of their ever-growing user base by improving both the performance and the user-friendliness of their products. As you'll see shortly, the tools we're going to use in this chapter are quite easy to acquire, install and configure, and you can be up and running with a PHP-enabled web server much more quickly than you might think.

Now, it may be that you're working in an environment in which there's *already* a web server equipped with support for PHP – you'll need to ask your system administrator if you're not sure – in which case you're free to go straight from here to the section headed *Your First PHP Page*. You might want to stick around, though, because between now and then I'll be explaining how to set up your own machine for developing and testing PHP code. Along the way, we'll also talk a little about the nature of PHP.

Our goal is to establish a development environment without requiring in-depth knowledge about how to configure it, and the two pieces of this solution will be PHP itself and the web server it will run on. Now, it's worth mentioning that unlike ASP, which only runs on Microsoft web servers, PHP places no constraint our choice in this respect. Among others, PHP works happily with Microsoft's Personal Web Server and Internet Information Server (IIS), and with Xitami server software. In this chapter, though, we'll be using it in conjunction with the web server it most frequently accompanies: **Apache**. Don't worry though – the principles covered here are equally applicable to other platforms, and the code has been tested on IIS, too.

> *Both Apache and PHP are included on this book's CD.*

> *If you want to use PHP with a web server other than Apache, you'll find that the instructions on the PHP web site (www.php.net) are clear and concise, and you should have little difficulty in 'going it alone'. Once you've got PHP up and running, you'll be able to follow the examples with no need for changes.*

The Apache Web Server

The Apache web server is freely available from the Apache Software Foundation's web site at www.apache.org. Since it's an open source product, it may not come as much of a surprise to you that a lot of what's available behind the Download link is pure source code. However, if you find your way to the binaries folder, you'll find precompiled versions of Apache for Windows, OS/2, and most flavors of UNIX (including Linux). You can also get a compiled Apache for Mac OS X, but this is the first release of Apple's operating system for which it's been made available. For our examples here, we'll use the Windows version.

Installation of the Windows version of Apache is pretty straightforward, as the distributions on the web site are almost completely self-configuring. You just need to download the latest version from the win32 folder and execute it – there's just one file that covers all versions of Windows. Accept all of the default options, and when installation finishes you should find a new item in your Start menu:

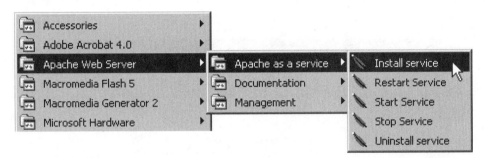

As the screenshot suggests, choose the Install service option and then restart your machine. This should ensure that when Windows returns Apache is running in the background, ready to serve web pages. To test this, open your web browser and navigate to http://127.0.0.1, where you ought to see something like this:

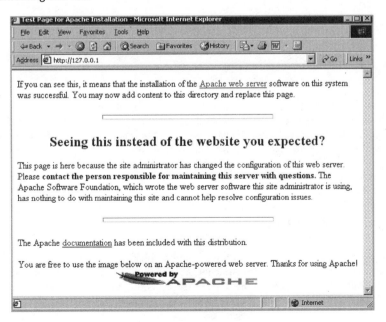

Congratulations! You now have a successfully installed Apache web server, and we're ready to move on to adding PHP functionality to it.

> *In case you're wondering,* 127.0.0.1 *is called the loopback address. When you type this into a web browser, it doesn't go out onto the Internet to search for a page. Instead, it looks for a web server on the local machine – and now that we have Apache installed, it finds one.*

If you're using IIS to work through this chapter, you need to ensure that you've started Personal Web Manager:

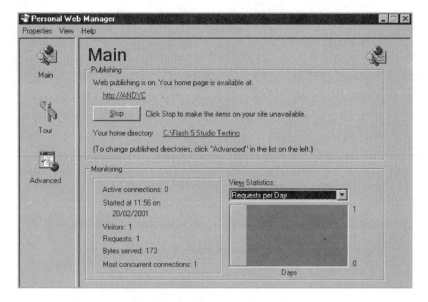

In this screenshot, you can see that my test machine is accessible by typing http://andyc into the URL box on a browser, and that any files that I want to display on the site will be placed inside the C:\Flash 5 Studio Testing folder. We can't cover all the setup procedures for IIS here, but you should be able to get the help you need from your system administrator or online from Microsoft.

Assuming that you've got a web server set up, let's move along and look at the mighty beast of burden that is PHP.

PHP4: The Hypertext Preprocessor

PHP's home page is to be found at www.php.net, and a quick visit to the downloads page reveals a situation similar to the one we had for Apache. Most of the products available to you are source code packages, but there are precompiled versions for Windows. Ever in search of an easy life, we'll be using the latter for our first foray into writing PHP code.

As is so often the case with open source software development, new versions of the PHP software are released weekly, and sometimes even daily. Because we'll really only be scratching the surface in this chapter, it's not hugely important that you have the very latest version, but there's no harm in getting the most recent one you can find. At the time of writing, the version number was 4.0.4pl1, but the only thing you really need to ensure is that you get the one that specifies Apache support (it will be around 3Mb in size). Clearly, if you're running IIS you'll need to download the appropriate version for that platform.

Once you have the PHP ZIP file, you should extract its contents to a folder called PHP on your C: drive. The file that's now located at C:\PHP\install.txt contains the instructions you need to effect the remainder of the installation procedure, but for the sake of clarity, I'll reproduce them here. It's a little trickier than installing Apache, but nowhere near as bad as you might have been expecting!

> *If you're running IIS, you should find that the installation program does all the work for you, and that once you've run it you should be ready to rumble.*

First of all, you need to move the file at c:\PHP\php4ts.dll to c:\Windows\System or c:\WINNT\System32, depending on whether you have a Windows 9x- or NT-based operating system. Then, go to the Start menu and choose Programs > Apache Web Server > Management > Edit configuration. This will result in the opening of a Notepad window containing a text file called httpd.conf; this is Apache's configuration file, and we need to make some changes to it.

There are five lines to add to this file, in four separate locations. The settings appear in groups, so you can find out where to add the following lines simply by searching for the first word in each line. (I'll also provide some context here, so that you can check you're on the right road.) Here's the first:

```
#LoadModule status_module modules/ApacheModuleStatus.dll
#LoadModule usertrack_module modules/ApacheModuleUserTrack.dll
LoadModule php4_module c:/php/sapi/php4apache.dll
```

And the second:

```
ScriptAlias /cgi-bin/ "C:/Program Files/Apache
Group/Apache/cgi-bin/"
ScriptAlias /php4/ "C:/php/"
```

And the third and fourth:

```
AddType application/x-tar .tgz
AddType application/x-httpd-php .php4
AddType application/x-httpd-php4 .php
```

And the fifth:

```
# Format: Action media/type /cgi-script/location
# Format: Action handler-name /cgi-script/location
#
Action application/x-httpd-php4 "/php4/php.exe"
```

Close the Notepad window (making sure to save the file as you do so), and we're almost there. The final action is to copy `C:\PHP\php.ini-dist` into your `Windows` (or `WINNT`) folder, rename it to simply `php.ini`, and restart your computer again, for luck. Then cross your fingers...

Your First PHP Page

To test that our Apache/PHP configuration is in order (you can also test this on your IIS setup if you wish), create a file called `test.php` and edit it to contain the following three lines:

```
<?php
        echo "Trying out some <B>PHP</B> content...";
?>
```

This simple code has two 'outer' elements that define this as a PHP script. These are the tags that contain the two question marks:

```
<?php
        ...
?>
```

These tags tell the server that anything found between these two tags is a PHP script, and should be run using the PHP CGI executable. The server configuration will define where the executable is and route any relevant script content to it.

Now for the actual *content* of the script. In this example we just have a single line of script between the PHP script delimiters, which just tells the server to send a stream of text and HTML tags back to the browser that invoked the script. This uses the PHP `echo` command, which essentially says 'invoking browser, please display the stuff that follows'. The text that's enclosed in the quote marks will be displayed as typed, with the HTML 'bold' tag emphasizing the PHP acronym. Finally, there's a semicolon, which is PHP's character for terminating a discrete chunk of script.

Place this simple PHP script in the `htdocs` folder under your Apache installation – if you used the default settings, this will be `C:\Program Files\Apache Group\Apache\htdocs`. (Unprompted, this folder is where Apache will always start looking for content.) Then, type http://127.0.0.1/test.php into your web browser, and if everything has gone to plan, this is what you should see:

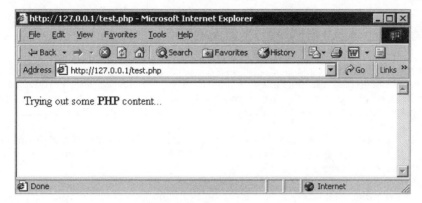

Voila – you're doing client-server, script-based dynamic content.

To test your basic configuration in IIS, save the `test.php` file into your web server's default folder – `Flash 5 Studio Testing` in my case – and then point your browser at it using the web server/file name combination. Like this:

PHP4 Documentation

To obtain the complete documentation for PHP, go to the documentation section of the PHP web site and download one of the numerous versions that are available. The frequently updated manual is very clearly structured, and it contains information that's essential to any PHP developer. Almost all aspects of PHP are explained, with good written examples that can easily be used to explore the possibilities of the features in PHP.

OK, we now have the server groundwork done, and we can move on to looking at how the PHP platform can make your Flash movies more powerful.

What you can do with PHP and Flash

With a little imagination and planning, PHP-driven Flash movies offer all manner of opportunities. However, to understand the principles of the advanced features we'll be introducing in this chapter, it's best first to examine PHP-powered Flash applications at a more general level. The tasks that PHP scripting can perform divide broadly into the three following categories:

- **Processing data** the user has entered over the course of a movie, and possibly *storing* the data. The information can be checked for validity, and the script can respond to the Flash movie accordingly.

- **Creating completely new data** using PHP functionality and passing it forward to a Flash movie. In common with other structured programming languages, PHP includes a large collection of algorithms and functions. It's easy to use PHP functions to create complex data sets (such as data trees) that can be used in conjunction with Flash movies.

- **Working as a bridge** between the Flash movie and some external data source or store. This includes server-side file systems, databases, external HTTP connectivity, e-mail, and other data access media.

A single PHP script can be a tailored mixture of any of these three categories. When you're dealing with a higher-end web application, you'll often find that the integral data handling features of Flash are just not powerful enough to carry out all the operations you need, especially if there's a large amount of data to be processed and responded to. When there's a lot of data, use a database: PHP has extensive support for all the popular ones, although sadly we don't have space here to deal with database usage in detail.

The more you learn about the features of PHP, the easier it will be to navigate the best route through problems and complex tasks. Try to keep your Flash movies and your PHP script code as modular as possible – it will pay off when you're planning or expanding the features of the application in the future. These principles will become clearer when you take a look at the example applications later on.

PHP Performance Issues

It's advisable to keep the execution time of individual scripts relatively short. On the whole, PHP code is quite fast to execute, especially if it's been optimized for best performance. The length of a script – in terms of the amount of code it contains – doesn't matter, but the execution time *does*. If the script can be logically 'sliced' into smaller pieces, it usually makes sense to do that to help ensure that the calling Flash movie doesn't suffer from long PHP execution timeouts.

> *The execution speed of PHP scripts can be greatly improved by optimizing them using the Zend optimizer. This tool has been developed for use only with PHP version 4 or higher, and it will not work with earlier versions. Take a look at* http://www.zend.com *for more information.*

Next, let's get our hands dirty and examine in more practical detail just how Flash and PHP interact at the level of exchanging information. We'll do that by working through a practical example that will pass information from the Flash front end, process it in a PHP script, and save the data in a text file that lives on the server.

Flash and PHP in Action

This simple example application is a PHP-powered Flash movie that gathers site visitors' names and e-mail addresses before writing them into a single server-side text file:

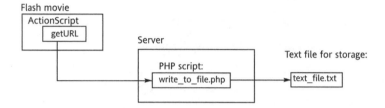

We're going to work through this in full-on detail, as it establishes the core practicalities of integrating Flash with PHP.

Writing Text into a Server-side File

The user interface of this small application is about as simple as it could be:

> Please enter your name: [   ]
>
> And e-mail address: [   ]
>
> Submit

Let's build it.

1. Open a new movie and set the stage dimensions to something suitable for a simple user input interface – ours is 300 by 150 pixels.

2. Now add two static text fields to act as labels for the input boxes:

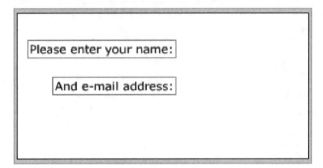

Next, we need two input text boxes for the user's input.

3. Add your two input text boxes, giving the top one a variable name of n, the bottom one a variable name of e, and giving them Max Chars values of 20 and 30 respectively. Ensure that you check the Border/Bg box too, so that the input box will be visible on the interface:

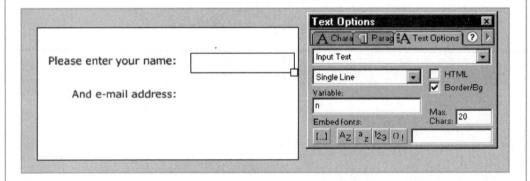

We've established the input environment for the user. The next step is to provide the movie with the ability to process that input by calling a PHP script on the server. We'll add that functionality to a Submit button that has some ActionScript attached.

4. Create yourself a submit button symbol of choice, and give it a suitable Hit state.

5. So that the content is always visible, add a `stop` action in the movie's single frame.

   You now have the front end elements built...

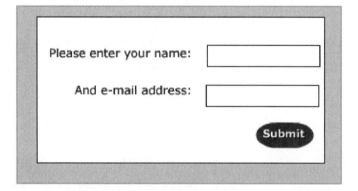

...so let's add the ActionScript that'll bring the movie to life.

The movie's real functionality is all located in the Submit button, but even this is quite straightforward. The ActionScript required for calling the external PHP module and passing the n and e variables (along with their typed values) is based on the `getURL` action.

6. Select the button on the stage and add this code in the Object Actions window:

```
on (release) {
    getURL ("write_to_file.php", "_self", "POST");
}
```

Here, the `getURL` function is being used to pass the variables of the movie to a PHP script called `write_to_file.php`.

Here, then, the three parameters taken by the getURL action are:

- "write_to_file.php" – this, as we've just said, is the name of the PHP script that we want to process the data that we're going to send to the server. The way that we've specified it here, just using the name of the script, tells Flash (and the server) that they should expect to find the PHP script in the same folder as the movie (SWF file) that's calling the script.

- "_self" – this parameter instructs Flash where to send the values returned from the PHP script. In this instance, we're effectively telling Flash that we want the values to be routed back to the calling HTML window.

- "POST" – this specifies the method that'll be used to transfer the variables between the browser and the server. The choice you make here between GET and POST will determine whether the variables are sent as part of the URL name, or as a discrete chunk in the data that streams between the browser and the server. It's particularly recommended that you use the POST method when you're passing large numbers of variables back and forth. Our preference is for using the POST method as a default, which is why we've chosen it here.

Once this ActionScript is run when the user clicks on the Submit button, the call is made to the server and the focus of execution passes to the PHP code (which, incidentally, can direct the user to some other Flash movie resource if you choose to do so). Note also that because we used _self as the target parameter in the getURL call, the Flash movie will be terminated in the browser window and replaced by whatever output the PHP generates. As an alternative, we could have specified _blank as the target parameter, which would display any output from the PHP script in a new browser window, leaving the calling movie running. Another option if we want the Flash movie to continue playing after sending the information to the PHP script is to use the loadVariables action instead.

> *In a real world application, you'd probably want to add some checking code to the button to ensure that both of the fields on the screen had been filled in by the user, but we'll omit that code here for the sake of clarity and simplicity.*

Let's build the PHP script file that the ActionScript calls – write_to_file.php.

7. Create a new text file, add the following PHP code to it, and save the file as write_to_file.php:

```php
<?php

$f=fopen("text_file.txt","a");

fwrite($f,"****************************************\r\n\r\n");
fwrite($f,"  Name:\t\t\t$n\r\n");
fwrite($f,"  E-Mail:\t\t$e\r\n\r\n");

fclose($f);

echo "<BR><BR><B>Submit successful!</B>";

?>
```

Don't worry about the syntax for now – we'll explain all that in a moment.

8. Publish your movie, and then place the HTML file, the SWF, and the PHP script file in the default web folder that you set up as your host – remember that mine was called Flash 5 Studio Testing, and that on the default Apache installation these files would go into C:\Program Files\Apache Group\Apache\htdocs.

9. In your browser, type in the URL for the HTML page that's hosting the SWF and enter your details into the boxes before hitting that Submit button:

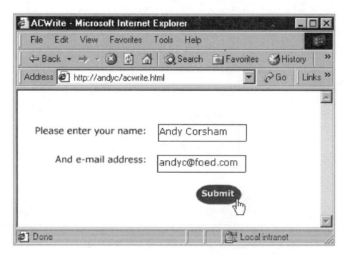

If everything works as advertised, you'll see this message pop up in your browser:

10. Now go back and have a look at your host web folder. You should see a new file there called `text_file.txt`:

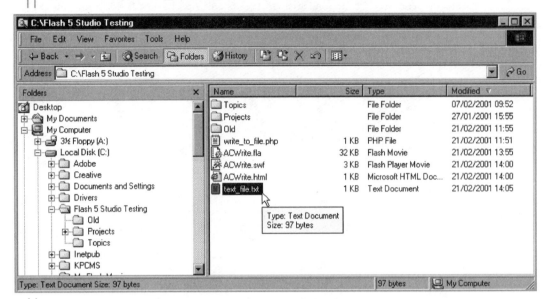

11. Double-click on that file and you'll see the fruits of PHP's (and your) labors:

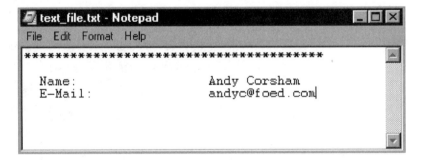

You can see here that the PHP script really has done its work, by transferring the information we keyed into Flash across into a text file on the server. Now we'll explain exactly how it all happened...

OK, Flash has issued the getURL command and POSTed the user's keyed variables to the server. On arrival, the PHP script is invoked and passed the variable names we defined for the input text boxes (n and e), plus the values that the user has keyed in and submitted – in this case, Andy Corsham for n, with andyc@foed.com for e. Fully equipped with this quota of variables, PHP can now process the information using the write_to_file.php script.

Here's a reminder of that script in full:

```php
<?php

$f=fopen("text_file.txt","a");

fwrite($f,"****************************************\r\n\r\n");
fwrite($f," Name:\t\t\t$n\r\n");
fwrite($f," E-Mail:\t\t$e\r\n\r\n");

fclose($f);

echo "<BR><BR><B>Submit successful!</B>";

?>
```

Like all PHP code, the code block starts with an opening tag that identifies it as a chunk of PHP script:

```php
<?php
```

The first substantive piece of code in the script opens up the text file on the server so that we can store the variables sent from Flash:

```php
$f=fopen("text_file.txt","a");
```

Here, $f is a variable name that we're going to use as a shorthand reference to the full file name – this reference is also known as a **file handle**. All variables in PHP are identified by prefixing them with a $ (dollar) sign. The value of the $f variable is assigned by invoking PHP's fopen function and passing it a couple of parameters. The fopen function will open up the file named in the first parameter inside the parentheses – "text_file.txt". If PHP can't find that named file, it will create one for us with that name. The second parameter – in this case, "a" – defines the mode (read, write, or append) in which the file will be opened. Here, we'll always open the file in 'append' mode so that each pair of values submitted will be added onto the *end* of the text file.

Now that we've opened up the text file on the server, it's time to store our Flash-derived values in it. The key player here is PHP's fwrite function:

```php
fwrite($f,"****************************************\r\n\r\n");
fwrite($f," Name:\t\t\t$n\r\n");
fwrite($f," E-Mail:\t\t$e\r\n\r\n");
```

fwrite's purpose in life is to write data to files – precisely what we want to do here. We need to supply this function with two parameters: the file handle that identifies the target file; and the string of information that we want written into the file.

The first line...

```
fwrite($f,"****************************************\r\n\r\n");
```

...calls the `fwrite` function and uses the `$f` file handle (reference) to point the `fwrite` function at our text file. Next, inside the quotation marks, we tell `fwrite` what we actually want it to write. In this case, we're writing a string of asterisks, followed by some return characters (`\r`) and line feeds (`\n`). The effect of this is to create a 'separator' line and some space in the text file, which will clearly delineate each separate pair of variable values that we want to store:

The next line is the one that actually does the work on the Flash-supplied variables:

```
fwrite($f,"  Name:\t\t\t$n\r\n");
```

Here again, we use the same `fwrite ($f,` combination, followed by the opening quotes, which indicate the start of the data string. Then we have some leading spaces followed by the text 'Name:', which will appear in the text file exactly as typed in the script. Next up are three tabs (`\t`), and then we have the very important `$n`. Remember that in PHP, the dollar sign denotes a variable, and the name of the variable follows the `$`. So the variable `$n` in this line of code *maps directly* to the variable n that we defined in the Flash movie's first input text box: we've named the variable `$n` in the PHP script so that we can feed the value of the Flash-defined n variable straight into PHP:

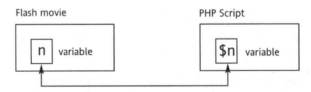

Matching variable names allow us to pass
data back and forth between Flash and PHP

Giving variables the same name in PHP and Flash (without the $ identifier) makes the implicit link that allows you to pass data between the two programs.

After writing the variable value pulled in from Flash, we then perform a carriage return and line feed to prepare for writing the next line.

At this stage in the script, our target text file will look like this:

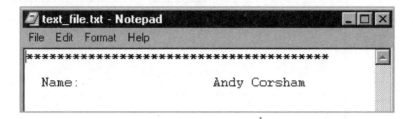

The next line of script...

```
fwrite($f,"   E-Mail:\t\t$e\r\n\r\n");
```

...uses exactly the same principle to write the $e variable (e in the second Flash input box) onto the next line in the text file:

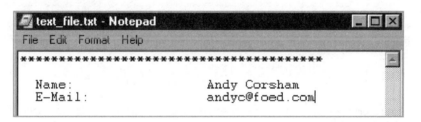

Then, after using the familiar carriage returns and line feeds, we close off the text file using PHP's fclose function:

```
fclose($f);
```

Finally, we use the echo command to send the user a confirmation message that the PHP script has run, and that their details have been added to the text file...

```
echo "<BR><BR><B>Submit successful!</B>";
```

...before terminating the script with the proper tag:

```
?>
```

After a couple of submissions by different users, our text file would start to look something like this:

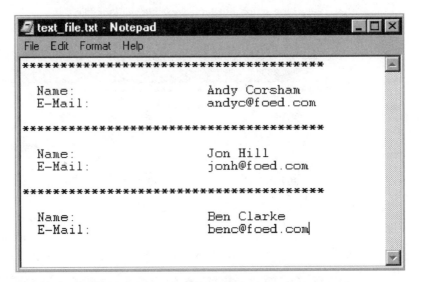

And that's it. With a few lines of simple PHP code and a single ActionScript statement, we've created a Flash application that's capable of manipulating the server-side file system.

Conclusion

In that simple example, we've already established the core principles you need to know to start building Flash-PHP applications. Of course, there's much, much more to the PHP language and what it can do with Flash than we've covered here, but we hope that this has given you the taste for exploring PHP for yourself and discovering what's possible.

One of the great things about using Flash with PHP is the relative simplicity of passing data back and forth – essentially, you match up variable names and use getURL and loadVariables commands to trigger the data transfer in either direction. This simple mechanism can be hooked up to your clever ActionScript in the SWF, and as much PHP programming as you want to do on the server. If you're more adventurous, you can also explore using database back ends and query languages to further enrich the interactivity that server-side scripting can bring to your Flash movies.

19
Flash and PHP

Section 4
Dynamic Content

18
Dynamic
Web
Applications

17
Dynamic Content
with Text files

Chapter 20
Flash and XML

The **Extensible Markup Language**, or **XML**, lies at the center of many visions of the future of computing. Depending on whom you listen to, it's a new way of typesetting documents, it's the glue that will hold the next generation of operating systems together, or it's just the *best* way of storing almost any kind of data. All of these claims have some truth in them, and the efforts being put into advocacy suggest either that XML really is important, or a lot of people have got it very wrong indeed. Certainly, Macromedia considers it significant enough to have introduced support for reading, writing, and generating XML into Flash 5 ActionScript, and it's that new functionality – and the uses to which it can be put – that we'll analyze in this chapter.

Before I go any further, it's worth setting down what XML is *not*. It's not a new set of tags for, or an extension of, HTML; yet I often hear it described like that. If you know who started this rumor, please scold them for me. Furthermore, XML is not a 'programming' language. You can't write a game, or a word processor, or a voice recognition system in XML. The way I usually explain it to clients is that there are no verbs in XML, only nouns; XML doesn't *do* things, it just *is* things. With those misconceptions out of the way, let's look at what XML really *is*, and how we can put it to use with Flash.

Just the Facts

As I suggested above, the most common misconception is that XML is some kind of 'upgrade' for HTML, which I suppose is understandable when you consider that a typical line of HTML might look something like this...

```
<A HREF="index.html">Go to the index</A>
```

...while the following is an example of a line that might appear in an XML document:

```
<BOOK isbn="1903450306">Flash 5 Studio</BOOK>
```

The resemblance between the two is down to the fact that both HTML and XML are **markup** languages that use **tags** of the form `<...>` to mark the beginning and end of individual pieces of information. The very big difference, though, is that while HTML is useful only for describing how information should be *displayed* in a web browser, XML can be used to *describe* anything you like about any kind of information – that's where the 'extensible' part of its name comes from. Of course, there are *some* rules that you must adhere to, but as a way of structuring data using nothing more than plain text, XML easily beats alternatives such as comma or tab delimitation.

Even if you've never come across XML before, you can probably see that the single line above contains some information about this book – or at least, that's a likely interpretation. In XML, and unlike HTML, there are *no* predefined tags. You are free to define an unlimited number of your own tags, based on the use to which you intend to put the information. I didn't have to make the tag name `<BOOK>`; it could have been `<TOME>`, or anything else I decided on. What's important is that the application reading your XML data must know what to do when it encounters a `<BOOK>` tag, just as your web browser knows to create a hyperlink when it comes across an `<A>` tag. In this way, it's possible to create a custom data model to deal with any situation.

Why Should You Care?

The almost total flexibility of XML is the reason for the diverse list of uses I mentioned in my introductory paragraphs. If you were creating a document to be printed, you could use the tags to stipulate the size and position of all the text on a page. In the design of an operating system, you could use XML to describe the information to be passed from one application to another. When it comes down to it, though, these and other uses are all about storing and communicating data in a way that enables easy creation and rapid access.

Of course, the need to be able to describe, store and communicate information is not a new one, and XML is not the first technology to attempt to address it. There are a number of common formats for storing data, and some of those created by companies like Lotus and Microsoft for use in their products have almost become 'standards' in their own right. However, XML scores over solutions like these in key ways:

- XML is free – you don't need to pay licensing fees to anyone in order to use it.

- XML is platform and technology-neutral – it doesn't care what kind of computer you have, or what operating system you're running.

- XML is quite easy for regular humans to read – this enables you to get a quick idea of what the data is about, and even find any simple errors.

Essentially, these boil down to the same thing:

- *XML is just text*. If you like, you can create it using no more than a text editor, and transmit it without the need to resort to encoding techniques.

Above all, XML has *caught on*, to the extent that people working in similar fields have agreed on sets of tags that best describe the data they have to deal with from day to day, enabling the quick and easy exchange of information between such organizations. Evidence for this kind of cooperation can be found in publishing, in finance, in science, and even in music. Furthermore, the companies that produce proprietary database software are increasingly providing options to load and save data in XML format, opening up their tools as ways of managing XML-formatted information.

All of this means that the amount of data out there in XML format is increasing day by day, and there's no indication of that trend letting up. As a consequence, the need to be able to read and write such data is of ever-greater importance to any application that prides itself in the presentation and dissemination of information. It is this need that has been addressed by Macromedia with its new support for XML in Flash 5, and this suggests that *now* would be a great time for you to learn about XML.

The Nature of the Beast

Although you're free to use whatever tags you like in an XML document, there are some quite strict rules that govern the overall structure of the data, and the syntax you use within your tags. This is in contrast to HTML, which has looser rules that allow browsers to 'guess' what the author intended, with varying degrees of success. (For example, if you don't end an HTML table with the </TABLE> tag, it won't display in some versions of Navigator, but Internet Explorer will always show the table and its contents.) When you think about it, this is sensible: HTML documents are intended to be viewed in a web browser, so the scope of any 'guessing' is automatically restricted to that purpose. An XML document could be used for anything at all, so there's no context in which a guess could be made.

The primary role of XML is the transmission of data, and the integrity of that data is therefore vitally important. As an example, imagine that your bank uses XML to transmit your transactions to its service bureau. Now say that you deposited three checks, but that in the middle of completing your transaction, the connection between the bank and the bureau is lost. The service bureau may get an XML document that looks like this:

```
<DEPOSIT account="900411557000"
              datetime="Fri Nov 17 16:11:29 EST 2000"
              tran="123">
    <CHECK num="123456">405.33</CHECK>
    <CHECK num="123457">29.99</CHECK>
```

It wouldn't be good if the bank's service bureau assumed that the next thing to do was close the <DEPOSIT> tag. If it did, your third check wouldn't get into your account. The existence of an opening tag without an accompanying closing tag (which in this case would be </DEPOSIT>) means that this document is not **well-formed**, and the rules of XML don't allow us to make a guess at how to 'fix' it. Instead, we assume that the document is broken because something went wrong, and what we really need to do is ask the bank for the record of this transaction again. There are a number of specific rules and guidelines regarding 'well formedness' in XML documents, and if you want to become an expert I suggest you take a deep breath and look around at http://www.w3c.org.

> *If you haven't come across it before, the W3C (World Wide Web Consortium) is a bit like the United Nations of the Web. Most notably, they create technical specifications that attempt to bring order to the chaos of the Internet through standardization. They 'wrote the book' (as it were) on HTML, XML, and a host of other protocols and file formats.*

For the remainder of this chapter, we'll just stick with the parts of XML that we need to know in order to get started using it in Flash 5. You'll be happy to know that this just made our complexity factor go *way* down.

Basic XML Syntax

I can't, in good conscience, leave your whole education up to the W3C – I'd feel as if I had thrown you to the wolves. Here, then, is a quick rundown on the anatomy of some XML that's along the same lines as the code we'll be using in our upcoming examples. Let's look again at the first piece of sample XML I gave:

```
<BOOK isbn="1903450306">Flash 5 Studio</BOOK>
```

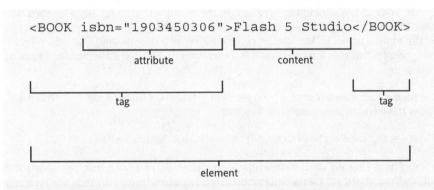

As the diagram shows, this XML **element** is made up of an **opening tag**, a **closing tag**, and some **content**, but it's worth analyzing that structure a little more closely, so that we can see exactly what's going on. What we have here is a `<BOOK>` element, but what exactly marks it out as such? Well, the opening tag starts with a `<`, so that's a good sign: all XML tags start that way. Immediately after the `<` is a four-character string, followed by a space. Those four characters, B-O-O-K, tell us the name of the element; this is no different from the way `<FONT` or `<TABLE` are used as the beginnings of valid HTML tags.

Moving on, we come to some more things that bring HTML to mind. After the element name, but before the end of the opening tag, we have `isbn="1903450306"`. This **attribute** appears inside the tag, and is therefore a part of the tag – and you may be familiar with its HTML corollary. Consider something like `<FONT face="arial" size="3" color="black">`. In HTML, this tag would denote the beginning of a block of text to be displayed in the Arial typeface, at size 3, and colored black.

Returning to our XML example, the **name** of the attribute is `isbn`, the **value** is `1903450306`, and I should add that attributes are *always* specified using this syntax. There's no compulsion for XML elements to have any attributes at all, but equally there's no ceiling on the number they may possess – it all comes down to what's appropriate for your purposes. However long the list of attributes is, though, the `>` character always terminates it and, by implication, the opening tag. We're ready to move on to the next part of the element.

Between the opening tag and the closing tag comes the **content** of the element. In this case, it's just the text `Flash 5 Studio`, but it could also be other XML elements – a situation that we'll examine in more detail in just a moment. A third possibility is that the element could contain *nothing at all*, and this is the basis of something approaching a religious war between the designers of XML documents: should the information held in an XML element be stored as content, or in attribute values? For example, it would be quite possible to represent exactly the same data this way:

```
<BOOK isbn="1903450306" title="Flash 5 Studio"></BOOK>
```

Once again, the choice you make here is entirely down to you. Because XML places no interpretation on your data, it doesn't care how you represent it, as long as you obey its rules. All the same, this kind of 'content-free' element *can* have an impact on the structure of your XML documents. Look at the closing tag here: inside the < and > characters are a forward slash, and the name of the element exactly as it appeared in the opening tag. Note that this really must be *exactly* the same – unlike HTML, XML is case-sensitive, so </book> and </Book> would *not* act as closing tags for this element, and you'd have an error. In XML, all elements must have opening and closing tags.

The alternative that using a 'content-free' element gives you is to use a tag that effectively opens and closes the element simultaneously, like this:

```
<BOOK isbn="1903450306" title="Flash 5 Studio" />
```

By including that forward slash before the > character, we're saying that this element has no content, and that there will be no dedicated closing tag of the form </BOOK>. We'll be using this shorthand technique extensively in the sample XML documents later in this chapter.

The final piece of XML syntax to look at before moving on is how to use *elements* as the content of other elements, and to find that out we can turn once again to HTML. If we wanted to put a cell in the row of a table, we'd use something like <TR><TD></TD></TR> – the <TD> element is completely enclosed by the <TR> element. We use this same syntax in XML, so adding an element inside our <BOOK> element would give us something like this:

```
<BOOK isbn="1903450306" title="Flash 5 Studio">
    <CHAPTER number="1" name="Introduction" />
</BOOK>
```

As we've described, the <CHAPTER> element forms the content of the <BOOK> element, and the former consists of a single, self-closing tag.

For the purposes of using XML with Flash, that's more or less all you need to know about XML elements and their components. Now, then, it's time to get more specific, so that you can apply your new skills to using XML within Flash 5.

Using XML in Flash 5 ActionScript

So far, I've been talking almost exclusively about using XML as a means for representing data while it's being stored, and as it's moved from one place to another. For the information to be *useful*, though, we're going to need some way of accessing and manipulating it from within our applications – in our case, from within our Flash movies – and that opens the door to a whole new bunch of jargon.

The **Document Object Model**, or just **DOM**, is just another of the many standards that are overseen by the W3C, but it's interesting for us because it provides a way of describing the structure of a document that's been marked up using XML (or one of a number of other markup languages) in an object-oriented format. When Flash receives an XML document, it makes it available to your ActionScript code in DOM form, and from that point on you're free to do with it pretty much what you will – you can use ActionScript to move things around, change them, alter the way they look, and so on, integrating the XML data into the Flash movie that the users are seeing in their browser.

The DOM organizes the entities in an XML document using a hierarchical relationship. From what you've already seen, you know that an XML element can contain nothing, or text content, or other XML elements. In the terminology used by the DOM, a single element, or a single piece of text context, is referred to as a **node**. When a node is contained by another node, the former is said to be a **child** of the latter. Predictably, the 'outer' node in this relationship is called the **parent**.

Although I used it just a moment ago, I'm actually sick to death of the phrase *object-oriented*, but we do need to talk about it just in case you haven't been assimilated yet. If you've used ActionScript in Flash 5, you've seen object orientation in use: it's the 'compartmentalized' approach to programming. An **object** (basically, just a variable) has **properties** and **methods** associated with it that you can access programmatically by typing the variable name, followed by a dot, then the name of the property or method you're interested in (myObj.xPos, for example). Properties can be used to retrieve information from an object (including other objects that are being 'contained' by the first object), while methods cause something to happen.

The XML Object

What we're building towards here is that Flash 5 ActionScript has a built-in XML object that includes all the properties and methods you'll need to read, write, and manipulate *any* XML document, by means of the Document Object Model. In ActionScript, you create an XML object by setting a variable equal to a new one, like this:

```
xmlObj = new XML();
```

The XML object itself is the common ancestor of the whole hierarchy: all nodes in the document are its children, or one of its children's children, or... you get the picture. A node can be the child of one node, and also the parent of another. With all that going on, it's about time we had another example that puts all this new information in context. Have a look at this section from an XML document:

```
<PERSON firstname="John" lastname="Doe">
    <CHUM firstname="Billy" lastname="Kid" />
    <CHUM firstname="Jane" lastname="Doe" />
    <CHUM firstname="Harry" lastname="Carry" />
</PERSON>
```

Imagine that we're writing a chat program on a planet where no two people have the same name. We want a user to be able to see if any of their favorite chat buddies are around. If we could persuade the chat server to send us a piece of XML like this one on demand, we'd have all the information we need to check for the availability of each of the user's friends.

Basic Properties

The first element (or node) in this document is `<PERSON>`, which is also the parent of the three `<CHUM>` elements it contains. By the rules given above, `<PERSON>` serves a second role as the first (and only) child node of any XML object containing the document, so if such an object were named xmlObj, we would refer to the node in ActionScript as `xmlObj.firstChild`.

If we wanted to know what kind of information was contained in the first child, we could tell by looking at the value of `xmlObj.firstChild.nodeName`. Note that nodeName is a property of all nodes, and it's simply the name of the element (or 'null', if it's a text node). If we check nodeName here, we'll know that we're dealing with a `<PERSON>` element, and therefore we'll know to look for the firstname and lastname attributes. (We know to look for those attributes because we sat through seven hours of meetings to work out the details of this data model, and the specification sheet says the PERSON tag always contains these two attributes, OK?)

Following the same pattern, the syntax for getting hold of the value of this attribute would be `xmlObj.firstChild.attributes.firstname`. If we wanted to, we could drop that value into a dynamic text box right now, but our ambitions are a little higher than that. We want to be able to search for and then extract information from child nodes – and to do that we'll need to be familiar with some more of their properties.

Properties of Nodes

One of the properties of nodes is hasChildNodes. This property is either true or false, and (predictably) tells us whether the node has any children. In code, we'd say something like this:

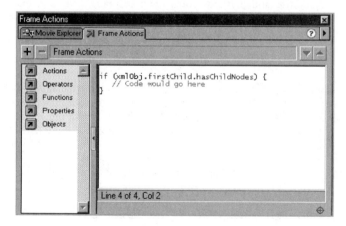

If it were true, we'd want to begin to cycle through those children, checking their node names and attributes, and possibly checking them for children of their own. To do that, we need to know how many children the first child node has, so that we can set up a loop to look at them all one by one. Here's how the code to do that might start:

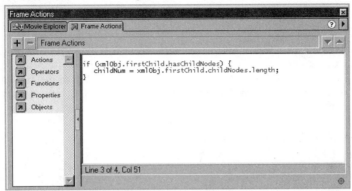

`childNodes` is another of a node's properties: it's a **collection** containing all the children of a node. Collections are useful because they make their contents available in a way that makes it particularly easy to search through them, using expressions like `collectionName[x]`. The value you put in the brackets here represents the position in the collection of the item you want to refer to, although you need to know that the numbering starts at zero (so the third item is at position 2). A collection's `length` property tells you the total number of items in the collection.

Once we've found out how many items the collection contains, it's time to write the loop that searches through it, as follows:

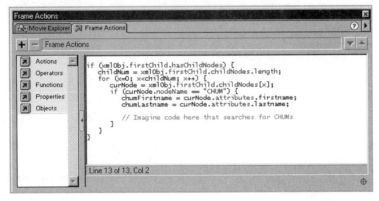

That's going to need some explanation. We start the loop with our counter variable, x, set to zero, because the collection of child nodes is zero-based. Because of that, we make sure to stop when the counter is one less than `childNum`, since our three child nodes will be numbered 0, 1, and 2.

Then comes the line that says:

```
curNode = xmlObj.firstChild.childNodes[x];
```

All that does is set the `curNode` variable to contain the child node object that has the index x – I didn't feel like typing `xmlObj.firstChild.childNodes[x]` any more than I had to. It didn't make much difference in this case, but it can, trust me. If we had to check and record ten attributes, you wouldn't think I was so silly.

The next thing we do is check the node name to see what kind of information is contained in this child node. If it's a `<CHUM>`, we extract the name from the node's attributes, and then we're free to do whatever we like – we could display it in a movie somehow, or maybe use some more code to fire off an automatic greeting. Once you've got your data, XML takes a back seat and you can get on with creating your movie.

Manipulating XML Documents

Although we haven't explored all of the properties available to us, we've at least had a little taste of the `XML` object and the DOM, and how they let us read XML documents. For the moment, just take my word that the code above will work – I'll prove it to you in a minute.

Of course, reading XML is only half the battle, at best. Sometimes, we're going to want to modify the information in XML documents, or even create our own. One way of doing this programmatically is to build them with some variables, some plus signs, and a whole bunch of quotation marks. But then, one way to make a Flash movie is to hand-draw a 500-frame animation, screen capture each frame, and make them all keyframes. I don't recommend either technique. A better way to roll your own XML document is to use the methods made available by the Flash `XML` object. Let's revisit the sample document we just *read* using the `XML` object, and see one way we could have written it in the first place. In case you forgot, here it is again:

```
<PERSON firstname="John" lastname="Doe">
    <CHUM firstname="Billy" lastname="Kid" />
    <CHUM firstname="Jane" lastname="Doe" />
    <CHUM firstname="Harry" lastname="Carry" />
</PERSON>
```

The two methods we'll need to write this document are `createElement` and `appendChild`, and we'll use them (along with some of the properties we saw above) to create a new XML document. Let's actually put this in a movie so you can watch it happen.

Open Flash and start a new movie. Select the Text tool, and then choose Dynamic Text and Multiline in the Text Options panel. Next, make a nice big text box that nearly fills the whole stage. Then go back to the Text Options panel and put `body` in the variable field, and check the Word wrap box if it's not checked already.

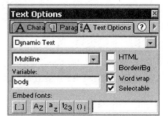

As a result of this procedure, when we set the variable `body` equal to something, we'll be able to see it in the text field. Double-click frame 1 to open the ActionScript editor, and then switch to Expert mode:

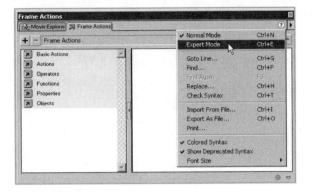

Enter the following code:

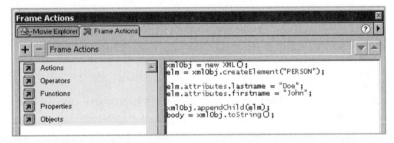

Run the movie, and you should see this:

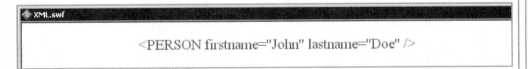

How did that happen? Well, in the first line we created an XML object named xmlObj. Line two uses the createElement method of that object to create an element named <PERSON>, and stores it in another new variable called elm. Lines three and four set the firstname and lastname attributes of the new node. Line five appends the newly created element to our XML document, and line six puts the XML document into the body variable, so we can see it in the text box.

> *Notice that in order to get the attributes in the same order as we had them in the document we're trying to duplicate, we had to set the* lastname *attribute first.*

Now let's add the <CHUM> elements – once we've done that, we can actually *make* something using all this stuff. Here's the code:

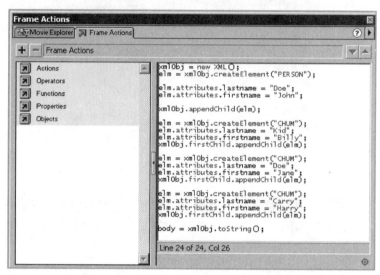

```
xmlObj = new XML();
elm = xmlObj.createElement("PERSON");

elm.attributes.lastname = "Doe";
elm.attributes.firstname = "John";

xmlObj.appendChild(elm);

elm = xmlObj.createElement("CHUM");
elm.attributes.lastname = "Kid";
elm.attributes.firstname = "Billy";
xmlObj.firstChild.appendChild(elm);

elm = xmlObj.createElement("CHUM");
elm.attributes.lastname = "Doe";
elm.attributes.firstname = "Jane";
xmlObj.firstChild.appendChild(elm);

elm = xmlObj.createElement("CHUM");
elm.attributes.lastname = "Carry";
elm.attributes.firstname = "Harry";
xmlObj.firstChild.appendChild(elm);

body = xmlObj.toString();
```

What you should see now when you play the movie is exactly the XML we had before, with the exception that it's not laid out particularly well. Mine looks like this:

```
<PERSON firstname="John" lastname="Doe"><CHUM firstname="Billy"
lastname="Kid" /><CHUM firstname="Jane" lastname="Doe" /><CHUM
firstname="Harry" lastname="Carry" /></PERSON>
```

Did you notice the important difference when we were adding the <CHUM> elements? When making the <PERSON> element, we appended it to our new XML document by calling the latter's appendChild method, making <PERSON> the first child. For the three <CHUM> elements, we called the appendChild method of xmlObj.firstChild – in other words, the <PERSON> element – making each <CHUM> element a child of <PERSON>.

Testing the XML Code

I did promise to prove to you that the code to read the <PERSON> and <CHUM> elements would work, and now that we have the complete XML inside Flash, that'll be possible. The process of 'running through' an XML document to analyze its contents is known as **parsing** the document, and that's what we'll be doing here.

Testing the Code

Let's step through this code testing as an exercise.

1. Since frame 1 of our example movie creates the document, you should start by inserting a new blank keyframe in frame 2.

   Because we created the source XML document, we're in the relatively unusual position of knowing exactly what it contains. We're going to take advantage of that fact and design our movie with exactly the right number of text boxes to display that content.

2. Make a Single Line text box somewhere near the upper left corner of your movie, and name it fcName (short for 'first child name'). Set the text options to Dynamic Text, and throw a border and background in there too. Here's what mine looks like:

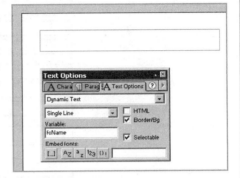

3. Now that we have a text box with all the properties set the way we want them, let's copy it to save some time. In all, we'll want four sets of three boxes, because we want to show the element name of each node, as well as its firstname and lastname attributes. I stacked mine straight down the left-hand side of the movie; it looked like this when I was done:

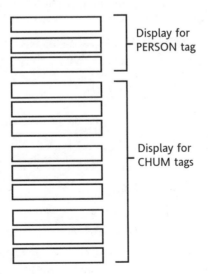

Display for PERSON tag

Display for CHUM tags

   Now comes the slightly tedious task of setting the variable names of all the text boxes – right now, all the boxes are set to fcName, but that's only the correct name for the *top* box.

4. Name the second text box `pFirstname`, and the third `pLastname`. These are the variables we'll put data from the PERSON element into.

To display the CHUMs, we want to use numbers in our variable names, so that we can easily access them inside a loop. Here's the rundown:

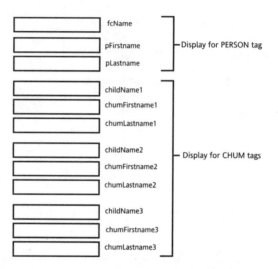

All we need now is the code, which will be a slightly modified version of what we had earlier. I'll cover it all again, though, so you don't have to go back. It goes like this:

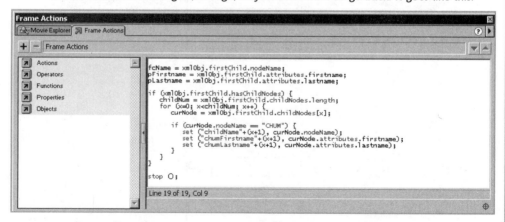

```
fcName = xmlObj.firstChild.nodeName;
pFirstname = xmlObj.firstChild.attributes.firstname;
pLastname = xmlObj.firstChild.attributes.lastname;

if (xmlObj.firstChild.hasChildNodes) {
    childNum = xmlObj.firstChild.childNodes.length;
    for (x=0; x<childNum; x++) {
        curNode = xmlObj.firstChild.childNodes[x];

        if (curNode.nodeName == "CHUM") {
            set ("childName"+(x+1), curNode.nodeName);
            set ("chumFirstname"+(x+1), curNode.attributes.firstname);
            set ("chumLastname"+(x+1), curNode.attributes.lastname);
        }
    }
}

stop ();
```

The first three lines here put the `nodeName` and the `attributes` of the `<PERSON>` element into the appropriate display variables – nothing fancy so far. Following on from there, the `if` statement begins just as we had it before: we check to see whether the PERSON node has any child nodes, and if it does, we count them and store them in `childNum`.

> *You may be thinking that we don't need the if statement at all, since we know there are three child nodes. That's true, but I wanted to do two things: show you as many properties and methods as possible with this simple example, and keep it close to real life. In the general case, we wouldn't know in advance how many children an element has, and a test like this would be essential.*

Moving ahead to the for loop, we start with the variable x equal to zero, and repeat as long as x is less than the number of PERSON's child nodes (remember that the childNodes collection is zero-based). The first line inside the for loop puts the node object we're currently evaluating into the curNode variable, so we don't have to type as much. Next is another (apparently) useless if statement, but if there were more than one element that could be a child of a PERSON element, we would need some way of differentiating between them.

The next three lines display the element name, and first and last names, of child x. Until now, we've been setting variables with the variable = value syntax, but inside this loop we're referring to the variables using expressions, so we must use the set command. If x is zero, the expression "childName"+(x+1) evaluates to childName1, which you should recognize as the variable name we associated with our first <CHUM> display field. When x is equal to zero, then, the command:

```
set ("childName"+(x+1), curNode.nodeName);
```

sets the childName1 variable to be equal to the nodeName of the first CHUM node, which is obviously CHUM. Similarly, these lines...

```
set ("chumFirstname"+(x+1), curNode.attributes.firstname);
set ("chumLastname"+(x+1), curNode.attributes.lastname);
```

...set the variables chumFirstname1 and chumLastname1. Add 1 to x, wash, rinse, repeat, and you've set all the variables, and all your text fields are full.

Please notice the stop() command on the last line of the script: we don't want to cause any seizures by flashing back-and-forth between frames 1 and 2, so we'll stop the movie on frame 2 after all our code has executed. If you view the movie now, you should see something like this, which should (I hope) convince you that everything I've said so far is true:

Loading an XML Document

Now that you know how to read and write XML documents inside Flash, it's time to put that knowledge to good use. Let's do another exercise, in which we'll make a Flash address book that loads addresses from an external XML file. After that, we'll create an Access database for addresses and load XML from an ASP page that searches the database. Do you think you're ready? Don't worry, there's nothing to it!

It's at this stage, as we begin to think about using external XML files, that we have to face up to the fact that Flash's support for XML isn't yet *quite* what it could be. We noted above that when Flash outputted the XML document we created, it wasn't laid out particularly well. However, we didn't worry about it very much, because the XML specification says that **whitespace** (that is, spaces, tabs, and carriage returns) between elements isn't important. If you want to lay out your documents neatly, you're welcome to do so, but it makes no difference to XML.

Sadly, when it comes to reading XML documents, Flash isn't quite so agnostic. It's important that any document intended for this purpose is free of all tabs and carriage returns, so while it would be nice to be able create something like the following in a text editor, for the time being it's only this way to make it easy for you to read:

```
<ADDRESSES>
    <ADDRESS fName="John"
                    lName="Doe"
                    address1="1313 Mockingbird Lane"
                    address2=""
                    city="Springfield"
                    state="MA"
                    zip="12345-6789"/>
    <ADDRESS fName="Billy"
                    lName="Kid"
                    address1="123 West St."
                    address2=""
                    city="Silver City"
                    state="NM"
                    zip="98765-4321"/>
    <ADDRESS fName="Sam"
                    lName="Sham"
                    address1="123 Street Road"
                    address2=""
                    city="Philadelphia"
                    state="PA"
                    zip="12345-6789"/>
    </ADDRESSES>
```

This file is available in Flash-friendly format (that is, all on one line!) on the accompanying CD, under the name `mydoc.xml`, and we'll be using it to help with designing and testing our Flash address book prior to adding its database back end. In other words, we're going to create a Flash movie that can open this XML document and let us view the information it contains.

Loading an External XML Document

1. Open Flash, start a new movie, and name it `xmlAddresses.fla`. While you're at it, take this opportunity to make sure that your publish settings include SWF and HTML output formats.

    This will be a one-frame, one-layer movie – so when I ask you to add something, it will always go in frame 1, layer 1.

2. The first things we need to add are seven dynamic text boxes, and their corresponding static labels. Try to keep these in the upper half of the movie. My layout looked like this:

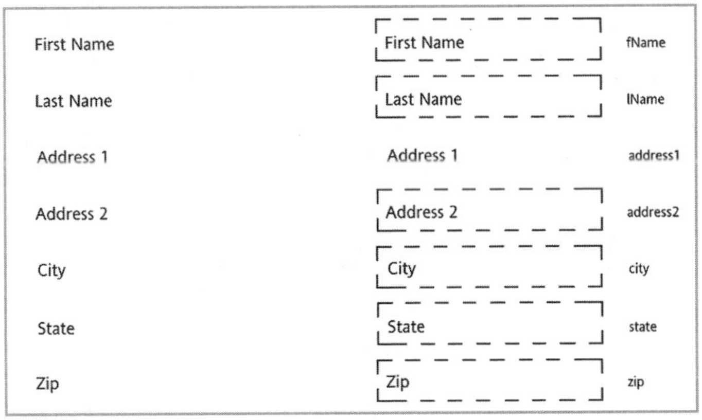

    | First Name | First Name | fName |
    | Last Name | Last Name | lName |
    | Address 1 | Address 1 | address1 |
    | Address 2 | Address 2 | address2 |
    | City | City | city |
    | State | State | state |
    | Zip | Zip | zip |

    Here, the labels at the far right are not part of the Flash form – rather, they are the variable names associated with the dynamic text boxes to their left. The bottom half of the movie will contain two command buttons, and some miscellaneous variable displays. I'll show you the layout you need to create first, and then explain:

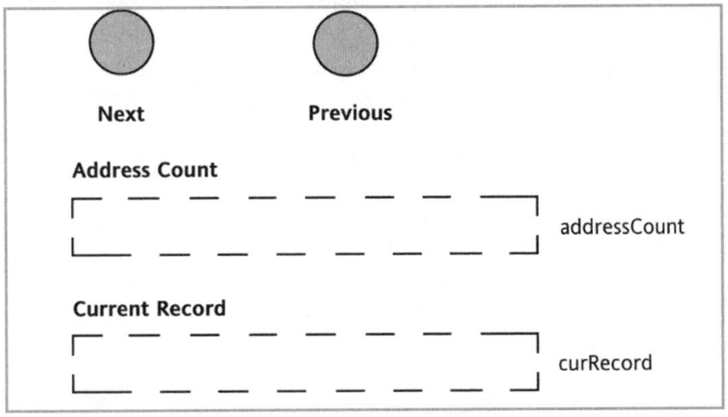

    Next   **Previous**

    Address Count

    addressCount

    Current Record

    curRecord

Again, the labels on the right are the variable names of the dynamic text boxes to their left. The two blue circles, on the other hand, are very much part of the movie: they're actually button symbols that will allow the user to move among the records in the database.

3. To that end, you need to add some very simple code to the Object Actions window for each button:

```
on (release) {
    showNext();
}

on (release) {
    showPrevious();
}
```

We'll be writing showNext and showPrevious in just a moment, but that's all there is to the display part of the movie.

4. Now you can open up the ActionScript window for frame 1. Switch to Expert mode, and enter the following code:

```
curRecord = 0;
```

This just creates a variable called curRecord, and sets its value to zero. This variable will act as a pointer to let us know which record we are currently in within the database.

5. Now add this:

```
// function for onLoad method of objXML
function getLoaded(success) {
    if (success) {
        addressCount = this.firstChild.childNodes.length;
        setDisplay(1);
    }
}
```

This is a function that accepts a parameter named success, which will be either true or false. If success is true, we'll set the variable addressCount equal to this.firstChild.childNodes.length (which I'll get to in just a second), and call the setDisplay function, passing it a 1 (which I'll get to slightly later).

6. To understand the whole this line, look at what comes next and add it to the frame-based script you've created so far:

```
// XML declaration and loading
objXML = new XML();
objXML.onLoad = getLoaded;
objXML.load ("mydoc.xml");
```

The first part of this should be old hat to you by now: we're creating a new XML object called objXML. The second line attaches the getLoaded function we defined above to a special method of the XML object, the onLoad method. The latter is called after the load method of an XML object either completes or fails within the allotted time. The default implementation of the onLoad method does nothing, but you can add custom functionality by writing your own function and doing what we did above. When we say to Flash objXML.onLoad = getLoaded, we're telling it to run the getLoaded function after every attempt to load an external XML file into the objXML object. Inside the getLoaded function, we can refer to objXML as this, because getLoaded has become a method of objXML. The last of the three lines, objXML.load ("mydoc.xml"), loads the external XML document named mydoc.xml that you made earlier.

7. Now add this next bit of script:

```
// function to be run by "next" button
function showNext () {
    if(curRecord == addressCount) {
        loadnum = 1;
    } else {
        loadnum = curRecord + 1;
    }
    setDisplay (loadnum);
}
```

This function is pretty straightforward: we'll be cycling through addresses, and if we're at the last record, we'll want to jump to the first record just for the sake of being user-friendly. curRecord keeps track of the current record being displayed, addressCount keeps track of the total number of addresses, and we'll be setting loadnum to the number of the record that should be displayed next. So, in English, what the function says is: "If the current record being displayed is the last record, display the first record next. Otherwise, display the next record in line."

8. Now you need to add this function:

```
// function to be run by "previous" button
function showPrevious () {
    if (curRecord == 1) {
        loadnum = addressCount;
    } else {
        loadnum = curRecord - 1;
    }
    setDisplay (loadnum);
}
```

This function is the same as showNext (), except that it checks to see if you're already at the *beginning*, and if so sends you to the *last* record. No big deal.

9. Now add this last piece of code:

```
// function to set variable names/display fields
function setDisplay (recnum) {
    var nodeObj = objXML.firstChild.childNodes[recnum-1];
    fName = nodeObj.attributes.fName;
    lName = nodeObj.attributes.lName;
    address1 = nodeObj.attributes.address1;
    address2 = nodeObj.attributes.address2;
    city = nodeObj.attributes.city;
    state = nodeObj.attributes.state;
    zip = nodeObj.attributes.zip;
    curRecord = recnum;
}
```

This function is the real meat of this example. It accepts a parameter named `recnum`, which will signify the record to be displayed. The first line of the function is then just another timesaver: we set a variable called `nodeObj` to the `<ADDRESS>` element we're interested in. (Remember, the `childNodes` collection is zero-based, so we use `recnum – 1` to get the correct node.) Next, we set all our display variables to the corresponding attribute values of `nodeObj`. Lastly, we set `curRecord` equal to `recnum`, so that the display is set correctly, and to keep track of the current record for the `showNext` and `showPrevious` functions.

10. Publish the movie in the same directory where you saved `mydoc.xml`, and then view it. You should see the following:

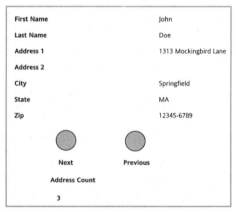

First Name	John
Last Name	Doe
Address 1	1313 Mockingbird Lane
Address 2	
City	Springfield
State	MA
Zip	12345-6789

Next   Previous

Address Count

3

11. Play with the Next and Previous buttons, and you should find that you're able to rotate through the three addresses fairly efficiently. If you don't get any results (or you get more than three results), your problem is most likely a tab or a carriage return in your XML file that should not be there.

We've included the FLA for this example on the CD – it's called `xmlAddresses.fla`.

Potential glitches aside, we've created our address-book client, and we can move on to trying to tie in a database.

Accessing a Database using XML

There are a few ways that we could go about getting the contents of a database into our Flash movies in XML format, but the one I'll demonstrate here is to use **ASP pages**. If you haven't come across it before, **Active Server Pages** (ASP) is a Microsoft technology that's usually employed to create web (that is, HTML) pages dynamically. In other words, rather than having a static file containing HTML, you write a script file that *generates* HTML from code, on the fly. If you use it well, this enables your web pages to reflect user input, or changes in underlying data, or the results of computations automatically, without your intervention.

However, there's nothing to say that ASP *must* generate HTML – far from it. For this application, instead of creating an HTML document, we're going to build an XML document that's based on the results of a database query.

To complete this example, you will need to have Microsoft's IIS (Internet Information Server) or PWS (Personal Web Server) installed on your server or machine. I'm also going to use Microsoft Access as the database. In general, and certainly in a production environment, I'd prefer to use Oracle or SQL Server, but I want to make this as generally useful as possible, and Access at least has widespread availability.

Creating the Database

Before we can even start to think about pulling information from a database, we'd better make sure that we have a database to work with. If you don't have Microsoft Access, don't worry: you can still use the file that I've provided on the accompanying CD – address.mdb. If you *do* have the software, you can follow along with the creation of a quick, one-table database.

1. Start off by opening Access and creating a new database named address.mdb. Then select the Tables section from the Objects pane, click the New button, and select Design View. (Alternatively, you could double-click the Create table in Design view option.)

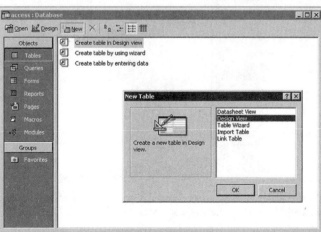

Our new table will have eight fields. The seven text fields will correspond to the seven display fields in our Flash movie, and we'll name them the same way so we don't get confused. The eighth field will be of the 'AutoNumber' type that creates a unique number to identify each record in the database. This number is automatically generated by the database every time a new row is added.

2. This next screenshot shows the eight fields you need to create:

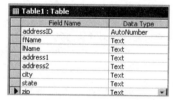

The fName, lName, and city fields can all remain at their default 50-character length. However, you should set address1 and address2 to 255 characters, state to 2, and zip to 10.

3. Next, arrange things so that the properties of all fields except address2 won't allow zero-length values. Then right-click on the addressID field and set it as the primary key:

4. Now, save the new table with the name myAddresses, then right-click on myAddresses in the UI, and select the Open option. Now, enter a few sample rows of data into the new database:

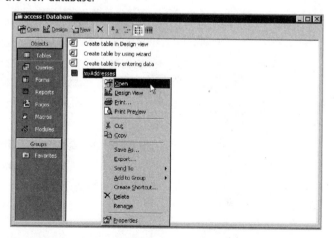

Once you feel like you have enough addresses in your database, it's time to make it available to ASP so that we can extract information from it programmatically.

Making the Database Available

To do this, we need to create a **Data Source Name (DSN)** that points to the database file – ASP will then be able to use this name to get access to the database.

1. The place to perform this task differs between Windows 9*x* and Windows 2000. In the former, you should go to Start > Settings > Control Panel and double-click the ODBC Data Sources icon. In the latter, follow the same path to the Control Panel, but then enter the Administrative Tools folder and double-click on Data Sources (ODBC). Either way, you should select the System DSN tab in the dialog that appears, and click the Add button:

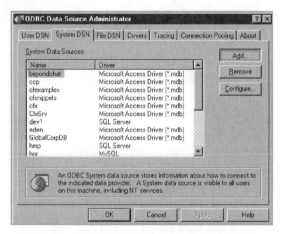

2. Select the Microsoft Access Driver (*.mdb) option from the list, and click Finish:

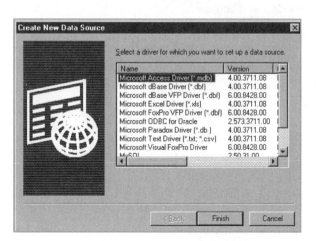

3. Name the new data source addressDSN, and give it any description you like. Click the Select button, and then browse to the location of the address.mdb database we created:

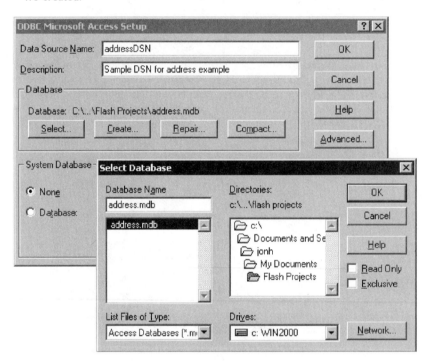

4. Now, OK your way back to the Control Panel, and everything should be ready to go – with one possible exception: if you're using Windows 2000, you'll need to change the security settings of your database so that ASP can access it. Talk to your system administrator if you don't know how to do this yourself.

We're now ready to try and retrieve some of the data we just entered, and so that we don't try to run before we can walk, we'll forget about Flash for a while and concentrate on ASP.

Writing ASP Code

1. Create a new ASP file named `testSearch.asp` using whatever program you like (I usually use either Microsoft Visual InterDev, or Notepad). Insert the following code:

```
<%@ Language=VBScript %>
<%
    Option Explicit

    Dim cn
    Dim cmd
    Dim rs

    Set cn = Server.CreateObject("ADODB.Connection")
    cn.ConnectionString = "addressDSN"
    cn.Open

    Set cmd = Server.CreateObject("ADODB.Command")
    cmd.ActiveConnection = cn
    cmd.CommandType = 1
    cmd.CommandText = "SELECT fName, lName FROM myAddresses"

    Set rs = cmd.Execute
%>
<HTML>
    <HEAD>
        <TITLE>No Title</TITLE>
    </HEAD>
    <BODY>

<%
    Do Until rs.EOF
        Response.Write rs("lName") & ", " & rs("fName") & "<BR>"
        rs.MoveNext
    Loop

    rs.Close
    cn.Close
    Set cn = Nothing
    Set rs = Nothing
    Set cmd = Nothing
%>

    </BODY>
</HTML>
```

This code is on the CD, in the `testSearch.asp` file.

You'll probably be pleased to hear that I'm not about to give you a tutorial in ASP on top of the one in XML, but it's not too difficult to explain what's going on here, starting with the first line:

```
<%@ Language=VBScript %>
```

When the web server encounters this line at the top of the page, it understands that the code is written in VBScript. In an ASP page, *anything* enclosed between `<%` and `%>` delimiters is script, and won't form part of the dynamically generated HTML that's eventually sent to the client.

```
Option Explicit
Dim cn
Dim cmd
Dim rs
```

Manipulating databases from code in an ASP page is not dissimilar to manipulating XML documents from within Flash: it's all a matter of using objects. For this example, we'll need three: one that represents the database itself, one for the request that we'll send to the database, and one to hold the data that's returned to us. The three variables created by the above code will be used to hold these objects; the VBScript command `Dim` is rather like from ActionScript's `var`.

> *The* `Option Explicit` *line is an aid to debugging: you'll get an error if you try to use a variable name that hasn't previously featured in a* `Dim` *statement. This prevents you from using new variables 'as you please', which is a recipe for confusion in large code files.*

In the next three lines of code, we create an `ADODB.Connection` object that will represent the link to the database, and then set it to the name of the data source we want to use – this is `addressDSN`, which we set up earlier:

```
Set cn = Server.CreateObject("ADODB.Connection")
cn.ConnectionString = "addressDSN"
cn.Open
```

Here, `Server` is a built-in object that ASP provides for us, in rather the same way that Flash 5 ActionScript supplies `Math` and `Date`. `ADODB.Connection`, on the other hand, is the name of an object provided by a Windows technology called **ActiveX Data Objects (ADO)**. Once we've *made* the connection, we *open* it with a call to the `Open` method of the `Connection` object.

```
Set cmd = Server.CreateObject("ADODB.Command")
cmd.ActiveConnection = cn
cmd.CommandType = 1
cmd.CommandText = "SELECT fName, lName FROM myAddresses"
```

In this part of the code, we set the variable `cmd` equal to a new `ADODB.Command` object, using the same technique as we used for the connection. This is the object we'll be using to make our request for some data. Once the command is created, we set its `ActiveConnection` property to `cn` to specify which connection it should use. (There's only one connection in our code, but the command still needs to be told – that may not always be the case.) The next property we set is `CommandType`, which goes to 1, indicating that this is a plain-text query. Finally, the `CommandText` property is set to the text of the request itself.

> *The query is written in a language called the* Structured Query Language (SQL), *and if you've never used it before, here's some real quick explanation.* SELECT *means, "Get records from the database". Right after* SELECT *are the names of two fields from our* myAddresses *table. Then comes the keyword* FROM, *followed by the name of a table.* cmd*'s* CommandText *property says, "Get me a recordset containing the* fName *and* lName *fields of all the records in the* myAddresses *table".*

```
Set rs = cmd.Execute
```

This line sets the variable `rs` equal to the recordset that's retrieved by calling the `Execute` method of `cmd`. The server goes away, interrogates the database, and comes back to us with this answer. We never actually used a `Server.CreateObject` call to make `rs` a recordset, but we didn't have to: the `Execute` method returns an `ADODB.Recordset` object when executing a `SELECT` query.

```
<HTML>
    <HEAD>
        <TITLE>No Title</TITLE>
    </HEAD>
    <BODY>
```

This is just some HTML to set up the page that will be presented to the visitor, up to and including the start of the `<BODY>` tag.

```
<%
Do Until rs.EOF
    Response.Write rs("lName") & ", " & rs("fName") & "<BR>"
    rs.MoveNext
Loop
```

This is the loop that cycles through all the records in the recordset that's been returned to us, and puts them into the ASP `Response` object. The HTTP protocol is request/response based: a client issues a **request** to a server, which in reply sends a **response**. The ASP `Response` object gives us the ability to manipulate the server's response in several ways. Among other things, it can be used to create the HTML that will be displayed in the client's browser dynamically, which is precisely what we're doing here with the contents of the recordset.

The `Write` method of the `Response` object accepts a string parameter, and appends that string to the HTML text. The reference to `rs("lName")` will return the value of the `lName` column of the recordset's current row, while `rs("fName")` returns the value of the `fName` column. The `MoveNext` method of the recordset object does just what you suspect it might: it changes the current row to the next record in line. Inside our loop, what we're doing is writing one row of the recordset to the response, then moving to the next record and writing the next row, and so on. Eventually we'll encounter the last record in the recordset, at which point the `EOF` ('end-of-file') property of the recordset object will become equal to `true`. Our loop is constructed in such a way that it continues *until* the `EOF` property of `rs` is true. That way, we'll output all the records, then exit the loop.

```
    rs.Close
    cn.Close
    Set cn = Nothing
    Set rs = Nothing
    Set cmd = Nothing
%>

    </BODY>
</HTML>
```

All that's left here is a great deal of tidying up. When you're dealing with databases, it's sensible to close and then delete all connections once you've finished using them, which is what the first five lines here achieve. Then we just provide closing `BODY` and `HTML` tags, so that our response is a well-formed HTML document.

And that's all it should take for us to check that we can, in fact, retrieve data from an Access database and put it in an HTML response. I made a directory called `AddressBook` in my `inetpub\wwwroot` directory and put all my files there, but you can call yours anything you like. The next screenshot shows the result, as displayed by the browser:

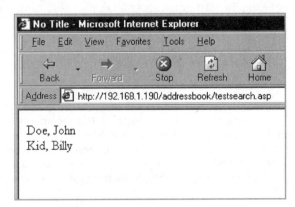

Here's the HTML source code generated by my ASP script:

```
<HTML>
    <HEAD>
        <TITLE>No Title</TITLE>
    </HEAD>
    <BODY>

Doe, John<BR>Kid, Billy<BR>

    </BODY>
</HTML>
```

All right. We've proved that we can handle the ASP side of things, but now we need to format our results as *XML* (rather than HTML), so we can read it directly into Flash 5.

Generating XML using ASP

1. Make a copy of testSearch.asp and rename it addressSearch.asp. Then edit addressSearch.asp to match the following listing (also available in the corresponding file on the CD):

```
<%@ Language=VBScript %>
<%
    Option Explicit

    Dim cn
    Dim cmd
    Dim rs
    Dim sXML
    Dim q


    ' q is a shorthand way of specifying the double quote character
    q = chr(34)

    Set cn = Server.CreateObject("ADODB.Connection")
    cn.ConnectionString = "addressDSN"
    cn.Open

    Set cmd = Server.CreateObject("ADODB.Command")
    cmd.ActiveConnection = cn
    cmd.CommandType = 1
    cmd.CommandText = "SELECT addressID,fName,lName,address1," & _
                          "address2,city,state,zip FROM myAddresses"

    Set rs = cmd.Execute
```

```
Do Until rs.EOF
    sXML = sXML & "<ADDRESS id=" & q & rs("addressID") & q & _
                    " fName=" & q & rs("fName") & q & _
                    " lName=" & q & rs("lName") & q & _
            " address1=" & q & rs("address1") & q & _
            " address2=" & q & rs("address2") & q & _
                    " city=" & q & rs("city") & q & _
                    " state=" & q & rs("state") & q & _
                    " zip=" & q & rs("zip") & q & "/>"
    rs.MoveNext
Loop

sXML = "<ADDRESSES>" & sXML & "</ADDRESSES>"
Response.Write sXML
%>
```

So what does all *that* mean? Well, starting at the top, we declared two new variables, both of which will hold some string data for us. sXML is where we'll build the XML document to send to Flash, while q will hold ASCII character 34, which is the double quote ("). This q variable is just another of my finger-savers: the double quote is used to enclose a string in VBScript, but we also need to build a string with double quote characters in it. To get around this, every time we need a double quote, we'll append q to the string.

The next change we made was to expand our SELECT statement to retrieve *all* the fields from the myAddresses table, instead of just the first and last names. We've had to alter the loop too: instead of writing directly to the Response object, we're concatenating a large string. Each individual row in the recordset will be turned into an ADDRESS element that contains each of the fields from that row as attributes. (The underscores at the ends of the lines in this statement indicate to the VBScript parser that this one logical line of code breaks over several physical lines.)

When the loop is done, we have a series of ADDRESS elements, one for each row in the recordset. Then we put all these ADDRESS elements inside an ADDRESSES element, and the XML string is ready.

> *I should mention in passing that we need the outside* ADDRESSES *tag because an XML document can only have one 'top level' element. If we just had three* ADDRESS *tags in a row, that would be a malformed XML document, and Flash wouldn't like us very much.*

The last line of this ASP page writes the contents of the sXML variable to the Response object. Since we took out the HTML code, what's in sXML is all that will be sent back to the browser.

2. Place this ASP page somewhere in your web server's search path, and open it up from your browser. If you see nothing but a blank, white page, it probably worked — don't forget there's no HTML here, so you wouldn't *expect* to see anything. If you view the *source* from your browser, however, the story is rather different. It should look something like this:

Interfacing Flash and ASP

We think that we're producing XML from our ASP page correctly, so it's time to try to open it up with Flash.

1. Make a copy of the `xmlAddresses.fla` file, and name it `xmlAddressesConcat.fla` (We'll call it that because this version will load from an ASP page that creates XML using string concatenation.) We'll only need one change to our Flash movie to make it work. Change the line of script that reads:

```
objXML.load ("mydoc.xml");
```

to:

```
objXML.load ("addressSearch.asp");
```

2. Publish the movie, and copy it into the same directory on your server that contains `addressSearch.asp`.

3. Then browse to `xmlAddressesConcat.html` and check it out.

Things should look exactly like they did when we loaded from the text file, but we know the difference: there is no text file here. We're using an ASP page as the source of XML data, and as we'll see, that opens the way to a whole range of new possibilities.

Improving the ASP Code

Building XML using string concatenation is all right for generating small pieces of XML, but the chance of us making a small syntactical error, and hence a nasty mess, is fairly evident. If only we had something like Flash's XML object that we could use in ASP! Well, we do. If your server has Internet Explorer 4 (or later) installed, then Microsoft's XML parser is installed as well. This is great for us, because Microsoft's object for parsing XML uses almost exactly the same set of properties and methods as Macromedia's. The name of the object we want to use is MSXML.DOMDocument.

Improving the ASP Code

1. Make a copy of addressSearch.asp, and name it properSearch.asp.

2. Now we'll build our XML document the proper way.

3. Edit properSearch.asp to match the following:

```
<%@ Language=VBScript %>
<%
    Option Explicit

    Dim cn
    Dim cmd
    Dim rs
    Dim objXML
    Dim elm

    Set cn = Server.CreateObject("ADODB.Connection")
    cn.ConnectionString = "addressDSN"
    cn.Open

    Set cmd = Server.CreateObject("ADODB.Command")
    cmd.ActiveConnection = cn
    cmd.CommandType = 1
    cmd.CommandText = "SELECT addressID,fName,lName,address1," & _
                      "address2,city,state,zip FROM myAddresses"

    Set rs = cmd.Execute

    Set objXML = Server.CreateObject("MSXML.DOMDocument)

    ' Set our top level element
    Set elm = objXML.createElement("ADDRESSES")
    objXML.appendChild elm

    Do Until rs.EOF
```

```
        Set elm = objXML.createElement("ADDRESS")
        elm.setAttribute "id", rs("addressID")
        elm.setAttribute "fName", rs("fName")
        elm.setAttribute "lName", rs("lName")
        elm.setAttribute "address1", rs("address1")

        If IsNull(rs("address2")) Then
            elm.setAttribute "address2", ""
        Else
            elm.setAttribute "address2", rs("address2")
        End If

        elm.setAttribute "city", rs("city")
        elm.setAttribute "state", rs("state")
        elm.setAttribute "zip", rs("zip")

        objXML.firstChild.appendChild elm

        rs.MoveNext
    Loop

    Response.Write objXML.xml
%>
```

The beginning of this file has changed little, although the q and sXML variables are gone, replaced by objXML and elm, which will store objects representing our XML document, and elements within that document, respectively. After the recordset rs has been opened, our first real piece of new code sets objXML to store a new DOMDocument object, using the Server.CreateObject method. Then we create the <ADDRESSES> element in almost exactly the same way we would in Flash. The createElement method of the DOMDocument object returns an element object, so this line...

```
    Set elm = objXML.createElement("ADDRESSES")
```

...sets elm to an element with the name ADDRESSES. Then we append the new node in elm to our objXML object using the appendChild method. Inside the loop that comes next, we set elm to contain another new element – an <ADDRESS> this time – and proceed to set all its attributes to the values in the recordset. This part is slightly different from the ActionScript equivalent, because instead of setting the value of an attribute directly, we call the setAttribute method, passing it the attribute's name and value as parameters.

> *Notice the* If *statement that deals with the* address2 *attribute. Since we've allowed this field to be zero length, it's possible that it may have a null value in the recordset.* IsNull *is a built-in VBScript function that returns* True *if the expression passed to it is null, and* False *otherwise.*

Once we've set all the attributes of our <ADDRESS> element in elm, we need to append it to our top-level element, <ADDRESSES>. There's some more Flash-like code here:

```
objXML.firstChild.appendChild elm
```

This simply appends the element in elm as a child of the <ADDRESSES> element. Once we're done looping, we write the xml property of objXML to the Response object – this is simply the string representation of the XML document. The output of this ASP page will therefore be identical to the output of addressSearch.asp, and for this relatively simple example, you might be tempted to think that we've used a sledgehammer to crack a nut. The more complex the XML documents you're creating become, however, the more you'll reap the benefits of this technique.

4. To view the results of your labor in Flash, make a copy of xmlAddressesConcat.fla, and name it xmlAddressesProper.fla. Once again, we need only change the line of code that loads the XML document. It should now read:

```
objXML.load ("properSearch.asp");
```

5. Save xmlAddressesProper.fla, publish it, put it in the proper directory, and then browse to xmlAddressesProper.html to gaze in wonder at your latest creation. Once again, it might *look* the same as it did before, but under the covers we're getting closer and closer to our goal of dynamic, searchable database access.

Adding Search Functionality

For the last part of this example, we're going to add the ability to search the addresses in the database for a particular entry, based on some simple criteria. Let's start on the Flash side this time, since we'll have to make some significant changes.

Search Functionality

1. Make a copy of xmlAddressesProper.fla and name it xmlAddressesParm.fla. Then, drag the keyframe in frame 1 into frame 2, and insert a new blank keyframe in frame 1.

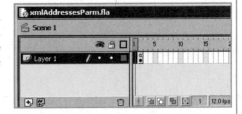

2. Next, cut all of the ActionScript out of frame 2, and paste it into frame 1. Now, since we want to perform a search, we don't want to load from the database as soon as the movie runs, so remove the line of code that reads:

```
objXML.load ("properSearch.asp");
```

3. Instead, we'll wait for the user to pick values to search for, and *then* load the data. Below the code in frame 1, add the following:

```
function doSearch (field, value) {
objXML.load ("parameterSearch.asp?field="+field+"&value="+value);
  searchVal = "";
  play ();
}

stop ();
```

The doSearch function will be called when the user clicks one of the search buttons that we're going to add to frame 2. As you can see, quite apart from the fact that we're using another different ASP page (the new one will be called parameterSearch.asp), the parameter being passed to the load method has become more complicated:

```
"parameterSearch.asp?field="+field+"&value="+value
```

What's happening here? Well, the string you supply here isn't *just* a filename – it's actually a URL, which means we can use a trick that you may have seen appearing from time to time in the Address line of your web browser. When a question mark appears in a URL, everything to its right becomes a set of parameters to the file being loaded, which in this case is our ASP page. This line will result in two variables called field and value becoming available to the VBScript in that page; field is the name of a database field, and value is the literal value the user wishes to search for.

Returning for now to the doSearch function, we'll assign the searchVal variable to the input box that the user will type search values into; setting searchVal to "" will clear the input box after the user has made their submission. We've added a stop command to the end of frame 1, which is also where we're going to put the search form.

Putting a play command in the doSearch function will send us into frame 2 (where our display is) upon initiating a search. Note that the load method is **asynchronous**, meaning that Flash won't wait for it to finish before continuing on to the next line of code. This means that we'll probably be in frame 2 before the XML is actually loaded, but although we haven't added any error handling to detect failure of the load method, you'll know if it hasn't worked.

4. With regard to the search form, we need a single-line input text box, four more buttons of the type we used in the other frame, and four one-line static text boxes. Set the variable name of the input box to `searchVal`. My form looks like this:

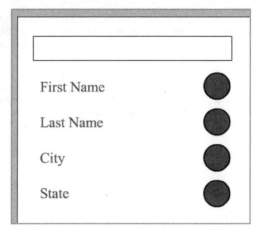

5. Put this code in the First Name button:

```
on (release) {
    doSearch ("fName", searchVal);
}
```

6. ...this code in the Last Name button:

```
on (release) {
    doSearch ("lName", searchVal);
}
```

7. ...this code in the City button:

```
on (release) {
    doSearch ("city", searchVal);
}
```

8. ...and this code in the State button:

```
on (release) {
    doSearch ("state", searchVal);
}
```

9. We're almost done now. Add a single `stop` command in frame 2's actions (we don't want to come all the way to frame 2 just to go back to frame 1 again), find some blank space on the stage in frame 2, and add a label that says Search and a button containing the following actions:

```
on (release) {
    gotoAndPlay(1);
}
```

This will allow the user to go back and perform another search, once they have reviewed their results.

That's all for Flash; now we just need some minor ASP work, and we can call it a day.

10. Make a copy of `properSearch.asp` and name it `parameterSearch.asp`. Then we just need to change the line where we set the command text of `cmd` to match the following:

```
cmd.CommandText = "SELECT addressID,fName,lName,address1," &_
                  "address2,city,state,zip FROM myAddresses " &_
                  "WHERE " & Request.QueryString("field") &_
                  " = '" & Request.QueryString("value") & "';"
```

We've added a WHERE clause to our SQL query that filters through the records in the `myAddresses` table and finds only the ones that match our additional criteria. If the Flash movie loads XML from an address like:

```
.../parameterSearch.asp?field=fName&value=John
```

then our WHERE clause would read like this:

```
...WHERE fName = 'John';
```

When that query was executed, any addresses of people with the first name John would be added into the XML document.

11. Congratulations: we're finally done. Publish `xmlAddressesParm.fla`, then put everything in the same directory on your server, and browse to `xmlAddressesParm.html`.

Being critical, we should probably work it over a little graphically, because it's not really too pretty at the moment. In terms of functionality, though, we've met the targets we started with.

Conclusion

What I've done in this chapter is introduce you to the basics of XML and how to use it in conjunction with Flash. From the examples that we've worked through here, I hope you'll have gathered that XML is a big player on the Web, and that anyone who wants to work on serious web applications should really know how it works. The potential for hooking up your Flash applications with XML is huge. We've only been able to scratch the surface here, but as Flash support and usage of XML spreads, they'll be great opportunities to extend your skills and knowledge. All that XML data is just waiting to be displayed in great-looking, functional Flash movies...

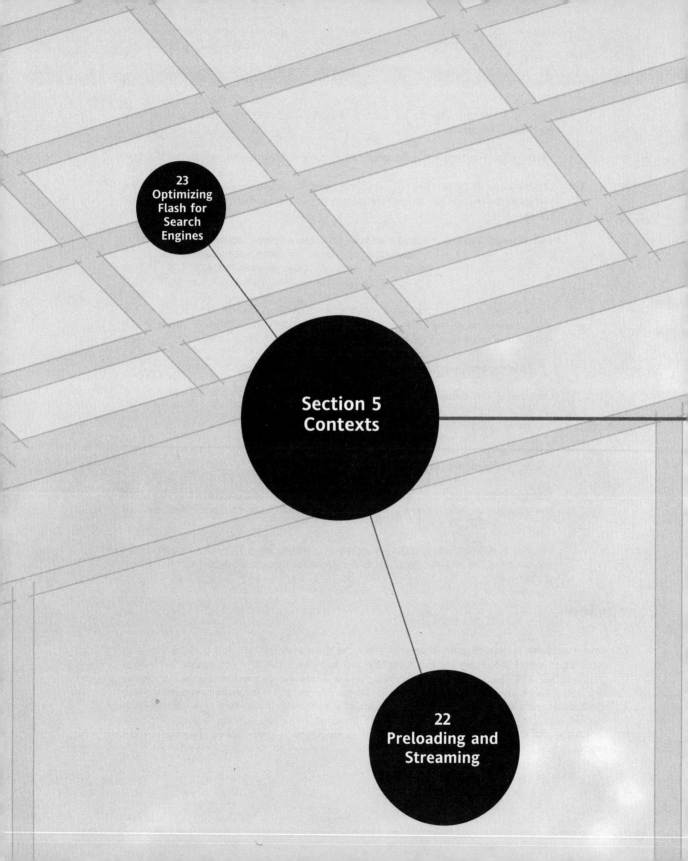

23
Optimizing
Flash for
Search
Engines

Section 5
Contexts

22
Preloading and
Streaming

Chapter 21
Combining Flash
and HTML

Flash movies don't live in a vacuum. Without a browser in which to view them, a page to put them in, and a web site to give them context, a Flash movie is just another computer file. To design a site that utilizes Flash wisely, it's essential to have an understanding of the principles of site architecture. This includes knowing how the movies will sit on a page, how they will interact with other elements on the page, and how that page will be displayed in various web browsers on various platforms.

Even the most beautifully executed animation or perfectly communicative piece of design is incomplete if you haven't also considered its context. In the simplest of situations, creating that context can be as easy as building and embedding a movie at an appropriate size. But it can be as complex as using multiple movies in several layers, embedded in HTML frames of various size, communicating with each other via JavaScript or Perl. By understanding the issues associated with the online viewing of Flash by various browsers, and even just by recognizing that there *are* issues to understand, you'll be on your way to creating web sites that utilize Flash in an elegant and complete way.

The first step in the design of any web site should be to establish a provisional **architecture** (outline) for the site. This architecture may change as the site design progresses, but without at least a preliminary plan, key decisions will be impossible to make. For example, the first decision is to determine whether to use Flash at all. Of course, for the purposes of this book, Flash is an essential, but it's not the be all and end all of web design. There is a lot that can be done on a site without Flash, so it's a bad idea simply to assume that it *should* be used. The following are some good reasons for choosing it:

- If scalability is important - the ability to resize your graphics without any loss of quality, to fill larger monitors and shrink to fit smaller ones

- If high levels of interactivity and animation will be used in the design

- If sound will be very important

On the other hand, if the site will largely feature textual content, or it will be database-driven and won't contain much animation, then Flash can be a burden to the design.

The expected user base of the site should also be carefully considered. If, for example, your intended audience is very 'web-savvy' and is likely to be keen to view your site, then you can probably insist that they have (or be expected to go and download) the Flash plug-in. If, however, the expected audience is of varying levels of computer expertise, or you feel that you must compete for their attention, then Flash might not be a good idea. If Amazon was based on Flash, a lot of users, especially those without Flash already installed, would be doing their shopping elsewhere. There are many other factors involved in choosing to use Flash (or any proprietary technology) on a web site, but a general rule should be that if you can't think of a good reason why you *need* to use the technology, then you probably shouldn't use it.

Once the decision has been made to use Flash in some capacity, the next stage is to decide whether there will be HTML content in addition to Flash content. If no HTML content is necessary, you then decide how Flash will be used. Will it fill the whole of the browser window, or just part of it? Will there be one movie, several linked movies, or several stacked movies? How will non-Flash visitors be dealt with? If there *will* be HTML content, then you have to start asking how it will co-exist with Flash – Flash headers, Flash as inline images, and Flash pages linked with HTML pages are all possibilities. Once these options have been decided upon, you can devise a plan, and design can begin on the site. You'll find that some of these decisions will change after you've started designing the site, and it's up to you, or your client, to decide how much of this feature-creep will be allowed. To make these decisions, it's handy to know how a Flash movie will be displayed in an HTML page.

An Introduction to HTML and Flash

The only way to fully grasp the concepts of embedding and working with Flash movies in context is to have at least a cursory understanding of HTML, and how to code web pages by hand. Applications such as Dreamweaver, while useful to the novice, can be limiting and constricting to the working professional who must regularly deal with a wide variety of situations. Flash is also capable of creating its own HTML pages – accessed through the Publish menu – to use for displaying movies in a browser. Given the relative simplicity of the HTML required and the limitations of these 'helper' tools (Dreamweaver, Flash's publish function, etc.), it's still recommended that designers understand the basics of hand-coded HTML and learn to create their own HTML documents. In most instances, for the purposes of working with Flash, complex HTML and esoteric tags aren't important, but knowledge of the basics most certainly is.

For a SWF file to be displayed in a web browser it has to be **embedded** into a page – that is, referred to from inside an HTML page. When a user arrives at the page, it then 'sends' them the SWF. The HTML code in the page dictates how the web browser will display that SWF.

For example, here's a simple HTML page that shows the embedded movie `mainpage.swf`. We've formatted the code for clarity:

```
<OBJECT CLASSID="clsid:D27CDB6E-AE6D-11cf-96B8-444553540000"
        WIDTH="100"
        HEIGHT="100"
        CODEBASE="http://active.macromedia.com/flash5/cabs/
                        swflash.cab#version=5,0,0,0">

    <PARAM NAME="MOVIE"    VALUE="mainpage.swf">
    <PARAM NAME="PLAY"     VALUE="true">
    <PARAM NAME="LOOP"     VALUE="true">
    <PARAM NAME="QUALITY"  VALUE="high">

<EMBED SRC="mainpage.swf"
        WIDTH="100"
        HEIGHT="100"
        PLAY="true"
        LOOP="true"
        QUALITY="high"

        PLUGINSPAGE="http://www.macromedia.com/shockwave/download/
                        index.cgi?P1_Prod_Version=ShockwaveFlash">

</EMBED>

</OBJECT>
```

Every piece of information in this page is repeated, once for Internet Explorer, and once for Netscape – the latter uses the highlighted <EMBED> portion. Internet Explorer will just ignore the code within the <EMBED> tags, and Netscape will do the same for the <OBJECT> tags. This may seem like a waste of time and file size, but it's just one of those little niggles that comes with having to write for two separate browser standards. It's not all bad though, as most of the instructions will stay the same over every page. The only attributes that'll change from document to document are the source file (SRC in <EMBED>; MOVIE in <OBJECT>) and the scale factors (WIDTH and HEIGHT in both sections).

Frames are another aspect of HTML that are vitally important when working with Flash. They allow you to display two or more HTML pages simultaneously in the same browser window. The height and width of the frame containing each page are dictated by *another* HTML document called a **frameset**, which also controls other features such as scrollbars. Frames are also the only way to ensure that a SWF file will fill the screen, no matter what browser it's running in.

Here's a sample HTML frameset for a page displaying two frames:

```
<FRAMESET ROWS="80%, 20%"
     MARGINWIDTH="0"
     MARGINHEIGHT="0"
     FRAMESPACING="0"
     BORDER="0"
     FRAMEBORDER="NO">

  <FRAME NAME="flash"
     SRC="flash.html"
     SCROLLING="NO"
     MARGINWIDTH="0"
     MARGINHEIGHT="0"
     FRAMESPACING="0"
     BORDER="0"
     FRAMEBORDER="NO">

  <FRAME NAME="bottom"
     SRC="bottom.html"
     SCROLLING="NO"
     MARGINWIDTH="0"
     MARGINHEIGHT="0"
     FRAMESPACING="0"
     BORDER="0"
     FRAMEBORDER="NO">

</FRAMESET>
```

In this example we've specified that the viewer's browser window should contain two frames arranged in horizontal rows: one at 80% of the overall height of the window, the other at 20%. The top frame will display the HTML page flash.html (which contains <EMBED> and <OBJECT>

elements for a Flash movie), while the bottom frame displays a page called bottom.html (which might be a blank placeholder, or might contain other content such as an advertisement or another Flash movie). This frameset would look like this on the user's screen:

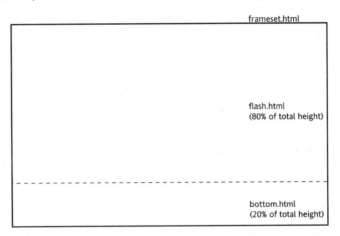

frameset.html

flash.html
(80% of total height)

bottom.html
(20% of total height)

Frames are an extremely useful, and simple, way of combining different technologies and media on one screen. As we said earlier though, frames don't necessarily have to split the screen up. They can have quite the opposite effect and allow one frame to take up the whole screen.

Full Window Embedding

One of the most common and effective ways to use Flash movies is to make them occupy the whole of the web browser's window. By using Flash in this manner, the designer has substantial control over what's actually being seen by the user. In an HTML environment, the content cannot scale to fit the user's window, and because of this it isn't possible to plan exactly how the page will appear.

In order to achieve a predictable, well-designed, full-window Flash experience however, several factors must be taken into account. The first is the browser's inherent misunderstanding of what "full window" actually means. If you simply embed your movie at 100% width and 100% height (which would be the obvious choice, given that 100% of the window size is your goal), the browser will usually put scroll bars on the window. Some browsers will also leave space at the top or right-hand side of the page when embedding at 100%, but this changes on different browsers and platforms.

A frameset that consists of a 1-pixel frame at the top or bottom of the browser window will allow you to embed a Flash movie at 100% (minus the almost invisible 1-pixel frame). Putting your Flash into a frame in this manner eliminates the scroll bars that appear and will allow for predictable embedding of Flash across all browsers and platforms. The 1 pixel that's lost is almost unnoticeable and is a small price to pay for a well-designed page. This invisible frame can also be a useful place to hide code such as hit counters or JavaScript.

Here's an example of a frameset built to contain a full-window Flash movie:

```
<FRAMESET ROWS="*,1"
        MARGINWIDTH="0"
        MARGINHEIGHT="0"
        FRAMESPACING="0"
        BORDER="0"
        FRAMEBORDER="NO">

    <FRAME NAME="flash"
        SRC="flash.html"
        SCROLLING="NO"
        MARGINWIDTH="0"
        MARGINHEIGHT="0"
        FRAMESPACING="0"
        BORDER="0"
        FRAMEBORDER="NO">

    <FRAME NAME="bottom"
        SRC="bottom.html"
        SCROLLING="NO"
        MARGINWIDTH="0"
        MARGINHEIGHT="0"
        FRAMESPACING="0"
        BORDER="0"
        FRAMEBORDER="NO">

</FRAMESET>
```

Notice the ROWS="*,1" in the opening <FRAMESET> tag. This allows the top frame (the one that holds the Flash movie) to expand to whatever height the user's browser window is set to. Here's an example of a web site that I designed called *Decontrol* that's set up in this way:

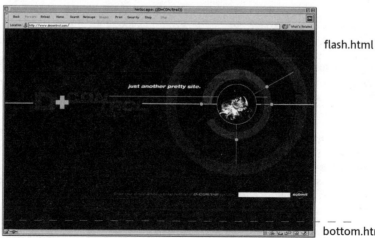

flash.html

bottom.html
(1 pixel)

The first step in planning Decontrol was to decide, in general terms, what look I wanted for the main page. The site had previously been contained entirely in a single pop-up window, but I knew I didn't want to repeat that format again. I wanted the initial appearance of the site to be slightly less jarring – to ease the user in a little bit. I also wanted the page to fill the user's screen as much as possible. The obvious choice was to use Flash in a standard browser window (no pop-up) and to embed it at 100% of window size. Before I even started designing the page, I set up a frameset and a working Flash file to embed in the top frame. By doing this, I basically had my 'raw canvas' in place and was free to design within the parameters that I'd laid out. It's not quite as easy as this though, because all the user needs to do is resize their browser, and my design as it stands will be ruined.

Movie and Window Proportions

If Flash movies were always viewed in browser windows that filled the screen, the question of what proportions to give them would be simple: you'd just build them with a 4:3 aspect ratio, and let them scale to fit any monitor that they might be viewed on. Unfortunately, it's much more likely that whoever's viewing your movie won't have their browser maximized, and this changes not only the *size* of the viewable area, but also its *shape* (from a horizontal rectangle, to a square or even a vertical rectangle). There's also the problem that if the user resizes their browser window while the movie is playing, the movie will scale and reposition itself to fill the new window size and proportion. As a designer, you have very little idea of the proportions of the browser that your movie will be viewed in.

All this means is that the question of what proportions to give your movies is one of design, rather than technical considerations. Factors such as page composition, legibility, and style must all be taken into account when determining the correct stage proportions for a given movie. With a solid understanding of the mechanics of scaling movies, and of how Flash reacts to different situations, you can make educated decisions that also satisfy these design criteria.

When Flash displays a movie, it will always scale it so that everything within the confines of the stage is visible. If a movie is embedded at 100% width and 100% height, it will scale in one of three ways – EXACTFIT, NOBORDER, and SHOWALL – depending on which option you select in the SCALE parameter of the <EMBED> and <OBJECT> tags, for example:

```
SCALE="showall" for <EMBED>, or:

<PARAM NAME="SCALE"  VALUE="showall"> for <OBJECT>
```

If you don't specify a SCALE value in your code, it will just be set to the default value, SHOWALL. This will make Flash maintain the movie's proportions and fit it at the largest size possible without cropping. For example, if your movie is 300 pixels wide by 150 pixels high, and you wish to display it in a window that happens to be 600 pixels wide by 400 pixels high, Flash will scale your movie to 600x300, leaving 50 pixels unaccounted for at the top and bottom of the page. If you choose EXACTFIT, Flash will stretch the movie so that the width and height fit exactly to the dimensions of the window, distorting your movie – generally an undesirable effect. If you select NOBORDER, Flash will fill the entire window with the movie, cropping where necessary so that no stretching is forced. This is also less than ideal though, as it's difficult to plan exactly *how* a movie will be cropped, making it impossible to position important content and guarantee that it will be seen.

SHOWALL is the only option that displays the whole movie at its correct proportions, and therefore is the preferred method to use. What this means in terms of planning a Flash movie though, is that you'll need to determine what users might see in the 'dead space' beyond the edges of your movie:

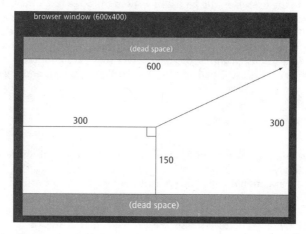

There are a few ways to deal with this dead space. When you're embedding a movie at 100%, any artwork that's put into a Flash movie but falls beyond the edges of the stage will show up, if there is extra room on the page. This is one of the most useful aspects of embedding at 100%, as it allows the designer to control with some confidence what viewers with almost any browser window size will see.

Assume, for example, that you want to create a movie with a stage size of 600x300. If that movie is to be displayed in a window with a 600x300 viewable area, then the user will see just what's on the stage, and nothing else. If that movie is displayed in a window with a 600x400 viewable area however, the viewer will see a further 50 pixels above and below the stage. Luckily, Flash allows you to place art off-stage, so that with careful planning those 50 pixels can be easily incorporated into your design strategy. The simplest way of doing this is just to extend the background colours of your movie for a fair distance outside the stage:

OVERFLOW ART

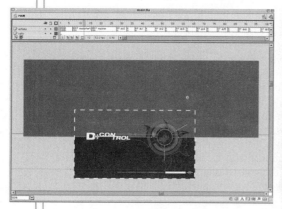

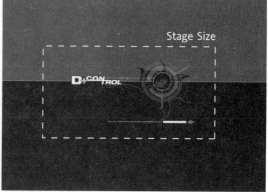

Another way to take advantage of this 'bleeding' feature is to create a mask around the area of the movie that you want people to see. This mask is useful in that it can hide the rough edges of your animation, or areas beyond the stage that you don't want to be visible when the movie is embedded. This includes things like animations that begin off-stage, or movie clips that you're going to use or duplicate later. This mask is just a black (or white, or any color) border around the edges of the movie, on the topmost layer and across all frames. It means that all a user will see if there's excess space, is a black frame. You're still putting art beyond the edges of the stage, but the visual effect is different:

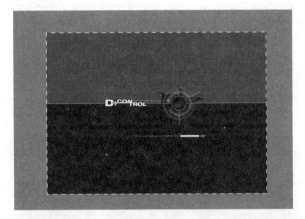

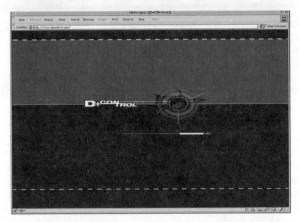

It's also possible to fill up the dead space with background images. Be wary of using this method though, as a background image can be very difficult to align correctly with a Flash movie, especially across browsers and platforms. Furthermore, it offers no real benefit (at least, in a full-screen situation) over placing the additional artwork in the movie itself. Therefore, as a general rule, it's more useful to use flat color masks than background images with full-screen Flash movies.

There is some considerable forethought required in planning the stage size of a full-window movie, depending on how you'd like the movie to appear to a variety of users. By experimenting with different stage proportions and different designs, you can control with some precision what users will see in their browsers, regardless of their individual window size. The best way to really understand how the process works is to make a movie and experiment with its size (by setting size parameters), and see how it appears in different window sizes. The one crucial rule to remember is that as long as you haven't set the SCALE parameter to NOBORDERS, then everything that's on the stage will definitely be seen, but visibility of content outside the stage depends entirely on the user.

To see this in action, use the sample code from above to create a frameset to hold full-screen Flash movies. Then, create a Flash movie that allows you to easily recognize where the edges of the stage are. Try changing the stage's height and width, and view the movie (in your frameset) in a browser. Notice what changing the proportions of the stage does to the amount of art you can see beyond the edges of the stage. Also, try modifying the size and shape of your browser window, and notice how that affects the way your movie appears on the page. Here's an example using the Decontrol web site that we looked at before:

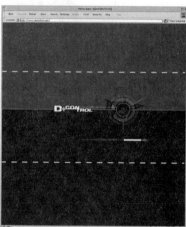

I wasn't sure of the exact proportions of the stage for the Decontrol main page until after the design was completed and viewed in a bunch of different browsers and window sizes. I wanted to get the page to appear as large as possible, but more importantly, due to the very horizontal nature of the design, I wanted to try and make it fill the screen horizontally. In order to achieve this, I chose a stage size that would scale to fit the horizontal aspect of all but the widest of windows, allowing there to be vertical space in most cases. I filled this vertical space with art inside the Flash movie, beyond the edges of the stage (basically just a large grey box).

There are times when, for one reason or another, you need to create a page (or an entire site) in Flash that can't be displayed in a full window. Perhaps your movie contains very complex animation that won't run well if it's shown at a large size. Or perhaps, for aesthetic reasons, you wish to insist that all users see your movie at a fixed pixel size, or at a percentage of their overall window size. In these cases, you have two options available to you, either a **percentage embed** or a **fixed-size embed**.

Percentage and Fixed Size Embedding

For a percentage embed, you specify what percentage of the total window size a movie should occupy. Where a movie at 100% will appear to 'bleed' beyond the edges of the window, a movie at 90% will *always* have a border equal to 10% of the total window size. It's worth noting that the way a movie retains its proportions is the same for percentage embedding as it is for full-window embedding – that is, it will scale to fit the smaller dimension to prevent cropping.

A fixed-size embed is the most straightforward way to embed a movie. If you specify that the movie should be 600 pixels wide by 400 pixels high, that's exactly the size it will appear on the page, regardless of window size, and regardless of the stage size that you used when building it. The movie doesn't scale, and therefore works like an inline image in this respect. If the size you specify is larger than the user's window, the window will scroll just like it would for a simple image.

A problem with percentage and fixed-size embedding is that Flash no longer allows viewers to see art placed beyond the edges of the stage. You must therefore work a little harder to account for the area of the page that's not occupied by the movie – your options are background images or simple background colors. Depending on how you choose to place the movie (using HTML), you may have a difficult time aligning a background image to it. The HTML formatting to align the movie precisely to a background image is by no means impossible (and is actually used quite often), but it can be difficult when dealing with several browsers on several platforms. It's also limiting in that it is impossible to center your movie and still have it align horizontally to a background image (since background images always begin at the left side of the page, there is no way to center the image in the way you center a movie). Here's an example of the Decontrol page percentage embedded within the browser:

PERCENTAGE EMBEDDING

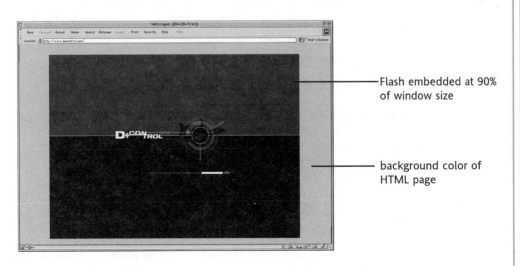

Flash embedded at 90% of window size

background color of HTML page

The only differences in the code for this method are that there's a new <CENTER> tag, which tells the browser to center the movie on the page, and the HEIGHT and WIDTH parameters are changed to reflect the percentage size of the embedded movie. In this case they are set to 90%:

```
<BODY BGCOLOR="#CCFF00" MARGINHEIGHT="0"
    MARGINWIDTH="0"   TOPMARGIN="0"
    LEFTMARGIN="0">

<CENTER>

<OBJECT CLASSID="clsid:D27CDB6E-AE6D-11cf-96B8-444553540000"
        WIDTH="90%"
        HEIGHT="90%"
        CODEBASE="http://active.macromedia.com/flash5/cabs/
            swflash.cab#version=5,0,0,0">

    <PARAM NAME="MOVIE"     VALUE="mainpage.swf">
    <PARAM NAME="PLAY"      VALUE="true">
    <PARAM NAME="LOOP"      VALUE="true">
    <PARAM NAME="QUALITY"   VALUE="best">
    <PARAM NAME="SCALE"     VALUE="showall">

<EMBED  SRC="mainpage.swf"
        WIDTH="90%"
        HEIGHT="90%"
        PLAY="true"
        LOOP="true"
        QUALITY="best"
        SCALE="showall"
    PLUGINSPACE="http://www.macromedia.com/shockwave/download/
                index.cgi?P1_Prod_Version=ShockwaveFlash"

</EMBED>
</OBJECT>

</CENTER>
```

This HTML will give a centered, inset movie, with a green border around it. This effect is fine if you're happy with a border from a design point of view, but if you want to display your movies at 100% but still in a smaller screen, it's best to turn again to frames.

Embedding in Frames

It's possible to utilize the advantages of embedding at 100%, such as the ability to view art beyond the edges of the stage, while still using less than the full size of the window. This is achieved by using frames. A frameset can be designed that'll contain a movie at a percentage of the total window size, or at a specific pixel size, but within which the movie itself is still embedded at 100%. For example, if you know that you want the Flash movie to occupy 40% of the total height of the browser window, you might build the following frameset:

```
<FRAMESET ROWS="40%,60%"   MARGINWIDTH="0"
     MARGINHEIGHT="0"  FRAMESPACING="0"
     BORDER="0"        FRAMEBORDER="NO">

  <FRAME NAME="flash"    SRC="flash.html"
     SCROLLING="NO"   MARGINWIDTH="0"
     MARGINHEIGHT="0" FRAMESPACING="0"
     BORDER="0"       FRAMEBORDER="NO">

  <FRAME NAME="bottom"   SRC="content.html"
     SCROLLING="auto" MARGINWIDTH="0"
     MARGINHEIGHT="0" FRAMESPACING="0"
     BORDER="0"       FRAMEBORDER="NO">

</FRAMESET>
```

Notice that the frameset is now divided into two rows – one row at 40% of the total window height and one row at 60%:

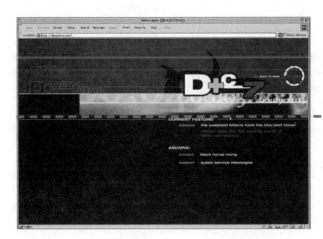

flash.html
(40% of total window height)

content.html
(60% of total window height)

In `flash.html`, you'd embed the Flash movie at 100%, which now relates to 100% of the size of the frame, rather than 100% of the total window size.

For the sub-pages on Decontrol, I originally had a design that put the page header in a frame by itself and the content in a frame at the bottom. This would have allowed for easy updating of the content frame as it would have been all HTML-based. It would also have allowed that frame to scroll with regular browser scroll-bars. In the end though, I scrapped the idea in favor of doing the sub-pages as part of the same Flash movie as the main page. In this way, I was able to easily carry information about the user's visit around with them as they navigated the site, giving me more control and making it possible to gray-out menu items that they had previously visited.

Using frames, you can almost always maintain 100% embedding of your movies, while forcing those movies to scale to percentages or fixed pixel sizes. For this reason, frames are often a better choice than percentage embedding for the flexibility in design that they allow. It's worth noting, however, that there are some problems with frames that should be considered. A frameset can take slightly longer to load than a standard HTML page since it's actually loading three or more pages to display the same information. It's also more difficult to make a site 'bookmarkable' when using framesets. It's not impossible, but the developer will need to put in extra effort to allow pages to be bookmarked easily. There are more files to contend with as well, which can present a logistical problem on very large sites. For example, a site that contains 1000 pages would actually need 3000 HTML files if it used frames. From a purely aesthetic point of view, frames are often the best choice, and their disadvantages are easily overcome. Another option for displaying your content, however, is through the use of pop-up windows.

Pop-up Windows

Pop-up windows are a common feature on many web sites. By using JavaScript, the designer can open a new window, sized according to their wishes, to display content. Other aspects of the new window, such as whether it contains a menu bar, a location bar, a status bar, or even the window's location on the user's screen, can also be specified in the JavaScript code. Given the level of control a designer has over the viewing environment when using pop-ups, it can be quite an attractive option in many instances.

> *It's worth noting that many people express a strong dislike for pop-up windows. They find the experience of a new window opening in front of the old one to be jarring and disorienting. The decision whether to utilize pop-ups should be one of design and of expected audience. There are also some compatibility issues with certain browser and platform combinations, so as always, thorough testing is essential.*

Here is a sample piece of JavaScript code that'll open the file popupwindow.html in a new pop-up window :

```
<HTML>
<HEAD>

<TITLE>decon</TITLE>

<SCRIPT LANGUAGE="JavaScript">

   <!-- Hide from older browsers
```

```
function OpenPopup()
  {
    window.open('popupwindow.html','window','toolbar=0,location=0,
➥directories=0,status=0,menubar=0,scrollbars=0,resizable=0,width=
➥  400,height=300');
  }

  //-->

</SCRIPT>
</HEAD>

<BODY TEXT="#FFFFFF"  LINK="#EE7C0B"
   VLINK="#7D0202"  ALINK="#7D0202"
   BGCOLOR="#000000" TOPMARGIN="0">

  <CENTER>
    <!-- Page content goes here -->
  </CENTER>

</BODY>
</HTML>
```

This is the code for the original page — the one that the pop-up will open *from*. Enclosing the JavaScript inside an HTML comment tag (<!-- -->) ensures that older browsers that don't understand JavaScript will safely ignore it, while the majority of browsers that do understand it will open up the pop-up window. Depending on whether you're opening the window from a Flash movie or from HTML, the code to make the link would be either:

```
getURL("javascript:OpenPopup()");
```

...to open the window from Flash, or:

```
<A HREF="javascript:OpenPopup()">
```

...to open it from an HTML page. It's also possible to open the window automatically when the user arrives at a page by putting the OpenPopup call inside an ONLOAD tag in the BODY tag for the page. This would look like:

```
<BODY ONLOAD="javascript:OpenPopup()">
```

From an embedding standpoint, using Flash in pop-up windows is a far simpler proposition than using it in a regular browser window. You know the exact size of the pop-up window because you opened it yourself using JavaScript, so you can very easily plan the size of your Flash movie accordingly. Here's an example from the Decontrol web site showing the use of a pop-up window to display information:

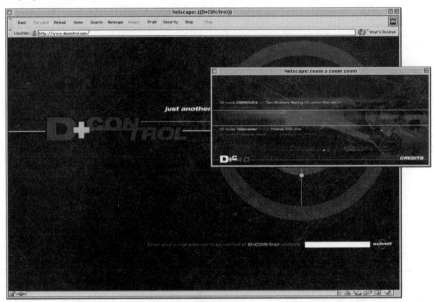

Decontrol uses pop-up windows to display all of its actual content. This proved to be a very practical solution since much of the content of the site is from outside contributors. We're able to tell them that their piece of work can be displayed in any size window they like, and that the window will open directly from the main site window. The pop-up window creates a semi-autonomous environment where artists are able to create their own work while still maintaining hints for the user that they haven't left the Decontrol site. It's also a way to instantly let the user know what is a featured piece of art and what's site navigation.

One Movie Versus Several Movies

The next decision in Flash site development is whether to use just one large movie for the entire site, or several movies for the different sections of a site. As usual, there are advantages and disadvantages to each option. All considerations should be explored before design begins, as it's sometimes difficult to convert a site from one movie to several movies once design has begun. Let's look at each option in more detail.

One Movie

Using one Flash movie for an entire site can be cumbersome. The file tends to get pretty large and, unless you're very well stocked with RAM, it can be slow to work on. It's also extremely difficult to work in a team when there is only one master file to work from. For example, if you're working on the main page of a site and another designer is working on a sectional page, you'll need to work in separate files and then combine your work into the single master file by copying frames or symbols. This is eased by Flash 5's new **shared library** feature, but it's still a less-than-ideal method of working together, and creates quite a few problems. Note that these are all issues faced by the developer and not the end-user. In an ideal situation, all site design would cater entirely to the user, but in a practical environment, issues like workflow and file management become very important.

There are a few very good reasons, however, for working past these problems and using a single movie for an entire site. If you've got the whole site contained in a single movie, you can dictate how it loads into the user's computer. This can be especially valuable if you expect your potential users to have slow connections. For example, you could display an interesting loading screen while the main page loads, then display the main page while the first sectional page loads, and so on.

Another significant advantage of using a single movie for an entire site is the ability to create transitions between sections and sub-sections. Since there is no real distinction between sections, you're able to animate out of one and into another quite easily. Taken a step further, putting all of the content of a site into one movie allows you to dispense with traditional site structure (main page, sections, sub-sections, etc.) and create a more fluid, non-linear structure. Pieces of content that open in areas of the page, floating windows, persistent content tools, etc., are all easily possible if a site is contained entirely in one movie.

This is not to say though, that all of these advantages can't be built into a site made up of several movies. It's much *easier* to incorporate them into a single movie site, but we'll look now at how they can be employed just as successfully in a multi-movie site.

Several Movies

Breaking a site into smaller individual movies that are based on sections provides distinct advantages too. It becomes much simpler for multiple designers to work on a single site. For example, one designer can build the main page in its own file, while another builds a sectional page in *its* own file – these files don't ever need to be physically combined into a single file, though they will, of course, need to work together when viewed on the site. Also, files are generally smaller, easing the burden on overworked processors.

If you decide that using multiple movies is appropriate, you must make some more decisions. Do you put each movie on its own HTML page, or embed the first movie and call the new ones into the same page using the loadMovie command? If all of the movies on the site are to be embedded full-window, then it's generally better to call new movies into the same HTML page. This eliminates some work in creating many identical HTML pages, as well as removing the brief 'hiccup' that occurs when jumping to a new page. This comes when linking movies where the background color of the page always stays on the screen before the new content is loaded.

If you need to embed several movies differently, or if the movies are built at different sizes, then you're stuck with using several HTML pages. This isn't necessarily bad though, as each page of the site can be easily bookmarked or e-mailed. Also, the Back and Forward buttons on the user's browser will remain functional. These are both features that are impossible (or at least very difficult) to maintain when using a single HTML page to contain all of a site's Flash movies.

While each of these methods has its own advantages and disadvantages, there is another way that combines elements of the two.

Stacked Movies

It's possible to create a hybrid of both of the above methods by using multiple movies that are 'stacked' — that is, they're loaded on top of one another, which is not to be confused with movies that are loaded in place of one another, as in the previous section. Usually, a controller movie is embedded onto the page that then loads the individual movies for the site onto layers above itself. These movies can be downloaded and then left until they're needed. In this way, you could load movies either as they are needed, all at once, or even a combination of the two. For example, if you were on the main page, you might begin loading all of the sectional pages (which are each in their own movies) onto separate levels, so that they're ready when the user clicks to go to them.

With stacked movies, it's also possible to create layers that are present throughout a site visit. Movies loaded into layers are transparent anywhere that there's nothing else on the stage, and because of this, it's possible to view two or more movies at the same time. So, if you had a movie with a basketball court on it in level 1, and a movie with a bouncing ball on level 2, the user would see the ball bouncing in the basketball court. Movies are stacked sequentially, based on their layer number: higher numbers at the top of the pile, lower numbers at the bottom. It's also worth remembering that stacked movies will inherit the stage properties of the lowest level movie; this includes background color, frame rate, and stage dimensions.

Since all sections or areas of a site are present at the same time, even though they are in different movies at different levels, the designer is able to provide planned transitions between sections or movies. Provided the site is properly designed, the user experience can be every bit as seamless as when using a single movie. Stacking movies provides all of the advantages of a single movie, without the drawbacks of the need for one large file. It also allows for the practical advantages of using multiple movies without the design issues associated with that method. Here's an example page from the Decontrol site, where four movies have been stacked in layers and combined to form a single user experience:

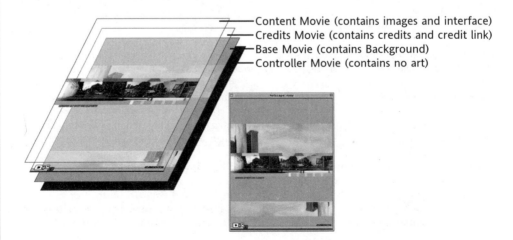

Content Movie (contains images and interface)
Credits Movie (contains credits and credit link)
Base Movie (contains Background)
Controller Movie (contains no art)

In this particular piece from Decontrol, I used several separate movies stacked on top of one another. The primary reason in this case was that a programmer was working on getting some functionality built at the same time that I was working on the design. By using separate movies, he was able to program and test what he was working on (code that was contained in the bottom Controller movie) while I was designing and testing the page. If the piece had been all one file, then one of us would have had to finish and then hand the file over to the other to do their part, taking twice as long as doing it concurrently.

After deciding all of this, and working with a star team to create the perfect Flash site, you're no doubt waiting for the countless millions of visitors to start rolling in. But for some reason, it's worryingly quiet. To ensure your site gets the maximum amount of traffic, it's sometimes worth including an alternative version of your site for those people who don't use Flash.

Flash Detection and Flat Sites

Although a majority of viewers do browse the Web with the Flash plug-in installed, there are still those who don't. For these people, you can implement a detection scheme that'll determine whether they have the plug-in (or even a specific version of the plug-in, if you desire) and send them to an alternative page without Flash content if they don't. It can also be worth offering viewers the choice of whether they'd like to view the Flash site or a flat site. Whether you implement an auto-detection system or give your visitors a choice is a matter of personal taste, but it can be influenced by such factors as your expected readership and the function of the site. In some cases, especially when content *must* be displayed using Flash, a flat page might consist simply of a message alerting the viewer that they don't have the necessary plug-ins, and that if they want to see the page they should probably go and download them. A link to the Macromedia site (where the user can download Flash) is also usually a good thing to include on this type of page. By giving users a choice, all viewers are accounted for, and nobody receives a plug-in error message or an ambiguously blank page. It's worth noting that it's also possible to generate a sequence of images from Flash to replace the movie. While this can obviously create huge numbers of files when used wrongly, it can be useful for creating GIF equivalents of simple animations such as logos.

The simplest method for detecting Flash involves using Flash itself to detect for the plug-in. To do this, you can build a page that contains a basic Flash movie that just has a getURL command to your main Flash site. The rest of the page would be the HTML version of your site. In this way, if you've got Flash installed on your computer, you'll immediately be sent to the Flashed site, and if not, you'll remain on the basic page. This method is perfectly reliable and very simple to implement, but can appear sloppy to a user due to the rapid flipping between two pages when they first arrive. For this reason, it may be worth investigating a JavaScript based solution.

When using a JavaScript detection scheme, the user often doesn't know that they've been 'detected' because the detection happens so quickly and seamlessly. Unfortunately, the code for accurate and dependable detection of the Flash plug-in via JavaScript has become progressively more complex and intricate with each new browser and plug-in version that's released. New detection scripts are written almost daily at many larger design studios and for this reason, it's impossible to give reliable working examples. Some relatively stable pieces of detection code can be found for free online from various sites – a good place to start is the Macromedia site.

FLASH/NON-FLASH REDIRECT

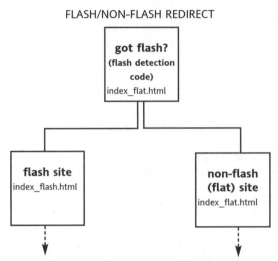

Flash movies can be used on pages in exactly the same way as static images, but they can provide far more interactivity and opportunity for design. In many cases, Flash files are also smaller in size than their GIF or JPEG counterparts. Flash can therefore provide even more benefit over static images, with little or no drawback.

Flash as an Inline Image

In many situations, site layout calls for a simple, self-contained image. Often, though, additional animation and interactivity would be desirable. In these cases, there is seldom a reason not to use a Flash movie – although it's generally a good idea to provide automatic detection for the Flash plug-in, and exchange the movie for an image if necessary. This method allows for a seamless experience for the user, as they don't know that anything has been detected or switched; they simply receive the content that's appropriate for them.

> *A disadvantage of this is that the user then may not know that a richer experience would be possible if they had the plug-in. For this reason, images are often labeled with a message to the effect of, "You're seeing a static image where you could be seeing a Flash movie. Please download the plug-in," with a link to the appropriate download site.*

Flash movies used in this manner on a page are generally not scalable. The only possible way to allow a Flash movie to scale with the page content would be to create an HTML table with scalable cells and embed the Flash into one of these scaling cells. It's unreliable to embed a movie in this way, however, so, movies are usually embedded at a fixed size. Here's an example of a static Flash image combined with a standard HTML page in the same way as a GIF or a JPEG would be:

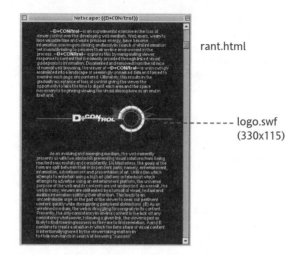

rant.html

logo.swf
(330x115)

Flash Headers

Page headers and menus can work very well as Flash movies. In the simplest example, what would normally be an image-mapped graphic on the page would become a Flash movie containing similar functionality (that is, linking to other pages on the site), but with more dynamic presentation of that functionality. Sounds, more robust animations, elaborate button rollovers, ease of development, and smaller file sizes are all good reasons to use Flash for page headers and menus rather than simple images. If executed correctly, there are few drawbacks to using Flash in this manner.

A page that's going to use Flash menus or headers can be designed just as it would be without Flash. Composition, hierarchy, and structure are the primary concerns in laying out a page, whether or not elements are to be created using Flash. Headers and menus are embedded in exactly the same way (fixed sizes, aligned using tables, etc.) as they would be if they were not Flash.

Using Frames for Flash Headers

A better way still to use a Flash movie as a page header is to employ frames. In this scheme, the page is divided into two frames: a top frame that'll contain the Flash movie, and the bottom frame that'll contain the content. If the site is structured appropriately, the top frame may never need to be reloaded. When users arrive at the site, they're greeted by a Flash header and some content. When they select a menu item from the top frame, only the content in the bottom frame needs to be replaced. The Flash movie can reflect the current content through methods such as graying-out or highlighting certain menu items.

It's sometimes difficult to create a site that works with this simplistic structure. Many sites, especially those that feature primarily HTML-based content, need to have a main page with a different look and feel (and consequently different architecture) than the sectional pages. In this situation, a problem arises. Do you build separate sectional pages and use individual movies as headers on each page – in which case you're forcing the user to load a brand new movie every time they switch pages – or do you use just one header movie for all of the sectional pages?

One interesting solution might utilize a scalable Flash main page, with a single Flash movie header on all of the sub-pages. This format would allow for an exciting full-screen experience for the main page, with easily updateable, HTML-based content pages. To make all this work, a single, unchanging header would need to be in place throughout the entire site. The problem lies in linking from the Flash main page to the mixed HTML-and-Flash sub-pages. These sub-pages would all contain the same movie, and that movie would contain menu information for all of the site sections. As the user goes from the main page to a sub-page, it would be necessary to pass information to the Flash header to tell it which section's menu information it should display.

There are many possible solutions to the problem of communicating between Flash movies on different pages. Each option has many subtleties that'll affect other aspects of the site's functionality. All of the methods to be explored have the same goal: communicating from a Flash movie to a page, then from that page to another, then from the second page to another Flash movie.

One technique involves making sure that you've got a persistent frame: one that'll be present on the main page, and in all of the sections. Using JavaScript, you then tell this frame where you're planning on going when you leave the main page. Once the sectional header loads, it will ask the persistent frame which section it should be displaying (by gathering information contained in the JavaScript in that frame), and display the appropriate sectional information. It's up to you how to tell the content frame which content is to be displayed.

The Flash header can go to an About section, for example, then tell the content frame to load the appropriate About page, or you could have separate frameset pages for each possible sectional page. It's also possible to load the About page, and then have *it* talk to the header and tell it what section to display. Another method might involve sending information to a CGI script that'll then direct both the content frame *and* the Flash header, and make sure everybody's on the same page. Any of these methods might be a viable option, and factors such as expected site traffic (and therefore server load), page content (simple pages or complex ones), and programming ability would affect the method to be chosen.

main.html

blank.html

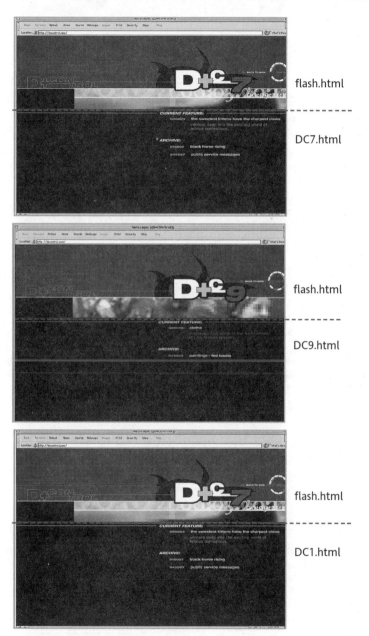

We experimented on Decontrol with doing the sub-pages as a header with a content frame (as I mentioned before). The problem was that we wanted to transfer information from the main page to those sub-page Flash headers. We worked with a lot of different methods for achieving this and, in the end, decided that they were all far too complex for what we were trying to do. In this case, it was far more practical to convert the sub-pages to an all Flash format, and include them in the same movie as the main page.

Flash Pages with HTML Pages

Another way to mix Flash with HTML involves having some pages of a site that are entirely in Flash, while other pages are entirely in HTML (or HTML with inline Flash movies).

A situation where this could occur is where you *want* to do a site entirely in Flash (for reasons such as scalability of Flash movies, or animation capabilities), but you *need* to have some pages entirely in HTML (such as a CGI-based message board or a database-driven content area). If you intended to create the Flash portion of the site as one large movie (or several stacked movies), you'd need to link to a new page that contained the message board. The problem with this solution occurs when the user attempts to return to the Flash part of the site from the message board: you'll be forcing the user to reload the entire Flash movie every time they do so. This would especially be an issue for users with slower connections.

There are a few possible solutions:

- You could open the message board in a pop-up window – this would work quite well, and would separate the message board from the Flash movie.

- You could link from the Flash movie to a regular HTML page with a message board on it – this would work well, but would cause the user to reload the entire site upon returning from the message board.

- You could break the site up into smaller movies so that every page was its own movie – this would mean that you'd load a new movie any time you switched pages, alleviating the strain of loading the entire site at once, but disrupting the experience by forcing lengthy loads any time you wanted to switch pages.

None of these possible solutions is ideal, but various factors such as desired user experience (would pop-up windows be jarring), expected readership (fast or slow connections), and site design (are there transitions between sections that would be lost when breaking the site up into many movies) will determine which compromise is best.

Flash Linked to HTML pages

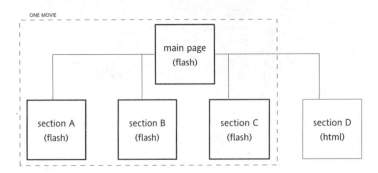

Conclusion

You should take many factors into consideration when thinking about the architecture of a web site. Three of the most important are:

- The content to be displayed on the site – for example, an informational site would have very different needs than a purely entertainment site. An entertainment site will probably focus on creating as immersive an experience as possible by using full-window Flash movies and large streaming animations, whereas an informational site would probably focus more on ease of use and quick, concise presentation of information. Considerations such as how often a site will be updated will also affect the planning of the architecture. If a site will be constantly updated, it's usually a good idea to build the updating parts in HTML and possibly build menus and other non-changing elements in Flash.

- The expected audience of the site – a site aimed at web developers would probably be put together differently than one aimed at hobbyists. One can safely assume that web developers will have the most current plug-ins and will be less adverse to elements such as pop-up windows, whereas groups that may or may not be web savvy can't be expected to have the latest technology. For the latter group, considerations such as simplicity of use and non-reliance on proprietary technologies (such as Flash) might be very important.

- The visual design of the site – the visual design is, of course, influenced by the other two factors, but should then affect the architectural decisions. In essence, the architecture of the site is very much a part of the visual design, so it's probably not accurate even to separate the two.

Establishing the architecture of a web site is one of the most important, and often overlooked, decisions a designer needs to make. An all-too-common practice is to assume that the site will be made with Flash and simply to begin designing, but this leaves out a very important step of the conceptualization process. Decisions such as whether to use Flash alone or with HTML, at what size to embed Flash movies, and how many individual movies should be used, are crucial to a site architecture that'll provide a compelling user experience. Even once a decision has been made about what should be used as an appropriate architecture, the question of how exactly to execute that plan still remains. The possibilities are nearly endless and are multiplying every single day with every new technology or software update that gets released. With at least a working knowledge of the possibilities available when using Flash, you can make an educated decision that'll enhance, and hopefully expand upon, the overall visual impact of the web site.

21
Combining
HTML and
Flash

Section 5
Contexts

23
Optimizing
Flash for
Search
Engines

Chapter 22
Preloading and Streaming

Flash can create enhanced web applications through the use of sound, images, and animation, but the majority of Internet users just don't have the capacity to accommodate the large file sizes that are inherent with the large-scale implementation of these media types. In today's web development environment, where you usually want to attract and retain as many visitors as possible, it's critical that these users are not overlooked. On the contrary, they should normally be a central design consideration.

At the moment, 50 kilobytes is still the size benchmark against which to judge the general accessibility of a web application. Anything larger than that will begin to try the patience and capacity of many users. Long download times are frustrating to the population of low-to-medium bandwidth modem users, and many will leave a site (often never to return) when they feel a download is taking too long. As a designer, however, it's sometimes difficult to forgo the stunning media potential of the Flash technology and concentrate on creating applications that come in beneath that threshold. Fortunately, there are techniques that can be used to push back the boundaries, and create higher bandwidth applications that a lower bandwidth audience will be willing to accommodate.

Preloading and **streaming** offer viable ways to distribute media assets in a way that makes optimal use of a web surfer's resources. These techniques do this by prioritizing the content elements required at each stage of the user's visit, and by ensuring that the flow of data to the user's machine keeps pace with their progress through a web application. Through preloading and streaming, the 50-kilobyte threshold can be manipulated to take fuller advantage of Flash's powerful media integration abilities, and without punishing the user with an excessive download wait. Preloading and streaming are not, however, panaceas for creating enormous Flash movies that will download quickly in a narrow bandwidth space. Flash's media assets must *always* be used in an intelligent and sparing manner – and that's a question of forethought and considered design.

Let's move on by considering streaming and preloading concepts in more detail. After that we'll look at how these concepts can be applied in Flash using a series of examples.

What is Streaming?

A stream, as it applies to web design and the Internet, refers to a **flow of data**. The process of 'streaming' describes the dynamics and mechanics of how data flows into a user's allotted **bandwidth**, which is a term used to describe the amount of data that can be transferred into a device per unit of time. A user sitting at the end of a phone line with a 56k modem, for example, is considered to have a 'low bandwidth' connection, because this type of device can only receive data at a relatively slow rate. (In this case, around 56,000 bits per second. Compare this with a typical office network, which will transfer data at between 10 and 100 *million* bits per second.)

> *Bandwidth is affected by a range of influences; most significantly by the type of Internet or network connection (modem, DSL, T1/T3, etc.), network traffic, geographical location, the physical composition of communications lines, and a variety of other technical factors that are beyond the scope of this chapter.*

Macromedia's helpful definition of the process of streaming in terms of Flash technology, and how it relates to this chapter, is as follows:

> *"The term streaming, as it relates to Flash Player, refers to the normal flow of data from a server over a network connection to the client machine that has requested it. The fastest speed at which data moves is limited to the slowest connection through which that data travels. Often, the slowest point in the connection is a user's modem (running at 28.8 kbits per second or slower).*
>
> *Since all data streams over a connection to the user's machine, what makes a Flash Player movie's stream different from a big GIF or JPEG file's stream? The difference is that the data in a Flash Player movie is stored sequentially by frame. When the Flash Player (plug-in or ActiveX control) receives all of the data for a single frame, it may then immediately render it to the screen without waiting for any more of the data to arrive. A Flash Player movie will play smoothly only if Flash Player is able to receive the data over the net connection at about the rate that the Flash Player movie is set to play in frames per second."*
>
> Source: Macromedia Flash TechNote ID: 12085

To summarize this second paragraph, an online Flash movie will start playing its frames as soon as they are downloaded to your computer, without requiring Flash to wait for the remainder of the movie to download. In Flash, this is considered 'streaming'. The advantage of streaming is that users with even quite limited bandwidth will not experience a delay before they start viewing a movie, and the movie will play back smoothly.

The *danger* inherent in this kind of streaming is that users with low-to-medium bandwidth (56k modem users are a good example of this audience) will see the Flash movie as it downloads, but face a risk that the movie will encounter dropped frames or pauses during playback. This event occurs when the user's network connection cannot keep up with the rate at which Flash is sending data to their computer. In cases where the amount of data required to display each Flash movie frame is small, streaming can work effectively for all users, but these are not terribly common – especially where a web designer has used Flash's powerful media integration abilities to combine sound, animation, video, and images to produce rich web applications. These types of media elements involve large files, making streaming a bad choice for the current web audience, where most users cannot accommodate high bandwidth media. To account for this problem, Flash's data stream needs to be regulated and optimized; this can be done through ActionScript, and the process known as **preloading**.

What is Preloading?

Preloading is almost the opposite of streaming. In preloading, media elements essential for successful playback are loaded *before* advancing to a given point in a movie, preventing Flash's default streaming from playing the movie as soon as frames are downloaded. This is a good technique to implement when a Flash movie has a large file size that makes streaming an unrealistic alternative. ,

Technically, this is accomplished through the ActionScript property `_framesloaded`, which allows you to specify the quantity of content elements that should be downloaded before Flash executes other actions or advances to a specified point in the movie. The `_framesloaded` property can be exploited in a variety of applications and scenarios to optimize a Flash application for both high and low bandwidth audiences.

A typical example of preloading might involve a reasonably large Flash web site, around 50 to 100 KB in size, which included a number of bitmap images, sounds, and animations. Preloading takes place during the appearance of a 'loading' screen, which is essentially a 'waiting room' area for the user. While the user waits, media assets are downloaded in the background, after which the movie can be accessed. Preloading deals with situations where a data stream is forced into a bandwidth space that can't otherwise accommodate the size of the data. By forcing the user to wait for content to download, the data stream 'gets ahead' of the user's bandwidth, and the user can access the movie without data transfer issues affecting playback performance.

The drawback of preloading large files, of course, is the problem we started with: the built-in wait period will frustrate Internet users who – like the rest of us – generally don't like waiting before receiving some form of feedback or reward. Users may leave your application or web site if the loading time exceeds their patience. To help deal with this problem, preloading screens should be as inviting and pleasurable as possible, offering multiple forms of user feedback to make the wait more tolerable. Furthermore, any delays you introduce should be no longer than absolutely necessary, and while that could seem like obvious advice, there are techniques for squeezing the wait period even harder than you might have thought. We'll discuss some of these strategies next.

Load Screens, Diversionary Tactics, and User Feedback

The **load screen** is the first impression of your application a user will receive and experience. First impressions are always a critical facet of successful, powerful design, and they'll often shape a user's perception of your whole product. It's important to recognize that waiting is *never* a pleasant experience for the Internet user, especially when they're entering a site for the first time and its benefits, rewards, or purpose are still unproven to them. It's therefore paramount to alleviate user frustration during this period by offering some reassurance that your site is going to be worth the wait. By crafting a load screen, you can help the user to understand that you are considerate of their needs, and give them a meaningful taste of your site's attitudes towards them.

Designers commonly overcome this challenge by presenting the user with an engaging animation, a movie, or an interactive toy that responds to the user's actions. Any of these will occupy the user's attention, which in turn can alter their perception of the loading time and site value. A user may, for example, get so involved playing with an interactive toy that the site has preloaded everything it needs before they realize no further waiting is necessary.

The use of **progress bars** is a different technique from feedback and diversion: one that provides the user with information about the status of the site they're visiting. Progress bars – accurate ones at least – indicate visually just how much of the application has downloaded, and how much longer the user can expect to wait. This is useful because it lets the user know that content is being transmitted to their computer, and the application is not just sitting in an idle or broken state. Many users automatically assume that a web application is broken if they can't see some form of feedback, and may leave as a result of that misconception.

An important point to note about Flash is that it departs from the conventional HTML loading patterns that users are accustomed to experiencing. In typical HTML pages, frames, text, and images are loaded in a cumulative manner that builds up the page over time. Images in HTML may appear as 'placeholder' icons initially, and fill in once the associated file has downloaded. This not only tells the user that information is being downloaded to their computer, but also yields visual cues demonstrating how much of the page is complete. In Flash, this feedback does not generally occur: pages often go from a blank state to being visible in their entirety, with no hint of what's going on in the interim. Combining a progress bar with an aesthetic diversion is often the most effective, professional approach to establishing successful user feedback.

Prelude to Construction

Before we go ahead and look at some examples and code, it's worth pointing out that techniques like streaming and preloading should be seen as the *last* stage in the process of optimizing Flash applications for your users. They are not a substitute for thoughtful design, and Flash provides a number of ways to improve the efficiency of your movies – intelligent use of symbols, and choosing appropriate image and sound formats can go a long way to reducing file size and improving your users' experience. Some of the best advice in this regard is probably that provided by Macromedia itself in the document *Using Flash 5*, which is available for download in PDF format from the Flash Support Center at www.macromedia.com. In particular, check out the section entitled *Optimizing Movies*.

Only when you're sure that you've streamlined as far as you can, and the demands of your movie are still such that preloading and streaming are required, should you start planning how best to implement them. With all of that in mind, we need now to take a quick look at some of the tools of the trade that will help us to identify the sections of our movies where solutions of this type may be necessary.

Using Flash Player's 'online simulation' mode and the bandwidth profiler in harness can help to demonstrate how the principles of streaming and preloading work, and aid your decision-making about which techniques are appropriate for each movie.

Testing Streaming Movies, and Flash's Bandwidth Profiler

To examine the streaming and preloading mechanisms of the example movies that we'll be building over the course of this chapter, you can open the FLA file for any one of them from the CD (say, `approximate.fla`), and invoke the Control > Test Movie command. When the movie opens in a new window, select View > Show Streaming to invoke Flash's online download simulation. In this mode, you'll see the preload bar fill up slowly, as Flash 'pretends' that data is arriving at the speed it would over a typical Internet connection. (If you just select Test Movie, Flash will not enter its online simulation, and will skip the display of the preloading or streaming process.)

Another aspect of Flash's online simulation is a tool called the Bandwidth Profiler, which can be accessed from the Flash Player's View menu:

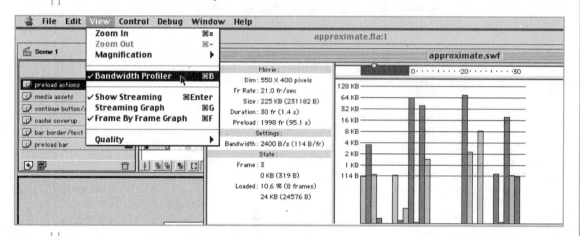

The 'state' portion of the bandwidth profiler's dialog box (on the left-hand side) contains information about the number of frames loaded, the percentage of the movie loaded, and the size of the frame currently loading. This information is often useful for diagnostic or troubleshooting purposes.

On the right-hand side of the window, the profiler provides a graph of Flash's data stream, with frame and file size information. This view changes depending on whether the View menu is set to Frame By Frame Graph or Streaming Graph. In the case of the former, the horizontal axis of the graph represents frames, while the vertical axis represents size. Tall, rectangular blocks on the graph are frames with large sizes, and any blocks that pass the horizontal red line are frames where Flash will pause playback until the frame has fully downloaded. This line is relative to the connection speed setting (14.4k, 28.8k, 56k, etc.) selected under the Debug menu, and will change position depending on the bandwidth of the selected connection setting.

When the 'Show Streaming' mode is activated, a green bar that grows from left to right (and sometimes pauses) appears above the bandwidth profiler:

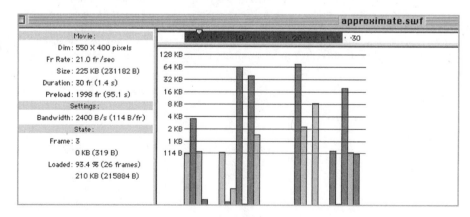

This bar represents Flash's data flow, and the total number of the movie's frames that have been downloaded so far. The relationship between the green bar and the playback arrow superimposed on it represents the dynamics of how the user's bandwidth is accepting Flash's data. If the playback arrow catches up with the end of the green bar, pauses or dropped frames will occur, offering important clues about the success or failure of a preloading or streaming loading technique. The general aim here is to always keep the right-hand side of the bar in advance of the playback arrow.

If you do manage to isolate streaming problems using these tools, possible solutions include making the data stream smaller by adjusting the file size of media assets, adding extra compression, or by lowering the movie's frame rate. In the case of preloading media, a hiatus may simply indicate that the playback arrow has paused at a certain frame until some more media assets have been loaded, at which point the arrow may advance to another frame. Before your site goes 'live', of course, you should also test it over a *real* Internet connection – the Flash simulator is good, but it's not perfect.

Modifying Load Order

When exporting or publishing movies, Flash offers two Load Order options: Bottom up, or Top down:

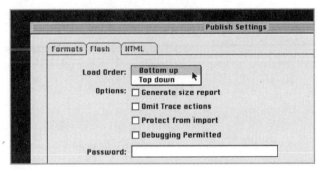

These options control the order in which Flash loads the layers for the first frame of the movie. If, for example, the Bottom up option is selected, and a user has a slow connection, Flash will render the bottom layers of the movie before rendering the top layers. This option can be used as a rudimentary preloading/streaming technique if graphics are present on the first frame of your movie. Media assets, for example, can be prioritized by layering graphics according to what you want the user to see first, and selecting the appropriate Load Order option:

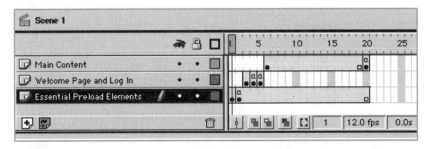

Keep in mind, however, that if the user has a fast connection, or the graphics have small file sizes, the assets may still appear simultaneously. In other words, don't count on any visual 'effects' that you obtain by tweaking the load order.

Generating Size Reports

Flash also has the ability to generate a text file called a **size report** that contains an analysis and breakdown of the content and media assets in a Flash movie. To obtain this report, you need to publish a movie with the Generate size report box checked. Size reports are an invaluable tool for gaining a frame-by-frame analysis of file size and general media usage in your movie, with the aim of identifying portions of the movie that may present a problem in terms of download time. By creating size reports it's easier to pinpoint potential trouble spots and therefore to make enlightened decisions regarding whether to stream or preload media.

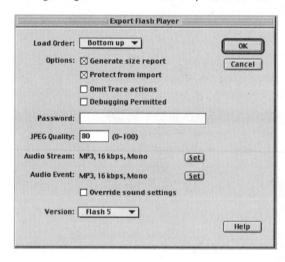

A typical size report looks like this (broken up for clarity):

```
Movie Report
_____
```

Frame #	Frame Bytes	Total Bytes	Page
1	131	131	Scene 1
2	3976	4107	2
3	301	4408	3
4	15	4423	4
5	2	4425	5
6	2	4427	6
7	270	4697	7
8	10	4707	8
9	39	4746	9
10	66386	71132	10

11	6	71138	11
12	43478	114616	12
13	1590	116206	13
14	2	116208	14
15	2	116210	15
16	2	116212	16
17	2	116214	17
18	2	116216	18
19	2	116218	19
20	81759	197977	20
21	2526	200503	21
22	2	200505	22
23	8762	209267	23
24	2	209269	24
25	2	209271	25
26	329	209600	26
27	6	209606	27
28	21374	230980	28
29	241	231221	29
30	117	231338	30

In this first section, column one contains the frame number; while column two contains the size of that particular frame in bytes. The third column contains a running total of the movie's size in bytes; while the fourth column reflects what scenes the associated frames are contained in. This portion of the report is useful for pinpointing large frames that may cause loading delays.

Now the second section...

Page	Shape Bytes	Text Bytes
Scene 1	0	380
Embedded Objects	244	0

Symbol	Shape Bytes	Text Bytes
g-image4	0	0
b-continue	35	44
g-acorn	223	0
g-bar border	39	0
g-image1	0	0
g-image2	0	0
g-image3	0	0
g-loadbar	38	0
g-tree	315	0
m-cover	39	0
m-loadbar	0	0

The second section of the report reveals shape byte and text byte sizes for the symbols and scenes contained in the movie. **Shape bytes** are the amount of memory taken up by a vector shape, while **text bytes** are the amount of memory taken up by text. Generally, shape byte sizes are small, unless a lot of control points are present (a complex, traced bitmap is a good example of this), in which case a vector shape can grow to a much larger size.

And the third section:

```
Bitmap          Compressed      Original      Compression
- - - - - - -   - - - - -       - - - - -     - - - - -
cloudcity.pct      21299        1500000       JPEG Quality=80
Bitmap 5           81684        1497000       JPEG Quality=80
Bitmap 3           43403        1497000       JPEG Quality=80
Bitmap 15          66311        1500000       JPEG Quality=80
```

This section of the report shows the compressed and original file sizes of any bitmap images contained in the movie, as well as the image compression settings. This is useful when comparing differences in image degradation and dithering between compression settings to differences in file size. By making a file size and compression setting comparison, you can come to a sensible decision over which compression setting is the best in terms of good image quality and reasonable file size.

```
Event sounds: 11KHz Mono 16 kbps MP3

Sound Name      Bytes           Format
- - - - - - -   - - - - - -     - - - -
apollo1.aiff        8751        11KHz Mono 16 kbps MP3
crash2              2511        11KHz Mono 16 kbps MP3
hat open2           1575        11KHz Mono 16 kbps MP3
```

The fourth section of the report contains the names and sizes of any sound clips present in the Flash movie, along with their associated formats. Sound file sizes vary depending on their sample rate, whether the files are mono or stereo, and the type of compression used. MP3 is the best compression format to use for streaming sound, and results in small file sizes with good sound quality. Similarly to the image quality settings, this section of the report is useful in comparing sound quality and compression settings to file size.

```
Font Name       Bytes           Characters
- - - - - -     - - - - - -     - - - - - -
Helvetica           3478        %.0123456789acdefgilmnoprstuy
```

The final section of the report reveals the names of any embedded fonts, the size of the font file in bytes, and any characters that are embedded in the movie. Embedded characters include any text fields with the 'embed fonts' option turned on, as well as any symbols containing text. As with vector shapes, file size increases with the number of control points, so complex fonts, multiple fonts, or fonts with the full range of characters embedded (numbers, punctuation, upper/lowercase characters) will take up more room, since there are more control points and data present.

Demonstration of Animation and Sound Streaming

As we discussed at the very beginning of the chapter, Flash streams its media by default, playing the movie's frames as soon as they're made available through the network connection. The movie on the CD entitled `soundstream.fla` is intended to demonstrate this dynamic, and contains a simple example of streaming sound and vector animation in Flash. It should be previewed online, or using Flash Player's 'show streaming' mode in order to witness the mechanics of streaming. (How Flash handles streaming is a prerequisite for the topics that come later in this chapter, and this movie will help demonstrate that handling process.)

The `soundstream` movie comprises just three layers: actions, which contains all the ActionScript code in this example; sound/anime, which contains a lengthy sound clip and a short motion tween; and static graphic, which contains exactly what its name suggests. Here's what the timeline looks like in the Flash interface:

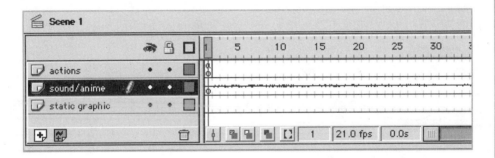

If you preview this movie in the show streaming mode of the Flash player, or over the Internet, the following streaming dynamic occurs: Flash waits on frame 1 until the sound buffer time is reached. (We'll have more to say about that in just a moment.) When this happens, the playhead jumps to frame 2, where it begins to play the streaming sound as the movie's frames are downloaded and made available. After the playhead reaches frame 650, the movie plays a streaming vector animation, eventually stopping at frame 690, where a `stop` action occurs.

> *Test this movie with the bandwidth profiler open, and at connection speeds of 56.6k, 28.8k, and 14.4k. It will become apparent at the 14.4k connection speed what happens to streaming media when the user's bandwidth cannot accept the data transfer quickly enough. It's also informative to watch the playback arrow and the green data transfer bar at various connection speeds in order to develop a mental model of the streaming concept as it relates to playback speed and data transfer.*

Movie Analysis

Frame one of our movie contains the following important line of ActionScript code:

```
_root._soundbuftime = 0;
```

This single line controls the **sound buffer time** for the root timeline (_root), a property that plays a critical role in how a streaming sound will operate. At the start of the streaming process, Flash will wait until it has received enough data to play the sound for the number of seconds specified in this line of code. By default, this property is set to five seconds, but in many cases that will be inappropriate. By setting this property to a higher or lower value, Flash's playback can be more effectively controlled for a specific 'target bandwidth' audience.

Try testing the soundstream.fla movie with _soundbuftime set to zero, and a 14.4k connection speed. You'll find that the playback head reaches the rate of data transfer rapidly, resulting in multiple pauses and stuttering sound for the majority of the playback period. This happens because the buffer time is set to zero, resulting in playback starting as soon as any data arrives. If, on the other hand, _soundbuftime were set to 17, the movie would wait until it had 17 seconds' worth of sound before commencing playback:

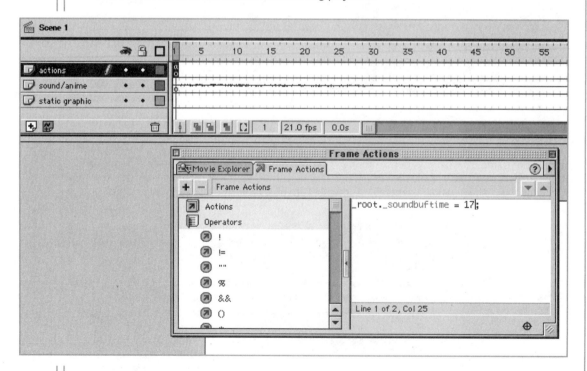

By forcing the playhead to wait until 17 seconds of sound has been received (approximately 53% of the movie), the offset between the data transfer and the playhead becomes large enough that the latter never catches the former, and no pauses occur. This single line of code therefore provides a convenient way to control Flash's playback and streaming capabilities by preloading a set amount of the movie, ensuring that the playhead and data transfer will remain offset and unconnected.

Of course, as you've probably realized, there are two sides to this story. When you tested this movie with a simulated 56k connection, a sound buffer time of zero was perfectly all right – in other words, the default sound buffer time of five seconds was too *high* for those circumstances. It makes no sense to make a user wait for five seconds to pre-buffer sound when a sound buffer time of zero works just as well.

The leveling factor here is that the Internet's physical network connections are often unstable, and can slow down or stop unexpectedly. This should always be taken into account when setting a sound buffer time, and it may be in your best interests to set the buffer time higher than is technically strictly necessary in order to account for network lulls, ensuring the stream will *always* work properly. Experimentation is the key with buffer time, and settings and content combinations should be tested under a variety of connection speeds (as well as on a real connection) to see which setting works best.

Streaming Vector Animations in Flash

Before we leave this section, we can make a few more points about the specifics of streaming animations and sounds, and draw some general conclusions. First, vector animation in Flash tends to work well, regardless of audience bandwidth – especially if the shapes are simple, and there are no overabundances of either shape tweens, or keyframes, or objects. Vector animations keep pace with any streamed sounds present, and if there's a halt in playback because of bandwidth issues, the vector animation will halt in conjunction with the sound.

Streaming Sound in Flash

Secondly, and as you may have noticed above, streaming a sound in Flash requires that its Sync should be set to Stream in the Sound panel:

Streamed sounds should *never* be looped, because the file size of the movie will increase by the frame span of the streamed sound, multiplied by the number of loops specified. When exporting movies, it's also useful to experiment with the bit rate and quality settings of the MP3 compression in order to lower file size without compromising the sound quality excessively.

With the groundwork done, we can move on to look at our first real example.

A Basic Preloading Technique

Here, we'll give the user something to look at while continuing to download content in the background. We'll also prevent the user from progressing in the movie until we're good and ready to let them – that is, when the appropriate content has downloaded.

This kind of basic preloading is the most fundamental technique for controlling Flash's data stream. It's accomplished by using Flash's `_framesloaded` property in a conditional statement that checks whether a specified frame is loaded, and it's precisely what you'll see if you take a look at the `basicpreload.fla` movie that's on the accompanying CD.

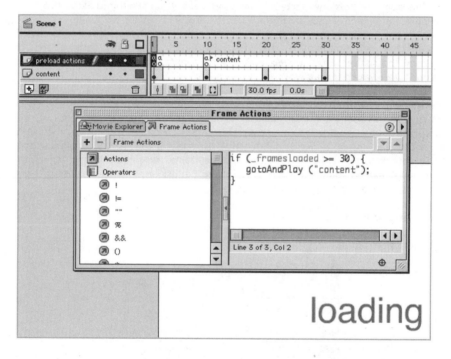

This movie has just two layers: one for content, and the other for ActionScript code. Our goal is that the four items in the content layer should be loaded before the user is allowed into our site, so that once they *are* in, they face no further delays. To that end, the first two frames in the code layer contain some very simple-looking commands.

Frame 1:

```
if (_framesloaded >= 30) {
    gotoAndPlay ("content");
}
```

Frame 2:

```
gotoAndPlay (1);
```

The code in frame 1 tells Flash to check whether frame 30 (our last content-carrying frame) is loaded, and to advance to frame 10 (which is labeled content) if this is the case. However, it's imperative to note that the code in frame 2 is also central to the effect we're trying to achieve. If the code in frame 2 were *not* included, and frame 30 were *not* loaded when the playhead reached frame 1, it would continue to frame 2, 3, 4, etc., until it reached the end of the movie (or encountered a frame with other ActionScript directions). By adding the code to frame 2, Flash is forced to loop back to frame 1 until the conditional statement becomes true.

> *There is a common misconception regarding the operation of ActionScript code with respect to the Flash playhead. The fact is that Flash plays all movies in linear order, from start to finish, unless explicitly instructed to behave otherwise. The playhead plays an integral part in supervising how ActionScript code is executed, sequenced and controlled.*
>
> *Flash differs from other programming languages in which conditional statements may loop or execute automatically. Flash needs to be instructed when to check variables or conditional statements by the inclusion of a frame that routes the playhead to the location where the checking code is located. This is especially applicable in situations where a variable or a conditional statement needs to be counted or checked multiple times.*

In this particular example, we've placed a movie clip spanning frames 1 and 2 that animates the word "loading", so the user is receiving feedback that movie content is still in fact being downloaded to their computer. Once the data is downloaded, the playhead advances to the frame entitled content at frame 10:

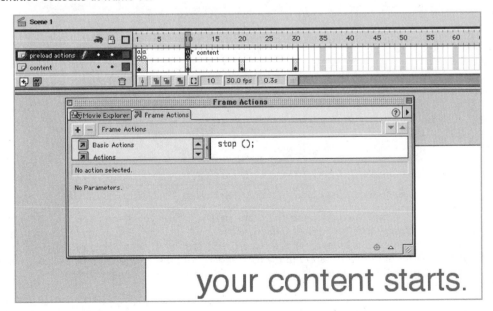

691

Frame 10 just contains a bitmap and a stop action here, but in general application this could be the beginning of your movie proper. Similarly, frames 20 and 30 contain bitmap images that represent any kind of content you might care to mention.

The simple technique demonstrated here is used in many web applications/scenarios, and should be considered as the basic ingredient for constructing the more complicated streaming and preloading techniques that we'll be discussing later in this chapter – starting with this next example.

An Approximate Preload Bar

The approximate preload bar is best suited to applications where it's important to give a user *some* feedback that Flash content is being downloaded to their computer, but where the absolute accuracy of that feedback isn't too important. The bar is generated by using Flash's built in _framesloaded and _totalframes properties; this is the most rudimentary form of preload bar to construct and code, and this example is intended as preparatory material on how to build more complex preload bars.

This screenshot shows the composition of approximate.fla, which of course you'll find on the CD:

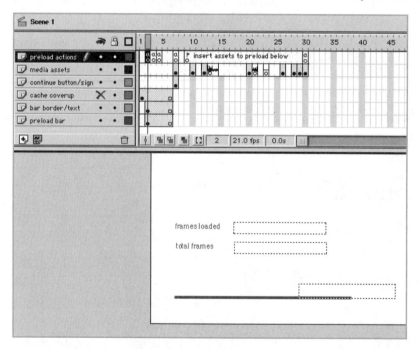

It *looks* rather complicated, because there are six layers, but you'll soon see that it shares a number of features with the simple initial preloader we just saw. For example, the top layer, preload actions, contains (almost) all the ActionScript code we'll need, while media assets has a couple of pieces of text we'll display to the user, and lots of other 'resources' that we'll be loading in the background. The continue button/sign layer is home to only a single button.

The bottom three layers form a set, of sorts. The bar border/text layer includes most of the things we'll be showing to the user as our content is downloading (see the boxes and labels in the screenshot), save for the preload bar itself, which resides in the layer with that name. The cache coverup layer, meanwhile, holds a movie clip named cover that contains a graphic of a white box that covers the entire stage. (In fact, the color of the clip is matched to the background color of the Flash movie.):

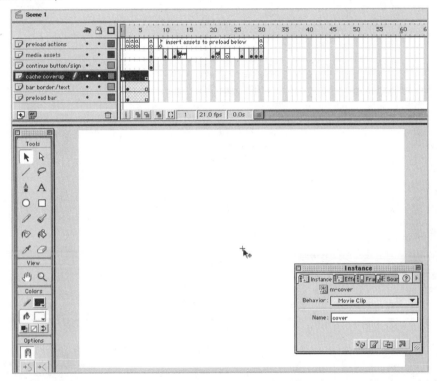

The purpose of this white box is to prevent users whose browsers have previously cached and stored the movie from viewing the preload bar (and associated graphics) again, should they return to our site or hit their Refresh button.

> Web browsers 'cache' data, meaning that a certain amount of recently accessed data is stored on the computer's hard disk. This makes web browsing quicker, because it allows you to 'return' to recently accessed sites without needing to download them again. In the case of Flash, browsers cache SWF files, so it's necessary to clear the cache if you've already visited the movie once and wish to see the operation of a preload bar again. Most browsers' caches can be cleared under their Preferences or Settings menus.

Precise details of how this trick works will be given a little later in this explanation.

Movie Analysis

The only thing to happen in frame 1 is that the `cover` movie clip is loaded, ready for use whenever necessary. The real action begins in frame 2, which features the following single line of ActionScript code:

```
wscale = loadbar._width / 100;
```

This sets the `wscale` variable to 1% of the width of the `loadbar` movie clip, in pixels. The purpose of this code is to establish a scaling factor that will be used in frame 3 to set the width of the bar, the aim being for the bar to reach its full width when the main movie is 100% loaded. In this case, the `loadbar` movie clip's width is 250 pixels, which makes `wscale` equal to 2.5. Setting this variable allows you to change `loadbar`'s full width to whatever you find visually appealing, without having to make further programming changes to ensure the code scales correctly. You must remember, however, to set the bar's *border* equal to the width of `loadbar` as well, so that the bar appears to fill up its border as content downloads. This can be done in the Info panel:

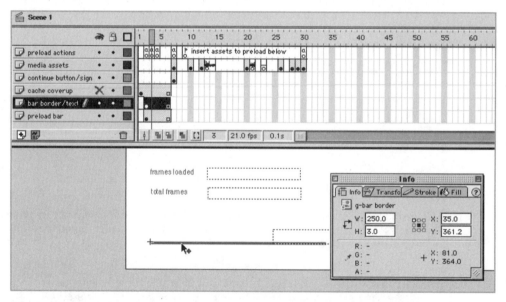

Frame 3 is labeled "calculation", and it contains the majority of the ActionScript code in this movie, dealing not only with the appearance of the preload bar, but also with what happens when the download is complete. Here it is in its entirety:

```
framesloaded = _framesloaded;
totalframes = _totalframes;

percentloaded = Math.floor (framesloaded / totalframes * 100);
pload = percentloaded + "% completed";
loadbar._width = percentloaded * wscale;
```

```
if (percentloaded == 100) {
   gotoAndPlay ("continue");
} else if (percentloaded < 100) {
   cover._visible = 0;
}
```

That's quite a lot all in one go; so let's take it in pieces, starting from the top:

```
framesloaded = _framesloaded;
totalframes = _totalframes;
```

The first job of these two lines is to set the values in the framesloaded and totalframes text boxes that appear in the bar border/text layer. We've seen _framesloaded in use before, while _totalframes returns the total number of frames in the current movie or movie clip. However, these variables are also used in our 'percentage loaded' calculation:

```
percentloaded = Math.floor (framesloaded / totalframes * 100);
```

This is the driving math routine of the preload bar. The expression inside the parentheses yields the exact proportion of frames loaded so far as a percentage value, and the Math.floor function rounds this precise value down to the nearest whole number (so 33.33 would become 33, 0.5 would become 0, and 9.99 would become 9). The percentloaded variable is then set to this whole-number value.

Now for the next line:

```
pload = percentloaded + "% completed";
```

In this line, pload is the third text box on our stage – it appears just above the preload bar. All we're doing here, then, is creating a string that supplies some numerical information to the waiting user, in addition to the visual feedback that's provided by the bar itself:

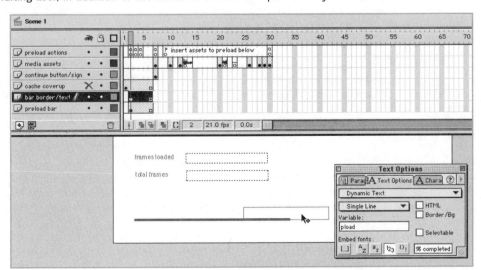

This is not an essential element of the user interface, but it's a nice touch, and the kind of thing that will help keep users on your side (and on your site).

Next up...

```
loadbar._width = percentloaded * wscale;
```

This line sets the width of `loadbar` in pixels to the percentage we calculated above, multiplied by our `wscale` variable. The important thing to be aware of here is that for this to work correctly, our preload bar graphic must be located on the *right* side of the origin mark in the m-loadbar movie clip. This will ensure that the preload bar grows from left to right:

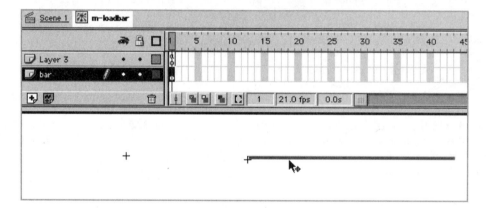

The last part of the code in this frame is a conditional statement that's used to determine what happens next:

```
if (percentloaded == 100) {
    gotoAndPlay ("continue");
} else if (percentloaded < 100) {
    cover._visible = 0;
}
```

If our `percentloaded` variable equals 100 (that is, the movie is fully loaded), Flash is directed to `gotoAndPlay` the frame labeled `continue` (actually, frame 7). This frame contains a continue button that advances the user to the content that begins in frame 30. If, however, the `percentloaded` variable is *less* than 100, then the visibility of the movie clip called `cover` is set to zero, revealing the elements on the layers beneath it.

By default, the `cover` movie clip's visibility is set to one, which means that everything behind it is hidden unless the ActionScript code instructs otherwise. In cases where the movie is fully loaded or cached, or the user has hit the Refresh button in the browser, Flash will skip directly to the `continue` frame, and the user will not see the preload bar or its associated graphics.

Thereafter, the example gets rather simpler. If frames 7 to 30 have not yet been loaded, we have the same situation we had in our previous example, and the ActionScript code in frame 4 must send the playhead back to frame 3:

```
gotoAndPlay ("calculation");
```

Looping will continue in this manner until such time as our conditional statement sends Flash to frame 7 (continue), which contains a bitmap, a button, and a stop command:

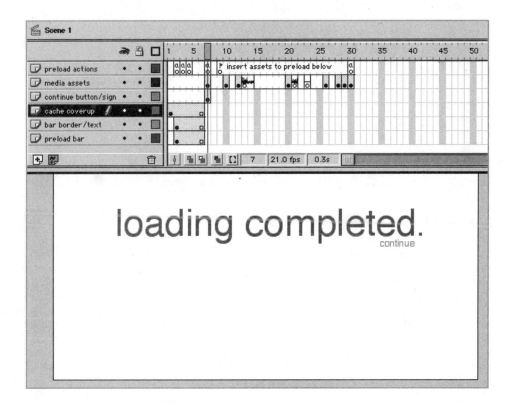

Finally, in the continue button, you'll find the following code that takes the user to the beginning of the content proper – in this case, no more than another bitmap-and-stop-action combination:

```
on (release) {
    gotoAndPlay ("content");
}
```

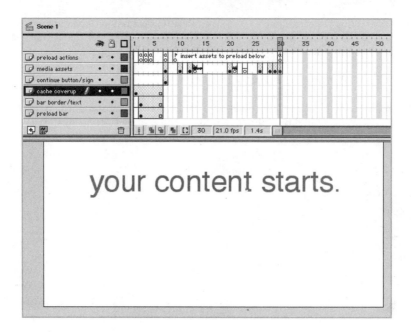

Closing Thoughts

This bar calculates its 'percentage loaded' value based on the number of frames loaded, and the total number of frames in the movie. However, while this gives an accurate account of the proportion of total *frames* downloaded, it says nothing about how much of the SWF file has actually been transmitted. For example, imagine that frames 1 to 99 contain no actual content at all, and frame 100 contains a 100 KB image. In this case, the first 99% of our bar will fill up immediately, showing that 99% of the movie has downloaded, but then pause on frame 100 while the image loads (which may take a while). The user will wonder why there is a pause, when the first 99% filled up so quickly. To remedy this situation when employing a solution like this one, try to distribute your media assets as evenly as possible across a frame span, so that the number of frames loaded will correlate more closely to the amount of data so far transmitted.

To advance in this respect, we need to find a way of providing more accurate information to the user on how much of the SWF file has *really* downloaded to their computer, and how much is left to load.

A More Accurate Preload Bar

Thankfully, Flash 5 does make this kind of more accurate data available, via the ActionScript functions MovieClip.getBytesLoaded and MovieClip.getBytesTotal. However, these functions only work on movie clips into which *external* SWF files are being loaded, a fact that will necessitate some changes to the architecture of our solution.

In this example, the substantive content of our Flash site is in a movie called `main.swf`. This is available on the CD in FLA and SWF versions, and if you examine it you'll find that, like the other examples of content we've used in this chapter, it's not much more than a placeholder. The `main.swf` movie has one frame, which features a large bitmap and a `stop` action. The preloading mechanism resides in a *second* movie, defined in `accurate.fla`, and it's into a movie clip in this movie that the content will eventually be loaded.

Because of this two-stage loading mechanism, the bandwidth profiler can no longer be used for realistic testing – the preload bar simply will not appear. When the time comes you'll need to place the three files `accurate.html`, `accurate.swf`, and `main.swf` on a web server, and view them through a real web browser. To see the preload bar in operation more than once, it'll be necessary to clear your Internet browser's cache. (If you take a look at this book's chapter on Flash and PHP, you'll find coverage of setting up the Apache web server on your machine.)

With the real content now located elsewhere, `accurate.fla` is actually a simpler proposition than the movie in the previous example. As you can see from this screenshot, it has only four layers:

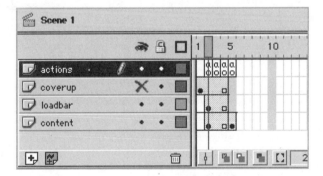

Better yet, you should be starting to get familiar with the structure of these solutions, in terms of what gets put on each layer. The coverup and loadbar layers, for example, are almost identical in construction and behavior to their equivalents in the 'approximate preload bar' movie, while actions contains the ActionScript code that we'll focus on shortly. The content layer has (in frame 2) the target movie clip (called loadtarget) that will eventually hold our content, and (in frame 5) some text for the user to read.

Movie Analysis

Once again, we can take the code in the actions layer as our cue, and run through what we have here frame-by-frame.

As before, things only start to happen in frame 2:

```
loadMovie ("main.swf", loadtarget);
wscale = loadbar._width / 100;
totalbytes = -1;
```

The first line of this code loads an external Flash movie entitled `main.swf` into our blank target movie clip, `loadtarget`. It's significant that the latter is located at the upper left corner of the Flash movie stage (x = 0.0, y = 0.0), ensuring that any graphic placements within `main.swf` will correlate with the stage coordinates in our preload movie (`accurate.swf`):

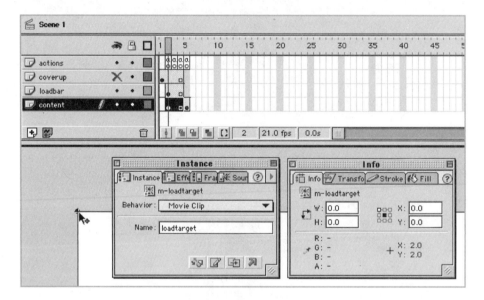

The second line of the code snippet shown previously sets up the `wscale` variable as a scaling factor for our loadbar movie clip, exactly as it did before, but after that we have another new line of code in this frame:

```
totalbytes = -1;
```

This sets a variable named `totalbytes` to -1, a nonsense value whose purpose will become clear when we start to analyze the code in frame 3, which is labeled `calculation`:

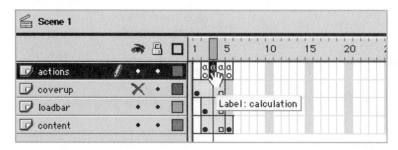

Here's the code:

```
if (loadtarget.getBytesTotal() == totalbytes) {

    percentloaded = Math.floor(loadtarget.getBytesLoaded()
        ➥totalbytes * 100);
    pload = percentloaded + "% completed";
    loadbar._width = percentloaded * wscale;

    if (percentloaded == 100) {
        gotoAndPlay ("content");
    } else if (percentloaded < 100) {
        cover._visible = 0;
    }
}

totalbytes = loadtarget.getBytesTotal();
```

In fact, you may have noticed – if you're watching carefully – that this code is exactly the same as we had in the last example, except for the three lines that feature our mysterious new totalbytes variable. The easiest of these to explain is the one where percentloaded is set to the result of our call to the Math.floor function: we're simply using bytes rather than frames for the calculation, as we said we would at the beginning. It's the brand new lines that are more interesting, and for ease we'll highlight them in isolation from the rest of the code, like this:

```
if (loadtarget.getBytesTotal() == totalbytes) {

    // ...The rest of the code

}

totalbytes = loadtarget.getBytesTotal();
```

The trouble is that when you're loading external files in Flash 5, and using the movieclip.getBytesLoaded and movieclip.getBytesTotal functions, there's a rather unfortunate 'up to dateness' issue – or 'latency problem'. Sometimes, and particularly as a movie is just beginning to load, these functions can return garbage values due to the time that it takes Flash to process the getBytesTotal command. Needless to say, this can be very nasty, because the garbage can interfere with the correct operation and expected performance of our application. What we really need to do is ensure that we're feeding the correct evaluation of getBytesTotal into our script.

The extra conditional statement in this code is designed to guard against this problem. When the playback head reaches this frame for the first time, it checks whether the number reported by the loadtarget.getBytesTotal function is the same as totalbytes. Of course, we set totalbytes to -1 in frame 2, so this condition is certain to be false the first time Flash executes the statement. *Because* the condition is false, Flash executes any commands *outside* the braces, thus setting the totalbytes variable to the value that's *now* returned by the loadtarget.getBytesTotal function.

As has been our habit in these examples, the ActionScript code in frame 4 loops straight back to this frame, where the check is performed again. This process continues until the statement is true, at which point the latency problem is resolved: `totalbytes` no longer reflects an inaccurate or changing value. Any statements inside the braces can then execute, and the main routine of our program becomes operational.

Once the `percentloaded` variable *is* equal to 100, and the movie is fully loaded, the playback head advances to the frame labeled `content` (frame 5), where your core content would start. In this movie, the preloaded content is never actually seen, since the `loadtarget` movie clip is not present in frame 5. Instead, your signal that everything has gone to plan is a screen that looks like this (remember, you'll need to view this through a web browser to get the full effect):

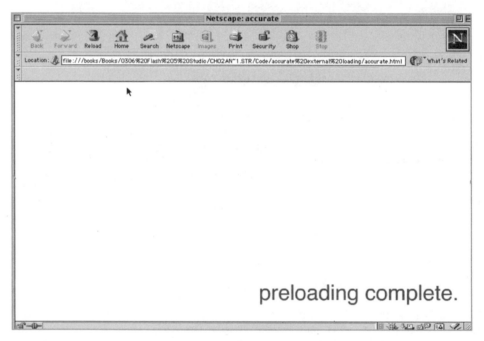

Closing Thoughts

The introduction of the `movieclip.getBytesLoaded` and `movieclip.getBytesTotal` functions in Flash 5 provides an indispensable tool for creating accurate loading bars that provide excellent user feedback on the *real* status of data transmission.

The only drawbacks in using these functions are the latency issue we've just mentioned and the fact that they only work when you're loading external Flash files. This is unfortunate, and somewhat inconvenient, but inevitably leads you to design systems and interfaces that behave in a modular manner by retrieving files and data on an 'as needed' basis. To some extent, this example movie is itself a modular system, since an external movie (`main.swf`) is being loaded into a host movie (`accurate.swf`).

A web site built in Flash is a good example of a modular system. The site's shell and menu features exist as a single Flash movie, while content areas and articles exist as separate Flash SWF files that are retrieved on demand. When a user triggers menu items on the site, external files load into blank movie clips or levels contained in the main Flash movie. With this type of system, files can not only be easily organized and separated, but the `movieclip.getBytesLoaded` and `movieclip.getBytesTotal` functions can be used with ease. Modular systems work extremely well in Flash, and we'll explore an expanded example of one such system in the next section.

A Modular Flash Site

In this final sample, we're going to explore a powerful, hybrid technique that combines an accurate preload bar with preloading and streaming functionality. An example of a situation in which this might be useful would be a web site where it's critical to *preload* only primary interface elements (to lessen load time), but to add or stream secondary assets like sound or animation once a user has gained access to the interface. The example movie for this technique (`hybrid.fla`) builds from our accurate preload bar example by *preloading* an external movie (`cloudcity.swf`) from frames 1 to 12, but *streaming* the remaining frames (13 to 411).

Movie Analysis

Although the techniques we're using are becoming ever more sophisticated functionally, our movies look as though they're actually getting simpler! With `hybrid.fla`, we're back down to just three layers, and a stage that looks like this:

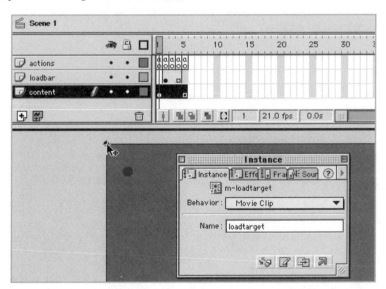

The actions and loadbar layers fulfill the same roles as in our other examples, and we'll again be looking through the ActionScript code shortly. You'll notice that we *don't* have a 'cover' layer this time round; that's because we've used an alternative method for hiding the preload bar when we don't want it to be visible, as you'll see.

The content layer contains a target movie clip for our `cloudcity.swf` movie, and a button that we'll use to set everything in motion. This time, the user will be in complete control of the moment when the movie begins.

Now that we have the button to control affairs, the ActionScript code in the first frame of `hybrid.fla` consists of nothing more than a `stop` command, halting the playhead at frame 1. The interesting code here, then, is attached to the button:

```
on (press) {
    loadMovie ("cloudcity.swf", loadtarget);
    gotoAndPlay (2);
}
```

When the button is pressed, Flash begins the process of loading `cloudcity.swf` into the `loadtarget` movie clip, which is again located at the top left corner of the stage. It also restarts the playhead by sending it to frame 2, where this happens:

```
wscale = loadbar._width / 100;
totalbytes = -1;
```

This is *exactly* what we had in the last example, so we don't need to dwell on it again here – especially when there are so many new and interesting things to discover in frame 3, which is again labeled `calculation`:

```
if (loadtarget.getBytesTotal() == totalbytes) {
    percentloaded = Math.floor(loadtarget.getBytesLoaded() /
preloadchunksize * 100);

    if (percentloaded >= 100) {
        _root.pbox.pload = "100% completed";
        loadbar._width = 100 * wscale;
        gotoAndPlay ("content");
    } else if (percentloaded < 100) {
        loadbar._alpha = 100;
        barborder._alpha = 100;
        pbox._alpha = 100;
        _root.pbox.pload = percentloaded + "% completed";
        loadbar._width = percentloaded * wscale;
    }
}

preloadchunksize = 17688;
totalbytes = loadtarget.getBytesTotal();
```

This is the main programming routine for our preload bar, and as you were probably expecting, it has a number of similarities with the `accurate.fla` example movie – its structure at least is likely to be familiar to you. But there are some differences too, and our investigations of these should begin with the `preloadchunksize` variable that appears in the first line of code inside the `if` statement:

```
if (loadtarget.getBytesTotal() == totalbytes) {
    percentloaded = Math.floor(loadtarget.getBytesLoaded() /
    ➡preloadchunksize * 100);
```

This variable represents the number of bytes of the `cloudcity.swf` movie that we wish to preload before streaming the remainder of its content. (Remember, we only want to *preload* frames 1 to 12, while *streaming* the remainder.) This new variable is used in place of the `movieclip.getBytesTotal` function, which returns the total file size of the movie, and isn't what we want here. The decision to preload this section of the movie was taken because it contains a large bitmap graphic and animation that most 56k modem users would not have the bandwidth to stream. For the sound that the movie also contains, we can take advantage of Flash's streaming technology, since the user's bandwidth *will* be able to manage the data flow needed for this purpose.

The `preloadchunksize` value was obtained by generating a size report and obtaining the file size for the desired frame span, in this case frames 1 to 12:

```
                          cloudcity.swf Report
Movie Report
-----------

Frame #   Frame Bytes   Total Bytes   Page
-------   -----------   -----------   ------
   1          46            46        Scene 1
   2        17522         17568          2
   3          12          17580          3
   4          12          17592          4
   5          12          17604          5
   6          12          17616          6
   7          12          17628          7
   8          12          17640          8
   9          12          17652          9
  10          12          17664         10
  11          12          17676         11
  12          12          17688         12
  13        3743          21431         13
  14          12          21443         14
  15         220          21663         15
  16          12          21675         16
  17         220          21895         17
  18          12          21907         18
  19         220          22127         19
  20          12          22139         20
  21         116          22255         21
  22          12          22267         22
```

Looking at the Total Bytes value for frame 12, it's quite clear that the cumulative size of frames 1 to 12 in the `cloudcity.swf` movie is 17688 bytes, and this is the value we give to `preloadchunksize`. The calculation that determines the value of `percentloaded` then uses it to establish what proportion of *the part of the movie we want to preload* has been downloaded so far.

The preload bar will reach 100% capacity when the number of bytes loaded is equal to the preload chunk size we've set. Note that 17688 bytes is only about one fourth of the total file size of the `cloudcity.swf` movie, since the cumulative sum of frames 1 to 411 is 64071 bytes:

```
                          cloudcity.swf Report
  406          12          63379         406
  407         220          63599         407
  408          12          63611         408
  409         220          63831         409
  410          12          63843         410
  411         228          64071         411

Page                  Shape Bytes   Text Bytes
-------------------   -----------   ----------
Scene 1                    0           247

Embedded Objects          61            0

Symbol                Shape Bytes   Text Bytes
-------------------   -----------   ----------
g-cloudcity                0            0

Bitmap                Compressed   Original   Compression
-------------------   ----------   --------   -----------
Bitmap 5                 17447      1500000   JPEG Quality=65

Stream sound: 11KHz Mono 16 kbps MP3
Font Name             Bytes     Characters
-------------------   -----     ----------
Helvetica             2984      ,.0123456789:abcdefghiklmnoprstuw
```

The remaining three fourths of the movie will therefore be streamed, and this represents a decent load balance. Load balancing depends largely on the target audience's bandwidth, and experimentation is critical in order to find results that seem right for your design and user base.

> *Note that the* `preloadchunksize` *variable is not (and could not be) derived through Flash's built in functions, and must be updated each and every time the movie is modified – the number will almost certainly change if new scripting or graphic elements are added. If the* `preloadchunksize` *variable is inaccurate, the preload bar will not reflect accurate values, and the movie may inadvertently end up preloading the wrong amount of content.*

Taking the anti-latency code as read, the next thing need to focus our attention on is the conditional statement that changes the appearance of the preload bar. It's a while since we saw that code on the page, so here it is again:

```
if (percentloaded >= 100) {
    _root.pbox.pload = "100% completed";
    loadbar._width = 100 * wscale;
    gotoAndPlay ("content");
} else if (percentloaded < 100) {
    loadbar._alpha = 100;
    barborder._alpha = 100;
    pbox._alpha = 100;
    _root.pbox.pload = percentloaded + "% completed";
    loadbar._width = percentloaded * wscale;
}
```

If all of the preloading is done, we need to be a little careful – you might have noticed that we now test whether `percentloaded` is equal to *or greater than* 100. When we were preloading whole movies, this wasn't an issue – we could never go over 100%. However, now that we've simply chosen a number of bytes to preload, it's possible that we'll already have gone slightly above our target when we perform the test. This change to the code logic handles that eventuality.

By the same reasoning, if we *have* reached our preload target, we make sure that `pload` and `loadbar` are set with values that reflect 100%, rather than 'just-over-100%'. With that done, we can `gotoAndPlay` frame 5, as usual.

If preloading is not yet complete, we reach the second part of the conditional statement, which begins by setting the alphas of `loadbar`, `barborder`, and `pbox` to 100. By default, these items are hidden by having their alphas set to zero, to prevent users whose browsers have previously cached the movie from viewing the preload bar and associated graphics:

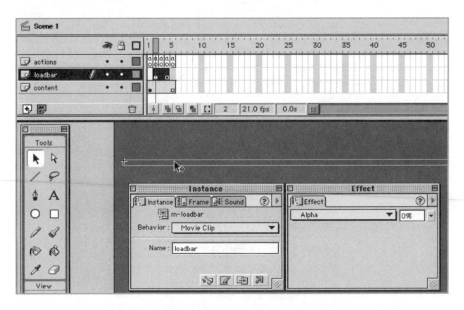

In earlier examples, we used a covering layer to achieve this effect; this is simply a different means to the same end. The code then ends by setting pload and loadbar.

To conclude the code in this movie, frame 4 contains the inevitable loop back to frame 3, while frame 5, which is labeled content, has this:

```
with (loadtarget) {
    gotoAndPlay (2);
}

stop ();
```

The with statement tells the loadtarget movie clip to gotoAndPlay frame 2, which is where the animation starts in the cloudcity.swf movie. The rest of our code has made sure that the external movie will begin playback only after frames 1 to 12 have been preloaded and the preload bar and associated graphics have disappeared.

Construction: cloudcity.swf

To complete our analysis of this example, we should take a quick look at the movie we've gone to such efforts to load efficiently. Here's that movie's timeline:

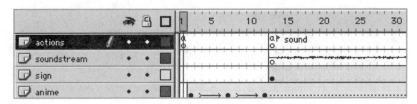

The movie is delimited by `stop` command bookends – one in frame 1, and the other in frame 411. The former prevents the movie from starting at all until the `hybrid.swf` movie instructs it to do so, while the latter brings things to an orderly conclusion. That just leaves the code in frame 13, which sets the sound buffer time for this movie, just as we did in this chapter's first example (see the section entitled *Demonstration of Animation and Sound Streaming*):

```
soundbuff = 2;
_root._soundbuftime = soundbuff;
```

From here, it's fairly plain sailing – certainly compared with some of the other things we've been looking at! The soundstream layer contains, from frames 13 to 411, a streaming sound file called an `intro.aiff`, with Sync set to Stream:

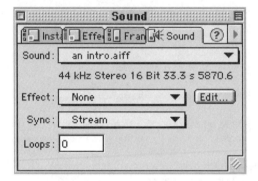

In the same frame range, the sign layer has a line of text that reads, "Graphics are now loaded, but a sound is streaming in the background..." It also includes a dynamic text box that displays the `soundbuff` variable that was set in the ActionScript code above.

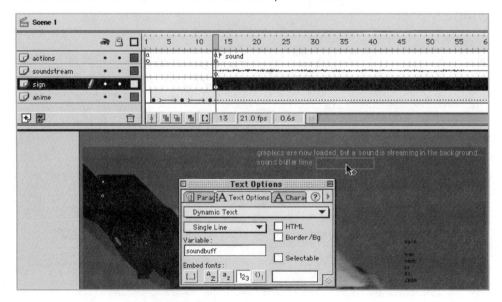

Last of all, the anime layer contains an animation of a bitmap graphic that plays from frames 2 to 12, and remains static for the remainder of the movie. This is the segment that's initially preloaded by the `hybrid.swf` movie.

When the button in the `hybrid.swf` movie loads this movie, the first 12 frames are preloaded. After these frames have been preloaded, the playhead starts to play the animation of the bitmap graphic until it reaches frame 13, where our sound begins to stream and play, eventually terminating at frame 411 where a `stop` frame action occurs.

Closing Thoughts

This technique can be altered to suit a wide spectrum of applications – the limits are your imagination, what you are trying to accomplish, and how the user might potentially navigate through your application. Balancing preloading and streaming is a highly effective method that can bridge high and low bandwidth audience gaps, while simultaneously providing user feedback. The only drawbacks to the method outlined in this section are the fact that external Flash files must (again) be loaded in order to implement an accurate preload bar, and the `preloadchunksize` variable must always reflect an accurate value. However, these are inexpensive prices to pay for optimizing the user experience.

Conclusion

Preloading and streaming offer a palette of solutions that cater for the potentially wide variations in user bandwidth. However, these solutions should always be considered secondary to the creation of small, clever, efficient Flash movies. The current web audience is not yet ready to handle the high bandwidth that many web developers seem to believe already exists – like me, you've probably been to sites that flash up 'loading 780k' and thought "I don't think so..."

Regardless of Flash's stunning media-handling capabilities, 50k is still the ideal threshold to gauge whether a web application is going to be accessible to the bulk of the mass-market audience. Flash media assets should always be utilized in a sparing and intelligent manner if user accessibility and usability is of primary concern.

The techniques that we've analyzed and discussed here should give you some pointers on how to apply generic download and streaming considerations to your own specific Flash movies, meaning that you can balance your desires as a designer with the bandwidth capabilities of the people that you want to stick to your site.

22
Preloading
and
Streaming

Section 5
Contexts

21
Combining
HTML and
Flash

Chapter 23
Optimizing Flash
for Search
Engines

When you've completed your Flash masterwork and published it on the Internet, you'll soon come to realize that this is by no means the end of your task. After countless hours of building a web site, testing it, and finally going live, there's still another step in the process of site creation: marketing! Simply putting a web site on the Internet is not going to get users to look at your site. Web marketing is a fast-growing area that requires significant skill and expertise, as well as a strong understanding of your products, services, and goals.

One of the fastest and least expensive ways to get users to your site is through **search engines**. This chapter is designed to give you an understanding of how to optimize a web site – and in particular, a Flash web site – for search engines, and to introduce the concepts and approaches necessary to get your site a prominent listing.

Types of Search Services

There are hundreds of search services on the Internet today, with more being created all the time. Just trying to keep track of them all is a full-time job, and that's certainly not our goal here. Fortunately for us, *most* user traffic is directed through the top ten engines, so simply targeting these will offer you the best results for the smallest outlay, and should significantly increase your site traffic.

From a functional perspective, search services can be broken down into two main types:

- **Directories.** These are filtered sites where a human being (yes, a real one) reviews each submitted page to determine whether it's appropriate for listing. Typically, directories are set up in categories, and subcategories allow users to drill down further into the structure. Popular directory services include Yahoo, the Open Directory Project (or www.dmoz.org), and LookSmart.

- **Search Engines.** These tend to use an automated process in which the database of web sites and pages is updated programmatically. Typically, search engines are powered by a **spider** (or **crawler**, or **robot**) that follows links on the Internet and records data about new pages. Popular search engines include AltaVista, Google, and Excite.

Predictably, there are also some search services that use a combination of technologies to produce results, making this kind of categorization rather difficult. Furthermore, a number of search services actually use the facilities of *other* search services to do their work. AltaVista, for example, has a directory-type search service that uses a structure provided by LookSmart's system. Later in this chapter, I'll be explaining more about the various search services out there, and how they relate to one another. If you want more information on search engines and their relationships, www.searchenginewatch.com and www.searchengineworld.com are great resources for obtaining detailed data.

Web Spiders

Spiders, crawlers, robots – call them what you will, these are automatic programs that roam the Internet looking for content to add to the search engine's databases. Each spider's criteria for identifying a page that should be indexed is different, and can change over time depending on the goal of the search service in question. What a spider sees is based on the information provided by the site being reviewed, and can be affected significantly if the site administrator plans and considers what a spider is looking for. Although there's no guarantee that a page will be viewed or indexed by a particular spider, designing pages to be spider-friendly greatly increases the chance that a page will be recognized and therefore become locatable using searches. If you feel the need to go find more information about the world of web spiders, try http://info.webcrawler.com/mak/projects/robots/robots.html.

Planning a Site that's Search Engine-friendly

How you structure your web site will affect the way you need to approach search engine optimization. A web site that uses small pieces of Flash content, but is predominantly HTML-based, offers a fair degree of flexibility in this regard. Web sites in which Flash is the only content, on the other hand, require rather more creativity. Let's start by examining some of the basic issues involved.

> *Currently, there are no web search engines that are capable of reading Flash movie content directly, although this may change in the not-too-distant future. Atomz (*www.atomz.com*) has a product that allows visitors to your site to search the text contained in Flash movies, and extensions of this functionality to the Web at large must be considered likely.*

Search engines index pages based on the text that comprises an HTML document. Anything that's not text within the HTML document is *invisible* to a search engine spider – a PNG image file that contains your company's logo, name, and address, for example, will be recognized by a spider as nothing more than a file with a name. For search engine optimization, web sites can usefully be broken down into the following categories:

- **HTML-based sites** contain some images and other types of content, but primarily they're just HTML documents. These sites may have small Flash animations, or a Flash menu, but the main content is in HTML.

- **Multimedia sites**, of which Flash is one type, are those where the content is primarily within an executable program or some other package that requires a plug-in for interpretation.

Often, particularly when HTML *frames* begin to enter the fray, a web site will turn out to be a 'hybrid' of these types, featuring many different kinds of content. When optimizing a site for search engines (or preferably, before the site is even created), it's necessary to consider the *layout* of the site as well as its substance.

Doorway Pages

Doorway pages are specifically designed to attract search engine spiders, and to relay information on the site to them. The idea is that they carry as much information about your site as possible, in as concise a manner as you can get away with – that's what spiders like. On arriving at your doorway page as a result of a search engine link, users should be able to move easily to other areas of interest.

Done poorly, doorway pages can look confusing to users, but a good site designer will create them in such a way that they're helpful to human and machine alike. As we look at different types of sites and content, we'll discuss the value of using doorway pages with each.

There are many tools on the market today that help with the creation of doorway pages. First Place Software's Web Position Gold, for example, includes a tool called Page Generator that serves precisely this purpose. You can visit the web site at www.firstplacesoftware.com for more information. For an extended tutorial on doorway pages, try: http://spider-food.net/doorway-pages.html.

Dealing with Standard HTML Sites

Standard HTML sites are the easiest to optimize for search engines, which base their ranking on the page content they can recognize. Later in this chapter we'll examine some tricks that can be used to improve your rankings regardless of the composition of your pages; these are useful with 'standard' content, and are almost *required* for other types of content.

> *If you're interested in seeing how a spider sees a web page, take a look at the Search Engine Spider Simulator located at* www.searchengineworld.com/cgi-bin/sim_spider.cgi.

Sites with Frames

Sites that use frames are more difficult to optimize for search engines. The problem is that spiders aren't capable of viewing the frame structure, so they'll either index your pages incompletely, or simply ignore them. When dealing with a framed site, doorway pages and a 'shadow' site that doesn't make use of frames are essential to achieving full success with spiders.

The problem with frames lies in the fact that by following a link in a search engine, a user may come into your site through a page that's intended to be just one component in a set of frames. At best, the reader will see an incomplete rendering of your site; at worst, they'll get an error. Spiders have no way of knowing that the 'pages' on your site are supposed to be viewed together, and they make no provision for it.

The easiest way to deal with this is actually to exclude the framed pages of your site from being indexed by spiders (we'll discuss how to do this in *Excluding Pages from Search Engines*, later on), and to create separate doorways for each page of content that uses the frame structure. There are also some JavaScript coding techniques that can help you to deal with some frame-related issues.

> *If you'd like some more information on how to work with frames and some of the issues concerning them, take a look at* http://searchenginewatch.internet.com/webmasters/frames.html.

Flash/Multimedia Sites

Sites that use a SWF file as their only content require significant attention if they're to be indexed by search engines. A single file that contains *all* of the content for a site may appear efficient to publish and manage, but from a search engine's perspective, there's not much to see. Remember: **spiders can't read the data in a Flash SWF file**. To compensate for this, there are two approaches you could consider:

- Although it may make the publishing process more complex, *breaking up some of the content into subsections* offers significant advantages to both the end user and search engine spiders. This method allows a user to be able to enter the site and download (and bookmark) only the sections that are relevant to them, without having to go through other levels of the site. In addition, employing separate sections allows us to utilize doorway pages in conjunction with each section, rather than having just a single page for the whole site.

- If the site *can't* be broken into sections, or you feel that it would hinder the development process, then the next best solution is simply to create doorway pages that point towards your main page, and to optimize your main page as efficiently as possible.

Selecting Keywords and Targeting Traffic

Before you can even begin to optimize a site for search engines, you need to determine exactly what kind of audience and attention you're trying to attract, and the first step in this process is to select your **keywords**. In search engines' terms, keywords are any words or phrases a user might enter into a search engine to find information on that topic. Choosing the right keywords for your site is vital, because picking poor ones won't help you to get traffic.

There are three areas that you should focus on as you select keywords:

- Understanding your products, services, and content

- Understanding your target market

- Understanding your competition

Understanding your products and services is a very important step in the keyword selection process, and you need to be careful that your experience of the industry doesn't prejudice this task. Often, site administrators will be exposed daily to the jargon of an industry, and they'll forget that the typical user may not be as familiar with it. This can work to your advantage if you're only looking for industry-savvy users, but otherwise the use of industry- (or even company-) specific keywords can result in a lot of work for little gain. You need to think like your *user* here.

If possible, gather a group of typical users together and brainstorm on what words *they* would look for if they wanted to find your web site through a search engine. You may even want to consider conducting a poll of users from the different demographics your site generally attracts. It's common to find wide variations in how different users approach looking for the same information. If the budget is available, conducting a customer survey to assist in the keyword selection process is a worthwhile use of resources.

Another way to find keywords that could bring more traffic to your site is to go and look at your competition. I'm not suggesting that you go to a competitor's page and take their information, but you'll often find that they have taken a different approach to targeting the same demographic as you. Keep in mind that your competition will also be looking at you, and often using the same keywords that you've chosen. It's dog eat dog out there...

Site administrators will try many different techniques to divert traffic to their sites from search engines, but as you'll soon see, applying them can be a time-consuming business, and you don't want to design pages to catch searches for words that no one searches for. On the other hand, if only four people a month search for a particular phrase, but they all result in a purchase from your site, you might judge that your work was well worth it. Estimating how many searches there might be on a keyword can help you determine the amount of time and effort that should be spent on it. Although there are no great resources for determining how many searches for a particular keyword are currently being conducted, there are some that can be used as the basis for an informed opinion.

GoTo, a pay-for-results search engine, offers an inventory list that allows site administrators to determine how often particular keywords are searched for. Although it only tracks users of www.goto.com, this information can be used to estimate how many searches would come from the same keywords on larger search engines. The GoTo Suggestion Tool (at http://inventory.go2.com/inventory/Search_Suggestion.jhtml) will also recommend keywords and phrases that may help you with your keyword selection process. I recommend that you enter all of your keywords into the Suggestion Tool, and use the information it returns to determine what keywords you want to target first (and perhaps find other keywords that will help target your demographic).

> *There are also tools and sites like Metaspy (www.metaspy.com) and Excite Voyeur (www.excite.com/search/voyeur) that allow you to view what users are searching on in real time. These sites may not be very helpful for determining how much traffic to expect for a keyword, but they may give you some ideas on how users think – scary as that can sometimes be!*

Other Considerations in the Keyword Selection Process

After brainstorming and determining what keywords are right for a web site, there are still more steps that can help to increase traffic. For example, you should consider trying to catch common misspellings of keywords – this is actually quite a common trick, and you can even see it in some URLs. Many companies purchase common typos or misspellings of the names of their web sites, in the hope of pulling in extra traffic.

If your products and services are limited by physical location, consider including that as a keyword too. For example, if a company provides automobile servicing in Phoenix, Arizona, then users from that area are the only ones it's interested in. Remember, the goal is to get the right users to the right information. There's no point in trying to sell ice to an Inuit.

Once you've Selected your Keywords

Once you've selected your keywords, the next step is to make sure that your pages are optimized for spiders to pick them up and determine that they should indeed be listed under the keywords that you've targeted. This process can be a time-consuming one, so before we get into the details of how to add and optimize the keywords on your pages, let's look at some of the measurements we can use to help determine whether the job has been done properly.

Some of the things that can help us to gauge our success in preparing pages for search engine inclusion are:

- Keyword placement

- Keyword prominence

- Keyword frequency

- Total words

- Keyword weight

As we'll discuss soon, different search engines rank pages according to different criteria. However, obtaining a high grade for each of these measurements will help obtain a better listing in most of them, and therefore increase the likelihood of your target market finding you.

- **Keyword placement** is simply *where* in an HTML page your keyword is situated. The closer to the top of the document your words are, the better. Typically, search engines will give a higher rating to pages that have the keyword in the title and/or the first line of text on the page.

- **Keyword prominence** is how close to the start of a *section* a keyword is placed, where a section is a part of your HTML document that's enclosed by tags such as <TITLE>, <H1>, or <BODY>. To obtain high prominence, you'll want your keyword to be at the beginning of as many sections as possible. (This can be difficult for 100% Flash sites, since they won't have any HTML-formatted text.) As an example, if we were targeting "Car Parts" as our keyword, example A below would have greater prominence than example B, since the keyword appears closer to the beginning:

  Example A: <TITLE>European Car Parts and Accessories</TITLE>

Example B: `<TITLE>Accessories for European Cars and Car Parts</TITLE>`

- **Keyword frequency** measures how often a keyword appears in an HTML document or section, but there's a fine line to be trodden here – it's all about keeping a balance. To obtain a good 'frequency' score, you shouldn't *overuse* your keywords, but just keep them coming naturally in sentences. Obtaining a high keyword frequency is challenging for Flash sites, because we're limited in our choice of where we can place text. Later on in this chapter, we'll discuss some possible routes around this problem.

- **Total words** is simply a count of the number of words on a page, not including HTML tags, etc. It's difficult for Flash sites to rank highly in this category, since the Flash file typically *is* the content, but we'll discuss ways around this later in the chapter too.

- **Keyword weight** is the percentage of *keywords* in a HTML document, compared to all other words. Again, this is important, but don't get carried away trying to obtain a high keyword weight. Follow the simple rule of thumb that you want to keep your content in a natural and readable writing style.

<META> Tags and Other Search Engine Specific Code

Having looked at how to select keywords, let's move on now to examine some ways of putting keywords into web pages. Obviously, the easiest way is simply to include them in the text of your pages, but what if (for example) your site uses Flash alone and doesn't have any real HTML text content?

There are many different things that a search engine spider can look at when reviewing a page to be indexed, and each spider will focus its attention according to the interests of its search engine. Some of the important features that most spiders examine when indexing a page are the `<TITLE>` tag and the `<META>` tags. We'll now review some of the pieces of information that spiders look for, and discuss ways to adjust these elements to improve our sites' ratings.

What is a <META> Tag?

Although there are no rules that force spiders to look at any particular element of a page, many of them will use `<META>` tags to help them understand the content. `<META>` tags contain **metadata** – that is, data about data – about your HTML pages. In other words, they hold information that describes the content (the data) of the web sites you create.

`<META>` tags can be used to describe almost anything – not only the content of your page, but also such things as the name of the author, or the version number of the file. If you use Microsoft FrontPage to create your HTML files, you may have noticed that it automatically adds the following in the `<HEAD>` tag:

```
<META name="GENERATOR" content="Microsoft FrontPage 4.0">
```

This tag, for example, tells us that the 'generator' (the creation tool) for this document was Microsoft FrontPage 4.0 – but that's just scratching the surface of what we can do.

Let's look at a slightly more detailed set of metadata: the following document is a blank HTML page with `<META>` tags explaining what the content will eventually be about.

```
<HTML>
    <HEAD>
        <TITLE>My Car Page</TITLE>
        <META http-equiv="Content-Type" content="text/html;
           charset=windows-1252">
        <META name="GENERATOR" content="Microsoft FrontPage 4.0">
        <META name="ProgId"
           content="FrontPage.Editor.Document">
        <META name="Keywords" content="cars, car, auto">
        <META name="Description" content="Information about cars.">
        <META name="Author" content="Andrew Zack">
        <META name="Copyright" content="2000 ZTech Consulting">
        <META name="Date" content="2000-12-26">
    </HEAD>

    <BODY>
    </BODY>
</HTML>
```

As you can see, the metadata is placed between the `<HEAD>` tags, which is where you should always place any metadata you specify. Don't worry about having to understand all the tags in this example — I just wanted to give an impression of the different types of information that you can use `<META>` tags for. You can probably see, though, that we have described the creation environment, stated what Keywords are relevant to the page, provided a Description of the content, and supplied some information about who wrote it, and when.

`<META>` tags can even be used to control the way a page *acts*. For example, the following HTML code would force the page that contains it to load another page automatically:

```
<META http-equiv="Refresh" content="0; URL=frame.htm">
```

While this next piece of HTML would make the page have a 'boxed-in' effect in Microsoft Internet Explorer:

```
<META http-equiv="Page-Enter"
content="revealTrans(Duration=5.0,Transition=0)">
```

> *If you're interested in finding out more about* `<META>` *tags, check out* http://vancouver-webpages.com/META *for a list.*

<META> Tags and Keywords

With a basic understanding of <META> tags under our belts, we can move on to look at what search engines focus on. The good news here is that there are only two varieties of the <META> tag that we really need to worry about: the ones with name="Keywords", and the ones with name="Description".

The Keywords <META> tag is, sensibly, where we place the keywords that we've decided are relevant to the document. As we discussed earlier, it's important to select your keywords carefully, and ensure that they relate appropriately to the content of the page. Don't repeat the same keyword in the hope of getting better results, as many search engines frown upon this behavior. You should structure them something like this:

```
<META name="Keywords" content="cars, auto ,car, car books,
auto manuals">
```

The Description <META> tag is where you place a brief description of the content of your site (or this particular page). This is usually the text that gets displayed in search engine results, so it should be written to attract potential web site visitors. The text should be short (typically, fewer than 25 words). There are three main goals that you should try to achieve here:

- Your description needs to be compelling, and make users want to click it

- Your description should consider keyword prominence

- Your description should fit well with the page title

Combining these three goals can be challenging, but be creative and try to keep the user in mind. The bottom line is that you want to be listed effectively, and you want search engine users to be interested enough to click on your link. To see how that might work, let's look at the final results from the users' perspective.

Typically, search engine results will display information from the <TITLE> tag, followed by information from the Description <META> tag. Often, the search engine will take only a certain amount of characters from the title and description. Ideally, of course, we'd like our site to be displayed at number 1, and be compelling to the user. Here's an example of a good link (provided, of course, that we were looking for golf clubs):

1. Golf Clubs and other golf accessories
   We have a complete line of golf clubs and golf accessories to meet all of your golfing needs.
   URL: www.yourgolfsite.com

Here, Golf Clubs and other golf accessories is likely to have been the content of the <TITLE> tag in the HTML document, while We have a complete line of golf clubs and golf accessories to meet all of your golfing needs would come from the <META> tag. This entry should come up fairly high under the keyword 'golf', since the word appears twice in the title and three times in the description. (The third count is 'golfing', which contains 'golf'.)

HTML Comments

Comments in HTML pages are usually placed there by developers in order to document their code. They aren't displayed when a page is viewed in a browser, but some search engines may recognize them. The structure of a comment tag is open, so there aren't really any guidelines to follow when using them as a search engine optimization technique. It's probably best, though, not to repeat keywords excessively, and to use them to support the content of the page. When possible, follow the same rules and guidelines that we suggested for <META> tags.

HTML comments are opened with <!— and closed with —>, and you can include whatever you like in between these two delimiters. There are no formal limits on their length, but don't overdo it. Here, for example, is a comment that would support our automobile page example:

```
<!— This page contains information on automotive manuals, cars,
car parts, car accessories, and auto guides. —>
```

In this example, we're still trying to emphasize the keywords we've been working with, and we've tried to leave our comment as a clear and well-structured sentence. Comments can be placed anywhere within an HTML document, so you're free to do things like this:

```
<HTML>
    <HEAD>

        ... code as before ...

        <!-- My Car Page is your best source for car parts.-->
    </HEAD>
    <BODY>
        <!-- This page contains information on automotive
manuals,cars, car parts, car accessories and auto
guides. -->
    </BODY>
</HTML>
```

Hidden Input Fields

Another technique that will allow you to add more keyword information to a web page is to use **hidden input fields**. These are normally used by web programmers to pass information between pages, but for search engine optimization purposes, you can enter keywords into the name and value attributes to help increase keyword prominence on your page. Here's an example:

```
<INPUT type="Hidden" name="auto" value="auto manuals,
        automotive manuals, car parts, auto accessories">
```

You should place hidden fields within the body of the document; they're hidden from display by all recent browser versions, and they won't affect the appearance of your page.

Here's our example again, with two hidden input fields:

```
<HTML>
   <HEAD>

       ... as before ...

   </HEAD>
   <BODY>
      <!—This page contains information on automotive manuals,
          ➥cars, car parts, car accessories and auto guides. —>
      <INPUT type="Hidden" name="auto"
             value="auto manuals, automotive manuals, car
      parts, auto accessories">
      <INPUT type="Hidden" name="car"
             value="car accessories, car parts, car shop
      manuals, accessories">
   </BODY>
</HTML>
```

Image Tags

The next aspect that we're going to discuss in this section is the alt attribute of the <IMG> tag, which is used to display an image within an HTML document. A typical <IMG> tag will look like this:

```
<IMG border="0" src="carparts.jpg" width="246" height="259">
```

Here we have an <IMG> tag that specifies the file to be used, as well as the height, width, and border size with which it should be displayed. There are many more attributes that can be applied to an <IMG> tag, but our primary focus will be on alt. In this context, alt is an abbreviation for *alternative*, and refers to the text that will be displayed instead of an image while the image is loading, or if the user has images turned off in their browser. In Microsoft Internet Explorer, the alt attribute is displayed in a 'tooltip' that pops up when you let the cursor hover above an image:

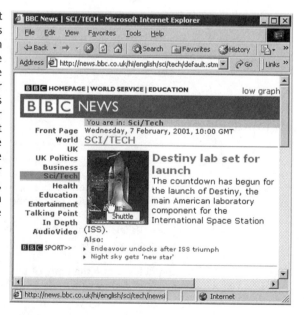

Here's an `<IMG>` tag with the `alt` attribute set for our automobile example:

```
<IMG border="0" src="carparts.jpg" width="246" height="259"
     alt="Auto manuals">
```

The `alt` attributes of `<IMG>` tags are often read by web spiders, and are yet another way to get your keywords recognized. If you don't have images on your page, you may consider adding an outline around your Flash movie, or simply attaching a 1x1-pixel graphic to your HTML document. You may have noticed that the word *car* appears in the name of our image file, too.

File names, URLs, and Links

Finally, the way you name your files and URLs can also help with your optimization strategy – and that includes the name of your SWF file! Any time that you can include your keywords in your file names, directories, links, and naming conventions, it is to your benefit. Most of the search engines will look at these items, and you will tend to increase your search engine ranking if you use this strategy. Naming a page `auto.htm` will increase the chances of your site appearing high up in the search engine ranking for the keyword *auto*. You can do the same with image files (`auto.gif`), or even directories (`/auto/auto.gif`).

We now have all the techniques we need to load a document with keywords without affecting its appearance. At the end of this chapter, we'll put them all together in an example that demonstrates how they might be applied to a typical Flash web site. Before we do that, though, there are a number of other things we need to consider, including whether we should allow spiders to examine a particular document *at all*. This decision, and the factors that affect it, are our subject for the next section.

Excluding Pages from Search Engines

Despite all that I've said so far, there are actually a number of reasons why you may *not* want to have your pages indexed by search engines. Such pages will typically fall into one of the following categories:

- **Administrative pages.** These are used by the administrator of a site to change or modify the site. Inviting users to browse straight here will likely result in an immediate 'no access' message (bad), or allow them to see data they shouldn't (worse).

> *Extremely important pages that may contain proprietary information, etc., should be placed in secure directories.*

- **Results pages.** These display the results from a query or form. Having your results pages indexed by a search engine will not benefit you, and may give a bad impression to your site's visitors.

- **Dynamically generated pages.** Many site administrators will use technology like PHP or ASP to generate pages dynamically. These may require prior input from a user, or a special code to be passed from the referring hyperlink. You don't want these types of pages to be indexed, since they would display incomplete information, and discourage the user from following other links to your site.

- **Incomplete or pre-publication pages.** Many web servers contain directories where pages are stored before they go live. Spiders can come at any time, and if you have such a directory on your site, these pages may be indexed prematurely. Be careful when barring access to these pages, though, since you may end up creating pages that are temporally labeled not to be indexed, and then forget to remove that code when you publish them. It's definitely a better decision to handle this at the directory level – or even to find another machine for your production work!

- **Sequenced pages.** You may have a group of pages that need to be viewed in sequence to obtain the proper user response – a presentation perhaps, or a linear narrative. In these cases, you would want to include the first page, but exclude any additional pages from being visited by a spider.

How do we arrange for certain pages to be kept from being indexed by web spiders? Basically, there are two techniques, but you should be aware that although they're recognized by *most* search engines, they're not foolproof. If you absolutely don't want a page to be indexed by a spider, make certain it's in a secure directory that spiders simply cannot access.

The techniques in question are the use of the robots.txt file, and a special version of the <META> tag.

The robots.txt File

The robots.txt file is the most convenient way for site administrators to keep spiders from indexing sections of their sites. The file uses the **Robots Exclusion Protocol**, which is a very simple way of explaining to a spider (a.k.a. a robot) what areas of a site not to enter.

> *For more detailed information on the Robots Exclusion Protocol, you could take a look at a useful site :*
>
> http://info.webcrawler.com/mak/projects/robots/exclusion.html*; as an introduction I'll provide a summary of the information in the documents available when you get there.*

There can be only a single robots.txt file on your site, and it should reside in the root folder. When a spider arrives at your site (say, www.myexamplesite.com), the first file it will look for is www.myexamplesite.com/robots.txt. Since URLs can be case-sensitive, you should be sure to use lowercase letters when naming it.

Here's an example of a basic robots.txt file:

```
# robots.txt for http://www.myexamplesite.com

User-agent: *
Disallow: /leftnavbar.htm
Disallow: /code.htm
Disallow: /backup/          # for backup purposes only
Disallow: /images/          # only contains images
Disallow: /includes/        # includes only
```

The first line in this example is commented out:

```
# robots.txt for http://www.myexamplesite.com
```

This fact is denoted by the # symbol, and the line is simply telling us what the file is for. It is recommended that your robots.txt files should also include this line. The other lines in the example clearly demonstrate that comments can be added anywhere within the file – doing so is generally held to be good practice.

The next line specifies which types of spiders should read this robots.txt file:

```
User-agent: *
```

The * symbol means that the file's contents apply equally to *all* spiders.

The other lines in the file (the ones that begin Disallow:) actually tell the spider what to exclude. In this example, the spider will omit the leftnavbar.htm document, the code.htm document, and the backup, images, and includes directories.

Here are some more examples of common robots.txt files. Keep in mind that if you'd like to see some more samples, you can go to any site's robots.txt file simply by typing it into your browser – you know that it should always be in the root folder.

To exclude all robots from the entire site:

```
# robots.txt for http://www.myexamplesite.com
User-agent: *
Disallow: /
```

To allow all robots access to the entire site:

```
# robots.txt for http://www.myexamplesite.com
User-agent: *
Disallow:
```

To exclude a particular, named robot:

```
User-agent: evilBot
Disallow: /
```

Robots and the <META> Tag

Another way to keep spiders from indexing your pages is to use the Robots <META> tag, which follows the same format as the Keyword and Description tags we discussed earlier in the chapter. By adding this between the <HEAD> tags, you can specify that an indexing spider shouldn't review this page. The <META> tag offers users who don't have control over the robots.txt file an option to prevent search engines from indexing their pages. Here's a simple example:

```
<HEAD>
    <TITLE>A Page I Don't Want In Search Engines</TITLE>
    <META name="Robots" content="NOINDEX">
</HEAD>
```

The Robots <META> tag can be used to specify the following options:

- NOINDEX, which tells the spider not to index the page, but also tells it that it can follow the links on the page:

```
<META name="Robots" content="NOINDEX">
```

- INDEX, which tells the spider to include this page in the search engine:

```
<META name="Robots" content="INDEX">
```

> *Currently, there is no reason to believe that this will actually increase the page's chances of getting listed, but it may be worth a try.*

- NOFOLLOW, which tells the spider to index the page, but not to follow any of the links on the page:

```
<META name="Robots" content="NOFOLLOW">
```

- FOLLOW, which recommends that the robot should follow the links on the page:

```
<META name="Robots" content="FOLLOW">
```

- NONE, which tells the robot to ignore the page completely. The page should not be indexed, and links should not be followed:

```
<META name="Robots" content="NONE">
```

Monitoring your Traffic and Listings

Throughout the process of optimizing your site for search engines, you should monitor the traffic coming to your site. If your site is new, you won't have much to go on, but if it's been around for a while the existing site traffic reports can be very helpful in determining what is (or is *not*) helping to bring users to your site. As you become more involved in search engine optimization, the analytical tools that you use to monitor web site traffic will become some of your most valuable applications.

There are many tools on the market today that help you to keep track of the users of your site. Based in part on the features and the detail that they provide, these tools range in price from free, to thousands of dollars. For the most part, these tools read the log files generated by your server and produce reports based on the information recorded therein. Exactly what information gets recorded depends on how the server is configured, and on the type of server being used.

> *These programs are typically only as good as the information recorded by the server. Often, the server can't track user information, so this may be incomplete. There's no way around this – it's all just part of the process.*

Most web analysis packages will produce reports that can be put to good use in the process of web optimization. Typically, the reports that you'll want to see are as follows:

- Reports on referring URLs

- Reports on referring search engines

- Reports on search engines by keyword

- Reports on top entry pages (that is, the pages through which your site is most frequently entered)

Once you've become familiar with these reports, you'll begin to notice trends in them, and how they relate to search engines. Don't be discouraged if it takes time to get the process working for you: it will pay off when you get your first top listing. Keep track of the pages that are currently bringing in traffic, and see how they can be improved. You'll often discover pages on your site that have been listed in search engines without you even knowing about it!

Two of the more popular web site statistical tools are:

- **WebTrends** (available from www.webtrends.com). This is the most widely used tool on the market, and comes in many different versions. It needs to be installed on your web server.

- **LiveStats** (available from www.mediahouse.com). This offers many of the features of WebTrends, as well as live statistical tracking.

In addition to the server-based products, there are a number of web-based products that require you to display a banner on your site, and add code to each individual page. Depending on your budget, though, these services can be very helpful. Some free traffic-tracking products include:

- HitBox (www.hitbox.com)

- StatTrack (www.stattrack.com)

You should take a look at their web sites, and see which (if any) of these products suit the way you do business. Ultimately, though, they're only useful once you've already begun to attract visitors, and the only way you're going to do that is to get your site listed on the search engines in the first place! *That* problem, then, is the one we need to address next.

Submitting Pages to Search Engines

Submitting your pages to search engines can be a grueling process. There are many services on the Internet that offer free or low-fee services to submit your pages to a whole range of sites, but for the most part these are of questionable value. The process of submitting is very important, and it's worth taking the time to submit to each and every one of the major search engines yourself.

> *Remember that over 90% of all traffic passes through the top search engines, so a #1 listing in any of the smaller ones will likely be worth less than (say) a #25 listing on AltaVista.*

There is, however, *some* purpose in using these tools of mass submission. Although many of the search engines out there won't get you much traffic by themselves, if *they* get indexed by the major search engines, your link popularity may go up. This isn't a priority, but if you're working hard at increasing site traffic, you may want to consider using one of these services or products. Good packages of this type include Trellian Software's SubmitWolf (www.trellian.com) for Windows machines, and VSE's Be Found (www.vse-online.com) for Macintosh.

> *Just to reiterate, if you try products or services that submit your pages to large numbers of sites, don't allow them to submit to the top search engines. It's worth taking the time to do the really important work by hand.*

Details on Specific Search Engines

Each search engine has its own criteria for accepting, indexing, and displaying web pages. Now that we've gone through the basics of the many general techniques that you can use to help get a web site indexed, we're going to look into specific search engines and directories to gain a further understanding of how they work. We can't possibly be comprehensive here, but we'll review a few of the top search services available on the Internet.

Yahoo

Yahoo is, quite simply, the most popular search service on the Internet. Yahoo's primary results come from its own human-filtered database, and they're displayed in the following order:

- Categories (from Yahoo's database)

- Web sites (from Yahoo's database)

- Web pages (from results provided by Google.com)

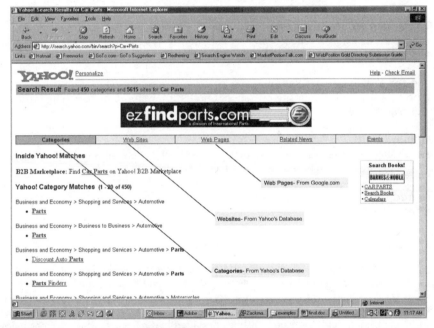

A good showing on Yahoo is probably the most important listing a web site can have in a search engine. Before you can even begin the submission process, however, you need to select the appropriate *category* for your site. It's important that you really study Yahoo's directory structure before you attempt this. To help you out, Yahoo has set up a good guide for what you need to do at http://docs.yahoo.com/info/suggest/appropriate.html.

Once you've found the appropriate category for your site, you should go to the bottom of that category page and click the Suggest a Site link. Yahoo records your position within its directory structure when you submit a site. Once you've done this, you need to be patient and wait for results. Yahoo rarely allows for multiple pages to be submitted from a single site, and you don't want to be labeled as a pest by Yahoo!

During the submission process, you'll be able to provide the title, URL, and description of your site. Be particularly careful not to let typos creep into this information, and try to write clearly while still including your keywords. Remember that this is only a *suggested* link, and Yahoo's reviewer has the option of rejecting it, relocating it, or even rewriting the description. Yahoo offers significant page submission advice at http://help.yahoo.com/help/url.

> **Don't submit doorway pages to Yahoo; only submit your home page.**

Yahoo Business Express Submission
Yahoo offers an expedited submission service called Business Express for $199. If this is within your marketing budget, it can be very useful: it guarantees that your site will be reviewed within seven days, and that you'll get a written response if your site isn't accepted for listing.

How Search Results are Displayed
When your site appears in Yahoo search results, it will typically be displayed the way you submitted it, although the Yahoo reviewer may modify it.

Checking for a Web Site on Yahoo
There is no trick to locating your site on Yahoo. Check for a web site by searching for it by title, by URL, or by category.

Link Popularity
Some search engines keep track of how often the links they contain are followed, and move popular ones up the order. Yahoo doesn't use this technique.

Page to Add URL
This depends on the category selected.

AltaVista

AltaVista is one of the older search engines, and has consistently been one of the largest indexers of pages. It's powered primarily by a spider called Scooter, and it has a number of other similar spiders that focus on particular tasks (such as reviewing existing links to make certain that they are still current). In addition to its own database, AltaVista offers directory-based searches powered by LookSmart, and 'sponsored' listings provided by GoTo.com, which appear below the AltaVista results on the first page of results for each search:

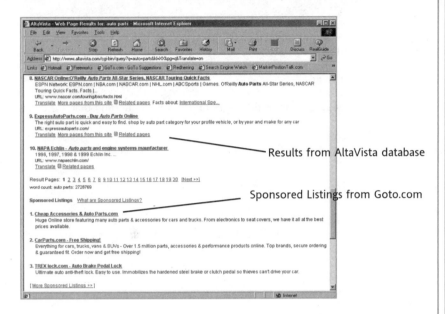

Results from AltaVista database

Sponsored Listings from Goto.com

AltaVista is another site that gives detailed advice on how to submit a link. For more information on AltaVista, try http://doc.altavista.com/adv_search/ast_haw_index.html.

How Search Results are Displayed

AltaVista search results display the title of the HTML document on a line of its own, followed by any description you supplied using <META> tags. If there's no such description supplied, it will display the first few lines of visible text on the page.

What Criteria are Used when Indexing?

AltaVista is a true search engine that indexes pages based on various criteria. The following are some simple points to consider when submitting or building a page for AltaVista:

- Consider waiting for AltaVista to find your site. It's believed that AltaVista will give higher ranking to pages it finds on its own. If you don't have time to wait, you may want to leave your top page to be 'found', but submit a doorway or some other page that links to many of the others on your site.

- When AltaVista ranks sites, it gives some weight to link *popularity*.

- Include your keywords in your page title, and if possible in your URL too.

- Longer pages are given more weight, so if possible include a reasonable amount of text on your doorway pages.

- AltaVista is aggressively combating spammers, so understand their rules before submitting pages. You can view AltaVista's spam policy at http://doc.altavista.com/adv_search/ast_haw_spam.html.

Checking for a Web Site's Pages on AltaVista

AltaVista provides a convenient way to check for pages in its index. To discover whether a site is listed, enter the following search:

url: www.yoursite.com

AltaVista will then display all of the pages on the site in question that are currently indexed.

Link Popularity

AltaVista uses link popularity to increase page rank. To check your link popularity, enter the following search:

link: www.yoursite.com

There are also some link popularity tools on the Internet that allow you to check a site's popularity on multiple sites. Two that I have tried are www.linkpopularitycheck.com and www.searchengineworld.com/cgi-bin/linkage.cgi.

Page to Add URL

http://doc.altavista.com/addurl

Google

Google is one of the newer players in the search engine industry, and it boasts one of the largest databases of links (currently well over a billion). Google has established a relationship with Yahoo, replacing Inktomi (q.v.) as Yahoo's secondary result provider. Google also offers directory-based searching, powered by dmoz.org (q.v.). Currently, when you enter a search on Google, the first link will be a *sponsored* link. Then it will display any relevant directory categories, and finally the results from its own engine:

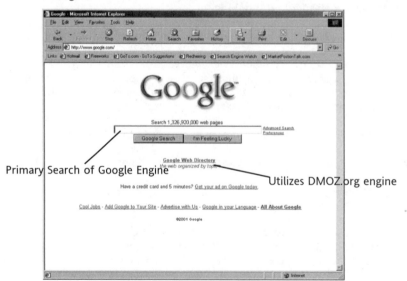

Primary Search of Google Engine

Utilizes DMOZ.org engine

How Search Results are Displayed

Google search results display the title of the HTML document, and then a description that's based on the words that appear around the keywords on your page. Typically, this will be one of the first lines of text that contains the search keyword. It seems that Google doesn't use <META> tags for this purpose.

What Criteria are Used when Indexing?

Google indexes pages using a spider called Googlebot, and it's currently one of the quicker sites to index new pages. Here are some simple points to consider when submitting or building a page for Google:

- Google searches are *not* case sensitive.

- For a page to be listed in the results for a Google query, *all* the words in the query must be on the page.

- Google gives higher ranking to sites with strong link popularity.

- Include your keywords in your page title, and if possible in your URL too.

Checking for a Web Site's Pages on Google

Currently, there's no easy way to check for a site on Google. One of the ways I've found to get an *idea* of how you're doing is to experiment with its free site search capability at http://services.google.com/cobrand/free_select.

This tool allows you to add Google search functionality to your site, including a site-specific search. You don't necessarily need to sign up for the service, but if you enter your domain name at the first step of the process, Google will return the total number of links for that domain. Another technique is to use the advanced search feature, and search for a word that's on every page of your site (your company name, perhaps), setting the domain as you do so.

Link Popularity

Like AltaVista, and as mentioned above, Google uses link popularity to increase page rank. To check your link popularity, enter the following search:

link: www.yoursite.com

Page to Add URL

http://www.google.com/addurl.html

dmoz.org – The Open Directory Project

The Open Directory Project (www.dmoz.org) is an Internet directory search service manned by volunteers who agree to maintain a specific content area. To submit a site, you should follow the same steps as for Yahoo. Obtaining a good listing here is important, because it's used by many of the top search engines. At the time of publishing, Google, HotBot, Netscape, and AOL Search were all using the Open Directory Project.

How Search Results are Displayed
Search results in the Open Directory Project are generally displayed the way you submitted them, although the reviewer may modify them.

Link Popularity
Since the Open Directory Project doesn't use a spider, there's no link popularity factor for this search directory.

Page to Add URL
This depends on the category selected.

Inktomi

Inktomi is a back-end provider of search engine services that are used by many popular sites. Currently, over 100 portals employ Inktomi as a primary or secondary provider of search results. Inktomi-powered sites include iWon, AOL Search, HotBot, GoTo, and NBCi (formerly Snap).

Unlike many of the other search engines, Inktomi has no 'front-end' service – it *only* resides behind the scenes of its many search engine partners. Most of these use the same database, but they may have different criteria for results, resulting in *similar* but different rankings, depending on the search engine in question.

The Inktomi spider gives high priority to keywords in the page title, and to <META> tags. Submissions to Inktomi should be made through one of its partners; you can find HotBot, for example, at http://hotbot.lycos.com/addurl.asp.

Search/Submit Paid Inclusion
Inktomi's Search/Submit inclusion program allows web pages to be submitted and included for a fee. The service is priced by the number of pages that you wish to include in the database, and includes being re-indexed every 48 hours to maintain a continuous update on your site. If you have the budget, this will gain you recognition with many large search engines very quickly. For more background information on this service, you could take a look at:
        http://www.inktomi.com/products/search/pagesubmission.html.

Checking for a Web Site's Pages on Inktomi Search Engines
To check for your web site's pages on an Inktomi-powered search engine, just enter the URL of your site. After you've located one of the links to your site, there will be an option to view more results from the same site. Clicking on this link will display all of the results for that site.

GoTo.com

The last search service that we're going to mention here is GoTo.com, which is the largest pay-per-click search engine. Webmasters are allowed to bid for top ranking spots on a real-time system – in other words, they can buy traffic, based on the popularity of the keyword. Results from GoTo.com are displayed on many of the larger search engines (including AltaVista, America Online, Lycos, and HotBot), typically as a 'featured site' or 'sponsor'.

Practical Exercise

We've at last covered all the theory you need in order to be able to make informed decisions about how best to get your web site noticed in the shifting sea of light that is the Internet. To close the chapter, we'll examine how to apply that knowledge to a freshly produced Flash site.

In our example, we'll be building a site that sells parts and accessories for 4-wheel-drive vehicles. The content will be entirely in Flash, so there'll be no visible HTML content elements.

After analysis, I've determined that our top keywords will be *4-wheel*, *4 wheel*, *truck parts*, and *truck accessories*. The front page of the site is index.html, which will contain a small Flash presentation that tells users about the site. We're now going to go through the process of optimizing that page.

> *You can probably think of some more keywords that might be appropriate here – the words four and drive come to mind – but by keeping the number low we can (hopefully) avoid repetition. You'll see that it wouldn't be hard to include additional keywords if we wanted to.*

Once you've produced the perfect movie, the next step is to publish the Flash file. The options in the Publish Settings dialog give us our first opportunity to perform some optimization.

Our server administrator has told us that the default home page must be called index.html, but that doesn't prevent us from renaming the SWF file to 4-wheel.swf, thereby getting one of our keywords into the document at the first opportunity:

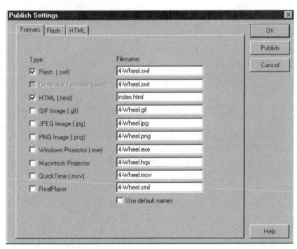

After making those changes, publishing the movie, and opening the `index.html` document in a text editor, you should have something roughly similar to the following listing, which we've formatted for clarity here:

```
<HTML>
    <HEAD>
        <TITLE>4-wheel</TITLE>
    </HEAD>
    <BODY bgcolor="#FFFFFF">
        <!- URLs used in the movie ->
        <!- text used in the movie ->
        <!- Keep Out ->
        <OBJECT classid="clsid:D27CDB6E-AE6D-11cf-96B8-444553540000"
          codebase="http://download.macromedia.com/pub/
            shockwave/cabs/flash/swflash.cab#version=5,0,0,0"
                  width="221" height="56">
            <PARAM name="movie" VALUE="4-wheel.swf">
            <PARAM name="quality" VALUE="high">
            <PARAM name="bgcolor" VALUE="#FFFFFF">

        <EMBED src="4-wheel.swf" quality="high" bgcolor="#FFFFFF"
                width="221" height="56"
                type="application/x-shockwave-flash"
                pluginspage="http://www.macromedia.com/shockwave/
                download/index.cgi?P1_Prod_Version=
                ShockwaveFlash">
        </EMBED>
        </OBJECT>
    </BODY>
</HTML>
```

Next, we want to work on modifying the `<TITLE>` tag. As discussed earlier in the chapter, this is extremely important, since it's typically the main piece of information displayed about a page in a search engine, and it's often weighted heavily for keywords. Since our site is about 4-wheel parts and accessories, and our company name is XYZ, we decided to make the title "XYZ - 4 Wheel Truck Parts and Accessories". Using the text editor, we change the `<TITLE>` tag to:

`<TITLE>`**XYZ - 4 Wheel Truck Parts and Accessories**`</TITLE>`

This new content emphasizes many of our keywords, including *4 Wheel*, *Truck Parts*, and *Truck Accessories*. (Although the phrase *Truck Accessories* doesn't appear verbatim, many spiders will pick this phrase up, since both words appear.) *XYZ Parts*, *4 Wheel Accessories*, and many other keyword combinations may also be indexed.

It's time to focus on our `<META>` tags. For this example, we're not concerned about author information or the publication date. Rather, we'll concentrate on the varieties that a spider is likely to look at: those that set `Keywords`, and the `Description`. The first of these should simply take into account all of our keywords, and some variations thereon. After some consideration, we decided to go with the following:

```
<META name="keywords"
    content="4-wheel, truck parts, 4 wheel,
            truck accessories, 4 wheel parts, 4 wheel accessories">
```

We based our keywords on the ones we identified in our earlier discussion, and also included a few variations on the theme (in the hope of increasing keyword frequency and bringing in searchers for phrases that are similar to our keywords). Selecting keywords is not a precise science, however, and each search engine will look at them differently. As you become more experienced with each search engine, you'll come to learn what they are looking for, and how to refine your Keywords <META> tags accordingly.

When it comes to the Description <META> tag, it's important to note that spiders may look at this to discover keywords too. However, we have to balance including keywords against making sure that the description is legible and appealing, since this is often the text that search engines will display. For this page, we'll add the following description, which contains our keywords and a good description of our Flash site:

```
<META name="description"
    content="XYZ is your source for 4 wheel truck parts,
    accessories and more.
    XYZ is the one-stop shop for all of your 4- wheel
    needs.">
```

This description tells the user what to expect from the site, and tells the spider our keywords (again): *4 wheel*, *4-wheel*, *truck parts*, and *accessories*.
All <META> tags are placed between the <HEAD> tags of an HTML document. After the new additions we've talked about here, the HTML document should look like this:

```
<HTML>
    <HEAD>
        <TITLE>XYZ - 4 Wheel Truck Parts and Accessories</TITLE>
        <META name="keywords"
            content="4-wheel, truck parts, 4 wheel,
                    truck accessories, 4 wheel parts, 4 wheel
accessories">
        <META name="description"
            content="XYZ is your source for 4 wheel truck parts,
accessories and more.
            XYZ is the one stop shop for all of your
4-wheel needs.">
    </HEAD>
<BODY bgcolor="#FFFFFF">

    ... as before ...

    </BODY>
</HTML>
```

We now have an HTML document with a few keywords and a lot more information for any visiting spider to see. The next step we'll take is to add a few comment tags. As you know, comment tags can be placed anywhere within the HTML document, since they are not read by browsers, but they may well be recognized by spiders. Comment tags are *supposed* to contain information for developers, so in order to make them look plausible in that respect too, we'll try the following:

```
<EMBED src="4-wheel.swf" quality="high" bgcolor="#FFFFFF"
       width="221" height="56"
       type="application/x-shockwave-flash"
       pluginspage="http://www.macromedia.com/shockwave
         /download/index.cgi?P1_Prod_Version=
            ShockwaveFlash">
    </EMBED>
    </OBJECT>
    <!- This page contains information on 4 wheel trucks,parts,
    accessories, and other 4-wheel
     information. ->
   </BODY>
</HTML>
```

That leaves just two more items in our list of techniques for optimizing the page for search engine recognition: hidden input fields, and <IMG> tags. As we discussed earlier in the chapter, hidden input fields can be used to include more content that won't be displayed by the browser, but *may* be recognized by spiders. Sticking with our current strategy, we'll simply add two hidden input tags repeating slightly modified versions of our "Keywords" and "Description" <META> tags.

These fields will be placed in the body of the document:

```
<INPUT type="Hidden" name="4 wheel"
       value="4-wheel, truck parts, 4 Wheel,
       truck accessories, 4 wheel parts, 4 wheel accessories">
<INPUT type="Hidden" name="4-Wheel"
       value="XYZ is your source for 4 wheel truck parts,
       accessories and more.
       XYZ is the one-stop shop for all of your 4-wheel needs.">
```

Finally, note that everything we've added to the page so far has been invisible. Any *images* we use will be 'visible', but if we want to, we can design them so they're not apparent to the eye. Since the background of this page is white, we'll make the graphic the same color as the background, so that it doesn't distract our users.

For this example, we created an image that's 1 pixel high and 10 pixels long, and the same color as our background. We named the file 4-wheel.gif, to match our keyword focus. Since the file won't easily be visible, we'll place it in the last line of the HTML body, so that it doesn't interfere with any other code that we work on in the future. In the alt attribute of the <IMG> tag, we'll also add our keywords one more time. Here's an example:

```
<IMG border="0" src="4-wheel.gif"
     width="10" height="1"
     alt="4 wheel parts and accessories">
```

That's it! We now have a page that is well optimized to be picked up by many search engines' spiders, and indexed under our keywords. Keep in mind, though, that this is an ever-changing process, and that this is simply an example. To truly be effective, you'll have to experiment with different techniques for different search engines. Here's the final code for our example:

```
<HTML>
  <HEAD>
    <TITLE>XYZ - 4 Wheel Truck Parts and Accessories</TITLE>
    <META name="keywords"
      content="4-wheel, truck parts, 4 wheel,
      truck accessories, 4 wheel parts, 4 wheel accessories">
      <META name="description"
      content="XYZ is your source for 4 wheel truck
      parts, accessories and more.
    XYZ is the one stop shop for all of your 4-wheel needs.">
  </HEAD>
  <BODY bgcolor="#FFFFFF">
    <!— URLs used in the movie —>
    <!— text used in the movie —>
    <!— Keep Out —>
    <INPUT type="Hidden" name="4 wheel"
        value="4-wheel, truck parts, 4 Wheel,
                truck accessories, 4 wheel parts,
                4 wheel accessories">
    <INPUT type="Hidden" name="4-Wheel"
        value="XYZ is your source for 4 wheel truck
        parts, accessories and more.
                XYZ is the one-stop shop for all of
                your 4-wheel needs.">
    <OBJECT classid="clsid:D27CDB6E-AE6D-11cf-96B8-444553540000"
            codebase="http://download.macromedia.com/pub/
            shockwave/cabs/flash/swflash.
              cab#version=5,0,0,0"
            width="221" height="56">
      <PARAM name="movie" VALUE="intro.swf">
      <PARAM name="quality" VALUE="high">
      <PARAM name="bgcolor" VALUE="#FFFFFF">

      <EMBED src="4-wheel.swf" quality="high"
bgcolor="#FFFFFF"
              width="221" height="56"
              type="application/x-shockwave-flash"
              pluginspage="http://www.macromedia.com/
              shockwave/download/index.cgi?P1_Prod_Version=
              ShockwaveFlash">
      </EMBED>
    </OBJECT>
    <!— This page contains information on 4 wheel trucks,parts,
        accessories, and other 4-wheel information. —>
```

```
        <IMG border="0" src="4-wheel.gif"
              width="10" height="1"
              alt="4 wheel parts and accessories">
    </BODY>
</HTML>
```

Conclusion

Remember that *building* your web site is just the beginning. Now that you have a better understanding of how to market your web site on the Internet you should be able to find many routes to take to increase site traffic. The simple techniques discussed here will hopefully help you get your site noticed, visited more frequently, and – critically – visited by the right people: your target audience.

As the specialized world of Flash becomes increasingly mainstream, and people search for Flash sites not just because they have cool Flash features, but because of their core content too, the principles we've discussed here will stand you in good stead. You'll be able to move with shifts in indexing technologies and track your audience as they shift. Because after all, nobody wants to run a site that no-one knows about or visits!

Index

The index is arranged hierarchically, in alphabetical order, with symbols preceding the letter A. Most second-level entries and many third-level entries also occur as first-level entries. This is to ensure that users will find the information they require however they choose to search for it.

freshfroot
motion web mindfood

stripes

warhol

seams & f

seven day itch

freshfroot is where friends of ED fertilise the designer mind. It's a visual search engine, a daily creative resource and a hard-to-kick addiction. Everyday the froot pickers, along with a select band of celebrity guest editors, search through the web's good, bad and ugly to bring you the diamonds – categorised, critiqued and instantly searchable. freshfroot rejects the usual search engine criteria in favour of daily themes that pull together stylistically similar works and images to provide the rock solid creative resource to complement the technical resource on offer in our books.

freshfroot is the place where Mike Cina, James Paterson, Golan Levin, Mumbleboy, Brendan Dawes and many other new and future masters go to share their inspirations and be inspired. It's the place everyone goes when they need fresh ideas fast. Submit your own found or created masterpieces, spout your opinions and share ideas in the discussion forum. Get involved, be inspired and escape the mediocre.

my froot

my froot

?

shee

archive

a-z   a-z

23   date

?   keyword

search for: inspiration

james pate

forward

hybrid   revolution

urban

playground

brendan dawes

friendsof
DESIGNER TO DESIGNER™

Books

D2D

Code

News

Authors

Interviews

Web

Events

Contact

Home

You've read the book, now enter the community.

friendsofed.com is the online heart of the designer to designer neighbourhood.

As you'd expect the site offers the latest news and support for all our current and forthcoming titles – but it doesn't stop there.

For fresh exclusive interviews and videos every month with our authors – the new and future masters like Josh Davis, Yugo Nakamura, James Paterson and many other friends of ED – enter the world of D2D.

Stuck with a design problem? Need technical assistance? Our support doesn't end on the last page of the book. Just post your query on our message board and one of our moderators or authors will make sure you get the answers you need – fast.

New to the site is our EVENTS section where you can find out about schemes brewing in the ED laboratory. Forget everything you know about conferences and get ready for a new generation of designer happenings with a difference.

Welcome to friendsofed.com. This place is the place of friends of ED – designer to designer. Practical deep fast content delivered by working web designers.

Straight to your head.

www.friendsofed.com

DESIGNER TO DESIGNER™

friends of ED writes books for you. Any suggestions, or ideas about how you want information given in your ideal book will be studied by our team.

Your comments are valued by friends of ED.

Freephone in USA 800 873 9769
Fax 312 893 8001

UK contact: Tel. (0121) 258 8858
Fax. (0121) 258 8868

feedback@friendsofed.com

Flash 5 Studio - Registration Card

Name _____

Address _____

_____

_____

City _____ State/Region _____

Country _____ Postcode/Zip _____

E-mail _____

Occupation _____

How did you hear about this book?

☐ Book review (publication) _____
☐ Advertisement (name) _____
☐ Recommendation _____
☐ Catalog _____
☐ Other _____

Where did you buy this book?

☐ Bookstore (name) _____
☐ Computer Store (name) _____
☐ Mail Order _____
☐ Other _____

What influenced you in the purchase of this book?

☐ Cover Design   ☐ Contents
☐ Other (please specify) _____

How did you rate the overall contents of this book?

☐ Excellent   ☐ Good
☐ Average   ☐ Poor

What did you find useful about this book?

What did you find least useful about this book?

Please add any additional comments

What other design areas will you buy a book on soon?

What is the best design related book you have used this year?

Note: This information will only be used to keep you updated about new friends of ED titles and will not be used for any other purposes or passed to any third party.

NB. If you post the bounce back card below in the UK, please send it to:

friends of ED Ltd.,
30 Lincoln Road,
Olton,
Birmingham.
B27 6PA